THE TSAR AND HIS FAMILY [Photo by Stanley

LETTERS OF THE TSARITSA TO THE TSAR 1914–1916

WITH AN INTRODUCTION BY
SIR BERNARD PARES, K.B.E.

ACADEMIC INTERNATIONAL

1970

INTRODUCTION

These letters are profoundly interesting human documents on one of the strangest of modern tragedies. But they are also a mine of information on the crisis which finally brought about the overthrow of the Russian Empire; on many points it is to them alone that we must turn for explanation of the deciding factors in this event. It is desirable, therefore, that, in spite of the respect due to their extremely intimate character, these letters, which were written in English and have already been published in Berlin, should be made accessible without delay to English readers. It will, however, be some time before anything like a complete critical study or elucidation of the letters is possible. This introduction can only be a general sketch, and the index—in the compiling of which I have to acknowledge very valuable help from Prince D. Svyatopolk-Mirsky and Baron A. F. Meyendorff—can only include the principal names mentioned and even then has some omissions and probably some inaccuracies.

One of the predominant features of the Empress's life, and at the same time one of the predominant features in the ruin of Russia, was the growing and finally almost complete isolation of the Imperial family circle from the Russian nation. In consequence there was an extraordinary ignorance both of the currents of public opinion on the side of the Emperor and Empress, and of the life of the Emperor and Empress on the side of Russian opinion. It is only such a cataclysm as the Russian Revolution that could have made the letters themselves public property; and it is at least fortunate from the reader's point of view that they can to a certain extent be checked by at least four records of persons within the extremely small circle of friends of the

Imperial family. But apart from the difficulty of penetrating this circle, the letters deal with matters of the most momentous interest which can only be fully understood when something like full materials are available for the whole history of this epoch.

The letters were discovered in a black box in the last prison of the Imperial family at Ekaterinburg after the tragedy of July 16, 1918. Their authenticity is not questioned by the Bolsheviks, and it has been equally taken for granted by the publishing firm Slovo, conducted in Berlin by Mr. Joseph Hessen, one of the most prominent leaders of the Russian Liberals. It is the Slovo edition which is now for the first time printed in England. According to a recent article published under Soviet conditions in Moscow, the Slovo edition is in some respects both inaccurate and incomplete. If this book claimed to be a collection of all the letters from the Empress to the Emperor, its incompleteness is obvious and indeed is stated in the introduction to the Slovo edition. Roughly speaking, the Empress wrote 630 letters to the Emperor. Of these, some 230 cover the whole period from their first acquaintance to the outbreak of war in 1914; as they were peculiarly devoted and were therefore very seldom parted, the letters in this period were far fewer than during the war, when the Emperor was at first engaged in frequent visits to his army and later, after he had assumed the chief command, was for months at a time at General Headquarters. After the death of Rasputin in December 1916, with which these letters end, the Emperor was only parted from his wife for the very short period of his last visit to Headquarters. That there were many other letters during this period, or that these have been seriously cut in the present edition, seems unlikely. The Empress wrote practically every day and sometimes twice a day. Many of the letters are so lengthy that it must have taken her very long to write them and even have taken the Emperor a considerable time to read them. Their object was not only to keep him in the closest touch with his family, but also, in the later part of this period, with public affairs in general; more than that, it seems clear that the Empress felt that only by enveloping him in a whole atmosphere of her counsels and of her love could she keep him steady in the political course which with such whole-hearted fervour she urged upon him. Inaccuracies in the Slovo edition there are several. A good deal of the misspelling was no doubt the Empress's own. But in several cases it is clear that the English words have been misread. We are told that a full edition is likely to be printed in Russia. This may contain the earlier letters before the war, which have also reached England but have not been published, and might also be supplemented with letters from the Empress to other persons than the Emperor from her captivity in Tobolsk.

That these letters are authentic will certainly be the conclusion of those who may read the other records of the Imperial family during this period. Of these I would put unquestionably first *Le Tragique Destin de Nicholas II et de sa famille* of M. Gilliard, published in French in 1921 and in Vienna in 1921 in a Russian translation authorised by M. Gilliard and supplemented with further pages from his diary.* M. Gilliard, or Zhilik, as the whole Imperial family affectionately called him, was one of its best and most devoted friends. Taking up the duties of preceptor of the Tsarevich in 1913, he was hardly ever again parted from him. He shared with the family their days of anguish at Tsarskoe Selo during the Revolution and their subsequent imprisonment; and with them he went into exile and was imprisoned with them in Tobolsk. Nothing but his forcible separation from them in the last stage at Ekaterinburg prevented him from sharing their fate. It is in every way a noble and honourable book. M. Gilliard seems to us unique in being probably the only person in this intimate family circle who had an understanding of the extraordinary narrowness of their perspective and of the fatal consequences of their isolation. But this is never emphasised. He does not write of politics, but only of the Imperial family.

Of much less value, but of a very peculiar interest, is the book

* Gilliard, Pierre. *Thirteen Years at the Russian Court.* A personal record of the last years and death of Czar Nicholas II and his family. Transl. by F. Appelby Holt. With 59 illustrations. London, 1921 (Hutchinson).

of the Empress's most intimate friend, the till now mysterious Anna Vyrubova, which appeared in Russian under the title *Stranitsy* (*Pages*) in 1923. This book is a mixture of ingenuous frankness and of equally ingenuous evasion and reticence. Whatever else one may gather from the book, it is clear that the author was a person of no intellect or force of character or distinction, and her very mediocrity has its value in making more lifelike the picture of the Empress's family life.* Very superficial, less a record of facts than of impressions, of little accuracy and with no qualities of judgment, is the book of another of the Empress's friends, Madame "Lili" Dehn, *The Real Tsaritsa*, published in English. There is also a small book of Princess Paley, second wife of the Empress's last remaining uncle, the Grand Duke Paul (*Souvenirs de Russie*: Paris), which has attracted attention by its fantastic attacks on Sir George Buchanan.

Far more valuable as checking the narrative of the Empress's letters is the brilliant journal of the French Ambassador of this period in Petrograd, M. Maurice Paléologue (*La Russie des Tsars*: Plon-Nourrit, 1921). This is not merely a political record, though it will be among the most valuable sources for the history of this period. M. Paléologue, who made many friends in Russian society, was particularly well acquainted with the Grand Duchess Maria Pavlovna, widow of the Emperor's eldest uncle, the Grand Duke Vladimir, and therefore one of the great ladies of the capital and one of the chief leaders of Russian society. He was also intimate with two other Grand Dukes, who each played a part in this period, the Grand Duke Paul already mentioned, and the

* This view is confirmed fully by M. Gilliard and also by Mr. Rudnev, who took part in the detailed investigation of the secret influences at the Court conducted, from May 1917, by the Provisional Government. It should be noted that Rudnev read a number of letters of the Empress and did not find in them any traces of her interference in public affairs. Mr. Rudnev says that he read a mass of letters of the Empress to Anna Vyrubova and to the Emperor extending over ten years. This would seem to cover the Empress's letters before the war. He gives no sign of having seen the letters during the war. These were presumably with the Emperor till his final return from the army.

Grand Duke Nikolay Mikhaylovich, a man of considerable learning and of relatively Liberal opinions who was credited with something like the attitude of Philippe Egalité in French society before the French Revolution. There is also the record of Sir George Buchanan (*My Mission to Russia*), who was not, however, so widely in touch with Russian society, though probably more in contact with the leaders of the Duma. If one follows M. Paléologue's journal from day to day and reads by the side of it the record of M. Gilliard, nothing in the letters of the Empress herself need come as a surprise.

The future Empress of Russia, Princess Alix of Hesse-Darmstadt, was born on June 5, 1872, at Darmstadt. Her mother was the beloved Princess Alice of England, who died while nursing her children in 1878 at the age of thirty-five. Princess Alix was brought up largely in England at the court of her grandmother, Queen Victoria, whose ideas and discipline she fully assimilated. A large portrait of the Queen hung later in one of the chief living-rooms at Tsarskoe Selo; "She was very tiny," said the Empress, "but she was very forceful." The whole *morale* of Princess Alix was English. English was the language which she always spoke and wrote to the Emperor. The housekeeping of Tsarskoe Selo was English; and the Empress always thought and spoke of herself as an Englishwoman. In her family there was hereditary the hæmophilic ailment. One of her uncles had his life cut short by it, and her sister, Princess Irena of Prussia, married to Prince Henry, lost several of her children by it. This malady appears only in males and is transmitted only by females. The Empress herself was therefore immune from it, and though later she suffered very much from her heart, she had health to support a life full of trials and at times full of activities. Her eldest sister, Princess Victoria of Battenberg, was married in England. Another sister, Ella, married the Grand Duke Sergius, younger brother of Alexander III of Russia, and became on her conversion to the Orthodox Church (which was anything but nominal), the Grand Duchess Elizabeth. It was on a journey to this sister that Princess Alix was first contemplated as a possible bride for the heir to the throne. But nothing came of the idea this time. The whole nature of the Princess was deeply religious. Her strong Protestant honesty of conscience did not allow her to change her faith without conviction. An Orthodox Bishop was sent to Darmstadt to explain to her the Orthodox confession, and, as in her sister's case, it proved capable of satisfying the deepest instincts of her nature far more than was possible for Protestantism. There was in her father's family and also, perhaps, in her mother's a tendency towards mysticism. On the sudden illness of the Emperor Alexander III, in his anxiety for his son's marriage, Princess Alix was hastily summoned to Russia, and her first appearance to the Russian people as the future Empress was at Alexander's funeral.

She was, of course, a woman of wonderful beauty, fair and tall, with the dignity of an empress. But she was from the first painfully shy. Though this shyness gave way when she was with her very few intimate friends, it cannot be denied that she not only was thought, but actually was, very awkward, ill at ease, and unsympathetic in her appearances at the court. One does not need to take the description of one who hated her, Count Witte. M. Paléologue also finds that conversation is an effort to her, that she can hardly get out a word of welcome ; and others too carried away the impression that her thought throughout court functions was, " When will this be over, and when will all these people be gone ? " The life which she and her family led throughout, a life particularly of her choosing, was remote, not only from the culture and intellect of the country, but even from the other members of the Imperial family. The Grand Dukes themselves complained that they had the greatest difficulty in getting to the Emperor. The extraordinary limitedness and isolation of this life gave the whole atmosphere and background to the part which the Empress was to play in politics. And at the same time they solve the riddle of the extraordinary contrast between her private life and her public influence. It is this isolation which makes so intelligible the wonderful resignation and complete absorption in religion which marked the family life during imprisonment. Mr. Gibbs, colleague of M. Gilliard, and English tutor to the Tsarevich, said the Empress was never so worthy of herself as after the abdication. It was as if her nature could onl expand in such a hermitage of remoteness and privation.

From the outset, the "funeral bride" seemed marked foı misfortune. The coronation festivities were completely marred by the terrible catastrophe on the Hodynsky Plain outside Moscow, where thousands were crushed through extraordinarily incapable arrangements for the distribution of presents to the people. The Emperor and Empress were not told of the extent of the disaster, and their decision to carry out their programme left with many the impression of heartlessness. The investigation which followed led to a conflict between the Court Ministry on one side and the Moscow administration of the Grand Duke Sergius on the other, and this was a signal for one of those wars of court intrigue which were to disfigure the whole reign. The Empress's ardent wish to give an heir to the throne was disappointed time after time by the successive birth of four daughters, and when at last, in the midst of the disasters of the Japanese War, the little heir arrived in 1904, it was found that he was marked by the hereditary ailment of his mother's family. He was hæmophilic; the slightest scratch might lead to internal bleeding which there was no known means of stopping. Full of spirit, he had to be deterred as far as possible from any childish games and sports. The radiant health of his four sisters seemed a mockery of his ailment, and the Empress could not herself forget that the disease was transmitted through her.

In the most striking contrast with this succession of misfortunes stands out the picture of the home life of the Imperial family. While one is reading this story, one seems almost as much cut off from the outside world as were the actors in it; they had no ambitions, their requirements were healthy and of the most modest kind; there was nothing to make them wish to look outside their own life, everything to deter them from doing so. The Emperor, who as an emperor was so conspicuous a failure, was the most tender and devoted of husbands, and in the home circle that strong natural charm which impressed everyone who met him had full, free play. The Empress adored him, as is clear from these letters. There was no feeling of superiority, but a deep pity for the burden which he had to bear and the unsuitability of it to his yielding and lovable character. The family was brought up on strictly English lines. The four girls, by a tradition of Alexander I, slept only on camp beds. They had a cold bath every day. There was nothing whatever of pomp in their relations with their servants, all of whom seemed to have become their friends. The presents which they received might have been those of an ordinary family in England; such were also their many family jokes. Though not at all mindless, they hardly seem to have had any intellectual requirements. In all the records of this life which we have, they stand out as a charming family. No two were very alike; Olga is perhaps the most determined, Tatanya the most industrious and helpful to her mother, the plump Marie is the good-natured "Tou-Tou," and little Anastasia is the maker of mischief. Anastasia on the imperial yacht hides under the table and pinches the calves of sedate admirals or ministers, who have difficulty in keeping their faces until the Emperor puts down his hand and drags the miscreant out by her hair. During the Revolution the whole family had measles one after the other, and their hair had to be cut off. Nice little caps were made for them and Olga induces Zhilik (M. Gilliard) to photograph them in these caps. Just as he pulls the catch, at a signal from Olga all the girls remove the caps and are photographed capless and hairless. All the four girls were absolutely devoted to the little Tsarevich, whose health was a constant source of anxiety to all of them. The boy himself shows plenty of mind and a remarkable sympathy for any suffering of others. He spends most of the day with his sailor-guardian Derevenko, who, after countless favours, was to desert the family disgracefully at the moment of the Revolution. Two doctors are in more or less constant attendance: Dr. Botkin, not an ordinary court physician, more like a family doctor, a man of Liberal opinions which did not prevent him from being devoted to the family. Dr. Botkin followed them to Siberia and into the dismal house at Ekaterinburg, where with them he met his death. He has an assistant, curiously also named Derevenko, who is equally devoted as Botkin. M. Gilliard, too, is a real friend of the family, and so is Mr. Gibbs, who, like M. Gilliard, followed the family to Siberia and then to Ekaterinburg, where they were turned back on the platform from accompanying their friends farther. Reading of their daily life, it is difficult to remember that the Emperor is emperor. It is not a question of his entire simplicity; it is that there seems hardly any place for the cares of State. The Emperor worked in a room apart like any other man of business, but he had time for walks with his children in the park once or even twice a day. Both he and the Empress took the closest part in the education of their children. The evenings he spent reading aloud to the family. The rooms themselves were cosy and simply furnished. Guests were seldom seen at the family table, though one of the greatest treats which the Emperor gave to those whom he really liked was to invite them to one of these simple meals. Even for most of the Imperial family access to the palace was comparatively rare. The real intimates can be counted on the fingers.

The chief of these is Anna Vyrubova, who lives just outside the park and comes in ordinarily after breakfast. This woman of mystery, if one reads her book and the other records about her, seems very simple indeed. The reader may be specially referred to two passages of M. Paléologue where he describes his meetings with her when she was sent to get his opinion by the Emperor and Empress. She strikes him by her complete mediocrity, and that indeed is how the court of Tsarskoe Selo struck all visitors. Later Maxim Gorky stated that the life of Tsarskoe, which was fully investigated by the Bolsheviks, proved to be of the most respectable bourgeois kind. "Ania," as she appears in the letters, was a daughter of General Taneyev, whose family for close on a hundred years had held the post of head of the Emperor's chancery. She is a weak and childish person, full of her own moods, and very selfish in her indulgence of them, as also appears in several passages from the Empress's letters. She does not seem to have been a person who could have dominated anyone. As to politics, as M. Gilliard says, she was quite incapable of understanding or directing them. Anna Vyrubova has nothing like the strength or the *morale* of the

Empress. She is usually a child to be petted, to be pitied and to be appeased. She was always in love with someone or other, says Madame Dehn, and the Empress has some bitter passages on the same subject. As to her relations with Rasputin, her own book gives no light, although she enters fully into the subject. What is clear is this, that Anna had no political importance except as transmitting to the Empress and Emperor the instructions of Rasputin.

The mystical tinge of the Empress's mind has already been mentioned. She had, we are told, " a very strong inner life " and could remain for hours absorbed in contemplation. She herself strongly disclaimed spiritualism. " It is a great sin," she said. But to everything mystic her miserable surroundings urged her strongly, and one cannot think that she saw any clear frontier between the two. A charlatan doctor of nervous diseases at Lyons, one Philippe, who worked in what he called " astral medicine " and had been fined three times for posing as a regular practitioner, was introduced to the Grand Duchess Militsa, the Montenegrin Princess who had married the Grand Duke Peter Nikolayevich, and to her sister Anastasia, the Stana of these letters, married first to the Duke of Leuchtenberg and after her divorce in 1907 to the Grand Duke Nikolay Nikolayevich. Philippe, who was in person insignificant but had a remarkable attraction of manner, was through the Grand Duchesses presented to the imperial couple in 1901 at Compiègne during their visit to France and was later taken by them to. TsarskoeWe read of séances in which Philippe called up the spirit of Alexander III (whose wishes always possessed an immense authority for his son). We read even of a claim of Philippe that he could fix the sex of children, and from Witte's *Memoirs* and elsewhere we understand that the Empress was strongly persuaded that she was enceinte in the autumn of 1902. In 1904, however, Philippe definitely interfered in politics, and as his first steps in this field were very indiscreet—for instance, he promised quick success in the war against Japan—he left Russia in disgrace and died in France in August 1905. Philippe had told the Empress that she would have a second friend who would talk to her of God. He also, as we learn from the letters, gave her a bell as a symbol that she was to warn the Emperor against those who wished to influence him.

Philippe's successor was the famous Rasputin. The name itself is not a surname, but a nickname given him by his fellow-peasants and meaning "the dissolute." Gregory, who was born in 1871, was a simple peasant of the village of Pokrovskoe, not far from Tobolsk in Siberia. After a most disorderly youth he retired to a neighbouring monastery, and on his return obtained among the peasants a reputation for wonderful spiritual powers. The disorders in his life did not cease; they broke out from time to time with extraordinary violence. But this, it was claimed, only gave the more force to his reiterated repentances. Rasputin was not a monk, but one of those "holy" men who wandered about among the people claiming a direct commission from God, a type of extravagant and unlicensed individualism of which there are many instances in the story of the Orthodox Church. Throughout he claimed to be the typical man of the people, and it was as such that he was welcomed in Petrograd by the Rector of the Theological Academy, Bishop Feofan, who was confessor to the Empress. Certified by Feofan, Rasputin entered the circle of the Montenegrin Grand Duchesses and the Grand Duke Nicholas, and it was from them that he was passed on to the Palace at Tsarskoe in the summer of 1907. Rasputin never sought to flatter the sovereigns; he even spoke roughly to them from the first. He was early associated with another charlatan, the Buryat doctor Badmayev, who was guilty of money frauds. Rasputin's visits to the place have been greatly exaggerated. M. Gilliard, who only once set eyes on him, says that Rasputin did not see either of the sovereigns more than once a month and sometimes much less frequently. According to Anna Vyrubova, it was only twice or thrice a year before the war and from four to six times afterwards; she maintains that Rasputin only saw the Emperor once throughout the critical year, 1916. Most of the meetings took place not in the palace but in the little house outside the park tenanted by Vyrubova. Far more often the messages from Rasputin to the Emperor and

Empress were, in the language of these letters, " handed over " by Anna and often they were in the form of telegrams to her. We must believe that the Empress never saw anything of the man's vileness, though once she mentions in the letters that " he was not tipsy." Both Madame Dehn and Anna Vyrubova strongly disclaim any knowledge of this side of his character. Madame Dehn is convinced that even for Anna Vyrubova Rasputin was nothing more than a holy man, though her book, like the Empress's letters, represents Anna as a person who would be in love with anyone. It is possible to believe this. But Petrograd itself could be in no doubt about the man's real character. He was a standing outrage on decencies. Even Vyrubova admits that during the war adventurers " took advantage of his simplicity," took him out to dinner and gave him too much drink. As to the sexual exploits there can be no question. They were innumerable, and several of them were openly vaunted by the women who fell victims to him. In March 1911, to counteract these public scandals, Rasputin made a visit to Jerusalem, but was back in Petrograd by November. There followed further orgies, and Rasputin was now openly condemned both by Bishop Feofan and by two others who had formerly been his strong supporters—Bishop Hermogen of Saratov and the monk Heliodore—who spat at him and struck him, and were very shortly afterwards relegated to monasteries. At this time the newspapers printed numberless instances of Rasputin's seductions. By the so-called press-reform made during the Revolution of 1904–7, the preliminary censorship had been abolished, and papers could print what they pleased at the risk of being arbitrarily fined by the local governors after publication. This risk they were glad to take in the case of Rasputin, but the Empress secured from the Emperor an order that there should be nothing printed at all on the subject. Thereby the Emperor broke his own law and the leader of the Duma, Alexander Guchkov, seized the occasion for an interpellation and a public debate on Rasputin. In March 1912 the Prime Minister, Kokovtsev, a strong but enlightened Conservative, urged the Emperor to send Rasputin away from Petrograd. Rasputin departed of himself with an insolent threat to Kokovtsev, and when the Prime Minister visited the sovereigns in Livadia in May the Empress turned her back on him. At the beginning of 1914 Kokovtsev was summarily dismissed without explanation.

It may be true, as is urged, that in the main the Empress confined her interventions in politics up to the war to obtaining the dismissals of those Ministers who were hostile to Rasputin. As to Rasputin himself, the part which he took in politics was soon an active one. The pleas of Vyrubova on this point will not hold good for an instant. There is no need to regard him as a champion of any particular view except that of autocratic absolutism, which alone could enable him to penetrate an ignorant palace as the voice of the Russian peasants. But his good offices were constantly sought by political adventurers, and he himself was probably not conscious of the extent to which he was being used as a tool.

The foundation of Rasputin's influence with the Empress is quite clear. Before 1912 he had been called in to help with his counsel, and more than that, even with his prophecies, at moments critical to the health of the Tsarevich. In the summer of this year the Imperial family was at one of the Emperor's shooting-boxes in Poland, when Alexis fell while getting out of a boat so that he bruised his groin against the gunwale. This and a subsequent piece of negligence brought on a most serious crisis, and the parents were half beside themselves with anxiety. The doctors declared themselves helpless. Of course anything like an operation was at all times out of the question, and the internal bleeding could not be stopped. Recourse was made by telegraph to Rasputin, who replied at once: "This illness is not as dangerous as it looks. Let the doctors not torture him." It was from that moment that the danger rapidly passed away. In December 1915, while the Tsarevich was with his father at General Headquarters, there was another serious crisis, and the Emperor was bringing him back to Tsarskoe with little hope that the boy would arrive alive. Medical help was again impotent, and Rasputin intervened with a message which again coincided exactly with the passing of the crisis. Rasputin was certainly believed by most of his admirers to have the gift of prophecy. Anna Vyrubova says he was never wrong and gives several instances, some of them surprising. M. Gilliard thinks that Rasputin, who was certainly very astute, took care to be excellently posted as to all matters in which he ventured to intervene. As his influence increased, this certainly became much easier for him. Some of his messages almost amount to threats that the child is in danger if he, Rasputin, is not listened to. From this it was an easy step to demand, for instance, the dismissal of a minister or the promotion of a protégé. The Empress looked upon everything that he said as coming from a "Man of God."

Rasputin, as has been seen, was well known in Petrograd society before he met the sovereigns, and had already been taken up by other members of the Imperial family. Petrograd society, as will have been understood, was a different world from that of Tsarskoe. We have throughout this story three different worlds: the palace, the higher aristocracy and the general public; and, strange as it may seem, the aristocracy seems to have known even less of Tsarskoe than it did of the general public. The Dowager Empress was on anything but good terms with the Empress. At the beginning of the reign the Emperor was guided chiefly by his mother's counsels, and friends of the Empress complain that she was always overshadowed. Later she had the Emperor to herself, but almost completely cut him off from his mother. In every record of any value—take, for instance, Count Witte and M. Paléologue—we have a tribute to the sound sense and patriotism of the Dowager Empress. She made many efforts to persuade her son of the fatal influence of Rasputin, but the only result was to complete the break. Not that the Emperor ever quarrelled with his mother; he was far too gentle for that; but intimacy more or less ceased. The Empress's elder sister, the Grand Duchess Elizabeth, after the assassination of her husband, the Grand Duke Sergius, in February 1905, became the mother-superior of a religious community which she founded, and lived always in Moscow. She, too, repeatedly warned her sister and with the same result. The Emperor's brother Michael, usually regarded as a man of Liberal opinions but of weak will, fell shortly before the war completely under the influence of a lady divorced, remarried, and divorced again to marry the Grand Duke. The marriage, which took place in 1913, was strictly against the wishes of the Emperor, who said that Michael had promised him not to do it. He was, however, persuaded to give to the wife the title of Countess Brassov. The Countess made a point of emphasising her Liberalism and gathered round her a society which could only be very distasteful to the Emperor.

Of the cousins the nearest branch were the family of the late Grand Duke Vladimir, brother of Alexander III, who married Princess Marie of Mecklenburg-Schwerin, one of the two Maria P.'s of these letters (the other being the daughter of the Grand Duke Paul). Of Maria Pavlovna we have a very full picture in the memoirs of M. Paléologue. Though German by birth, she was strongly against the Hohenzollerns and entirely for Russia in the war. She at one time asked the hand of the Grand Duchess Olga for her dissolute son, Boris, and the Empress's very natural opposition was thought to have rankled afterwards. One of the principal leaders of Petrograd society, Maria Pavlovna stands out as a constant critic of the hopeless isolation and the growing discredit of the Imperial couple. Her elder son Cyril took a prominent part in the family movement of indignation or more, shortly before the Revolution, and was one of the first to offer his sword to the Imperial Duma. Boris is responsible for a capricious outburst against the English friendship, which led to his receiving a well-deserved rebuke from the Emperor. The allusion to this incident in the letters is one of the innumerable proofs of the strong English sympathies of the Empress. The Emperor had one remaining uncle, the Grand Duke Paul, whose part throughout this period was also that of a critic. Like nearly all other members of the Imperial family who possessed any consequence, he gave his warning against the fatal rule of the Empress on the eve of the Revolution. His son Dmitry, though not actually the assassinator of Rasputin, was one of those who was present. The second wife of the Grand Duke Paul was the Princess Paley, authoress of the book on this period which has been mentioned.

Farther removed from the throne were the Grand Duke

Sergius Mikhaylovich, who was at the head of the Russian Artillery and is described as a hard worker and capable organiser, and his brother Nikolay Mikhaylovich, who has his part in these letters. He had written serious historical works on the Napoleonic period and was regarded as a Liberal Grand Duke, almost as a Philippe Egalité. He had no strength of will, but his protest was not lacking during the last crisis.

For energy and character, far the most distinguished of the Grand Dukes was Nikolay Nikolayevich, whose father was the third son of the Emperor Nicholas I. The Grand Duke had long taken a distinguished part in public affairs. He was head of the Council of Imperial Defence during the Japanese War. In October 1905, at a moment of Imperial wavering, he strongly insisted on the issue of the constitutional manifesto of that date. We are told that he even threatened to shoot himself at once if an immediate decision were not taken. The Grand Duke came in for a good deal of criticism from the Duma in the notable session of 1908 when the military scandals of the Japanese War became the chief plea for the programme of patriotic reform introduced in the Duma by its leader Alexander Guchkov. The two men, though later almost forced to work together, had little sympathy for each other. Several writers, among others Count Witte, agree in describing Nicholas as extremely excitable. Witte tells us of an avowal of Nicholas in which he declared that he looked upon his sovereign as God. There is no doubt that he too, like his wife, was one of the early protectors of Rasputin. This explains repeated references in the letters where the Empress condemns the Grand Duke as "one who has abandoned a man of God." Nicholas had long, however, held the position of a critic. The two Montenegrin Princesses, who came in for a great deal of abuse from Witte as having brought all sorts of misfortunes upon Russia, certainly came to be in sharp opposition to the Imperial couple. One thing comes out clearly as to the Grand Duke Nicholas. He was a man, perhaps as we understand it the only man in the Imperial family. He was also a splendid soldier. His merits as Commander-in-Chief will not yet be fixed, though his antagonists

Hindenburg and Ludendorff both had a very high opinion of his ability. But as a man with will and with complete honesty of purpose, the Grand Duke was anyhow an enormous asset in the post of Commander-in-Chief of the Russian Army. Many of his best remarks are unprintable. But they were always to the point and always deserved. In the story of Russia's tragedy there may be moments where he made mistakes, but there is nothing which does not do him honour.

There were a few persons whose honesty of intention enabled them to serve as links between the three isolated worlds of which I have spoken: the Court, the aristocracy and the public. Such was General Dzhunkovsky, Commander of the Guard, earlier City Prefect of Moscow, a devoted servant of the Crown and of the Imperial family, but fearless enough to tell it the full truth. Such also was General Orlov, described by Vyrubova as the only friend the Emperor ever had, Commander of his Military Chancery, equally loyal and equally fearless. Such again was Samarin, Marshal of the Moscow nobility, devoted to the Orthodox Church and to the autocracy, full of the old Slavophil tradition, and for that very reason distressed that any barrier should separate the Emperor from his people.

The Ministers themselves did not as such possess any credit at Court nor necessarily in Petrograd society, nor yet of course could they claim, except in individual cases, such as those of Sazonov, Krivoshein and Samarin, to be in any way representative of public opinion. A greater importance perhaps attached during the war to the Ambassadors of the two principal Allied States, M. Paléologue and Sir George Buchanan. M. Paléologue's admirable book is, among other things, a self-revelation. He is his own critic, for he tells time and time again how incessantly he harried the Ministers for military and other steps in support of the French. One cannot but think that this was the surest way of exhausting the credit of the alliance. The attitude of Sir George Buchanan was quite different. I can remember his saying in the spring of 1915: "I wish we did not ask them to do too much." I know of no one else in Russia who was capable of saying this at the time, but the sequel has proved that Sir George was entirely right. M. Paléologue probably knew better than Sir George the ins and outs of the higher Petrograd society, but from his book I should judge that he had not so close an acquaintance with the currents of public opinion or the aims of the chief political parties. His book is remarkable for a knowledge, most unusual for a foreigner, of Russia's past history and of Russian culture. Both the Ambassadors had every opportunity of putting their desires before the Emperor, which he almost invariably did his best to carry out. It was, for instance, a great deal that M. Paléologue asked when he requested the amnesty of the revolutionary Burtsev, who had been associated with successful plots against members of the Government.

It remains here only to mention the relations of the Imperial couple with two of their royal kinsfolk. The Empress, as is clear both from the letters and from other records, had the greatest dislike for the Emperor William. She considered that he was responsible for the war and that in making it he made the greatest mistake of his life. Her feeling towards him was certainly shared by many of the princes of Germany, but her own feeling was prompted by her Russian patriotism and her strong English sympathies. The Princess Victoria of Battenberg, sister of the Empress, was credited with having a great deal of influence with the Emperor, and we are told that she also gave her warning before the Revolution.

From the almost complete isolation of the Imperial couple, from the thin top stratum of Petrograd society, we will turn to the life of the country as a whole. Russia at the beginning of the war had reached a critical stage in her history, of which the importance is even now hardly realised at all. The emancipation of the serfs in 1861 was itself a most belated reform forced on all classes by sheer necessity and leaving all sorts of arrears to be made up. It completely altered the basis of the Russian community. It set rolling masses of free peasant labour; it initiated the formation of a town proletariat; it created the beginnings of Russian industry; it made the old class basis of Russia an anachronism and an absurdity.

In particular, it necessitated the creation of a whole new system of local government based on the principles of election and responsibility to the public. These principles, applied to local government by Alexander II, were desperately resisted by the central authorities up till the bankruptcy of government credit and the national catastrophe of the Japanese War. The movement of the public which followed this failure affected all classes and all nationalities of the empire and at least brought the institution of a national representative assembly, the Duma. The first two Dumas tried to make the system of government frankly and completely constitutional. Each of them was dissolved after a life of a few months, and the franchise was drastically altered to assure the predominance in the Assembly to the gentry class. But no national representation in Russia at that time could fail to be critical; and starting with a sober sense of the failures of 1906 and 1907, the Third Duma, unrepresentative as it was, came more and more to embody the good sense of the nation, which was in hopeless conflict with the extremely incompetent bureaucracy. The Emperor William on several occasions threw his influence at the Russian Court into the scale against representative institutions, and when the challenge of Germany was taken up by Russia in July 1914, this was of itself a great victory for Russian constitutionalism. All the more so because the beginnings of constitutionalism in Russia had been inevitably accompanied by a strong movement of attraction towards France and England, which were now Russia's allies against Germany. The victory of constitutionalism was now possible, but it was not as yet by any means won.

When the war began, the Russian ministers might be divided into three groups: the Prime Minister, Goremykin, was a thorough Russian patriot, but a thorough Conservative or even a Reactionary in home affairs; with him one may perhaps class the Minister of Communications, Rukhlov, who was not much more than a business minister. Goremykin's views in home politics were shared and exaggerated by the Director of the Holy Synod, Sabler, the powerful Minister of the Interior, N. Maklakov, the Minister of Justice, Shcheglovitov, who, himself formerly a Liberal, was the leader of the reactionary extremists, and the Minister of War, General Sukhomlinov, who after co-operating with the Duma in army reform was now its adversary. But these four Ministers went further, and practically had no sympathy for the war at all. Sukhomlinov showed his indifference by a complete failure to equip the army adequately and by sheer dishonesty in concealing this neglect.

But the Ministry also included some who were both eager champions of the war and the Alliance, and convinced believers in the necessity of constitutional rule. Of these the principal was Sazonov, Minister of Foreign Affairs, whose whole public life had been bound up in these two causes. He was a warm personal friend of both the British and the French Ambassadors, and these were inevitably brought by the war into some participation in the internal issues of Russia. He was supported by Krivoshein, the very able Minister of Agriculture, by Kharitonov, the Imperial Comptroller, and to a certain extent by Bark, the Minister of Finance, and Admiral Gregorovich, the Minister of the Navy.

When the war crisis was in progress, Rasputin sent a telegram to the Emperor strongly asking " Papa " " not to plan war," for " from that war will come the end of Russia and yourselves ; we shall lose to the last man." The Empress was of course much afflicted at the thought of war, and the Emperor did not inform her of the order for mobilisation. But she at once set herself to do her full duty for Russia, and Russian patriotism glows in her letters, not least in those which she wrote after the abdication from her captivity in Tobolsk. Rasputin's interference annoyed the Emperor, and in the first period of the war he had no influence. The Empress with her four daughters went through a thorough course of training in nursing ; and when we realise that she had a very weak heart which was constantly giving her trouble, we must be astonished at the enormous amount of work which she did for the wounded. This was not mere official patronising of Red Cross organisations. She herself took a frequent part in the most disagreeable details of dressing and nursing, and travelled from one part to another to promote the work of the Red Cross.

The Emperor's acceptance of the German challenge occasioned

a scene of public enthusiasm which seemed almost unbelievable to many of those who witnessed it. When he appeared on the balcony of the Winter Palace, the enormous crowd outside was on its knees. The Emperor himself was extremely invigorated, as he said many times, by this close contact with his people. After a short session full of the liveliest patriotism, the leading members of the Duma in most cases went to the front to take an active part in the subsidiary services of the Army. Goremykin himself asked the Union of Zemstva Red Cross to supplement the quite inadequate provision of the Government for the wounded. This organisation had been persecuted during the Japanese War. Prince George Lvov, who was at its head, almost within the first month of the war, had organised provision for a million wounded. The Union of Zemstva was invaluable in supplementing not only the inadequate medical service of the Army (there were five surgeons only to every 4,000 men, very often less), but also the defective arrangements for food-supply and for transport. It must be remembered that this Union was the equivalent of a Union of all the County Councils of England, and was therefore a more representative body than any other in the country except the Duma.

The great epic period of the war on the Russian front was the first chapter of it. Believing that the whole issue could be settled in a few months, the Russians, to whom the war was more popular than any other could have been, made the greatest sacrifices, suffered the most overwhelming casualties and won, on one side at least, brilliant results. The battle of Tannenberg was a tremendous reverse for Russia, involving a loss of something like 250,000 men. Very heavy also were the losses in the battle of the Mazurian Lakes, where defeat was due, as at Tannenberg, largely to the incompetence of General Rennenkampf. But in Galicia, on a front of something like 150 miles, General Alexeyev, the Chief of the Staff of the South-western front, completely outplayed an invading Austrian army of close on a million men, and by allowing it to advance its centre and meanwhile outflanking it with large masses from either side, he drove it in headlong flight, not only back into Galicia but almost out of that great province.

In May 1915 opened a new period. The Austrian Army was nearly broken and there was already talk of a separate peace. Count Tisza's Hungarian country house was already in the hands of the Russian Army and he hurried to Berlin to demand immediate help. There followed what seems to have been the first of those tremendous concentrations of artillery at a given point, of which there was to be a succession in ever greater proportions throughout the war. The southern Russian armies were almost entirely without heavy artillery. Worse than that, through the criminal neglect of Sukhomlinov, at the end of 1914 the supplies of ammunition had almost ceased. The victorious Russian infantry entrenched along the top of the Carpathians and in Western Galicia was overwhelmed with metal, and the remainder of this heroic host, retreating slowly and always showing a firm countenance to the enemy, was driven out of Galicia and far into Russia. This brought with it the fall of Warsaw, and the Germans advanced all along the front till in the autumn of 1915 they took up their winter quarters in the Pinsk marshes. It was only by vigorous countermeasures of General Plehve and others that some of the most important remaining strategic railways of Russia were secured from the Germans. All this created an entirely new situation in home affairs, bringing Russia nearer to a real constitution than she had ever been before.

The country was attached to the Army with a devotion which cannot be forgotten by anyone who saw it, and of which there is a wonderfully good picture in Mr. Hugh Walpole's book *The Dark Forest*. The Russian losses up to June 1915 amounted to 3,800,000.* Meanwhile there were splendid records of heroism, such as the routing of two Austrian divisions by one Russian with the bayonet at Krasnustaw after all the Russian ammunition was expended. Men had even been sent under fire without rifles in their hands. Officers had been punished for firing more than three shells a day. Batteries had been reduced throughout the Army from six guns to four. There was an irresistible movement of indignation. The

* The figure which was then given to me by the Russian War Office for communication to our own Government. I have reason to think that it was an understatement.

Emperor himself was devoted to his Army. On June 25 he summoned his Ministers to General Headquarters and there dismissed Sukhomlinov, at the same time calling the Duma for August 1 and appealing for a great effort of the country as a whole. Maklakov, Shcheglovitov and Sabler were also dismissed as being out of sympathy with the war. The new War Minister was General Polivanov, who had always worked in the most cordial collaboration with the Duma, in particular with the leader of the largest party in it, Guchkov. The new Minister of the Interior was Prince Shcherbatov, a practical administrator of moderate Liberal opinions, frank and plain-spoken. The new Minister of Justice was a respected member of the Upper House, Alexander Alexeyevich Khvostov. The new Procurator of the Holy Synod was the most distinguished member of the Moscow nobility, Samarin, like all his family closely associated with the Slavophil tradition, which, while supporting the Russian autocracy, claimed that the autocrat should be in the closest union with his people, and well fitted to co-operate with the other new Ministers in the national effort called for by the Emperor. The Duma met on August 1 and voted by an enormous majority for the trial of Sukhomlinov. This was accorded. It also asked for the establishment of a central Committee of War Industries for the supply of munitions, which should include representatives of the two legislative chambers. This was also granted, and the most prominent men both of the Duma and of the Zemstva Union became active workers on this committee. Inevitably the Allies were brought into the question of munitions. Lord Kitchener, unable to get from Sukhomlinov the information which he asked, had entered into direct communication with the Commander-in-Chief, the Grand Duke Nicholas, and was actually appointed agent of the Russian Army with a free hand to purchase munitions. To help the munitioning of Russia there was established a special department in the British War Office, and later in the year Colonel Knox, our able military attaché in Petrograd, visited England and France with results which were of the first importance to the Russian Army.

There was no question as to the tendency which all these

changes emphasised. Closer union with the Allies inevitably meant the progress of the constitutional cause in Russia. An appeal to the Duma and to the people had inevitably the same bearing. There was no question whatever as to the Empress's loyalty to Russia during the war, nor as to her devotion to the Russian Army; but constitutionalism was to her anathema. It meant the limitation of absolute power for her son. Since October 1905, no one could have stated exactly whether the Emperor had accepted that limitation of his authority which seemed the logical inference of the manifesto of October 30, 1905; nor could one say that the manifesto itself had ever been carried out with any sincerity. In any case this was the moment when the Empress abandoned all restraint and threw herself heart and soul into a battle with Russian constitutionalism. Rasputin had for some time been absent from Petrograd, but after the reverses of May his influence was stronger than ever. He was very fully informed and at first proceeded cautiously. The Empress herself at first, while urging his opinions on the Emperor, still offers excuses for her own interference. Rasputin on July 22 went to his Siberian home. He returned in the middle of August and threw himself more and more into the fight with the Duma. The Duma at this time with practical unanimity declared for a ministry which should have the full confidence of the people. This formula was a concession of the Liberal majority to those Conservatives who were not ready to demand that the Ministers should be chosen by the Duma. The great majority of the Duma, including nearly all the brains in it, formed into a single Progressive Bloc, for which the way had long been prepared, and was even able to propose a detailed unanimous programme of long-deferred reforms.

From July 11 the Emperor spent two months in Tsarskoe. This of course gave the Empress her opportunity, and the crisis of the struggle is not recorded in the letters. For her, even more odious and more dangerous than the Duma was the Grand Duke Nicholas. In her earlier letters we see that she is morbidly fearful that he would acquire a moral authority replacing that of the Emperor. Madame Vyrubova was always ready to repeat malicious gossip from officers at General Headquarters against the Grand Duke. She even at one time bunches together the names of all the foreign military attachés (including General Hanbury Williams, who was devoted to Nicholas II) as conspirators against the Emperor. The Grand Duke may have let fall the suggestion that the Empress should retire to a convent. This and more than this was current gossip at the time. Some even accused him of having allowed himself to be spoken of as Nicholas III. It can only be said that everything in the conduct of the Grand Duke (and there is plenty of light thrown on this question) is a flat contradiction to any possible doubt as to his loyalty. In any case, on August 24, the Ministers were summoned to Tsarskoe and there informed that the Emperor had decided to take over the Command in Chief. They were astounded; and particularly Sazonov used every effort to dissuade him. Vyrubova relates how on his return to his family he says: "I was firm; see how I have been perspiring"; and tells how he held fast in his left hand throughout the interview the little ikon given him before it. The decision was received with connsteration on all sides, but there was at least one point which it finally cleared up. By going permanently to the Army, and still more by the remarkably vigorous manifesto which he then issued, the Emperor showed friends and foes alike that he was absolutely committed to war to the end—a decision in which he never for a moment wavered.

With the Emperor at Headquarters, the Empress assumes an altogether new rôle in the Government. She describes herself later as "his wall in the rear." The Ministers, with a growing regularity, come to her with their reports. She herself remarks later that she is the first Russian Empress to have received them regularly since Catherine the Great—hardly a tactful thing to write to the new Catherine's husband. The change did not come all at once; but from the very outset she was in constant communication with Goremykin for the dismissal of the new more Liberal Ministers. The record of her letters here hardly needs any supplement or explanation. In letter after letter she urges the dismissal of Shcherbatov and of Samarin and more than suggests that of Polivanov and Sazonov.

Sazonov's Memoirs, when they appear, will no doubt clear up one episode in this story. The Liberal Ministers had seen the leaders of the Duma. They addressed in September a joint memorial to the Sovereign which directly or indirectly supported the Duma formula of a Ministry possessing the confidence of the country, that is of course of the legislature. They definitely expressed their difficulty in serving under the premiership of Goremykin. We gather that those who signed this memorial explained that they could not effectively do their work under the existing conditions. The Ministers of War and of the Navy abstained from signing on grounds of service discipline, but supported the view of those who signed.* Anyhow, the Emperor summoned the Ministers to Headquarters on September 29, and there told them that he would not allow of any "strike" against the Premier Goremykin. He ordered them to continue in their work, but is believed to have told them that he would relieve any who had signed the memorial when he found more suitable successors. The Empress's letters are full of the details of this search for substitutes in which clearly most of the suggestions came from herself.

The Duma had been prorogued (September 16), and a meeting of the Union of Zemstva and Towns again calling for a Ministry which commanded the public confidence had been silenced (September 20); its deputies to the Emperor were refused an audience. There followed a notable scandal in the affairs of the Church. A comrade of Rasputin, Varnava, had been made Archbishop of Tobolsk, and had on his own initiative announced the canonisation of a new saint, Bishop John of Tobolsk. This was against all Church law, and the Synod vigorously protested. Samarin sent Varnava and his supporters to seclusion in monasteries. Varnava, however, over the head of the Synod, secured a direct approval of his act from the Emperor. This was a plain triumph of the influence of Rasputin. Samarin did his utmost to bring home to the Emperor the evil of Rasputin's influence in Church

* The memorial was signed by Sazonov, Krivoshein, Bark, Shcherbatov, Samarin, and Shakhovskoy.

affairs, and this is the text of several indignant letters from the Empress. It was not long before she prevailed, and both Samarin and Shcherbatov were dismissed (October 9). The same fate befell Krivoshein on November 9. The dismissal of Samarin infuriated the most Conservative body of opinion in Russia, the nobility of Russia, and laid bare the open degradation of the Church, which lay at the mercy of Rasputin.

The new Procurator was a nonentity and even he, it would seem, was not a willing instrument; to all intents and purposes from this time onwards the Procurator was Rasputin. The new Minister of the Interior was Alexis Nikolayevich Khvostov, a strongly Conservative member of the Duma, chosen by the Empress mainly because he might know how to deal with that body. This nomination was entirely her work, as is made evident by the letters. Khvostov owed his elevation to Rasputin, but being a man of very independent character it was not long before he tried to cut himself free from his trammels. There followed, then, after some months a bitter conflict between Khvostov and Rasputin. Khvostov had recourse to the help of the fanatical monk Heliodore, formerly a friend, now an enemy, of Rasputin, and dispatched an agent to the monk, who was then living in Copenhagen. Heliodore had recently threatened the Emperor directly that he would publish in the United States an exposure of Rasputin. Khvostov's agent, it was later reported, was to plot with Heliodore the assassination of Rasputin. The agent was intercepted by the Director of the Department of Police, Beletsky, who was one of Rasputin's supporters. The scandal never came fully before the public; both Khvostov and Beletsky ultimately lost their posts.*

Already in the autumn of 1915 it was clear that Rasputin was the most powerful man in Russia. For instance, General Mishchenko, with whom I was staying at that time, sent an A.D.C. to Petrograd to find out what was going wrong with army supplies, and the officer, who returned during my visit, explained that nothing at all could be done now without Rasputin's support. He

* A full explanation of this incident is given by Rudnev, who regards the plot as a police provocation on the part of Beletsky.

did not assume the direction of affairs. He was still careful in his interventions, but that his approval was the first qualification for a ministerial post was already clear. The shame of this domination led to protests from two honest servants of the Emperor, already mentioned, General Dzhunkovsky and Prince Orlov. Rasputin had in the spring visited the tombs of the Metropolitans at Moscow and spent the evening at the most notorious place of entertainment in the town, a kind of Moulin Rouge, called by the name of Yar. Here he was both drunk and disorderly, and on being challenged used words which were deeply insulting to the Empress herself—"as to the old woman, I can do what I like." Dzhunkovsky, we are told, presented the police record of this scene to the Emperor, and he was dismissed from all Court appointments (September 8). Prince Orlov had more than once urged the dismissal of Rasputin. Now, we are told, he did so upon his knees, with the result that he was called upon to resign (September 5). Both these episodes have several echoes in the Empress's letters. One sees that the separation of the Sovereigns from the people is gradually becoming complete. Even the Moscow nobility, even the Imperial family, even the most loyal servants of the Palace are affronted, and from this time onwards we read in these letters, as a kind of running comment on every appointment or dismissal, "he venerates Our Friend" (that is, Rasputin), or, "he does not like Our Friend."

The prorogation of the Duma was from time to time prolonged. Old Goremykin, nearly ninety years of age, frankly feared to face it under the new conditions, and it was definitely his fear of the Duma and the Empress's own feeling of his weakness that led her in the end to recommend his resignation. The new appointment made on February 2, 1916, on the eve of the meeting of the Duma, was more astonishing than any that preceded it. The new Prime Minister, obviously the choice of the Empress, was Stürmer. He had been Governor in Yaroslavl and had conducted a savage repression of the Liberal County Council in Tver. He was also a Master of Ceremonies at the Court. He was simply known to the public for large defalcations, and typical enough was the report current at this time that at the outset of his premiership he informed his colleagues that a large sum was reserved to him for uncontrolled disposition, to which he asked their signatures. He was of course an obsequious follower of Rasputin. Stürmer himself was not really a man of any strength of character or of will. He was a puppet. With the most various of persons he left the impression of weakness and dishonesty. Stürmer was regularly received by the Empress for the conduct of affairs. The Duma was called for February 22, and on the suggestion of no other than Count Fredericks, who certainly wished the Emperor to stand well with his people, Nicholas took the occasion of the opening to pay his first visit to it. He was rapturously received. For the first time he addressed the Duma as " representatives " of his people, and there was a great and unanimous outburst of patriotism. Rasputin, we are told, greatly deplored this incident. The Emperor the same day left for the front.

The great hopes thus aroused were soon to be disappointed. Of the constitutionalist Ministers there still remained Polivanov, Bark and Sazonov. Military testimony, including, for instance, that of General Knox and of Field-Marshal von Hindenburg, agrees that Polivanov had effected a most remarkable reorganisation of the Russian Army, which might be regarded as entirely saving the position. Munition work had proceeded apace with the energetic collaboration of the Allies. Drafts for the front were now much better trained. But Polivanov, as will be seen from the letters, was to the Empress *persona ingratissima*. It is true he had not signed the memorial of his colleagues, but he was working closely with Guchkov, the principal figure behind the representative Central Munitions Committee, and that was enough. After letter on letter the Empress at last persuaded the Emperor to dismiss him. This blow fell on April 2. Polivanov was directly informed that the cause of his fall was his Liberal opinions and his co-operation with the Munitions Committee. Nicholas did not accept the Empress's recommendation of General Ivanov as a successor. He chose an honourable but mediocre officer, General Shuvayev, who himself bemoaned his own incapacity.

Worse was to follow. One question raised in its most radical form by the war was that of Poland. All Poland was now lost to Russia, nor could it be recovered except by a joint effort of all the Allies, and this of itself tended to make the Polish question an international one. At the outset of the war the Emperor had himself proposed to issue a promise of autonomy to the Polish people. In deference to his more reactionary Ministers he left this initiative to the Grand Duke Nicholas. But when asked by Marquis Wielepolski, he assumed full responsibility for the manifesto. The Empress was entirely opposed to anything of the kind, on the usual ground that it was a robbery of the hereditary rights of her son. More than once the Emperor himself gave a further push to the business when it was hung up by the disinclination of some of his Ministers. Now he again took up the question with Sazonov. He summoned him to Headquarters, entirely approved of his views and ordered him to draft a detailed manifesto on Polish autonomy. It reserved to the Russian Government the control of customs, army and foreign policy, but otherwise the autonomy was to be practically complete. Debated points were to be settled by a special sub-committee to be appointed from the Senate, consisting equally of both nationalities. Sazonov came back and told the British and French Ambassadors that he had triumphed all along the line. He went straight off for a holiday to Finland and there heard on July 21 the news of his dismissal. Both Stürmer and the Empress had visited the Emperor at Headquarters and induced him to reverse his decision. The two Ambassadors made a joint effort to prevent Sazonov's fall, but were unsuccessful. The Ministry of Foreign Affairs was entrusted to Stürmer, that is, practically to Rasputin.

In the summer of 1916 Rasputin made another journey to Siberia in connection with the canonisation of Varnava's new saint, and by the Empress's desire both Anna Vyrubova and Madame Dehn accompanied him. Both have given records of the journey. Madame Dehn maintains that she did everything to persuade him to remain in Siberia, but in vain.

Rasputin's control of Russia was now complete. His reception-room was more than ever the rendezvous of all charlatans and adventurers. Rasputin would give them ill-written notes on slips of paper to the various authorities, who were simply requested to execute his wishes. Rasputin had all along predicted the greatest disasters from the war, so it was not surprising that he became the mouthpiece of a group of persons who wished to put an end to it. He even interfered in military operations, for instance discountenancing an offensive on the side of Riga or dictating, or trying to dictate, arrangements as to transport of food or even of troops. He imposed on Bark, who had remained at his post, an enormous loan. The Synod, of course, was entirely in his hands, and so were all Church appointments. There were few sides of the administration of the Empire with which he did not deal. His instructions, handed over by " Ania," were sent on by the Empress to the Emperor. She sometimes even wrote them out for him or actually drafted a form of telegram for him to send to her with his signature. She herself complains more than once that her head goes round with the complications of the matters with which she deals. Yet she receives from the ante-room of Rasputin a man whom she had so far detested, Bonch Bruyevich, to hear his complaints against his chief, General Ruzsky, to which she begs the Emperor to listen. She is furious because Guchkov has written a letter to Alexeyev in which were the words " all depends on you," and she successfully urges that Alexeyev should be sent for a holiday.

At the beginning of July a party of members of the Duma, sent to England and France to promote closer contact with the Allies, returned to Russia. Its leader was Protopopov, Vice-President of the Duma, who had been picked by the President Rodzianko for this task. I had known him well in the summer of 1915 as right-hand man of Guchkov in the patriotic work for munitions. In England and France he had still maintained the same rôle, as he told me himself on the way back. Directly afterwards, while passing through Stockholm, he entered into long conversations on the subject of peace with a German diplomatist. In Petrograd he indeed maintained an appearance of loyalty to the Allies; but suddenly, through the agency of Rasputin, whom he had earlier met in connection with his taste for spiritualism, he was appointed Minister of the Interior (October 3). Of course after that, practically no one in the Duma would speak to him. Again the Empress imagined that a member of the Duma would be the best weapon for suppressing the Duma.

Protopopov himself was no strong man, though he posed to the Emperor as such. He was simply a mouthpiece of Rasputin. The direct slap in the face which had been given both to the Russian people and to the Allies was bitterly resented. Public affairs were now managed from some mysterious subterranean chamber and scandals of every kind flourished. There was the scandal of Manussein-Manuilov, a member of the secret police, journalist and speculator, who had actually been nominated by Stürmer as his principal private secretary. There were the financial scandals connected with the names of Manus and Rubenstein, big speculative financiers unquestionably favourable to Germany. Rasputin in a visit to Moscow is reported even to have asked the Lefts why they too did not use his good offices. The case of Sukhomlinov was arbitrarily withdrawn on the repeated instances of the Empress contained in these letters. Sukhomlinov himself was removed from prison to a hospital on what seemed quite an insufficient plea of ill-health. She urges the same favour for Rubenstein. The Empress again demands that her husband shall contravene the ordinary course of law, and demand back all the papers on the case of Manuilov. Lines which were always ringing in one's head at this time of national abasement were those which immediately follow Shakespeare's magnificent description of England in *Richard II* : " Is now leased out Like to a tenement or pelting farm."

It is interesting that the Empress herself recognised the inevitableness of the Duma. She would advise the Emperor to " cleverly shut it " ; but it was only tentatively that she hinted at its abolition. Stürmer, even more than Goremykin, was in mortal fear of the Duma. After all he, a weak and obsequious opportunist, would have to go there and answer for all the iniquities

of Rasputin. After long delays the Duma met on November 14. 1916
Stürmer had arranged that immediately after the opening speech the Ministers followed by the Ambassadors would walk out. The crowded public remained, and the empty benches of the Ministers were assailed by a storm of national indignation. All along, it had been the policy of the Liberals to endeavour in every way to postpone revolution till after the war, and the Duma endeavoured by the vigour of its protests to represent, and thus to keep in hand, the wholesale indignation of the country. The Cadet leader, Milyukov, made use of a remark of the amiable and incompetent Shuvayev, who had said, " I am perhaps a fool, but traitor never." Turning this round, Milyukov exposed all the sins of the Government, concluding each item in his indictment with the question : " Is this folly or treason ? " No less vigorous was Shulgin, the Nationalist ; and in a later debate even the most brilliant of the Reactionaries, Purishkevich, came out with a terrible comparison between Rasputin and an earlier " Grishka," the monk Otrepyev, a pretender who in the seventeenth century actually ascended the throne of Moscow. Stürmer never dared to go to the Duma again ; he asked of the Emperor and was refused leave to dissolve it and arrest Milyukov, and, with the agreement of the Empress and Rasputin, was dismissed.

Stürmer's successor was appointed by the Emperor at Headquarters without the Empress and against her wishes (November 23). He was an honest, capable, plain-spoken Conservative, Trepov, who had done good work in putting some degree of order into the chaotic administration of the railways. [Trepov, who was a man, had demanded the dismissal of Protopopov as a condition to his own acceptance of the premiership.] There follows the most feverish period in the Empress's correspondence. Letter after letter she writes to save Protopopov, and ultimately goes down with him to Headquarters herself. [The Emperor kept Protopopov, and ordered Trepov to continue in office.] On the other hand, Trepov, whose position was little understood by the public, had no success in the Duma, where three times he was shouted down. Trepov dragged on as best he could till January. Ultimately his resignation was accepted and with him went the last chance of saving the dynasty.

The administration was already really in the hands of Protopopov and his puppets. It is impossible that the Empress understood or approved of the outrageous swindles which her authority covered. Her letters show her to have been peculiarly ignorant of public affairs. She complained to a friend that honest Ministers could not be found—repeating a constant excuse put forward by the Russian Reactionaries for choosing the most dishonest. Clearly she had only one thing in mind: that no Minister must stand except by the approval of Rasputin. This comes out plainly in all the letters. Evidently she looked upon herself as saving Russia.

The Emperor, after his last feeble flicker of will in the appointment of Trepov, according to all evidence simply sank into a hopeless apathy. He was eating and sleeping badly; he looked miserable. He had come to the Army to win the war and, so far from thinking of peace, the hope of victory was his sole obsession. At times he spoke of making reforms after the war, but there should be nothing while a German army remained in his territory. The rear he evidently left to itself. There was at this time a curtain between front and rear. The front, as many of us can testify, was still clean; the rear was putrid. Not only the Emperor, but Alexeyev, the Generals, and all of us who were there, felt quite sure that the spring offensive of 1917 would be successful. Hindenburg was evidently almost inclined to the same opinion. The rear, therefore, was allowed to go its own way.

Most certainly there were now in the rear strong symptoms of defeatism. Who were exactly the pro-German clique, whether they had anyone of consequence leading them (M. Paléologue mentions Shcheglovitov, and the Empress received N. Maklakov), how far Rasputin was consciously in their hands, are some of the questions of this most confused final period which can hardly yet be answered. There was a very distinct change of attitude towards the Allies, typified by the earlier outbreak of the Grand Duke Boris, who told the English Colonel Thornhill that Russia's next war would be against England. One felt throughout 1916 that the credit of the Allies was being overdrawn and in a measure exhausted. If we count up how many times M. Paléologue went to the War Office to press French demands for help, if we realise that Russians while they appear to yield may resent the more, one can readily understand this gradual change. But the leaders of nearly all sections of society and the public remained the same. In the Army serious signs of defeatism were very few—even Hindenburg bears this testimony ; but in the rear the gospel of defeat was making great progress in the Petrograd garrison, the drafts for the front and the factories, and at the end of October soldiers brought out to repress a street riot joined the people.

Warning after warning streamed in on the isolated Emperor. Samarin, Dzhunkovsky and Orlov had spoken earlier. In this last period there was hardly a member of the Imperial family who possessed any political credit who did not have the courage to say his or her word. Among those who warned the Emperor were the Grand Duke Paul ; his son Dmitry ; the Grand Duke Nikolay Mikhaylovich, who came to Headquarters for the purpose ; the Grand Duke Alexander Mikhaylovich, husband of the Emperor's sister Xenia, who was heard in the Emperor's cabinet at Tsarskoe arguing hotly with him ; the Empress's sisters, Princess Victoria of Battenberg and the Grand Duchess Elizabeth, the latter of whom made an appeal on her knees, was cut short by the Empress and advised to return at once to Moscow ; the new Minister of Foreign Affairs, Pokrovsky, who pleaded with clasped hands ; a leading Nationalist with Court rank, Balashev ; Princess Vasilchikova, wife of a former Conservative Minister ; Admiral Nilov, an old servant and friend ; and both the Allied Ambassadors, M. Paléologue and Sir George Buchanan. M. Paléologue's warning was, it is true, only a tentative one ; but Sir George Buchanan began by saying that when he saw someone of whom he was very fond going over a precipice, he felt bound to warn him, and urged on the Emperor that his only safety lay in making peace with his people.

It is in the middle of these warnings that the last chapter begins with the murder of Rasputin on December 30. Latterly

Rasputin had been guarded by the Palace police and seldom went out. At his last meeting with the Emperor he said: "This time, you bless me!" Passing the Neva one day he declared that he saw it red with blood; there would be many Grand Princes killed and hundreds of nobles. He had declared more than once that his own death, which it was not difficult for him to foresee, would be the beginning of the end. On December 30 Prince Felix Yusupov, married to a niece of the Emperor, came to fetch him in a motor on the plea of introducing him to his wife, who at that time was in the Crimea. In Yusupov's house were gathered a company of strongly Conservative patriots, among whom were the Grand Duke Dmitry Pavlovich and the ultra-Conservative of the Duma Purishkevich. They tried to poison him, but the poison did not take effect. Yusupov shot him, but Rasputin was yet crawling away into the garden, when he was finally killed by Purishkevich.

The Empress was in an agony of distress and lost all hope. Rasputin's body was found near one of the mouths of the Nevka and buried early one morning in grounds adjoining the Palace park in the presence of the whole Imperial family. [The Emperor, who returned in time for this to Tsarskoe, spent some two months at the Palace, but he saw hardly anyone from outside, and was as much cut off from his relations as from the public.] He spent whole days in his cabinet or in the billiard-room. Outside, everyone was talking of a palace revolution. The Imperial family signed a joint letter asking that the Grand Duke Dmitry Pavlovich should be released from house arrest and not be punished. In Moscow at the top of society, as elsewhere, there was open talk of the end of the Emperor Paul by assassination; noisy dinners in Petrograd society repeated the same refrain. The general programme was the deposition of the Emperor, the banishment of the Empress to a monastery, and the accession of the Tsarevich under the regency of the Grand Duke Nicholas. It is known that a patriotic general, Krymov, was planning measures to this end and that he had the sympathy not only of many of the Imperial family, but of some of the Liberal members of the Duma. Protopopov, almost the only visitor to the Empress, boasted that he had the situation well in hand, and spent his evenings in spiritualist séances in which he seems to have invoked the spirit of Rasputin. It was generally thought that he was suffering from the beginnings of mental paralysis. He often spoke boldly of challenging and suppressing the Revolution. There are reasons for thinking that his programme was to provoke an outburst, and after repressing it to turn round to the Allies and to say that with whatever regret Russia could not continue the war in the midst of so many home difficulties. In February there was certainly a distinct shortage of food in Petrograd. This the Palace put down to the revolutionaries. Others with more reason put it to the account of Protopopov. These were the circumstances in which the outburst ultimately came.

The Emperor had called the Duma, he had adjourned it, and it was known that he would prorogue it or dissolve it. It was also known that the Duma would refuse to go. The Emperor had left Tsarskoe again for the Army. Crowds were on the streets calling for bread. The police from the best points of vantage in the city fired with machine guns on these crowds. The soldiers very soon joined with the people against the police (March 12). The Duma out of a belated loyalty contented itself with telegraphing to the Emperor and asking for constitutional reforms. The control meanwhile slipped out of its hands. The Emperor acceded to the Duma's request only when it was too late. Leaving Headquarters, he tried to make his way back to his family, found the line blocked by revolutionaries and turned aside to the Headquarters of General Ruszky at Pskov. There, on March 15, far from the Empress, he acceded without any reluctance to the request unanimously made by all the principal generals, and reinforced the same evening by Guchkov and Shulgin in the name of the Duma. He abdicated not only for himself, but for his son, after consulting Dr. Feodorov, who told him that the Tsarevich's ailment was incurable. The comment of the Empress when she heard the news was : " Et lui tout seul là-bas ! "

This is the end of her public significance. All evidence is

agreed that she, the Emperor and all the family bore all the trials which followed with a resignation which was almost heroic. The Emperor, when he got back to his family, broke down in a terrible scene, but from that time onwards it was as if they set themselves to endure anything that came to them. There was practically no complaint. From extant papers of the Empress found after the tragedy of Ekaterinburg, it is clear that she found in religion the strength to bear all that was sent to her. This is also made clear by the evidence of M. Gilliard and Mr. Gibbs and by her letters to her friends in Russia, which there is no reason to question, for they are in complete agreement with all other testimony. "He will help us," she writes, "and save this unhappy country." "O God, save Russia, this is the cry of my soul day and night." "We must endure, be purified, be born again." "The worse it is here, the better and brighter it will be there" (in Heaven). "Have mercy, O God, on our long-suffering country." "My faith is strong, my spirit is bold, I feel the nearness of God." "All life is a fight, or else there would be no effort and no reward." "The Bridegroom cometh; let us prepare to meet Him." And on April 2, 1918, in one of the last letters received from her: "Our crosses are only the shadow of His Cross. O God, help me not to lose that which Thou hast given me" (meaning her faith and resignation). And again, on April 21: "Though the storm is drawing near, I have peace of mind."

The Imperial family were moved to Siberia in August 1917 by the Provisional Government, unquestionably in order to save them from a possible attack of the Bolshevik mob in Petrograd. They had not unsympathetic guardians at Tobolsk, and were not treated with any greater rigour than was necessary. On the fall of the Provisional Government in November 1917, the change was not at once apparent at Tobolsk. In April orders were received that the Emperor was to be moved. The Empress insisted on going with him and the Tsarevich too; the four girls remained behind at Tobolsk and joined them later. It appears that the train at first actually travelled eastwards, but on orders received from Moscow turned in the opposite direction towards Europe.

The Emperor seems to have had a fixed idea that he would be approached by the Germans that they might obtain his sanction to the disgraceful Treaty of Brest Litovsk, a sanction which he was utterly determined not to give. It is stated that the Emperor's journey towards Moscow was a result of representations of the German Ambassador to the Bolshevik Government, Count Mirbach, and that the local Soviet of Ekaterinburg, in stopping the Emperor there, was executing a secret order given by the Moscow Soviet with the object of defeating Count Mirbach's purpose. There is evidence that a member of the Ekaterinburg Soviet went to Moscow for further instructions and that on his return all arrangements were made for the assassination of the whole Imperial family. It was carried out on July 16, 1918, with no more warning than a summons to the whole family to descend to the cellar. The Emperor's last act, it is said, was to stand forward to cover the Empress from attack. All were shot down, and their bodies with the other traces of the crime were taken to a clearing in the forest near Koptyaki, some twelve miles north-west of Ekaterinburg, and destroyed with fire. The following day, at the not far distant town of Alapayevsk, there were murdered the Grand Duchess Elizabeth, the Grand Duke Sergius Mikhaylovich, the three sons of the Grand Duke Constantine and the son of the Grand Duke Paul, Prince Paley.

BERNARD PARES.

No. 1.

Livadia, April 27-th 1914

My sweetest treasure, my very Own one,

you will read these lines when you get into your bed in a strange place & unknown house. God grant that the journey may be a pleasant & interesting one, & not too tiring nor too dusty. I am so glad to have the map, as then can follow you hourly. I shall miss you h o r r i b l y, but I am glad for you that you will be away for 2 days & get new impressions & hear nothing of Anias stories. My heart is heavy & sore — must one's kindness & love always be repayed thus? The black family & now she? One is always told one can never love enough — here we gave our hearts our home to her, our private life even — & this is what we have gained! It is difficult not to become bitter — it seems so cruelly unjust. —

May God have mercy & help us, the heart is so heavy! I am in despair that she gives you worries & disagreeable conversations, no rest for you either. Well try & forget all these two days. I bless you & cross you & hold you tightly in my arms — kiss you all over with boundless love & devotion. I shall be in Church to-morrow morning at 9 & try to go again on Thursday — it does me good to pray for you when we are separated — cannot get accustomed, for ever so short, not to have you in the house, tho' I have our 5 treasures. —

Sleep well my Sunshine, my own precious one & thousand tender kisses fr. yr. own old Wify.

God bless & keep you.

No. 2.

Petergof, June 29-th 1914

My beloved One,

It is very sad not to accompany you — but I thought I would better remain with the little Ones quietly here. Heart & soul are e v e r near you with tenderest love & passion, all my prayers suround you — I am therefore glad to go at once to evening service when you leave & to-morrow morning at 9 to mass. I shall dine with Anna, Marie & Anastasia & go early to bed. Marie Bariatinsky will lunch with us & spend her last afternoon with me. —

I do hope you will have a calm sea & enjoy yr. trip wh. will be a rest for you — you need it, as were looking pale to-day. —

Shall miss you sorely, my very Own precious One. — Sleep well my treasure, — my bed will be, oh, so empty.

God bless & kiss you. Very tenderest kisses fr. yr. own old

Wify.

No. 3.

Tsarskoje Selo, Sept. 19-th 1914

My own, my very own sweet One,

I am so happy for you that you can at last manage to go, as I know how deeply you have been suffering all this time — yr. restless sleep has been even a proof of it. It was a topic I on purpose did not touch, knowing & perfectly well understanding your feelings, at the same time realising that it is better you are not out at the head of the army. — This journey will be a tiny comfort to you, & I trust you will manage to see many troops. I can picture to myself their joy seeing you & all your feelings — alas that I cannot be with you to see it all. It is more than ever hard to bid goodbye to you my Angel — the blank after yr. departure is so intense! Then you, I know, not withstanding all you will have to do, will still miss yr. little family & precious agoo wee one. He will quickly get better now that our Friend has seen him & that will be a relief to you.

May the news only be good whilst you are away, as to know you have hard news to bear alone, makes the heart bleed. Looking after wounded is my consolation & that is why the last morning I even wanted to go there, whilst you were receiving, so as to keep my spirits up & not break down before you. To lessen their suffering even in a small way, helps the aching heart. Except all I go through with you & our beloved country & men I suffer for my »small old home« & her troops & Ernie & Irene & many a friend in sorrow there — but how many go through the same. And then the shame, the humiliation to think that Germans should behave as they do! — egoistically I suffer horribly to be separated — we are not accustomed to it & I do so endlessly love my very own precious Boysy dear. Soon 20 years that I belong to you & what bliss it has been to be your very own little Wify! —

How nice if you see dear Olga, it will cheer her up & do you good. — I shall give you a letter & things for the wounded for her. —

Lovy dear, my telegrams cant be very warm, as they go through so many military hands — but you will read all my love & longing between the lines. — Sweety, if in any way you do not feel quite the thing, you will be sure to call Feodorov, wont you — & have an eye on Fredericks.

My very most earnest prayers will follow you by day and night. I commend you into our Lord's safe keeping — may He guard, guide & lead you & bring you safe & sound back again.

I bless you & love you, as man was rarely been loved before — & kiss every dearly beloved place & press you tenderly to my own heart.

For ever yr. very own old

Wify.

The Image will lie this night under my cushion before I give it to you with my fervent blessing.

No. 4.

Tsarskoje Selo, Sept. 20-th 1914

My own beloved One,

I am resting in bed before dinner, the girls have gone to church and Baby is finishing his dinner. He has only slight pains sometimes. Oh my love! It was hard bidding you goodbye and seeing that lonely, pale face with big sad eyes at the waggon-window — my heart cried out, take me with you. If only you had had *N. P. S. or Mordv.* with you, a young loving face near you, you would be less lonely and »feel warmer«. I came home and than broke down, prayed, — then lay down and smoked to get myself into order. When eyes looked more decent I went up to Alexei and lay for a time near him on the sopha in the dark rest did good, as I was tired out in every sense. At 4¼ I came down to see *Lazarev* and gave him over the little Image for the regiment — I did not say it was fr. you, as then you would have to give to all the other newly formed regiments. The girls worked in the *stores.* At 4½ Tatiana and I received Neidhardt about her committee — the first will be in the Winterpalace on Wednesday after a *Te Deum,* I shall again not assist. It is a comfort to set the girls working alone and that they will be known more and learn to be useful. During tea I read *reports* and then got a letter at last from Victoria, dated the 1/13 Sep. it has taken long coming by messenger. I copy out what I think may interest you: »We have gone through anxious days during the long retreat of the allied armies in France. Quite between ourselves (so lovy don't tell on better) the French at first left the English army to bear all the brunt of the heavy german out flanking attack, alone, and if the English troops had been less dogged, not only they but the whole French forces would have been crumpled up. This has now been set right and two French generals who were to blame in the matter, have been deposed by Joffre and replaced by others. One of them had 6 notes from the English Com. in chief French, unopened in his pocket — the other kept sending as answer to an appeal to come on and help, that his horses were too tired. That is past history however, but it has cost the lives and liberty of many good officers and men. Luckily it was kept dark and people here in general dont know about it.« — »The 500 000 recruits asked for are nearly complete and hard at work drilling all day long masses of gentlemen joined the ranks and set a good example. There is a talk of raising a fourther 500 000 including the contingency from the colonies. I am not sure I like the idea of Indian troops coming to fight in Europe, but they are picked regiments and when served in China and in Egypt kept perfect discipline so that those who ought to know best are confident they will behave perfectly well no leeting or massacring. The superior officers are all English. Ernies friend the Maharagah of Biskanir is coming with his own contingent — last time I saw him was as Ernie's guest at Wolfsgarten. — Georgie wrote us an account of his share in the naval action of Helgoland. He commands the fore-turret and fired quite a number of shots and his captain says with coolness and good judgement. S. says that the attempt to destroying the docks of the Kiel Canal (the bridges alone would be little good) by aeroplanes is always in the admiraltys mind — but it is very difficult as all is well defended and one has to wait for a favorable opportunity or the attempt has no chance of success. It is distressing that the only passage into the Baltic for men-of-war, wh. is at all possible of being used, is through the Sound, wh. is not deep enough for battleships or big cruisers. In the North Sea the Germans have strewn mines far out all over the place recklessly endangering neutral trading ships and now that the first strong autumn winds are blowing, they will drift (for they are not anchored) on the Dutch and Norwegien and Danish shores (some round the German, one must hope) «She sends much love. — The sun shone so brightly this afternoon — but not in my room — tea was sad and strange and the armchair looked mournful without my precious One in it. — Marie and Dmitri dine, so I will stop writing and shut my eyes a little — and finish to-night. — Marie and Dmitri were in good spirits, they left at 10 so as to go to Paul. Baby was restless and only got to sleep after 11, but no strong pain. The girls went to bed, and I to surprise Ania who lay on her sopha in the big palace — she has now *obliteration of veins,* so Princess Gedroytz had been again to her and told her to keep quiet a few days — she had been by motor to town to see our friend and that had tired her leg. I returned at 11 and went to bed.

My face is tied up, as the teeth, jaw ache a bit; the eyes are sore and swollen still, and the heart yearns after the dearest being on earth who belongs to old Sunny. — Our Friend is happy for your sake that you have gone and was so glad to have seen you yesterday. He always fears Bonheur, that is to say, the *crows* want him to get the P. throne or in *Galicia* that that is there aim but I said she should quieten him, even out of thanks you would never risk such a thing. *Gr.* loves you jealously and cant hear N. playing a part. — Xenia answered my wire — is sad not to have seen you before you left — her train arrived. I miscalculated, Schulenburg cannot be here before to-morrow afternoon or evening, so I shall only get up for Church, a little later too. —

No. 5. *Tsarskoje Selo,* 21th Sept. 1914

My very own beloved One,

What joy to receive your 2 dear telegrams — thank God for the good, such a comfort to receive it upon your arrival. God bless your presence there. Do so wonder, hope and trust that you will see the troops. — Baby had a rather restless night but no real pain. I went up to kiss him before Church, at 11. Lunched with the girlies on my sopha, Bekker arrived. Then lay near Alexeis bed for over an hour and then off to the train — not very many wounded. Two officers of one regiment and *rota* died on the journey and one soldier. Their lungs are much attacked after the rain and having gone through the *Nieman* in the water — no acquaintances army regiments — one soldier remembered seeing us at Moscou this summer at the *Khodynka*. *Paretzky* got worse from his ill heart and overstrain, looks very bad, sunken in face, staring eyes, grey beard, — painful impression poor dear — not wounded. — Then we 5 went to Ania and took tea early there. At 3 went to our little hospital to put on our *chalat* and off to the big hospital, where we worked hard. At 5½ I had to return with M. and A. as received an *otriad* with Masha *Vassiltchikov's* brother at the head. Then back to the little hospital, where children were working and I did 3 new officers — then showed *Karangosov* and *Zhdanov* how to really play domino. After dinner and prayers with Baby, went to Ania where the 4 girls already were and saw *N. P.* who had dined with her. He felt comforted to see us, as very lonely and feels himself so useless. Princess Ged. came to see Anias leg wh. I then bandaged and we gave her a cup of tea. Dropped *N. P.* in the motor near the station. Bright moon, cold night. Baby is sleeping fast. All the little family kiss you ever so tenderly. Miss my Angel quite horribly, and at night whenever woke up tried to be silent not to wake you up. So sad in Church without you near me. Goodbye Sweetheart — my prayers and thoughts follow you everywhere. Bless and kiss you without end, every dearly beloved place

Your own old

Wify.

N. Gr. Orlova is going off to morrow to *Baranovitchi* see her husband 2 days. *Ania* heard from *Saschka* — and 2 letters from her brother. —

No. 6.

Tsarskoje Selo, 23rd Sept. 1914

My own beloved Darling,

I was so sorry not to be able to write to you yesterday, but my head ached hideously & I lay all the evening in the dark. In the morning we went to the *Grotto church* for half of the service & it was lovely; I had been before to see Baby! Then we fetched the Pss. G. at Anias.

My head already ached & I cant take any medecins now, neither for the heart. We worked from 10—1, as there was an operation wh. lasted long.

After luncheon I had Schulenburg who left again to-day, as Rennenkampf told him to hurry back. Then I came up to kiss Baby & went down & lay on my bed till tea-time, after wh. I received *Sandra Schouvalov's otriad*, after wh. to bed with a splitting headache. Ania was offended I did not go to her, but she had lots of guests, & our Friend for three hours. The night was not famous & I feel my head all day — heart enlarged — generally I take drops 3 or 4 times a day, as otherwise I could not keep up, & now I cant these days. — I read *Doklady* in bed & got on to the sopha for luncheon. Then received the couple Rebinder from *Kharkhov* they have my *stores* there & she had come from *Vilna* where she had been to bid goodbye to her brother *Kutaissov.* He showed her the Image I had sent the battery from Baby & it looked already quite used it seems they daily have it out for prayers & before every battle they pray before it — so touching. —

Then I came to Baby & lay near him in the half dark whilst *Vlad. Nik.* was reading to him, now they are playing together, the girls too, we have had tea up here too. — The weather is bright, in the night almost frost. —

Thank God the news continues being good & the Prussians retire. The mud hurried them away. *Mekk* writes that there are a good many cases of cholera & dissentry in *Lvov* but they are taking sanitary measures. — There have been difficult moments there, according to the papers; but I trust there wont be anything serious — one cannot trust those Poles — after all we are their enemies & the catholics must hate us. — I shall finish in the evening, cant write much at a time. — Sweet Angel, soul & heart a r e e v e r with you.

I am writing on Anastasias paper. Baby kisses you very much — he has no pains at all, lies, because the knee is still swollen, do hope he can be up then by your return. — I got a letter from old M-me *Orlova,* to whom *Ivan* wrote that he wants to continue the military service after war — he told me as much too — he is *Flyer Orlov, 20th Corps, active Army* — he received the St. George's cross, has the right to another decoration, but perhaps he might receive the grade of *praporstchik* (or *podporoutchik*). He did his *»reconnoitring under heavy fire of the enemy«* — one day he flew alone particularly high up & the cold was so intense, he did not know what to do — the hands freezing — machine stopped working — he did not care what would become of him, so numbed he felt — then he began praying & all of a sudden the machine went off working again alright. When it pours they cannot fly so sleep & sleep. Plucky boy to fly so often alone — what nerves one needs; indeed his father would have been proud of him therefore the Grandmama asks for him. — I write abominably to-day, but my brain is tired & heavy. — Oh my sweetheart, what an i n t e n s e joy it was when your precious letter was brought to me, & I thank you for it from all my heart. It was good of you writing — I read parts of it to the girls & Ania, who had been permitted to come to dinner & remained till 10½. How interesting it must all have been. — *Rouzsky* for sure was deeply moved that you made him general adj. Wont agoo wee one be happy you wrote! He has no more pain, thank God. You are probably now off in the train again — but how short you remain with Olga. What a recompense to the brave garnison of *Ossowetz* if you go there; — perhaps *Grodno,* if some troops are still resting there. — *Schulenburg* saw the lancers, their horses are completely done up, the backs sore to blood — hours in the saddle — & their legs quite weak. As the train stood near *Vilna* several of the officers came & slept change about several hours on his bed, & they enjoyed this luxury of a train-bed even, & to find a real W. C. was exquisite joy to them, *Kniajevitch* did not want to come out any more he was so comfortable there! (this *Sch's* wife related to *Ania*).

And beloved huzy misses his little Wify! And do I not you too! But I have the nice family to cheer me up. — Do you go into my compartment sometimes? Please give Fred. many kind messages. Have you spoken to Feodorov about the military students & Drs? — No telegram from you to-day, that means that you did nothing in particular, I suppose. —

Now my own sweetest one my Nicky dear, I must be trying to sleep & lay this letter out to be taken at 8½. —

I had no more ink in my pen, so had to take another.

Goodbye, my Angel, God bless & protect you & bring you safe & sound back again.

Ever possible tender kiss & caress fr. yr. foundly loving & truly devoted little Wify.

Wify.

Ania thanks for your message & sends much love. —

No. 7.

Tsarskoje Selo, Sept. 24-th 1914

My beloved Darling,

From all my heart I thank you for your sweet letter. Your tender words touched me deeply and warmed my lonely heart. I am deeply disappointed for you that one advises you not to go to the fortress — it would have been a real recompense to those wonderfully brave men. One says Ducky went there for the thanksgiving Te Deum and that she heard the cannons firing in the distance. — At *Vilna* there are many troops resting as the horses are so worn out, I hope you can see them. Olga wrote such a happy telegram after having seen you — dear child, she does work so bravely, and how many grateful hearts will carry home pictures of her bright sweet being into the ranks again and others home into their villages and her being your Sister will make the link yet stronger between you and the people. — I read such a pretty article out of an English paper — they praise our soldiers so much and say that their deep religiousness and veneration for their peace-loving monarch makes them fight so well and for a holy cause. — How utterly shameful that the Germans have shut the little Grandduchess of Luxemburg in a castle near Nürnberg — such an insult! — Fancy only I got a little letter from Gretchen without signature or beginning, written in English and sent from England and the adress written in another handwriting — I cannot imagine how she got it sent. — Ania's leg is much better to-day, and I see she intends to be up for your return — I wish she had been well now and the leg next week bad, then we should have had some nice quiet evenings cosily to ourselves. — We only went at 11 to the hospital, fetched the Pss. at Anias. We assisted at 2 operations — she did them sitting, so as that I could give her the instruments sitting too. The one man was too amusing when he came to himself again in bed — he began singing away at the top of his voice and very well, and conducting with his hand, upon wh. I concluded he was a »*Zapievalo*« — and so he was most cheery and said he hoped he had not used rude language — he wishes to be a hero and soon go back again to the war as soon as his foot heals up again. — The other one smiled mischivously and said: »*I was far, far away, I walked and walked, — it was nice over there. Almighty God, we were all together you don't know where I have been!*« and thanking God and praising him — he must have seen wonderful sights whilst one was extricating the ball out of his shoulder. She did not let me bind up anyone, so as to keep quiet, as felt my head and heart. After luncheon I lay in Babys room till 5, Mr. G. read to him and I think I took a short nap. Then Alexei read 5 lines in French aloud, quite nicely. Then I received Uncle *Mekk* after wh. I flew for a half an hour with Olga to Anias house, as our Friend spent the afternoon with her and wanted to see me. He asked after you and hoped you would go to the fortress. — Then we had our lecture with Pss. G. — After dinner the girls went to Ania where *N. P.* was, and I followed after prayers. We worked, she glued and he smoked. She is not over amiable these days and only thinks of herself and her comfort and makes others crawl under the table to arrange her leg on lots of cushions, and does not trouble her head whether others sit comfortably — spoilt and badly brought up. She has lots of poeple coming to see her all day long, so she has no time to be lonely, tho' when you return she will groan that she was wretched the whole time. — She is surrounded by several big photos of you enlarged ones of hers — in every corner and heaps of small ones. — We dropped *N. P.* near the station and were home at 11. — I wanted to go to Church every day and only got there once, such a pitty, as it is such a help when the heart feels sad. We always place candles before we go to the hospital and I like to pray for God and the holy Virgin to bless the work of our hands and to let them bring healing to the ill. — I am so glad you are feeling better again, such a journey is beneficient, as still you feel yourself nearer to all and could see the chiefs and hear all from them directly and tell them your ideas. —

What joy for Keller — he really has deserved his cross and now he has repayed us for everything, it was his ardent wish all these years. — How dead-tired the French and English troops must be, fighting without ceasing for 20 days or more. — And we have the big guns from Koenigsberg against us. To-day Orlov sent no news, so I suppose nothing in particular has occurred.

To be away from all the petty talks must do you good — here there are such rumours always, and generally without foundation. — Poor old Fredericks, the other one, had died. How sad our poor old one got worse again — I was so afraid it might happen again when out with you, and it would have been more delicate had he remained behind — but he is so deeply devoted to you, that he could not bear the idea of your going alone. I fear we shall not keep him long amongst us, his time is near at hand — what a loss it will be — there are no more such types to be found and such an honest friend is difficult to replace. — Sweetheart, I hope you sleep better now, I cannot say that of myself, the brain seems to be working all the time and never wanting to rest. Hundreds of ideas and combinations come bothering one. — I reread your dear letters several times and try to think its Lovy speaking to me. Somehow we see so little of each other, you are so much occupied and one does not like to bother with questions when you are tired after your »*doklady*« and then we are never alone together. — But now I must try and get to sleep, so as to feel stronger to-morrow and be of more use — I thought I should do so much when you were away, and Bekker spoilt all my plans and good intentions. — Sleep well wee One, holy Angels guard your slumber and Wify's prayers and love suround you with deep devotion and love.

25-th. Good morning my treasure. To-day the Feldjeger fetches the letter later so I can write still a little. This may be the last letter if Fredericks is right, that you are returning to-morrow, but it seems to me you wont, as you are sure to be seeing the hussars, lancers, artillery and other troops resting at *Vilna*. There were 2 degrees of frost this night — now there is again glorious sunshine. — We shall be at 11 at the hospital, I still cannot take medicins wh. is a great nuisance, as my head daily aches tho' not very strongly and I feel my heart, tho' it is not enlarged, but I must keep still rather quiet to-day. I have not been for a real airing since you left. — Sergei is a little better — Pss. Orlov too feels quite alright, only weak. — Baby slept and feels well. One continues speaking of that property in the Baltic provinces where the place is marked white and a hydroplane rested upon their lake there — as tho' officers, ours, had dressed in plain clothes and seen it — nobody is allowed to go there. — I do wish one could have it seriously enquired into. — There are so many spies everywhere that it may be true, but it would be very sad, as there are still many very loyal subjects in the Baltic provinces. This miserable war, when will it ever end. William, I feel sure must at times pass through hideous moments of despair, when he grasps that it was he, and especially his antirussian set, wh. began the war and is dragging his country into ruin. All those little states, for years they will continue suffering from the after-effects. It makes my heart bleed when I think how hard Papa and Ernie struggled to bring our little country to its present state of prosperity in every sense. — With God's help here all will go well and end gloriously, and it has lifted up spirits, cleansed the many stagnant minds, brought unity in feelings and is a »healthy war« in the moral sense. Only one thing I long that our troops should behave examplarily in every sense, and not rob and pillage — leave that horror to the Prussian troops. It is demoralising, and then one looses the real control over the men — they fight for personal gain and not for the country's glory, when they reach the stage of high-way robbers. — No reason to follow bad examples — the rearguard, »*obozy*« are the curse in this case all speak in despair of them, nobody to hold them in hand. — There are always ugly sides and beautiful ones to everything, and so is it here. — Such a war ought to cleanse the spirits and not defile them, is it not so? — Some regiments are very severe I know and try to keep order — but a word from above would do no harm, this is my very own idea, Darling: because I want the name of our russian troops to be remembered hereafter in the countries with awe and respect — and admiration. Here people do not ever quite grasp the idea that other peoples property is sacred, and not to be touched — victory does not mean pillage. — Let the priests in the regiments say a word to the men too on this topic. —

Now I am bothering you with things that do not concern me, but only out of love for your soldiers and their reputation.

Sweetest treasure, I must be ending now, and get up. All my prayers and tenderest thoughts follow you; may God give you courage, strength, and patience, — faith you have more than ever and it is this wh. keeps you up — yes prayers and implicid trust in God's mercy alone, give one strength to bear all. And our Friend helps you carry yr. heavy cross and great responsabilities — and all will come right, as the right is on our side. I bless you, kiss your precious face, sweet neck and dear loving handies with all the fervour of a great loving heart. How lovely to have you soon back again. Your very own old

Wify.

No. 8.

Tsarskoje Selo, Oct. 20-th 1914

My love of loves, my very own One,

Again the hour of separation is approaching & the heart aches with pain. But I am glad for you that you will get away, see other things & feel nearer to the troops. I hope you can manage to see more this time. We shall eagerly await your telegrams. When answering to the *Headquarters* I feel shy because I am sure — lots of officers read the telegrams & then one cannot write as warmly as one would wish to. That *N. P.* is with you this time, is a comfort to me — you will feel less lonely as he is bit of us all & you understand many looks & things together which warm one up, & he is intensely grateful & rejoicing to go with you, as he feels so useless in town, with all the camrades out at the war. — Thank God you can go away feeling quiet about Baby sweet — if there should be anything the matter, I shall write »*rutchka*«, all in the diminutive, then you will know I write about agoowee one. — Oh, how I shall miss you — I feel so low these days already & the heart so heavy — its a shame as hundreds are rejoicing to see you soon — but when one loves as I do — one cannot but yearn for ones treasure. Twenty years to-morrow that you reign & that I became orthodox! How the years have flown, how much we have lived through together. Forgive my writing in pencil, but I am on the sopha & you are confessing still. Once more forgive your Sunny if in any way she has grieved or displeased you, & believe it never was willingly done. — Thank God we shall have the blessing of Holy Communion together to-morrow

— it will give strength & peace. — May God give us success on shore & at sea — our fleet be blessed. — Oh my love, if you want me to meet you, send for me & O. & T. — Somehow we see so little of each other & there is so much one longs to talk over & ask about, & at night we are tired out & in the morning are hurrying. I shall finish this in the morning. 21-st. How lovely it was to go to Holy Communion together on this day — & the glorious sunshine — may it accompany on yr. journey in every sense. My prayers & thoughts & very, very tenderest love will follow you all the way. Sweetest of loves, God bless & protect you & the Holy Virgin guard you from all harm. My tenderest blessing.

Without end I kiss you & press you to my heart with boundless love & fondness.

Ever, Nicky Mine, yr. very own little

Wify.

I copy out *Gr.*'s telegr. for you to remember:

»Having been administered the sacred mysteries at the communion cup, beseeching Christ, tasting of His body and blood, there was a spiritual vision of Heavenly Beautiful rejoining. Grant that the Heavenly Power be with you on the road, that angels be in the ranks of our warriors for the salvation of our steadfast heroes with joy and victory.«

Bless you.
Love you.
Long for you.

No. 9.

Tsarskoje Selo, Oct. 21-st 1914

My own sweet Love,

It was such an unexpected joy to get your dear telegram, and I thank you for it with all my heart. Thats nice that you and *N. P.* took a turn at one of the little stations, it will have freshened you up. — I felt so sad seeing your lonely figure standing at the door — it seems so unnatural your going off all alone — everything is queer without you, our centre, our sunshine. I gulped down my tears and hurried off to the hospital and worked hard for two hours. Very bad wounds; for the first time I shaved one of the soldiers legs near and round the wound — I worked all alone to-day, without a sister or Dr. — only the Princess came to see each man and to what was the matter with him and I asked her if it was right what I intended doing — tiresome Mlle Annenkov gave me the things I asked for. Then we went back to our little hospital and sat in the different rooms with the officers. From there we went and looked at the little *Pestcherny Chapel* under the old *Palace Hospital* once — in Catherin's time there was a Church there. This has been done in remembrance of the 300 years Jubilee — it is quite charming all chosen by *Viltchkovsky,* purest and ancient Byzantine style, absolutely correct

— you must see it. The consecration will be on Sunday at 10, and we shall get our officers and men who are able to move, to come to it. There are tables with the names of those wounded who have died in all our hospitals of *Tsarskoje Selo,* and those officers too who received St. George's crosses or the *gold arms.* After tea we went to M. and A.'s hospital — they have several very gravely wounded men. Upstairs are 4 officers in most cosy rooms. — Then I received 3 officers who return to the *Active Army* — one lay in our hospital and the other 2 in my redcross *station* here; then I rested. Baby said his prayers down here, as I was too tired to go up. Now O. and T. are at Olga's Committee — before that *Tatiana* received Neidhardt alone for half an hour with his *report* — its so good for the girls and they learn to become independaat and it will develop them much more having to think and speak for themselves, without my constant aid. — I long for news from the Black Sea — God grant our fleet may have success, I suppose they give no news, so as the ennemy should not know their whereabouts by wireless telegraphy. —

It is very cold again to-night. I wonder whether you are playing domino! Oh, my love, how lonely it is without you! What a blessing we took Holy Communion before you left — it gave strength and peace. What a great thing it is to be able to take holy Sacrement at such moments and one longs to help others to also remember that God gave this blessing for all — not as a thing that must be done obligatorily once a year in lent — but whenever the soul thirsts for it and needs strength. When I get hold of people alone who I know suffer much — I always touch this subject and with God's help have many a time succeeded in making them understand that it is a possible and good thing to do and it brings relief and peace to many a weary heart. With one of our officers I also spoke and he agreed and was so happy and courageous afterwards and bore his pains far better. It seems to me this is one of the chief dutys of us women to try and bring people more to God, to make them realise that He is more attainable and near to us and waiting for our love and trust to turn to Him. Shyness keeps many away and false pride — therefore one must help them break this wall. — I just told the Priest last night that I find the clergy ought to speak more with the wounded in this way — quite simply and straight out, not sermonlike. Their souls are like children and only at times need a little guiding — with the officers its far more difficult as a rule. —

22-nd. Goodmorning my treasure. I prayed so much for you in the little Church this morning — I came for the last 20 min: — it was so sad kneeling there all alone without my treasure, that I could not help crying. But then I thought of how glad you must be to get nearer to the front and how eagerly the wounded will have awaited your arrival this morning at *Minsk.* We bound up the officers from 10—11 and then went to the big hospital for three operations — serious ones rather, 3 fingers were taken off as bloodpoisoning had set in, and they were quite rotten. Another had an »*oskolok*« taken out of his — another lots of *fragments* (bones) out of his leg. I went through several *wards.* Service was going on in the big hospital-church and we just knelt down on the top balkony during the prayer to the Kazan Virgin's Image. Your *Rifles* feel sad with you away. — Now I must be off to my *supply* train No. 4.

Goodbye my Nicky love, I bless and kiss you over and over again. Slept badly, kissed your cushion and thought much of you.

Ever your very own little

Wify.

I bow to all and specially to *N. P.* whom I am glad you have with you — more warmth near you. —

No. 10.

Tsarskoje Selo, Oct. 22-nd 1914

My own beloved One.

It is 7 o'clock and as yet no news from you. Well, I went to see my *supply-train* No. 4 with *Mekk* — they leave to-night for *Radom* I think and from there *Mekk* will go to see *Nikolasha,* as he must ask him some questions. He told me privately from Ella that she wants to go and see my *store* at *Lvov,* without anybody knowing about it — she will come here so as that the Moscou public should know nothing, the first days of November! We envy her and Ducky fearfully — but still hope you will send for us to meet you. It will be hard leaving Baby, whom I have never been long away from, but whilst he is well and M. and A. are there to keep him company, I could get away. Of course I should like it to be a useful journey — best if I could have gone with my train, one of the sanitary ones — out to their destination to see how they take in the wounded and bring them back again and look after them. Or meet you at *Grodno, Vilna, Bielostok* where there are hospitals. But that I all leave in your hands, you will tell me what to do, where to meet you — or to *Rovno* and *Kharkov* — whatever suits you — the less one knows I come, the better. — I received *Schulenburg* who leaves to-morrow, (my train which *Loman* and Co. arrange) leaves the 1-st I think. Then we had the P-ss. for our lecture. We have finished a full surgical course, with more things than usual, and now shall go through anatomy and interior illnesses as its good to know that all for the girls too. —

I have been sorting out warm things for the wounded returning home — and going back to the army again. *Ressin* has been to me and we have settled to go to *Luga* to-morrow afternoon to my »*Svietelka*«. It was a *country-house* given to *Alexei* which I took and arranged as a »dependance of my *school of popular art,*« — the girls work, make carpets there and teach the village women how to make them — then they get their cows and poultry and vegetables, and will be taught *housekeeping.* Now they have arranged 20 beds and look after the wounded. — We have to take a short train, as the ordinary ones go slower and at inconvenient hours — Ania, Nastinka and *Ressin* will accompany us three — nobody is to know anything about it. M-elle Schneider only knows A. and N. are coming, — otherwise she might just be away. — We shall take simple *cabs* and go in our nurses' dresses to attract less attention and as its a hospital we visit. — M-me Becker is a bore, should be much freer without her. — How vile one having thrown bombs from aeroplans on to King Albert's Villa in which he just now lives — thank God no harm was done but I have never known one trying to kill a sovereign because he is ones enemy during the war! —

I must rest a ¼ of an hour before dinner with shut eyes — shall continue to-night. —

What good news! *Sandomir* ours again and masses of prisoners heavy guns and quickfiring ones — your journey has brought blessings and good luck again. — Baby love came down to say prayers again, as I felt so tired in every sense. My Image was in Church this morning and hangs now in its place again. — It is warmer this evening so I have opened the window. — Ania is in splendid spirits and enjoys her young operated friend — she brought him your »*Skopin S.*« to read. — Ago wee one wrote out for me during dinner on the menu j'ai, tu as etc. so nicely; how you must miss the little man! Such a blessing when he is well!! I gave my good night kiss to your cushion and longed to have you near me — in thoughts I see you lying in your compartment, bend over you, bless you and gently kiss your sweet face all over. — oh, my Darling, how intensely dear you are to me; — could I but help you carrying your heavy burdens, there are so many that weigh upon you. But I am sure all looks and feels different now you are out there, it will freshen you up, and you will hear lots of interesting things. — What is our blacksea fleet doing? The wife of my former »Crimean« *M. Lichatchev* wrote to Ania from Hôtel Kist, that a shell had burst quite near on the place there. She pretends the German ship got one shot from us, but that he was not blown up by our mines, over which she went, because Eberh. had them (how does one say it?) ausgeschaltet, I can't find the word, my brain is cretinised. Probably our squadron was intending to go out, she said they were heating the boilers when the shots flew — well, this is lady's talk, may or may not be true. I enclose a telegram from Keller sent through *Ivanov* to Fredericks for me — an answer to mine probably of congratulations for his St. Georges Cross. — In what a state of nervousness *Botkin* must be, now that *Sandomir* is taken; — wonder whether his poor son is yet alive. — Ania sends you rusks, a letter and newspapers open. — I shall have no time to write to-morrow in the day, as we go for half an hour to Church, then to the hospital, and at 1½ to Luga, back by 7 — shall lie in the train, takes 2 hours there and 2 back. — Goodnight my sunshine, my very Own one, sleep well, holy Angels guard your bed and the blessed Virgin keeps watch over you. My very tenderest thoughts and prayers hover ever around you — yearning and longing, feeling your moments of loneliness accutely. Bless you.

23-rd. Good morning Lovy mine! Bright and sunny! We had little to do this morning and so I sat nearly all the time and did not get tired. — We went a moment to Mme Levitzky to see her 18 wounded, all our old friends. Now we must eat and fly — too bad, C-ss Adlerberg has found out we go and wants to come — but I have told Iza to answer that she knows nothing and once I say nothing, it means I wish it to be kept secret, so as better to see things than when all is prepared. — Goodbye Sweetheart, I bless and kiss you over and over again.

Your very own

Wify.

My love to *N. P.* to whom we send this card. —

No. 11.

Tsarskoje Selo, Oct. 23-rd 1914

My sweetest Love,

Thank God for the good news that the Austrian army is in full retreat from the river San, and what good news in Turkey — *Endigarov* is wild with joy and my »*Crimeans*«. — I beg your pardon for having forgotten to send Ania's rusks, but I had to seal up my letter in such a hurry before we left, that I forgot sending them, but shall forward them to-morrow. Our expedition to *Luga* was most successful. When we arrived at the station we were met by old Mlle Sheremetiev (sister of Mme *Timashev*) who told me that there were two hospitals, and she thought I had come on purpose — so I told her we should go there after the »*Svietelka*«. We went off in three *cabs,* with the *chief of police* in front in a charming cart. The 3 hospitals were very far from each other, but we enjoyed the primitive drive through the streets and sandy roads into the pinewood — quite near the place where we took a walk then near a lake years ago ... Mlle *Schneider* got an awful shock when she saw us, as she never received Ania's telegram, and laughed nervously, excitedly the whole 20 m. we were there. 20 men lie in the little *country house* — they had been wounded near *Suvalki* end of Sept., but light wounds — they were evacuated from *Grodno.* They all came by the same train, 80 men on the whole, mostly regiments from the Caucasus. One »*Erivanetz*« who had seen us at Livadia. — One *Timashev* daugther was in one hospital as nurse and a younger sister M-lle *Sheremetiev* at the head of another near the Artillery barracks. — Friede I suddenly discovered there. Many of the men were soon going off again to the army. They have a *Kitchen* at the station since 2 months and not one sanitary or military train has stopped there. On our way back we took tea. We knitted a lot and Ressin kept us company. — The weather was fine and not too cold. It is nearly 1. I think I ought to try and sleep — I had very little sleep these nights, tho' I kept the window open till 3 o'clock in the night. — Baby sweet motored in the garden, M. and A. drove with Isa, went to their hospital and then worked in the *supply store.* I received Alia who accompanys her husband on Sunday till where Misha is. — Goodnight my Sunshine, my huzy sweet, sleep peacefully and feel wify's presence ever near you full of love.

24-th. I must finish my letter, then lunch, change and be off to town to my *store* and if headache not much worse, then to my *Krestov. Red Cross Station.* — We worked all the morning and were very sad to bid goodbye to my 5 *Crimeans,* and lancer *Ellis* who are off with 3 others in a waggon with a nurse and 1 sanitary to *Simferopol* and *Kutchuk-Lambat.* — *Mme Muftizade* returned from the Crimea and brought me roses and apples. — God bless you my Angel love.

I kiss you ever so tenderly,

your very own

Sunny.

Thank God my *Alexander* squadron has turned up. I was so anxious about them. Our love to *N. P.*

No. 12.

Tsarskoje Selo, Oct. 24-nd 1914

My own precious Darling,

Well we got through everything alright in town. Tatiana had her Committee which lasted 1½ hour; she joined us at my *Krestov. Red Cross Station,* where I went with Olga after the *supply store.* Lots of people were working in the Winter Palace and many came to fetch work and others to bring back their finished things. I saw the wife of a Dr. there, who just had a letter from her husband from *Kovel,* where he is in a military hospital, where they have very little linnen and nothing to dress the men in, when they leave the hospital. So I quickly told them to put lots of linnen and *warm undergarments* to send to *Kovel* and a biggish Image of Christ painted on linnen (and brought as a gift to the *store)* as its a little jewish town and they have no Image in their hospital which is in barracks. I wonder how you spend your days and evenings and what your plans are. Our Friend was very pleased we went to *Luga* and in sisters dresses and wants me to go about more and not to wait for your return to go to *Pskov,* so I shall spin off again, only this time must tell the Governor I suppose, as its a bigger town — but that makes it always shyer work. I shall take then linnen with me to the military hospital which Marie said needed things, or send it after. — There were many wounded at the *Red Cross Station* to-day, one officer had been 4 days in Olga's hospital and said there was not such a second sister. Some men had very serious wounds. They had mostly been wounded near *Suvalki,* or been lying since some time at *Dvinsk.* — We read the discription of your visit to Minsk in the papers; I received a wire from the Governor thanking for the Images and gospels you had left there from me. — Now I must try and sleep, which I do very badly all these nights — cannot get off to sleep before 3 or 4. Goodnight my Sunshine, I bless and kiss you as tenderly and lovingly as is only possible. —

25-th. Goodmorning my love! I slept much better this night, only need to begin more heartdrops I feel, as chest and head ache. Thermometer is on zero this morning. — Ania is in excellent spirits this time. — Our Friend intends leaving for home about the 5-th and wishes to come to us this evening. Paul has asked to take tea and Fred. to see me, so we will lunch and then we have to go to the consecration of the hospital in the »*Mixed Regiment*«, which has got already wounded out of M. and A.'s hospital, who were already better and had to leave to give place for severely wounded. — Now must get up and dress for the hospital — and place candles at *Znamenia* before.

God bless and keep you, my Treasure. Have no time for more. Kisses without end. Ever your own old

Wify.

The girls kiss you fondly. — Our love to *N. P.*

No. 13.

Tsarskoje Selo, Oct. 25-th 1914

My own sweet Treasure,

Now you are off to *Kholm* and that will be nice and remind you of ten years ago. Loving thanks for your telegram — it was surely pleasant seeing your dear hussars, and the G. à Cheval in Reval. — After the hospital this morning we went into 2 private houses to see the wounded — always old patients of ours. Fredericks came to luncheon, really he had nothing to tell, brought several telegrams to show and looked pretty well. At 1/4 to 2 we were at the barracks of the *Mixed Regiment* looked at the hospital arranged and had a *Te Deum* and blessed the rooms — the men looked very contented and the sun shone brightly upon them. From there we went to *Pavlovsk,* picked up Mavra who showed us over four hospitals. — Paul came to tea. He longs to go to the war, and so I am writing this to you with his knowledge, so as for you to think it over before you meet him again. All along he hoped you would take, but now he sees there is little chance, and to remain at home doing nothing drives him to exasperation. He would not like to go to *Russky's* staff as would be inconvenient, but if he might begin by going out to his former comrade *Bezobrazov* he would be delighted. Wont you speak this question over with *Nikolasha?* — Then we went to the evening service in the new *Pestcherny Chapel* under the existing one in the big *Palace* hospital. There was a Church there in Catherin's time; after that we sat with our wounded; many of them and all the nurses and ladies had been in Church. *Gogoberidze* the »*Erivanetz*« had just arrived. — Our Friend came for an hour in the evening; he will await your return and then go off for a little home. — He had seen M-me *Muftizade* who is in an awful state, and Ania was with her — it seems *Lavrinovsky* is ruining everything — sending off good Tartars to Turky and most unjust to all — so that they begged her to come to their Valideh to pour out their complaints, as they are truly devoted subjects. They would like *Kniazhevitch* to replace *Lavrinovsky,* and our Friend wishes me quickly to speak to *Maklakov,* as he says one must not waste time until your return. So I shall send for him, pardon my mixing in what does not concern me, but its for the good of the Crimea and then *Maklakov* can at once write a *report* to you to sign — if you cannot let *Kniazhevitch* leave the army now (tho' I think he would be of more use in the Crimea) then another must be found. I shall tell *Maklakov* that you and I spoke about *Lavrinovsky* already. He seems to be most brutal to the Tartars and its certainly not the moment when we have war with Turky to behave like that. Please don't be angry with me, and give me some sort of an answer by wire — that you »*approve*«, or »*regret*« my mixing in — and whether you think *Kniazhevitch* a good candidate, it will quieten me; and I shall know how to speak to *Masha Muftizade.* — You remember he was angry she wished to see me about sending things to the regiment, and founded that Tartars must not show themselves in their dresses before us, and so on offending them constantly. He may do better in another government; I know *Apraxin* is of the same opinion, and was deeply grieved by the change he found. —

Its nearly one, must try and sleep. I saw Alia and husband at 10½, he joins *Khan* and Misha. —

26-th. We just returned from 2 hospitals, where saw wounded officers and the old Priest of your rifles from here, who got overtired and was sent back. — I enclose a letter from *Olga* for you to read (privately) and if you see her, can you give it back to her. I got another sweet letter from her to-day, so full of love, Dear Child, she does work so hard. Now, *Loman's* train (my name) will only be ready later, am so sorry. Wonder whether you will send for us anywhere, or whether we can get into Schulenburg's train, think he must return soon. — The weather is mild to-day and its gently snowing. Baby motored and then made a fire which he enjoyed. — The Children told you probably all about the Consecration of the Church (you must see it) and that we visited our officers afterwards. *Egor* gave me news you had seen him. — Thank God all goes so well in Turky — would that our fleet could have success. — I received M-me *Kniazhevitch* (wife lancer) who offered me money for 10 beds from my lancer ladies — and through her husband I got money from all the squadrons and shall get monthly too, to keep up 6 beds — too touching. —

Then M-me *Dediulin* came to thank for my note and you for the telegram which came so unexpected and touched her very deeply. —

Must end now my treasure. Goodbye and God bless you, sweetest, deeply missed one. I cover your precious face with tender kisses.

Ever your very own wife. Alix.

Our love to *N. P.*

No. 14. *Tsarskoje Selo,* Oct. 26-th 1914

My very own precious One,

I fear my letters are somewhat dull, because my heart and brain are somewhat tired and I have always the same thing to tell you. Well, this afternoon I wrote what we did. After tea we went with Alexei and Ania to the hospital and sat there for an hour and a half — several officers had gone to town as they did not know we would come. — Just this minute Tudels brought me a wire from *Botkin,* thank God he has news that his son recovered very well and was well looked after, but taken to Budapest Oct. 1-st — *Botkin* returns here over *Kholm.* — How nice that you were there for Church; do so wonder, whether you can get for a peep to *Lublin* or anywhere else to see some troops. — I am so glad it has been settled by the Princess and Zeidler that *Shesterikov* and *Rudnev* need not be operated, one can leave the bullets in them — its safer as they sit very deep in, and cause no pain. Both are enchanted, walk about again and went to the Consecration of the little Church this morning. — *Kulinev* we found less well, grown pale and suffers more from his head, poor boy. Young Krusenstern returned to his regiment. *Genig* lies in the red cross station; he is also contusioned in the head, lies with dark spectacles in a half dark-room. — The »*Erivanetz*« *Gogoberidze* has come to us now. — Baby says his prayers of an evening down here, so as for me not to go up, as I do much now and feel my heart needs caring after. — To-morrow its a week we parted, and the longing that fills my heart is great. I miss my Angel terribly, but get strength by remembering the joy of all who see you and your contentment at being out there. Do you play domino of an evening I wonder! We intend going to Georgi to-morrow to see his wounded, he only knows the big girls go, about myself I did not say — then I shall ask to see Sergei a minute — and go to some smaller hospitals. Now, after blessing and kissing you fondly in thought, I must put out my lamp and get to sleep — am very tired. —

27-th. I am so glad you are contented with your expedition. — We have had a busy day — 3 operations this morning, and difficult ones too, so had no time to be with ours in the little house, this afternoon were in town — went to *Georgi* — the wounded lie in the big room and looked contented. Sat with Sergei — find him much changed, greyish complexion, not thin face, eyes strange — is a little bit better, had been very bad; saw old Zander there. Then went to the *Palace Hospital* where wounded (and usual ill) lie — found Mr. Stuart there, lies there since 6 weeks, had typhoid. — Then off to the *Constantin School* on the *Fontanka.* There 35 men some *Izmailov* officers. — Am tired, have *Taneyev* at 6, and *Svetchin* with *report* at 6½. — Miss you always, my Sunshine, think of you with yearning love. — God bless and protect you, Nicky dear, big agoowee one. I kiss you over and over again.

Ever your very own Wife

Sunny.

All the girls send you lots of love.

We also send our love to *N. P.*

No. 15.

Tsarskoje Selo, Oct. 27-th 1914

My own sweetest Nicky dear,

I have come earlier to bed, as am very tired — it was a buisy day, & when the girls went to bed at 11, I also said goodnight to Ania, her humour towards me has been not amiable this morning — what one would call rude & this evening she came lots later than she had asked to come & was queer with me. She flirts hard with the young *Ukrainian* — misses & longs for you — at times is colossaly gay; — she went with a whole party of our wounded to town (by chance), & amused herself immensely in the train — she must play a part & speak afterwards of herself the whole time & their remarks about her. At the beginning she was daily asking for more operations, & now they bore her, as they take her away from her young friend, tho' she goes to him every afternoon and in evening again.

Its naughty my grumbling about her, but you know how aggravating she can be. You will see when we return how she will tell you how terribly she suffered without you, tho' she thoroughly enjoys being alone with her friend, turning his head, & not so as to forget you a bit. Be nice & firm when you return & don't allow her foot-game etc. Otherwise she gets worse after — she always needs cooling down.

Her Father came with a *report* to me, then *Svetchin* about more motors he has got for our trains. — How is the news to-day, I wonder — she says our Friend is rather anxious — perhaps to-morrow He will see all better again, & pray all the more for success. My Becker wired from Varsovie telling about my squadrons 5 weeks amongst the enemy. They lost 1 officer & 23 men. I always kiss & bless your cushion in the evening & long for my Lovy.

I quite understand you had no time for writing & was grateful for your daily telegrams — & I know you think of me, & that you are occupied all day long. Dearest Treasure, this is my 7-th letter, I hope you get them alright. — Does *N. P.* photograph? He took his apparatus I think with him. — We had a letter from Keller again. — Css. Carlow's second daughter Merica is engaged to a Chevalier C. Orjevsky, who is only 22 — the mother is not contented. —

I saw in the papers that Greek Georgie & wife have left for Greece from Copenhagen via Germany, France & Italy — I am astonished one has let them through. —

What is Eberhardt doing? They have been bombarding Poti. —

Oh this miserable war! At moments one cannot hear it any more, the misery & bloodshed break one's heart; faith, hope & trust in God's infinite justice & mercy keep one up. — In France things go very slowly — but when I hear of success & that the Germans have great losses, I get such pang in the heart, thinking of Ernie & his troops & the many known names.

All over the world losses! Well, some good must come out of it, & they wont all have shed their blood in vain. Life is difficult to understand — »*It must be so — have patience*«, thats all one can say. —

One does so long for quiet, happy times again! But we shall have long to wait before regaining peace in every way. It is not right to be depressed but there are moments the load is so heavy & weighs on the whole country & you have to carry the brunt of it all.

I long to lessen your weight, to help you carry it — to stroke your brow, press you to myself. But we show nothing of what we feel when together, which happens so rarely — each keeps up for the others sake & suffers in silence — but I long often to hold you tight in my arms & let you rest your weary head upon my old breast. We have lived through so much together in these 20 years — & without words have understood each other. My brave Boy, God help you, give strenght & wisdom, comfort & success.

Sleep well, God bless you — holy Angels & Wify's prayers guard your slumber.

28-th. Good morning Darling! I slept very badly, only got off after 4 & then constantly woke up again, so tiresome, just when one needs a good rest. Its warmer to-day & grey weather. — Just before going to the hospital received your beloved letter — it was sweet of you to have rejoiced my heart like that — & I thank you from all my loving heart. — Certainly we shall come with greatest pleasure & let *Voyeikov* arrange all & say exactly, when to meet you — perhaps we can stop on the way out & see some hospital at *Dvinsk* or so — I have sent for *Ressin* to talk all over. — We shall then go off to *Pskov* to-morrow, sleep this night in the train, & be back to-morrow for dinner. Probably Babys train will arrive Thursday. — We saw Marie's at *Alexander* station — the most were wounded in the legs — came from Varsovie hospitals & Grodno. —

We are going to another hospital now directly. — I think, if its possible to stop perhaps at *Dvinsk* on the way to you, if there is time. R. is finding out about the hospitals (privately) — there we shall go as sisters (our Friend likes us to) & to-morrow also. But being with you at *Grodno* we shall dress otherwise, not to make you shy driving with a nurse. —

M. is coming at 9, & I shall tell him also your wish about *Lavrinovsky*.

Feeling myself a wound-up mashine which needs medicins to keep her up — seeing you, will help mightily.

I think of bringing Ania & Iza & *O. Evg.* & perhaps one maid for the 2 girls & me, & one for the ladies (to meet you) — the less people the better & to hang less on to your train afterwards. — Its best taking *Ressin* I think, as a military man. — Now must end.

Blessings & kisses without end. The joy of seeing you will be intense — but hard leaving my Sunbeam. — Instead of *Pskov,* perhaps we might stop with you still in some other town. — I bless you over & over again — a whole week already to-day! Work is the only remedy. —

Ever your

very own old

Sunny.

Love to *N. P.*

Nr. 16.

Tsarskoje Selo, Nov. 17-th 1914

My own beloved One,

The train will be carrying you far away from us when you read these lines. Once more the hour of separation has come — & always equally hard to bear. — The loneliness when you are gone, tho' I have our precious Children, is intense — a bit of my life gone — we make one.

God bless & protect you on your journey & may you have good impressions & shed joy around you & bring strength & consolation to the suffering.

You always bring »*revival*« as our Friend says. I am glad his telegram came, comforting to know His prayers follow you. —

Its good you can have a thorough talk with N. & tell him your opinion of some people & give him some ideas. May again your presence there bring goodluck to our brave troops. —

Our work in the hospital is my consolation & the visiting the specially suffering ones in the big palace. — I only dread Ania's humour — last times our Friend was there, once a bad leg, & then her little friend.

Lets hope she will hold herself in hand. I take all much cooler now & don't worry over her rudenesses & moods like formerly — a break came through her behaviour & words in the Crimea — we are friends & I am very fond of her & always shall be, but something has gone, a link broken by her behaviour towards us both — she can never be as near to me as she was. — One tries to hide one's sorrow & not pride with it — after all its harder for me than her, tho' she does not agree — as you are all to her & I have the children — but she has me whom she says she loves. — Its not worth while speaking about this, & it is not interesting to you at all.

It will be a joy to go & meet you, tho' I hate leaving Baby & the girlies. And I shall be so shy on the journey — I have never been alone to any big town — I hope I shall do all properly & your wife wont make a mess of herself. — Lovy my dear, huzy my very, very own — 20 years my own sweet treasure — farewell & God bless & protect you & keep you from all harm.

My light & sunshine, my very life & being. For all your love be blessed, for all your tenderness be thanked. I bless you, kiss you all over & gently press you to my deeply loving old heart.

Ever, Nicky my Own,

your very own

Wify.

I am so glad N. P. accompanies you, it makes me quieter knowing him near you and for him its such a colossal joy. —

Our last night together, its horribly lonely without you — and so silent — nobody lives in this story.

Holy Angels guard you and the Sweet Virgin spread her mantle of love around you. — Sunny.

No. 17.

Tsarkoje Selo, Nov. 18-th 1914

My own beloved One,

As a Feldjeger leaves this evening, I profit to write & tell you how we spent the morning. Such pain fills the heart without my Sweetheart being here — so hard to see you having all alone. — We went straight to the hospital after Fredericks had given me a paper to sign at the station. We had a good deal to do, but I sat long whilst the children worked. A. was in a stupid, unamiable mood. She went off earlier to see Alia who arrives, & will only come back at 9 & not to our lecture. She never asked what I would do — once you are not there, she is glad to get out of the house. Its no good running away from ones sorrow. But I am glad to see less of her when she is unamiable.

What dirty weather! I am going to the Childrens' hospital & then to the big palace.

Marie & Olga go rushing about the room, Tatiana has a lesson, Anastasia sits with her — Baby is going out after resting. The Governor calls me quickly. — I just received M-me *Muftizade* & then the *business manager* of my *Tsarskoje Selo* red cross of *Suvalki.* He has come to fetch things & ask for 2 motors. —

Beloved One, my very own Huzy dear — me wants kiss you, to cudle close & feel comfy.

Now the children call me to the hospital, so I must be off. The man goes at 5. Goodbye lovy mine, God bless & keep you now & evermore.

All the children kiss you tenderly

Ever your very own

Wify.

No. 18.

Tsarskoje Selo, Nov. 19-th 1914

My very own beloved One,

Your letter was such an intense joy, consolation to me, God bless you for it and a thousand tender thanks. I love to read all the dear things you say, it warms me up because I cannot help feeling your absence greatly, the »thing« is missing in all the life of my home. I lunch now always on the sopha when we are alone. How lucky one has taken Rennenkampf away before you came, I am glad may they only find a good one instead — it wont be *Mistchenko* by any chance? He is so loved by the troops and a clever head, is he not? — One says the blue curassiers are enchanted to have my *Arseniev* and well they may be. — Really it was an excellent idea your arranging your stick for gymnastics — good excercise when you will be shut up for so long, except standing in hospitals which is horribly tiring. — At 9 Olga, Anastasia,

Baby and I went off to his train. We have very heavy wounded this time, the train was at *Sukhatchev, 6 versts* from the battle, and the windows shook from the artillery. Aeroplanes were flying there and over Varsovie. *Schulenburg* says that the 13 and 14 Sib. were hideously afraid off all and thought God was with the Germans, not grasping what the aeropl. were and so on, and one could not get them to advance — all new troops, and not real Siberians. They have discovered our 6 motors of his train, which had disappeared since the 1-st — they are at *Lodz* only cant get away, otherwise may be taken, but they do still bring wounded. Lots came on foot now so have their lungs in a precarious state. *Yagmin* arrived *(»Nizhegorodsky«)* I get no news — in town one says it was bad yesterday — in the papers lots are white, not printed; — probably we retreated near *Sukhatchev*. Some of these wounded had been taken by the Germans and then ours got them after 4 days back again. Dear me what wretched wounds, I fear some are doomed men; — but I am glad we have them and can at least do all in our power to help them. — I ought to have gone now to see the rest, but am too awfully tired, as we had 2 operations besides, and at 4, I must go to the big palace, as I want the P—ss also to have a look at the poor boy, and an officer of the 2-nd rifles whose legs are already getting quite dark and one fears an amputation may be necessary. —

I was with the boy yesterday during his *dressing* awful to see, and he clung to me and kept quiet, poor child. — We have some heavy cases in the big Palace. —

It was grey and rainy yesterday and warm, this morning the sun shone, but its grey. A. has gone for a walk and then will come to me — she was in a disagreable mood the whole evening, so I went to bed ad 11 — this morning she continued, but we succeeded in breaking her. Its doubly painful when one feels sad, and she pretends being the »chief mourner« before others. I keep up and talk — and she might do the same. She continues asking about the Feldjeger, I suppose intends writing — whether you have allowed it — I do not know. — Olga and Tatiana have gone to town to receive donations in the Winter-palace. — *Boris* is at Varsovie for a week, *Schulenburg* took him to wash and clean up, as he has the *itch* — well Miechen is in good time. — Yesterday we went also to the Children's hospital — sat with *Nikolaiev* and *Lazarev*. — A »*Volynetz*« officer lay in the train to-day — they have only 12 officers in the regiment and few men left. —

The Children all kiss you fondly, daily one of them will write, Marie has begun now. — Please give *N. P.* my love. — Did you hear whether »*Giants*« are wounded, there are such *rumors* from town. — Oh yes, it would indeed have been lovely to have gone together, but I think your journey to the Caucasus at such a time, is better undertaken alone — there are moments when we women must not exist. — Yes, God has helped me with my health and I keep up — tho' at times am simply deadtired — the heart aches and is enlarged — but my will is firm — anything only not to think. —

My Sweetheart, my very own Treasure, I must end now, the messenger leaves earlier to-day. —

When you return, you must give me my letters to number, as I have no idea how many I have written. Once more, endless thanks for your dear letter, which is very well written, tho' the train moved. —

I press you to my yearning breast, kiss all the dear places I so tenderly love. God bless you and guard you from all ill.

Ever Nicky my Angel, my own treasure, my Sunshine, my life —

your very own old

Wify

Messages to *Dmitri Sheremetiev.*

No. 19.

Tsarskoje Selo, Nov. 20-th 1914

My own beloved Nicky dear,

There is a belated gnat flying round my head whilst I am writing to you. — Well, I went to the big Palace to that poor boy's dressing, and somehow it seems to me as tho' the border of the great bedsore wound were getting firmer — the P—ss did not find the tissue too dead looking. She looked at the rifle's leg and finds one ought at once to take it off before it is too late, and it must be done very high. Vladimir Nikolaievitch and Eberman find one must first try another operation of the veins ancurism and if that does not help, then take the leg off. His family want some celebrity to consult — but all are away except Zeidler, who could not come before Friday. I am going to have a talk still with B. v. Huk — the evening I read Rost's papers till 10 o'clock. Before dinner I received Mme Zizi and then I got a nap. Ania wants us to go off to Kovno, as we cannot menage the Sanitary train this time, to our regret, and Vojeikov's joy. But that means also Vilna. I cant pass without stopping there. The children like that idea, as hope to see our »friends« — she says there are heaps of wounded there. Ella arrived Monday — really don't know what to do — wish you were here to ask and this letter will reach you only Saturday at earliest, and then we ought to be off. I shall think it over still. Am so tired and don't much care to go off now, and then here is much work and our Children, whom I must leave on the first. But perhaps it would be good to go there. Ania wants change and »Dr. Armia« as she always says. Dearest Beloved — I kiss yr. cushion morn and evening and bless it and long for its treasured master. — I enclose a postcard of us at Dvinsk. I think it might amuse you to have for yr. album. Its quite mild weather. Baby is going in his motor and then Olga who is now walking with Ania, will take him to the big palace to see the officers, who are impatient for him. I am too tired to go and we have at 5¼ an amputation (instead of lecture) in the big hospital. This morning we were present (I help as always, giving the instruments and Olga threaded the needles) at our first big amputation (whole arm was cut off) then we all had *dressings* (in our small hospital) very serious ones in the big hospital. — I had wretched fellows with awful wounds ...., scarcely a »man« any more, so shot to pieces, perhaps it must be cut off as so black, but hope to save it — terrible to look at. I washed and cleaned, and painted with iodine and smeared with vaseline and tied them up and bandaged all up — it went quite well and I feel happier to do the things gently myself under the guidance of a Dr. — I did three such — and one had a *little tube* in it. Ones heart bleeds for them — I wont describe any more details, as its so sad, but being a wife and mother I feel for them quite particulary — a young nurse (girl) I sent out of the room — Mlle Annenkov is already older — the young doctor so kind — Ania looked on so cooly, quite hardened already, as she says — she astonishes me with her ways constantly — nothing of the loving gentle woman like our girlies — she ties them up roughly when they bore her, goes away when she has had enough — and when little to do, grumbles. Sedigarov noticed that they already bore her — and she fidgets and hurrys one. — I am disappointed in her — must always have something new like *Olga Evgenievna*. At 4 she goes off to her sister instead of coming to the amputation, once we go — she might have spent the evening at her sister. P—ss. Gedroitz said to me she soon noticed how A. does not care doing or knowing things à fond and she feared we might be so, but is grateful its not the case and that we do all thoroughly. Its not a play — she wanted and fidgeted for the cross, now she has it, her interest has greatly slakened — whereas we feel now doubly the responsability and seriousness of it all and want to give out all we can to all the poor wounded, with slight or serious wounds, equally lovingly. — Marie saw an officer of her regiment. — You will give *N. P.* our love please, and tell him the news we give you, as all we do interest's him. — My nose is full of hideous smells from those blood-poisoning wounds. — One of the officers in the big palace showed me German frabricated dum-dums, very long, narrow at the tip, red copper like things. — Me misses you, me wants a kiss badly. Lovy my child, I long for you, think and pray for you incessantly. Sweetest One, goodbye now and God bless and protect you.

I press you tenderly to my heart, kissing you fondly, and remain for ever your deeply loving own old wify Sunny.

The Children all kiss you. —

No. 20.

Tsarskoje Selo, Nov. 21-st 1914

My Lovebird,

I don't want the Feldjeger to leave to-morrow without a letter from me. This is the wire I just received from our Friend. »*When you comfort the wounded God makes His name famous through your gentleness and glorious work.*« So touching and must give me strength to get over my shyness. — Its sad leaving the wee ones! —

Iza suddenly had 38 and pains in her inside, so *Vladimir Nikolaievitch* wont let her go. Fullspeed we telephoned to Nastinka to get ready and come. —

We are taking parcels and letters from all the naval wives for *Kovno.*

We are eating, and the Children chattering like waterfalls, which makes it somewhat difficult to write. —

Now Light of my life, farewell. God bless and protect you and keep you from all harm. I do not know when and where this letter will reach you. — Blessings without end and fondest kisses from us all. Your very own

Sunny.

We all send messages to *N. P. — and Dmitri Sheremetiev.*

No. 21.

Tsarskoje Selo, Nov. 21-st 1914

My own beloved Treasure,

Its nice that we were together at *Smolensk* 2 years ago (with C. Keller) so I can imagine where you were. Alexei's »*committee*« wired to me after you had been there to see them. I remember them giving Baby an Image at that famous tea there. — Still no news of the war through fat Orlov since you left. One whispers that Joachim has been taken by our troops — if so, where has he been sent to, I wonder. If true, one might have let *Dona* know through Vicky of Sweden that he is safe and sound (not saying where) but you know better, its not for me to advise you, its only a mother pittying another mother. —

I remained at home in the afternoon yesterday, and lay in bed before dinner, being dead-tired. The girls went to the hospital instead of me. After dinner I received *Schulenburg* rather long; he leaves Saturday again. The bombs were being thrown daily over Varsovie and everywhere and at night. Baby's train stuck an hour and 1/2 on the bridge (full of wounded, over 600) and could not get into the station (coming from *Praga)* on account of the other trains, and he feared every minute that they would be blown up. — Then I received *Ressin* — quick man — in an hour he settled all the plans, and we leave this evening at 9, reach *Vilna* Saturday morning at 10—15. — Then continue to *Kovno* 2.50—6, back *Tsarskoje Selo* Sunday morning at 9. *Ressin* only lets the Gov. of *Vilna* know, because of motors or carriages and he is not to tell on — from there he will let the Gov. at *Kovno* know (or its the same man). Ania has telephoned privately to *Rodionov* — I hope we may catch a glimpse of them somewhere. — A. is very proud she kept me from going to the hospital as tiring — but its her doing this expedition which is tiring — 2 nights in the train and 2 towns to visit hospitals — if we see the dear sailors, it will be a recompense. — I am glad we can manage it so quickly and wont be long away from the Children. — Excuse this dirty page, but I am quite ramolie and my head is weak, I even asked for a little wine. 100 questions, papers — beginning by *Viltchkovsky* in the hospital, every morning questions to answer, resolutions to be taken and so on — and my brain is not as strong or fresh as it was before my heart got so bad all these years.

I understand what you feel like of a morning when one after the other come bothering you with questions. — At the hospital I received a »*Khansha*« who gave M-me *Mdivani* motors and was going to send an *unit* for the Caucasian troops on the German frontier — now she asked my permission to change, and have it in the Caucasus where sanitary help is yet more deficient. — I could not get to sleep this night, so at 2 wrote to A. to tell her to let the naval wives know there is an occasion safely to forward letters or packets — then I sorted out booklets, gospels (1 Apostel), prayers to take for the sailors, goodies and sugared fruits for the officers — perhaps shall find still warm things to add. — For your second dear letter, thanks without end. It was a joy to receive it, sweetheart. It is such anguish to think of our tremendous losses; several wounded officers, who left us a month ago, have returned again wounded. Would to God this hideous war could end quicker, but one sees no prospect of it for long. Of course the Austrians are furious being led by Prussians, who knows whether they wont be having stories still amongst each other. — I received letters from Thora, Q. Helena and A. Beatrice, all send you much love and feel for you deeply. They write the same about their wounded and prisoners, the same lies have been told them too. They say the hatred towards England is the greatest. According to the telegrams Georgie is in France seeing his wounded. — Our Friend hopes you wont remain too long away so far. — I send you papers and a letter from Ania. — Perhaps you will mention in your telegram, that you thank for papers and letter and send messages. I hope her letters are not the old oily style again. — Very mild weather. At 9½ we went to the end of mass in the *Pestcherny Chapel* — then to our hospital where I had heaps to do, the girls nothing and then to an operation in the big hospital. And we showed our officers to Zeidler to ask advice. — Olga and Tatiana went in despair to town to a concert in the Circus for Olga's committee — without her knowledge one had invited all the ministers and Ambassadors, so she was obliged to go.

Mme Zizi, Isa and Nastinka accompanied them, and I asked Georgi to go too and help them, — he at once agreed to go — kind fellow. — I must write still to Olga with the eatables I send her. Her friend has gone there for short, as he is unwell, like *Boris* with *the itch,* and needs a good cleaning. — A. says she has looked through the newspaper and its very dull, she begs pardon for sending it, she thought it was a nice one. Just back from the big Palace and *dressings* I looked at, and sat with officers.

Now *Malama* comes to tea to say quite goodbye.

Goodbye my Angel huzzy.

God bless and protect you.

1000 fond kisses from your own old

Wify.

The Children all kiss you. We all send heaps of messages to *N. P.* — Long for you!

No. 22.

Tsarskoje Selo, Nov. 23nd 1914, Sunday

My own beloved Darling.

We returned here safely at 9¼, found the little ones well and cheery. The girls have gone to Church — I am resting, as very tired, slept so badly both nights in the train — this last we tore simply, so as to catch up an hour. Well, I shall try to begin from the beginning. — We left here at 9, sat talking till 10, and then got into our beds. Looked out at *Pskov* and saw a sanitary train standing — later one said we passed also my train, which reaches here to-day at 12½. Arrived at *Vilna* at 10¼ — Governor and military, red cross officials at station, I cought sight of 2 sanitary trains, so at once went through them, quite nicely kept for simple ones — some very grave cases, but all cheery, came straight from battle. Looked at the *feeding station* and ambulatory. — From there in shut motors driven (I was just interrupted, Mitia *Den* came to say goodbye) to the Cathedral where the 3 Saints lie, then to the Image of the Virgin, (the climb nearly killed me) — a lovely face the Image has (a pitty one cannot kiss it). Then to the Polish *Palace* hospital — an immense hall with beds, and on the scene the worst cases and on the gallery above officers — heaps of air and cleanly kept. Everywhere in both towns one kindly carried me up the stairs which were very steep. Everywhere I gave Images and the girls too. — Then to the hospital of the red cross in the Girls gymnasium, where you found the nurses pretty — lots of wounded — *Verevkin's* both daughters as nurses. His wife could not show herself, as their little boy has a contagious illness; his aids wife replaced her. No acquaintances anywhere. The nurses sang the hymn, as we put on our cloaks; the Polish ladies do not kiss the hand. Then off to a small hospital for officers (where *Malama* and *Ellis* had layn before). There one officer told Ania he had seen me 20 years ago at Simferopol, had followed our carriage on a bicycle and I had reached him out an apple (I remember that episode very well) such a pitty he did not tell me — I remember his young face 20 years ago, so could not recognise him. From there back to the station we could not go to more, as the 2 sanitary trains had taken time. *Valuyev* wanted me to see their hospital in the woods, but it was too late. *Artsimovitch* turned up at the station thinking I would go to a hospital where sisters from his government were. I lunched and dined always on my bed. At *Kovno* the charming commandant of the fortress (no Governor counts there now, as it is the active front) and military authocraties, some officers, *Shirinsky* and *Stchepotiev* stood there too. The others had been just sent out to town expeditions, close to Thorn to blow up a bridge and the other place I forget, such a pitty to have missed them. *Voronov,* we passed at *Vilna* in the street. Again off in motors, flying along to the Cathedral (from *Vilna* we let know we were coming) — carpet on the stairs, trees in pots out, all electric lamps burning in the Cathedral, and the Bishop met us with a long speach. Short *a Te Deum,* kissed the miraculous Image of the Virgin and he gave me one of St. Peter and St. Paul, after whom the Church is named — he spoke touchingly of us »the sisters of mercy« and called wify *a new name,* »the mother of mercy«. Then to the red cross, simple sisters, skyblue cotton dresses — the eldest sister, a lady just come there, spoke to me in English, had been a sister 10 years ago and seen me there, as my old friend *Kirejev* had asked me to receive her. Then to another little wing of the hospital in another street. Then to a big hospital about 300 in the bank — looked so strange to see the wounded amongst such surrounding of a former bank. One lancer of mine was there. Then we went to the big military hospital, tiny service and wee speech. Lots of wounded and 2 rooms with Germans, talked to some. From there to the station, on the platform stood the companies (I had begged for them, I must confess), so difficult to recognise them, and not many acquaintances, you saw them. *Simonin* looked a dear. The boatswain of the »Peterhof« with the St. George's cross -- all well, *Shirinsky* too looks well. *The Commandant* is such a nice simple kind, not fussy man. Begged me to send still 3000 Images or bibles. He blessed us when the train left, touching man — to be cheered by our sailors at a fortress-station, they dressed as soldiers, we as nurses, who would have thought that possible a few months ago. At *Landvarovo* we stopped and looked at the feeding station and barracks hospital at station and service in wee Church. Some heavy cases. *The Livland committee* — (Pss. *Schetvertinskaya* at the head, her property is close by), the daugther as nurse. — At 2 we stopped at a station, I discovered a sanitary train and out we flew, climbed into the boxcars. 12 men lying comfortably, drinking tea, by the light of a candle — saw all and gave Images — 400. An ill Priest too was there — »Zemsky« train, 2 sisters (not dressed as such) 2 brothers of mercy, 2 doctors and many sanitaries. I begged pardon for waking them up, they thanked us for coming, were delighted, cheery, smiling and eager faces. So we were an hour late and cought it up in the night, so that I was rocked to and fro, and feared we should capsize.

So now I saw *Irina,* after which must meet my Sanitary train. Ella arrives to morrow evening. God bless and protect you — no news from you since Friday. Very tenderest, fondest kisses from your very own old wify

Sunny.

Victoria sends love, living Kent House Isle of Wight.

Messages to *N. P.*

No. 23.

Tsarskoje Selo, Nov. 24th 1914

My very own beloved One,

I am so glad you had such a touching reception at *Kharkov* — it must have done you good and cheered you up. The news from out there make one so anxious — I don't listen to the gossip of town which makes one otherwise quite nervous, but only beleive what *Nikolasha* lets know. Nevertheless I begged A. to wire to our Friend that things are very serious and we beg for his prayers. Yes, its a strong enemy we have facing us and a stubborn one. —

Sashka is coming to us to tea, on his way to the Caucasus — one says he married an actress and therefore leaves the regiment, he denied it to A. and said it was his bad health which obliged him to ask for leave and he wanted to see his parents. — *Malama* took tea before leaving too. — Ella arrives this evening. — We had 4 operations this morning in the big hospital and then officers dressings — My 2 »*Crimeans*« from *Dvinsk* arrived — they happily look better than they did then. — Almost daily I receive officers returning to the army or leaving to continue a restcure in their family. — Now we have placed officers in the big palace on the opposite side too; General Tancray (the father of mine) lies there too. — I am going off to see them at 4, the poor little fellow with the terrible wound always begs me to come.

The weather is grey and dull. — Do you ever manage to get a run at the stations? —

Fredericks was again ill two nights ago and spat blood — so he is kept in bed — poor old man, it is so hard for him — and he suffers morally terribly. — Masses of your Mamas IIth Siberian regiment came in my train, 7 of her officers lie here in different trains. — Yesterday we received three »*Pavlovtsi*« to congratulate us on their feast-day, and *Boris* wired from Varsovie in the »*Atamantsi*« name. — *Petia* looks alright, told us a lot, smelt of garlic, as he has injections of arsenic made him. — The Children are well and cheery. — Such a pitty I cannot get off now in a sanitary train — I long to be nearer the front, as you are so far away — that they should feel our proximity and gain courage. — A. Eugenie has 100 wounded in the hall and adjoining room. —

I do so long for you, my treasure — to-morrow a week that you left us — heart and soul are ever near you. I kiss you as tenderly as I only can and hold you tightly in my arms.

God bless and strengthen you and give consolation and trust. —

Ever, Nicky my own, your very own deeply loving old Wify

Alix.

Wonder whether you saw my *supply store* at *K.;* the Gov. is on bad terms with the *Rebinders* and so does not give a penny to my *store,* alas. — Please, give *N. P.* our best love. — The Children kiss you 1000 times. I wonder where this letter will reach you! —

No. 24.

Tsarskoje Selo, Nov. 25th 1914

My own beloved One,

In great haste a few lines. We were occupied all morning — during an operation a soldier died — it was too sad — the first time it had happened to the Princess and she has done 1000 of operations already; *Hemorrhage.* All behaved well, none lost their head — and the girlies were brave — they and

Ania had never seen a death. But he died in a minute — it made us all so sad as you can imagine — how near death always is! We continued another operation. To-morrow we have the same one again and may end fatally too, but God grant not, but one must try and save the man.

Ella came for luncheon, remains still to-morrow. We had her *report* and the 2 *Mekk's,* Rost. and *Apraxin* — for 2 hours, that is why I had no time to write a real letter. — *Yedigarov* dined cosily with us yesterday, he leaves in a day or 2 and has left the hospital already — fancy my having had courage to invite him — he was a dear and so simple. —

Weather very mild. — Must end, man waits, others drinking tea around. —

Blessings and very fondest kisses from your own old

Sunny.

Remember me to *Vorontsov* and *N. P.* Ella and Children kiss you. Ella says General *Schwartz* adores you. —

No. 25.

Tsarskoje Selo, Nov. 26-th 1914

My very own precious One.

I congratulate you with the St. George's feast — what a quantity of new cavaliers — heroes we have now. But ah me, what heartrending losses, if one can believe what town says. *Ambrazantzev* is killed, Mme Knorring (his great friend, née Heyden) got the news. One says terrible losses in the hussars, but I cannot trust to it being true. But I have no right to fill your ears with »les on dit«, I pray they may not be true. Well, we all knew that such a war would be the bloodiest and most awful one ever known, and so it has turned out to be the case, and one yearns over the heroic victims martyrs for their cause! — A. has twice been to se Sashka, I told her it was very wrong, but she does not heed me in the least. Ella went in the afternoon with Olga and me to the big palace and she spoke to all the wounded; one of them was wounded last war and lay at Moscou, and remembers her having come to see him. Its difficult finding time to write these two days whilst she is here. — Sweet Treasure, its ages since you left and me longs for »Agoobigweeone«. We went to early mass in the »*Pestcherny Chapel*« and from there Ella went to town till 3 — and we till 1 to the little hospital — a small operation and 19 dressings, people I mean, as some had many wounds to be seen after. Very warm again. At 4 I am going to the big palace, because they daily wait for the motor and are disappointed if we dont go, which happens rarely and the little boy begged me to come earlier to-day. — I feel my letters are very dull, but am ramolie and tired and the thoughts wont come. The heart is full of love and boundless tenderness for you. I eagerly await your promised letter, long to know more about you and how you spend the time in the train after all receptions and inspections. — I hope you have fine weather and lots of sun, here its so grey and wet. Have not been out since you left, only in shut motors. My Angel goodbye now and God bless you. May St. George bring special blessings and victories to our troops. — The Children and I kiss you ever so tenderly. — Count Nirod is just coming to speak about the Xmaspresents for the troops. Ania sends you a funny newspaper.

Fondest kisses, Nicky love, from your very own

Wify.

The Children and I send *N. P.* many messages. Well, the Xmas presents cannot be got in time, so we shall do it for Easter — then 10 years ago for 300,000 it took from 3—4 months collecting and now its much more needed. —

No. 26.

Tsarskoje Selo, Nov. 27-th 1914

My own beloved One,

In great haste a few lines — we are at once off to the mass for and with the »*Nizhegorodtzy*«, our wounded and other officers, General *Bagration*, old *Navruzov* and ladies of the regiment. Worked the whole morning and had a big operation. At 9½ had a mass at *Znamensky* church, as its the feast of the Church's Image. Its pouring and very dark. All of us are well. We are taking all 5 children to Church as Baby is inscribed into the regiment. —

Well, all went off well. From there we went to the big palace to all the wounded — they wait for the motor daily, so there is no way of keeping away. I find the young boy gradually getting worse, the temp. is slowly falling, but the pulse remains far too quick, in the evenings he is off of his head and so weak. The wound is much cleaner, but the smell they say is quite awful. He will pass away gradually — I only hope not whilst we are away. Then we went to the one house of my red cross community. — Now have drunk tea and *Goremykin* waits and then the P-ss. Can't write any more. Blessings and kisses without end.

Ever Sweetheart, your very own

Sunny.

Its pouring hard.

No. 27.

Tsarskoje Selo, Nov. 28-th 1914

My very own precious One,

I could not manage to write to you by to-day's messenger, I had such a lot to do. We were at the hospital all the morning & as usual *Viltchkovsky's* report there. Then quickly changed, lunched & off to town to the *Pokrovsky Committee* on *Vasiliev Island.* The 3 Buchanans & some more English of the committee & nurses received us. A big ward for officers & a nice saloon for them with chintz & 3 rooms for men, quite simple & nice. Then we went through the wards & saw more wounded, & in the yard there was a big building belonging to the *Committee of the City Hospital* — in the upper story were 130 wounded. — From there we rushed to my *store* — masses of ladies working I am glad to see & heaps of things prepared. Then to *Anitchkov* to tea; — Mother dear looks well, I think my journeys alone astonish her. — but I feel its the time to do such things, God has given me better health & I find that we women must all, big & small, do everything we can for our touchingly brave wounded. At times I feel I cant any more & fill myself with heart-drops & it goes again — & our Friend wishes me besides to go, & so I must swallow my shyness. The girls help me. Then we came home I lay & read heaps of papers from Rost. — Lovy dear, I hope you wont be displeased at Fred.'s telegram to *Voyeikov,* we spoke it over by telephone, as he may not go out yet. You see its a national thing this exhibition with trophies of the war, & so its better the entry should be gratis — one can stand *collection-boxes* near the door, then it obliges nobody to pay. I do not wish *Sukhomlinov* harm, on the contrary, but his wife is really most mauvais genre & has made every body, the military especially, angry with her as she »put me in« with her collect on the 26-th. The day was alright & that singers wished to sing gratis in restaurants so as to get money for her *store.* And I allowed it. To my horror I saw the anouncement in the papers, that in all the restaurants & cabarets (of bad reputation) d r i n k s would be sold for the profit of her *branch store* (my name in big letters) till 3 in the morning (now all restaurants are closed at 12) & that Tango & other dances would be danced for her profit. It made a shocking impression — you forbid (thank Heaven) wine — & I, so to speak, encourage it for the store, horrid & with right all are furious, the wounded too. — And the ministers aides de camp were to collect money. There was no possibility any more to stop it — so we asked Obolensky to order the rest to be closed at 12 except the decent ones.

The fool harms her husband & breaks her neck. — She receives money & things in my name & gives it out in hers — she is a common woman, & vulgar soul, therefore such things happen, tho' she works hard & does much good — but she is harming him very much, as he is her blind slave — & all see this — I wish one could warn him to keep her in hand. When Rost. told them my displeasure, he was in despair, & asked whether she ought to close her *store,* so Rost. said of course not, that I know the good she does, only here acted most wrongly. — Enough of this, only I want you to know the story, as there were strong articals in the papers about it. — Therefore another collect for her now would make things worse. One wished my *store* to collect at Xmas, & I declined the project, one cannot go on begging incessantly, its not pretty. —

The Commandor of my 21-st Siberian regiment arrived to-day — happily his wounds are but slight. — Now I must get to sleep, its 1 o'clock. For the first time 2 degrees of frost to-day. — 29-th. How can I thank you enough for your sweetest letter of the 25-th which I received this morning. We follow with interest all you are doing — it must be a great consolation to see these masses of devoted happy subjects; I am glad you managed to go to yet two other towns where the Cosacks are. — We went to the *local hospital* & there I gave 4 medals to amputated soldiers — there were no very heavy cases otherwise. —

Then we went to the big palace to see all our wounded — they are already sorrowing that they wont see us so long. — This morning both »*Nishegorodtzy*«, *Navruzov* and *Yagmin* were operated — so we want to peep in this evening & see how they feel. They were mad with joy over your telegr. which they read in the papers — that you called them »*incomparable*« is the greatest recompense, as such a word was never used before.

Kniazhevitch comes this evening about affairs. — Are going to Church, so must end, & want to rest before. — Very tenderest blessings & kisses, Nicky mine, from your very own Wify.

Our love to *N. P.* — glad, you two sinners had pretty faces to look at — I see more other parts of the body, less ideal ones!! —

No. 28.

Tsarskoje Selo, Dec. 1-st 1914

My own beloved One,

This is my last letter to you before we meet — God grant in 6 days. To-morrow its two weeks since you left & I have missed my Sweetheart m o r e than I can say. The joy to meet will be intense, only the pain to leave the little Ones for a whole week is great — I cant get accustomed to separations — sweet Agoo-weeone. — Thank God he is well, that is my consolation. —

Oh I am so tired — so much to do & people to see the last days, therefore I could not write yesterday. — Then I went to the *local hospital* on Saturday, yesterday to the Invalides, to-day to our big hospital (took Alexei) & gave medals in your name — they were so awfully happy & grateful poor miserable fellows. — We shall miss our sick & they were sad to bid us goodbye. —

Petia lunched, & yesterday Paul took tea — he yearns for a nomination.

Rostof. comes now, I want to find out why *Maklakov* wont allow the Americans to see how our prisoners are kept — they have been sent to Germany to see, France & England, & I find it wrong one does not show ours. — Cannot write any more. Blessings — kisses without end. —

Ever, Nicky love, your very own deeply loving old Sunny.

Our Friend wired: »*Be crowned with earthly happiness, the heavenly wreaths follow you.*«

No. 29.

Moscou, Dec. 12-th 1914

My beloved Angel,

Once more we separate, but God grant shall meet again in 5 days. — I want to remind you to speak to Nikolasha about alowing officers to go on leave home to be treated and not to have them kept in towns, where by chance the sanitary train has brought them. — They will recover far quicker if can be near their families and some must finish their cures in the south to get their strength back, especially those wounded through the chest. — I am glad you will get one days rest in the train and being at the »Stavka« will freshen you up after these awful fatigues and endless receptions. One consolation, you have made 1000 wounded endlessly happy. — I shall try and keep a little quiet these days, more or less — as M. B. will be coming and the heart has been much enlarged these days. —

Lovy dear, why dont you nominate Groten for your hussars, they sorely are in need of a real commander.

Goodbye my treasure and sleep well, shall miss you horribly again. God bless and keep you. —

If you can, speak with Voyeikov and Benk about the Xmas-trees, for the wounded, and I shall to Viltchkovsky. Press you to my heart and kiss you ever and ever again with deepest tenderness.

Ever yr. very own

Wify.

In my glass cupboard over the writing table are candles in case you need any.

No. 30.

Tsarskkoje Selo, Dec. 14-th 1914

My very own beloved One,

A Feldjeger is leaving, so I hasten to send you a few lines. Agooweeone's foot is really alright, only hurts him to put it down, so he prefers not using it and for prudence's sake keeps on the sopha. Marie's angina is better, she slept well and has 37, *Tatiana* has Mme Becker, so only gets up for luncheon. *Botkin* has put me to bed as heart still very much enlarged and aches and I cannot take medicins; and feel still horribly tired and achy all over. Yesterday remained on the sopha, except when went up to Marie and Baby. Alia came to me for half an hour in the evening as feels sad and lonely without her husband — she spent the night at Anias. The girls went to the hospitals after luncheon and sledging — and in the evening. To-day they will go again, and to-morrow begin their work there. — I cant, alas, as yet and am very sorry about it, as it helps me morally. — Our Friend arrives to-morrow and says we shall have better news from the war — Ania goes to meet him in town. — Miechen is in town laid up with influenza; Paul one says, neither well. —

A. received 2 letters from *Tchakhov,* 2 from Jedigarov and *Malama* so touching all of them — I begged them always to give us news through A. I shall see *Afrosimov* to-morrow he leaves back to the regiment which soon goes to the »*Stavka*«, and longs to see its beloved »*chef*« (and family) there. Won't you speak about Kirill to *Nikolasha?* and then tell your *Mama;* it wld. really be good to settle all, and now during the war its easiest being done.

— Where are all the sailors now united? — Poor *Botkin* continues being in great anguish about his eldest son — always hopes still that he may be alive. One says the sisters (ladies) in the »*otriad*« of *Sandra* have received medals on St. Georges ribbons, as were working under fire, taking out the wounded, I think. — Sunbeam has just gone out in the donkey sledge — he kisses you — he can put the foot down but prefers being careful so as to be soon quite alright again. — How horrid it was saying goodbye to you in Moscou, seeing you stand there amongst heaps of people (all so unlike you in every respect) and I had to bow and look at them too and smile and could not keep my eyes fixed on you, as should have wished to. — You know before our arrival to Moscou, three military hospitals with German and Austrian wounded were cleared out to Kazan — I read the description of a young gentleman (Russian) who took them — many half dying who died on the road and never should have been moved with fearful wounds, smelling poisonously, not having been bandaged for several days — and just during their Xmas being tortured like that in no lovely sanitary trains. From one hospital they were sent even without a Dr. to bring them, only sanitaries. — I have sent the letter to Ella to enquire into this and make a good row, its hideous and to me utterly incomprehensible. At Petrograd one says scarcely a vacant bed. Babys train arrives from Varshau to-day — Loman found no wounded there, so has gone to look for them elsewhere. Does that mean all is quiter these days (their Xmas and we like Christians don't profit) and therefore less losses? One longs to know something clearer. — Must stop now as my head aches yet fr. the cold, tho' the nose no longer runs. — Sashka has returned fr. the Caucasus again, one says. — Its so lonely here without you my Treasure, tenderly, beloved One, always expect the door to open and see you enter from yr. walk. Its gently snowing. Give our love to N. P., so happy he is with you. — The Children kiss you endlessly and so does your wify. I hope you feel more rested now. — One says the Sinod gave an order there should be no Xmas trees — I am going to find out the truth about it and then make a row, its no concern of theirs nor the Churches, and why take away a pleasure fr. the wounded and children, because it originally came from Germany — the narrowmindedness is too colossal. — I saw Olga Evg. she has quite broken down after her brothers death, the nerves have given way and phisically her strength fails her, wretched soul — so she needs a month's good rest and hopes then to set to work again. — God bless and keep you my very own precious Nicky dear, I kiss you and press you lovingly to my old heart, and gently stroke yr. weary brow.

Ever yr. very own old

Sunny.

Can you find out whether it is true that little Alexei Orlov is wounded? It may be again gossip — I do not know where the regiment is, and why one is at the *General Quarter* now. — Wont you ask *Shavelsky* to send out the Priest in the regiments more *Saint Sacrements* and wine, so as that more can take Holy Communion — I send what I can with our *store* trains, — Ella too. —

No. 31.

Tsarskoje Selo, Dec. 15-th 1914

My beloved Darling,

Fredericks let me know that you are only returning on Friday as are going to see the troops — I am delighted for you and them, a great consolation for you all and will give them new strength. And this morning *Selenetzki* let me know and then Kiryll wired from town, that our dear *Butakov* had been killed — it is too sad, that kind good man, loved by all. How wretched his little wife will be, she who is only one bit of nerves already. Another one of our yacht friends gone already, how many more will this terrible war yet claim! — And now *Botkin* got the news from the regiment that his son was killed as he would not surrender — a German officer, prisoner told the news; poor man is quite broken down. — I saw Afrosimov who soon returns to the front, but I think its too soon, he was contusioned long ago and one sees his eye blinks and he suffers from giddyness. — The Children began their work to-day and had heavy cases. My heart is still enlarged and aches, as does my head and feel so giddy — I had to come over onto the sopha as Aunt Olga comes at 4½. — Marie and Dmitri wished to come to dinner, but I cant have them, feel too rotten still. — Marie has not yet come down as her throat is not quite in order, temp. normal. Baby goes out twice daily in his little donkey-sledge. — I have much to do thinking over Xmas-presents for the wounded and its difficult when one feels rotten. — I am glad you get a walk, it will have done you good. — Ella wrote in despair, trying to get to the bottom of the things about the trains and hospitals — she beleives the orders came from Petrograd. Often the orders from there are very cruel towards the wounded in the military hospitals. When she knows all, she will write to Alek. — In town there are scarcely any vacancies, don't know where I shall send my trains if they dont give me Finland. — Bright sunny day, He must have arrived, A. has gone to meet him, I only saw her a second, she was with the Children in the hospital and then lunched with them. Olga and Anastasia are sledging with Isa, Tatiana has lessons — *Shura* reads to Marie, Baby is out and I feel rotten. — Precious one, its lonely without you, but am glad for your sake that you are out and will see the troops. — I want so much to go to Holy Communion this *Lent,* if I can manage with my health. — My precious one. Goodbye now and God bless — and protect you and keep you from all harm. I press you to my heart and kiss you over and over again with gentle tenderness.

Ever your very own Wify.

Give my love to *N. P.* — he will be sad about *Butakov.* Make Feodorov go unexpected to small hospitals and poke his nose everywhere.

No. 32.

Tsarskoje Selo, Dec. 16-th 1914

My own beloved One,

A glorious, sunny day. The girls are in the hospital, Baby has just gone out, Anastasia has a lesson & Marie has not yet been let come down. — I slept badly & feel giddy & rotten, tho' just now the heart is not enlarged — am to keep lying as much as possible, so shall only go over onto the sopha after luncheon, like yesterday. A. Olga took tea with me & was very sweet & dear — she kisses you. — Have been reading through lots of papers & feel quite idiotical. — Here I am on the sopha, had *Viltchkovsky* with a *report,* heaps of questions as he tells me everything of the evacuation committee of *Y. C.* wh. he is at the head of — then questions about Xmas-trees. —

Mavra sent you a letter of Onors to Vicky of Sweden, to give over her love to us & to say that Ernie came for quite short after 3 months, that he left again & is well. — I enclose a letter of Keller — as it will interest you to see what he says — happily he seems not badly wounded.

From my *store* trains good news & begging always for more things, as the troops know them already, & when in need, turn up. — Glad my letter smelt nicely, when you got it, it was to remind you quite especially of your very own wify, who misses you awfully. —

At last Xenia is out of quarantine she let know. —

I feel still not famous, such a nuisance not to work, but I go on with my brain doing business. — I have nothing interesting to tell you, alas. Long for news of the war — so anxious. —

It seems masses of sanitary trains were sent here to town instead of Moscou, whilst we were there & there are no more Vacancies at *Petrograd.* There is something wrong about this evacuation question, Ella is trying to clear it up on her side. — *Loman* has not returned, as thank God there are few wounded at the present moment. — The Children kiss you very tenderly, Wify clasps you fondly to her lonely heart, & blesses you with fervour.

Ever yr. own old

Sunny.

Messages to *N. P.* please & the little Admiral. — I spoke a second to *Gr.* by telephone, sends: *Fortitude of spirit, — will soon come to you, will discuss everything.* —

No. 33.

Tsarskoje Selo, Dec. 17-th 1914

My own precious One,

This will probably be my last letter, if you return on Friday. Now you are with the troops — what a joy for you and them — tho' painful to see masses of known faces missing.

The Children are working & then go to *Anitchkov Palace* to luncheon before receiving donations in the Winter Palace. The train with poor *Butakov's* body is 24 hours late, so the funeral can only be to-morrow morning.

I scarcely slept a wink this night, perhaps from 4—5 & 6—7. The rest of the time could not, & in despair kept always looking at the watch, hundred of sad thoughts coursed through my tired brain & gave it no rest. The heart again enlarged this morning — to-morrow hope to rebegin my medicines again, then I shall get quicker right again. —

6 degrees this morning — *Olga* walks through the garden to *Znamenia* & fr. there on foot to the hospital, *Tatiana* follows in a motor after her lesson, Olga feels the better for air & short exercise in the morning. — Sonia sat with me yesterday & chattered a lot whilst I lay on the sopha & threaded Images. — Ania's brother returns to-morrow, so he asked to see me a minute at 4. — Anastasia & *Ania* have gone for a turn, they say its beastly cold & windy; Baby's foot hurts a wee bit, Marie is coming down at last. Thoughts so much with you — what joy to see the dear brave troops. — This morning our Friend told her by telephone that He is a little more quiet about the news. — The papers say we took German quickfiring guns at — it does indeed seem strange! — Excuse a mighty dull letter, but feel quite cretinised & good for nothing. — Just a wee bit of scent again to remind you quite, particularly of your Wify, who is impatiently awaiting yr. return. You remember I left candles for you in my compartment in the glass cupbord over my writing-table. Now my sweet Treasure goodbye & God bless & protect you. I kiss you ever so tenderly & bless you. Ever my Nicky yr. very. own tenderly loving

Sunny.

Ania kisses yr. hand. All the Children kiss you.

No. 34.

Tsarskoje Selo, 21. Jan. 1915

My very own beloved One,

Once more I pen a letter to you wh. you will read when the train carries you away from us to-morrow. It's not for long, & yet it is painful, but I wont grumble, knowing it brings you comfort & a change & others intense joys. — I hope that Baby's leg will be alright again by yr. return — it looks like it did in Peterhof & then alas it lasted long. I shall always give you news about the *little foot* & about Ania, — either »A.« or »the invalid«. Perhaps you will think some times in yr. telegram to me to ask after her health, it will touch her, as she will miss yr. visits sorely. —

I shall try & go to the hospital to-morrow morning, as I get up to go to Church with you & see you off, hate that moment & can never get accustomed to it. — Darling, you will think of speaking about the officers of the different regiments, that they should not loose their places & speak over those different questions with *Nikolasha;* perhaps you wish to mention the Manifest to him. If you want to do another kind act, telegraph once to Fredericks, or tell *Vojeikov* who wires to him daily, to give a message from you.

In prayers & thoughts I shall accompany you, alas not in reality — feel my presence & incessent love hovering around you, tender & caressing.

Goodbye, Sweetheart, treasure of my soul, God bless & protect you & bring you safe & sound back to us again. I kiss you fervently & remain, huzy dear, yr. very own old wify

Alice.

In the glass cupboard in my compartment you will find candles, in case you need any; think I am lying there at night & then you wont feel so lonely. —

No. 35.

Tsarskoje Selo, Jan. 22-nd 1915

My beloved One,

I have just heard that a Feldjeger leaves, so hasten to send a few lines. Baby spent the day alright & has no fever, now he begins to complain a little of his leg & dreads the night. — From the station I went to him till 11 & then to hospital, to 1, sat with Ania who is alright — she begs me to tell you what she forgot giving over to you yesterday fr. our Friend, that you must be sure not once to mention the name of the *commander in Chief:* in your manifest — it must solely come from you to the poeple. — Then I went in to see the wound of our *standard-bearer* — awful, bones quite smashed, he suffered hideously during the *bandaging:* but did not say a word, only got pale & perspiration ran down his face & body. — In each ward I photographed the officers. After luncheon say goodbye & then I rested & got a wee nap, after wh. I went up to Alexei, read to him, played together & then had tea near his bed.

I remain at home this evening, enough for one day. — Sweet treasure, I am writing in bed, after 6 — the room looks big & empty, as the tree has been taken away. — Sad without you, my Angel & seeing you leave was nasty. —

Tell *Fedorov* I have told *Viltchkovsky* — to find out whether *G. Martinov* would like to lie in the big palace as he wont be able to move for very long — & here we can get him out fine days into the garden in his bed even — I want to let the sick lie out, I think it will do them much good.

Now the man waits, so I must end. — I miss you & love you, my own Nicky dear. Sleep well. God bless & keep you. 1000 kisses fr. the Children & fr. old

Wify.

Baby kisses you very much. He did not complain in the daytime.

No. 36.

Tsarskoje Selo, Jan. 23-d 1915

My own beloved Nicky dear,

I am lying on the sopha next Baby's bed in the sunny corner room — he is playing with Mr. Gillard. Benkendorf came to me & before that M-me Scalon *(Homiakova)* — she told me how much one needs sisters out in the *front flying-detachment* as the poor wounded are often very badly cared for, having no real doctors & no means of sending off their wounded — its all well arranged to the east & north, but in Galicia & the *X.* armycorps much ought yet to be done. This morning I sat with Baby; he had not had a famous night — slept fr. 11—12 then woke up constantly, not from very great pain happily. So I had sat with him in the evening — whilst the girls were in the hospital, Isa came to me. In the morning I gave instruments during the operation, & felt happy to be at work again, then I watched the girls a little at work, after which I sat with Ania — met her brother & nice looking bride there. The sun is shining brightly, so I have sent the girls for an hour's walk. — According to the agency telegrams, such a heavy fighting has begun again, & I had so much hoped there would have been a little quiet. — Ania had slept better, 38.2 yesterday evening, this morning 37.8 — but that does not matter, she hopes you will give over the news of her health to *N. P.* — I think you both must be glad to hear no more grumbling.

Sweetest one I miss you very much & long for your tender love. Its so silent & empty without you. The children have lessons or are in hospitals, I have lots of papers fr. *Rostovtzev* to finish. — Forgive a dull letter, but my brain is tired. — Baby kisses you many times, but wify yet much more. — Goodbye & God bless you my treasure, my sweetest one — my tenderest thoughts suround you. I am glad you got a little airing at the stations. —

I bless you & kiss you, & remain Y. very own old

Sunny.

Give my love to *N. P.* & *Mordvinov.*

If there is any interesting news, do tell fat Orlov to let me know, please.

No. 37.

Tsarskoje Selo, Jan. 24-th 1915

My beloved Darling,

A glorious sunny morning again — I have to keep the white curtain down, as the sun shines straight into my eyes as I lie. Baby slept well, thank God, woke up 5 times, but soon went to sleep again, & is merry. Ania slept also with interruptions, 37.4 yesterday evening 38.6. The girls were in the hospital in the evening, but she was sleepy so did not keep them. I go earlier to bed now, as got up earlier too, on account of Alexei & the hospital. — Now I am next to Baby's bed again — I had an endless *report* with *Rostovtzev.* Then Isa with affairs, & before that Georgi lunched. —

In the morning I made two *bandages* & sat with Ania who finds an hour always too little & wants me in the evening, but I remained because of Baby & that she understood — besides I have been feeling so tired of an evening. — Only seeing suffering makes a bit weary. — Such sunny weather, & *Vojeikov* wired to Fred: you have it too, thats nice. I am sure *Vesselkin* tells you lots of interesting things. I sent you a letter fr. *Ella* wh. I got. — Baby is better & wishes me to tell you so; the dogs romp in the room. —

Several of our officers are off to the Crimea to get stronger. The children walked & are off to the big palace; Marie stands at the door & alas! picks her nose. *Vladimir Nikolaievitch* and Baby are playing cards until I finish. I feel my letters are mighty dull, but I hear nothing worth repeating. My train arrives now. — My treasure, I miss you so much. But I hope you can get some good walks to brace you up, give apetite & sleep. — I went into *Znamensky church* a moment before this hospital & placed a candle for you, huzy mine. —

Are you really having that dull *Shipov* for yr. hussars?

My ex — *Shipov* has received the St. George's Cross — Sandra P. telephoned to Tatiana to share the news with us. —

All the children kiss you ever so tenderly — I enclose letters from Olga & Alexei, our love to *N. P.* & *Mordvinov.*

Goodbye my very Own, God bless & protect you — Ever yr. very own

Sunny.

No. 38.

Tsarskoje Selo, Jan. 25-th 1915

My very beloved One,

Again a gloriously sunny morning, 10 degrees. Only got to sleep after 4 & then woke up still several times. Ania had last night 38.8, leg hurt — slept better, this morning 37.3. Now she suddenly likes the sister *Shevtchuk* & wants her in the room at night to send her to sleep. The girls went there in the evening, but she wished to sleep, so they sat in the other ward. Baby sweet was quite cheery yesterday & asleep before 10. — Motherdear feels depressed getting no news of the war since you left. —

Such intense joy, I received yr. yesterdays' precious letter, thank you for it with all my loving heart. — Don't be anxious about me, I am very careful & my heart is behaving well these days, so that *Botkin* only comes in the morning. Fancy, I just heard that *M-me Pourtzeladze* received a letter from her husband fr. Germany — thank God he was not killed — she adores him so, poor little woman — I can imagine how interesting *Vesselkin* was — God grant his expeditions further success. So *Piaterkin* remains with N. lets hope he will use him thoroughly & send him about to wake him up. — Yes, its lucky your people get on well together, it makes all the difference — I shall tell Ania her book has such success. —

Were at the wedding — sat with Ania (who sends this note) from 1—2 & then again — & then to the big palace. Baby has been twice in the wee sledge in the garden & thoroughly enjoyed it. — I send you our very tenderest love, kisses & blessings, my one & all, my muchly missed treasure. —

Ever yr. very own

Sunny.

Messages to *N. P.*

No. 39.

Tsarskoje Selo, Jan. 26-th 1915

My own beloved One,

How happy Olga must be to have you with her to-day a sunny day & recompense for her hard work. — Fredericks sends me the copies of *Voyeikov's* telegrams, so I got the news of all you do, & whom you see. — This morning I went to *Znamensky church* & the hospital, dressed several wounds & sat a little with Ania. She had the coiffeur so as to get her hair untangled, to-morrow he will come again & clean it. *Zina* is again ill, so nobody can do it well. She looks alright, complains only always about the right leg. Longs to go over to her house, & if the temp. gets quite normal, the Pss. has nothing against it. — How tiring it will be for us — but lovy, from the very first you must then tell her that you cannot come so often, it takes too much time — because if now not firm, we shall be having stories & love-scenes & rows like in the Crimea now, on account of being helpless she hopes to gain more caresses & old time back again — you keep fr. the first all in its limits as you did now — so as that this accident should be profitable & with peaceful results. She is much better, morally, now. — I have heaps of petitions our Friend brought her for you. — Here I enclose the telegr. you received before leaving. — Fat Orlov might find out through Buchanan what sort of a man this son of Steads is. —

Boris came here for 3 days to fetch Miechen — she cannot come to see me as she has not yet been out & there in Varsovie the warm air is to her good. She goes to see her hospital & train & motors. Its a great pitty, as the Poles neither care for the way in wh. she invites herself to their houses to meals — its so tactless of her arranging a second Paris. — *Tatiana* received the St. George's medal for having been under fire, soi disant, in her motor, when she went to bring presents to the *Erivantzy* — the General there gave it to her — that's not right, it makes the order too cheap — if a bomb, a shall burst near the motor & you are simply driving by chance with presents, not working under fire, you get it — & others who work for months, as Olga, quietly in one place, & therefore have by chance not got under fire, won't receive it. — Next Miechen will be returning with it, you will see — then Hélène & Marie deserve it much more for their work in Prussia at the beginning of the war. — Baby was out twice again & has rosy cheeks & does not complain of his leg nor of his arm — but he lies in bed. We take tea there, wh. is cosy & not so sad as down in my mauve room without you. One misses you dreadfully my love, have such bad nights — get to sleep only after 4 these three nights and wake constantly again, but the heart is keeping decent for the present.

Just got yr. telegram from *Rovno* & rejoice for you both Dears — I hope all will go off well at *Kiev* & *Rovno.*

Precious one, my tenderest thoughts always suround you longingly, lovingly & I rejoice for those that see you & to whom you bring new energy and courage. You brighten up all always by your serenity.

Lets hope you will have daily warmer, sunnier weather & will return browner, than when you went. —

Please, give kindest messages from us all to *N. P.* and *M.* — Do you sit sometimes in my compartiment?

Now I must give my letter out, as the man has to take it to town, — & then I shall get a little rest before dinner.

Do not worry, that you have no time for writing, I understand it perfectly well, & not for a moment am hurt — Goodbye my precious One, I bless you & kiss you over & over again — ever so tenderly, all the favourite places. —

Ever yr. very own

Wify.

No. 40.

Tsarskoje Selo, Jan. 27-th 1915

My own beloved Nicky,

I just received yr. wire from *Kiev,* am sure it is a tiring day you are having. — How disgusting the Breslau having shelled *Jalta* — only out of spite — thank God no victims. I am sure you will long to fly off by motor to see the damage done. — The fighting is strong again at the front & heavy losses on all sides; — these dum-dums are infernal! —

I saw Betsy Shuvalov, who is arranging a front detachment for Galicia, — she is still full of your visit to her hospital & the joy it brought to all hearts. —

We had an operation this morning — rather long but went off well. — Ania gets on alright tho' her right leg aches, but the temp. is nearly normal in the evening. Only speaks again of getting into her house. I foresee my life then! Yesterday evening I went as an exception to her, & so, as to sit with the officers a tiny bit afterwards, as I never have a chance. — She is full of how thin she has grown, tho' I find her stomach & legs colossal (& most unapetising) — her face is rosy, but the cheeks less fat & shades under her eyes. She has lots of guests; but dear me — how far away she has sliped from me since her hideous behaviour, especially autumn, winter, spring of 1914 — things never can be the same to me again — she broke that intimate link gently during the last four years — cannot be at my ease with her as before — tho' she says she loves me so, I know its m u c h l e s s than before & all is consecrated in her own self — & you. Let us be careful when you return. How I wish one could sink that odious little Breslau! —

The weather continues being glorious. Baby is daily better, lunched with us & will come down to tea, now he has a French lesson, so I came down again. —

Two more of my Siberians arrived, nice officers. — Have no answer fr. *Martinov.* — Give my love to *N. P.* Ania got his wire fr. the *Stavka* but dawdled about answering. Shall give her over yr. love. Girls have a committee this evening. — I slept 3 hours from after 4½ till 7½ this night, so tiresome I cannot get to sleep early. —

Must end now, Treasure, my Sunshine, my Life, my Love — I kiss & bless you. —

Ever yr. very own

Sunny.

Baby wishes us to come up to tea.

Think of me at Sebastopol & all known places. —

Feel *Jalta* will tempt you — don't mind on our account being a day late. —

No. 41.

Tsarskoje Selo, Jan. 28-th 1915

My beloved One,

Such loving thanks for yr. dear telegram. *Voyeikov's* to Fredericks I read with great interest as they tell in detail where you have been. How tired you must be after all you did at *Kiev,* but what a sunny remembrance you leave with all — you our Sunshine, Baby our Sunbeam. I was just now in the big palace with Marie and Anastasia, 2 of my Siberians arrived there & 2 in our hospital, then an officer of the 2-nd Siberian regiment *(comrade* of *Matznev)* with an amputated leg & a priest of the 4-th S. regiment wounded in the soft part of his leg, made a charming impression & spoke of the men, with such love and deepest admiration. — In the morning I made three *dressings.* A little *Crimeans,* whom I received in autumn after his promotion, is wounded in the arm — already in the Carpathian hills. — Ania's lungs are quite alright again, but she is weak & giddy, so is to be fed every two hours. I fed her personally, & she ate a good luncheon, more than I eat. —

I read two short stories of Saints to her & I think it was good & has left her something to think over, & not only of herself, wh. is my aim with her. —

The big girls went to town to Css. Carlov's small hospital in her house & to the Winter Palace to receive donations. — Baby has his lessons, goes out in the donkey sledge twice a day; he says your tower has dwindled somewhat. We take tea in his room, he likes it, & I am glad not to have it here without you. — Some regiments get their *rewards* awfully slowly, how I wish one could hurry it up. — And they do complain so, *Viltchkovsky* said about those 6 weeks as they loose so much & it makes them bitter, because if they go back too soon, they quite loose their health & if they remain over their term of 6 weeks, they loose so much. —

Nikolasha's long telegram fills one's heart with admiration & deepest emotion — what bravery to withstand 22 attacks in one day.

Really saints & heroes all of them. But what ghastly losses the Germans have & they don't seem to care. — Thanks so much for letting me get these telegrams. —

One says *Rodzianko 's* speech was splendid, especially the end, I have not had time to read it yet. —

Isa's Mother comes to me this afternoon, as she is going to Denmark, tho' her husband does not want her. — What do you think Madelaine told me, fr. people she knows, whose acquaintances returned just now fr. Jena, where they had lived several years. At the frontier one undressed the couple in separate rooms & then searched their *b* to see whether they had hidden any gold there. Too shameful & mad. — In the goldmines, niggers hide away gold there, but you see Europeans doing such a thing — ridiculous if not so degrading! — I daily place my candles at *Znamenia*. —

Yesterday I was in bed at 11¼ & got to sleep after 2 — slept till 8 with interruptions — an Orenburg shawl on my head helped me to get to sleep — but waiting so long for sleep is a wee bit dull, but not to be complained of as have no pains. — Thank God my heart keeps decent & I can do more again with care. —

Marie has a bad finger since several days, so *Vlad. Nik.* cut it to-day in my room — she was very good about it & did not move — those things hurt — it reminded me of Pss. Gedroitz whose 2 fingers I had to cut & bandage & the officers looked on through the door. —

Sweet Manny mine, beloved One, huzy my very own Treasure, goodbye. God bless & protect you. I kiss you ever so tenderly & fondly & bless you, yr. own old

Sunny.

You will receive this already on yr. homeward journey. — Many messages to *N. P.* & *Mordv.*

Glorious, sunny weather continues. —

Goodbye wee one, me's awaiting you with open, loving arms! I enclose a letter fr. Marie.

No. 42.

Tsarskoje Selo, Jan. 29-th 1915

My own beloved One,

Loving thanks for two dear telegrams. I can imagine how emotioning it was going on board our dear ships, & how your precious presence will have given them new courage for their difficult work. How one longs for them quickly to get hold of the Breslau before she does any more harm. How lucky there were only so few wounded still in the hospital. — Over & over I thank you for your dearest letter from *Rovno* — it came as a very great & most pleasant surprise whilst I was still in bed. Fancy Olga going to be the eldest sister now of the red Cross community out there — with God's help I am sure she will manage well. —

Petia has turned up & comes to-morrow to luncheon. I shall be having to see his mad father, as I sent Loman twice to him with questions about our trains, & he received before others & screamed at him & insulted him & understood everything wrong, tho' he had the paper wh. I had seen before he got it. He is so impossible rushing about the room, giving others no time to speak & screaming at all. — This night I went to sleep after 4½ & woke up early again — such dull nights! Then we had *Troitzky's* Operation, it went off well, thank God — hernial rupture & then I had to do several pensements, so scarcely saw Ania. Our Fr. came there, as He wanted to see me a second. — Fredericksy & Emma lunched, I photographed them. Olga & Tatiana only returned near 2, they had so much to do. In the afternoon I rested & slept half an hour. Then we took tea with Alexei upstairs, then I saw *Loman*, — *Viltchkovsky's report* is always at the hospital. — Baby stands — & I hope, by the time you return, that he will be able to walk again. Marie's finger is not yet right. — Ania is better, but the humour not famous — I fed her, so she ate alright & she sleeps quite decently now. — The most of the wounded I could not see to-day, there was no time. — I am so glad you had good talks with N. Freder: is rather in despair (rightly) about many orders he gives unwisely & wh. only aggravate, & things one had better not discuss now — others influence him & he tries to play your part wh. is far from right — except in military matters — & ought to be put a stop to — one has no right before God & man to usurp your rights as he does — he can make the mess & later you will have great difficulty in mending matters. Me it hurts very much. One has no right to profit of one's unusually great rights as he does.

The weather continues being glorious, but I cannot venture out into the garden. —

Do you remember one of our first wounded officers *Strashkevitch* who had his head tied up & spoke so long to you, until you felt quite faint? Well poor man, he returned to his regiment & has been killed. Sad for his poor family — he served in a bank. — I said to *Loman* that some of the wounded might also come with us to Church & take Communion with us — it would be such a consolation for them, & I hope you do not object. *Lòman* will speak with *Viltchkovsky*, & you can warn *Voyeikov*, if you don't forget. — How the »noises« this night will remind you of the Yacht — that clang clang of *Sebastopol*.

Sweetheart, what joy to have you back in four days! Now I must send off my letter. Goodbye & God bless & protect you my dearest darling Treasure.

I kiss you ever so tenderly & hold you tight in my loving old arms.

Ever, Lovy, yr. very own

Wify.

No. 43.

Tsarskoje Selo, Jan. 30-th 1915

My own beloved One,

This is probably my last letter to you. So interesting all the news of *Sebastopol*, I regret not being with you. How interesting all you saw, you will have a lot to tell us. Thank God so few wounded. But it must have seemed to you like a dream going out in the steamlaunch round the squadron — & so emotioning — God bless the dears & may he give them success. The darkness at night must be rather uncanny I should say. — Alas! the news fr. East Prussia are not so good & we have had to go back for a second time — well we shall have all our forces stronger together then — I just read a very interesting letter Sonia received fr. Lindenbaum, thanking for the things we sent. He loves his regiment which only exists half a year — *Korotojaktsi,* I think; he was in Prussia, & wrote the 22-d whilst battles were going on. — *Nikolasha* sent *Petia* here to look after his leg — *Karpinsky* thinks it has been contusioned & so must be treatened according; but *Petia* cannot imagine when it happened as he felt no pain for ages. — Alek has a stiff back & so could not come & sent *Petia* with papers, & I gave him mine, & *Viltchkovsky* to help him explain all. — Then I had Rost: & B. Witte about Xenia's committee. In the morning I came to a *Te Deum* before the Image at *Znam.* wh. was nice — then I did several *dressing's* & sat with Ania — our Friend's girls came there to see us. Her throat is much better, 37.1 — but last night 38.5 — dont know why. I did not go, as too tired. — She speaks in an extinguished voice & is dull poor soul, scarcely opened her mouth, except to eat, wh. she did well. Her poor back is sore again from lying. To-day its 4 weeks. — I must go this evening, as did not see all the wounded. To-morrow we have an operation. No sun to-day for the first time. —

Now goodbye & God bless you my Sunshine. I kiss you very tenderly & lovingly, longingly, Ever yr. own old

Wify.

No. 44.

Tsarskoje Selo, Jan. 31-st 1915

My beloved One,

This is Marie's paper, because I am beginning on Baby's sopha & did not bring up my thing for writing. — Just received yr. dear telegram fr. *Ekaterinoslav* I had quite forgotten that you were stopping there. Can imagine how interesting the *plate workshop* must be — & yr. visit will encourage all to work quicker.

The operation went off alright this morning. — The officer *Kubatov* has invented a *machine gun,* wh. he watched being made at *Tula* & the navy has ordered. In the afternoon we went to the big palace & sat sometime with my *Rifles,* 2 fr. our hospital had also come to see them.

Xenia & Ducky lunched — both are well. At 6 I received M-elle Rosenbach, who has the Invalid house. — I said goodbye to 5 officers who are going back to the war — amongst them *Schevitch* he was sad not to be able to await your return — he leaves to-morrow, as otherwise fears loosing the regiment. Zeidler said he might leave, but he has not even tried to ride

& his foot will always I am sure remain weak, as the sinews were torn — jumping off his horse will always be risky & walking on enemi ground — his foot is tightly bandaged. But he felt tho' ashamed to remain here any longer. — Its much milder to-day & snowed hard this morning. Baby & *Vlad. Nik.* are dining O. & A. are shooting soldiers. Ania is impatiently awaiting yr. return. She has grown really much thinner, & as she sits better one notices it more. — Now my very own one I must end, as the messenger leaves early.

Goodbye & God bless you beloved Nicky dear, such joy to think that in two days you will be here. I kiss you over & over again & remain yr. very loving

Sunny.

You understand I can't come so early to the station?

No. 45.

Tsarskoje Selo, Feb. 27-th 1915

My very own deeply beloved One,

God bless you quite particularly on this journey, & give you the possibility of seeing our brave troops nearer. Your presence will give them new force & courage & be such a recompense to them & consolation to you.

The *Stavka* is not the thing — you are for the troops, when & where possible — & our Friend's blessing & prayers will help.

Such a comfort for me that you saw Him & were blessed by Him this evening. Sad I cant follow you out there — but I have the little ones to look after. I shall be good & go once to town before *M. B.* comes & visit some hospital, as they are impatiently awaiting us there. — My Angel sweet, me no likes saying goodbye — but I wont be selfish — they need you & you must have a change.

My work & prayer must help me over the separation — the nights are so lonely — & yet you are far lonelier, poor agooweeone! —

Goodbye Lovy, I bless you — & kiss you without end, love you more than word can say.

All my soul will follow & suround you everywhere. —

I press you tenderly to my old loving heart & remain yr. very own

Wify.

Oh such pain saying goodbye! Feel so sad to-night — me does love you so intensely. God be with you. —

No. 46.

Tsarskoje Selo, Feb. 28-th 1915

My very own One,

It was sad seeing you go off in the train all alone, & my heart ached. — Well I went straight to Ania for 10 minutes & then we worked in the hospital till 1. After luncheon we received 6 officers who return to the army —

those wh. we had sent to the Crimea look splendid, round & brown. — Then *little John* called Olga to the telephone to tell her, that poor *Struve* is killed — he is awfully sad, because he was his great friend. He told J. that if he should fall in war, he was to be sure to tell you, that he had never once taken off his *achselbant* since you gave them to him — poor, kind, cheery, handsome boy! His body is being brought back. Then I went to the big palace & sat for some time with the worst, I took the lovely postcards of Livadia to show & they were greatly admired — then the Children joined me & we went through all the wards. — I shall go for a little to church, it does one good; that and work, looking after those brave fellows, are one comfort. In the evening we shall go to Ania — she finds I am too little with her, wants me to sit longer, (& alone) but we have not much to speak of — with the wounded one always can. —

My Angel, I must finish because the messenger has to leave. —

I bless & kiss you over & over again, my Nicky dear — a lonely night awaits us.

Ever yr. very own

Wify.

The Children kiss you very much. Hope tiny Admiral »behaves« himself. —

No. 47.

Tsarskoje Selo, March 1-st 1915

My very own Huzy dear,

What an unexpected joy yr. precious letter was, thank you for it from all my loving old heart. Yes, lovy mine, I saw you were happy to be home these 2 days again & I too regret that we cannot be more together now that A. is not in the house. It reminds one of bygone evenings — so peaceful & calm, & no one's moods to bother & make one nervous. —

I went to Church last night at 7, the cosacks sang well & it was soothing & I thought & prayed much for my Nicky dear — I always think you are standing near me there. — Baby madly enjoyed yr. bath, & made us all come & look on at his pranks on the water. All the daughters beg too for the same treat some evening — may they? — Then we went to Ania, I worked, Olga glued her Album, Tatiana worked — M. & A. went home after 10 & we remained till 11. I went into the room where the *Strannitza* (blind) was with her lantern — we talked together & then she said her *prayer.* —

The Com. of the O. fortress *Schulman* knew us when he was at *Kronstadt* to put order there & then at *Sebastopol* he commanded the *Brest* regiment, wh. behaved so well during the stories — I remember his face very well. — After luncheon shall finish — now must dress. Ortipo has been rushing all over my bed like mad & crushed *Viltchkovsky's reports* I was reading. — The weather is quite mild, zero. —

I had *Olga E.* to say goodbye, she leaves for a quiet sanatorium near Moscou for 2 months. Then we went to the cemitry, as I had long not been there, & then on to our little hospital & the big palace. Upon our return found your dear telegram for wh. tenderest thanks. — We all kiss & bless you over & over again. Our love to *N. P.*

Ever, my Treasure, yr. very own

Wify.

Who misses her sweetheart very much. —

No. 48.

Tsarskoje Selo, March 2-nd 1915

My beloved One,

Such a sunny day! Baby went in the garden, he feels well, tho' has again a little water in the knee. The girls drove & then joined me in the big Palace. We inspected the sanitary train 66, its an endlessly long one, but well arranged — it belongs to the Ts. Selo district.

In the morning we had a hernial rupture operation of a soldier. Yesterday evening we were with Ania — *Schwedov* & *Zabor* too. — I got a letter fr. Ella's Countess Olsufiev — she has been placed at the head of 16 Comités de bienfaisance des 22 hospitaux militaires de Moscou. They need money, so she asks whether she might get the big theater for a big representation May 23-rd — (second Easter holiday) she thinks they might gain about 20,000 (I doubt) for those hospitals. They give them things the ministery (military) cannot give them. If you agree, then I shall tell Fredericks & he can send you the official paper. — On the affiches they will print that the theatre has been given by a special grace of yours. — The idea of going to town to a hospital is rather awful, but still I know I must go, so to-morrow afternoon we shall be off. In the morning *Karangosov's* appendicitis will be cut off. — How glad I am you get yr. walks daily. — God grant you will really be able to see lots & have talks out there with the Generals. — I have told *Viltchkovsky* to send fat Orlov a printed paper one of the wounded received from his chief — far too hard orders & absolutely unjust & cruel — if an officer does not return at the time mentioned he must be disciplinied punished etc.: I cant write it, the paper will tell you all. One comes to the conclusion that those that are wounded are doubly badly treated — better keep behind or hide away to remain untouched & I find it most unfair — & I dont beleive its everywhere the same, but in some armies. — Forgive me bothering you my Love, but you can help out there, & one does not want bitterness setting in their poor hearts. — Must end. — Blessings & kisses without end.

Ever yr. own

Sunny.

No. 49.

Tsarskoje Selo, March 2-nd 1915

My own sweet one,

I am beginning my letter this evening, as I want to talk to you. Wify feels hideously sad! My poor wounded friend has gone! God has taken him quietly & peacefully to Himself. I was as usual with him in the morning & more than an hour in the afternoon. He talked a lot — in a wisper always — all about his service in the Caucasus — awfully interesting & so bright, with his big shiny eyes. I rested before dinner & was haunted with the feeling that he might suddenly get very bad in the night & one would not call me & so on — so that when the *eldest nurse* called one of the girls to the telephone — I told them that I knew what had happened & flew myself to hear the sad news. After M. & A. had gone off to Ania, (to see Ania's sister in law & *Olga Voronov*) Olga & I went to the big palace to see him. He lay there so peacefully, covered under my flowers I daily brought him, with his lovely peaceful smile — the forehead yet quite warm. I cant get quiet — so sent Olga to them & came home with my tears. The elder sister cannot either realise it — he was quite calm, cheery, said felt a wee bit not comfy, & when the sister, 10 m. after she had gone away, came in, found him with staring eyes, quite blue, breathed twice — & all was over — peaceful to the end. Never did he complain, never asked for anything, *sweetness* itself as she says — all loved him — & that shining smile. — You, Lovy mine, can understand what that is, when daily one has been there, thinking only of giving him pleasure — & suddenly — finished. And after our Friend spoke of him, do you remember, & that »*he will not soon leave you*« I was sure he would recover, tho' very slowly. And he longed to get back to his regiment — was presented for golden sword & St. G. Cross & higher rank. — Forgive my writing so much about him, but going there, & all that, had been a help, with you away & I felt God let me bring him a little sunshine in his loneliness. Such is life! Another brave soul left this world to be added to the shining stars above. — And how much sorrow all around — thank God that we have the possibility of at least making some comfortable in their suffering & can give them a feeling of homeliness in their loneliness. One longs to warm & help them, brave creatures & to replace their dear ones who cant come. — It must not make you sad what I wrote, only I could not bear it any longer — I had to speak myself out.

Benkendorf has asked to accompany us to town to-morrow, so I had to say yes, tho' I had only thought of taking Ressin & Isa. — Baby dear's leg is better — he sledged to *Pavlovsk* to-day, *Nagorny* & the man of the donkey sledge worked alone at the hill. —

If by any chance you ever happen to be near one of my *stores tram* (of wh. I have 5 in all directions), it wld. be very dear if you could peep in, or see the *com.* of the train & thank him for his work — they honestly are splendid workers & constantly have been under fire — I am writing to you now in bed, I am lying since an hour already, but cant get to sleep, nor calm myself, so it does me good talking to you. I have blessed & kissed your dear cushion as always. — One says *Struve* is going to be buried in his country place. —

To-morrow we receive 6 officers going back to the war, two of my Siberians, *Vykrestov* & the Dr. *Menschutkin* — & *Kratt* for the second time, God grant he may not be wounded again. First time the right arm — the next time left arm & through the lungs — the Crimea did him no end of good. — The *Nijegorodtzy* are wondering whether their division wont be sent back again, as they have nothing to do now. — Shulman thinks of his *Ossovets* with anguish & longing — this time the shots are bigger & have done more harm — all the officers houses are already quite ruined. — One does so long for detailed news.

I heard *Amilachvari* is wounded, but slightly only. —

Igor has gone to the regiment, tho' the Drs. found him not well enough to leave. — Now I must try and sleep, as to-morrow will be a tiring day — but I don't feel like it. You sleep well my treasure, I kiss & bless you.

March 3-rd. We have just returned from town — were in M. & A.'s hospital in the new building of the Institute of *Rucklov's*. *Zeidler* showed us over all the wards 180 men — & in another building 30 officers.

Karangozov's operation went off well — he had a rotten appendicitis & the operation was done just in time.

At 12½ we went to the *funeral service* in the little hospital Church below, where the poor officer's coffin stands — so sad no relations there — so lonely somehow. — Its snowing hard. — Must end. God bless & protect you — kisses without end, my treasure. Ever yr. very own

Wify.

Messages to *N. P.*

No. 50.

Tsarskoje Selo, March 4-th 1915

My own beloved Darling,

With what joy I received yr. dear letter, thanks over & over for it. I have read it already twice over & kissed it several times. —

How tired all those complicated talks must make you. God grant the coal question may soon be settled satisfactorily & the guns too. But they too must soon be running short of everything. — About Misha I am so happy do write it to Motherdear, it will do her good to know it. I am sure this war will make more of a man of him — could one but get her out of his reach, her dictating influence is so bad for him. — I shall tell the children to fetch your paper & send it with this letter — Baby has written in French, I told him to do so & he writes more naturally than with *Peter Vass.* His leg is almost alright, does not limp — the right hand is bandaged as rather swollen, so wont be able to write probably a few days. But he goes out twice daily. — The four girls are going to town — Tatiana has her committee, M. & A. will look on whilst *Olga* receives money & then they will all go to Mary — the little ones have never seen her rooms. —

Botkin has put me to bed, heart a good deal enlarged & have rather a cough — I felt rotten, in every respect, these days & now Mme Becker arrived & prevents me from taking my drops. — Am glad I managed the hospital in town yesterday — we did it quickly 1 hour & 1/4 & one carried me up the stairs — the 4 girls helped giving the Images & talking, & Ressin arranged those well enough to be stood in a row in the corridor — tell this to *N. P.* as he thought I wld. overtire myself in town — its the strain of these weeks, 2 a day to Ania, who never finds it enough, wrote now she had wanted to see me more to talk (have nothing to say, hear only of sad things, Nini brightens her far more up with her »bavardage« & gossip) & to read to her — have a cough these days, so could not. And she cant understand this death having upset me so — Zizi does, wrote so kindly. — I cannot do a thing by halves & I saw his joy when I came twice daily — & he all alone, others were not at in — he had no family here. — She grudges me to the others, I feel, & they so touchingly always ask me not to tire myself — »*you are only one for us, we are many*«. — He told me too still the last afternoon that I overtire myself — so on — awfully kind — so how cannot I try & give them everything of warmth & love — they suffer so & are unspoiled — she has all, tho' of course her leg is a great worry to her & does not grow a bit together yet — the Pss. looked yesterday. But A. one never can satisfy & that is the most tiring, & she does not understand Botkin's hints at all about me. —

The sun is shining & its snowing a little. — I got *nurse Liubuscha* (the eldest sister of big Palace) to come & sit with me for half an hour, she is cosy, told me about the wounded & more details about the other. To-morrow one buries him — our Friend wrote me a touching little letter about this death. — I can imagine *Svetchine* makes you wild — me he drove to distraction a few years ago in the Crimea with these half French anecdotes — one says he is the son of old *Galkine-Vrassky*. — Send him about to look at motors or hospitals close by. — Now I wonder what you will do — dont tell, where you intend going, then you can get through unawares & I am sure, he knows far less where you can go, then when you are nearer out there already in the train. — To-morrow is N. Willy's death day — 2 years!

My precious one, my muchly missed one, I must end now. — God bless & protect you & keep you safe from all harm.

I kiss you over & over again with deepest tenderness.

Ever yr. very own

Wify Sunny.

I bow to yr. people. —

No. 51.

Tsarskoje Selo, March 5-th 1915

My very own beloved One,

I enclose a paper fr. Ella wh. you can sent to *Mamantov,* or fat *Orlav* & then a letter from Ania. She is very put out, that I do not go to her again, but *B.* keeps me again in bed till dinner, like yesterday. The heart is not enlarged this morning, but I feel still rotten & weak & sad — when the health breaks down its more difficult to hold oneself in hands. Now he is being buried.

I dont know whether they will leave him here or not, because the regiment intends burying all the officers after the war in the Caucasus, — there have marked the graves every where — but some died in Germany. I got a telegr. fr. my *Vesselovsky* that they had all just enjoyed the *bania* train & clean linen & are off to the *okopi.* — Then I got a report (according to my wish) from him. He returned Feb. 15-th. But of the heaps who are to receive decorations, only one *Pr. Gantimurov* got the *Georg Sword* as yet — he himself is not presented to anything, as *in the absence of his chiefs who commanded over; the Divisionnary General von Hennings was dismissed from his post, and the Brigadier-Gen. M. Bykov is taken prisoner.*

A terrible worry & sorrow is that they have no flag, they entreat you to give them a new one, *representations regarding this have already been made to the War-Minister by the commander-in-chief on February 7, under No. 9850.* Their losses were quite colossal, 4 times the reg. has been filled up again, *during the battles above vil. B.,* but I better write this on an extra paper, instead of filling up my letter with it; I shall copy out bits for you. — My Image reached them just after 30-th, their Lieut. Colonel Sergeiev, burned their flag. After he was wounded then, *the chief of the supply service* took the regiment & during 3 months did all splendidly. — I fear this letter is mighty dull. — Have let off Madelaine for the day to town — 6 weeks Tudels has not turned up. Sunny again. — I had Isa for affairs — & then Sonia. — Just got yr. dear telegram. Ania wrote that Fredericks is intensely happy over your letter, of course she envies him. Perhaps you will put in your telegram to me that you thank for inclosed letter & send love or messages — she said I was to burn hers if I thought you would be angry — how can I know, I answered her that I would send it, so I hope she does not bother you with it — she can not grasp that her letters are of little interest to you, as they mean so much to her. — I have send the little ones to her — she wanted them in the evening; but they said they wished to remain with me then, as don't see them all day. — Dont you tell *N.* & go off where it suits you & where nobody can expect you — of course he will try to keep you back, because one won't let him move — but if you go, *I know that* God will hold you in safe keeping & you & the troops will feel comforted.

Now my very own Sunshine my treasure beloved, I will close my letter. God bless & protect you now & ever, I cover your dear face with tenderest kisses, & remain,

Ever yr. very own Wify.

I wish I were near you as I am sure you go through many difficult moments, not knowing who speaks the exact truth, who is partial & so on — & personal offenses etc., which ought not to exist at such a time, just show themselves, alas, now in the rear, I fear. — Where are our dear sailors? What are they doing & is Kirill with them? —

No. 52.

Tsarskoje Selo, March 6-th 1915

My very own Sweetheart,

A bright sunny day again, but 12 of frost. This morning the heart is not enlarged, but it has slipped to the right, so the feeling is the same. Yesterday evening it was again enlarged. I get over onto the sopha for dinner till 10½ or 11. Feel still so weak, A. fidgets for me to come to her, but *Botkin* is going there, so as to tell her, that I cannot yet, & need quiet still some days. Thank God, the wounded officers in both hospitals are pretty well, so that I am not absolutely necessary this moment & the girls were at soldiers' operations again yesterday. They so touchingly ask after me through the girls, Zizi or *Botkin.* I miss my work, & all the more so that you, my Angel, are not here. —

Do so wonder where & when you will be able to move on — standing so long at the *Headquarters* must be rather despairing. — Lovy dear, people want to send gospels to our prisoners, prayerbooks they (the Germans) do not allow to be forwarded to *Germany* — Loman has 10,000 — may they be sent with an inscription that they come from me, or better not, kindly answer by wire »gospels yes — or not«, then I will understand how to have them sent. — Sonia sat with me yesterday afternoon ¾ of an hour, shall ask Mme Zizi to-day, as children must go out & to hospitals. — Please give the enclosed letter to *N. P.* through your man, it's one from O, T. & me together. —

My lancer *Apukhtin* is for the moment commanding an infantry regiment (forget which), because only a *captain* was left eldest there. — Just got your precious letter — such an unexpected intense joy, thanks ever so tenderly! warm words comfort my tired heart. — That is nice your having named yourself »*chef*« & *Georgi* too — with what force & cheer those brave »*Plastuni*« will now be off — God bless their voyage & give them success. —

Your walks are surely refreshing, & the different falls must cheer up the monotony (when not too painful). — Lovy mine, your letters are just as a ray of Sunshine to me!

Yesterday they buried the poor fellow & *sister Liubusha* said he had still his happy smile — only a little changed in colour, but the expression we knew so well, had not faded. Always a smile, & he told her he was so happy

& wanted nothing more — shining eyes which struck all & after a life of ups & downs, a romance of changes, thank God he was happy with us. —

How many »*plastuni*« regiments go? as I might send them quickly Images — how many officers in each regiment? Make *Drenteln* cypher the wire through *Kira* to me, please. — Ania's Mother was very ill with a colossal attack of stones in the liver, but is now better — another such strong attack, our Friend said, would be her end. — Again she fidgets I am to telephone & come in the evening, when we daily explain I can't yet; so tiresome of her, & heaps of letters every day — its not my fault, & I must get quite right & only by quiet lying (as can't yet take medicine) can help me — she only thinks of herself & is angry. I am so much with the wounded — they do me good & their gratitude gives me strength — whereas with her, who complains about her leg always, it's more tiring — one gives out so much of oneself, moral & physical all day, that in the evening little is left. —

Got again a loving letter from our Friend, wants me to go out in the sun, says it will do me good (morally) more than lying. But its very cold, I have still a cough, the cold I keep down, then feverish again & so weak & tired. — Got a wire from my *Tutchkov* from *Lvov (Lemberg) supply train* who arranged (have 4) a flying one so as to help more, it will become our 5-th. »*The flying train finished its 2-nd trip by touring the region of the Stry, Skole and Vigoda, some military units and sanitary sections received their supplies in the neighbourhood of the front positions of Tukhli, Libokhori and Koziuvki, at the same time distributing gifts and images (from me). The attentions bestowed by Your Majesty everywhere provoked the sincerest enthusiasm and limitless joy. On the return trip the empty cars furnished with portable stores carried from Vigoda about 200 wounded, the evacuation of whom considerably lightened the task of the hospital, etc.*« So the nearer these little trains go in front, the better it is — *Mekk* is a wee genius, inventing & setting all this going — all he does is really well & quickly done & he had the chance of getting good gentlemen for these *supply trains.* — Zizi sat an hour & was very dear.

The girls walked & now have gone to the big palace. —

A man leaves for Olga, so must send her a line. — Please tell *Drenteln* that we send messages & hope his leg is better. Bow to *Grabbe* & *N. P.* & wee Admiral & my friend *Feodorov.* Goodbye now, my own precious one, my huzy dear, my sweet Sunshine, I cover you with very tenderest kisses, Baby too.

The girls are wild that they may bathe in your bath.

God bless & protect you & keep you from all harm — prayers & thoughts are ever with you. Messages to the family.

Ever your own — Sunny.

No. 53. — *Tsarskoje Selo,* March 7-th 1915

My own beloved One,

A week to-day you left us — it seems much longer. Your telegrams and precious letters are such a comfort and I constantly read them. — You see

I am looking after my tired old self, and to-d a y again only get up for 8. Ania won't understand it, the Dr., children and I explain it to her, and yet every day 5 letters and begging me to come — she knows I lie in bed, and yet pretends to be astonished at it — so selfish. She knows I never miss going to her when I only can, and dead tired too she still grumbles why I went twice daily to an unknown officer and does not heed *Botkin's* remark, that he needed me and that she always has guests all day long almost. My visits to her are as a duty she finds (I think) and therefore even o f t e n d o e s not seem to appreciate them, whereas the others thank for every second given to them. It is quite good she does not see me some days — tho' last night 6-th letter complained she had had no good-night kisses nor blessings for so long. If she would kindly once remember who I happen to be, then she might learn to understand that I have other duties except her. — 100 times I told her about you too, who you are, and that an E. (Emperor) never goes daily to a sick person — what would one think otherwise, and that you have your country first of all to think of, and then get tired from work, and need air and its good you should be with Baby out, etc. It is like speaking to a stone — she w o n ' t understand, because she goes before everybody. — She offers to invite officers in the evening for the children, thinking to get me like that, but they answered that they wished to r e m a i n with me, as its the only time we are quietly together. We have too much spoiled her — but I honestly find, as a daughter of our friends, she ought to grasp things better and the illness ought to have changed her. Now enough about her, it's dull — it has stopped worrying me as it used to, and only aggravates one, because of the selfishness. — It's cold, grey and snowing. — The girls wildly enjoyed your swimming bath — first the 2 little ones and then the eldest — I could not go. — I slept badly and feel weak and tired — so far the heart is not enlarged, it becomes so every afternoon — so I think I won't see anybody and remain completely quiet, then it may behave itself! — Had heaps of papers to read this morning from *Rostovtsev* etc.: *Shulman* was so grateful to hear about *Osovetz,* I told the children to tell him. — Baby's »*Moscouits*« are not far from there. *Galfter* wrote. Hope *Drenteln's* leg is better, bow to him and *N. P.*

Goodbye and God bless and protect you my precious Angel. Kisses without end from your own wify

Alix.

No. 54.

Tsarskoje Selo, March 8-th 1915

My own beloved One,

I hope you get my letters regularly, I write and number them daily, also in my little lilac book. — Forgive my bothering you, by sending a petition, but one would like to help those poor people — I think it's the second time they write — kindly put a decision and send it to the minister of Justice. —

I copied out a telegram it might amuse you to read, thanking our *store* for presents; I don't need it returned. Then a note from Marie to *Drentein*.

What a good thing Memel has been taken, they did not expect this, I am sure, and it will be a good lesson to them. And everywhere the news, thank God, seem good, I have time to read up all now, lying in bed. — I am going over onto the sopha for 4½ already, bit by bit a little more, tho' every evening the heart is enlarged, and every day Ania asks me to come. — Glorious sunshine but very cold, they say. —

Ducky had a correspondant with her, and he wrote most interesting all she had done at *Prasnish* — she really does a lot with her *unit,* and is really under fire. Miechen promenades with her decoration to all exhibitions etc; you ought to find out really how she got it, and that such things don't happen again, and Tatiana neither. Ducky deserves it certainly. —

How sad the losses of the »Bouvet«, »Irresistible« and »Ocean«, so hideous to be sunk by floating mines and so rapidly too — not as tho' in battle. —

I had a letter from Victoria from Kent House — nothing new in it. Have, alas, nothing interesting to tell you. The children are lunching next door and making an unearthly noise. —

What joy sweetheart to have got another letter from you — it was just brought to me, and the nice postcards and the children's cards — we all thank over and over again and are very deeply touched you find time to write to us. —

I see now why you did not go more forward, but surely you could go still to some place before returning, it would do you good and cheer the others up — anywhere. That drive must have been nice, but I understand the sad impression of those empty houses, probably many of them never to be inhabited by the same people again. Such is life — such a tragedy!

Did Sergei L. make a better impression upon you, less sure of himself and simpler? I at once sent Ania your message, it will have given her pleasure. She probably thinks that she alone *is lonely* without you. — Ah, she is greatly mistaken! But I know it's right you should be there and the change is good for you. only I should have wished more people to have profited and seen you. — I suppose you had service to-day. — The children went this morning. Just heard *Irene* had a daughter (thought it would be a girl) glad it's over, poor Xenia worried about it all along. — It would have seemed more natural, had I heard that Xenia herself had borne a Baby. —

Such sunshine! The girls drove, now have gone to my red cross *community,* then to Ania and after tea the eldest go to Tatiana. Alexei has three of Xenia's boys. I am going to be up by ¼ to 5. —

Goodbye my Sunshine — don't worry if you can't write daily, you have much to do, and must have a little quiet too — and letter-writing takes you so much time.

God bless you, Nicky treasure, my very own huzy, I kiss and bless you and love you without ceasing.

Ever your very own wify

Alix

No. 54 a.

Tsarskoje Selo, March 9-th 1915

My Huzy sweet Angel,

What happiness to know, that the day after to-morrow I shall be holding you tight in my arms again, listening to your dear voice and looking into your beloved eyes. Only for you I regret, that you won't have seen anything. If I could only be decent by the time you return. This night I only got to sleep after 5, felt such pressure on the heart, and the heart rather much enlarged. Yesterday it kept normal, and I was also from 5—6 on the sofa and 8—11 — Irene and Baby are well — she suffered a good deal, but was brave — she likes her name, and so wished the child to be called by it, funny little thing. — Dmitri, Rostislav and *Nikita* came to Alexei, and the latter dined with us. —

It is cold, but bright sunshine. —. I enclose a letter from *Masha,* (from Austria) which she was asked to write to you, for peace's sake. I never answer her letters, of course, now; then a letter from Ania; — I don't know whether you agree to her writing, but I can't say no, once she asks me, and better like this than through the servants. She sent for *Kondratiev* yesterday — so foolish to get the servants to talk to —, in the hospital she already wanted to see them — only to make a fuss —, it's not quite ladylike, I must honestly say. Now she will be sending for your men, and that will be quite improper; — why can't she then sooner ask, after the poor wounded she knows, and with whom she won't have anything to do! —

Just got your telegram, it came in 15 min; thank God *Przmysl* taken, congratulate you with all my loving heart — this is good — what joy for our beloved troops! They did have a long time of it, and honestly speaking I am glad for the poor garrison and people who must have almost been dying of hunger. Now we shall have those army corps free to throw over to more weak places. I am too happy for you! —

From *Olga* good news, likes *Lvov (Lemberg),* she feels sad Misha is with wife there and she has never seen him for 4 years.

Now goodbye my treasure, I bless and kiss you over and over again — your very own Sunny.

No. 55.

Tsarskoje Selo, April 4-th 1915

My very own Treasure,

Once more you are leaving us, and I think with gladness, because the life you had here, all excepting the work in the garden — is more than trying and tiring. We have seen next to nothing of each other through my having been lain up. Full many a thing have I not had time to ask, and when together only late in the evening, half the thoughts have flown away again. God bless your journey my beloved One, and may it again bring success and encouragement to our troops. You will see a bit more I hope before you get to the

Headquarters and should *Nikolasha* say any thing to *Voyeikov* in form of a complaint, have it at once stopped and show that you are the master. Forgive me, precious One, but you know you are too kind and gentle — sometimes a good loud voice can do wonders, and a severe look — do my love, be more decided and sure of yourself — you know perfectly well what is right, and when you do not agree and are right, bring your opinion to the front and let it weigh against the rest. They must remember more who you are and that first they must turn to you. Your being charms every single one, but I want you to hold them by your brain and experience. Though *Nikolasha* is so highly placed, yet you are above him. The same thing shocked our Friend, as me too, that *Nikolasha* words his telegrams, answers to governors, etc. in your style — his ought to be more simple and humble and other things. — You think me a medlesome bore, but a woman feels and sees things sometimes clearer than my too humble sweetheart. Humility is God's greatest gift — but a Sovereign needs to show his will more often. Be more sure of yourself and go ahead — never fear, you won't say too much. — Dear old Fredericks, may all go well with him — I feel he goes for your cause as he alone can allow himself to say anything to *Nikolasha*. *Grabbe* will amuse you at domino and when *N. P.* is with you, I feel always quiet, as he is quite our own and nearer to you than the rest, and is young and not as heavy as Dmitri Sh: — That reminds me, what about Dmitri P. is he ever going to stick here?

Look what a letter, but it seems I have not talked to you simply for ages (and Ania imagines hourly we do)!

Perhaps you can find time to go to one of the hospitals at *Bielostok* as very many wounded pass there and see that Fredericks does not insist upon accompanying you upon bad roads, *Feodorov* must keep a severe watch over him. —

How lonely it will be without you, my Sunshine! Tho' I have the children — but lying without work now is difficult and I long to get back to the hospital. To-morrow the Dr. wont come, (unless I should feel worse) as he wishes to be at the funeral of a friend of his. — It's a rest not seeing poor Ania and hearing her grumbling.

You open the windows nicely in my compartment then yours won't be so stuffy. —

Sweetheart, you will find some flowers (kissed by me) upon your writing-table, it cheers up the compartment.

Goodbye and God bless you, Lovy my very Own dear One — I press you tenderly to my heart and kiss you all over and hold you tight, oh so tight.

Ever yr. very own wify Alix.

No. 56.

Tsarskoje Selo, April 4-th 1915

My Own precious One,

A Feldjeger leaves this evening at 5, so I must write to you, tho' have no news to give. Thanks sweety for sending Baby back to rest with me, so

I had to keep my tears back, not to grieve him — I got back into bed and he lies for half an hour near me. Then the girls returned. —

It is so hard every time — it wrenches at one's heart and leaves such an ache and endless longing — Ortipo too feels sad, and jumps up at every sound and watches for you. Yes Deary, when one really loves — one indeed loves! Dreary weather too. I am looking through masses of postcards from soldiers. — Ania sent me lovely red roses as goodbye from *N. P.* — they stand near my bed and smell too divinely, do thank him for his awfully kind thought and that I was very sad not to have been able to say goodbye to him. She gave him a letter for you, as wrote it late and he went straight to church from her. All the girls have gone to M. and A.'s hospital to the concert arranged by Marie's friend D. — Baby was going to play near the white tower with D.'s children. —

Each child brought me your message — ah lovy mine, I cry now like a big baby — and see your sweet, sad eyes, so full of love before me. —

Keep well, my treasure — wify is ever near you in thoughts and prayers. 1000 kisses. God bless and protect you and keep you from all harm.

Ever yr. very own old

Sunny.

No. 57.

Tsarskoje Selo, April 5-th 1915

My own huzy darling,

Just got your telegram. This is wonderful. You left at 2 and arrived at 9. When you leave at 10 you reach there only at 12! Bright, sunny weather, I hear the birdies chirping away. Wonder why you changed your plans. — The girls have just gone to church; baby moves the arms better, tho' water in the elbows still he says. Yesterday he went with *Vladimir Nikolaievitch* to Ania, and she was mad with joy, he goes again to-day to see *Rodionov* and *Kozhevnikov*. Now she has *Vladimir Nikolaievitch* to show how to electrify her leg — every day a new Doctor. *Tatiana* and *Anastasia* were there in the day and found our Friend with her. He said the old story that she cries and sorrows as gets so few *caresses*. So *Tatiana* was much surprised and He answered that she receives many, only to her they seem few. Her humour seems not famous (the chief mourner) and notes cold, so mine too. —

I did sleep alright, as so awfully tired — but feel the same so far. Yesterday again 37.3, this morning 36.7, and morning's headache — the empty cushion beside me makes me, oh so sad! Dear sweet One, how is all aranging itself? You will let me have telegrams through fat Orlov when there are news, won't you? — Spent the evening lying quietly and the girls each reading a book. Olga and Tatiana went for ½ an hour to the hospital to see how all were. — I hear Shot barking before the house. — I send you your Image from our Friend of *St. John the Warrior,* wh. I forgot to give yesterday morning.

I have been rereading what our Friend wrote when he was at Constantinopel, it is doubly interesting now — quite short impressions. Oh, what a day when mass will again be served at St. Sophie. Only give orders that nothing should be destroyed or spoiled belonging to the mahomedans, they can use all again for their religion, as we are Christians and not barbarians, thank God! How one would love to be there at such a moment! The amount of churches everywhere used or destroyed by the Turks is awful — because the Greeks were not worthy to officiate and have such temples. May the Orthodox Church be more worthy now and be purified again. — This war can mean so colossaly much in the moral regeneration of our Country and Church — only to find the men to fulfil all your orders and to help you, in all your immense tasks! —

Here I am back again — lay two hours on the sopha, had Mme Zizi half an hour with petition — feel rottenly weak and tired and she did not approve of my looks. — My dear, Ania has been wheeled by *Shuk* as far as *Voyeikov's* house, Dr. *Korenev* near her and was not a bit tired — now to-morrow she wants to come to me! Oh dear, and I was so glad that for a long time we should not have her in the house, I am selfish after 9 years, and want you to myself at last and this means, she is preparing to invade upon us often when you return or she will beg to be wheeled in the garden, as the park is shut (so as to meet you) and I wont be there to disturb. Shall give *Putiatin* the order to let her in to the big park, her chair wont spoil the roads. — I should never have ventured out — what a sight! Covered by a *shuba* and shawl on her head — I said better a tennis cap and her hair plaited tidily will strike less. The man is needed in the *Feodorov* hospital and she uses him constantly. I told her to go to *Znamenia* before coming to me — I foresee lots of bother with her; all hysteria! Pretends to faint when one pushes the bed, but can be banged about in the streets in a chair.

The children went out before one, and I shant see them till 5 for quite short, then they go off to Ania to see our officers, Baby after his dinner. I was up fr. 1—3. — Fancy your having had snow in the night! Sweetest treasure — how I miss you! Long and lonely days — so when head aches less copy out things of our friends, and then the time passes quicker. Please give my love to *N. P.* & *Grabbe.*

What a lot of prisoners we have taken again! Now this must go. — Goodbye, Nicky love, I bless and kiss you over and over again with all the tenderness of wh. I am capable.

Ever yr. very own old

Wify.

No. 58.

Tsarskoje Selo, April 6-th 1915

My own beloved Darling,

Ever such tender thanks for yr. precious letter, I just received. It is such an intense joy to hear from you, Sweetheart & comfort, as I miss you awfully! — So that is why you did not travel as intended! But the idea of

L. & *P.* already now, makes me anxious, is it not too soon, as all the spirits are not much for Russia — in the country, yes, but not at *L.* I fear. — Well, I shall ask our Friend to quite particularly pray for you there — but, forgive my saying so — its not for N. to accompany you —you must be the chief one, the first time you go. You find me an old goose, no doubt, but if others wont think of such things, I must. He must remain & work as usual — really don't take him, as the hate against him must be great there — & to see you alone will rejoice those hearts that go out to you in love and gratitude. — Such sunshine! The little girlies drove between their lessons — & I am going to have Ania's visit!! The Dr. lets me get up more, only to lie when the temp. rises, heart nearly normal, but feel horribly weak yet, & my voice like Miechens when she is tired. — One just brought me an endless letter fr. the Countess Hohenfelsen — I send it you to read through in a free moment, & then return it to me. Only speak to Fredericksy about it. Certainly n o t o n m y namesday or birthday as she wishes — but all can be alright in her wish, excepting the »*Princess*«, that is vulgar to ask for. You see it will sound well when one announces them together, almost as *Grand Duchess.* Only what reason to Misha later — both had children before, whilst married to another man, tho' no, *Misha's* wife was already divorced. And she forgets this eldest son — if one acknowledges the marriage fr. the year 1904, this Son, clear to all, was an illegal child — for them I don't mind, let them openly carry their sin — but the boy? You speak it over with the old man, those things he understands, & tell him what yr. *Mamma* said when you mentioned it to her. Now perhaps people will pay less attention. —

My love to N. P. & tell him the roses are still quite fresh. —

Here I am back into bed again, was 3 hours on the sopha — so stupidly weak & tired. Well, Ania came, & she has invited herself to luncheon one of these days. Looks very well, but did not seem so overjoyed to see me, nor that had not seen me for a week, no complaint, thank goodness — but those hard eyes again wh., she so often has now. — The Children are all out, Baby's arms are better, so he could write to you Sweetheart. — Mary Wassiltshikov's son-in-law *Stcherbatov* (ex naval officer) died suddenly yesterday. He had recovered from typhoid & was taking tea with his wife, nice Sonia, when suddenly died from a failure of the heart — poor young widow! You remember her last baby was born the day of Ducky's gardenparty for the English naval officers — the grandmother came straight there.

I wonder how Fr. conversation with N. went off. Our Friend is glad for the old man's sake that he went, as it gave such intense pleasure, & perhaps its the last time he can accompany you on such a journey — well, as long as he is prudent. —

Have been choosing, as yearly, summer stuffs for my ladies and the maids and housemaids. —

Au fond, our Friend wld. have found it better you had gone after the war to the conquered country, I only just mention this like that. —

The man is waiting for my letter. —

Beloved Nicky, my, very, very own treasure, I bless & cover yr. sweet face & lovely big eyes with the tenderest of kisses,

Ever yr. very own

Sunny.

No. 59.

Tsarskoje Selo, April 7-th 1915

My very own sweet One,

Every possible tender wish for to-morrow. The first time in 21 years we dont spend this anniversary together. — How vividly one remembers all! Ah my beloved Boy, what happiness & love you have given me all these years — God verily richly blessed our married life. For all your wify thanks you from the depths of her big loving heart. May God Almighty make me a worthy helpmate of yours, my own sweet treasure, my sunshine, Sunbeam's Father! —

Tudels just brought me your dear letter, & I thank you for it with all my heart — such joy when I receive it, & many a time it is reread. I can imagine what a funny sight *Grabbe* sticking in the bogg, must have been; those walks I am sure do all no end of good. — How interesting all you are going to do. When A. told Him in secret, because I want His special prayers for you, he curiously enough said the same as me; that on the whole it does not please Him »*God will help; but it is* (too early) *to go now, he will not observe anything, will not see his people, it is interesting, but better after the war.*« —

Does not like N. going with you, finds everywhere better alone — & to this end I fully agree. Well now all is settled, I hope it will be a success, & especially that you will see all the troops you hope to, it will be a joy to you, & recompense to them. God bless & guard this voyage of yours. Probably you will see both Xenia & Olga & *Sandro.* In case you see a sister all in black anywhere, its Mme Hartwig (von Wiesen) — she is at the head of my *stores* & often at the station. — I am feeling much the same, 37.2 in the evening, 36.6 this morning — a little redness is still there. —

I am glad you send Fred. by rail to *L.* — Grey, rainy morning rather. — My letters are so dull, have only *report* to read & that is all, seeing people tires me too much, tho' I long for a glimpse of *Koj. Rod* & *Kubl.* who will be at Anias from 3—4, they leave this evening for O. Tell Fred. I send him my love & beg of him to be very good & prudent, & to remember he is no longer a wild young *cornet!* — I send you some lilies of the valley, I kissed, & wh. are to perfume yr. little compartment. The note for *Olga* yr. man can send her at *Lvov,* as you wont have time to think about it. I saw *Rod* & *Kubl* both look well & brown — longing I think to go with the *Plastuny special force* & not only for the end (they are to be spared one says) but this they did not tell me. Now all & Baby take tea at Anias. She came this morning. My blessings, tenderest prayers suround you. 1000 of kisses. Ever yr. old

Wify.

Of course I understand if you are a day or two later back. You also may like a fly to Livadia! — All the children kiss you — they & I send love to *N. P.* —

Have sent *Ropsha* strawberries.

No. 60.

Tsarskoje Selo, April 8-th 1915

My very own beloved Husband,

Tenderly do my prayers & grateful thoughts full of very deepest love linger around you this dear anniversary! How the years go by! 21 years already! You know I have kept the grey princesse dress I wore that morning? And shall wear yr. dear brooch. Dear me, how much we have lived through together in these years — heavy trials everywhere, but at home in our nest, bright sunshine!

I send you in remembrance an Image of *St. Simeon* — leave it for always as a guardian angel in your compartment — you will like the smell of the wood. —

Such a sunny day! — Poor Mme *Viltchkovsky* is going to have her apendicitis cut out — she lies in our little room, where Ania was the first night. They say she looks so clean & apetising in white & lace with pretty ribbons in jacket & hair — *Navruzov* who is there again — comes & looks after her, writes down her temp. & is most touching with her — am in despair not to be with her. — Lovy mine, how can I thank you enough for that i d e a l l y lovely cross? You do spoil me, I never for a second imagined you would think of giving me anything. How lovely it is! Shall wear it to-day — just what I like, & this one we had not seen. And yr. note & the dear letter — all came together after the Dr. He lets me go on the balkony, so I shall get Ania to come out there. — I see now why you take *N.* with you, thanks for explaining deary.

The sweet flower has gone into my gospel — we used to pick those flowers in spring on the meadow at Wolfsgarten, before the big house always. — Am sure you will all return nicely bronzed. — My throat is almost in order, heart still not yet quite normal, tho' I take my drops & keep so quiet.

I hear the Churchbells ring, & long to go to *Znamenia* & pray there for you — well my candle burns here too for you, my very own treasure.

I am finishing my letter to you on the sopha. The big girls are in town, the little ones walked, then went to their hospital & now have lessons, Baby is in the garden. I lay for 3/4 of an hour on the balkony — quite strange to be out, as it happens so rarely I get into the fresh air. The little birdies were singing away — all nature awakening & praising the Lord! Doubly it makes one feel the misery of war & bloodshed — but as after winter cometh summer, so after suffering & strife, may peace & consolation find their place in this world & all hatred cease & our beloved country develop into beauty in every sense of the word.

It is a new birth — a new beginning, a »Läuterung« & cleansing of minds and souls — only to lead them aright and guide them straight. So much to do, may all work bravely hand in hand, helping instead of hindering work for one great cause & not for personal success & fame. — Just got your dear telegram, for wh. a tender kiss. — Mme *Viltchkovsky's* operation went off alright. — My stupid temp. is now already 37.1, but I think that does not matter. —

I wear your cross on my grey teagown & it looks too lovely — yr. dear brooch of 21 years ago I have also got on. — Sweet treasure I must end now.

God bless & guard you on yr. journey. You will no doubt receive this letter in *Lvov*. Give my love to Xenia, Olga & *Sandro*. I send you a wee photo I took of agooweeone on board last year. A fond blessing & thousands of very tenderest kisses, ever, Nicky sweet,

yr. own old

Wify.

No. 61.

Tsarskoje Selo, April 9-th 1915

My own Sweetheart,

Such a sunny morning again. Slept badly, heart more enlarged. Yesterday at 6 temp. 37.3½ at 11. 37.2. This morning 36.5; — such an infection generally acts upon a not strong heart, & as mine was again so tired, of course I feel it more. *Botkin* turned up to my surprise, to-morrow *Sirotinin* comes for the last time. — I send you a French letter from Alexei, & one from *Anastasia*. — I wore yr. lovely cross the evening in bed still. — My thoughts are the whole time with you, & I keep wondering what you are doing & how getting along. What an interesting journey. Hope somebody will photograph.

Had news fr. my *flying stores* train No. 5, that *Brussilov* inspected it, & was very contended with the help it gives — they bring out presents, medicaments, linnen, boots, & return with wounded. The bigger ones have the kitchen & Priest; — all this is thanks to little *Mekk*. — It grew so dark & now there has been a good downpour & more to follow, so I wont go on the balkony & its windy besides — Ania still intends coming, tho' I strongly advised her not to — why get wet & have *Juk* soaked, (only so as to come to me) its selfish & foolish, she might as well be a day without seeing me, but she wants more, says an hour is too little already. But I want little at a time, as get so tired still. — Fond thanks for yr. letter from *Brody*. How glad I am you have fine weather. Our Friend blesses your journey. — I keep thinking of you the whole time. It got fine this afternoon, but I was too tired to go out. Received *Khlebnikov*, my exlancer who has civil service in the Crimea because of his health, but whom I helped to get into the regiment as soon as the war began (he looks & feels flourishing) — told me about the lost *platoon* of the 6-th squadron. 10 men ran away & got back to the regiment after wandering about in the forests & dressed as peasants. Then *Apraxin* came, whom I had not seen for four months. — Ania sat for an hour. Now she has our Friend & the girls, after walking & driving have gone to the big Palace; Baby is in the garden. I wear your ideal cross.

God's blessing be upon you, guard & guide you. Very fondest kisses fr. yr. very own

Wify.

My love to the old man & to *N. P.* & give him news of my health. — Just now 37.1 again.

No. 62.

Tsarskoje Selo, April 10-th 1915

My very own Treasure,

I wonder when and where this letter will reach you. Such fond thanks for yesterday evening's telegram. Indeed your journey must be very interesting — & so emotioning seeing all those dear graves of our brave heroes. Wont you just have a lot to tell us upon your return. Difficult writing yr. diary, I am sure, when there are so many different impressions. How happy Olga dear will be to see you — Xenia wired upon yr. arrival so kindly. —

Wonder whether you took Shavelsky with you. —

Ania gave over what you telegraphed to our Friend, He blesses you & is so glad you are happy. — This morning the weather is going to be finer, I think, then can lie out. Heart still enlarged, temp. rose to 37.2 — now 36.5, & still so weak, they are going to give me iron to take. —

Gr. is rather disturbed about the »meat« stories, the merchants wont lessen the price tho' the goverment wished it, & there has been a sort of meatstrike one says. One of the ministers he thought, ought to send for a few of the chief merchants & explain it to them, that it is wrong at such a grave moment, during war to highten the prizes, & make them feel ashamed of themselves. —

Have read through the papers & found nothing of interest. — Marie is going to the cemetry to lay flowers on poor *Grabovoy's* grave, 40 days to-day! So the time flies by. — Mme *Viltchkovsky* is getting on nicely. I saw *Aleinikov* (& wife) 5 months he lay in the big palace — he longs to continue serving, only his arm aches still so (right to the top the right one is off) & he has to take mudbaths. Then *Koblev* who goes back to his regiment, & then Grünwald with messages fr. you, Sweetheart. I lay half an hour on the balkony, quite mild. — Now Ania is coming, so goodbye & God bless you. I cover yr. sweet face with tenderest kisses, Nicky love, & remain

Ever yr. very own

Sunny.

No. 63.

Tsarskoje Selo, April 11-th 1915

My very own Darling,

Your dear telegram yesterday made us all so happy. Thank God, that you have such beautiful impressions — that you could see the *Caucas. corps* & that summer weather blesses your journey. — In the papers I read Fred: short telegram fr. *Lvov,* telling about the Cathedral, peasants etc. dinner, and nomination of *Bobr.* into yr. suite — what great historical moments. Our Friend is delighted and blesses you. — Now I have read in the *Novoie Vremia* all about you, & feel so touched & proud for my Sweetheart. And your few words on the balkony — just the thing. God bless & unite in the fully deep, historical & religious sense of the word, these Slavonie Countries to their old Mother Russia. All comes in its right time & now we are strong enough to uphold them, before we should not have been able to — nevertheless we must in the »interior« become yet stronger & more united in every way, so as to govern stronger & with more authority. — Wont E. N. I. be glad! He sees his greatgrandson reconquering those provinces of the long bygone — & the revenge for Austria's treachery towards him. And you have personally conquered thousands of hearts. I feel, by your sweet, gentle, humble being & shining, pure eyes — each conquers with what God endows him — each in his way. God bless yr. journey on — I am sure it will revive the strength of our troops — if they need this. I am glad Xenia & Olga saw this great moment! — How nice you went to Olga's hospital — a recompense for her infatigable work! —

This moment got yr. wire fr. *Perem.* & plans for to-day — & now yr. sweet letter fr. the 8-th, for wh. 1000 of tender thanks; such joy to get a letter from you, love them so!! — Here is Ella's telegram unciphered; I return it, in case you wish to mention anything about it, or find out from the railway officials, whether true. — Had masses of *report* to read through, & now must get up & finish later on. —

I received an awfully touching telegram from Babys' *Georgian* regiment. *Akhmisury* arrived back & told them he had seen you, & gave over our messages — & thanking for my looking after their officers etc. —

Mme Zizi came after luncheon with papers — then my Siberian *Geleznoi* to say goodbye. Then I lay on the balkony ¾ of an hour, & the eldest sister *(Liubusha)* of the big Palace, sat with me. Ania came from 12—1 as usual. — My train No: 66 has just been to *Brody* to fetch wounded — lots of men, over 400, but only two officers. —

Goodbye Lovy mine — I do so wonder where you are going to see *Ivanov* and *Aleksejev* & can you get at them this time. — Goodbye & God bless and keep you. Very tenderest kisses fr. yr. very own old

Wify.

The Children all kiss you, & with me send love to the old man & *N. P.* —

No. 64.

Tsarkoje Selo, April 12-th 1915

Beloved One,

I wonder where you are? Xenia wired that you had dined together before leaving. Must have a look at the papers. Till now I go to bed at 6 & dont get up any more, & am up from 12—6. — The Children have gone to Church. Baby's foot is not quite the thing, so he is carried & drives, but does not suffer — he played Colorito on my bed this morning before his walk. — The weather is very sunny, tho' at times dark clouds hide all — hope to lie out again. Take lots of iron & arsenic & heartdrops & feel a little stronger now at last. —

We saw dear little Madame *Pourtzeladze* & her adorable baby boy yesterday — brave little soul! — She gets letters fr. him, but does not know whether he is severely wounded & how treated, that he dare not write — but thank God he is alive. —

2 hours I lay on the balkony, & Ania kept me company — Baby drove about in his motor & then in a little carriage.

I received my *Kniajevitch,* who intends going back to the lancers — over the *Headquarter* — but poor man doubts he can continue commanding the regiment, as fears he cannot ride on account of his kidneys — if so, he will return & seek some other service, as finds it dishonest towards the regiment. — Precious mine, quite spring, so lovely. —

I bless you & kiss you without end from the full depth of my great love. Goodbye Sweetheart.

Ever yr. very own old

Sunny.

About 16 lancers have escaped — 2 got on German officers horses & flew back — they had been well treated.

Many messages to the old man, the little Admiral, *Grabbe* & *N. P.* — The Children all kiss you tenderly. — Miss you sorely, precious Sunshine of our little home! —

Is it true *Mdivani* receives another nomination, & who is his successor? —

No. 65.

Tsarskoje Selo, April 13-th 1915

My very own Life,

Such a glorious, sunny morning! Yesterday I lay two hours out — shall lie out at 12 & I think after luncheon again. — The heart is not enlarged, the air & medicins are helping & I decidedly am feeling better & stronger, thank goodness. — To-morrow 6 weeks I worked last in the hospital. — The Commander of Baby's *Georgian's* sat with me for half an hour yesterday — such a nice man. Was before in the General staff, over *the frontier guards* in the Caucasus, singing highly the praises of his regiment & of poor *Grabovoy* —

seems *Mistchenko* mentioned the young man 2 in his *orders* (he was to get the St. George's cross & sword, — the Commander presented him for both) — I got onto the sopha for dinner & remained till 1. —

Fancy only, there was a youngster in Olga Orlov's hospital *Shvedov* with the St. George's cross — there was something at the end louche about him, how cld. a *Volunteer* have an officer's cross, & to me he said he had never been a *Volunteer* quite a boy to look at — he left — one found german chiffres on his table — & now I hear he has been hung! Too horrid — & he begged for our signed photos. I remember; — how could one have got hold of such a mere chap! — Baby just brought one of those German arrows one drops fr. aeroplans — how hideously sharp — *Romanovsky* brought it (is he a flier?) & asked for Baby's card — the aeroplan lies somewhere out here, Baby forgot fr. where it was brought. —

So now you are off to the South — did not get hold of your Generals? To-day perhaps in Odessa already — how brown you will get — I whisper a wish of Kirylls, wh. he told *N. P.* who repeated it, en passant to Ania (because thought he could not tell you) — that he hoped you would take him to *Nikolaiev* & *Sebastopol* — I only mention it like that, because I don't think you have any place for him.

Our dear sailors, how glad I am you will see them. —

Now you will find out how many *plastuni* battalions — & then I can send Images. —

Our Friend is glad you left for the South. He has been praying so hard all these nights, scarcely sleeping — was so anxious for you — any rotten vicious jew might have made a scandal.

Just got yr. wire fr. *Proskurovo* that is nice that you will see the *Zaamursky frontier guards* at *Kamenetz—Podolsk.* Really, this journey at last gives you more to see & brings you into contact with the troops.

I love to know you do and see unexpected things, not everything wh. is planned & marked out before — à la lettre — spontanious things (when possible) are more interesting. — What a lot you will have to write in your diary & only during stoppages. —

We only remained half an hour on the balkony, it got too windy & fresh. Received two officers after luncheon then Isa, after wh. Sonia over an hour, then Mme Zizi & at 4½ *Navruzov,* as want so much to see him again. —

I hope the rest of your journey will go off alright.

Goodbye & God bless & keep you, my Angel. I cover yr. dear face with kisses, & remain yr.

Ever very fondly loving old wife

Alix.

Bow to yr. Gentlemen.

On the 16-th is *N. P.'s* birthday.

Ask *N. P.* whether *Nic. Iv. Tchagin* who died, was brother of *Iv. Iv. (General of Infantry)* it says in *Petrogr.* I only know he had a brother in Moscou & one who died — an architect. —

No. 66.

Tsarskoje Selo, April 14-th 1915

My own beloved One,

Fancy only, it is snowing slightly & a strong wind. Thanks so much for yr. dear telegram. That was a surprise you saw my *Crimean reg.* am so glad & shall eagerly await news about them & why they were there — what joy for them! — Poor Ania has got again flebitis in her right leg & strong pain, so one has to stop massage, & she must not walk — but may be wheeled out, as the air is good for her — poor girl, she now really is good & takes all patiently & just as one was hoping to take off the plaster of Paris *(gypsum).*

Yesterday morning for the first time she walked alone on her crutches to the dining room without being held. Awful bad luck. —

Navruzov sat half an hour with me yesterday & was sweet; — to-day *Pr. Gelovani* will come, as I only saw him once en passant & it does one good seeing them — freshens one up.

Am feeling better & shall put on my stays for the first time. — Well, Ania came for 2 hours & now *Pr. Gelovani* comes to me, Tatiana arranged this. Very windy, but sunny. — All my love & tenderest thoughts follow you. God bless & protect you, my Sunshine.

Fondest kisses fr. yr. very own old

Sunny.

Bow to all. —

I send you some lilies of the valley to stand on yr. writing table — there are glasses one always brought for my flowers; I have kissed the sweet flowers & you kiss them too. —

No. 67.

Tsarskoje Selo, April 15-th 1915

My own beloved Treasure,

A windy, cold day — there was frost in the night, the *Ladoga* ice is passing, so shall not be able to lie out again. Temp. 37.2 again yesterday evening, but that means nothing, am feeling decidedly stronger, so will go to Ania this afternoon & meet our Friend there, who wishes to see me. At 11½ I have *Viltchkovsky* with a *report* wh. is sure to last an hour — then Schulenburg with his papers at 12½; & at 2 *Witte* with his affairs, sent by Rauchfuss. —

Yesterday *Gelovani* sat ½ an hour with me, spoke much about the regiment. — You must have felt very tired at Odessa doing so much in such a short time And our dear sailors! & 2 hospitals, that is nice indeed & will have rejoiced all hearts. —

I wonder, what that *woman's legion* wh. is being formed in *Kiev* is? If only to be as in England, to carry out the wounded & help them like sanitaries, then it can be alright — but I should personally not have allowed women to go out there »en masse« — the sister's dress is still a protection & they hold themselves otherwise — but these will be what?

Unless in very severe hands, well watched they may do very different things. A few of them with sanitary *detachements* cld. be good, but as a band -- no — that is not their place — let them nurse out there, from nurses *detachements.* There is an English lady who does wonders in Belgium in her warkit & short skirts — rides & picks up wounded, flies about to get vehicles to transport them to the nearest hospital, binds up their wounds — & once even read the prayers over the grave of a young English officer who died in a garret in a Belgium town taken by the Germans, & one dared not have a regular funeral. — Our women are less well educated & have no discipline so I don't know how they will manage »en masse« — wonder who allows them to form themselves. —

I think you may get these lines before leaving *Sebastopol* — the dear black sea!

And the fruit trees all in blossom — a flying visit to *Livadia* & *Jalta* would be lovely, I am sure! —

Ania's leg is not at all good, such red spots — fear this flebitis can last some time! Her Mother too is again ill, & Alia & the Children. —

Well, that was a surprise yr. precious letter & the dear little flower, thanks ever so much. Too interesting all your journey, everything you wrote — one sees it all before one. From *Olga* I also got a letter with her impressions — how happy she was to see you! —

It is so cold! And the wind howls down the chimny — Baby drove in the morning & will now again. His motor has a stronger mashine & so goes very quickly — Mr. Gillard & *Der.* follow him in a big one. —

Precious One, I suppose you are at *Nikolajev* now — interesting all you will see, & give the men energy to build on quickly & get our ships done. —

Goodbye, my own huzy love, God bless & protect you, I kiss ever so tenderly & with deepest devotion.

Ever yr. very own old

Wify.

Messages to Fred.

No. 68.

Tsarskoje Selo, April 16-th 1915

My Sweetheart,

I have just been eating up the newspapers with Freder. long telegrams about your journey. You have done & seen a lot, I am delighted — & been to hospitals too. Some of our wounded officers are now at Odessa & will surely have seen you there. But you must be very tired.

Pitty you cannot have one quiet day's rest in the South, to have quietly enjoyed the sunshine & flowers. Life once back here is so awfully tiring &

fidgety for you always, my poor treasure. I want the weather to get again warm & nice for yr. return & Baby's foot.

He is very careful with it I think on purpose.

This morning he is out driving with Mr. Gibbs. —

I had hoped to go to our hospital to sit a bit there but the heart is again a little enlarged, so have to remain at home. —

Our Friend was not long at Anias yesterday, but very dear. Asked lots about you. — To-day receive three officers returning to the war, yr. *Kobilin* too, & then Danini & two others, whom I sent to *Evpatoria* to choose a sanatorium. We have taken one for a year — the money you gave me covers the expenses. There are mud, sea, sun, sandbaths there, a Zanderroom, electricity, watercures, garden & plage close by — 170 people, & in winter 75 — its splendid.

Duvan, who has built a theatre, streets etc. there, I am going to ask to be the *Burser, Kniazhevitch* thinks he may help materially then too. — Xenia has returned one says. —

How glad you will be to see your *plastuni* to-day. —

Well, my treasure, I must say goodbye now. —

God bless & protect you — I kiss you over & over again with tenderness, & remain yr. ever fondly loving old

Wify.

How is Fred. I wonder!

Bow to him & *N. P.*

No. 69.

Tsarskoje Selo, April 17-th 1915

My own sweetest One,

Bright, sunny but cold, lay an hour on the balkony & found it rather too fresh. — Yesterday Paul came to tea. He told me he had just received a letter from Marie, telling him about your talk in the train concerning Dmitri. So he sent for the boy last night and was going to have a serious talk with him He too is greatly shocked at the way the boy goes on in town etc. —

In the evening at 8.20 there was this explosion — I send you Obolensky's paper. Now I have had telephoned to Sergei for news — one says 150 severely wounded — how many killed one cannot say, as one collects the bits — when the remaining people are assembled together, then they will know who is missing. Some parts in town & streets heard absolutely nothing — here some felt it very strongly, so that they thought it had occured at Tsarskoe. Thank God its not the powder-magazine as one at first had said. —

I had a long, dear letter fr. Erni — I will show it you upon your return. He says that »if there is someone who understands him (you) & knows what he is going through, it is me«. He kisses you tenderly. He longs for a way out of this dilema, that someone ought to begin to make a bridge for discussion.

So he had an idea of quite privately sending a man of confidence to Stockholm, who should meet a gentleman sent by you (privately) that they could help disperse many momentary difficulties. He had this idea, as in Germany there is no real hatred against Russia. So he sent a gentleman to be there on the 28 — (that is 2 days ago & I only heard to-day) & can only spare him a week. So I at once wrote an answer (all through Daisy) & sent it the gentleman, telling him you are not yet back, so he better not wait — & that tho' one longs for peace, the time has not yet come. —

I wanted to get all done before you return, as I know it would be unpleasant for you.

W. knows of course absolutely nothing about this. — He says they stand as a firm wall in France, & that his friends tell him, in the North & Carpathians too. They think they have 500.000 of our prisoners. —

The whole letter is very dear & loving; — I was intensely grateful to get it, tho' of course the question of the gentleman waiting there & you away, was complicated; — & E. will be disappointed. —

My heart is again enlarged, so I don't leave the house. *Lilly D.* is coming to me for half an hour. — I do hope you have warmer weather to-day, *Sebastopol* is not amiable both times. —

Xenia is coming to-morrow to luncheon.

Ania sat with me this morning for an hour. — 2 Girls are riding & 2 driving — Alexei out in his motor. — I wonder whether you return 21-st or 22-d.

Ressin has gone to town to see the place & bring me details, as I should like to help the poor sufferers. —

Now Lovebird, I must end, as I have to write for the English messenger & to sister Olga. —

God bless & protect you. I kiss you over & over again in tenderest love

Ever, Nicky dear, yr. old

Sunny.

No. 70.

Tsarskoje Selo, April 18-th 1915

My own sweet precious One,

A grey, cold, damp morning — the barometer must have fallen, feel such a pressure on my chest. — Yesterday evening Hagentorn took off Ania's *gypsum* from round her stomach, so that she is enchanted, can sit straight, & back no longer aches. Then she managed to lift her left foot, for the first time since 3 months, wh. shows that the bone is growing together. The flebitis in the other leg is very strong — so massage cannot be done on either leg, wh. is a pitty. She lies on the sopha & looks less of an invalid; she comes to me, as I remain at home on account of my heart. —

This morning I receive *Mekk* — he will, entre autre, tell me about *Lvov,* where he saw you in Church. My little *flying stores* trains have hard & useful work in the Carpathans, & our mules carry the things in the mountains — hard fighting, ones heart aches, — & in the North too again. — There, the kind sun is peeping out. Yr. little plant stands on the piano & I like looking at it — reminds me of the Rosenau 21 years ago!!

Our Friend says if it gets more known that that catastrophy happened from an *attempt to set fire,* the hatred towards Germany will be great. —

(Hang those aeroplans in the Carpathans now too?) I am going to send money to the poorest families & Images to the wounded. —

Olga wrote you the details; & I suppose others do officially, so I wont any more. —

My temp. rose to 37.3 in the evening & this morning 37; heart just now not enlarged. — Shall finish this in the afternoon, Xenia & Irina lunch with us, — & perhaps I may find something more interesting to tell you by then.

Well, now they have gone, Irina looked pretty, only much too thin. — It seems there was a fire in Ania's house, the little blind woman's candle fell down & things took fire, so the floor in the back room burned a little & two boxes with books, Ania got a nice fright — bad luck always. —

Now goodbye & God bless you — soon, soon I shall have you back, what joy!! 1000 fond kisses.

Ever yr. old

Wify.

No. 71.

Tsarskoje Selo, April 19-the 1915

My own darling Huzy dear,

Such a gloriously sunny morning! Shall lie out on the balkony at last again. Yesterday Mme *Janov* sent us flowers from beloved *Livadia* — glycinias, *golden rain-drops,* lilac iris wh. have opened this morning, lilac & red Italians anemonies wh. I used to paint & now want to again — *Judas tree* little branches, one pioni & tulips. To see them in ones vases makes me quite melancholy. Does it not seem strange, hatred & bloodshed & all the horrors of war — & there simply Paradise, sunshine & flowers and peace — such a mercy but such a contrast. Do hope you managed to get a nice drive beyond *Baidary.*

Well, Baby & I went at 11½ to Church, & came just during *the Credo* — so nice being in Church again, but missed you, my Angel, awfully — & was tired & felt my heart. — Blind Anisia took holy Communion — she upset the lantern in Ania's house & set the room on fire. After luncheon I lay knitting for an hour on the balkony, but the sun had gone & it was cold. Ania sat with me from 1½—3¼. — Such tender thanks for the divine lilacs — such perfume!

Thanks over & over again from us all — I gave Ania some too. —

The Children are giving medals in a hospital (with Drenteln) & then they & Baby go to Ania to meet the 2 cosacks & Marie's friend. —

How dear you named Baby chef of one of those splendid battalions, *Vorontzov* sent me a delighted telegram. Eagerly awaiting your return — lonely without you, my Sweetheart; & you will have such a lot to tell. —

Schwibzik is sleeping near me.

Now Goodbye, my very Own, God bless & protect you & bring you safely home to us.

Very fondest kisses fr. yr. own

Sunny.

Messages to everybody!

No. 72.

Tsarskoje Selo, April 20-th 1915

My own beloved Darling,

This is my last letter to you. For your precious & unexpected one & lovely flowers, tenderest thanks. One feels homesick for the beautiful Crimea — our earthly Paradise in spring! — All you write is so interesting — what a lot you have done — must be tired I am sure, dear precious One, Huzy mine!

Yes, my heart, I know you are lonely, and that makes me always so sad, that Sunbeam is not old enough to accompany you everywhere. The family is alright, but none of them are near to you, — or really understand you. — What a jubilation when you return. — Ania's Aunt returned full haste from *Mitave,* & the Governor with all the documents — a panic — the Germans coming! No troops of ours! — German *scouts.*

I think near *Libau* — I feel sure they want to make a *landing* with their heaps of sailors (doing nothing) & other troops, to push down from there towards Varsovie from the back, or along the coast, to get the Germans onto their side — that has all along been in my head since autumn. — Our Friend finds them awfully slie — looks at all seriously, but says God will help. — My humble opinion, why does one not get some cosack regiments along the coast, or our cavalry a little bit up more towards *Libau,* to keep them fr. ruining everything & finding basis for settling down with their devilish aeroplans. — We dont want them ruining our towns, not to say killing innocent people. —

Baby enjoyed himself at Ania's yesterday. — To-day the young couple *Voronov* are coming to us to tea, they have come for a few days from Odessa. I receive 7 officers returning, amongst others the General, Commander of Baby's *Georgians,* then *priest* fr. the Standart to say goodbye before leaving & Benkendorf, & then Ania.

I went for 3/4 of an hour at last to the hospital. *Gogoberidze* suddenly appeared to our surprise, he was only a month in the regiment & then went to *Batum* as was quite ill — now he looks brown as a nut — he returns to the regiment in a few days. —

It rained again, so I shall not lie out. — Sweetest one, I have got to see all those people now, so cannot write any more. The Children all and I kiss you ever so tenderly and warmly, beloved One. —

God grant in two days I shall have you back again in my longing arms. — The Children go to an exhibition to-morrow and then take tea at *Anitchkov*.

God bless & keep you. Ever yr. very own tenderly loving old wife

Alix.

No. 73.

Tsarskkoje Selo, May 4-th 1915

My own sweetest of Sweets,

You will read these lines before going to bed — remember Wify will be praying & thinking of you, oh so much, & miss you quite terribly. So sad we shall not spend your dear birthday together — the first time! May God bless you richly, give you strength and wisdom, consolation, health, peace of mind to continue bravely bearing your heavy crown — ah it is not an easy nor light cross He has placed upon yr. shoulders — would that I could help you carrying, in prayers & thoughts I ever do. I yearn to lessen yr. burden — so much you have had to suffer in those 20 years — & you were borne on the day of the longsuffering Job too, my poor Sweetheart. But God will help, I feel sure, but still much heartache, anxiety, & hard work have to be got through bravely, with resignation & trust in God's mercy, and unfathomable wisdom. Hard not to be able to give you a birthday tender kiss & blessing! — One gets at times so tired from suffering & anxiety & yearns for peace — oh when will it come I wonder! How many more months of bloodshed & misery? Sun comes after rain — & so our beloved country will see its golden days of prosperity after her earth is sodden with blood & tears — God is not unjust & I place all my trust in Him unwaveringly — but its such pain to see all the misery — to know not all work as they ought to, that petty personalities spoil often the great cause for wh. they ought to work in unisson Be firm, Lovy mine, show yr. own mind, let others feel you know what you wish. Remember you are the Emperor, & that others dare not take so much upon themselves — beginning by a mere detail, as the Nostitz story — he is in yr. suite & therefore N. has absolutely n o right to give orders without asking your permission first.

If you did such a thing with one of his aide de camps without warning him, wld. he not set up a row & play the offended, etc. & without being sure, one cannot ruin a man's career like that. — Then, Deary, if a new Com. of the *Nijegorodtzy* is to be named, wont you propose *Jagmin?*

I meddle in things not concerning me — but its only a hint, — (& its your own regiment, so you can order whom you wish there).

See that the story of the Jews is carefully done, without unnecessary rows, not to provoke disturbances over the country. — Dont let one coax you into unnecessary nominations & *rewards* for the 6-th — many months are yet before us! — You cant fly off to *Cholm* to see *Ivanov* or stop on the way to see soldiers waiting to be sent to refill the regiments.

One longs that each of yr. journeys should not only be the joy for the *Headquarters* (without troops) — but for the soldiers, or wounded, more need strength from you & it does you good too. Do what you wish & not the Generals — yr. presence gives strength everywhere. —

No. 74.

Tsarskoje Selo, May 5-th 1915

My own beloved One,

I send you my very, very tenderest goodwishes & blessings for yr. dear birthday. God Almighty take you quite particularly into His holy keeping. — I hope the candlesticks & magnifying glass will be useful for the train — I could not find anything else suitable, alas. — Ania sends you the enclosed card. —

This morning I went to *Znamenje,* then to her for half an hour. At 10 to the hospital, operation & *dressings* — no time to write details. Got back at 1¼ — left at 2 for town. Xenia & Georgia were also at the committee — lasted an hour & 20 m. then went to *stores* got home at 5½ — now must receive peasants from *Duderhof* & *Kolpino* with money. The Feldjeger must leave at 6. — Sunny, but cold. Am ramolie, so cannot write much & awful hurry. —

Slept badly — so lonely. —

My Angel Darling, I kiss & bless you without end — awfully sad not to spend dear 6-th together. Goodbye my love, my huzy sweet.

Ever yr. own old

Sunny.

No. 75.

Tsarskoje Selo, May 6-th 1915

My very own precious One,

Many happy returns of this dear day. God grant you may spend it next year in peace and joy, and the nightmare of this war be over. I cover you with tender kisses — alas, only in thoughts — & pray God to protect and quite particularly bless you for all your undertakings.

Such a sunny morning — (tho' fresh) may it be a good omen. — Our Friend's lovely telegram will have given you pleasure — shall I thank him for you? And for Ania's card, wire me a message to give over to her. — We sat with her in the evening as she had spent a lonely day, by chance nobody, except mother & son *Karangozov* came to see her. — We had a tiring day, so I did not take Olga to town, because of her cold & Becker's visit; Tatiana replaced her at the Committee. At the *stores* Marie Bariatinsky & Olga were making stockings, the same as they had been doing at Moscou so far. —

Everybody asks for news — I have none to give — but the heart is heavy — through Mekk's telegrams one sees the movements more or less. — *Navrusov* spoke with us by telephone, the sinner only leaves to-night — as he said to me, he had »fasted« for six months, now he must enjoy town. I called him a hulligan, wh. he did not approve of, — too bad, he says my health is better now, because he has been drinking for my health. I told him Pss. Gedroitz who is very fond of him, calls him our enfant terrible; then I spoke with *Amilakhvari* by telephone, & he will come to say goodbye to-day. — Bobrinsky has left full speed to *Lvov.*

They sang beautifully in Church. We had all my ladies, Benkend. & Ressin to lunch, then I received *Kotchubey, Kniazhevitch, Amilakhvari* then went to Ania & read to her, after wh. to the big palace for 10 m. — Now Xenia & Paul come to tea, so must end, — always a hurry. — Blessings & kisses without end — no news, so anxious.

Sweetheart, yr. very own, longing for you Wify.

No. 76.

Tsarskoje Selo, May 7-th 1915

My very own Angel,

Again I write in full haste, no quiet time. — Yesterday evening were at Ania's.

Slept not famously — heart heavy of anxiety, hate not being with you when trying times. — This morning after *Znamenje* peeped in to Anias, her sweet nieces & Alia overnighted in her house so as to get good air. — Then we had an operation — anxious one, serious case — & worked till after I. Before 2 said goodbye to *Karangozov* & *Gordinsky,* then Tatiana's committee — big group 2¼ to 4.

Went to A. till 5, saw our Friend there — thinks much of you, prays, *»we sat and talked together, — and still God will help.«*

Its horrid not being with you at a time so full of heartache & anxiety — would to God I could be of help to you — one comfort *N. P.* is near you & then I am quieter — a natural, warm heart & kind look helps when worries fill the soul; not a fat O. or *Drent.* As the cosacks begged everytime so much, have said two or 1 officer may come with us. — Fear it will be very official still, but our Fr. wants me to go on such journeys. —

Treasure of my soul, Angel beloved, God help you, console & strengthen & help our brave heroes. —

I kiss you over & over again & bless you without end. Must finish.

Ever yr. very own Wify.

No. 77.

May 8-th 1915

My beloved One,

Artsimovitch will meet you at *Dvinsk* to-morrow, and has proposed to bring you a letter. But I have the feeling that if the news continue not being good, that you will probably be remaining on still at the *Headquarters*. Such splendid weather & all quite green, a great difference after *Tsarskoje*. — So far all has gone beautifully & we are having three hours rest, wh. is splendid, as my back aches a lot. — We went to the Cathedral, a *Te Deum* of 5 minutes, the Bishop *Cyrill* seemed ramoli, I must say. Then went to four hospitals, the sisters of my *Krestovozdvijensky Community* work in one since August — in another, sisters & Drs. from *Tashkent* — everywhere good air, clean & nice; & not fussy. A group was taken of us with masses of wounded in a garden. Masses of Jews, & trains arrive with them from *Curland* — painful sight with all their packages & wee children.

The town is pretty when one crosses the river. The Children had the Governor & *Mezentzev* to luncheon & then the latter came & sat with me — such a nice man & works well one sees.

Now we shall be going to one of his *stores* & to three hospitals & to the Palace where the Gov. lives as there is a *store* under my protection there. We leave again at 7. I did not sleep very well. Wonder what news, feel so anxious far from you. — Now my Lovy, Goodbye & God bless you.

I kiss you from the depths of my loving heart

Ever yr. very own old

Wify.

The girls kiss you. —

I got your wire, that you have put off yr. journey, wh. is more than comprehensible — easier to be nearer these trying days — would to God that that »ray of light« might brighten into sunshine — one yearns for success — & now Essen's death, the one that the German's feared has died! Ah, what trials God sends — whom do you name in his place I wonder, who has the same energy as he for the time of war? I hate not being near you, knowing your suffering. But God Almighty will help, all our losses wont be in vain, all our prayers must be heard, no matter how hard it is now — but being far away, with scarce news is trying & yet you cannot get nearer. Sweet one, I know yr. faith & trust in God. — St. Nicolas feast to-morrow may that holy Saint intercede for our brave, struggling troops. — I had my wish & saw a sanitary train wh. brought fresh wounded of four days ago, of the *sixth infantry division the Muromtzevsky and Nizovski*. There were no very severe cases, thank God, tho' bad wounds, to many I said I should tell you I had seen them & their faces lit up. — We went over my *store* of the red cross wh. *Mesentzev* has, still 3 hospitals & the *stores* in the Governor's palace & took a cup of coffee wh. gave one new strength. My back hurts awfully — kidneys, I think crystals again wh. always cause pain. The pavement vile, glad, had our motors. Ortipo climb onto my lap, have sent her off several times without success — so yet more difficult writing on the top of her back in a shaking train. All the *convalescent* stood near the station when we returned, & school-children.

Glorious sunset — quite summer — such dust. Shall finish this at Tsarskoe to-morrow.

May 9-th. We got here alright, the *Pavlovsk* line, as near *Gatchina* their had been an explosion on the train going with ammunitions — such a horror — 12 waggons they managed to save — one sees it was done on purpose; just what one so soreley needs, it does seem cruel. — The little ones met us at the station. Worked as usual in the hospital, was at Ania's, placed candles in Church.

After lunch received *Apraxin, Hartman* the Com. of the *Erivantzi* & a wounded officer. —

Yr. *Taube* lies still at *Lomzha* & one was obliged, alas, to amputate his leg above the knee. Now I have got Ania coming, Sonia lunched with us — one says news a wee bit better? —

The a. d. c. of the blue curassiers brought us flowers — they love *Arseniev* & highly appreciate him. —

The wife of one of the *Georgian* officers is coming to me as its their feast — & later I want to take flowers to *Grabovoy's* grave.

God bless you my Sunshine I cover yr. sweet face with kisses —

Ever yr. very own

Sunny.

I have got hold of a rotten pen.

Hope to go to Church — sad to-morrow's great feast not together. —

Bow to all yr. people.

No. 78.

Tsarskoje Selo, May 10-th 1915

My own precious One,

A lovely, warm, sunny morning; yesterday too it was fine, but so cold lying on the balkony after the summerweather at *Vitebsk*.

Our Church is so prettily decorated in green — do you remember last year at *Livadia* how lovely our little Church was — & once this day on board in Finland too!

Dear me, how much has happened since the peaceful, homely life in the *fjords*.

Edigarov writes that they have 35 degrees of warmth. —

Sister *Olga* wrote that all their wounded had to be sent off in full speed with deep sorrow on both sides — the very worse were transferred to another hospital wh. must remain. — God grant still *P.& L.* wont be taken & that these great feastdays may bring us luck. This journey of yours I get no telegrams alas, & so have to hunt in the papers for news — one lives through a time of grave anxiety — so I am glad you are not here, where everything is taken in a different tone, except by the wounded, who understand all much more normally. —

Drive with A. to *Pavlovsk* — my first drive since autumn — lovely, only one feels so sad at heart — & my back aches awfully since 3 days — then remained on the balkony & we are drinking tea there too. Thanks for yr. telegram Deary, — thank God the news are better. I saw 3 of Olga's ladies, its the regiment's feast, then Kostia & Commander of Izmail. reg. — *Sister Ivanova* (Sonia's Aunt) fr. Varsovie — interesting all she told about the hospitals there. —

Miechen heard through the Pss. Oginsky & told Mavra to tell me, that the prisoners (wounded) catholics are allowed to confess to Priests *(Vilna)* but not have holy Communion — thats quite wrong, but is *Tumanov's* order — if they are afraid of the Priests, then why allow confession — I suppose those are Bavarians, I don't know how the protestants are treated — can you speak to somebody to enquire into this? Thank old man & bow fr. me, & bow to *N. P.* — A. sends her love & kisses yr. hand. — Blessings & kisses without end, beloved One.

Ever yr. very, very own

Wify.

No. 79.

Tsarskoje Selo, May 11-th 1915

My own precious Nicky,

Again quite fresh and grey, & in the night only one degree — extraordinary for the month of May. — We spent the evening at Ania's yesterday, some officers were invited 8—10½ & they played games — Alexei came fr. — 9¼ & enjoyed himself greatly; I knitted. She gave me then letters fr. the wretched Nostitz couple to read — it seems this hideous intrigue was written to her relations to America, by a Gentleman of the American embassy, instigated by her enemies — the Ambassador is a friend of theirs. She thinks it is all done by Mme *Artzimovitch* (an American by birth) a story of jealousy. But it was sad to read their despairing letters of lives ruined — but I feel sure you will see that this story is cleared up satisfactorily & justice done them. I care for neither, but the whole thing is a crying shame & N. had no right to act as he did with a member of your Suite, without asking first your permission — so easy to ruin a reputation & more than difficult to reestablish it. — I must dress now. — I ordered service at 9½ in the *Pestcherni chapel* of the *Dv. hospital,* so that we can work at once in the hospital when mass is over. My heart keeps decent (drops always) but back aches very strongly — for sure kidneys. —

I had *Engalitchev* to-day & he told me many interesting things. — Went to the big palace & then lay on the balkony reading to Ania, tho' cold. Our

Friend saw *Bark* for 2 hours & they talked well together. — God be thanked that the news is better, may it only continue thus. What joy, you are writing to me.

To-day its a week you left us. — The Children all kiss you & so do I, my lovebird. Send blessings without end,

Ever, huzy love, yr. very own old

Sunny.

Bow to old man & *N. P.*

No. 80.

My own beloved One,

When we returned from the hospital I found your beloved letter, & thank you for it from the depths of my loving heart. Such joy to hear from you, Sweetheart. Thanks so much for all details, I was so longing to get real, exact news from you. How hard those days were, & I not near you & such hard work, much to do. Thank God that all is better now & may Italy draw some of the troops away. I remember *Savitch,* did he not come to the Crimea? The new Admiral's face I don't remember, he is a cousin of *N. P.* — Have the *Eriv.* & all the Caucasian division been sent to the Carpathans, or is it not true? They were asking me again. —

Engal. said one expects the next heavy battles will be near Varsovie, but he finds our 2 Generals (don't remember the name) weak & not the types to meet heavy *attacks* he told N. & *Janoushk.* so.

Am so glad about the paper you sent of my *Crimeans* — they are then again in another division. — My *Alexand.* have also been doing well near *Shavli.* Wonder how my *Kniazhevitch's* health is, have no news since he left. — Just now received 2 officers — the most going off to *Evpatoria* — that law of 8 or 9 months is fearfully hard — we have some with broken limbs wh. can be healed only after a year, impossible before, but then alright for service — & as they cannot possibly now return to their regiments, they loose their pay — & some are so poor, have no fortune of their own — it does seem unjust. Crippled, not always for life, but for a time, doing their duty bravely, wounded & then left like beggars — their moral sufferings becomes so great. Others hasten back too early, only not to loose all & may completely loose their health fr. that. Certainly some types (few) must be hurried off to their regiments because are fit for work already. — Its all complicated. —

My back still aches & now higher up, a sort of Hexenschuss wh. makes many movements very painful — still I managed to do my works. Now I shall lie on the balkony & read to Ania, as driving been shaken, makes the back worse. —

What joy if we meet really on Thursday!

Goodbye my Love, God bless & keep you from all harm.

Ever such tender kisses from us all. Yr. very Own.

No. 81.

Tsarskoje Selo, June 10-th 1915

My very own precious One,

It is with a heavy heart I let you leave this time — everything is so serious & just now particularly painful & I long to be with you, to share your worries & anxieties. You bear all so bravely & by yourself — let me help you my Treasure. Surely there is some way in wh. a woman can be of help & use. I do so yearn to make it easier for you & the ministers all squabbling amongst each other at a time, when all ought to work together & forget their personal offenses — have as aim the wellfare of their Sovereign & Country — it makes me rage. In other words its treachery, because people know it, they feel the government in discord & then the left profit by it. If you could only be severe, my Love, it is so necessary, they must hear your voice & see displeasure in yr. eyes.; they are too much accustomed to your gentle, forgiving kindness.

Sometimes a word gently spoken carries far — but at a time, such as we are now living through, one needs to hear your voice uplifted in protest & repremand when they continue not obeying yr. orders, when they dawdle in carrying them out. They must learn to tremble before you — you remember Mr. Ph. & Gr. say the same thing too. You must simply order things to be done, not asking if they are possible (you will never ask anything unreasonable or a folly) — for instance, order as in France (a Republic) other fabrics to make shells, cartridges (if guns & rifles too complicated) — let the big fabrics send teacher — where there is a will there is a way & they must all realise that you insist upon yr. wish being speedily fulfilled. It is for them to find the people, the fabricants, to settle all going, let them go about & see to the work being done, themselves. You know how talented our people are, how gifted — only lazy & without initiative, start them going, & they can do anything, only dont ask, but order straight off, be energetic for yr. country's sake!

The same about the question wh. our Friend takes so to heart & wh. is the most serious of all, for internal peace's sake — the not calling in the *Second class* — if the order has been given, you tell N. that you insist upon its counterordering — by your name *to wait,* the kind act must come fr. you — dont listen to any excuses — (am sure it was unintentionally done out of not having knowledge of the country). Therefore our Friend dreads yr. being at the *Headquarters* as all come round with their own explanations & involuntarily you give in to them, when yr. own feeling has been the right one, but did not suit theirs. Remember you have reigned long, have far more experience than they — N. has only the army to think of & success — you carry the internal responsabilities on for years — if he makes faults (after the war he is nobody), but you have to set all straight. No, hearken unto our Friend, beleive Him, He has yr. interest & Russians at heart — it is not for nothing God sent Him to us — only we must pay more attention to what He says — His words are not lightly spoken — & the gravity of having not only His prayers, but His advise — is great. The Ministers did not think of telling you, that this measure is a fatal one, but He did. — How hard it is not to be with you, to talk over all quietly & to help you being firm. — Shall follow & be near you in thoughts & prayers all the time. May God bless & protect you, my brave, patient, humble one. I cover yr. sweet face with endless, tender kisses, — love you b e y o n d words, my own, very own Sunshine & joy. — I bless you. — Sad not to pray together, but *Botk.* finds wiser my remaining quiet, so as soon to be quite alright again.

Yr. own

Wify.

Our Marie will be 16 on the 14-th, so give her diamond-necklace fr. us, like the other two got. —

No. 82.

Tsarskoje Selo, June 11-th 1915

My very own precious One,

All my tenderest thoughts surround you in love and longing. It was a lovely surprise, when you suddenly turned up again — I had been praying & crying & feeling wretched. You don't know how hard it is being without you & how t e r r i b l y I always miss you. Your dear telegram was such a consolation, as I felt very low & Ania's odious humour towards me (not to the Children) did anything but enliven my afternoon & evening. — We dined out & took tea on the balkony — this morning its glorious again — I am still in bed, resting you see, as heart not quite the thing, tho' not enlarged — I have been sorting out photos to be glued into albums for the exhibition-bazar here. — Fancy, big Marie *Bariat.'s* husband died from a stroke on the 9-th at *Berejany* in a property named Raï — one carries his body to *Tarnopol.* He was *Commissioner* of the *red cross at the 11-th Army,* can imagine Marie & Olga's despair, as they loved so their brother *Ivan.* Then the old C. Olsufiev has died — they lived as turtledoves, she will be brokenhearted. — One hears of nothing but deaths it seems to me. — Fancy, what I did last night in bed? I fished out yr. old letters & read through many of them, & those few before we were engaged — & all yr. words of intense love & tenderness warmed up my aching heart, & it seemed to me, as tho' I heard you speaking.

I numbered yours, the last 176 fr. the *Head-Quarters.* You number my yesterdays please, 313 — I hope my letter did not displease you but I am haunted by our Friend's wish & k n o w it will be fatal for u s & the country if not fulfilled. He means what He says, when speaks so seriously — He was much against yr. going to *L.* & *P.* — it was too soon, we see it now — was much against the war — was against the people of the *Duma* coming, an ugly act of *Rodz.* & the speeches ought not to have been printed (I find).

Please, my Angel, make N. see with your eyes — dont give in to any of the *2-nd class* being taken — put it off as long as only possible — they have to work in the fields, fabrics, on steamers etc.; rather take the recroutes for next year now — please listen to His advise when spoken so gravely & wh. gave Him sleepless nights — one fault & we shall all have to pay for it. — I wonder what humour you found at the Head-Quarters & whether the heat is very great. —

Felix told Ania that one threw (then) stones at Ella's carriage & spat at her, but she did not wish to speak to us about it — they feared disorders these days again — don't know why. — The big girls are in the hospital, yesterday all 4 worked in the *stores* — *bandages* — & later went to *Irina*. — How do you feel, my Love, your beloved sad eyes haunt me still. Dear Olga wrote a sweet letter & kisses you & asks sweetly how you bear all, tho' she knows you will always wear a cheery face & carry all hidden inside. I fear often for yr. poor heart — it was so much to bear — speak out to yr. old wify — bride of the bygone — share all with me, it may make it easier — tho' sometimes one has more strength carrying alone, not letting oneself get soft — the phisical heart gets so bad from it, I know it but too well. Lovebird, I kiss you without end, bless you, cover yr. precious face with kisses & long to let your dear head rest upon my old breast, so full of unutterable love & devotion.

Ever yr. own old

Alix.

I recieve Mme Hartwig, Rauchfuss, the 4 Trepov daughters (2 married). Remember to speak about the wounded officers being allowed to finish their cures at home befor returning for 2,3 or 4 time to battle, its cruel & unjust otherwise, N. must give Alek the order.

My love to the old man & *N. P.*

No. 83.

Tsarskoje Selo, June 12-th 1915

My very own precious One,

With such anxiety I wait for news & eagerly read the morning papers so as to know what happens. —

Glorious weather again — yesterday during dinner (on the balkony) there was a colossal downpour, seems it must daily rain, personally I have nothing against it, as always dread the heat & yesterday it was very hot & Ania's temper beastly, wh. did not make me feel better — grumbling against everybody & everything & strong hidden pricks at you & me. — This afternoon I may drive & to-morrow I hope to go (after a week's absence) to the hospital, as one of the officers must have his apendicitis cut off. —

Dmitri had his leg put in plaster of Paris *Gypsum* & to-day they are going to look with Röntgen-rays to see whether the leg is really broken, crushed or strained — what bad luck always!

Sweet one, please remember the question about the *Tobolsk Tatars* to be called in — they are splendid, devoted fellows & no doubt would go with joy & pride. — I found a paper of old Marie Feod. you once brought me, & as it is funny, I send it to you. —

I saw Mme Hartwig yesterday — she told me many interesting things when they left *Lvov* — & sad impressions of soldiers being depressed & saying that they wont return to fight the enemy with empty fists — the rage of the officers against *Soukhomlinov* is quite colossal — poor man — his very name they loathe & yearn for him to be sent away — well for his sake too, before any scandle arises, it would be better to do so. It is his adventurer wife who has completely ruined his reputation — because of her bribes he suffers & so on; — one says it is his fault there is no ammunition wh. is our curse now etc. I tell you this to show you what impressions she brought back. —

How one craves for a miracle to bring success, that ammunition & rifles should do double work! —

Wonder how the *spirit* in the *Head-Quarters* is? — Would to God N. were another man & had not turned against a man of Gods, that always brings bad luck to their work & those women wont let him change; he recieved decorations without end & thanks for all — but too early — its pain to think he got so much & nearly all has been retaken.

But God Almighty will help & better days will come, I feel convinced. Such trials for you to bear my own Sunshine. I long to be with you, to know how you are feeling morally — brave & calm as usual, the pain hidden away as usual. God help you my very own sweet Sufferer & give you strength, trust & courage. Yr. reign has been one of sore trials, but the recompense must come some day, God is just. — The little birdies are singing away so cheerily & a soft breeze comes in by the window. When I finish my letter, I shall get up; — these quiet days have done my heart good.

Give many kind messages to the old man & *N. P.* I am glad the latter is near you, I feel a warm heart with you & that makes me quieter for your sweet sake. —

Try & write a wee word for Marie, her 16 birthday being on Sunday. —

Tatiana went for a ride yesterday, I encouraged her, the others were of course too lazy & went to the Nurse's school to play with the babies. —

A Pr. Galitzine *Serg. Mikh.* died at Lausanne — I suppose its the man of many wives. —

Now my own Nicky darling, I must say goodbye. I regret having nothing of interest to tell you.

The 4 *Trepov* daughters beg to thank you ever so deeply for having permitted their mother to be buried next to their Father — they saw his coffin, still quite intact. —

Blessings without end be yours, my Love, I cover yr. sweet face with kisses, & remain

Ever yr. very own

Sunny.

No. 84.

Tsarskoje Selo, June 12-th 1915

My very Own,

I begin my letter still to-night, as to-morrow morning I hope to go to the hospital & shall have less time for writing. Ania & I took a nice drive to *Pavlovsk* this afternoon — in the shade it was quite cool; we lunched & took tea on the balkony, but in the evening it got too fresh to sit out. From 9½—11½ we were at Anias, I worked on the sopha, the 3 girls & officers played games. I am tired after my first outing. — My *Lvov stores* is now at *Rovno* near the station for the time — God grant we shant be driven back fr. there too. — That we had to leave that town is hard, but still it was not quite ours yet — nevertheless its sad to have fallen into other hands — William will now be sleeping in old Fr. J's bed wh. you occupied one night — I don't like that, its humiliating, — but that one can bear — but to think that once more the same battle-fields may be strewn with the bodies of our brave men — thats heartrending. But I ought not to speak to you in this tone, you have enough sorrow — my letters must be cheery ones, but its a bit difficult when heart & soul are sad. I hope to see our Friend a moment in the morning at Anias to bid Him goodbye — that will do me good. Serge *Tan.* was to leave tonight over *Kiev* but got a telegram that the *Akhtirtzy* are being sent elsewhere & he must leave to-morrow. I wonder what new combination. — How one wishes Alexeiev had remained with *Ivanov,* things might have gone better — *Dragomirov* set all going wrong. One prays & prays & yet never enough — the Schadenfreude of Germany makes my blood boil. God must surely hearken unto our supplications & send some success at least; — now shall be having them turn towards Varsovie & many troops are near *Shavli,* oh God, what a hideous war! Sweet, brave Soul how I wish one could rejoice your poor, tortured heart with something bright & hopeful. I long to hold you tightly clasped in my arms, with yr. sweet head resting upon my shoulder — then I could cover Lovy's face & eyes with kisses & murmer soft words of love. I kiss your cushion at nights, thats all I have — & bless it. — Now I must go to sleep. Rest well, my treasure, I bless & kiss you ever so fondly & gently stroke your dear brow.

June 13-th. How can I thank you enough for your beloved letter, I received upon our return from the hospital. Such an intense joy hearing from you, my Angel, thanks thousands of times. But I am sad your dear heart does not feel right, please let *Botkin* see you upon yr. return as he can give you drops to take from time to time when you have pains. I feel so awfully for those who have anything with the heart, suffering from it myself for so many years. Hiding ones sorrow, swallowing all, makes it so bad & it gets besides phisically tired — your eyes seemed like it at times. Only always tell it me, as I have after all enough experience with heart complains & I can perhaps help you. Speak about all to me, talk it out, cry even, it makes it phisically too, easier sometimes. —

Thank God N. understood about the *second class.* — Forgive me, but I don't like the choice of Minister of war — you remember how you were against him, & surely rightly & N. too I fancy. He works with Xenia too — but is he a man in whom one can have any confidence, can he be trusted? How I wish I were with you & could hear all yr. reasons for choosing him. I dread N.'s nominations, N. is far from clever, obstinate & led by others — God grant I am mistaken & this choice may be blest — but I like a crow, croak over it rather. Can the man have changed so much? Has he dropped *Gutchkov* — is he not our Friend's enemy, as that brings bad luck. Make dear old *Goremykin* thoroughly speak with him, morally influence him. Oh may these 2 new ministers be the right men in the right place, ones heart is so full of anxiety & one yearns for union amongst the ministers, success. Lovy mine, tell them upon their return from the *Headquarters* to ask & see me, one after the other, & I shall pray hard & try my utmost to be of real use to you. Its horrid not helping & letting you have all the hard work to do. —

Our Friend dined (I think) with *Shakhovskoy* again & likes him — He can influence him for the good. Fancy how strange! *Schtcherbatov* wrote a most amiable letter to *Andronnikov* (after having spoken against him to you). —

There is another minister I don't like in his place, *Stcheglovitov,* (to speak to pleasant) he does not heed to your orders, & whenever a petition comes wh. he thinks our Friend brought, he wont do it & not long ago tore one of yours through again. *Verevkine* his aid *(Gr.'s* friend) told this — & I have noticed, that he rarely does what one asks — like *Timiriasev* obstinate & »by the letter« not by the soul. Its right to be severe — but one might be more just than he is & kinder to the small people, more lenient. —

Our apendicitis operation went off well; saw the new officers — the poor boy with *tetanos* is a little better — more hopeful. — Such fine weather, am lying on the balkony & the birdies are chirruping away so gaily. — A. just sat with me, she saw *Gr.* this morning, he slept better for the first time since 5 nights & says its a little better at the war. He begs you m o s t i n c e s s a n t l y to order q u i c k l y that on o n e day a l l o v e r the country there should be a *church procession* to ask for victory, God will sooner hear if all turn to Him — please give the order, any day you choose now that it should be done — send yr. order (I think) by wire (open that all can read it) to *Sabler* that this is yr. wish — now is *Petrovski Lent,* so it is yet more apropriate, & it will lift the *spirit* up, & be a consolation to the brave one's fighting — & tell the same thing to *Shavelsky* Deary — please Darling, & just that its to be an order from y o u , n o t from the Synod. — I could not see Him to-day — hope to-morrow.

A., Alia & Nini have gone by motor to *Krasnoje* to talk with *Groten.* Now I must quickly send off this letter. Marie Bariatinsky dines with us & leaves to-morrow with Olga for *Kiev* I think. —

God bless & protect you — heart & soul with you, prayers without end surround you. Feel sad & lowspirited, hate being separated fr. you, all the more so when you have so many worries.

But God will help & if these *church processions* are done, am sure He will hearken unto all prayers of your faithful people. God guard & guide you, you my very own Love.

If you have any question for our Fr. write at once.

I cover you with fondest kisses, Ever yr. own old

Wify.

Love to old man & *N. P.*

No. 85.

Tsarskoje Selo, June 14-th 1915

My own beloved One,

I congratulate you with all my loving heart for our big Marie's 16-th birthday. What a cold, rainy summer it was when she was borne — 3 weeks I had daily pains until she turned up. Pitty you are not here. She enjoyed all her presents, I gave her her first ring from us made out of one of my Buchara diamonds.

She is so cheery & gay to-day.

I am writing on the balkony, we have just finished luncheon after we had been to Church. Baby is going to Peterhof for the afternoon & later to Ania. Such lovely weather & the wind keeps it from being too hot — but the evenings are fresh. Marie Bariatinsky dined with us & remained till 10½ & then I went to bed as had a headache.

The girls had a repetition in the »little house«. —

Beloved one, all my thoughts & prayers are with you the whole time & so much sorrow and anxiety fills the heart. — I hope you will say about the *church processions.* Old Fred. of course made a confusion & gived O. Ebr. on her money she got as my lady, not her Father's pension (wh. was much less) & she asked for. She feels quite confused at. yr. great kindness. —

Yesterday I looked at the 10 English motors — quite splendid, much better than ours, for four lying & a sister or sanitary can sit inside with them & always hot water to be had for them — they hope to get yet 20 more for us, yr. Mama & me together. As soon as she has seen these, they ought to be sent off I find at once where the cavalry is most in need of them n o w, I don't know where, perhaps you could ask, & then I can hint it to Motherdear. She is now at *Elagin.*

Paul comes to tea & then the children go to Ania, perhaps I too for a bit if not too tired. I see our Friend this evening or to-morrow morning.

We are going out driving this afternoon, A. & I; the girls will follow in two small carriages.

Now I must end dear Love. How I long to know how the news really are, such anxiety fills the soul. —

Goodbye Nicky mine, my very, very own.
God bless & protect you. I cover your precious face with kisses.

Ever yr. very own

Sunny.

No. 86.

Tsarskoje Selo, June 14-th 1915

My own beloved Nicky,

So many thanks for yr. dear telegram. Poor Darling, even on Sunday a council of ministers! — We had a nice drive to *Pavlovsk,* coming back, little Georgi on his small motor (like Alexeis) flew into our carriage, but luckily he did not upset & his machine was not spoiled. — Paul came to tea & remained 1 & 3/4 hours, he was very nice & spoke honestly & simply, meaning well, not wishing to meddle with what does not concern him, only asking all sorts of things wh. I now repeat to you, with his knowledge. Well, to begin with, Paleolog dined with him a few days ago & then they had a long private talk & the latter tried to find out from him, very cleverly, whether he knew if you had any ideas about forming a seperate peace with Germany, as he heard such things being spoken about here, & as tho' in France one had got wind of it — & that there they intend fighting to the very end. Paul answered that he was convinced it was not true, all the more, as at the outset of the war we & our allies had settled, that peace could only be concluded together on no account separately. Then I told Paul that you had heard the same rumour about France; & he crossed himself when I said you were not dreaming of peace & knew it would mean revolution here & therefore the Germans are trying to egg it on. He said he had heard even the German mad conditions posed to us. — I warned him he wld. next hear, that I am wishing peace to be concluded. —

Then he asked me whether it was true that *Stcheglovitov* was being changed & that rotten *Manukhin* named in his place — I said I knew nothing, wh. is the truth, & neither why *Stchegl.* has chosen the moment now to go to the *Solov. convent.* Then he mentioned another thing to me wh. tho' painful its better to warn you about — namely, that since 6 months one speaks of a spy being at the *Headquarters* & when I asked the name, he said Gen. *Danilov* (the black one), that from many sides one has told him this »feeling« & that now in the army one speaks about it. Lovy mine, *Vojeikov* is sly & clever, talk to him about this, & let him slyly & cleverly try & have an eye upon the man & his doings — why not have him watched — of course as Paul says one has the spy mania now, but as things are at once known abroad wh. only very wellinitiated people at the *Headquarters* can know, this strong doubt has arisen, & Paul thought it honest to ask me whether you had ever mentioned this to me — I said no. — Only dont mention it to *Nikolasha* before you have taken information, as he can spoil all by his excited way & tell the man straight out or disbelieve all. But I think, it would only be right, tho' the man may seem perfectly charming & honest, to have him watched. Whilst you are there the yellow men & others can use eyes & ears & watch his telegrams & the people he sees etc. One pretends as tho' he often receives big sums. I only tell you all this, knowing nothing whether there is any foundation in it, only better to warn you. Many dislike the *Headquarters* & have an uncomfortable feeling there & as, alas, we have had spies & also innocent people accused by *Nikolasha,* now you can find out carefully, please. — Paul says *Schtcherbatov's* nomination was hailed with delight; he does not know him. — Forgive my bothering you so, poor weary Sweetheart, but one longs to be of help & perhaps I can be of some use giving over such messages. —

Mary *Vassiltchikov* & family live in the green corner house & fr. her window she watches like a cat all the people, that go in & out of our house & makes her remarks. She drove Isa wild asking why the children one day went out of one gate on foot & next time on bicycles, why an officer comes with a portfolio in the morning in one uniform & differently dressed in the evening — told Css. Fred. that she saw *Gr.* driving in — (odious). So to punish her, we went to A. this evening by a round about way, so she did not see us pass out. He was with us fr. 10—11½ in her house — I send you a stick (fish holding a bird), wh. was sent to Him fr. *New Athos* to give to you — he used it first & now sends it to you as a blessing — if you can sometimes use it, wld. be nice & to have it in yr. compartment near the one Mr. Ph. touched, is nice too. He spoke much & beautifully — & what a Russian Emperor is, tho' other Sovereigns are anointed & crowned, only the Russian one is a real *Anointed* since 300 years. Says you will save your reign by not calling out the *2nd class* now — says *Shakhovskoy* was delighted you spoke about it, because the ministers agreed, but had you not begun, they did not intend speaking.

Finds, you ought to order fabricks to make *Ammunition,* simply you to give the order even choose wh. fabrick, if they show you the list of them, instead of giving the order over through commissions wh. talk for weeks & never can make up their minds.

Be more autocratic my very own Sweetheart, show your mind. —

The exhibition-bazar began to-day in the big Palace, on the terrace — not very big (have not yet been there) & our works are already bought up, it's true we had not done very much & we shall continue working & sending things there; they sold over 2100 entrance tickets à 10 kop., soldiers (wounded) need not pay, as they must go & see what works please them & wh. they can make.

I gave a few of our vases & two cups, as they always attract people.

Tell the old man I saw his family a moment yesterday, when I went to fetch Ania at Ninis, & found the three ladies looking well. Tell *Vojeikov,* that I find his cabinet quite charming (happily not smelling of cigars).

Now I must go to sleep & finish to-morrow. —

So fresh, we dined out & there were only 9 degrees. Baby enjoyed *Peterhof* & then the games with the officers. Dmitri is better & hopes to leave on Thursday, if even on crutches — is in despair to have remained behind.

The last Dolgoruky, *Alexei* died in London. — Sleep peacefully & rest well, my treasure — I have blessed & kissed your cushion, as alas have not you here to tenderly caress & codle. Goodnight my Angel. —

June 15-th. Very fine again, am writing on the balkony, we have lunched, then I must receive some officers & hereafter go to Mavra. We photographed at the hospital in the garden & sat on the balkony after we had finished everything. —

Do so long for news. — Wonder how long you will remain away.

Ania has gone for the first time to town by motor to her Parents, as her Mother is ill, & then to our Friend. —

Now goodbye my very own, longed for Treasure, my Sweetheart, I kiss you ever so fondly & pray God to bless, protect & guide you

Yr. own old

Wify.

Have you the patience to read such long letters?

No. 87.

Tsarskoje Selo, June 15-th 1915

My own beloved One,

Before going to sleep, I begin my letter to you. Thanks for yr. wire, I received during dinner — we dined in, as there were only 9 degrees & I had just had my head washed. I am sorry fat O. no more sends me telegrams, I suppose there is nothing particular to tell. When you are not there, one gets no direct news & feels lost. I am eagerly awaiting your promised letter. —

Town is so full of gossip, as tho' all the ministers were being changed — *Krivoshein* first minister, *Manukhin* instead of *Stcheglovitov, Gutchkov* as side to *Polivanov* & so on & our Friend, to whom A. went to bid goodbye, was most anxious to know what was true. (As though also *Samarin* instead of *Sabler,* whom it is better not to change before one has a very good one to replace him, certainly *Samarin* wld. go against our Friend & stick up for the Bishops we dislike — he is so terribly Moscovite & narrowminded.) Well, A. answered that I knew nothing. He gave over this message for you, that you are to pay less attention to what people will say to you, not let yourself be influenced by them but use yr. own instinct & go by that, to be more sure of yourself & not listen too much nor give in to others, who know less than you. The times are so serious & grave, that all your own personal wisdom is needed & yr. soul must guide you. He regrets you did not speak to Him more about all you think & were intending to do & speak about with yr. ministers & the changes you were thinking of making. He prays so hard for you and Russia & can help more when you speak to Him frankly. — I suffer hideously being away from you. 20 years we shared all together, & now grave things are passing, I do not know your thoughts nor decisions, & its such pain. God help & guide you aright, my own sweet Darling. — I too am much quieter when you are here — I dread their profiting of yr. kind heart & making you do things, wh., when calmly thought over here, you wld. perhaps do otherwise.

I went to Mavra for an hour, she is calm & brave — Tatiana looks awful & yet thinner & greener. — How too horribly sad that accident is that occured to the young couple *Kazbek.* They were going at a terrific speed in their motor & flew against a Schlagbaum, wh. they did not see was closed. He was killed on the spot & she has her arm broken, at first they said her both legs & head, but now one says only the arm & not so bad & one has not told her about her husband. The wretched Father has now lost his third son — ghastly. — We went to the exhibition-bazar — very nice works made by the wounded were shown & I hope it will prove useful & encourage all learning some handicraft. — My head ached again rather, so I better try & sleep now — it is 12½. All my prayers & tenderest thoughts surround you in deepest love & compassion. Oh, how I long to help you & give you faith in yourself. — How long do you remain still? Sleep well & peacefully, holy Angels guard yr. slumber.

June 16-th. Just received yr. precious letter, for wh. heartfelt thanks. Glad you were contented with the work & sitting. Yes, Lovy, about Samarin I am much more than sad, simply in despair, just one of Ella's not good, very biggoted clique, bosom friend of *Sophie Iv. Tiutchev,* that bishop *Trifon* I have strong reason to dislike, as he always spoke & now speaks in the army against our Friend — now we shall have stories against our Friend beginning & all will go badly. I hope heart & soul he wont accept — that means Ella's influence & worries fr. morn to night, & he against us, once against *Gr.* & so awfully narrowminded a real Moscou type — head without soul. My heart feels like lead, 1000 times better *Sabler* a few months still than *Samarin.*

Have the *church procession* now, don't go putting it off, Lovy, listen to me, its serious, have it quicker done, now is lent, therefore more appropriate, chose Peter & Paul day, but now soon. Oh, why are we not together to speak over all together & to help prevent things wh. I know ought not to be. Its not my brain wh. is clever, but I listen to my soul & I wish you would too my own sweetest One. —

I don't want to croak, but I only say all straight out to you. — Goodbye my own & all, God bless & help you — I kiss you without end.

Ever yr. own sad

Wify.

No. 88.

Tsarskoje Selo, June 16-th 1915

My beloved One,

Just a few words before the night. Your sweet smelling jasmin I put in my gospel — it reminded me of Peterhof. Its not like summer not being there. We dined out this evening, but came in after 9 as it was so damp. The afternoon I remained on the balkony — I wanted to go to Church in the evening, but felt too tired. The heart is, oh, so heavy & sad — I always remember what our Friend says & how often we do not enough heed His words.

He was so much against yr. going to the *Headquarters*, because people get round you there & make you do things, wh. would have been better not done — here the atmosphere in your own house is a healthier one & you would see things more rightly — if only you would come back quicker. I am not speaking because of a selfish feeling, but that here I feel quieter about you & there am in a constant dread what one is concocting — you see, I have absolutely no faith in N. — know him to be far fr. clever & having gone against a Man of God's, his work cant be blessed, nor his advice be good. — When *Gr.* heard in town yesterday before He left, that *Samarin* was named, already then people knew it — He was in utter despair, as He, the last evening here, a week ago to-day, begged you not to change him Sabler just now, but that soon one might perhaps find the right man — & now the Moscou set will be like a spiders net around us, our Friend's enemies are ours, & Schtcherbatov will make one with them, I feel sure. I beg your pardon for writing all this, but I am so wretched ever since I heard it & cant get calm — I see now why *Gr.* did not wish you to go there — here I might have helped you. People are affraid of my influence, *Gr.* said it (not to me) & *Voyeikov,* because they know I have a strong will & sooner see through them & help you being firm. I should have left nothing untried to dissuade you, had you been here, & I think God would have helped me & you would have remembered our Friend's words. When He says not to do a thing & one does not listen, one sees ones fault always afterwards. Only if he does accept, N. will try & get round him too against our Fr. thats N.'s campaign.

I entreat you, at the first talk with S. & when you see him, to speak very firmly — do my Love, for Russia's sake — Russia will not be blessed if her Sovereign lets a man of God's sent to help him — be persecuted, I am sure.

Tell him severely, with a strong & decided voice, that you forbid any intrigues against our Friend or talks about Him, or the slightest persecution, otherwise you will not keep him. That a true Servant dare not go against a man his Sovereign respects & venerates.

You know the bad part Moscou plays, tell it him all, his bosom friend *S. I. Tiutchev* spreads lies about the children, repeat this & that her poisenous unthruths did much harm & you will not allow a repetition of it. Do not laugh at me, if you know the tears I have cried to-day, you would understand the gravity of it all. Its not woman's nonsense — but straight forward truth — I adore you far too deeply to tire you at such a time with letter like this one, if it were not that soul & heart prompt me. We women have the instinct of the right sometimes Deary, & you know my love for yr. country wh. has become mine. You know what this war is to me in every sense — & that the man of God's who prays incessantly for you, might be in danger again of persecution — that God would not forgive us our weakness & sin in not protecting Him. — You know *N's* hatred for Gr. is intense. Speak once to *Vojeikov,* Deary, he understands such things because he is honestly devoted to you.

S. is a very conceited man, in summer I had occasion to see it, when I had that talk with him about the evacuation question — Rostov. & I carried off a most unpleasant impression of his selfsufficiency — blind adoration of Moscou & looking down upon Petersburg. The tone in wh. he spoke shocked Rost. greatly. That showed me him in another light, & I realised how unpleasant it wld. be to have to do with him. — When one proposed him for Alexei before, I unhesitatingly said no; for nothing such a narrowminded man. Our Church just needs the contrary — soul & not brain. — God Almighty may He help & put things aright, & hear our prayers and give you at last more confidence in yr. own wisdom, not listening to others, but to our Friend & yr. soul. Once more excuse this letter written with an aching heart & smarting eyes. Nothing is trivial now — all is grave. I venerate & love old *Goremykin* had I seen him, I know how I should have spoken — he is so franck with our Friend & does not grasp, that S. is your enemy if he goes & speaks against *Gr.* —

I am sure your poor dear heart aches more, is enlarged & needs drops. Please deary, walk less — I ruined mine walking at the shooting & in Finland before speaking to the Drs. & suffering mad pain, want of air, heartbeating. Take care of yourself — agoo wee one I hate being away fr. you, its my greatest punishment at this time especially — our first Friend gave me that Image with the bell to warn me against those, that are not right & it will keep them fr. approaching, I shall feel it & thus guard you from them — Even the family feel this & therefore try & get at you alone, when they know its something not right & I wont approve of. Its none of my doing, God wishes your poor wify to be your help, *Gr.* always says so & Mr. Ph. too — & I might warn you in time if I knew things. Well, now I can only pray & suffer. I press you tightly to my heart, gently stroke your brow, press my lips upon yr. eyes & mouth, kiss with love those dear hands wh. always are pulled away. I love you, love you & want yr. good, happiness & blessing. Sleep well & calmy — I must try & sleep too, its nearly one oclock.

My train brought many wounded — Babys has fetched a lot from Varsovie where they empty out the hospitals. Oh God help. —

Lovy, remember, quicker the *church procession,* now during lent is just the most propicious moment, & absolutely from you, not by the new *Chief Procurator of the Synod* — I hope to go to holy Communion this lent, if B. does not prevent me. — Reading this letter you will say — one sees she is Ella's sister. But I cant put all in three words, I need heaps of pages to pour all out & poor Sunshine has to read this long yarn — but Sweetheart knows & loves his very own old wife. —

The boys from the *college* come & make *bandages* every morning at our stores here from 10—12½ & now will make the newest masks wh. are far more complicated but can be used often. — Our little officer with tetanos is recovering, looks decidedly better — his parents we sent for fr. the Caucasus & they live also under the colonnades — we have such a lot living there now. —

The exhibition-bazar goes very well, the first day there were over 2000, yesterday 800 — our things are bought before they appear — *beforehand* already people write down for them & we manage to work a cushion or cover each, daily. — Tatiana rode this evening 5½—7 — the others acted at Anias — the latter sends you the enclosed card she bought to-day at our exhibition — tell me to thank her. —

Poor Mitia Den is quite bad again & cannot walk at all, Sonia is going to take him near Odessa, Liman for a cure — so sad. —

June 17-th, Good morning, my Pet. Slept badly & heart enlarged, so lie the morning on bed & balkony — alas, no hospital, head too rather achy again. Churchbells ringing. — Shall finish after luncheon. Big girls go to town, *Olga* receives money then go to a hospital & tea at *Elagin.*

It is very hot & heavy air, but a colossal wind on the balkony, probably a thunderstorm in the air & that makes it difficult to breathe. I brought out roses, lilies of the valley & sweet peas to enjoy their perfume. I embroider all day for our exhibition-bazar. — Ah my Boy, my Boy, how I wish we were together — one is so tired at times, so weary from pain & anxiety — nigh upon 11 months — but then it was only the war, & now the interior questions wh. absorb one & the bad luck at the war, but God will help, when all seems blackest, I am sure better, sunnier days will come.

May the ministers only seriously work to-gether fulfill your wishes & orders, & not their own — harmony under your guidance. Think more of *Gr.* Sweetheart, before every difficult moment, ask Him to intercede before God to guide you aright. —

A few days ago I wrote to you about Paul's conversation, to-day the Css. H. sends me Paleologue's answer: »Les impressions que S. A. S. le Gr. D. a rapportées de son entretien & que vous voulez bien me communiquer de sa part me touchent vivement. Elles confirment avec toute l'autorité possible, ce dont j'étais moralement certain, ce dont je n'ai jamais douté, ce dont je me suis toujours porté garant envers mon Gouvernement. A un pessimiste qui essayait récemment d'ébranler ma foi, j'ai répondu: »Ma conviction est d'autant plus forte qu'elle ne repose sur aucune promesse, sur aucun engagement. Dans les rares occasions, ou ces graves sujets ont été abordés devant moi, on ne m'a rien promis, on ne s'est engagé a rien; parceque toute assurance positive eut été superflue; parceque l'on se sentait compris, comme j'ose esperer avoir été compris moi-même. A certaines minutes solennelles, il y a des sincérités d'accent, des droitures de regard, où toute une conscience se révèle & qui valent tous les serments«. — Je n'en attache pas moins un très-haut prix au témoignage direct qui me vient de S. A. S. le Gr. D. Ma certitude personnelle n'en avait pas besoin. Mais, si je rencontre encore des incrédules, j'aurai désormais le droit de leur dire, non plus seulement: »Je crois, mais je sais«. — This was about the question of a separate peace negociation. Have you spoken to *Vojeikov* about *Danilov,* please do so — only not to fat *Orlov,* who is N. colossal friend — they correspond the whole time when you are here, B. knows it.

That can mean no good. He grudges no doubt about *Gr.'s* visits to our house, & therefore wants you away from him, at the *Head-Quarters*. If they only knew how they harm instead of helping you, blind people with their hatred against *Gr.!* You remember dans »Les Amis de Dieu« it says, a country cannot be lost whose Sovereign is guided by a man of God's. Oh let Him guide you more.

Dmitri is feeling better, tho' his leg hurts him still. — The poor little *Kazbek* one answered, does not suffer from her broken arm too much, but is I think in a rather dazed state, therefore one has not yet told her about her husband's death. How full of life they were when *N. P.* was at their Wedding. — Now this letter has become volumes & will bore you to read, so I better end it. God bless & protect you & keep you from all harm, give you strength, courage & consolation in all trying moments. Am in thoughts living with you my Love, my one & all. I cover you with kisses & remain ever yr. tenderly & deeply loving old

Sunny.

All the Children kiss you. — Many messages to the old man & *N. P. Khan Nahitchevanski* comes to say goodbye to-morrow. —

No. 89.

Tsarskoje Selo, June 17-th 1915

My very own Darling,

I had just finished my letter, when yr. dear one was brought to me — thanks ever so tenderly for it. You don't know the joy yr. letters give me, as I know you have little time for writing & are so tired. Wify ought to send you bright & cheery letters, but its difficult, as am feeling more than lowspirited & depressed these days — so many things worry me. Now the Duma is to come together in August, & our Friend begged you several times to do it as late as possible & not now, as they ought all to be working in their own places — & here they will try to mix in & speak about things that do not concern them. Never forget that you are & must remain authocratic Emperor, — we are not ready for a constitutional government, N's fault & Wittes it was that the *Duma* exists, & it has caused you more worry than joy. Oh I do not like N. having anything to do with these big sittings wh. concern interior questions, he understands our country so little & imposes upon the ministers by his loud voice & gesticulations. I can go wild at times at his false position. Why did the ministers ask that to be changed, that was their first duty. He has no right to meddle in other affairs & one ought to set ones fault to rights & give him only all the military things — like French & Geoffre. Nobody knows who is the Emperor now — you have to run to the *Head-Quarters* & assemble yr. ministers there, as tho' you could not have them alone here like last Wednesday. It is as tho' N. settles all, makes the choices & changes — it makes me utterly wretched. He did not like *Kriv.* speaking about *Danilov* & the man did his duty — there must be a reason, except his bad character, that the whole army & old *Ivanov* hate him — all say he holds N. & the other Grand Dukes completely in hand. Forgive my writing all this, but I feel so utterly miserable, & as tho' all were giving you wrong advises & profitting of your kindness. Hang the *Head-Quarters* no good broods there. Thank God you may get a good day at *Bieloviezh* in God's glorious nature, away from intrigues — could you fly off another day to *Ivanov*, another somewhere where the troops are, not to the guard again but where others are massed together waiting. You are remaining still long away, *Gr.* begged not — once all goes against His wishes my heart bleeds in anguish & fright; — Oh, to keep & protect you fr. more worries & miserys, one has enough more than the heart can bear — one longs to go to sleep for a long rest. —

Lovy, wont you wire to poor old Gen. *Kazbek* who has now lost his third son, it would be a true consolation to the poor old Father. —

The heat is colossal to-day & the air heavy & sultry & the wind very strong, the curtains on the balkony went flying about. — Daisy heard fr. Vicky of S. from Karlsruhe, that when the French threw bombs onto the palace — they all fled into the cellars in the morning at 5.

Sad, just their palace, next will be ours at Mainz & the splendid old museum; each country by turn. — *Ivan Orlov* has to fly daily for a week over *Libau* I am so glad you spoke about all helping, working to prepare ammunition etc. in yr. rescript — now at last they must do it. — Do my long, grumbling letters not aggravate you, poor wee One?

But I only mean all for yr. good & write fr. the depths of a very suffering, tormented heart. — My lancer *Kniazh.* has come for 2 days & I shall see him to-morrow, also make Pr. *Schterbatov's* acquaintance. —

N. P. must be very unhappy about poor *Kasbek.*

Dear me, what an amount of misery on all sides! When will once again peace & happiness reign in the world? —

The nice, young, pretty *Kalzanova* who works with us in the hospital always, has to leave for 2 months — she overworked herself, & her always ailing heart has become so bad that one has sent her to the country & thence to *Livadia.* Kind Heyden gave the »*Strela*« to-day to take Mme *Taniejev* to *Peterhof* as she is too ill to go by motor or rail. Our Friend said they were not to go there this summer, but they could not bear the air any longer in town, poor woman suffers so hideously fr. stones in the liver & now I think she has jaundice. As Ania can bear the motor, she will go there to-morrow after luncheon & return on Friday, as its wiser to stop the night there. —

Do you think you could tell me where my *Crimean's* are now — I heard as tho' one had sent them fr. the Bukovina elsewhere. —

Such grateful thanks for dear telegram, have at once asked *Goremykin* to come to-morrow, Thursday, & shall be happy to listen to the dear old man, & to him I can speak quite frankly, I know him ever since I married & he is so utterly devoted to you & will understand me. — Such a downpour suddenly at 9 & twice very distant thunder, now its raining steadily for four hours — it will refreshen the air wh. was so close all day. *Gr.* telegraphed to A. from *Viatka: »I travel quietly, sleep, God will help, kiss all.«* Goodnight wee One, sleep peacefully — holy Angels guard your slumber and loving Wify's earnest prayers for her very own precious sunny, big eyed Darling.

18-th. Good morning my Treasure — no sun, grey, rained a little, warm hot & heavy thunderstorming air — heart still enlarged, so remain again quiet, shall go over onto the balkony towards 12 like yesterday. I have told them to put electric strings wires, then we can have lamps & spend the evenings out, when it is warm. — Think of us at *Bieloviezh!* Such remembrances of many years ago when we were younger & went about to-gether — & of the last awful time, when poor suffering Baby lay hours on my bed & my heart also was bad — remembrances of pain & anguish — you all away — the days endless & full of suffering. — My name you will find on the bedroom window leading out onto the balkony under my initials in wire covering the windowpane. — Lovy, I saw my *Kniazhewitch* & we spoke about *Maslov*. In Aug. it will be 25 years that he is in the regiment — he managed very well indeed whilst the commander was ill, yet there are many questions difficult to him & if he got another regiment, he wld. loose the lancer uniform & probably not be a very perfect commander. He feels sticking in the regiment, that he keeps others fr. advancing. Could you not have made him *your aide-de-camp* it would have been a kindness, as he is such a really honest & good fellow; only then better sooner — *Kniazh.* has kept the papers back all along, about whether he should accept a regiment — this wld. enable him to stay on without harming anybody. There are lots of old Colonels in the Chev. G. regiment, they manage it somehow. —

I saw Pr. *Schtcherbatov* who made me a pleasant impression, as far as I can judge after one talk. —

The girls have gone to the Invalid hospital — & Ania to Peterhof, so am alone. Am surrounded by masses of roses (just sent fr. *Peterhof)* & sweet-peas — the smell is a dream, wish I could send them to you. —

Just got yr. sweet telegr. for wh. thanks; thank heavens you feel better; only don't overdo things by walking too much, its never advisable when the heart is not quite in order, too much of a strain at a time, phisical & moral. — Must send this off. Saw in the papers our torpedoboats acted well. —

Goodbye & God bless you, beloved Sunshine, caress & kiss with unboundless love & tenderness.

Ever, Nicky mine, yr. very own wify

Sunny.

No. 90.

Tsarskoje Selo, June 18-th 1915

My own Darling,

Real summer weather very hot in the daytime, & in the evening delicious; I hope tomorrow the lamps will be ready, then we can sit out longer, if not eaten up by gnats. The girls motored after dinner, before that they went to see Tatiana. — Dear old Goremykin sat for an hour with me & I think we touched many questions.

God grant him life! — I asked about *Polivanov,* he said when one proposed him for Varsovie, Nikolasha made an awful grimace & now at once proposed him, & when *Goremykin* asked him why he mentions his name now, he answered that he had changed his opinion. He told me what *Samarin* said to him & what he hadn't written to you, I told him my opinion about him & Stcheglovitov & then he pleasantly surprised me by saying that you had told him yr. intention to change him — he thinks Khvostov will be a good choice. — He sees & understands all so clearly, that its a pleasure speaking to him — we spoke about the question of the Germans & Jews & the wrong way all had been managed & orders given by generals & *Nikolasha.* The way they have treated *Ekesparre* for instance. — I wish others had his sound mind. — Am very tired, so will end & try to sleep. God bless yr. slumber. —

19-th. Goodmorning my Treasure. Lovely weather again, such a Godsend after the late summer & much rain. The »*Enginaer Mechanic*« has come to me, & I should like to send him flying. — I wonder what news from the war, one hears so little. Our steady retreat will in the long run make the line very long & complicated for them & that be our gain, I hope. How about Varsovie? The hospitals are being emptied out & even some quite evacuated — is that only as an extreme precaution, because surely in months one has had time to well fortify the town; they seem to be rebeginning their autumn move, only now they will bring their very best troops & it will be easier, as they know the ground by heart. My dear Siberians with their comrades will have the mass coming in upon them — & may they once more save Varsovie. All lies in God's hands — & as long as we can drag on till sufficient amunition comes & then fall upon them with full force. Only the perpetual great losses make the heart very heavy — they goe as martyrs straight to their heavenly home, its true, but still its ever so hard. —

Pay attention to Baby's signature in his letter — its his own invention & it seems his mood at his lesson this morning was somewhat wild, & he only got 3. — The girls have some of their lessons on the balkony. — Benkendorf suddenly had a fainting fit in town & hurt himself when he fell — they say it may be fr. his stomach, but I fear worse things — we shall see what the Drs. say this morning. It would be a loss, as he is far more worth than *Valia* — & one of the old style still wh. now, alas, no longer exist. —

I have an immense bunch of jasmin standing near me on the balkony — Mme *Viltchkovsky* picked it in the hospital garden. —

Goodbye Sweetheart, my light, my joy. I bless, & kiss you incessantly with deepest love.

Ever yr. very own

Wify.

No. 91. *Tsarskoje Selo*, June 20-th 1915

My beloved Nicky dear,

All my thoughts are ever near you in tender love & loneliness. I hear the churchbells & long to go and pray for you there, but the heart is again enlarged, so must keep quiet. Weather again splendid. Our corner on the balkony is so cosy & pretty in the evening with two lamps, we sat out till after 11. — Ania saw the Alexandrie, »*Dozorny*« & »*Razvedchik*« & »*Rabotnik*« from far — lots of public, music, everything looking lovely. It seems sad & strange for the first time since 20 years not to go there — but here there is more work to do & to run over fr. *Peterhof* constantly, I could not have managed. Then people can be sent for & got at quicker when one needs them. — Do so wonder what you settled with *Samarin*, whether you let him off — if so, then don't hurry getting another & lets talk it quietly over here. I told the old man all, & I think he understood me, tho' being very religious he personally knows little about Church affairs *(Goremykin)*.

This wire A. got today from our Friend from *Tiumen:* »*Encountered singers, we sang in praise of Easter, the abbot was jubilant, remember it's Easter, suddenly a telegram reaches me that my son is being drafted, I said in my heart, am I like Abraham, of ages past, having one son and supporter, I hope he will be allowed to rule under me as with the ancient czars.*« Beloved One, what can one do for him, whom does it concern — his only son ought not to be taken. Cannot *Voyeikov* write to the *local military chief*, I think it concerns him — will you say, please. —

The train with your Feldjeger is 8 hours late, so shall only get your letter at 7. This moment *Varnava* telegraphs to me fr. *Kurgan.*

»*Our own empress, the 17-th on the day of the Saint Tikhon the Miracle Worker, during the procession around the church in the village of Barabinsk, there suddenly appeared on the sky a cross, which was seen altogether for 15 minutes, and as the Holy Church is praying »the Cross of the Czar is the support of the kingdom of the believers«, I felicitate you with this vision and believe that God sent this vision and sign in order to uphold visibly with love his devoted ones. I pray for all of you.*«

God grant it may be a good sign, crosses are not always. —

Benkendorf came to me, he looks alright, feels only a bit weak still. — He said one had written that you were perhaps returning the 24-th — is it really true? What joy to have you safely back again. — I bless & kiss you with all the strength of my great love.

Ever, Sweetheart, yr. very own Sunny.

No. 92. *Tsarskoje Selo*, June 21-th 1915

My sweetest One,

Ever such fond thanks for your dear letter, I received yesterday before dinner — Baby thanks for the candlestump. I gave yr. man an extracandle on the way. Here I return you cascara. I am so glad yr. Drachenschuss is better, I have it continually & generally fr. a false movement & the left side, wh. makes the heart worse. — Today my heart is not enlarged, but I keep quiet. Costia (to say goodbye) & Tatiana come to tea before the Children go to Ania's to play — Baby has gone to *Ropsha* before for a few hours — he enjoys these expeditions. Such air, quite divine & delicious breeze & birdies singing away so brightly. — Shall think of you so much to-morrow & hope you will enjoy our dear *Bielovezh.* — Yesterday evening we went to Anias, there were the 2 *Grabbes,* Nini, Emma, Alia, *Kussov* of the *Moscov. Dragoon Regiment* (ex »*Nighegorodtzi*«) — the first time I saw him & we were quite at home together as tho' we had known each other for years — I lay working on the sopha & he quite close chatting away busily. I am going to invite him here too once, so nice to speak about all our wounded friends. —

I congratulate you with yr. Curassiers' feast — little *Vick* came with a bouquet of yellow roses in the regiments name, so touching. — The giving over of Mme Souchomlinov's (my *stores*) to me is going alright & with tact luckily — because I dont want them to suffer in this, as she really did a lot of good. — Just got a telegram from Romanovsky (why he signs G. M. *Romanov* I can't think), that he leaves the 20-th *Gal(ician) Regiment* has a nomination in the *Staff of the Army.* I suppose this is my last letter to you, unless I hear a man goes to meet you. — What joy to have you back again! You precious One, Wify is lonely & has a heavy heart. — S.'s nomination makes me sad, can't help it as he is an enemy of our Friends & that is the worst thing there can be, now more than ever.

Blessings & kisses without end & such love, love

Ever my Nicky yr. very own old

Sunny.

No. 93.

Tsarskoje Selo, June 22-nd 1915

My own beloved One,

I wonder how you got to *Bielovezh* & whether the weather is as beautiful as here. — So you have put off your return back — well, nothing is to be done; — if you could at least profit & see some troops. Cant you flie off again, as tho' to *Bielovezh* but go another way, without telling anybody. — *Nikolasha* need neither know, nor my enemy *Dzhunkovsky.* Ah dear, he is n o t an honest man, he has shown that vile, filthy paper (against our Friend) to Dmitri who repeated all to Paul & he to Alia. Such a sin, & as tho' you had said to him, that you have had enough of these dirty stories & wish him to be severely punished.

You see how he turns your words & orders round — the slanderers were to be punished & not he — & that at the *Headquarters* one wants him to be got rid of (this I beleive) — ah, its so vile — always liars, enemies — I long knew *Dzhunkovsky* hates *Gregory* & that the »*Preobrazhensky*« clique therefore dislikes me, as through me & Ania he comes to the house.

In winter *Dzhunkovsky* showed this paper to *Voyeikov* asking him to give it over to you & he refused doing anything so disgusting, thats why he hates *Voyeikov* & sticks with *Drenteln* I am sorry to say these things, but they are bitter truth, & now *Samarin* added to the lot — no good can come out of it.

If we let our Friend be persecuted we & our country shall suffer for it — once a year ago one tried to kill him & one has slandered him enough. As if they would not have called the police straight in to catch him in the act — such a horror! Speak, please to *Voyeikov* about it, I wish him to know *Dzhunkovsky's* behaviour & false using of yr. words. *Voyeikov* not a fool, without mentioning names can find out more about it. It dare not be spoken about. I don't know how *Stcherbatov* will act — probably also against our Fr. therefore against us. — And the *Duma* dare not broach this subject when they meet — *Loman* says they will, so as to force one to get rid of *Gregory* & *Ania,* I am so weary, such heartache & pain fr. all this — the idea of dirt being again spread about one we venerate is more than horrible.

Ah my Love, when at last will you thump with your hand upon the table & scream at *Dzhunkovsky* & others when they act wrongly — one does not fear you — & one must — they must be frightened of you, otherwise all sit upon us, & its enough Deary — don't let me speak in vain. If *Dzhunkovsky* is with you, call him, tell him you know *(no* names) he has shown that paper in town & that you order him to tear it up & not to dare to speak of *Gregory* as he does & that he acts as a traitor & not as a devoted subject, who ought to stand up for the Friends of his Sovereign, as one does in every other country. Oh my Boy, make one tremble before you — to love you is not enough, one must be affraid of hurting, displeasing you. You are always too kind & all profit. It cannot go on like that Deary, beleive me once, its honest truth I speak. All, who really love you, long that you should be more decided & show your displeasure stronger, be more severe — things cant go well so. If your Ministers feared you, all would be better. The old man, *Goremykin* also finds you ought to be more sure of yourself & energetically speak, & show more strongly when you are displeased. — How much one hears complaints against the *Headquarters,* these surrounding *Nikolasha.*

Now another affair — don't know how to explain it well, wont mention names, so as that nobody should suffer. — The »*Erivantzi*« are perfect — where there is a difficult place — one sends them & keeps them to the last, as one is so sure of them. Now one intends taking of their own officers & putting them into other regiments to make those better. This is quite wrong & breaks their hearts. If you take their old ones away, then the regiment will no longer be what it was. They have lost enough killed, wounded (made prisoners) & cannot spare their own. Please do not let the regiment thus be ruined, & leave those officers, they love their regiment & keep up its fame. One does it with other officers of the *2-nd Brigade* & they fear their turn is coming too & it worries the Commander & all — but they dare not say anything, have no right — therefore they want their *chief* to know it, & not to allow their *Veteran officers* to be taken fr. them into other regiments. »*We shall be able to stand up for the country's cause in the ranks of our own regiments, we will not waver about sacrificing our lives for it. This is so urgent a situation that one must hurry if our own nest is not to be broken up. I think that the regiment has some right to claim such attention (not like the others), for its fighting service in the past, and as to the present, the order to the Division is eloquent enough. All the brunt of the rearguard battles, from the 31-st of May to the 6-th of June were carried by its shoulders, which has been recognized at the top.*«

Only do not let *Nikolasha* or others guess that the regiment asks this, otherwise they will suffer f o r i t. — Do try & do something & give me an answer, they are very anxious — one sent a delightful pettyoffice fr. there with a letter here. Must end, man waits. Blessings & kisses without end fr. own

Wify.

Ania kisses your hand. — Excuse beastly dull letter

No. 94.

Tsarskoje Selo, June 22-nd 1915

My very own beloved One,

The letter I wrote in such haste to-day, I fear will have caused you little pleasure & I regret, that I had no time to add nothing nice.

It was a joy to get your telegram from *Bielovezh* — I am sure it did you good seeing the splendid forest — but yet a sad feeling seeing the old places & realising that now a terrible war is raging not so very far off from that peaceful place. —

This morning I went in my »*droshki*« with Alexei to our hospital & we remained there over two hours. Spoke to the wounded, sat in the hospital embroidering & then in the garden whilst the others played croquet. But my heart felt bad & ached so — too early probably for such a visit yet — but I was so glad to see them all. *Kolenkin* turned up after commanding the »*Alexandrovtzi*« only a month, he had to come away because of terrible abscesses in the ear — they burst the drum of the ear too, so he hears nothing on the left ear, poor fellow. —

I had Rostoftzev for an hour & a half talking over the *store* of Mme *Sukhomlinov* — all is arranging itself satisfactorily & without any scandal. — To-morrow I shall receive *Polivanov* — *Stcherbatov* leaves very great freedom to the press — *Maklakov* was far severer, but now the result is one speaks & gets too excited about the *Duma* wh. is not a good thing. —

One longs sometimes to go to sleep & to awake when all will be over & peace once more reign everywhere — external & internal. —

Everywhere *Samarin's* name is already mentioned — so disagreable before his nomination comes out — how that fills me, with d e e p e s t anxiety. I fear I aggravate you by all I write, but its only honestly & well meant, Sweetheart — others will never say anything, so old wify writes her opinion frankly, when she feels its right to do so. One longs to help keeping of any disaster, but often ones words, alas, come too late, when already nothing can be done. Now I must try & sleep, its late. God bless yr. slumber, send you rest & strength, courage & energy, calm and wisdom. —

June 23-rd. Just got the *report* of my »*Alexandrovtzi*« you kindly sent me — thanks Deary, even an envelope is a nice thing to receive with sweet handwriting upon it. — I remain quiet to-day, as heart again enlarged, pulse rather weak & head aches.

Am lying on the balkony — all are out & away & Ania gone to *Peterhof*.

I enclose a letter from Victoria wh. you may like to read.

Css. Hohenfelsen wrote to A. asking, whether she thinks we & the children would have accepted a luncheon at their house after Church — on Paul's namesday, with the people living in their house & whomsoever we wld. wish. I told her to answer (this was to be found out in case of a refusal, so that it should not follow upon a regular invitation), that I do not know when you return & that my heart troubling me again it is doubtful I could sit at a big luncheon. So foolish & tactless to ask. If we liked we might call upon him to congratulate — but not like this, with *Babake* & *Olga Kreutz*, & the Countess! —

Sweetheart, me is so lonely without you, agoo wee one! —

Goodbye Lovebird, I bless & kiss you with fervour & great love. — Hope so much to go Friday morning to Holy Communion, if well enough, otherwise one of the last days of this Lent. — Wonder what you have settled for the day of the cross, hope you have said its to be done by *your* order. —

God bless & protect you, I cover you with kisses,

Ever yr. own old

Sunny.

Love to old Man & *N. P.* —

No. 95.

Tsarskoje Selo, June 24-th 1915

My beloved Nicky dear,

Again a splendid day. Slept little this night & at 3 looked out of the window of my mauve room. A glorious morning, one felt the sun behind the trees, a soft haze over all, such calm — the swans swimming on the pond, steam rising from the grass — oh so beautiful, I longed to be well & go for a long, long walk as in bygone days. — Sergei M. comes to tea, it seems he is quite well again & *Petia*.

Saw *Polivanov* yesterday — don't honestly ever care for the man — something aggravating about him, cant explain what — preferred *Sukhomlinov,* tho' this one is cleverer, but doubt whether as devoted. *Sukhomlinov* has made the great mistake of showing your private letter to him, right & left, & others have copies of it. Fred. ought to write him a word of reprimand. I understand he did it to show how kind you are to him to the end — but others need not know the reasons he left, except that he told an untruth at the famous sitting at *Peterhof,* when he said that we were ready & had enough to hold out, when we had not sufficient ammunition — this is his only very great fault, the *bribe* of his wife the rest. Now others can think that public opinion is enough to clear out our Friend etc. a dangerous thing before the Duma. — You cannot imagine the cruel suffering of not being with you — I know I could help & guard off things sometimes & here I am, eating out my heart fr. far, feeling my inability of being any use, only writing disagreable letters to you, my Love. — From the outset *Goremykin* must speak to *Samarin* & *Stcherbatov* how they have to behave about our Friend, to prevent any calumnies & stories. — Alas, have nothing cheerful or interesting to tell you. Spent day & evening on balkony, to-day too as don't feel well, tho' heart not yet enlarged & can begin my medicins again. Eagerly awaiting yr. letter about *Bielovezh.* —

Its true one is completely evacuating Varsovie? (for prudence sake!) —

Hope to go to holy Communion, depends upon health, wh. day, think Sunday at early mass downstairs with Ania; when do you return? to-day two weeks — seems at least a month — (& our Friend begged for quite short, knowing things wld. not be as they ought if one kept you & profitted of your kindness). — Are you going off unaware to *Bielostok* or *Kholm* to see the troops? Do show yourself there before returning — give them & yourself the joy. The *Active Army* is not tho' *Headquarters* thank God — surely you can see some troops. *Voyeikov* can arrange all (not *Dzhunkovsky),* nobody need know, only then it will succeed — say you are going off again for a trip; — had I been there, I should have helped you going off — Sweetheart needs pushing always & to be reminded that he is the Emperor & can do whatsoever pleases him — you never profit of this — you must show you have a way & will of yr. own, & are not lead by N. & his staff, who direct yr. movements & whose permission you have to ask before going anywhere. No, go alone, without N., by yr. very own self, bring the blessing of yr. presence to them — don't say you bring bad luck — at *Lemberg* & *Przmysl* it happened, because our Friend knew & told you it was too early, but you listened instead to the *Headquarters.*

Forgive my speaking so straightforwardly, but I suffer too much — I know you — & Nikolasha — go to the troops, say not a word to N.; you have false scruples when you say its not honest not telling him — since when is he your mentor, & in what way do you disturb him? *Let* at last one see that you do after yr. own head, wh. is worth all theirs put together. Go Lovy — cheer up *Ivanov* too — such heavy battles are coming — bless the troops by your precious Being, in their name I beseech you to go — give them the *spiritual rise,* show them for whom they are fighting & dying — not for Nikolasha, but for you. 1000 have never seen you & yearn for a look of yr. beautiful, pure eyes. Such masses have moved down — one can't lie to you, that none are to be got at. Only if you say it to Nikolasha the spies that are at the *Headquarters* — who? — will at once let the Germans know & then their aeroplans will set to work. But 3 simple motors otherwise wont be seen, only wire to me something that I can understand & let our Friend know to pray for you. Say like that: going to-morrow again for an expedition — please Lovebird. Trust me, I mean yr. good — you always need encouraging & remember, not a word to Nikolasha let him think you go anywhere, *Bielovezh* or wheresoever it pleases you. Its a false *Headquarter* wh. keeps you away, instead of encouraging you to go. But the soldiers must see you, they need you, not the *Headquarters,* they want you & you them.

Now goodbye my Sunshine, kisses & blessings without end.

Ever yr. very own

Sunny.

No. 96.

Tsarskoje Selo, June 25-th 1915

My Sweetheart,

I thank you ever so fondly for yr. dear, long letter I was overjoyed to receive. How nice that yr. expedition was so successful — tho' you were lonely without yr. »Benoitons« to keep you company.

I never knew that Neverle had died, good old man! —

What luck you saw the *Moose* & could drive through the *thick-woods.* —

Ah my love! What anguish you must have gone through when *Nikolasha* got that bad news. Here I hear nothing & live in anguish & suspension, yearning to know what is going on out there. God will help, only we shall have still much misery & heartache I fear. That ammunition question can turn ones hair grey. —

Deary, I heard that that horrid *Rodzianko* & others went to *Goremykin* to beg the *Duma* to be at once called together — oh please dont, its not their business, they want to discuss things not concerning them & bring more discontent — they must be kept away — I assure you only harm will arise — they speak too much.

Russia, thank God, is not a constitutional country, tho' those creatures try to play a part & meddle in affairs they dare not. Do not allow them to press upon you — its fright if one gives in & their heads will go up. —

You know *Gutchkov* is still *Polivanov's* friend — that was the reason there, that *Polivanov* & *Sukhomlinov* went apart. I dont like his choice — I loathe yr. being at the *Headquarters* and many others too, as its not seeing soldiers, but listening to N.'s advice, wh. is not good & cannot be — he has no right to act as he does, mixing in your concerns. All are shocked that the ministers go with *report* to him, as tho' he were now the Sovereign.

Ah my Nicky, things are not as they ought to be, & therefore N. keeps you near, to have a hold over you with his ideas & bad councels. Wont you yet beleive me, my Boy?

Cant you realise that a man who turned simple traitor to a man of Gods, cannot be blest, nor his actions be good — well, if he must remain at the head of the army there is nothing to be done, & all bad success will fall upon his head — but interior mistakes will be told home upon you, as who inside the country can think that he reigns besides you.

Its so u t t e r l y false & wrong. —

I fear I anger & trouble you by my letters — but I am a l o n e in my misery & anxiety & I cant swallow what I think my honest duty to tell you. —

Yesterday evening I invited *Kussov* (ex Nizhegorodetz) of the Moscou reg. from *Tver* — & I was struck how exactly he spoke as I think, & he does not know me, only second time we have met — so how many others must judge like him. He was 3 days at the *Headquarters* & did not carry away a pleasant impression, neither do *Voyeikov* & *N. P.*, who are the most devoted to you. — Remember our Friend begged you not to remain long — He sees & knows *Nikolasha* through & through & your too soft & kind heart. — I here, incapable of helping, have rarely gone through such a time of wretchedness — feeling & realising things are not done as they should be, — & helpless to be of use — its bitterly hard; & they, *Nikolasha* knows my will, & fears my influence (guided by *Gregory)* upon you; its all so clear. — Well, I must not tire you any longer, only I want my conscience to clear, whatever happens. — Is it true *Yussupov* has had the half of his duties taken fr. him, so that he plays a secondary part? —

Sergei does not look famous — we touched no subjects — he is going to *ask permission* to go on Saturday to the *Headquarters.*

Petia full of secrets & his »heart«. —

How nice you could bathe, so refreshing. Here the heat is not great, always a breeze & ideal on the balkony — don't feel well enough to drive. Paul has invited himself to tea. Girls are in hospital, lessons. —

Please answer me, are the *cross Processions* going to be on the 29-th, as such a great holiday & the end of lent? Excuse bothering you again, but so eager to know, as hear nothing. — To-day I receive the Gentlemen of my committee for our prisoners in Germany & an American (of the young Christian's men's association like our »*Mayak*«) who undertakes to bring all our things personally to the prisons. He has travelled & photogr. in many places, especially Siberia, where we keep our prisoners & wh. are well arranged, those he will exhibit in Germany, hoping it will help ours in return. —

What answer about the »*Erivantzi*«?

Now goodbye, my very own tenderly beloved one. I cover you with kisses & ask God's blessing upon you. —

Ever yr. own old Wify.

No. 97. *Tsarskoje Selo,* June 25-th 1915

My very Own,

Oh, what joy, if you really return on Sunday & the news are better. I was just so miserable, as had a telegram fr. the com. of my Siberian regiment that they had very heavy losses in the night 23—24 fr. 10—3 — & I wondered what great battle was going on — because the wire came from a new place. — Well I saw that American fr. the young Men's Christian Association & was deeply interested by all he told me of our prisoners there & their here. I enclose his letter wh. he is also going to have printed & shown in Germany (& photos, wh. show our excellent barracks). He intends only telling the good on either side & not the bad things, & hopes thus to make all sides work humanely. This evening I got a letter fr. Vicky wh. I send you with Max letters (I fear I worry you, but you are free'er of an evening there than here please read it & you may like to mention some things there). I have let the American who leaves for Germany to-morrow know that I wish him to send the papers to Max & to go & see him & tell him all, so as to rectify all their false impressions upon the way we keep our prisoners.

I never heard about so many illnesses in Russia. — I think he said (the American) that 4000 had died at Cassel from *spotted typhus,* awful! — Chiefly read Max' English paper; & in Vickys fr. Max you will see our paper wh. my Dear is idiotically worded & without any explication — & abominable German. »Es ist befohlen die 10 ersten deutschen Kriegsgefangenen — als Erfolg (all wrong) der mörderischen Thaten, die sich einige deutsche Truppen erlauben, zu erschiessen.« One might have written it in decent German; explaining that in the spot where one finds a man had been tortured one will shoot 10 men just taken. Its badly written— Erfolg (means result — success) one says als Folge, but even that sounds wrong. Let it be decently worded in proper, grammatical German & more explanitarily written.

Then its not meant every time to shoot men down, you never meant that, its all wrong, somehow & therefore they dont understand what one means. —

Please dont mention fr. where the letters came, except to *Nikolasha* about Max, as he looks after our prisoners; — & they sent the letters through a Swede to Ania, not to a lady in waiting on purpose — nobody is to know about this, not even their embassy — don't know why this fright. I wired openly to Vicky that I thank her for her letter & beg her to thank Max fr. me for all he does for our prisoners & that he is to rest assured that one does ones best for their prisoners here. I don't compromise myself in that — I don't do anything personally & as I intend doing all for our prisoners & this American will take our things there & tell as where & what is needed & will help as much as he can. — Please, return the papers, or bring them on Sunday, if you really come then. —

I had Paul to tea & we chatted a lot. He asked whether Sergei would be relieved of his post as all are so much against him, right or wrong — & *Kchessinska* is mixed up again — she behaved like Mme *Sukhomlinov* it seams with *bribes* & the Artillery orders — one hears it fr. many sides. Only he reminded me, that it must be by your command, not *Nikolasha's* as you can only give such an order, (or hint to ask for his resignation) to a Grd. Duke who is no boy, as you are his Chief & not *Nikolasha,* that wld. make the family very displeased.

He is so devoted, Paul, & putting his personal dislike to *Nikolasha* aside, — finds too that people cannot understand his position, a sort of second Emperor, mixing into everything. How many (& our Friend) say the same thing. —

Then I enclose a letter fr. Count Pahlen, rectifying himself — *Goremykin* (or *Stcherbatov)* also found one had acted wrongly towards him (I think *Goremykin* told me; — the paper Mavra gave me). —

Look through it Deary & forgive me bothering you again. —

You will »hang her« when you get such long epistles from me — but I must write all. — I did not see the Siberian soldier, *Petia* let me know one forbade him coming to me, because he had run away from Germany — I dont understand the logic, do you? —

26-th. Then this will be my last letter to you, fear even it may not reach you before you leave, as trains so slow. — Heart enlarged so cant go to Church, hope still for to-morrow evening, so as to go Sunday at 8 or 9 to mass & holy Communion in the little Church below with Ania. Sweety, from heart & soul I beg your tender forgiveness for any word or action of mine wh. may have hurt or grieved you; & beleive it was not intentional. Am longing for this moment, to get strength & help. Am not without courage, Lovy, oh no, only such pain in heart & soul from so much sorrow all around & misery at not being able to help. —

There must be woods burning, smells strong since yesterday; & to-day very warm but no sun — shall lie out as usual if no rain. —

Fear can't meet you at station, as Church will already be a great exertion & do feel so rotten still!

What intense happiness to having you back soon — but I still tremble it may not be — God give success to our troops that you can leave there with a calmer heart. Wonder if you can manage to see troops on yr. return route. —

Xenia has announced herself to tea after her lunch at *Irina's* — am so glad to see her at last again.

Another »*Erivan*« officer had been brought to our hospital — what answer to their demand, I wonder?

Goodbye, my own beloved One, my Nicky sweet. God bless & protect you & bring you safely home again into the loving arms of your Children & your yearning old Wify.

Baby & I are going to see *Galfter* & then 3 wounded of. — Miss my hospital & feel sad not to be able to work & look after our dear wounded. — Love to old Man, *Dmitri Sh.* & *N. P.*

No. 98. *Tsarskoje Selo,* Aug. 22-nd 1915

My very own beloved One,

I cannot find words to express all I want to — my heart is far too full. I only long to hold you tight in my arms & whisper words of intense love, courage, strength & endless blessings. More than hard to let you go alone, so completely alone — but God is v e r y near to you, more then ever. You have fought this great fight for your country & throne — alone & with bravery & decision. Never have they seen such firmness in you before & it cannot remain without good fruit.

Do not fear for what remains behind — one must be severe & stop all at once. Lovy, I am here, dont laugh at silly old wify, but she has »trousers« on unseen, & I can get the old man to come & keep him up to be energetic — whenever I can be of the smallest use, tell me what to do — use me — at such a time God will give me the strength to help you — because our souls are fighting for the right against the evil. It is all much deeper than appears to the eye — w e , who have been taught to look at all from another side, see what the struggle here really is & means — you showing your mastery, proving yourself the *Autocrat* without wh. Russia cannot exist. Had you given in now in these different questions, they would have dragged out yet more of you. Being firm is the only saving — I k n o w what it costs you, & have & do suffer hideously for you, forgive me, I beseech you, my Angel, for having left you no peace & worried you so much — but I too well know yr. marvelously gentle character — & you had to shake it off this time, had to win your fight alone against all. It will be a glorious page in yr. reign & Russian history the story of these weeks & days — & God, who is just & near you — will save your country & throne through your firmness.

A harder battle has rarely been faught, than yours & it will be crowned with success, only believe this.

Yr. faith has been tried — your trust — & you remained firm as a rock, for that you will be blessed. God anointed you at your coronation, he placed you were you stand & you have d o n e y o u r d u t y, be s u r e, quite s u r e of this & He forsaketh not His anointed. Our Friend's prayers arise night & day for you to Heaven & God will hear them.

Those who fear & cannot understand your actions, will be brought by events to realise your great wisdom. It is the beginning of the glory of yr. reign, He said so & I a b s o l u t e l y believe it. Your Sun is rising — & to-day it shines so brightly. And so will you charm all those great blunderers, cowards, lead astray, noisy, blind, narrowminded & (dishonest false) beings, this morning.

And your Sunbeam will appear to help you, your very own Child — won't that touch those hearts & make them realise what you are doing, & what they dared to wish to do, to shake your throne, to frighten you with internal black forebodings — only a bit of success out there & they will change. They will (?) disperse home into clean air & their minds will be purified & they carry the picture of you & yr. Son in their hearts with them. —

I do hope *Goremykin* will agree to yr. choice of *Khvostov* — you need an energetic minister of the interior — should he be the wrong man, he can later be changed — no harm in that, at such times — but if energetic he may help splendidly & then the old man does not matter.

If you take him, then only wire to me »tail *(Khvostov)* alright« & I shall understand. —

Let no talks worry you — am glad Dmitri wont be there now — snap up *Voyeikov* if he is stupid — am sure he is afraid meeting people there who may think he was against *Nikolasha* & *Orlov* & to smoothe things, he begs you for *Nikolasha* — that would be the greatest fault & undo all you have so courageously done & the great internal fight would have been for nothing. Too kind, don't be, I mean not specially, as otherwise it would be dishonest, as still there have been things you were discontented with him about. Remind others about Misha, the Emperor's brother & then there is war there too. —

All is for the good, as our Friend says, the worst is over. — Now you speak to the Minister of war & he will take energetic measures, as soon as needed — but *Khvostov*, will see to that too if you name him. — When you leave, shall wire to Friend to-night through Ania — & He will particularly think of you. Only get *Nikolasha's* nomination quicker done — no dawdling, its bad for the cause & for *Alexejev* too — & a settled thing quieten minds, even if against their wish, sooner than that waiting & uncertainty & trying to influence you — it tires out ones heart.

I feel completely done up & only keep myself going with force — they shall not think that I am downhearted or frightened — but confident & calm. —

Joy we went to those holy places to-gether — for sure yr. dear Father quite particularly prays for you.

Give me some news as soon as you can — now am afraid for the moment *N. P.* wiring to Ania until am sure nobody watches again.

Tell me the impression, if you can. Be firm to the end, let me be sure of that otherwise shall get quite ill from anxiety.

Bitter pain not to be with you — know what you feel, & the meeting with *N.* wont be agreeable — you did trust him & now you know, what months ago our Friend said, that he was acting wrongly towards you & your country & wife — its not the people who would do harm to your people, but *Nikolasha* & set *Gutchkov, Rodzianko, Samarin* etc. —

Lovy, if you hear I am not so well, don't be anxious, I have suffered so terribly, & phisically overtired myself these 2 days, & morally worried (& worry still till all is done at the *Headquarters* & *Nikolasha* gone) only then shall I feel calm — near you all is well — when out of sight others at once profit — you see they are affraid of me & so come to you when alone — they know I have a will of my own when I feel I am in the right — & you are now — we know it, so you make them tremble before your courage & will. God is with you & our Friend for you — all is well — & later all will thank you for having saved your country. Don't doubt — believe, & all will be well & the army is everything — a few *strikes* nothing, in comparison, as can & shall be suppressed. The left are furious because all slips through their hands & their cards are clear to us & the game they wished to use *Nikolasha* for — even *Shvedov* knows it fr. there.

Now goodnight lovy, go straight to bed without tea with the rest & their long faces. Sleep long & well, you need rest after this strain & your heart needs calm hours. — God Almighty bless your undertaking, His holy

Angels guard & guide you & bless the work of your hands. — Please give this little Image of *St. John the Warrior* to *Alexeiev* with my blessing & fervent wishes. You have my Image I blessed you with last year — I give no other as that carries my blessing & you have *Gregory's* St. Nicolas to guard & guide you. I always place a candle before St. Nicolas at *Znamenje* for you — & shall do, so to-morrow at 3 o'clock & before the Virgin. You will feel my soul near you.

I clasp you tenderly to my heart, kiss and caress you without end — want to show you all the intense love I have for you, warm, cheer, console, strengthen you, & make you sure of yourself. Sleep well my Sunshine, Russia's Saviour. Remember last night, how tenderly we clung to-gether. I shall yearn for yr. caresses — I never can have enough of them. And I still have the children, & you are all alone. Another time I must give you Baby for a bit to cheer you up. —

I kiss you without end & bless you. Holy Angels guard your slumber — I am near & with you for ever & ever & none shall seperate us. —

Yr. very own wife

Sunny.

No. 99.

Tsarskoje Selo, Aug. 23-rd 1915

All my thoughts & prayers surround you in tenderest love. Such calm filled my soul (tho' terribly sad) when I saw you leave in peace and serene. Your face had such a lovely expression, like when our Friend left. God verily will bless you and your undertakings after this moral victory. Wonder how you slept — I went straight to bed, deadbeat & very lonely.

Dear Girlies proposed to sleep by turn in the room next door, as I am all alone on this floor — but I begged them not to, am quite accustomed to it & don't mind. I feel you near me, bless & kiss your cushion. Slept midling. Such a sunny morning — the three girls went at 9 to Church, as Olga & Tatiana wish to work in the hospital till 12½. — Wonder how the spirits around you are — your peace must spread itself upon them. I had a talk with *N. P.* & begged him not to heed to *Voyeikov's* varying moods. — The whole time those odious trains make a noise to-day, the wind comes from that side, but to me it seems that that big new chimney (where the electric mashenes are) makes the same noise, as it continues since a long time with intervals. — The Churchbells are ringing, I love the sound, with the windows open; I shall go at 11, as till now, tho' the heart & chest ache, it is not enlarged & I take many drops. The body feels very beaten & achy. Have got *Botkin* to allow Anastasia to sit in the sun on the balkony, where there are 20 degrees, it can only do the child good. It is 10 & Baby has not yet turned up, took a good sleep no doubt.

Such peace in the soul after those anxious days — & may you continue feeling the same. — If you have the occasion, give *N. P.* our love & give him news as I don't let A. wire now for a time, after one was so nasty & she gave him news of my health always. — I hope old Fred. is not too gaga & wont beg for fieldmarshal etc., wh. can only be given after the war, if at all. — Remember to comb your hair before all difficult talks & decisions, the little comb will bring its help. Dont you feel calm now that you have become »sure of yourself« -- its not pride or conceit — but sent by God & it will help you in the future & give strength to the others to fulfil your orders. Have let the old man know, that I want to see him today, & he is to choose the hours. —

Well, Deary, I just had the old man for half an hour. He was so glad to get your message, that you left quiet & calmly & Frederick's letter (I did not know he had written). But shocked & horrified with the ministers letter, written by *Samarin* he says. Finds no words for their behaviour & says how awfully difficult it is for him to preside, knowing they all go against him & his ideas, but he wld. never think of asking to leave, as he knows you would tell him if it were yr. wish. He has to see them to-morrow & will mention what he thinks about this letter, wh. is so false & untrue in saying »all Russia« & so forth — I begged him to be as energetic as possible. He will also talk before with the minister of war, to know what you told him. About *Khvostov* he says better not, it is he who spoke in the *Duma* against the government & Germans (is a nephew of the minister of justice), finds him trop léger, probably not quite sure person in some respects. He will think over names and send or bring me a list for you of people he thinks might do. — Finds certainly *Stcherbatov* cannot remain, already that he took no hold on the press is a sign what an incapable person he is for that place. — He says, he would not be astonished, if *Stcherbatov* & *Sazonov* asked to be released from their places, wh. they have no right to — *Sazonov* goes about crying (the fool) & I said I was convinced, that our allies will immensely appreciate yr. action, with wh. he agreed too. —

I told him to look at all as a miasm of *St. Petersburg* & Moscou & that all need a good airing to see all with fresh eyes & hear no gossip fr. morn to night. — He says, the *Duma* cannot be dispersed before the end of the week as they have not finished their work — he & others especially fear the left may outpass the *Duma* — I begged him not to worry about it, that I am convinced its not so serious & more talking than anything else & that they wanted to frighten you & now that you have shown a strong will of your own, they will shut up. It seems *Sazonov* called them all together yesterday — fools. I told him that the ministers were all des poltrons & he agreed — thinks *Polivanov* will work well. Poor man, it hurt him reading all the *heresies* of those, who signed against him & I was so pained for him. He so rightly says, each must honestly tell you his opinion, but when you have said yr. wish, all must fulfill it & forget their own desires, they don't agree, neither did poor Serge! —

I tried to cheer him up, & a wee bit I think I did, as I showed him how little serious, au fond, all this empty noise is. Now the Germans & Austrians have to occupy minds & all & nothing else — & a good minister of the interior will keep order. — He says, in town good mood & quiet after yr. speech & reception — & so it will be, I told him what our Friend said. — He begged me to see *Krupensky* to hear, what he has to say about the *Duma,* as he knows everybody — do you agree, then I certainly will, & without any noise. Only wire »agree«. — I told him *Ivanov* also begged you to come, through me. —

Finds the more you *show* yr. energy, the better, to wh. I agreed, & he also found the idea good, that you should send your eyes to the fabrics, even if the suite don't understand much, but to show they come from you is good — not only the *Duma* who looks after all. — I went with Baby to Church & prayed so fervently for you. The Priest spoke beautifully & I only regretted the ministers were not there to hear it & the men listened with deepest interest. What this 3 days lent means — & how all must cling & work together around you & so on, beautiful & so true & all ought to have heard it. — Anastasia remained out till 4 — & I writing on the balkony. Baby returned fr. *Peterhof* & has gone to Ania, where *Olga, Tatiana* & *Maria* are. — Here is a letter from old *Damansky,* he left it at Ania's when she was out — he came with his old sister half paralised & scarcely able to speak — am so pleased you gave that honest man this happiness, it will console him in his sorrow. —

I copy out 2 telegrams from our Friend. If you have an occasion, show them to *N. P.* — one must keep him up more about our Friend, as in town he hears too much against him, & begins to heed less to His telegrams. *Goremykin* asked whether you would be back this week (to disperse the *Duma* then) I said you could not possibly yet tell. —

The Children & I went to *Znamenje* at 3¼ & I placed a very big candle, wh. will burn very long & carry my prayers to God's throne for you & before the Virgin & St. Nicolas. — Now, my love, I must end. — God bless & protect you & help you & all you undertake. Kisses without end on all dear places, for ever yr. very own trusting proud

Wify.

Only a word en passant, Alia's husband returned & each time speaks against *Brussilov* as does also Keller — you enquire other opinions about him still. — The *Headquarters* has given the order, that all officers with German names serving in the staffs are to be sent out to the army, so Alia's husband too, tho' *Pistolkors* is a Swedish name & more devoted servant you scarcely have. *According to me,* it is again wrongly done — gently each general ought to have been told to hint to those to go back to their regiments, that they want others & these are to have their turn to fight. All is done so clumsily. I shall write to you always all I hear, (if think right) as may be of use to you to know now & to prevent injustices — can imagine what *Kussov* will write, so as to help the good cause.

Now I must lie down, as very tired — am feeling better & spirits up & full of trust, courage & hope — & pride in my Sweetheart. Good bless, guard & guide you. —

Hope *Voyeikov* did not tell you the rot he told A. he wld. beg you to make *Nikolasha* give his word of honour not to stop at Moscou — coward *Voyeikov,* & fool, as tho' you were jealous or frightened — I assure you I long to show my *immortal* trousers to those poltrons.

If Paul should ask to see me, can I tell him that you wish to take him next time. It will touch him & change his thoughts into the right current; he is sure to come — wire about *Krupensky* agree or don't agree I shall understand — tell Paul, or don't tell Paul. —

Smell the letter.

No. 100.

Tsarskoje Selo, Aug. 24-th 1915

My own beloved One,

Thank God all is done & that the meeting went off so well — such a relief. Bless you my Angel & yor brave undertaking & crown it with success & victory, interior & exterior. So emotioning telegram No. 01 *Imper-H.* — I have kept the envelope too as remembrance of that memorable day; Babykins is so happy, & interested in all, Ania too at once crossed herself & I directly called Nini to the telephone to quieten her, that all went off well, she had her Mother & Emma with her, & I knew it would soothe them.

The evening was so lovely, 13 degr. that I drove 20 m. with the three big girls in a half open motor. This morning it is very damp, grey & drizzling. — A. said Nini told her, that fat O. took it very decently, thats all I know about him, that Emma cried as she was fond of him, & Nini feared it was an intrigue of her husbands', but A. quietened her. —

Whilst Mitia *Den* is with you, he might also do duty, when there is no walking about to be done. Oh how I should love to see how you do all, altogether I should like a *concealing-fairy-cap* to peep into many a house & see the faces!!! — Baby enjoyed himself very much in the »little house« with *Irina Tolstoy* & *Rita Hitrovo,* they played games together. —

I went with Marie to the *Cath. S.* to mass, so nice, & from there at 12 to our hospital to sit with our wounded. Then we lunched upstairs in the corner room & remained there till 6.

Baby dear's left arm hurts & is very swollen, hurt fr. time to time in the night & to-day — the old thing, but he has not had it for very long, thank God. Mr. Gillard read aloud & then showed us the magic lantern. I received 7 wounded; & Ordin. A. was at Peterhof a few hours. Out such a drizzle. I see nothing had appeared yet in the papers, so suppose you intend telling it be known to-morrow when N. leaves. — I wonder. —

Did you appreciate *Volodia's* success in the black sea?

I got a charming letter fr. Nicolai about yr. having taken over the command & shall send it you to-morrow — this evening I must answer it. — Ania sends her love & kisses yr. hand & is always thinking of you. —

We all send our love to *N. P.*

God bless & protect you my Treasure — miss you very, very much, as you know cannot be otherwise; press you tenderly to my heart & cover you with caresses & kisses. I bless you & pray for God's help.

Ever yr. old

Wify.

Ella's prayers are with you — she is going for these last days to *Optin convent.*

This is just about another injustice *Taube,* Pss Gedroitz & our young Dr. back fr. the war were telling me.

It has just come out, that henceforth the Drs. are only to get *3 military rewards,* wh. is unfair, as they expose themselves continually to danger — & till now masses received rewards. *Taube* found quite wrong, people fr. the *ordnance* who sit behind in the *rear* should receive the same, as those under fire. The Drs. & sanitaries do marvels, are constantly killed — whilst the soldiers have to lie flat, these walk upright carrying out the wounded. —

My little Dr. *Matushkin* of the 21 *S. Regiment* has again been commanding a *company.* — One cannot recompense those enough, that work under fire. — One of your young curassiers was wounded by an officer, a quite young boy something like Minkwitz, Hessian reserve reg., such pain to hear that. — Am sure shall hear much now, hoping that I will repeat all to you. —

Longing for news from you & the war. God help you. —

This is gossip.

Aug. 24 1915. Only one word, one says, that on Wednesday in the *Duma* all parties are going to address themselves to you to ask you to change the old Man. I hope still, that when at last the change is made officially known things may get right, if not, I fear the old man cannot continue working when all are against him. He will never dare ask to leave, he said, but, alas, I don't know how things will work. To-day he sees all the ministers & intends speaking firmer to them, it can finish him off poor dear, honest Soul. —

And whom to take at such a moment firm enough? Minister of war, so as to punish them for (don't at all like the idea) a short time, as he understands nothing of interior questions, but will look like dictator ship. How is *Kharitonov?*

I don't know. But better to wait still. They of course aim at *Rodz.,* wh. wld. be the ruin & spoil all you have done & never to be trusted — but *Gutchkov* is behind *Poliv.* & you have no minister of the Interior yet. — Forgive bothering you, but its only a rumour, wiser to know. —

No. 101.

Tsarskoje Selo, Aug. 25-th 1915

My own Sweetheart,

Thanks for your dear telegram, Lovy. I am glad the country near *Mohilev* is pretty — *Glebov* always said it was very picturesque — but that was natural, as he was born there. But still I suppose you will choose a nearer place, so as that you can quicker & easier move about. When do my letters reach you? I give them out at 8 & they leave town at 11 at night. — Am anxiously awaiting when the change will be made public. It is pouring again & quite dark. — Baby's night was not famous, slept little, but pain not too strong. Olga & Tatiana sat with him fr. 11½—12½ & they kept him cheery. — In the papers, there was an article as tho' people, 2 men & a woman had been cought near Varsovie, who were going to make an attempt upon *Nikolasha's* life — people say *Suvorin* invented it to be more interesting (the censor told A. those were »*canards*«). A month ago all the redacteurs from *St. Pbg.* were at the *H.-Q.,* & *Janushkevitch* gave them his instructions, — this the military censor, under *Frolov* told A. — *Samarin* seems to be continuing to speak against me, well all the better, he too will fall into the pit he is digging for me. Those things dont touch me one atom & leave me personally cold, as my conscience is clear & Russia does not share his opinions — but I am angry, because it indirectly touches you. We shall hunt for a successor. —

How do you find work with *Alexeiev?* Pleasant & quick I am sure. Have no particular news; only *Mekk* let me know that my central *stores (Lvov, Kovno)* fr. Proskurov will probably have to move in 5 weeks to *Poltava* — I cannot grasp why, & hope it will not be necessary. Marie's ladies fr. *Jitomir* ask if one has to evacuate that town, where her hospital is to move to — all this is a bit early to decide, I think. — How very sad *Molostvov's* death is, I hear you have made Velepolsky your a. d. c. I suppose *Voyeikov* begged for him — he is not a very sympathetic man & such a »saloon« fellow. I suppose his health obliges him to leave the regiment & therefore you take him — but the Suite ought not to be a place like the *honor. curator,* where one pokes people into it. I alas, begged for my *Maslov,* but he had commanded the reg. for several months at the war already. Vel. is Olga O's sweetheart (a great secret she had to make a fausse couche fr. him a few years ago) he was not nice to her after — not a famous type, but *Vojeikov's* friend, so suppose good officer. —

The enclosed picture is for *N. P.* —

Is not this ugly, again somebody wishing to be nasty to *N. P.,* so you better tell Fred. to have printed (privately not fr. his name) that there wont be a *lieutenant* as you have now the big chancellry & *Dr.* & *Kira* remain on; it comes I am sure fr. the same source as the story of the telegr. then at the *H.-Q.* I fastened so, for you to show *Vojeikov* as easy to slip out — one need only let the military censor *Vissarionov* know what to write, as he is *Frolov's* chief censor & a good man; — its *Suvorin's* doing, last night & this morning. — So anxious no telegram yet, c a n n o t imagine why the change has not been officially anounced, it would have cleared & uplifted the minds & quicker have changed the current of thoughts in the *Duma*. I thought to-day was already the longest to wait as N. leaves — now yr. yesterday's wire was fr. *H.-Q.,* — on Sunday evening *Imp. H.-Q.,* it sounded so nice & promising. These are fasting days approaching fr. to-morrow on, so the news ought to have come before & the *Te Deum,* its a mistake all falling to-gether, was necessary beforehand, forgive my saying this — who again begged you put off the official anouncement, did wrong — no harm N. being there, as it will be known you were working already with *Alexeiev*. It was a bad council — how against it one party is, one sees it by this. The q u i c k e r o f f i c i a l l y known, the calmer all spirits, all get nervous awaiting the news wh. never comes — its never good such a situation & false — & only cowards can have proposed it to you, as *Voyeikov* & *Fred.* they think of N. before you — its w r o n g being kept secret, none think of the troops who are yearning for the good news — I see my black trousers are needed at the *H.-Q.,* too bad, idiots — & such perfection the jubilation & then fasting to pray for your success — & Tuesday passes & nothing; out of despair I wired this morning early, but got no answer & its already 7 o'clock. — Marie, A. & I went to *Cath. C.* again & then to the hospital, where I talked with the wounded. We lunched upstairs & will dine there too. The rain & darkness make one quite ramolie. Baby has much less pain & slept in the morning.

Helene & *Vsevolod* came to tea & then I received my lancer Toll with more photos. He says *Kniazhevitch* entreats to receive our brigade instead of *Schwedov*. Then I sent for the *Commandant Ossipov* to speak about the cemetry & Church I build for the dead of this war in our hospitals, to clear up that question. —

Mme *Lopukhin,* wife of the *Vologda* gov. wrote to me, because her husbands heart is so much worse again. *Botk.* & *Sirotinin* find too that his health cannot stand the strain of work he has. If you made him Senator, he could serve there & it would be a rest for a time, & perhaps later cld. get more to do if heart improves. He has served 25 years. It would be good if you could have this done. —

My Sunshine, I miss so very much, but am glad you are away. — You can let yr. ministers come by turn with their *report* — it will freshen them up too. I hope you sleep well. — Don't forget to wire to Georgie etc. when at last all is official. Goodbye my treasure, I bless & kiss you without end, every precious, dearly beloved place.

Ever, Nicky mine, yr. very own old

Wify.

The stories about *Varnava,* a monk fr. there came to let me know, are untrue. *Samarin* wants to get rid of him. —

Orlovsky is the name our Friend wld. like as gov., he is the *president* of the *Etchequer chamber* at *Perm*. You remember he gave you a book he wrote about *Tcherdyn* where a *Romanov* is buried & one considers him a saint.

No. 102. *Tsarskoje Selo,* Aug. 26-th 1915

My very own Sweetheart,

I am writing in the corner room upstairs, Mr. Gillard is reading aloud to *Alexei.* Olga & Tatiana are in town this afternoon. Oh Lovy, it was beautiful — to read the news in the papers this morning & my heart rejoyced more then I can say. Marie & I went to mass in the upper church, Anastasia came to the *Te Deum. The priest* spoke beautifully, I wish a good big crowd in town had heard him, it would have done them no end of good, as he touched the inner currents so well. With heart & soul I prayed for you my treasure. It lasted fr. 10½—12½. Then we went to Ania to meet her dear big *Lili* returning from church. She had been hunting for her mother whose husband has been killed & she was looking for his body. She could no more get to Brest, the Germans were at 18 fr. where she was. Fancy, *Mistchenko* asked her to lunch — she amongst 50 officers. She spent the night at Anias & leaves again to join her Boy; she has no news from her husband. — We lunched, took tea & shall dine here. I went for a short turn in a half opened motor with Ania & Marie to get a little air — quite like September. — Kostia comes at 6 & then I go to church — a consolation to be in church & pray with all together, for my huzy. — And *Ivanov's* good news was indeed a blessing for the beginning of your great work. God help you, Sweetheart. All seems small now, such joy reigns in my soul. — I have had no news from the old man since Sunday. — *Samarin* goes on speaking against me — hope to get you a list of names & trust can find a suitable successor before he can do any more harm. — How are the foreigners? I see Buchanan to-morrow, as he brings me again over 100,000 p. from England.

I got a letter from M-me Baharacht, who begs her husband should not be sent away till after the end of the war. He is of limit of age, but he does a lot at Bern for the Russians & tries his best — perhaps you will remember when his name may be mentioned by *Sazonov.* — The gramophon is playing in the bedroom for Marie & Anastasia. — Baby slept on the whole(?) hours — with interruptions — is cheery & suffers little. I told Fred.: it was unnecessary to arrange anything for the wounded at present at Livadia, as there are still very many empty places at *Jalta* — & now fr. all the sides fr. the Crimea one tells me all is being arranged. — Do ask Fred: why? — as I do n o t find it as yet necessary; perhaps later — soon my sanatorium, the military one, & the Livadia hosp. will be ready — enough for the present.

No. 103.

Tsarskoje Selo, Aug. 27-th 1915

My very own beloved One,

I wonder wheter you get my letters every day — pitty so far away & all the trains passing now stop the movement. — Again only 8 degrees, but the sun seems to wish to appear. Do you get a walk daily, or are you too much occupied? Baby slept very well, woke up only twice for a moment, & the arm aches much less I am happy to say; no bruise is visible, only swollen, so I think he might be dressed to-day. When he is not well I see much more of him, wh. is a treat (if he does not suffer, as that is worse than anything). Olga & Tatiana returned after 7 from town, so I went with Marie to the lower church 6½—8. This morning I go with the two little ones upstairs at 10½, as the others have Church before 9 below. — My fasting consists now of not smoking, as I fast since the beginning of the war, & I love being in Church. I do want to go to Holy Communion & the Priest agrees, never finds it too early to go again & it gives strength — shall see. Those soldiers that care, will also go. — Saturday is the anniversary of our stone! — Css. Grabbe told Ania yesterday, that Orlov & wife were raging in town, at being sent away, turned out — wh. shocked others — he told her too that *N. P.* was going to replace him (I was sure he had had it put into the papers) an ugly trick, after his wife having begged *N. P.* to come & talked with him — such are people. Many are glad, who knew his dirty money affairs and the way he allowed himself to speak about me. — Will you find time to scrawl a line once? We get no news, as I told *N. P.* better not to wire nor write for the present, after that ugly story at the *H.-Q.*

Wonder what news. You will let them send me telegr. again, wont you, Deary. — Baby dear is up & half dressed, lunched at table with us & had the little boys to play with. He would not go out, said he did not feel strong enough, but would to-morrow — he did not write yet, because he could not hold the paper with his left hand. We dine up there again — its cosy & not so lonely as down here without you. Well, this morning I went with the two youngest at 10½ to mass & *Te Deum* with lovely prayers for you to the Virgin & St. Serafim — from there we went to our hospital, all were off to the *Te Deum* in the little *grotto church* there so we went again — & now at 6½ to evening service. I hope very much to go to holy Communion on Saturday, I think many soldiers go too, so Sweetheart please forgive yr. little wify if in any way I grieved or hurt you, & for having bored you so much these trying weeks. I shall wire if sure I go, & you pray for me then, as I for you — its for you somehow this fasting, church, daily *Te Deum,* & so Holy Communion will be a special blessing & I shall feel you one with me, my dearly beloved Angel, very, very own Huzy. — Here I enclose a pretty telegr. fr. *Volodia* I want you to read. — Paul came to tea, very quiet & nice. About himself he spoke, & I said what we had spoken about, that you hoped taking him or sending him about. He wants in n o way to be pushy or forward, but l o n g s to serve you, wont bother you with a letter, asks me to give all this over to you. Or if you wld. send him to some armycorps under a good general — ready for anything & full of good intentions. Wont you think it over & speak with *Alexeiev* & then let me know please. — We spoke about Dmitri, d o n t r e p e a t it to him — it worries him awfully & he is so displeased, that he stuck for ever in the *H.-Q.*, finds he ought absolutely not to stay there, as its very bad for him, spoils him & he thinks himself then a very necessary personage. Paul was greatly discontented that he came now & sorry you did not shut him up quicker, instead of allowing him to try & mix up in things about wh. he understands nothing. —

Best if he returned into the regiment wh. uniform he has the honour to wear & in wh. he serves. In speaking about the G. a Cheval, Paul said that he found a new commander ought to be named, this ones wound does not heal, he has received everything, done all he could & the regiment cannot get along with only youngsters & no real Commander — as he says any good one fr. the war, no matter who he is, only that he should be good, so you will perhaps also talk this over (not with Dmitri) with *Alexeiev.* Buchanan brought me over 100.000 p. again, he wishes you also every success! Cannot bear town any more. Says what difficulty to get wood, & he wants to get his provisions now already & is waiting since 2 months & now hears it wont come. One ought to get a good stock beforehand, as with these masses of refugees who will be hungry & freezing. Oh, what misery they go through, masses die on the way & get lost & one picks up stray children everywhere.

Now must be off. I bless & kiss you a 1000 times very, very tenderly, with yearning love. Ever yr. own old

Alix.

Wont the *Duma* be shut at last — why need you be here for that? How the fools speak against the military censors, shows how necessary.

All our love to *N. P.*

No. 104.

Tsarskoje Selo, Aug. 28-th 1915

My beloved Nicky dear,

How can I thank you enough for your very precious letter wh. came as a most welcome surprise. I have reread it already several times & kissed the dear handwriting. You wrote the 25-th & I got it 27-th before dinner. —

All interested us immensely, the children & A. eagerly listened to some parts I read aloud — & to feel that you are at peace fills our hearts with joyful gratitude. God sent you the recompense of your great undertaking — yes, a new responsability, but one particularly dear to yr. heart, as you love all that is military & understand it. And having shown such firmness must bring blessings & success. Those that were so frightened at this change & all that nonsence, see how calmy & naturally all took place, & have grown quieter.

I shall see the old man & hear what he has to tell.

The *P. Municipal Council* needs smacking, what right have they to imitate Moscou? *Gutchkov* again at the bottom of this & the telegr. you got — would they but mind their own business, look after their wounded, fugitives, fuel, food & so forth — they need a sharp answer, to mind their own business & look after the sufferers of the war — nobody needs their opinion, cant they see to their canalisation first. I shall tell that the old man — I have no patience with these meddlesome chatterboxes. Oh Sweetheart, I am so touched you want my help, I am always ready to do anything for you, only never liked mixing up without being asked — only here I felt too much was at stake. —

Such glorious sunshine & 18 in the sun & cool breeze — curious weather this summer.

Certainly, its wiser you have settled down in the Governor's house if its damp for everybody in the woods — & here you have the staff close by, but still a bore being in town for you. Wont you come nearer as V. proposed, then you can be up & done here if necessary & get yr. ministers to come — this is yet further than *Baranovitchi* is it not? & there you could reach *Pskov* & sooner get at the troops. — We all go to Church again, the big ones early, we at 10½ & then to the hospital if *the priest* wont speak again, he held a sermon yesterday evening & again a good one. Then at 2 we go to the christening of *Underlieuten. Covb's* child, I christened his first child last autumn (he was our wounded & then served in Marie's train) so Marie & *Jakovlev* (ex lancer, com. of her train) christen the boy in the lower Hospital church.

Georgi met the train & gave the sisters medals — I am sure *Schulenburg* will be in despair, as they were also under fire last year. —

Then we shall drive & peep into the little house, as our Friend's wife will be there with the girls whom she has brought for their lessons. Then *Schulenburg* at 5¾ — Church — 7¾ *Goremyk.* before he has a sitting.

We have got 3 of Tatiana's lancers in our hospital & a fourth lies in the big palace — there are 25 vacant places there, happily again. —

I enclose a letter of C. Kellers you may like to read, as it shows his way of looking at things, sound & simple as the most who are not in *St. B.* & Moscou. He did not know of the change at the *H. Q.* then. To-day he returns to the army — I fear too early — but certainly he is needed there. — Rumours say the *Novik* had a battle & successful, but I do not know what is the truth about it. —

I hope I don't make you wild with my cuttings — is this naval news true or not? I cut it out. — We had a lovely drive, divine weather & ones souls singing, surely it means good news. — In the village of the *Pavlovsk* farm we stopped at a *shop* & bought two big *flasks* with strawberry-jam & *redberries* then met a man with mushrooms & we bought them for Ania — we drove along the border of *Pavlovsk* park — such weather is a real treat, & we are having tea on the balkony — & miss you, my very own Angel, to make it perfect. — *Gr.'s* wife sends you her love & ask *Archangel Michael* to be with you — says he had no peace & worried fearfully till you left. He finds it would be good the people should be let out of prisons & sent to the war, there are a catagory, I am sure, of harmless ones sitting, whose moral saving it would be to go; I can hint it to the old man to think over — he comes at ¼ to 8 so I must send my letter off before. — His governor has quite changed towards him (has returned you), he says will have our Friend stopped as soon as he leaves. You see, that others have given him this order — more than wrong & shameful.

There is *confession in common,* so *the priest* asked us to come to it in the upper Church, as lots of soldiers are going & to-morrow morning too with all upstairs. All the Children & Baby will come too — oh, how I wish you could have been there too — but I know you will be in hearts & thoughts. Once more forgive me, my Sunshine. God bless & protect you & keep you fr. all harm & help you in everything. To-morrow the day of the stone! I kiss you without end with deepest love & devotion. Ever yr. very own

Wify.

Baby hopes to write to-morrow, he is thin & pale, been out all day. Slept till 10.5 this morning, very cheery & happy to go with us to holy Communion. Such a nice photo you bathing. A few words for you fr. A. & from me for *N. P.*

No. 105.

Tsarskoje Selo, August 28-th 1915

Beloved One,

I just saw the old man, he must see you, so will leave to-morrow. He has thought about a minister of the Interior, he finds no one except perhaps Neidhardt & I think he would not be bad (Papa *Taneiev* mentioned him too) — of Tatiana's committee, he is a splendid worker, has shown it now, most *clear-headed* energetic — that he is snob, cant he helped, his »grandness« may be effective towards the *Duma* — then you know him well, can speak as you like with him, you need not se gêner with him — hope he is only not in the *Dzhunk.* — Drent. set. I think he wld. hold the other ministers in hand & thus help the old man. He finds it almost impossible to work with the ministers who wont agree with him, but also finds like us, that now he ought not to be sent away because they wish it — & once one gives in they will become worse — if you wish, then of y o u r o w n accord a little later. You are *Autocrat* & they *d a r e n o t* forget it. He says alright shutting *Duma,* but Sunday holiday, so better Tuesday, he sees you before. F i e n d s ministers, worse than *Duma.* Infections about censure — one allows rot to be printed, also says »*canards*« about the 2 attempts against *Nikolasha.* Finds *Schtcherbatov* is impossible to keep, better quick to change him. I think Neidhardt would be possible to trust — his rather german name I dont think would matter, as one praises him everywhere about Tatianas committee. Cons. de l'Emp. can finish the question about refugees. Will do dear old *Goremyk.* good to see you —, he is such a dear. Just back fr. *confession in Common* — most emotioning, touching & all prayed so, so hard for you — Must quickly sent this off. Blessings kisses without end — pray incessantly for you — such a joy in one 's soul all these days — one feels God near you my Sweetheart. Ever Y. very own

Sunny.

No. 106.

Tsarskoje Selo, August 29-th 1915

My own beloved One,

One just now brought me your sweet letter of the 25-th. I thank you for it with all my heart, sweetest Pet. It is such a comfort to know that you are contented with *Alexeiev* & find work with him easy. Is *Dragomirov* going to be his help? A man may fall ill & its safer one who knows the affairs a little — wont it be easier if you come nearer — where there are more railway lines. — *Mohilev* is so far & with all the crowded trains passing. One ought really to do something more for the *refugees* — more *food stations* & flying hospitals — masses of children are homeless on the highroad & others die — all returning from the war — one says its bitterly painful to see. The governement is working out questions for the fugitives after the war, but its more necessary to think of them. — But God grant soon the enemy wont any more advance & then all will go on smoother. The news is most consoling wh. I read in the papers & much better editied, one feels another person writes it. — But Friend finds more fabrics ought to make amunitions, where goodies are made too. — I love all the news you give, the children & A. listen with deepest interest, as we live with you, for you from far.

Let *M. Den* be at the head of the garage for the moment, perhaps one can get him a place later in the navy again, as he loves & understands the work. Yes, do invite the foreigners, its far more interesting with them & one finds more topics for talking. I am glad Dmitry is alright — give him my love — but remember he ought not to remain there, its bad for him, of your own accord let him go, its unhealthy doing nothing, when all are at the war, & now he lives in gossip & plays a part. Only dont say Paul and I think so. Paul begs you to be more severe with him, as he gets spoilt & imagines he can give you advice. — Bless you Sweetheart for fasting.

Perhaps you better give Samarin the short order that you wish *Bishop Varnava to chant the laudation of St. John Maximovitch* because *Samarin* intends getting rid of him, because we like him & he is good to *Gr.* — We must clear out C: & the sooner the better he wont be quiet till he gets me & our Friend & A. in a mess — its so wicked & hideously unpatriotic & narrow-minded, but I know it would be so & therefore they begged you to name & I wrote in such dispair to you. Poor *Markosov* has returned I must try & see him. It was lovely in church, only two hours, masses went to Holy Communion, every sort of person, lots of soldiers, 3 cosacks, Zizi, Isa, Sonia, Ania, M-me *Dedjulin* & sister, Baby's friend, *Irina, Jonk, Shah Bagov, Jussupov, Tchebytarev, Russin, Perepelitza, Kondratiev etc.* We went below to kiss the images before service, upstairs the children found too shy work. Then we got your telegram to rejoice us & feel you with us the whole time — missed you awfully & still felt your sunny presence. Breakfast, luncheon (with Isa & Zizi) & tea on balkony. I made the *dressings* in the hospital, felt so energetic & full of inner joy. — Drove to *Pavlovsk.* Baby alright, cought wasps again. *Vict. Erast.* left to day for *Mohilev.* We are not going to church this evening, as are tired, the services twice dayly these four days were very long, but so lovely. The day of our stone to-day! —

I saw M-me *Paretzki* & she spoke much of you — she goes over to town for winter again — I gave her our groop & said I shall ask you to sign it when you return. Have you any ideas of your plans?

This evening is a week you left — & how different are the feelings since — peace, trust & the new fresh pure beginning. That reminds me, wont you have the *com. of Kovno Grigoriev* quicker judged — it makes a very bad impression his wandering about like that, when one knows he gave up & left the fortress. *Schulenburg* hints this to me & another thing about the *Semenovtsy* — a sure thing, not gossip, *Ussov,* whom he can trust, told it him with tears — they simply bolted & therefore the *Preobr.* lost so many. Do find them a good brave commander. I hope, you do not mind my telling you all these things, they may be of use — you can have it found out & altogether make a clearing.

Many splendid, brave youngsters received no rewards — & high placed ones — having got the decorations. As *Alex.* cannot possibly do all, my weak brain imagines, some special people might see to this, to look through the immense lists & watch that injustices are not done. — In case (as I dont a bit know whether you approve of Neidhardt) you name him & he presents himself, have a strong & frank talk with him — see that he does not go *Djunk.* line. Put the position of our Friend clear to him from the outset, he dare not act like *Stcherb.* & *Sam.* make him understand that he acts straight against us in persecuting & allowing him to be evil written about or spoken of. You can catch him by his amour propre. And forbid the continuing of cutting down the Barons mercilessly, have you remembered about dispersing the *Lett.* bands amongst the regiments? Is nice *Dimka* with you? I am going to see *Maximov* who returned from Moskow. Sweety, remember to use the suite (other pen dried up) to be sent to the different fabrics in your name — please do it, it will have an excellent effect & show you watch all & not only the *Duma* pokes her nose into all — make a careful choice. Beloved, A. just saw *Andr.* & *Khvostov* & the latter made her an excellent impression (the old man is against him, I not knowing him, dont know what to say.) He is most devoted to you, spoke gently & well about our Friend to her, related that to morrow has to be a *question* about *Gr.* in the *Duma* one asked for *Khvost's* signature, but he refused & said that if they picked up that question, amnestie would not be given — they reasoned & abolished again asking about him. He related awful horrors about *Gutchk.,* was at *Gorem.* today, spoke about you, that by taking the army you saved yourself. *Khvost.* took the question about German *over powering influence* & *dearth of meat,* so as the left ones wld. not take it — now the right ones have this question it is safe — she feels taken by him & has good impression. *Gorem.* wanted to present *Kryjanovsky* but I said you would never agree. Do talk him over except Neidhardt — I did not see his article then — I mean his speech of the *Duma* its difficult to advise. Are others against him, or only the old man, as he hates all the *Duma.* Awfully difficult for you to decide again, poor Treasure — I cant say as I dont know the man. — She had a very good impression indeed. Talk him over with *Gorem.* Now I must sent this off. Hope you will clear out the *Duma,* only who can close it, if the old man is affraid of being insulted. I long to thrash nearly all the ministers & quickly clear away *Stcherb.* & *Sam.* back to his serious evacuation questions — you see the metrop. is against him. I hope to send you a list of names to-morrow for choice of decent people. Goodbye, Lovy, God bless & protect you, I kiss you without end & press you to my breast with infinite tenderness. Ever, Nicky mine, your very, very own

Wify.

Love to old man & *N. P.* Excuse rotten writing, but am in a great hurry & pen not famous. — If you could find a place for Paul out at the front, wld. be really a good thing & would not fidget you, under a real good clever general.

Is *Bezobrasov's* story cleared up? —

No. 107.

Tsarskoje Selo, Aug. 30-th 1915

My own beloved Darling,

Again a lovely sunny morning with a fresh breeze — one appreciates the bright weather so much after the grey weather we had & darkness. With eagerness I throw myself every morning upon the *Novoje Vremic,* & thank God every day good things are to be read about our brave troops — such consolation, ever since you came God really sent His blessing through you to the troops & one sees with what new energy they fight. — Could one but say the same thing about the interior questions. *Gutchkov* ought to be got rid of, only how is the question, *war-time* — is there nothing one could hook on to have him shut up. He hunts after anarchy & against our dynasty, wh. our Friend said God would protect — but its loathsome to see his game, his speeches & underhand work. On Thursday their *questions* in the *Duma* are coming out, luckily a week late — could one not shut it before — only d o n t change the old man n o w, later when it p l e a s e s y o u, *Gorem.* agrees to this, *Andron.* & *Khvostov* — that it would be playing into their hands. They cannot get over yr. firmness, as had sworn they would not let you go — now you keep on in this *spirit.* You are still as full of energy & firmness, tell me Lovy?

Its horrid not being with you. Have so many questions to ask & things to say & alas, we have no cypher together — cannot through *Drent.* & by telegraph do not dare either — as others watch them — am sure the ministers who are badly intentioned towards me, will keep an eye upon me, & then that makes one nervous what to write. — We went to Church & then had luncheon on the balkony, Sonia too. — I received 5 of my *Alexandr.* as its their visit. — Then *Maximovitch* & we had a long talk about everything — he was glad to see my spirits up & my energy, & I begged him also to pay attention, &

when he hears things that are not nice, to stop & to pay attention at the club — he has not been there for 5 months; when he is there of course nobody ventures to say anything, but he has been told, that not nice talkings were going on there & will pay attention — the same Css. Fred. told him about Orlov who before him neither dares say anything incorrect. O. now spreads that our Friend had him sent away — others say he lives at *T. S.,* as before they said we had Ernie here.

I saw Mme *Ridiger,* the widow of one of the *Georgian* officers, he is buried at Bromberg — I have asked her to look after my Sanatorium at *Massandra.* Here is wire A. got from our Friend just now. —

»*On the first news of the Ratniki being called, inquire carefully when our* (his) *government is to go. Gods will, those are the last crumbs of the whole. Gracious St. Nicolas, may he work miracles.*« — Can you find out when those of his government *(Tobolsk)* are taken & let me at once know. — I suppose in yr. staff all is marked down exactly. Does it mean his boy, but he is not a *ratnik.* So strange, when *Praskovia* left, he said she would not see her boy again. —

Maksim. found hospitals in good order, but the atmosphere needing a strong hand to keep order — he finds *Yussupov* ought to go back again & not stick here, with wh. I agree. —

Botkin told me, as *Gardinsky* (Ania's friend) was returning fr. the south, where he had been to see his mother, in the train he heard two gentlemen speaking nasty about me & he at once smacked them in the face & said they could complain if they liked but he had done his duty & would do it to all who allowed themselves to speak so. Of course they shut up. — Just energy & courage are needed, & all goes well. — Am anxious, no wire from you, whether you got my telegram last night about the Tail — *Khvostov* — he made such an excellent impression upon her, & I should like you to have read my letter before settling with *Gorem.* & did you get both letters on Saturday. — You are too far away, one cant get at you quickly. —

Only quickly shut the *Duma* before their »*question*« can come out. Continue being energetic. *Maksim.* was delighted. To *Botk.* I told a lot to make him understand things, as he is not always as I should wish — he saw I know all & could make him understand things he was unclear about. I talk away, its necessary to shake all up & show them how to think & act. —

Can you give, or send through yr. man the enclosed letter to *N. P.* — not through Dmitri only — as he wld. make remarks that we write. It will amuse you how Anastasia writes to him. — I enclose a petition from our Friend, you write your decision upon it, I think it certainly might be done. — Aeroplans are flying overhead, I am in bed, resting before dinner. — If there is anything interesting, can yr. Mama & I get the news in the evening as its long waiting till the next morning. — Now must end. Goodbye & God bless you my Beloved, my Sunshine, my life. Miss you greatly. Kiss you over & over again. Ever yr. very own wify

Alix.

Bow to old man. — It seems La Guiche when here shortly, spoke against *N.* being changed, in the club *(Sandro L.* heard it) so be a little careful what sort of man he is. — All look upon yr. new work as a great *exploit.*

A. kisses you very tenderly. Please quickly give me an answer.

No. 108.

Tsarskoje Selo, Aug. 31-st 1915

My sweet Beloved,

Again a sunny day — I find the weather ideal, but Olga freezes, its true, the »fond de l'air« is fresh. — I am glad you had a good talk with the *old one* as our Friend calls *Gorem.* — what you mention as having put off till your return, I suppose means the change of the Minister of the Interior — how good if you could see *Khvostov* & have a real talk with him & see whether he would make the same favorable, honest, loyal, energetic opinion on you as upon A. — But the *Duma,* I hope will at once be closed. —

Paul is not well, suffers, has fever, a colique wh. he has not had for many months, so is in bed — besides he is worried about D. If I could get some sort of an answer about himself, if you can make use of him at the front or *H.-Q.* & whether you are not sending D. to his regiment — I could go & tell him this. — Wont you send for Misha to stay a bit with you before he returns, would be so nice & homely for you, & good to get him away from her & yr. brother is the one to be with you. I am sure, you feel more lonely since you left the train — alone in a house for breakfast & tea must be sad. Will you come nearer? — And when about do you think of returning for a few days — difficult to say no doubt, but I meant on account of changing *Stcherbatchev* & »macking« the Ministers, whose behaviour to the old man & cowardice, disgust me. — I went this morning to *Znam.* with my candels, there I picked up A. & we went to the red Cross. She sat for an hour with her friend, whilst I went over both houses. The joy of the officers, that you have taken over the command, is colossal, & surety of success. Groten looks well but pale. Then I went to our hospital & sat in the different wards. After lunch I received, then went to A.'s to see Alia's husband who leaves for the war again to-morrow, & she with her Children to town. We took a nice drive — lunched & had tea on the balkony.

Now Baby has begged me to take him to Anias to see *Irina T.* & *Rita H.,* but I wont remain there & shall finish this when I return.

Well, I sat there 20 m. & then I went to pray & place candles for you my Treasure, my own sweet Sunshine. »One says« you are returning on the 4-th for a committee of ministers?! Aeroplans are flying again overhead with much noise. — Baby has written his letter quite by himself, only asked *Peter Vass.* when not sure about the spelling. *Gr.s* wife has quickly left, hoping to see her Son still is so anxious for *Gr.'s* life now. —

Goodbye my Angel. God bless, protect you & help you in all. Very tenderest kisses Nicky love, fr. yr. own old

Sunny.

How nice that you saw Keller, such a comfort to him I am sure.

No. 109.

Tsarskoje Selo, Sept. 1-st 1915

My own sweet Nicky dear,

Grey and dark & I am writing by lamp light. Slept badly. — Looked through the papers — what terrible hard work for our troups, such concentrated strength against us — but God will help on. It is pleasure to read how much clearer better the news is written now & it strikes all — it explains everything easier. — Is the *Duma* being closed? Every day articles, that its impossible one will send it away when so much needed etc. but you see the papers too — high time 2 weeks ago to have closed it. —

But they do go on persecuting the German names, *Stcherbatov,* who told me he would be just and not harm them, now bows down to the wishes of the *Duma,* clears away all German names, — poor *Gilhen* hunted away one, two, three from Bessarabia, he came crying to old Mme *Orlov.* Really he is a mad coward — all those honest people, completely Russian besides — kicked out — why, Lovy, did you give the sanction?

Change him quicker, one only gains enemies instead of loyal subjects — the mess he makes in a day will take years to correct.

A. got a charming telegram from *Kussov intensely happy* having heard the news about you. — She saw *Bezak* at Nini's, & he spoke splendidly, enchanted that *Dg. Orl.* & *Nik.* have left & Nikolai agrees too, says it right & left, & spoke so well about *Goremykin.* — One says the *prorogation of the Duma* till Oct. 15, pitty date is fixed so early again, but thank goodness it now dispersed — only one must work firmly now to prevent them doing harm when they return. The press must really be taken better in hand — they intend launching forth things soon against Ania — that means me again, our Friend was for me too, so A. sent a letter she received to *Vojeikov* to-day, that he must insist *Frolov* should forbid any articles about our Friend or A. being written, they have the military power & its easy for them — *Vojeik.* must take it upon himself, yr. name has not got to be mentioned — in his place, *V.* has to guard our lives & anything that harms us, & these articles are against us; nothing at all to be afraid of, only very energetic measures must be taken — you have shown yr. will & no slacking in any direction — once begun its easy to continue. —

The operation went off well & then I did some *dressing.* Little *Ivan Orlov* was very interesting, he has 3 St. George's crosses is presented to the officers cross & has *St. Stanislav with Swords.* He was a little contusioned & two men killed, bombs were thrown on his mashene, when it was on the ground. He has come for another. Throws bombs & arrows & papers warning them. — *Kniazhevitch* came for a few days — looks well. —

Then we drove, became sunny & nice. Met Baby in *Pavlovsk* park in his big motor with the boys. —

Thats nice Kirill is now too at the *H.-Q.*, can have good talks with him. Egg him on to get rid of *Nic. Vass.*

I shall go with the big girls to town to-morrow to see our wounded, who returned from Germany, & then to tea to *Elagin*, & hope to place a candle at the *Saviour Church* for your. — We were yesterday evening at Anias to see *Shourik* & *Yusik*. — I have nothing interesting to tell you my Sweetheart. God bless & protect you & help you in your very hard work & send force & success to our troops. A thousand kisses, Nicky mine, fr. yr. very own deeply loving old

Wify.

Our Friend is in despair his boy has to go to the war, — the only boy, who looks after all when he is away. —

Fat Orlov says he has been told not to leave before you return & he still hopes to remain. — His amour propre is hideously wounded — forgets all he has said & done no doubt, & all his dirty money affairs. — Zinaïda one says rages, that the 3 have left, & in the next room Papa Felix tells Bezak he is delighted they have gone. —

Tell the old man I saw his wife & 2 daughters at the door & they look well & have left for *Siverskaja*. —

No. 110.

Tsarskoje Selo, September 2-nd 1915

My Own beloved One,

Such a glorious sunny morning, both windows were wide open all the night & now too. I have new ink now, it seems the other is at an end now, it was not Russian. — It always grieves me to see how bad things one makes here, all comes from abroad, the very simplest things, as nails for instance, wool for knitting, knittingneedles in metal & any amount of necessary things. God grant, that after this terrible war is ended, one can get the fabrics to make leather things, & prepare the fur themselves — such an immense country dependant upon others. Young Derfelden (the brother of the G. à cheval you know), Paul's son in law returned with G. Kaufmann; the administration sent from France, he says, was without the *key*, so that they are no good & must be arranged here, wh. will take very long, the French say we must do it, — the boy wired to France & got that answer. *Sandro* wrote such a contented letter to Olga after having seen you on his first *report* with you. Was at first too anxious & I think against you taking over the command & now sees with other eyes. *N. P.* wrote a charming letter to A. & it was agreable to see how he has grasped all, as one has frightened him too, tho' he held his tongue till now about it, he marveled at you having gone against everybody & it has proved itself you were wise & right, his spirits are up again. Certainly being away *fr. Petr.* & *Moscou* is the best thing, pure air, other scenery, no vile gossip. — In town one says you return on Saturday? — We go to town (an aeroplane is passing, for the first time in the morning) — I want to see our poor fellows who came back from Germany & then we take tea at *Elagin* at 4½. — One says Paul keeps to his room & is in an awfull state. His boy leaves & only longs to be with you or in the army, & now is frightened you will sent for him & he is just feeling ill, so his humour is most depressing. I thought I would look in & cheer him up, only I wish I had some sort of an answer for him. The photos Hahn did of Baby were not successes, & the idiot did him sitting on the Balkony as tho' he had a bad leg, I have forbidden it to be sold & shall have him done again. Lovebird, good news again, thank God. One terrible hard fighting, they push on, but constantly beaten back again. — Now the *members of the Duma* want to meet in Moscow to talk over everything when their work here is closed — one ought energetically to forbid it, it will only bring great *troubles*. — If they do that — one ought to say, that the *Duma* will then not be reopened till much later — threaten them, as they try to the ministers — & the gouvernement. Moscow will be worse than here, one must be severe — oh, could one not hang *Gutchkov?*

You can not imagine what a joyful surprise it was to receive your sweet letter. I perfectly well understand how difficult it is for you to find time for writing therefore it touches me deeply, Sweetheart. — That is a name *Piltz!* — but at least the mushrooms are agreable to eat. — Now I understand you find *Moghilev* alright & that it does not disturb there. Just got your wire. — Thank God, news on the whole better, one feels so anxious their trying to cut off *Vilna,* but perhaps we can catch them in a trap, & then *Baranovitchi* — strange towards that place now — there too military people think in two weeks time it will be better. With much skill *Kniazhevitch* finds the losses might be less, as where the heavy firing goes on, one must quickly go under their range, as they are for great distances & cannot change quickly. The mans now are of a far less good cathegory. We just met a train going out & they waved their caps to us as we waved to them. Those heavy losses are hard — but theirs are yet worse.

Of course, you are more needed there now & Motherdear understands it perfectly. Its good you get out of an afternoon. We had divine weather to-day, like summer. I went with A. in my *droshka* to the cemetry, as I wanted to put flowers on the grave of the *Georg.* officers, who died 6 months ago to-day in the big palace — & then took her to *Orlov's* grave, where she has not been since her accident. Then to *Znamenia* I remained through half a mass & then to our hospital, where I sat with our wounded. Luncheon on the balkony, then Baby was photographed on the grass. Then at 2½ off to town to the *Hospital of Hel. P.* to see our prisoners back from Germany & Austria — the last arrived this month. Your *Mamma* had been there this morning. We saw several hundreds & 40 from another hospital, because they cried so she had not seen them. They did not look too bad on the whole, several poor blinds, lots without legs & arms — one with galloping consumption, alas; & the joy to be back. — I told them I should write to you, that I had seen them. Then to *Elagin* — *Feodor* has grown so thin, that I at first took him for *Andriusha* & very weak. *Irina* is in bed in the Crimea, also ill with the stomack. — Motherdear looks well, *Xenia* fidgets, knowing the children not well & separated. *Feodor, Nikita, Rostislav and Vassja* are here, the other three in the Crimea. — I do wish *Yussupov* wld. go back to Moskow, Zinaïda I beleive keeps him from fright. — Masses of movement in town, one gets quite giddy. I feel tired. At Elagin, our *runner* & your Mama's (ex sailor) carried me up on their hands. — Lovely air, window wide open. We always dine in the play room, but to-day I prefer remaining down as am tired & limbs ache. Think incessantly of you my Angel, pray heart & soul for you & miss you more than I can say — but happy you are out there & know at last all. —

Now goodbye, Lovy mine, the man must leave. God bless & protect you I kiss every dear spot over & over again & hold you tight in my arms.

Ever your own very own wify

Alice.

I receive *Kulomsin, Ignatiev* to-morrow & your *Eristov* lunches with us. — Dona received our 3 Russian nurses & Motherdear said she would not the Germans & now she feels, she must & fears being rude to them. Miechen & Mara could not in consequence, but then they too will. Now, if they ask me, what shall I answer. Every kindness shown them will make them sooner ready to be kind to ours & they would never understand, if I dont see them. if they ask; — & here one will no doubt rage against me. The red cross nurses make a difference, it seems to me. What do you think, tell me Sweetheart, please; I find, I might, as they are women, & I know Ernie will or *Onor* see ours, & *Grd. Dchs. of Baden* for sure. —

How this new ink stinks, shall scent the letter again.

No. 111.

Tsarskoje Selo, Sept. 3-rd 1915

My own beloved Nicky dear,

Grey weather. Looking through the papers I saw that *Litke* has been killed — how sad, he was one of the last who had not once been wounded, & such a good officer. Dear me, what losses, ones heart bleeds — but our Friend says they are *torches* burning before God's throne, & that is lovely. A beautiful death for Sovereign & country. One must not think too much about that, otherwise it too heartrending. — Paul's Boy left yesterday evening after having taken Holy Communion in the morning. Now her both sons are in the war, poor woman & this one is such a marvelously gifted boy, wh. makes one more anxious — he is sooner ready to be taken from this world of pain. — Wont you get *Yussupov* & give him instructions & send him off quicker to Moscou, its very wrong his sitting here at such a time when his presence can be needed any moment — she keeps him.

But one must have an eye on Moscou & prepare beforehand & be in harmony with the military, otherwise disorders will again arise. *Stcherbatchev* being a nullity, not to say worse, wont help when disorders occur, I am sure. Only quicker to get rid of him & for you to get a look a *Khvostov,* whether he would suit you, or Neidhardt. — (who is such a pedant).

Thank God, you continue feeling energetic — let one feel it in everything & in all yr. orders here *in this horrid rear.* — We take tea at Miechens.

Here are the names of Maia *Plaoutin's* sons — she entreats to get news of them — can somebody in yr. staff, or *Drenteln* try to find out their whereabouts? —

Well, I placed my candles as usual, ran in to kiss A. as she was off to *Peterhof* — then hospital, operation.

Your *Eristov* lunched with us, has grown older, limps a little, was wounded in the leg & lay at *Kiev.* Then I received *Ignatiev* (minister) & talked long with him about everything & gave him my opinion about all, they shall hear my opinion of them & the *Duma.* I spoke of the old man, of their ugly behaviour towards him, & turned to him as a former *Preobr.,* what would one do to officers who go behind their commanders back & complain against him & hinder & wont work with him — one sends them flying — he agreed. As he is a good man I know, I launched forth & he I think understood some things more rightly afterwards. — Then I had Css. Adlerberg; after wh. we made *bandages* in the *stores.*

O, T. & I took tea at Miechen, Ducky came too, looking old, & ugly even, had a headache & felt cold & was badly coiffée. — We spoke much & they looked at things as one ought to; also angry at the fright & cowardice & that none will take any responsability upon themselves. Furious against the *Nov. Vremia,* finds one ought to take strong measures against *Suvorin.* Miechen knows that a correspondence goes on between *Militza* & *Suvorin,* make the police clear this up, it becomes treachery.

I send you a cutting about *Hermogens* — again *Nicolasha* gave orders about him, it only concerned the *Synod* & you — what right had he to allow him to go to Moscou — you & Fredericks ought to wire to *Samarin* that you wish him to be sent straight on to *Nicolo* Ugretsk — as remaining with *Vostorgov,* they will again cook against our Friend & me. Please order Fred, to wire this. — I hope they wont make any story to *Varnava;* you are Lord & Master in Russia, *Autocrat* remember that. —

Then I saw Gen. *Shulmann* of *Ossovetz* — his health is still not yet good, so he cannot yet go to the army. — Uncle *Mekk* was long with me & we talked a lot about affairs — & then about all the rest. He finds *Jussupov* no good. Miechen said Felix told him his Father had sent in his demission & got no answer. —

Big *strikes* in town. God grant *Rouzsky's* order will be fulfilled energetically. — *Mekk* is also very much against *Gutchkov* — he says the other brother also talks too much.

Lovy, have that *assembly* in Moscou f o r b i d d e n, its impossible, will be worse than the *Duma* & there will be endless rows. —

Another thing to think seriously about is the question of wood — there wont be any fuel & little meat & in consequence can have stories & riots.

Mekks railway gives heaps of wood to the town of Moscou, but its n o t enough & one does not t h i n k s e r i o u s l y enough about this. —

Forgive my bothering you Sweetheart, but I try to collect what I think may be of use to you. — Remember about *Suvorin's* articles wh. must be watched & damped. —

A great misfortune, one cannot get the *refugees* to work, they wont & thats bad, they expect one to do everything for them & give & do nothing in exchange. —

Now this must go. The Image is fr. *Igumen Serafim* (fr. whom St. Seraphim came, wh. you held in your hand). The goodies, toffee is from Ania. —

Weather grey & only 8 degr.

Lovy, please send of your suite to the different manufacturies, fabricks to inspect them — your eye — even if they do not understand much, still the people will feel you are watching them, whether they are fulfilling your orders conscientiously — please dear. —

Many a tender kiss, fervent prayer & blessing huzy mine, fr. yr. very own old

Sunny.

God w i l l help — be firm & energetic — right & left, shake & wake all up, & smack firmly when necessary. One must not only love you, but b e a f r a i d of you, then all will go well. —

Is it true nice Dimka also goes to *Tiflis* — a whole suite of yours follow, thats too much, & you need him with the foreigners & for sending about.

All the children kiss you. —

No. 112.

Tsarskoje Selo, Sept. 4-th 1915

My very own Sweetheart,

I have remained in bed this morning, feeling deadtired, & having slept badly. My brain continued working & talking — I had spoken so much yesterday & always upon the same subject until I became cretinized; & this morning I continued to *Botkin,* as its good for him & helps him put his thoughts to right, as they also did not grasp things as they were. One has to be the medicine to the muddled minds after the microbes from town — ouff! She got his telegram yesterday, perhaps you will copy it out & mark the date Sept. 3-rd on the paper I gave you when you left with his telegr. written down: »*Remember the promise of the meeting, this was the Lord showing the banner of victory, the children or those near to the heart should say, set us go along the ladder of the banner, our spirit has nothing to fear.*«

And your *spirit* is up so is mine & I feel enterprising & ready to talk away. It must be alright & will be — only patience & trust in God. Certainly our losses are colossal, the guard has dwindled away, but the spirits are unflinchingly brave. All that is easier to hear than the rottenness here. I know nothing about the *strikes* as the papers (luckily) don't say a word about them. —

Ania sends her love — wont you wire to me to, »thank for letters, Image, toffee« — it would make her happy.

Aunt Olga was suddenly announced to me yesterday evening at 10½ — my heart nearly stood still, I thought already one of the boys was killed — thank God it was nothing, she only wanted to know whether I knew what was going on in town & then I had to let forth again, for the fourth time in one day, & put things clearer to her, as she could not grasp some things & did not know what to believe.

She was very sweet, dear Woman. — Here is a paper for *Alexeiev,* you will remember the same officer asked some time ago about forming a *legion;* well, you will think about it — perhaps it would do no harm to form it & keep it in reserve in case of disorders or let it replace another regiment wh. might come more back as a rest. — The *legion* of Letts, are you having it disbanded into other existing regiments, as you had intended & wh. would be safer in all respects & more correct.

The Children have begun their winter-lessons, Marie & Anastasia are not contented, but Baby does not mind & is ready for more, so I said the lessons were to last all 50 instead of 40 minutes, as now, thank God, he is so much stronger. — All day long letters & telegrams come — but its yours I await all day with intense longing. —

I want to go to Church this evening. — Ania sends you her fondest love. Got finer after luncheon & we drove. The girls had a concert. — So anxious for news. — Kiss you endlessly, my love & long for you. When you come, I suppose it will only be for a few days? — Have nothing interesting to tell you, alas. All my thoughts incessantly with you. Send you some flowers, cut the stalks a little, then they will last longer.

God bless you

Ever yr. very own old Wify.

Love to Kirill & Dmitri & Boris. —

No. 113.

Tsarskoje Selo, Sept. 5-th 1915

My own beloved Darling,

Grey weather. Again *Ivanov* & S. army had success — but h o w hard it is to the north — but God will help, I am sure. Are we getting over more troops there? The misery of having so few railway lines! —

I have nothing of interest to tell you, was yesterday in our lower church fr. 6½—8 & prayed much for you, my Treasure; the evening we spent knitting as usual & soon after 11 to bed. — I must get up & have my hair done before *Botkin,* as have sent for *Rostovtsev* at 10 o'clock. — Me kisses zoo. — Well I had Rostovtsev & told him we were going to town & he was to meet us at the station with *Apraxin, Neidhardt, Tolstoy, Obolensky* & so it was at 3 (& M. D. with the motors met us) & at the station *Rostovtsev* told them I wished to go & see the *refugees.* So we went, quite unexpectedly to different, 5 places to see them, a nighthouse wh. stands empty *near the Narva gate* (as people dont drink & so can find where to sleep) — & there women & children sleep in two lairs, — next a house where the men are. Many were out looking for work. Then the place they are first brought to, *bathed,* fed — written down & looked at by the Dr. Then another place, former chocolate fabric, where women & children sleep, all kissed my hands, but many could not speak being Letts, Poles. But they did not look too bad nor too dirty. The worst is to find them work when they have many children. There is an excellent new wooden building with large kitchen, dining passage, baths & sleeping rooms, built in 3 weeks near Packhouses & where the trains can be brought straight. — But now I am tired & cant go to Church. — I wonder if you understood my telegram, written in Ella's style rather — but Ania begged me do it quickly as *Massalov* spoke to her by telephone & said *Stcherbatov* would see you today. — The papers intend bringing in our Friend's name & Anias — here *Stchenbatov* promised *Massalov* that he wld. try to stop them, but as it comes fr. Moscou, he did not know how. But it must be forbidden; & *Samarin* will go on for sure — such a hideous shame, & only so as to drag me in too. — Be severe. And what about *Yussupov* — he does not intend returning & gave in his demission tho' one never does during war. Is there no capable general who might replace him? — only he must be energetic indeed. All men seem to wear peticoats now! —

Mme Zizi lunched as its her namesday — & then we talked & I explained a lot, at wh. she was most grateful, as it opened her eyes upon many unclear things. You know ramoli Fredericks told Orlov (who repeated it to Zizi) that I felt he disliked me — so he went only disculpiating himself & proving his innocence. Countess Benkendorf told Ania she was delighted he leaves & ought to have long ago, as the things he allowed himself to say were awful. — It was the kind couple Benkendorf that hinted last night to Ania that I shld. go & see the *refugees,* so I at once did it, as I know meant well & may help people taking more interest in those poor creatures. —

The fabrics began working again — not so in Moscou I fear. —

Kussov wrote (he gets none of Ania's letters & feels very sad we shld. have forgotten him). Is full of the news about You & he explained it all to his men. He longs to say heaps, & things you for sure don't know & wh. are not right, but he cannot risk writing frankly. — Zizi asked me who the General *Borissov?* is with *Alexeiev* as she heard, he was not a good man in the Japanese war! —

I was half an hour in Church this morning & then at the hospital (without working) — there were 8 of yr. *3d Rifles* fr. here wounded on the 30th — one of them, the first I have ever heard, said one longs for peace; — they chattered a lot! —

Now my Sunshine, dearly beloved Angel, I kiss & bless you & long for you

Ever yr. very own old

Wify.

I told *Mitia Den,* that you thought of sending the Suite to as many fabricks & *workshops* as possible, & he found it a brilliant idea & just the thing, as then all will feel your eye is every where. — Do begin sending them off & make them come with *reports* to you. — It will make an excellent impression & encourage them working & spur them on. — Get a list of your free Suite (without German names), *Dmitri Sheremetiev* as he is free. *Komarov* (as he spoke to you), *Viazemsky, Zhilinsky, Silaiev,* those who are less »able men« send to quieter & surer places; *Mitia Den, Nikolai Mikhailovitch* (as he is in a good frame of mind), Kirill — *Baranov*. But do it now Deary. — Am I boring you, then forgive me, but I must be yr. *note-book.* Now Miechen writes about the same man as Max & Mavra, Fritzie vouches for him not being a spy & a real Gentleman. — The papers concerning him I think lie in town at the general-staff; it was *Nikolasha* ordered him to be shut up. He is since beginning of the war in a real cell with a wee window, like a culprit — only let him be kept decently like any officer we have, if one wont exchange him for Costia's a. d. c. He writes to Adini that he was auf einer Studienreise durch den Kaukasus begriffen up in the mountains he heard rumours of impending war, & so he flew off on the shortest road. He reached *Kovel* July 20 & at the station heard of the declaration of war. The train did not continue. He announced himself as officer & begged to be permitted to pass over Sweden or Odessa; instead one took him prisoner in a cell at Kiev, where he is still now, regarding him as spy. He gives his word of honour to Adini that he »was only traveling without any ugly sidedeeds, & that he kept himself far from anything like spying«. He suffers away fr. wife & children & not being able to do his duty. — He begs to be exchanged, or at least a better position. Poor Photo, if one has wrongly shut him up in a cell, the quicker one takes him out & treats him as a German officer taken as being in Russia when war was declared, that would only be decent. When Miechen enquired, one said they had *(nothing?)* against him, *Sazonov* only said that he had given out he was unmarried or on his honeymoon, in any case not correct, but that means nothing (perhaps there was a croocked novel) & when they begged again, I think *Nikolasha* or *Yanushkevitch* one answered that one did not remember why he was shut, but probably they had a reason & therefore he must remain there — that's »*weak*« as the children would say. — Ah, here Miechen sends me a letter of his wife to Adini. They wanted to travel & he wanted to show her Petrograd & Moscou & take a rest, after hard work & freshen up his Russian. They left beginning of July 1914 Stettin. For safety sake her husband took a diplomatic Pass (?). The last moment friends in Kurland told them not to visit them, so they spent 8 days in Petrograd & 8 in Moscou & did sightseeing. There they separated because of her bad health wh. prevented her accomp. him to friends in the Caucasus. She daily got news fr. him, & fr. *Tiflis* & near there he went to a H. v. Kutschenbach, who during the war was murdered with his wife. Through the german Consul at *Tiflis* he got a ticket to Berlin over Kalish — but only reached *Kovel.* — The only red cross German sister, von Passow is his sister in law — she is now here to see the prisoners. Do have him well placed, please he can have his health for ever ruined — & Fritzy vouches for him. If you cant have him exchanged, then at least lodged & with light & good air. Excuse my writing all this, but its good you should know what Adini heard, & one cant be cruel, its not noble & after the war one must speak well of our treatment, we must show that we stand higher than they with their »kultur«. —

How I bother you, am so sorry, but its hard for others & you don't persecute as *Nikolasha* & *Yanushkevitch* did mercilessly in the Baltic provinces either, & that does not harm the war nor mean peace. —

Goremykin comes to me to-morrow at 3 — tiresome hour, but is only free then. — Tell *N. P.* that we thank him very much for his letters of thanks & — messages. —

God bless you, once more thousand warm, warm tender kisses Sweetheart. —

Cold & raining.

My love & goodwishes to Dmitri. —

My yesterday's letter I marked wrongly, it must be 344, please correct it. —

No. 114.

Tsarskoje Selo, Sept. 6-th 1915

Beloved Nicky dear,

Every morning & evening I bless & then kiss your cushion & one of your Images. I always bless you whilst you sleep & I get up to draw open the curtains. Wify sleeps all alone down here, & the wind is howling melancholy to-night. How lonely you must feel, wee One. Are your rooms at least not too hideous? Cannot *N. P.* or Drenteln photo them? All day impatiently I await your dear telegram wh. either comes during dinner or towards 11. —

So many yellow & copper leaves, & alas also many are beginning to fall — sad autumn has already set in — the wounded feel melancholy as they cannot sit out but rarely & their limbs ache when its damp — they almost all have become barometers. We send them off as quickly as possible to the Crimea.

Taube left yesterday with several others to *Yalta* as a surgeon must watch his wound & my little *Ivanov's* too. — Ania dined with us yesterday upstairs. To-day is Isa's birthday, so I have invited her with Ania to luncheon. — Oh beloved One — 2 weeks you left, — me loves you so intensely & I long to hold you in my arms & cover your sweet face with gentle kisses & gaze into your big beautiful eyes — now you cant prevent me from writing it, you bad boy.

When will some of our dear troops have that joy? Wont it be a recompense to see you! *Navruzov* wrote, he at last tried to return to his regiment after 9 months, but only got as far as *Kars,* his wound reopened again *a fistula* & he needs *dressings,* so once more his hopes are frustrated — but he begged *Jagmin* for work & he has sent him to *Armavir* with the young soldiers to train them & look after the youngest officers.

It is so nice to feel ones dear wounded remember one & write. Madame Zizi also often hears from those that lay in the big palace. —

Have you news from Misha? I have no idea where he is. Do get him to stop a bit with you — get him quite to yourself. — *N. P.* writes so contented & spirits up — anything better than town.

It seems Aunt Olga before coming to me had flown half wild to Paul saying the revolution has begun, there will be bloodshed, we shall all be got rid of, Paul must fly to *Goremykin* & so on — poor soul! To me she came already quieter & left quite calm — she & Mavra probably got a fright, the atmosphere spread there too from *Petrograd.* —

Grey & only 5 degrees. — The big girls have gone to Church at 9 & I go with the others at 10½. — Isa has cought cold & 38 this morning, so has to keep in bed. The news is good again in the south, but they are quite close to *Vilna* wh. is despairing — but their forces are so colossal. — You wired you had written so I am eagerly awaiting your letter, Lovy — its sad only with telegrams in wh. one cannot give any news, but I know you have no time for writing, & when working hard to have still to sit down to a letter, thats dull & wearisome work; & you have every moment taken too, Sweetheart.

I had *Markozov* from 6¼ to 8 so have to write whilst eating — most interesting all he told & can be of use to abolish misunderstandings, cant write about anything of that to-night. — Old man came to me — so hard for him, ministers so rotten to him. I think they want to ask for their leave & the best thing too. —

Sazonov is the worst, cries, excites all (when it has nothing to do with him), does not come to the conseil des Ministers, wh. is an unheard of thing — Fred. ought to tell him fr. you that you have heard of it & are very displeased, I find. I call it a *strike* of the ministers. Then they go & speak of everything wh. is spoken of & discussed in the Council & they have no right to, makes him so angry. You ought to wire to the old man that you forbid one talking outside what is spoken of at the Council of Ministers & wh. concerns nobody. There are things that can & wh. are known later, but not everything. —

If in any way you feel he hinders, is an obstacle for you, then you better let him go (he says all this) but if you keep him he will do all you order & try on his best — but begs you to think this over for when you return to seriously decide, also *Stcherbatov's* successor & *Sazonov*. — He told *Stcherbatov* he finds absolutely a person chosen by *Stcherbatov* ought to be present at Moscou at all these meetings & forbid any touching of questions wh. dont concern them — he has the right as Minister of the Interior; *Stcherbatov* agreed at first, but after having seen people fr. Moscou he changed his mind & no more agreed — he was to tell you all this, *Goremykin* told him to — did he? Do answer. — Then he begs *D. Mrazovsky.* should quickly go to Moscou, as his presence may be needed any day. — I don't admire *Yussupov* leaving (its her fault) but he was not worth much. — And now we have left *Vilna* — what pain, but God will help — its not our fault with these terrible losses. Soon is the Sweet Virgin's feast 8-th (my day, do you remember Mr. Philippe) — she will help us. —

Our Friend wires, probably after her letter his wife brought, telling about all the interior difficulties. »*Do not fear our present embarassments, the protection of the Holy Mother is over you — go to the hospitals though the enemies are menacing — have faith.*« Well I have no fright, that you know. — In Germany one hates me now too He said & I understand it — its but natural. —

How I understand, how disagreeable to change your place — but of course you need being further from the big line. But God will not forsake our troops, they are so brave. —

I must end now, Lovebird. — Alright about *Boris,* only is it the moment? Then make him remain at the war & not return here, he must lead a better life than at *Warshaw* & understand the great honour for one so young. — Its a pitty, true, that not *Misha.*

The German nurses left for Russia & Maria had no time to see them, me they did not ask to see, probably hate me. —

Oh Treasure, how I long to be with you, hate not being near, not to be able to hold you tight in my arms & cover you with kisses — alone in yr. pain over the war news — yearn over you. God bless help, strengthen, comfort, guard & guide. —

Ever yr. very own

Wify.

No. 115.

Tsarskoje Selo, Sept. 7-th 1915

Beloved Huzy dear,

Cold, windly & rainy — may it spoil the roads. I have read through the papers — nothing written that we left *Vilna* — again very mixed, success, bad luck & it cannot be otherwise, & one rejoices over the smallest success. It does not seem to me that the Germans will venture much more further, it would be great folly to enter deeper into the country — as later our turn will come. — Is the amunition, shells & rifles coming in well? You will send people to have a look — your Suite? — Your poor dear head must be awfully tired with all this work & especially the interior questions? Then, to recapitulate what the old man said: to think of a new minister of the interior, (I told him you had not yet fixed upon Neidhardt; perhaps, when you return, you can think once more about *Khvostov);* a successor to *Sazonov,* whom he finds quite impossible, has lost his head, cries & agitates against *Goremykin,* & then the question, whether you intend keeping the latter or not. But certainly not a minister who answers before the *Duma,* as they want, — we are not ripe for it & it would be Russia's r u i n — we are n o t a Constitutional country & d a r e n o t be it, our people are not educated for it & thank God our Emperor is an *Autocrat* & must stick to this, as you do — only you must show more power & decision. I should have cleared out quickly still *Samarin* & *Krivoshein,* the latter displeases the old man greatly, right & left & excited beyond words.

Goremykin hopes you won't receive *Rodzianko.* (Could one but get another instead of him, an energetic, good man in his place wld. keep the *Duma* in Order.) — Poor old man came to me, as a »soutien« & because he says I am »l'énergie«. To my mind, much better clear out ministers who strike & not change the President who with decent, energetic, well-intentioned cooperates can serve still perfectly well. He only lives & serves you & yr. country & knows his days are counted & fears not death of age, or by knife or shot — but God will protect him & the holy Virgin. Our Friend wanted to wire to him an encouraging telegram. — *Markozov* — no I must finish about *Goremykin,* he beggs you to think of somebody for Moscou & besides get *Mrozovsky* to come quicker, as these sessions may become too noisy in Moscou & therefore an eye & voice of the Minister of Interior ought to be there, & one has the right to, as Moscou is under the minister of Interior. *Neratov* he finds no good for replace *Sazonov* (I only like that mentioned his name), he knows him since he was a boy & says he never served out of Russia, & that is not convenient at such a place. But where to get the man. We had enough of Isvolsky & he is not a very sure man — Girs is not worth much, Benk. — the name already against him. Where are men I always say, I simply cannot grasp, how in such a big country does it happen that we never can find suitable people, with exceptions! —

My conversation with *Markozov* was most interesting (a little too sure of himself) & he can tell one many necessary things & clear up misunderstandings. *Polivanov* knows him well & already he has cleared up one thing. It seems there was an order to take off of the prisoner officers their *epaulets,* wh. created an awful fury in Germany & wh. I understand — why humiliate a prisoner & that is one of those wrong orders of 1914 fr. the *Headquarters* — thank God one has now changed it. — He also understands that we must always try to be i n t h e r i g h t, as they at once otherwise repay us equally — till for that — & when this hideous war is over & the hatred abated, I long that one should say, that we were noble. The horror of being a prisoner is already enough for an officer & one wont forget humilations or cruelties — let them carry home remembrances of christianity & honour. Luxury, nobody asks for. They are really improving the lot of our prisoners, I saw a photo, Max did of our wounded at Saalem (A. Maroussia's place) in the garden, near a Russian toy hut, Max used to play in & they look well fed & contented. Their greatest hatred has passed, & ours is artificially kept up by the rotten »*Novoye Vremya*«. — I must fly & dress, as we have got an operation & before that I want to place my candles & pray for you as usual; my treasure, my Angel, my Sunshine, my poor *much-suffering Job.* I cover you with kisses & mourn over your loneliness. —

The operation went off alright — in the afternoon we went to the big Palace hospital. *Kulomzin* came to me to present himself & bring lists, to show me what the *Romanovsky* committee has done; — most interesting talk about all sorts of questions. —

Well, Dear, here are a list of names, very little indeed, who might replace *Samarin.* Ania got them through *Andronnikov* who had been talking with the *Metropolitan* as he was in despair Samarin got that nomination, saying that he unterstood nothing about the Church affairs. Probably he saw *Hermogen* at Moscou, in any case he sent for *Varnava,* abused our Friend, & said that *Hermogen* had been the only honest man, because he was not afraid to tell you all against *Gregory* & therefore he was shut up, & that he, *Samarin* wishes *Varnava* to go & tell you all against *Gregory;* he answered that he could not, only if the other ordered him to, & as coming from him. So I wired to the old man to receive *Varnava* who would tell him all, & I hope the old man will speak to *Samarin* after & wash his head. You see, he does not heed what you told him — he does nothing in the *Synod* & only persecutes our Friend, i. e. goes straight against us both — unpardonable, & at such a time even criminal. He m u s t leave. — Well here: *Khvostov* (minister of justice) very religious knowing much about the Church, most devoted to you & much heart. *Guriev (Director of the Chancellary of the Synod)* very honest, serves long in the *Synod* (likes our Friend). He mentioned *Makarov* ex minister, but he would never do, & a small unknown man. —

But he goes on singing a praise of *Khvostov* & tells it to *Gregory* as he wants to bring him round to see, that this is a man ready to have himself chopped to pieces for you (will stand up for our Friend, never allow one mention him); his manque de tacte after all don't mind so much now, when one needs an energetic man who knows people in every place, & a Russian name, *Kulomzin* also hates the »*Novoye Vremya*« & finds the M o s c o v. V i e d. & »*Russkoye Slovo*« much better. I am a bit anxious what they are producing in Moscou. The *Petrograd strikes, Andronnikov* says, are thanks to colossal gaffes of *Stcherbatov* who shut up people who had nothing to do in that respect. — I hope *Voyeikov* listens less to *Stcherbatov* — he is such a nullity & weak & by that does harm. — What dull letters I write, but me wants to help zoo so awfully, Sweetheart, & so many use me as an organ to give over things to you. —

Sonia *Den* took tea with us, she leaves for *Koreiz,* as needs a better climate, is so happy you are out there & understands perfectly well that you went now when all is so difficult. —

Yesterday we took tea at *Pavlovsk* with Mavra — Aunt Olga turned up too — she looks unwell, worked in Sunday fr. 10—2½ in the hospital — she overtires herself, but wont listen to reason. I understand her — myself of experience have realised one must do less, alas, so I work rarely, to keep my strength for more necessary things.

Yesterday evenig we were at Ania's, also *Shurik, Yuzik* Marie's friend & *Alexei Pavlovitch,* who told us about the *Headquarters* — he leaves for there again to-morrow. —

I enclose a letter from Ania about her brother, tho' I advised her not to send it as if the name comes to you, of yr. own accord I know you will do what is right for the boy who worked so hard. —

Now I must dress for Church. Cold, wet and rainy, — may it spoil the roads thoroughly at least. — Awfully anxious to get news — God will help. —

Goodbye & God bless you my sweetest of sweets. —

I cover your precious face with tenderest, warmest kisses & long to hold you in my arms & forget everything for a few moments.

Ever yr. very own old

Sunny.

Here is Babysweets letter too. —

No. 116.

Tsarskoje Selo, Sept. 8-th 1915

My own beloved One,

Am so anxious what news — its 10½ & the »*Novoye Vremya*« has not come & I don't know what is going on, as never get the telegr. any more as before were sent me, when you were at the *Headquarters.* So cold, 3 degr. only in the night, grey & windy. The eldest went to mass at 9 & the little ones now, I shall follow, have been reading through an immense fat *report* fr. Rostovtsev. — There is *Prince Ukhtomsky* in the 4-th rifles & his wife is terribly worried, as some of the comrades said they had seen him fallen, wounded, whereas no sanitary has yet brought him. Did *Boris* bring the lists? But it may have happened since. In town one says all the guard was surrounded, but I wont believe anything that is not official. I must dress for Church. Service was nice last night & they sang well. —

Dear one, it is so difficult when there are things one must tell you directly — & I dont know whether anybody reads our telegrams. Again I have had to wire an unpleasant thing to you, but there was no time to loose. I have asked her, as well as she can, to write out *Suslik's* conversation in the *Synod.* Really the little man has behaved with marvelous energy, standing up for us & our Friend, & gave back slapping answers to their questions. Tho' the Metropolitan is very displeased with *Samarin,* yet at this interrogation he was feeble & held his tongue, alas. — They want to clear *Varnava* out & put *Hermogen* in his place, have you ever heard such an impudence! They dare not do it without yr. sanction, as by yr. order he was punished. Its once more *Nikolasha's* doing (egged on by the women) he made him come out of his place, without any right, to *Vilna* to live with *Agafangel* & of course this latter, *S. Philip* & *Nikon* (the awful harmbringer to *Athos)* attacked *Varnava* about our Friend for 3 hours; *Samarin* went to Moscou for 3 days I think, no doubt to see *Hermogen* — I sent you the cutting about his having been allowed to spend 2 days in Moscou at *Vostokov's* by *Nikolasha's* order — since when was he allowed to mix in such questions, knowing that by yr. order the punishment was inflicted upon *Hermogen!* How dare they go against yr. permission of the »*salutation*« — what have they come to, even there anarchy reigns & once more *Nikolasha's* fault, as he (purposely) proposed *Samarin,* knowing that that man would do all in his power against *Grgeory* & me, but here you are dragged in, & that is criminal, & at such a time quite particularly. Several times the old man told *Samarin* not to touch that subject, therefore he is fearfully hurt & said so to *Varnava* & that he found *Samarin* must at once leave, other-wise they will drag it into the public. I find those 2 bishops ought at once to be taken out of the *Synod* — let *Pitirim* come & sit there, as our Friend feared *Nikolasha* would harm him if he heard that *Pitirim* venerates our Friend. Get other, more worthy Bishops in. *Strike* of the *Synod* — at such a time, too unpatriotic, unloyal — what does it concern anybody — may they now pay for it & learn who is their master. Here is a cutting »again« you will say, but *V. J. Gurko* says (I will write it better out instead of sending you the paper). In Moscou, *Lvov* allowed him to speak: »*We want a strong authority — we mean an authority armed with extraordinary powers, authority with a horse-whip* (now you show it them in every way, where you can, you are their *autocrat* master) *but not such an authority which is itself under whip.* A slandering pun, directed against you & our Friend, God punish them for this; — its not Christian to write this, then better, God forgive them, but above all make them repent. —

Varnava told *Goremykin* all about the Governor — how nice he was with *Gregory* until he came here & got horrid orders fr. *Stcherbatov, i. e. Samarin.* About me he said to *Suslik* »*a foolish woman*« & about Ania abominable things wh. he cld. not even repeat. *Goremykin* says he must at once be changed. Look through my letters of about 5 days ago, there I named one, our Friend would have liked to have. Only all this must be done quickly, the effect is all the greater. *Samarin* knows yr. opinion & wishes & so does *Stcherbatov* & they don't care, thats the vile part of it. Give orders to the old man, that is then easy for him to fulfil. He told *Varnava* how hard it was to have all against him, if only you would give him new ministers to work with. — *Samarin* had ordered *Varnava* to go to you — now it would have been good, he could have told you all, only it will take up your time & one must hurry with ones decisions. You see he is like *S. I.* incorrigible & narrowminded. He ought to think of his churches, clergy & convents & not of whom we receive. That is his bad conscience now. Once more »who digs a pit for others, falls into it himself«, like *Nikolasha.* — Quicker also change the ministers, he cannot work with them — if you give him categorical orders, then he can give them over, thats easier — but to talk with them he cant. Excellent to send several flying & keep him, serves them right, *please* think of it.

Despairing not to be with you & talk all over quietly together. —

About the war news our Friend writes (add it to yr. list of telegrams) *Sept. 8: »Don't fear it will not be worse than it was, faith and the banner will favor us.«* — I enclose a telegram of E. Witgenstein, born *Nabokova* (Groten's great friend, was in Marie's train). She wants medals, perhaps you would give Fred. the order — & the telegram too. The Images I can send her straight. — Here my love is *Khvostov's* speech in reading you will understand why Paul disapproved because he openly speaks against *Dzhunkovsky.* You better keep it, in case one makes remarks about him, you can always fall back upon it; its clever & honest & energetic — a man longing to be of use to you. — Are you having more justice done in the Baltic provinces, one would like that, I must say poor people suffer enough. — *Khvostov's* speech I have just read through, very clear & interesting, but I must say our own lazy slave natures without any initiative have been at fault, we ought to have kept the bank in hand before — earlier nobody paid attention, now all eyes hunt for the German *influence,* but we brought it on ourselves, I assure you by our lazyness. Pay attention to page 21, 22 about *Dzhunkovsky,* what right had he to telegraph such a thing, it was only possible in quite particular cases — & that sounds rotten. I think it will interest you as it shows you his ideas about the banks etc. Then Ania's paper I enclose about *Varnava* & the *Synod.* Anastasia kisses you & begs pardon for not having written but we went for a little drive (of course the girls froze) & then to the Invalid-house where it lasted 1½ hour talking to all. We picked up Ania again at Css. Schulenburg's ideal little cottage. Then they went to their hospital & after tea to Ania's to play with some young girls. — One's head is ramolished fr. conversations — but *the spirit is good,* Lovy, & ready for anything you need. *Varnava* comes to me to-morrow. Go on being energetic Sweetheart, use your broom — show them your energetic, sure, firm side wh. they have not seen enough. Now is the fight to show them who you are, & that you have enough — you tried with gentleness & kindness, but that did not take, now you will show the contrary — the Master-will. *Kussov* wrote to Ania amongst other things, sad that a man like *Miheyev* came in yr. name as he represents nothing & does not know how to represent — nor to speak.

Manny mine, Angel Sweetheart, so sorry to daily bore you with things, but I cant otherwise. — I long to kiss you & gaze into yr. beloved eyes. I bless & kiss you without end in true & deep devotion. God bless, guard, guide & protect you.

Ever yr. very own old Wify.

Are you thinking of sending Dmitri back to the regiment? Dont let him dawdle about doing nothing, its his ruin, he will be worth nothing, if his caracter does not get formed at the war — he was not out more than one or 2 months.

No. 117.

Tsarskoje Selo, Sept. 9-th 1915

My very own Sweet One,

At last a sunny morning, & »of course we go to town«, as *Olga* says; but I must go to hospitals, there is nothing to be done. Yesterday we went to the Invalid-hospital, I spoke to 120 men 1½, & the rest en gros as they stood in one room, — why I told you all this yesterday, I am quite foolish. Thank God the news is a bit better, I find, to the north, i. e. *Vilna—Dvinsk,* You said we left *Vilna* the other night, but they have not yet entered, have they? Am eagerly awaiting your promised letter to-day, such a joy always. —

There! I have got your precious letter & I thank you for it from the depths of my heart, I hold it in my left hand & kiss it, Sweetheart. Wont Mme *Plautin* be mad with joy to have news that her sons are safe, thanks so much for enquiring. What a lovely telegr. from our Friend. —

Thats good you use Kirill now after *Georgie,* so that each goes in turn, only don't send Dmitri, he is too young & it makes him conceited — wish you would send him off! — Only don't say its I who ask this. — Well, you have a lot to do. You had a better impression of *Stcherbatov,* but he is not good, I fear at all, so weak and wont work properly with the old man. Well look what they spoke about at Moscou, again those questions, wh. they had come to the conclusion to drop, & asking for an answerable minister wh. is quite impossible, even *Kulomzin* sees this clearly — did they really have the impertinence of sending you the intended telegram? How they all need to feel an iron will & hand — it has been a reign of gentleness & now must be the one of power & firmness — you are the Lord & Master in Russia & God Almighty placed you there & they shall bow down before your wisdom & firmness, enough of kindness, wh. they were not worthy of & thought they could hoist you round their finger. What they said at *Moscow* was printed yesterday. — I saw poor *Varnava* to-day my dear, its abominable how *Samarin* behaved to him in the hotel & then in the *Synod* — such cross-examination as is unheard of & spoke so meanly about *Gregory* using vile words in speaking of Him. He makes the Gov. watch all their telegrams & send them to him — vicious about the *salutation* that you have no right to allow such a thing — upon wh. *Varnava* answered him soundly & said that you were the chief protector of the Church, & *Samarin* impertinently said you were its *servant.* Colossal *insolence* & more than ungentlemanlike — lolling back in his chair with crossed legs crossexamining a Bishop about our Friend. When Peter the Great of his own accord also ordered a »*salutation*«, it was at once done, in the place & round about. After *the salutation, the funeral services* cease (as when we were at *Sarov, the salutation* & *glorification,* were done together) — & they have reordered *funeral services* & said they would not heed what y o u said. Lovy, y o u m u s t be firm & give the strict order to the *Synod* that you i n s i s t u p o n y o u r order being fulfilled & the *Synod* that yr. order has to be fulfilled and the *salutation* is to continue — more than ever one needs those prayers now. They ought to know that you are most displeased with them. And please do not allow *Varnava* to be sent away, he stood up splendidly for us & *Gregory* & showed them how they on purpose go against us in all this. Old *Goremykin* was more than hurt & horrified & beyond words shocked, wenn he heard that the Gov. (whom *Dzhunkovsky* had made change his opinion & instigated) said to *Varnava* that I was a *crazy woman* & Ania a *nasty woman* etc. — how can he remain after that? You cannot allow such things. These are the devil's last trials to make a mess everywhere & he shant succeed. *Samarin* said highest praise of *Feofan* & *Hermogen,* & wants to put the latter in *Varnava's* place. You see the rotten game of theirs. Some while ago I begged you to change the Gov. he spies upon them, every step *Varnava* took at *Pokrosvk* & what our Fr. does & what telegrams are written, thats *Dzhunkovsky's* work & *Samarin's* excited on through *Nikolasha* by the black women. — *Agafangel* spoke so badly (fr. *Yaroslavl)* — he ought to be sent away *on the retiring list* & replaced by *Sergei F.* who m u s t leave & get out of the *Synod* — *Nikon* ought to be cleaned out of the *Council of the Empire,* where he is a *member* & also out of the *Synod,* he has besides the sin of *Mt. Athos* on his soul. This *Suslik* rightly all said, so as to give the *Synod* a good lesson & strong reprimand for their behaviour, therefore quickly change *Samarin.* Every day he remains, he is dangerous & does mischief, old man is of the same opinion, it is not woman's stupidity — therefore I cried so awfully when I heard they had forced you to name him at the *Headquarters* & I wrote to you in my misery, k n o w i n g *Nikolasha* proposed him because he was my enemy & *Gregory's* & through that yours. —

In conversation Metropolitan Vladimir said (they have made him mad too), when *Varnava* said that *Samarin* was breaking his neck by behaving thus, & that he is not *Over-Procurator* yet. »*The Emperor is no boy and ought to know what he is doing*« & »that you *earnestly begged Samarin* to accept« (I told *Goremykin* then that it was wrong) — well let them see & feel that you are n o t a *boy* & who calumniates people you respect & insults them — insults you, that they dare not call a Bishop to account for knowing *Gregory* — I cant repeat to you all the names they gave our Friend. Pardon my boring you again with all this, but its to show you, that y o u m u s t quickly change *Samarin.* — I shall have to suffer for it if he remains, as I shall get it onto my head, you heard what the Governor said, & here one is not kindly intentioned towards me in some sets & its not the time to drag ones Sovereign or his wife down. Only be f i r m (he begged not to remain long, you remember) & d o n ' t put him into the *Council of the Empire* as a bonbons after he behaved & spoke openly like that about whom we receive & such a tone about you & yr. wishes — that cannot be borne, you have not the right to overlook it. These are the last fights for yr. internal Victory, show them yr. mastery.

Remember, in 6 days he kicked out old *Damansky* (because of *Gregory)* & gave 60.000 for his successor to arrange the appartments — hideous actions.

I invented to-day the aid to the new one — *Prince Zhivakha* you remember him, quite young, knows all about the Church questions, most loyal & religious *(Bari-Bielgorod)* don't you agree?

Clean out all, give *Goremykin* new ministers to work with & God will bless you & their work.

Please Lovebird, and quickly. I wrote to him to give a list, as you asked but he begged you to think of *Sazonov's* successor & *Stcherbatov* he is far too weak, tho' you liked him better this time. I am sure *Voyeikov* (his bosom friend) told him how to be — dont listen to *Voyeikov,* he has been wrong all this heavy time & a bad adviser. — it will pass, he is conceited & got a fright for his own skin. — Oh dear, humanity!

My Image of yesterday, of 1911 with the bell has indeed helped me to »feel« the people — at first I did not pay enough attention, did not trust to my opinion, but now I see the Image & our Friend have helped me grasp people quickly. And the bell would ring if they came with bad intentions & wld. keep them fr. approaching me — there, Orlov, *Dshunkovsky, Drenteln* who have that »strange« fright of me are those to have a special eye upon.

And you my love, try to heed to what I say, its not my wisdom, but a certain instinct given by God *beyond myself* so as to be your help. —

Precious one, I send you the paper one of our wounded wrote by my request, as I was afraid of giving over the wish wrongly — it wld. be good if the regiment could get that bit of ground for building a mausoleum for their fallen officers. —

Perhaps you would tell Fred. to give the order from you to *Stcherbatov* you have not the time for doing all yourself. — The little Image is fr. Ania she went to the Chapel today whilst we were visiting hospitals, both under my protection. The one for 60 officers on the *Horse. Guards Boulevard,* very nice indeed & then to the *Vyborg suburb* between the prisons (a new hospital for the prisoners) wh. was now at once used for 130 men. — so nice & clean — several *Semenovtsi* fr. *Kholm* & rifles etc. & one who had been for a year in Germany. The pavement was atrocious. You see I choose the smart & quite poor places to turn up in — they shall see that I don't care what one says & shall go about as always. Now that am feeling better, I can do it. — Such sunny weather. From *Znamenia* I went in my *Droshki* round the Boulevard to the hospital to get good air in the morning. — Is there a chance of your coming now? — I was thinking about *Novgorod* (don't tell *Voyeikov)* & *Ressin* is making inquiries. By boat, or motor even fr. the broad railway too far, 60 *Verst* — so one must get into the narrow gauged waggon. Sleeping here in the train — reaching there in the morning, lunching there etc. back by 10½ in the evening — because must look at the Cathedral. The new soldiers are there & that makes me doubt whether I ought not rather await yr. return. If so, wire to me, »wait about *Novgorod*« & I shall then. — Our Friend wants me to go about more, but where to? —

Did you copy out his telegr. for yourself on the extra sheet? If not, here it is again:

»*Sept. 7, 1915. Do not fall when in trouble God will glorify by his appearance.*« — *Olga* has a committee this evening. — *Alexei's* train *(Schulenburg)* sticks at *Opukliki* since 4 days, was stopped there *until called to Polotzk;* he asked the Comm. of *Polotzk* by wire, but received no answer yet — are we cut off from there? —

My train returned, said there were lots of sanitaries waiting out there without being able to move, I hope it means that our troops are being brought up there? Then masses of women were brought to work near the lakes, but not told for how long, so that they had no time to take warm clothes, got *wages per day* for the journey, 30 *Kopeeks* & the journey lasted 5 days — are the Governors mad. Never any order here, it drives me to distraction — that lesson we ought to learn fr. the Germans.

Sister Olga's train is bringing many wounded officers & men & 90 *refugees.* I told them always to pick them up on the way. —

Dear me, what a lot one might do — I long to poke my nose into everything (Ella does it with success) — to wake up people, put order into all & unite all forces. All goes by fits & starts — so irregular — so very little energy (my despair, as have enough, no matter if I feel ill even, wh. thank God I don't just now) — am wise & don't do too much. — Now the endless letter must be finished. Do I write too much? Courage — energy — firmness will be rewarded by success, you remember what He said, that the glory of yr. reign is coming & we shall fight for it together, as it means the glory of Russia — you & Russia are one. —

Beloved one, yes, my bed is much softer than yr. camp-bed — how I wish you were here to share it. Only when you are away I dream. 2 weeks & ½ since you left. I bless you & cover you with kisses, my Angel, & press you to my heart. God be with you.

For ever yr. very own old

Sunny.

No. 118.

Tsarskoje Selo, Sept. 10th 1915

My own Sweetheart,

Yes, indeed the news is better — I just looked through the papers. What a blessing if the reinforcements from the south can soon get to their destination; one prays and prays. —

The article about *Varnava* in the papers is untrue, he gave exact answers to all questions and showed yr. telegram about the *salutation.* Last year the *Synod* had all the papers about the miracles and *Sabler* would not have the *salutation* this summer. Your will and order count, make them feel it.

Varnava implores you to h u r r y with clearing out *Samarin* as he and *Synod* are intending to do more horrors and he has to go there again, poor man, to be tortured. Goremykin also finds one must hasten (alas, no list from him yet). One praises the redfaced *Prutchenko* too — only his brother and wife horrid about our Friend. *Goremykin* wants quickly to see you, and before any others when you return, but if you dont soon — he wants to go to you, he is ready to scream at the bishops, *Varnava* said and to send them off. You better send for the old Man. — As one wants a firm Government, instead of the old Man going; clear out the others and get strong ones in. Please, speak seriously about *Khvostov* as Minister of the Interior to *Goremykin* am sure he is the man for the moment, as fears nobody and is devoted to you.

Again an ugly thing about *Nikolasha* I am obliged to tell you. All the Barons sent to the *Headquarters* a B. Benkern to *Nikolasha.* He begged in all their names that these persecutions should cease, because they could not bear them any more. *Nikolasha* answered that he agreed with t h e m , but could do nothing as the orders came from *Tsarskoje Selo.* Is not this too vile. S. Rebinder of the Artillery told it to Alia — Reutern was astonished to see *Suvorin* being received by *Nikolasha.* T h i s m u s t be cleared up, such a lie dare not lie upon you; they must be told that y o u are just to those that are l o y a l and never persecute the innocent. A man who wrote against *Nikolasha* was shut up for 8 months now, there they know how to stop the press, when it touches *Nikolasha.* — When the prayers for you were being read those 3 fasting days, fr. the *Synod,* in front of the *Kazan Cathedral,* 1000 of portraits of *Nikolasha* were being devided out to the crowds. What does t h a t mean? They had intended quite another game, our Friend read their cards in time, and came to save you by entreating you to clear out *Nikolasha* and take over the Command yourself. One hears always more and more of their hideous, treacherous game. *M.* and *S.* spread horrors about me in *Kiev* and that I was going to be shut up in a Couvent — the married daughter of one of the Trepovs was so hurt when they spoke, that she begged to leave tne room. He wrote this to the Css. Schulenburg. Oh Lovy, *Ivanov's* army (some) heard these rumours — is not that a mean scandal? I see *Dzhunkovsky* has gone for an unfixed time to the Caucasus — there: »birds of one feather flock together« what new sin are they preparing? They better take care of their skin there. —

We, i. e. *Olga, Ressin,* Ania and I went to *Peterhof* — we left her at her Parents and drove on to the *local hospital* — clean this time and no very heavy wounded — then to the tiny red cross *station* near the English Embassy, where there were a few officers — then to the new Rathhouse near the lake, where were also wounded — nothing very bad. Took a cup of coffee at the *Taneyev's* and came home. Then *Tatiana Andreievna* came to say goodbye, after wh. Mère Catherine and the Abbess, and talked without end. She brought a paper about flying machines wh. the inventor showed before at the *Headquarters* — it was *approved* and the papers now stick somewhere, so I enclose a paper about it and can you have the thing hurried up. There is a Rubinstein who has given 1000's already, who is willing to give 500.000

for this invention being made, if he receives the same as Manus — pretty these beggings at such a time, charity cant go unbought — so ugly. — Then Mary came and now I am writing and quite gaga — the road tired me in motor. The sea, my sea! Felt, oh, so sad, reminded me of happy peaceful times, our house without you — we passed it — pain in my heart and full of remembrances. — I received sweet letters from Ernie, Onor and Frl. Textor. He gave them Sister Baroness Uxkull who came — he hoped I would see and help her — yr. Mama did not receive her and then I was not asked — a great mistake of hers. These Sisters could have told us about our Prisoners. Ernie thinks so much of you too — I enclose his letter. — Frl. Textor lives at W. to give the children German and English lessons. The heather blooms and it is lovely they say — I will show you his letter, when you come — asks for nothing only full of love. Yr. regiment has better luck than the red Dragoons, who have only one officer not wounded. Moritz youngest son is slowly recovering fr. wounds. V. Giedesel (who was with Sandro in Bulgaria — a dear) has lost 3 sons already. — Onors nephew has also been killed. — The weather was divine to day. I was in the hospital this morning — another *Crimean* is coming. —

Now must send off my letter, high time. —

Every blessing and fondest, tenderest, warmest kisses and endless love fr. yr. own old

Sunny.

Am glad you will see Misha. —

Have you a list of the losses in the guard? All are so anxious, the wives anxious about their husbands — cannot somebody copy them out and send them me. — Tell Fredericksy that young Mme *Baranov* (he was just killed) is fearfully poor, you kept him in the regiment by paying him, now she looses that and *Shulgin* begged me whether something could be done for her, as he was such a good officer. Mme *Lütke* thanks for the flowers I had sent from us both. —

Maria Plautin thanks colossaly. —

No. 119.

Tsarskoje Selo, Sept. 11-th 1915

My own beloved Darling,

It was so grey, that I felt quite sad, but now the sun is trying to pierce its way through the clouds. The colouring of the trees is so lovely now, many have turned yellow, red & copper. Sad to think summer is over & endless winter awaits us soon. It was strange to see the beloved sea, but so dirty — pain filled my heart when I saw the Alexandrie from far & remembered with what joy we always saw her, knowing that she was the means for taking us to our beloved »*Standart*« & *fiords!* Now all but a dream. What are the

Bulgarians up to, why is *Sazonov* such a pancake? It seems to me that the poeple want to side with us & only the Minister & rotten Ferdinand mobilize to join the other countrys so as to squash Servia & throw themselves greedily upon Greece. Get rid of our Minister at Buccarest & the Rumaniens cld. be got to march with us, I am sure. — Is it true that they intend sending *Gutchkov* & some others from Moscou as a deputation to you? A strong railwayaccident in wh. he alone wld. suffer wld. be a real punishment fr. God & well deserved, they go too far, & that fool *Stcherbatov* gained nothing by only blotching out parts of what they said — indeed a rotten governement — wh. wont work with, but against its leader. — I am remaining in bed till luncheon, the motordrive shook me too much & I am tired from seeing i. e. visiting hospitals three days running. — Do so much wonder when you will be able to return & for how many days — how you have arranged with *Alexeiev,* when you leave? — The old man has asked to see me this evening, & as I know he must see you, I have already wired to you. He finds it absolutely indispensible *Sazonov* should at once leave, he told it to *Andronnikov* — another man they propose is *Makarov,* but that won't do, as he did not show himself at all well in the story of *Hermogen.* Now another is the *editor of the »Government Bulletin« Marshal of the Horse, Prince Urussov* an other man, very loyal to you, religious (made our Friend's acquaintance) — that would be best I think & at once. I write all this for you to have it clearly in yr. head — now I suppose he may bring yet candidates. The story of *Varnava* is going too far — he did not go again to the *Synod,* because he will not hear yr. orders mocked at — the *Metropolitan* calls yr. telegram »*foolish telegram*« — such impertinence cannot be borne — you must set yr. broom working & clear out the dirts that has accumulated at the *Synod.* — All this row about *Varnava* is only so as to drag our Friend's name into the *Duma.* When *Samarin* accepted this place he told his set at *Moscou* that he takes it only because he intends to get rid of *Gregory* & that he will do all in his power to succeed. — One betted in the *Duma,* that they would prevent you fr. going to the war. — you did go — they said nobody dare close the *Duma* — you did — now they have betted that you cannot send *Samarin* away — & you will. The Bishops too, that sat there & mocked at yr. orders — you have not had time no doubt to read the articles about the accusation against *Varnava* at the *Synod* about the *worship.* You show yourself the master. We cleared *S. I.* out & her friends shall flie too & with this ridiculous, unloyal, mad idea of saving Russia. Lots of grand words. *Goremykin* must tell him, that you chose him believing him to be a man, who would work for you & the Church & he has turned out a spy upon the doings & telegr.: of *Varnava* & *Gregory* & has posed as an accusing advocate & persecutor — & doubter of your wishes & orders. You are the head & protector of the Church & he tries to undermine you in the eyes of the Church. At once my Love, clear him out & *Stcherbatov* too. This night he sent out a circular to all the papers, that they may print anything they like against the Governement (your governement) — how dare he — only not against you. But they do all in a hidden way, des sousentendu — and he plays fast & loose a very fool indeed. — Please take *Khvostov* in his place. Did you look through his book? He wants very much to see me, looks upon me as the one to save the situation whilst you are away (told it *Andronnikov)* & wants to pour out his heart to me & tell me all his ideas. — He is very energetic, fears no one & is colossally devoted to you, wh. is the chief thing now a days. — His gaffes, one can warn him against making them — he knows the *Duma* poeple well, will not allow them to attack one, he knows how to speak; please Sweetheart seriously think of him, he is not such a coward & rag as *Stcherbatov.* The Government must be set to right & the old man needs good, devoted & energetic men to help him in his old age working; he cannot go on like this.

You must tell him all, ask everything — he is too discreet & generally waits to be asked & then says his impressions or what he knows. Keep him up, show him you need & trust him & will give him new workers — & God will bless the work. — Take a slip of paper & note down what to talk over, last time you forgot about *Khvostov,* & then let the old man have it as a help to remember all questions. — 1) *Samarin,* 2) *Stcherbatov-Synod,* 3) *Sazonov,* 4) *Krivoshein* who is an underhand enemy & false to the old man the whole time. — 5) How to let the Barons know that it was a great untruth *Nikolasha* told them, that he got the orders from *Tsarskoje* to persecute the Barons — that must be cleared up cleverly, delicately. — The old man begs always you should hasten & be decisive; when you give him categoric answers or orders to fulfil its far easier for him & they are forced to listen. — I do bother you, poor wee one, but they come to me & I cant do otherwise for your sake, Baby's & Russias. Being out there, your mind can see all clearly & calmly — I am too calm & firm, only when changes must be made to save further horrors & filth, as that at the *Synod* headed by the soi disant »gentleman« *Samarin* — then I get wild & beg you to hasten. He dare not treat your words like dust, none of the Ministers dare behave as they do after the way you spoke to them. I told you *Samarin* is stupid *insolent fellow* — remember how impertinently he behaved to me at Peterhof last summer about the evacuation question & his opinion of Petersburg in comparison to Moscou etc., he had no right to speak to his Empress as he did — had he wished my good, he would have done all in his power for me, to take it as I wished, & he would have guided & helped me & it would have been a big & popular thing — but I felt his antagonism — as *S. I.* 's friend; & that why he was proposed to you, & not for the Churches good. — I am inconvenient to such types, because I am energetic & stick to my friends wherever they may be. When the *Duma* closed, in a private sitting there, they said filth about *Gregory* Ania & her poor father — so loathsome.

Is that devotion, I ask you? Show yr. fist, chastisen, be the master & lord, you are the *Autocrat* & they dare not forget it, when they do, as now, woe into them. — Over & over let me thank you for your very sweet & dear letter, I was overjoyed to receive it & devoured it up. How glad I am you get lots of nice telegrams. — Thats the proof & your recompense, God will bless you for it, you saved Russia & the throne by that action. — I wish you could have a real good talk with *Shavelsky* about all that has been &

about our Friend — get him to tea à 2. — Ania spoke to him once, but he had his ears filled with horrors & I am sure *Nikolasha* continued thus. —

Olga thanks *Mordvinov* for his letter. — I fear Misha will ask for his wife to get a title — she cant — she left two husbands already & he is yr. only Brother, Paul is of no consequence. — Why is Boris still with you, he ought to be back with his regiment, not so? *Gregory* wrote despairing wires about his son & begged him to be taken into the *United Regiment* wh. we said was impossible, Ania begged *Voyeikov* to do something, as he promised to before & he answered he could not. I understand the boy had to be called in, but he might have got him to a train as sanitary or anything — he always had to do with his hous in the country, an only son, its awfully hard of course. One longs to help without harming Father or Son. — What lovely telegrams he wrote again. — I had old Rauchfuss — we have got masses of *cribs* in these three last months all over Russia for our Society for Mothers & Babies — its a great joy to me to see how all have taken to it so quickly & have realised the gravity of the question, now especially every Baby must be cared for, as the losses are so heavy at the war.

One says the guard has again lost colossally now. —

We drove to *Pavlovsk,* lovely air & so sunny, the beautiful Cosacks with St. George's Crosses follow one. —

Now I must end, Sunshine my beloved One. I long for you, kiss you without end, hold you tightly clasped in my arms.

God bless you & protect you, give you strength, health, courage, surety of your opinion, wisdom & peace.

Ever Nicky mine yr. very own old Wify

Alice.

The Children's joy over your letters is intense, they are all well, thank God.

No. 120.

Tsarskoje Selo, Sept. 12-th 1915

My own beloved One,

It is pouring and dreary. Slept very badly, head aches rather, am still tired from Peterhof & feel my heart, am awaiting Becker. — How I wish the time would come for me to write only simple, nice letters, instead of bothersome ones. But things dont a t a l l go as they should, & the old Man who came to me yesterday evening, was very sad. He longs for you to come quickly, if only for three days, to see all & to make the changes, as he finds it m o r e than difficult working with ministers who make opposition. Things must be put clearly — either he leaves, or he remains & the ministers are changed, wh. of course would be best. He is going to send you a *report* about the press — they go after orders *Nikolasha* gave in July, that one may write whatsoever one likes about the government, only not touch you. When *Goremykin* complains to *Stcherbatov* he throws the fault upon *Polivanov* & vice versa. *Stcherbatov* lied to you when he said one would not print what is said at Moscou. — They go on writing everything. Am so glad you declined seeing those creatures. They don't dare use the word constitution, but they go sneeking round it — verily it would be the ruin of Russia & against your coronation oath it seems to me, as you are a *autocrat,* thank God. — The changes must be made, cant think why the old Man is against *Khvostov* — his Uncle does not much care for him & they say he is a man who thinks he knows everything. But I explained to the old Man that we need a decided caracter, one who is not afraid, he is in the *Duma,* so has the advantage of knowing everybody & will understand how to speak to them & how to protect & defend your government. He proposes nobody, au fond, & we need a »man«. — He begged me to let *Varnava* know that he must not appear at the *Synod* but say he is ill — wh. is the best thing, tho' the papers are furious that he wont appear. But he has told them all & answered everything — great brutes, I cannot call them otherwise. If you could only come, then at once see the Metropolitan & tell him you forbid that subject to be touched & that you insist upon your instructions being fulfilled. He cried of despair when *Samarin* was appointed & now he is completely in his hands — but he must have a strong word from you. Yr. arrival here will be a *punitive expedition* & no rest, poor Sweetheart, but its necessary without delay, they go on writing without ceasing. But they cant propose anybody — *Makarov* — no good — *Arseniev* fr. M. screams against our Fr. — *Rogozin* — hates our friend. — *Prince Urussov* (don't know him) — knows our friend, one says much good of him. My head aches from hunting for men, but anybody rather than *Samarin,* who openly goes against you by his behaviour in the *Synod.*

Can you really not return soon, Lovy, things seem taking a better turn, thank God & will still. Wonder what troops you saw pass. Old man has a sitting of Ministers on Sunday, thats why he cant leave to-day. If you come Thursday, he says he need not go there before, but I find you can see him quieter now & speak over & prepare all for yr. return.

He says *Sazonov* is pitiful to behold, like »une poule mouillée« — what has happened to him? He tells *Goremykin* nothing at all & he m u s t know what is going on. The ministers are rotten & *Krivoshein* goes on working underhand he says — all s o ugly & ungentlemanly; — they need your i r o n w i l l wh. you will show, won't you. You see the effect of yr. having taken over all, well do the same here, i. e. be decided, repremand them v e r y s e v e r e l y for their behaviour & for n o t having listened to yr. orders given at that sitting here — I am more than disgusted with those cowards. — Can Alex. spare you 3 days, soon? Do answer this if you can. You cannot imagine how despairing it is not being able to wire all one would & needs too & not to get an answer. You have not time to answer my questions of wh. there are 100, but always the same ones, as they are pressing

& my head is weary from thinking & seeing things so badly — & beginning to spread in the country. Those types go talking against the government everywhere, etc. & sow the seed of discontent. Before the *Duma* meets in a month, a new strong cabinet must be formed & quicker, so as that they have time to work & prepare together beforehand. — He proposed I should see *Samarin* but what good? The man will never listen to me, & just do the contrary out of opposition & anger — I know him also but too well by his behaviour now, — wh. did not surprise me, as I know he would be thus. — *Goremykin* wants you to return & do all this, but waste no time. You are calm out there, & that is right, but still Sweetest, remember you are a bit slow too in deciding & dawdling is never a good thing. The big girls have gone to the hospital, the 3 young ones are learning, A. is going to town to Alia & her mother till 3, & I shall lie again till luncheon as heart a little enlarged & feel so tired. — Now *Yuzik* must be already at the *Headquarters.* Is it true that we are only 200 *Versts* from *Lemberg* again. Are we to hurry on so much & not come round and squash the Germans? What about Bulgaria? To have them in our flank will be more than rotten, but they have surely bought Ferdinand. —

How is Misha's humour? Kiss the dear boy from me. Have no news yet from Olga somehow her visit was sad — we scarcely got a glimps of her & she left sad & anxious. —

Just received a perfumed letter fr. *Olga Palei.* Paul is better — she at last had news fr. their boy, it took him a week to get to the *transport* of his regiment & now he hopes to find the regiment. — I beleive the lancers are not far fr. *Baranovitchi;* a river one speaks of near there, where was heavy fighting — w h a t fighting everywhere!

Mackensen is not the one we knew. There is a Fürst Bentheim at *Irkutsk* (a sort of relation of Marie Erbachs). Ernie asks in Max name whether there would be any possibility for him to be exchanged — he seems to be the last of his family — perhaps somebody of ours cld. be returned in exchange. He only asks like that, not knowing whether its possible. I shall let Rostovtzev know the same thing, — I doubt it being possible unless he gives his word of honour not to fight any more against any of the allies — only under that condition, I find, one can change him. I shall write this to Rost. & whom it concerns will know what to do, I have no idea whom one can ask for in return, nor whether its allowed. — About the gasses Ernie is also disgusted, but he says that when he was near Reims beginning of Sept. last year, the English used the gasses there — & German chemical industries being better, they made worse gasses. — Ania was at *the Church of »Joy to all grieving«* in town & brought this little Image for you. — Fancy our surprise — suddenly *Kussov* turned up. All his cavalry is being sent down to *Dvinsk* & during their move he flew off here, arrived in town this morning, probably goes on to-morrow, meets his wife & off to *Dvinsk* to meet his regiment. He had heavy losses — is in despair with Yuri Trubetskoy who makes fault upon fault & others dare not say anything, because one says you particularly care for him (wh. Kussov doubts).

Thanks to him Kussov's men got surrounded, because Yury took the three battalions of infantry away wh. guarded them, for himself — but they got through & only many horses were taken, as it was the place where they were standing together — he told his mind rather clearly to *Trubetskoy.* He came flying off to know how things were going, as letters never reached him & he wanted to hear all. Is already disgusted with town & furious with the »rotten atmosphere«. Was sorry you sent *Mikheyev,* because he is so very unrepresentive & does not know how to collect all round him & speak & thank in yr. name. — He saw the *Kabardintsi* passing a little while ago. Asked questions without end & says the »*spirit*« in the army splendid. It does one good & refreshes one seeing such a man straight from there — one also gets musty fusty here, tho' I fully trust & believe all must go well, if God will give us the necessary wisdom & energy. — Don't you find Baby's writing is getting very nice & tidy? I remained quietly at home to-day, saw Mme Zizi too. — Why is Boris not with his regiment? 3 of our Cav. Divisions got the order to break through the Germans wh. they did & are in their rear now, *Tatiana's* regiment is there too. —

Blessings & kisses without end & tenderest love, Sweetheart, lovy mine, fr. yr. very own old

Wify.

No. 121.

Tsarskoje Selo, Sept. 13-th 1915

My very own Treasure,

I am glad you have fine weather, here it is real autumn, there was a little sun an hour ago and now there is again a grey haze. — The 4 Girls have gone to early Church — »*Engineer Mechanic*« came, so keeps me company. So you cannot come before the end of the week, I feared so, as things are still very serious near *Dvinsk* — but how brave both sides are — God help and strenghten our dear troops. — The papers continue aggravating me, discussing and groaning that there will be a censure — and that ought to have been regulised months ago. — There is a messenger leaving for England this afternoon, so I must quickly profit to write to Victoria — this I will finish later in the day, as usual. — *Sazonov* says it concerns *Alexeiev* the exchange of prisoners, so I don't know what to do about Fürst Bentheim, I cannot ask for a German (and I believe not wounded or long ago well by now) — whom could one exchange him with? — I am glad you wrote a good letter to the old Man, it will help him in his difficult task. — 3 weeks to-day that you arrived at the *Headquarters* — when is *Nikolasha* going to *Tiflis?* To-day it is put in the papers that *Dzhunkovsky* is going to the Army and not any more under *Alexeiev's* orders for Sanitary questions.

Sweet Manny mine — am always in thoughts with you, yearning to see what you look and feel like; I have no doubt much better than when you were here. I told you about *Y. Trubetskoy* yesterday, so as that one should have an eye upon him, if he really is so very little famous and confuses them all. Am I meddling? I don't mean to, I only repeat what *Kussov* said, as I know he tells me things in the hope I give all over. — What news fr. the Black Sea and Baltic?

I spent the afternoon on my sopha in the corner of my big room and Ania read to me, tea we had at 4 and then the 5 Children went to Ania for an hour to see some Children. I have crawled into bed, so as to go to church, service to-day is from 6—8, and I shall go at about 7, more I have not the strength for, as cannot take drops and feel tired, but to-day the heart was not enlarged. A dreary day. — In Moscou Mme *Gardinsky* finds the things better than they expected, *Petrograd* she finds horrid just now and I think all agree. — I gave Zizi papers about *John Maximovitch* and how they found his tomb, and she was grateful and emotioned as it showed her all in quite another light, and now I made Ania send it to O. *Father Alex.* — I want others to understand the thing and the wrong behaviour of the *Synod.* If they choose to find you had not the right to give such an order, nevertheless, all the more they ought to have stood up for it, legalised it still from their side, instead of purposely going against your orders — and all that simply out of opposition and to harm *Varnava* and throw again a bad light on our Friend. —

My letter is dull, I have seen nobody interesting. — A. is going over to the big Palace for a week, so as to have her rooms cleaned, the shaky plafond seen to and windows arranged for winter. Danini is going to see it! She can meanwhile go through a cure of electrifying and strong light wh. we have next door in the hospital and *Vladimir Nikolaievitch* will do it, and her *Feodosia Stepanovna* works there too and does massage for the wounded officers. —

I enclose a letter fr. Olga, and am sending you flowers again — the frezia last very long and every bud will open in your vase. —

The leaves are turning very yellow and red, I see it from the windows of my big room. — Sweetheart, you never give me an answer about Dmitri, why you dont send him back to his regiment, as Paul had hoped; — he worrys so about the boy wasting his best years and at such a grave moment, doing nothing. It does not look well, no Granddukes are out, only Boris from time to time, the poor Constantins boys always ill. — I do so hope to get your letter before closing this, so I will rest and then finish it up. —

Well I must send it off. I kiss and bless you over and over again, my very own beloved Treasure, Sunshine.

I cover you with tender kisses — God bless and keep you.

A tender kiss

fr. yr. very own old

Wify.

No. 122.

Tsarskoje Selo, Sept. 14-th 1915

My own beloved Darling,

I found your dear telegram this morning upon getting up, I was so grateful as had been anxious getting no news all day. Being very tired I went to bed at 11.20. yr. wire left the *Headquarters* at 10,31 and reached here 12.10. Thank God the news is better. But what will you do for the army, so as not to have *Alexeiev* the only responsible one? Do you get *Ivanov* to come here and *Stcherbatov* to replace him out there? You will be calmer and *Alexeiev* wont have to carry the responsability all alone. — So after all you have to move to *Kaluga* — what a nuisance, tho' from here I should say the distance is less than now, only you are so far from the troops. But if *Ivanov* helps *Alexeiev* then you could go straight from here to see some troops at least. —

What has been going on at sea, I know nothing and read this morning of the losses of *the Captain of the 1-st rank, S. S. Viazemsky (heroic death in battle)* and the officers and men of the *ship* announce it, and his body is being brought *from the Baltik Station.* Then *Capt. of the 2-nd rank, Vl. Al. Svinin* also *fell as a hero.* What does this mean? *Peter Vasilievitch* told the Children some days ago that the *Novik* had been in battle, but as one keeps the naval news out of the papers, one feels anxious to know what it means. When you are not here of course I only get my news in the morning out of the »*Novoye Vremya*«. If there should be anything good, do wire it, as one hears often false news wh. of course I tell all not to believe.

How is *Voyeikov,* I cannot forget his madness here and horrid behaviour to Ania. Do take care that he does not take things too much in hand there and does not meddle, as poor old Fred. is old and, alas, becoming rather foolish, the other with his dominating spirit and being most ambitious and sure of himself, and try to fulfil functions wh. don't concern him. Don't you need somebody else still because of the foreigners, or deputations, or orders to be given over, wh. you have not the time to do yourself — a General aide de camp or something like that? — Have you got rid of useless people there? I am glad Boris has gone back again. — I hope he can get the lists of the losses as the wives are in all states. —

One says *Leichtenberg* is wounded, I forget what regiment he commands but its the Preobr. ladies especially who are nervous. — I wonder what troops you saw the other day. — Now the old Man is with you. Its stupid one prints when he comes to me, thats fr. town, my people don't know it even, as people get angry I mix in — but its my duty to help you. Even in that I am found fault with, sweet Ministers and society, who criticise all, and themselves are occupied with things not concerning them at all. Such is the unedifying world. — Still I am sure you hear far less gossip at the *Headquarters* and I thank God for it. — Church began at 6—8 yesterday, Baby and I came at 7¼.

Slept badly, am tired and my head rather aches, so keep in bed till luncheon. Paul's asked to come for tea.

Oh my sweet One, thanks and thanks ever so tenderly for yr. sweet letter of the 11-th, I received it with intensest gratitude and joy. It has been kissed over and over again and reread any amount of times. Yes indeed, when will that happy moment arrive, when we shall be cosily seated together in my mauve room! We continue drinking tea in the big room, tho' by the time Paul left at 6¼, it was already quite dark. —

Yes, the changes of ministers. In the train *Kussov* went with *Stcherbatov* and he called the old man »*crazy old man*« thats going far; some in the *Duma* want *Stcherbatov* in *Goremykin's* place, and I understand them because they could do whatsoever they like with him.

Paul was disgusted with the goings on at Moscou and the deputation that wished to present themselves to you! —

For the old woman's letter, warmest thanks — it pleased me very much and I read it aloud to Ania — Paul does not care for *Mrazovsky,* said he is such a *cad,* he remembers him fr. his service — I remember he screamed at the *Guard's Convoys* once, because a man cld. not say the words of the anthem by heart; the poor Grenadier divisions were so very little famous at the war now. Is it true *Kuropatkin,* got it, or are those gossips? Wonder how he will show himself this time — God grant alright — being in a lawer position it may go better. Paul asked why *Nikolasha* is still in the Country and whether it was true you wrote he was to rest in the Caucasus, at *Borjom* — I said yes, and that you had allowed him 10 days at *Pershino.* Lovy, order him south quicker, all sorts of bad elements are collecting round him and want to use him as their flag (God wont permit it) but safer he should be quicker in the Caucasus, and you said 10 days and to-morrow its 3 weeks he left the *Headquarters.* — Be firm in that too, please. I am so glad, that Paul has realised the game *Nikolasha* was to play — he rages about the way *Nikolasha's* a. d. c. speak. — I am glad you made *Voyeikov* understand things — he is so obstinate and selfsure and a friend of *Stcherbatov's.* — How happy I am you saw some artillery — what a recompense to them. — Keep Misha with you still, do. — Paul again repeated, that he hopes very earnestly that you will send D. to his regiment, he finds the life he now leads his ruin, as he has absolutely nothing to do and wastes his time, wh. is perfectly true. —

If ever you get any news of the hussars, do let me know, as Paul is anxious, his boy being now in the regiment. Paul is now well, but very weak, pale and thin. — Old *Aunt Sasha I.* has come to town and will take tea with us on Wednesday, Xenia and *Sandro* lunch that day with us too. —

The news to-day about our allies is splendid, if true — thank goodness if they are beginning to work now, it was hard time. And to have taken 24 artillery and made thousands of prisoners, but thats quite beautiful! — I do find it so wrong, that the Ministers do not keep to themselves all the discussions, wh. go on in the *Council of Ministers.* Once questions are decided, its early enough to know about them. But our uneducated, tho' they imagine themselves intellectual public, read up everything, only grasp a quarter and then set to discussing all, and the papers find fault with everything — hang them!

Miechen wrote to ask again about Plotho, whether anything can be done. — I do thoroughly bore you. — In sweet *Petrograd* one said you were here some days — now — that *Gregory* is at the *Headquarters,* — they are really becoming always more cretinised, and I pitty you when you return. But we shall be wild with joy to have you back again, if ever so short — just to hear your precious voice, see yr. sweet face and hold you long, long in my yearning arms. — My head and eyes ache, so I cant write any more now. Goodbye, Sweetheart, Nicky love. God bless and protect you and keep you fr. all harm. I cover you with kisses.

Ever yr. very own old wify

Alix.

I feel quite sad without our hospital, where I have not been since Thursday. —

Ania has gone over to the big palace. — Lovy, are you sending people of your suite to the fabrics? Please don't forget it. —

My »*Alexandrovtsi*« are near *Dvinsk* and have rather heavy losses amongst the men. —

The Children all kiss you, Marie is overjoyed with your letter. —

Yuzik never went to the *Headquarters,* the children imagined it. —

I like the story about the hunt for the germans near *Orsha;* our Cosacks would have found them fast enough. Are they aiming at *Riga* again? Lovy sweet, me wants you, oh so, so much, precious Darling. Your letters and telegrams ary my life now. — Kiss dear Misha, Dmitri.

My love to the old Man and *N. P.*

Think over about *Ivanov* sweet one — I think you would feel calm — or if he were with *Alexeiev* at the *Headquarters* and then you would be free to move about — and when you remain longer at the *Headquarters* he could go round inspecting all and give you news how things are going and have an eye on all, and his presence would be good everywhere. —

Sleep well, I bless and kiss you!

No. 123.

Tsarskoje Selo, Sept. 15-th 1915

My very own precious Darling,

Grey and raining & quite cold. Am still not feeling famous & head continues aching rather — nevertheless I have a committee for our prisoners in Germany. A private society all over Russia now has begun the same thing, instigated by *Suvorin,* as he finds Pr. Galitzin does not work enough — I do not like the idea as its only so as to hinder me, instead of asking to become part of our society. —

Not feeling well, I have been unable to go to old *Arseniev's services* but shall go either to-morrow evening to the *funeral* & *service* at *Znamenia* or to the funeral there Thursday morning. I sent a cross of flowers from us both & wrote to poor little Nadinka & sent expression of your sympathy to her brothers. — A bit of old history dies with him. I at once gave over yr. order about the papers & letters he had, wh. belonged to yr. library. —

To-day it was put in the papers about the naval losses & now I understand all. And how good the French & English at last began — & with success, may they continue thus — it is as they had promised in September. But what obstinate fighting on our side, despairing feeling that taking & retaking of places & positions several times running. —

Its sad you will have to go to *Kaluga,* wh. is such a big town & yet further away — but I suppose on account of the railway line? — So strange you should have lived at different places & gone through so much there & that I do not know them & had no share on yr. life there. —

Lovy, can one have an eye upon what is going on at *Pershino* not good rumours come from there. —

How I wish I had something interesting, cheery to tell you, instead of harping always on the same subject. —

Remember to keep the Image in yr. hand again & several times to comb yr. hair with His comb before the sitting of the ministers. Oh how I shall think of you & pray for you more than ever then, Beloved One. — Ania sends you her love. — One says Theo *Nirod* has left the service so as to follow *Nikolasha.* I find he is taking far too big a suite of a. d. c. yr. g. ad. & Orlov — its not good coming with such a court & clique, & I very much dread they will try to continue making messes. — God grant only that nothing shld. succeed in the Caucasus, & the people show their devotion to you & allow no playing of a grand part — I fear Militza & her wickedness — but God will protect against evil.

Well, the sitting went off allright, 10 people. I took Olga to sit near me & then she will get more accustomed to see people & hear what is going. She is a clever child, but does not use her brains enough. Before that I had *Kussov* for an hour, because he would not go away without having seen me once more. Quite disgusted with town & so pained by everything & that my name is always mentioned, as tho' I had cleared *Orlov* & *Dzhunkovsky* away because of our Fr. etc. He began to have a constant eye upon the going on in the Caucasus, that they should not spoil everything there & to send people to find out fr. time to time to »feel the atmosphere« — he certainly, one sees, has a very bad opinion of them all. *Stcherbatov* told him in the train that *Goremykin* is a *decrepit old man* (not »mad« as Ania said) & that he finds one must make *concessions,* wh. *Kussov* said to him would be most dangerous, as one gives a finger & the whole arm is cought hold of. People want *Stcherbatov* instead of *Goremykin,* I understand them, as he is weak & one can do anything & he is like a weathercock, alas. — Benkendorf let me know, that he is sending Gerbel to Moscou on account of the demenagement — that means yours I suppose. How sad, that you really have to go so far away & be near that rotten Moscou. — Ania went to town to her Parents till 5 — she took Groten to *Nat. Br.* and back again, he enjoyed the change after the sick room. —

Am s o anxious, how it will be with the ministers — now you cant change them once they come there & its so essential, only you must get a look at the others first. Please remember *Khvostov.* —

You know my committee will have to ask the government for big sums for our prisoners, we shall never have enough, & the number will be, alas, several millions — its most necessary, otherwise bad elements will profit & say we are not thinking of them, they are forgotten & many bad things can be inculcated into them, as amongst our prisoners for sure there are rotten red creatures.

The *organisation. of the Union of Cities* are also forming a society for the same thing, that makes 3 — we must keep in contact with them. Do take everything in hand, so as to say afterwards that the government does nothing, & they everything, the same for the wounded & *refugees* — they turn up & help everywhere — & their deligates need w a t c h i n g. —

Now goodbye my love, I am tired & head & eyes ache. —

Goodbye, dear Beloved, my own sweet husband, joy of my heart — I cover you with tender longing kisses. —

Ever yr. very own old Wify.

Please, give this other letter enclosed to Misha.

My love to old man & *N. P.* How are you contented with *Vilna,* & *Dvinsk,* & *Baranovitchi,* — are things going as you wish?

Sleep well & feel my warm presence. —

No. 124.

Tsarskoje Selo, Sept. 16th 1915

My very own beloved Darling,

Ever such tender kisses and thanks for your treasure of a letter. Ah, how I love to hear fr. you, over and over I reread your letters and kiss them. Shall we really soon have you here — it seems to be too good to be true. It will then be four weeks we are separated — a rare thing in our lives, we have been such lucky creatures and therefore one feels the parting all the more. And now when times are so very hard and trying, I long quite particularly to be near you with my love and tenderness, to give you cheer and courage and to keep you up to being decided and energetic. — God help you my beloved One, to find the right issue to all the difficult questions — this is my constant earnest prayer. But I fully believe in our Friend's words that the glory of your reign is coming, ever since you stuck to your decision, against everybody's wish — and we see the good result. Continue thus, full of energy and wisdom, feeling more sure of yourself and heeding less to the advice of others. *Voyeikov* did not rise in my opinion this summer, I thought him cleverer and less frightened. He has never been my weakness, but I appreciate his practical brain for simple affairs and orderliness. But he is too selfsure and that has always aggravated me and his mother in law. All this must have been a good lesson to him, lets hope. Only he sticks too much to *Stcherbatov,* who is a null — tho' he may be a nice man — but I fear that he and *Samarin* are one. — Heart and soul I shall be praying for you — may the committee go off well — they made me mad last time, and when I looked through the window I did n o t like their faces and I blessed you over and over again from far. God give you force, wisdom and power to impress them, and to make them realise how badly they have fulfilled your orders these three weeks. You are the master — and not *Gutchkov, Stcherbatov, Krivoshein, Nikolai III* (as some dare call *Nikolasha) Rodzianko, Suvorin* — — they are nothing and y o u a r e a l l , *anointed by God.* —

I am too happy that Misha is with you, thats why I had to write to him — your very own brother, its just his place, and the longer he stops with you, away from her bad influence the better it is and you will get him to see things with your eyes. Do speak often about Olga, when you are out together, don't let him think badly of her. As you have much to do, tell him simply to write for you to her to tell her what you are doing — that may break the ice between them. Say it naturally, as tho' you never imagined it could be otherwise. I hope he is at last nice with good *Mordvinov* and does not cut that devoted, loving soul who tenderly loves him.

I do so wonder, what the English wrote after you took over the command, I see no Engl. papers, so have no idea. They and the French really seem continuing to push forwards; thank goodness, that they at last could begin and let us hope it will draw some troops away from our side. After all its colossal what the Germans have to do, and one cannot but admire how well and systematically all is organised — did our »mashene« work as well as theirs, wh. is of long training and preparation and had we the same amount of railways, war would for sure already have been over. Our Generals are not well enough prepared — tho' many were at the Japanese war, and the Germans have had no war since ages. How much there is to learn from them, wh. is good and necessary for our nation and other things one can turn away from with horror. There was little news in the papers, and you wired last night that the news was good, so that means that we are firmly keeping them at bay. — There are 9 degr. this morning, and it is grey and rainy, not inviting weather. —

Little Nadinka Arseniev is coming to me this morning — poor girl, she was so touched by my letter and yr. sympathy I expressed them all, that she begged me to see her, as none had written so kindly. Poor, foolish child, what will become of her and her brother with all their old nurses and governesses. Her Father was everything to her in life. —

All my thoughts are with you, Sweetheart and those odious Ministers, whose opposition makes me rage — God help you to impress them with yr. firmness and knowledge of the situation and yr. great disapprouval of their behaviour — wh. at such a moment is nothing else but treacherous. But personally I think you will be obliged to change *Stcherbatov, Samarin* probably longnosed *Sazonov* and *Krivoshein* too — they wont change and you cannot keep such types to fight against a new *Duma.*

How one is tired of all these questions — the war is quite enough and all the misery it has brought and now one must think and work to set all to rights and see that nothing is wanted for the troops, wounded, cripples, families and *refugees.* — I shall anxiously await a telegram fr. you, tho' you wont be able to put much in it. —

I am glad my long letters don't bore you and that you feel cosy reading them. I cannot not talk with you on paper at least, otherwise it would be too hard, this separation and all the rest wh. worries one. —

Gregory telegraphed that *Suslik* shld. return and then made us understand that *Khvostov* wld. be good. You remember, he went once to see him (I think by yr. wish) to *N. Novgorod.* — I do so long for at last things to go smoother and let you feel you can quite give yourself up to the war and its interests. — How do you think about what I wrote of *Ivanov* as aid, so as that *Alexeiev* wont carry all the responsability when you are off and on away, here or inspecting the troops, wh. I do wish you could soon do — en passant, without preparation by motor fr. a bigger place — nobody will watch 2 motors or 3 even and you could rejoice yr. heart and theirs. — Xenia and *Sandro* lunch, *Aunt Sasha* comes to tea and then, I think, I must go for the *carrying out of the body* of *Arseniev* as thats not long and then to-morrow to the funeral at *Znamenia.*

I am so glad the flowers arrive fresh — they cheer up the room and they come out of my vases with all my love and tenderness. — I wonder, whether you asked *Stcherbatov* what he meant by telling you that. nothing wld. be printed in the papers about the speeches at Moscou, when they wrote whatsoever they wished. Coward that he is! —

I am choosing photos. I made, so as to have an album printed for Xmas (like A. Alex.'s) for charity, and I think it will sell well, as the small albums with my photos sold at once here this summer — and in the Crimea. —

Went for a drive to *Pavlovsk* with Anastasia, Marie and Ania, — the weather was lovely, the sun shone and all glittered like gold, a real treat such weather. At first I placed candles before the Virgin's Image, and St. Nicolas at *Znamenia* and prayed fervently for you. Church was being cleaned up, palms being stood and blue carpets arranged for poor Arseniev. *Aunt Sasha* took tea and chattered a lot and abused nobody, I could not keep her long as wanted to go with *Olga* to the *funeral procession* — of course because of the old woman we were late and they were just carrying him out, so we followed with Nadinka till the street and he was put on the funeral car and then we came home, as I go to-morrow to the funeral. Stepanov, — Ella had sent, — *Skariatin,* her old brother was there, Balashov; the 2 sons, *Benkendorf, Putiatin, Nebolsin* and 2 officers of the Naval corps. — Nadinka had been with me in the morning — talked a lot and did not cry, very caressing and grateful. She begs you whether she might remain on living in the little house with her poor brother, as they lived there so long with the Parents and their graves are at *Tsarskoje.*

— Perhaps one might for the present at least, don't you think so? Ella wrote and wishes me to give over how much she thinks of you and with what love and constant prayers. I send you a paper of hers wh. read through and find out the truth about it, please — *Voyeikov* can do that, or still better from your new staff. — I don't need the paper again. —

How one longs to fly away together and forget all — one gets at times so weary — my *spirit* is *good* but so disgusted with all one says. I fear *Gadon* is playing a bad part at *Elagin,* because one says the conversations there against our Friend are awfull — old Mme Orlov had heard this — she knows ladies who go there. When you see poor Motherdear, you must rather sharply tell her how pained you are, that she listens to slander and does not stop it, as it makes mischief, and others wld. be delighted, I am sure, to put her against me — people are so mean. — How I wish Misha could be a help in that. — Precious one we met some of the Cosacks riding at Pavlovsk and I loved them not only for themselves, but because they had seen and guarded you and been in battle. —

Beloved, I must end. God Almighty bless and protect, guard and guide you now and ever.

I kiss you with endless tenderness and fathomless love, ever yr. very own

Sunny.

Xenia looks better, they told nothing interesting.

So anxious how all went off.

No. 125.

Tsarskoje Selo, Sept. 17-th 1915

My very own beloved Darling,

It was with a feeling of intense relief, that I got your dear telegram telling me that the committee went off alright & that you strongly told them your opinion into their faces. God recompense you for this my treasure. You cannot imagine how hard it is not being with you, near you at such times, not knowing what is being discussed, hearing such horrors here.

Deary, *Khvostov* came to Ania again & entreated to see me, so I shall to-day. From all he told her one sees he thoroughly understands the situation & that with skill & cleverness, he thinks, one can manage to set all to rights. He knows that his Uncle & *Goremykin* are against him, i. e. they are afraid of him as he is very energetic. But he is above all devoted to you & therefore offers his services to you, to try him & see whether he cannot help. He esteems the old man very much & would not go against him. Once already now he stopped the question in the *Duma* about our Friend in time — now they intend bringing it up as one of the first questions. *Samarin* & *Stcherbatov* spread so much about *Gregory* & *Stcherbatov* showed your telegrams, our Friends & *Varnava's* to heaps of people — fancy the hideousness (about *John Maximovitch)* of such an act — private telegrams — this *Khvostov* told — &

Varnava too, how did they dare take the telegrams, when the people at the telegr. office have to take oaths — consequently it came through *Dzhunkovsky* before, the governor, *Stcherbatov* & *Samarin* (just as *Varnava* already told me) — he will put a stop to this, knows all the parties in the *Duma* & will know how to talk to them. He proposes his Uncle (Minister of Justice) instead of *Samarin* being a very religious man & knowing much about the Church, & in his place *Senator Krasheninnikov,* whom you have sent to *Moscou* to investigate things & they say everybody praises him highly. Now that *Gregory* advises *Khvostov* I feel its right & therefore I will see him. He got an awful shock as in the evening papers one said *Krizhanovsky* (is that the name) had left for the *Headquarters,* he is a very bad man & you very much always disliked him & I told the old Man so — God forbid him having advised him again.

Did you look through *Khvostov* book? only as soon as you can come & quickly make the changes, they will go on working against our Friend & that is a great evil. He will not play fast & loose with the press like *Stcherbatov* but watch it & stop whenever necessary wrong articles. Its madning not to know what you think, what you are deciding — its a cross going through this anguish fr. far — & perhaps you are making no changes until you return & I am uselessly worrying. Only wire a word to quieten me. If no ministers yet changed — simply wire »no changes yet«, & if you are thinking about Khvostov say »I remember the tail« & if not »dont need the tail«, but God grant you will think well of him — therefore I receive him as he begs for it quicker — why he believes in my wisdom & help I don't know, it only shows he wishes to serve you & yr. dynasty against those brigands & screamers. — Oh my Love, how dear you are to me, how infinitely do I long to help you & be of real use — I do so pray to God always to make me be yr. Guardian Angel & helper in everything — some look at me as that now — & others cannot find nasty enough things to say about me. Some are afraid I am meddling in state affairs (the ministers) & others look upon me as the one to help as you are not here *(Andronnikov, Khvostov, Varnava* & some others) that shows who is devoted to you in the real sense of the word — they will seek me out & the others will avoid me — is it not true, Sweetheart?

Do read the 36-th Psalm, it is so lovely & strengthening & consoling. — Ah me loves Zoo so, so, so much & so passionately.

Only 6 degrees, but such a glorious, sunny morning — a real gift of Gods. — Slept midling, got off only after 3, sad thoughts haunted me. — Why was *Kaluga* chosen, so far to the south? Do you pass by *Pskov* coming here, so as to see *Russky* & perhaps some troops?

How disgusting that *Gutchkov, Riabushinsky, Weinstein* (a real Jew for sure) *Laptev, Zhunkovsky* have been chosen into the *Council of the Empire* by all those brutes. Indeed one will have nice work with them. *Khvostov* hopes that in 2,3 months one can put all into order with cleverness & decision.

Ah, if he could but be the one to do it, even if the old man is against him — from fright. One can be sure he will act carefully, & once he intends standing up for our Friend, God will bless his work & his devotion to you. — the others *Samarin* & *Stcherbatov* sell us simply — cowards!

I see also *Prince Tumanov* instead of *Frolov* will be here — thats surely a good choice. Keep always an eye on *Polivanov,* please.

The painter *Makovsky* has had a horrible accident, his horse bolted & flew into a tram — he lies in a hospital with concussion of the brain & a cut on his head. — Now I must quickly get up & dress for the *service* of old *Arseniev.*

Mass begins at 10, so we shall go at 11 — I take *Olga* & *Tatiana* too. — Well. Sweetie, I have talked with »the tail« for an hour & am full of the best impressions. I was honestly, rather anxious, as A. is sometimes carried off for a person — but we talked over every possible subject & I came to the conclusion, that to work with such a man would be a pleasure. Such a clear head, understanding so perfectly the gravity of the situation, & understanding h o w one must fight against it. That is much, as here one criticises & rarely proposes antedotes. He is also of course horrified that *Gutchkov* & *Riabushinsky* have got into the *Council of the Empire* — it is indeed a scandle — & one knows *Gutchkov's* work is against the dynasty. I wish you could get him for a good talk. — Entre autre he told me, that *Stcherbatov* shows about all yr. telegr. & our Friends to whomsoever he wishes — many are disgusted & others enchanted. W h a t right has he to potter in his E.'s private affairs & have the telegraphs shown him? How do I know if he wont watch ours to, after that you can, alas, never more call him a gentleman or honest. *Krivoshein* is too well acquainted with *Gutchkov* being married to a lady fr. Moscou (also of the merchant families & that makes one). — I have so much in my head, that I don't know what to begin with nor what to tell. —

In any case he finds you must quicker change the ministers, above all *Stcherbatov* & *Samarin* as the old man cannot stand with them opposite to the *Duma.* Now, having spoken with him — I can honestly advise you to take him w i t h o u t a n y fear. He talks well & does not hide this fact, wh. is a plus, as one needs people to speak easily & be ready with a word to answer back at once & to the point. He could fight that duel with *Gutchkov* & God would bless him, I think. Of course he had too much tact & was too clever to hint about himself — he only thanked me many times for having allowed him to pour out all that was on his soul, as he puts his hope & trust on me to help for the good cause for you & Baby & Russia. All is in *Moscou* & *Petrograd* wh. is bad — but, the government must look ahead & prepare for after the war & this question he finds one of the most serious. And if he stands in the *Duma,* he must for his country's sake say all this things & then unwillingly again he will show up the weakness & not thinking beforehand (what abominable English) of the Government. When the war is over, all those 1000 of men working in fabrics for the army will sit without work & of course be a discontented lot to do with — therefore already now that must all be thought of, all the places, fabrics written down, the quantity of working hands etc. & settled what one will give them then to do, not to leave them in the street — & that will take long to prepare & think out & is of greatest gravity wh. of course is absolutely true. Then will be so many discontented elements, now they have money, then the troops return, the men to the villages, many ill & maimed, many whose patriotism & *spirit* now keep them up, will then be lowspirited & dissatisfied & act badly on the workmen, therefore it is of them one must think — & one sees he would do it. Wonderfully clever, does not matter if he is a bit selfsure, its not offensively noticed — only an energetic devoted man, who yearns to help you & his country. Then the preparations beforehand for the elections into the *Duma* (later) — the bad prepare, & so must the good »canvass«, as one says in England. — He says Mme *Stolypin* is trying hard for Tatiana's Neidhardt, hoping to play a part again herself — but he finds him quite incapable. You would enjoy working with this man & you would not have to be keeping him up, pushing him on — with you here or there, one feels he wld. work just as honestly. He got safely through in his governments during the revolution (& shot at). It seems it was he who asked to have the *relics* of *Paul Obnorsky* arranged, I had quite forgotten. — He says the old man is afraid of him because he is old & cannot bend into new ideas (as you yourself told me) & does not realise that one cannot do without new things & must count with them & cannot ignor them. The *Duma* exist — there is nothing to be done, & with such a hard worker, the old man would get on alright. — Excellent you did not see *Rodzianko,* at once their noses went down — you shut the *Duma* wh. they thought you wld. not dare to — all quite right. Now you dont, thank God, receive the Moscou deputation, all the better — again they intend asking, & don't you give in, else it looks as tho' you acknowledge their existence (whatever you may even say to them). That you went to the war was splendid, & he is horrified that people dared be so blind & unpatriotic & frightened as to be against it. Sees the way how to act with the press, & not as *Stcherbatov* has been playing with it. —

Now I must end, Lovy, its 7 o'clock — I have written all this in half an hour so excuse atrocious writing.

Really, my Treasure, I think he is the man & our Fr. hinted to A. in his wire; — I am always careful in my choice — but I have not the feeling wh. I had to *Stcherbatov* when he came to me. And he understands one must watch *Polivanov* since *Gutchkov* has got into the *Council of the Empire,* is not oversure of him. He sees & thinks like us — he did nearly all the talking. — Try him now, because *Stcherbatov* must leave, a man who openly shows about your telegrams & *Gregory's* wh. he has kidnapped & *Samarin* too — are utterly unworthy ministers & no better than *Makarov* who showed my letter to our Friend, to others too — & *Stcherbatov* is a rag & stupid. — If the old man grumbles — does not matter — wait & see how he proves himself to be, worse than *Stcherbatov* he cannot be, but I think 1000 time better, God grant, that I am not mistaken & I honestly believe I am not. I prayed before seeing him, as was rather frightened of the talk. Looks one straight into the eyes. —

I drove with my 5 girls to *Pavlovsk,* glorious weather.

Were $1\frac{1}{2}$ hour in Church, Nadinka held herself well. — *Petia* hopes still to see you here, then must go South for his lungs. —

Blessings & kisses without end. *Khvostov* has refreshed me, my spirit was not down, but I yearned to see a »man« at last — & here I saw & heard him. And you together would keep each other going. —

I bless you my Angel, God bless you & the holy Virgin.

Cover you with longing, loving, tender kisses,

Ever, huzy mine, yr. very own old

Sunny.

Nobody is any the wiser I saw him. —
Anastasia intensely proud & happy with yr. letter. —
Bow to Fredericks & *N. P.*
Love to Misha & Dimitri.

No. 126.

Tsarskoje Selo, Sept. 17th 1915

My own beloved Angel,

Only a word before going to sleep. Have been so anxious all evening because I got no telegram from you, at last whilst my hair was being done it came at 5.m to 12 — think, how slow it went, it left the *Headquarters* at 9.56 & reached here 11.30, & I fool got nervous & anxious. I sent you two wires because of *Khvostov* & hoped you would mention a wee word. I asked you by letter some days ago about seeing him as he wanted it & you did not answer, & now he begged again before going to the country & therefore I wired it in the morning, & at 8.30 after seeing him. — So thankful, you say news continues good — that means very much, & people's spirits will rise. — Misha wired, to thank for my letter, from *Orsha* — thats good you will have him with you afterwards again. Marie said Dmitri wrote that he comes here with you, why Darling, Paul earnestly begs for you to send him to the regiment, he asked again when he took tea with me on Monday. — Marie looks alright, her hair is growing thick — she has worries with her chief Dr. & wants to get rid of him. — The Orlovs are still in town it seems & continue talking — Fredericks must forbid it, its disgraceful, only the old man must not use any name again. — Fancy, Stana has sent away her faithful Mlle *Peterson* — I suppose she suddenly found the name too German & will choose a Caucasian lady to help her & be popular. Oh, wont she try to charm all there! — Now I must try and sleep. I have blessed & kissed & laid my head upon your empty cushion as usual. It only can receive my kisses, but, alas, cannot respond to them. — Sleep well, Sweetheart & see wify in your dream & feel her arms caressingly around you. God bless you, holy Angels guard you, good-night my Treasure, my Sunshine, my long-suffering Job. —

18th. Good-morning wee One — grey & pouring — I found the evening so lovely, moon & stars shining, that I even opened half the window *(ventilator* always) — & then now, when I drew up the curtains, I was quite disappointed & only 6 degrees again. — As am feeling better, want to peep in to Ania in the big Palace (after *Znamenia)* on my way to a new young officer who has just come — only 20 years old, with a bad wound in the leg, *Vladimir Nikolaievitch* thinks it ought to be taken off, as blood-poisoning is setting in there & in the wound in the shoulder — he feels well, does not complain, that is always a bad sign — so difficult to decide when death is so near leave him to die in peace or risk it, I should, as there always is a flicker of hope when the organism is so young, tho' now very weak & high temp. — seems 7 days he was without having his wound dressed, wretched boy, — & so I want to have a look at the child. I have not been into that room for 6 months — no, I was there once since my poor *Grabovoy* died. — From there I will go to our hospital, as have not been there for a week & I miss them & they even old me. One says one of my lancers, a *volunteer Lüder* (something like that) has come to us — not wounded but squashed somehow, they could not explain it properly. —

With pleasure I continue thinking over *Khvostov's* talk & wish you had been there too — a man, no petticoats — & then one who will n o t let a n y t h i n g touch us, & will do all in his power to stop the attacks upon our Friend, as then he stopped them & now they intend beginning again, & *Stcherbatov* & *Samarin* wont certainly oppose, on the contrary for popularity's sake. I am bothering you with this talk, but I should like to convince you, having honestly, calmly the opinion that this (very fat young man of much experience) is the one you would approve of & that old woman who writes to you I should say too — He k n o w s the Russian peasant well & closely having been much amongst them — & other types too & does not fear them. — He knows too that fat Priest, now *archimandrite.* I think, *Gregory's* & *Varnava* friend, as he helped him 4 years when he was governor during the bad years, & he spoke so well to the peasants & brought them to reason. He finds a good Priest's influence should always be used & he is right — & they arranged together for *St. Paul Obnorsky* & he is now at *Tobolsk* or *Tiumen* & therefore *Samarin* & company told *Varnava* they do not approve of him & will get rid of him — his body is colossal Ania says, but the soul high & clear. —

I told *Khvostov* how sad I find it, that evil intentioned have always far more courage & therefore sooner success — upon wh. he rightly answered, but the others have the *spirit* & feeling to guide them & God will be near them, when they have good intentions & guide them. —

The *Zemstvo Union,* wh. I too find has spread too far & taken too many things in hand, so as that later one can say, the Government did not enough look after the wounded, *refugees,* our prisoners in Germany etc. & the *Zemstvo* saved them, ought to have been held in bounds by *Krivoshein,* who set the things going — a good idea, only needed watching carefully as there are many bad types out at the war in their hospitals & *feeding stations.* Finds *Krivoshein* too much in contact with *Gutchkov.* — *Khvostov* in his paper never attacked german names of the Barons or devoted servants, when they speak of this *German influence* but drew all the attention upon the banks, wh. was right, as nobody had yet — (& the Ministers saw their faults). He spoke of the food & fuel question — Gutchkov, member of the *Petrograd Duma,* even forgot that, probably intentionally so as that one should throw the fault upon the government. And it is its very criminal fault not having thought — months ago of getting big stocks of wood — we can have disorders on that account & quite comprehensible — so one must wake up & set people working. Its not your busines to go into these details — it is *Stcherbatov,* who ought to have seen to that with *Krivoshein* & *Rukhlov* — but they occupy themselves with politics — & try to eat away the old man. — Well, I was happy to receive your dear letter from yesterday, & thank you for it from the depths of my heart. I understand how difficult it is for you to find time to write, & I am therefore doubly happy, when I see your dear handwriting & read your loving words. You must miss Misha now — how nice that you had him staying with you, & I am sure that it must have done him good in every sense. — I am enchanted, if you need not have to change the *Headquarters,* I was quite sad about it, just on account of the moral side of it, and as God blesses the troops & really things seem to be going better, & we keep firm where we are — then no need for you to move. — But what about *Alexeiev* remaining alone — you wont get Ivanov to share the work & responsability with him & there you can be more free in your movements to *Pskov* or wherever you wish. — Well dear, there is nothing to be done with those Ministers, and the sooner you change them, the better. *Khvostov* instead of *Stcherbatov* & instead of *Samarin* there is another man I can recommend devoted old *N. K. Shvedov,* — but of course I do not know if you find a military man can occupy the place of *Over-Procurator of the Holy Synod.* — He has studied church history well, has a known collection of Churchbooks — in being at the head of the Accademy for Oriental studies, he studied the Church too — is very religious & devoted beyond words (calls our Friend *Father Gregory)* & spoke well of him when he saw & had occasion to speak to his former scholars in the army, when he went to see *Ivanov.* He is deeply loyal — now you know him much better than I do & can judge whether its nonsense or not — we only remembered him, because he longs to be of use to me, to make people know me & be a counterbalance to the »ugly party« — but such a man in a high place is good to have, but as I say, you know his caracter better than I do, otherwise — *Khvostov* of the justice & the other one in his place, whom I mentioned to you the other day, who clears up the stories at Moscow, but whom instead of longnosed *Sazonov,* if he will be an opponent the whole time! —

I received this from Ella to-day, as she read in the papers that *Yussupov* is *retired from the service:* — not said, that according to his petition wh. wld. have sounded prettier & this makes people probably think he did not act well. He wld. gladly (I believe) have returned, had one given him the military power he asked for, but she spoiled all. Well, he is no loss there, tho' I am sorry it was not better worded, & he meant honestly — you might have written a wee word if you had had time but its true, one does not ask ones demission in time of war: »Just read old Felix officially *suspended,* when he wrote asking demission, must be an error, cant one do something as most painful impression, even people sent away one puts *»in accordance with request«.* I have also wired it to you, as don't know what to answer her. One must make the difference, I find, between a *Dzhunkovsky* & a *Yussupov,* the one utterly false — the other stupid but honestly devoted. —

Paul's wife was alright, but bored me with her way of saying how devoted she is etc.: Ladung's lovely daughter marries on Sunday, my Godchild, so I blessed her to-day! The afternoon I remained quiet & Ania read to me. In the morning I was with that poor boy & then in our hospital, sat knitting and talking. — Wet, grey day. — Ania had a long conversation with Mme Zizi about our Friend & Orlov & cleared up many things to her. She made her promise not to tell on the story of *Orlov* at the *Headquarters* & *N. P.* telegr.: — she was horrified & went green — and said she remembers, all the a. d. c. used daily to write their reports during the war to (she did not understand quite, to Anpapa or Motherdear). — She will see her again & clear up many more things for the old lady to know, as she is utterly devoted to us & can be of use if she sees the things rightly. I explained lots of other things the other day wh. she was, most grateful to know. — Is it true what Pss *Palei!!* says that *Bark* telegraphed he cannot make the *loan* without the *Duma* being called to-gether? That is a catch I fear. *Khvostov* entreated that one should n o t t h i n k of calling it together before 1-st of Nov: as was anounced. He knows people are working at this, but finds it would be a w r o n g *concession,* as one must have time to prepare ones actions clearly before they assemble — & be ready to meet all attacks with answers.

Fat *Andronnikov* telephoned to Ania that *Khvostov* was very contented with his talk, & other amiabilities wh. I shan't repeat. — Have you any place for my letters? I write such volumes — Baby sweet gently began speaking again, whether you would take him back to the *Headquarters* & at the same time he feels sad to leave me. But you would be less lonely — for a bit at least, & if you intended to move & see the troops, I could come & fetch him. You have *Feodorov,* so he would only need Mr. Gilliard, & you could let still one of the aide de camp accompany him out motoring. He could have his French lessons every morning & drive with you in the afternoon — only he cant take walks — he could remain behind with the motor playing about. Have you a room near you, or he could share yr. bedroom. — But that you must think over quietly. — Our Friend always wires about *Pokrov* — I am sure Oct. 1-st. will bring some particular blessing, & the Virgin help you. To-morrow its four weeks that you left us — shall we really have the intense joy of getting you back by Wednesday? Ania is mad with joy. I carry it in me. And, alas, you will have more disagreable than pleasant things to do; — but what a joy to hold you again in my arms, caress you kiss & feel your warmth & love I so long for. You don't know h o w I miss you, my Angel Dear.

Now my letter must be sent off. — God bless you. Goodbye my own sweet Nicky dear, my husband, my joy & light, the sunshine & peace of my life. I bless & kiss you over and over again. —

Ever yr. very own tenderly loving old wife

Alix.

P. S.

How are the foreigners? Is the nice young Irishman still there, ? — Messages to the old man & *N. P.* Nini is now here again, reasonable & clever & still in despair at her husband's behaviour last month & anxious how is behaving now & hopes he tells you things rightly & honestly. Don't you tell him this Lovy. —

All the children kiss you. Baby bakes potatoes & apples in the garden. The girls went to hospitals.

Why Boris is again here, I do not know. —

Frolov was in despair. All abused him for allowing the articles about our Friend, tho' it was *Stcherbatov's* fault & was watching now carefully to avoid anything again, & now he has been changed. *Khvostov* also has ideas about the press. You will think, that I have now got a »tail« growing. — *Gadon* does great harm to our Friend speaking horrors about him wherever & whenever he can. —

1000 thanks for the well written cuting about the *general situation.* This morning's papers with the news fr. the *Headquarters* pleased me, not dry & explaining the situation so well to all readers. —

No. 127.

Tsarskoje Selo, Sept. 19-th 1915

My own sweet Darling,

To-day its four weeks you left us, it was a Saturday evening — Aug. 22-nd. Thank God we may hope to see you soon back again, in our midst — oh what a joy that will be!

Grey & rainy again. —

Thanks for having at once answered me about *Yussupov,* I directly telegraphed it on to Ella, it will quieten her. —

I am glad *Vorontzov's escorts* were so nice. How will it all be there now — that nest collecting again together — & *Stana* has taken there *Krupensky's* wife as her lady — her husband did the most harm in the talking set at the old *Headquarters* — & is not a good man. One must have an eye on their behaviour the whole time, they are a dangerous foe now — & as not being good people, our Friend ends your telegr.: »*In the Caucasus there is little sunshine*«. — It hurts one that he should have changed so, but those women turn their husbands round their fingers. —

I see Ducky has been to Minsk to visit hospitals & *refugees!* Boris is coming to tea. — I placed my candles at *Znamenia* & prayed so earnestly for my Love. Then I went to our hospital & sat knitting in the different wards — I take my work so as to keep from being in the *dressing station,* wh. always draws me there. I only did one officer. — In the morning I finished Rost. papers, wh. I could not get done with before, tho' I read till 2 in the night in bed. —

I saw Dr. *Pantiukhin* fr. *Livadia* & we spoke about all the hospitals, sanatoriums, wh. he hopes can begin their work in Jan., it will be a great boon when they are ready. —

We drove to *Pavlovsk,* mild, fr. time to time rained. —

Boris told me about his new nomination, wh. has overjoyed him I think, as he will have a lot to do — then I had Isa with papers. At 7 I shall go to Church with Baby. *Grabbe* wrote to his wife that the ministers' sitting had been *stormy* & that they wont do as you bid, but that you had been very energetic, a real *Tsar* — & I was so proud when Ania told me this — ah Lovy, do you feel yr. own strength & wisdom now, that you are yr. own master & will be energetic, decisive & not let yourself be imposed upon by others. — I liked the way Boris spoke of you & the great change in the *Headquarters,* & how one always gets news there now from all sides, & how cheerful you are.

God be blessed — our Friend was right. — I had a wire fr. my *Vesselovsky,* that he is ill & had to go from the regiment to look after his health. — Perhaps you are in Church at the same time as we are, that will be a nice feeling. — My *supply* train No. 1 is at *Rovno* & fr. there goes out & with a motor column, wh. a Prince *Abamelek* (fr. Odessa) formed & gave me (he is with it) they take things linnen etc. along the whole front — & they continued without harm under heavy firing — I am so glad *Mekk* wired fr. *Vinnitsa* where my big *store* is. — *Varnava* has left for *Tobolsk,* our Friend said we were to send him back. The old man said he was no more to show himself at the *Synod.* One anounces *Samarin's* return fr. th. *Headquarters* & that he at once began the work about *Varnava* & that he must be *dismissed.* Please forbid this if it is true & should reach you. — I must end now & dress for Church. Every evening fr. 9—9½ Marie, Baby, I and either *Mr. Gillard* or *Vladimir Nikolaievitch* play »*Tishe Yedesh, Dalshe Budesh.*« — Dinner is very cosy in the middle of the playroom. — Goodnight my beloved One, God bless and protect you guard & guide you & I cover you with kisses.

Ever, Nicky, mine yr. very own loving

Wify.

I see the French people Monday at 4½, as they lunch at *Elagin.* Its such scandle — no flower to be had in town nor here — people stand in long files in the streets before the shops.

Abominably organised, Obolensky is an idiot — one must foresee the things — not wait till they happen. —

No. 128.

Tsarskoje Selo, Sept. 20-th 1915

My own beloved Darling,

I read the papers this morning with much interest — the promised explanation of our position at the war, clearly put & the work of a month that you are there keeping the enemy at bay. —

A grey, rainy morning again but not cold. — This afternoon we have a *Te Deum* in the red cross & then I give the diplomas to the ladies who have finished their courses as nurses & received the red cross. We are always in need of nurses, many get tired, ill, or wish to go out to the *front positions* to receive medals. The work here is monotonous and continual — out there, there is more excitement, constant change, even danger, uncertainty & not always much work to be done; certainly it is far more tempting. One of our Trepov's daughters worked nearly a year in our Invalid's hospital — but after her Mother's death she always felt restless, so off she went — & has already received the medal on the St. George's ribbon. — I send you a letter from *Bulatovitch* he sent you through Ania & a summary of her talk with *Beletzky* — that does indeed seem a man who could be most useful to the minister of the Interior, as he knows everything — *Dzhunkovsky* eat him out; just when one needs to have all the threads in hand. He says everywhere one complains of *Stcherbatov's* inactivity & not understanding of his work & duties. Has very bad opinion of fat Orlov & feels sure that my long lost letter from the Standart in C.(rimea) to Ania in the country is in Orlov's hands. Says *Dzhunkovsky* gave over those filthy papers about our Friend to *Maklakov's* brother, as they intend bringing up that question in the *Duma* & papers. — But God grant, if you find *Khvostov* suitable, he will put a stop to all.

Luckily he is still here & even went to *Goremykin* to place all his ideas before the old man. *Andronnikov* gave Ania his word of honour, that nobody shall know, that *Khvostov* comes to Ania (she sees him in her house, not in the palace) or *Beletzky,* so that her & my name will remain out of this. — Alas *Gadon* & *Sherv.* seem to spread very many bad things about *Gregory,* as *Dzhunkovsky's* friend of course — & knowing poor Ella's ideas & wishing to help — thus he does mischief — before others' eyes sets *Elagin* against *Tsarskoje Selo* & that is bad & wrong — & its he who ennervates *Xenia* & Motherdear, instead of keeping them up bravely & squashing gossip.

It was with deepest joy that I received your precious, tender letter — your warm words did my yearning heart good. Yes, my treasure, separation draws one yet closer together — one feels so greatly what one misses — & letters are a great consolation. Indeed he foretold most accurately the length of time you would remain out there. Still I am sure you long to have more contact with the troops, & I shall be glad for you when you will be able to move a bit. Of course this month was too serious — you had to get into your work & plans with Alexeiev & the time has been such an anxious out there — but now thank God, all seems going satisfactorily.

Tell *Grabbe* I am delighted with his proposition — *Viltchkovsky* wanted the new barracks badly & wrote I believe to him & *Voyeikov* about it — I said I could say nothing until you came. Long ago I had my eye upon it — but discreetly held my tongue — now I can only say I am enchanted — it is near the station — so big & lofty & clean, brand new & we have an *red cross station* waiting to be placed. Thank him v e r y much from me. — The old man has asked to see me at 6 to-morrow, probably to give over things to you, or to tell about *Khvostov's* talk. — It will be interesting what he will tell about the sitting at *Moghilev*. What a beautiful telegram from our Friend & what courage it gives you to act firmly. — Certainly, as soon as *Samarin* goes, one must clear out the members of the *Synod* and get others in. Our Friend's wife came, Ania saw her — so sad & says he suffers awfully through calumnies & vile things one writes about him — high time to stop all that — *Khvostov* & *Beletzky* are men to do that. — Only one must get the 2 *Khvostov* to work well together — all must unite. But about *Sazonov* what do you think, I wonder? I believe, as he is a very good & honest (but obstinate) man, that when he sees a new collection of Ministers who are energetic, he may draw himself up & become once more a man — the atmosphere around him cought hold of him & cretinised him. There are men who become marvels in time of anxiety & great difficulties — & others show a pittiful side of their nature. *Sazonov* needs a good stimulant — & once he sees things »working well« instead of fomenting & at the same time dropping to pieces — he will feel his backbone grow. I cant believe he is as harmful as *Stcherbatov* & *Samarin* or even my friend *Krivoshein* — what has happened to him? I am bitterly disappointed in him. Lovy, if you have an occasion in the train, speak to *N. P.* & make him understand, that you are glad to make use of me. He wrote to me once very upset that one mentions my name so much & that *Goremykin* sees me etc. & he does not understand that its my duty, tho' I am a woman, to help you when & where I can, once you are away, all the more so. Don't say I mentioned it, but bring the conversation onto that topic à deux. He has a cousin's husband in the *Duma* & perhaps he sometimes tries not rightly to tell him things or influence him. He told Axel Pistolkors that I give officers *Gregory* prayer belts — such rot, one loves those belts with different prayers & I give them to every officer that leaves to the war fr. here — & two whom I never saw begged for them fr. me with a prayer to *Father Seraphim*. — One told me that those soldiers that wore them in the last war were not killed.

I see *N. P.* so rarely to talk to longer, & he is so young & I always lead him all these years — & now he suddenly comes into quite a new life — sees what hard times we are going through & trembles for us. He longs to help & of course does not know how to. I fear *Petrograd* will fill his ears with horrors — please tell him not to heed what one says, because it can make one wild — & nasty ones drag my name about a good deal. —

We were in Church this morning, later drove & after the red Cross called on *Silaiev*. — His wife is so like her son *Raftopulo,* too amusing — their little Children are sweet. Now our 5 chicks are at Ania's in the big palace, playing with *Rita Khitrovo* & *Irina Tolstaya.* —

What intense joy — on three days, God grant, we shall have you back again — its too beautiful. My love, my joy, I await you with such eagerness.

Goodbye, Sweetheart, I bless & kiss you without end with deep & true devotion, better, better, every day. Sleep well, agooweeone. — I shall still write to-morrow, if a man goes to meet you, as may have something to tell after my talk with *Goremykin.*

Ever, precious Nicky mine, yr. own, tenderly loving old wife

Alix.

No. 129.

Tsarskoje Selo, October 1-st 1915

My own Beloved,

You will read these lines when the train has already carried you from us. This time you can part with a quieter heart, things, God blessed, are going better — exteriorly as interiorly our Friend is here to bless your journey. The holy feast of *Pokrov* may it shed its blessings upon our troops and bring us victories and the holy Virgin spread her *mantle* over your whole country. —

Its always the same pain to see you leave & now Baby too for the first time in his life, its not easy, its awfully hard. But for you I rejoice, at least you wont be quite alone & wont agoo wee one be proud to travel with you without any of us women near him. Quite a big boy. I am sure the troops will rejoice, when the news reaches them that he is with you — our officers in the hospital were enchanted. If you see troops beyond *Pskov,* please, take him also in the motor, — awfully much hope you can see some no matter how few, but it will already create joy & contentement. Wire a word from *Pskov* about your plans, so that I can follow you in thoughts & prayers.

Lovy my Soul! Oh how hard it is to let you go each time, tho' now I have got the hope to see you soon, but it will make you sad as I come to fetch Alexei — but not before 10 days, I suppose. —

Its so lonely without Your caresses wh. mean everything to me — ah how me loves oo, »better better every day, with unending true devotion, deeper than I can say«. But these days have been awfully tiring for you & the last evening we could not even spend quietly together — its sad. — See that Tiny does not tire himself on the stairs, I regret that he does not sleep near you in the train — but at *Moghilew* it will be cosy — *it is not neccesary* — even, too touching & sweet. I hope you will like my photo of Baby in the frame. *Derevenko* has got our presents for Baby — the tipe writing mashene he gets here & a big game when he returns — a bag in train. You will give him some writing paper & a silver bowl to have near his bed when he eats fruits in the evening, instead of a china saucer. — Ask him from time to time whether he says his prayers properly, please Deary. — Sweet One, I love you & wish I could never be parted from you & share everything with you. — Oh the joy it was having you here, my Sunshine, I shall feed on the remembrances. — Sleep well huzy, wify is ever near you, with & in you. When you remember the picture books think of old wify for ever & ever. —

God bless you & protect you, guard & guide you.

Ever Your very own old

Sunny.

I bless you.

I kiss & caress every tenderly beloved place & gaze into your deep, sweet eyes wh. long ago conquered me completely.

Love ever grows. —

No. 130.

Tsarskoje Selo, Oct. 1-st 1915

Sweet precious One,

It seems a messenger leaves this evening, so I profit to send you a word. Well there we are again separated — but I hope it will be easier for you whilst Sunbeam is near you — he will bring life into your house & cheer you up. How happy he was to go, with what excitement he has been awaiting this great moment to travel with you alone. I was afraid he might be sad, as when we left for the south to meet you in Dec. he cried at the station, but no, he was happy. Tatiana & I felt very hard to be brave — you dont know what it is to be without you & the wee one. I just looked at my little book & saw with despair that I shall... the 10-th... to travel & inspect hospitals the two first days I really cant, as otherwise shall get again one of my raging headaches — is it not too stupid! —

We drove this afternoon to *Pavlovsk* — the air was very autumnal — then we went into *Znamenia* & placed candles & I prayed hard for my darlings. Hereafter Ania read to me. After tea I saw Isa & then I went to the poor boy he has changed, a good deal since yesterday. I stroked his head a while & then he woke up — I said you & *Alexei* sent messages wh. delighted him & he thanked so much — then went to sleep again — that was the first time he had spoken to-day. My consolation when I feel very down & wretched is to go to the very ill & try & bring them a ray of light & love — so much suffering one has to go through in this year, it wears one out.

So *Kira* went with you, thats good & just — may he only not be stupid & sleep. Do so hope you can manage to see some troops to-morrow. Sweet Huzy mine, I kiss & bless you without end & long for your caresses — the heart is so heavy. God be with you & help you evermore. Very tenderest, fondest kisses, sweet Beloved, fr. yr. very own

Wify.

Sleep well, dream of old Sunny. —

I hope Paul will be allright & not fidgety. Did the little Admiral answer you?

No. 131.

Tsarskoje Selo, Oct. 2-th 1915

My own beloved Sweetheart,

Goodmorning my precious ones, how did you sleep, I wonder! I did not very well its always so when you are away, Lovy mine. So strange to read in the papers, that you & Baby have left for the front. I am sure you felt cosy sitting & playing with Baby, not this perpetual loneliness; for *N. P.* I too am glad, as he feels lonely there often, none are such particular friends, tho' he likes most of them & they get on splendidly but he misses us all — & now Alexei being there, it will warm him up & he will feel you nearer to him too. Mr. Gillard will enjoy all & he can speak with the French. — You did have such hard work here, that I am glad it is over now, more or less, & you see the troops to-day!

Oh, how pleased I am, the heart of a soldier's daughter & soldier's wife rejoices for you — & I wish I were with you to see the faces of those brave fellows when they see for whom & with whom they go out to fight. I hope you can take Alexei with you. — The impression will remain for his wole life & theirs.

Oh how I miss you both! The hour for his prayer, I must say I broke down, so hurried off into my room & said all his prayers in case he should forget to say them. — Please, ask him whether he remembers them daily. — What it will be to you when I fetch him! You must go off too somewhere, not to remain alone. — It seems to me as tho' you were already gone ages ago, such yearning after you — I miss you, my own Angel, more than I can say. — I went to A. this morning & took her to *Znamenia* & the big Palaces fr. whence she left for town, & I went to the poor boy — he had recognised nobody & not been able to speak, but me he did at once & even spoke a little. From there I went to our hospital. Two new officers have come. The one poor fellow has the ball or splinter in his eye — the other deep in his lungs & a *fragment* probably in the stomach — he has such a strong internal *hemorrhage* wh. has completely pushed his heart to the right side so that one clearly sees it beat, hear his right niple. Its a very serious case, & probably he must be operated to-morrow — his pulse is 140 & he is awfully weak, the eyeballs so yellow, the stomach blown up — it will be an anguishing operation. — After luncheon we received 4 new *Alexandrovtsi* just promoted going off to the war — 2 *Elisavetgradtsi* & 4 *Vosnesentsi?* — 4 wounded & *Arseniev's* son. Then we drove, eat a pear & apple — & went to the cemetry to have a look at our wee *temporary Church* for our dead heroes. From there to the big Palace to a *Te Deum* before the Image of the Virgin, wh. I had told them to bring fr. *Znamenia* it passed through all the wards — it was nice. —

After tea I saw *Russin* & gave him letters for Victoria & Toria — then *Ressin* about our journey — only what date to settle, because of *Bekker,* wh. spoils everything. — Got your telegram at 5½ & we all enjoyed it, thank God you saw the troops, but you do not mention whether — Tiny accompanied you. — Wont you let the soldiers, wh. stand now at *Moghilev,* show you some exercises & then they can see Baby. His having gone to the army will also bring its blessing our Friend told Ania; even agoo wee one helps. He is furious with the way people go on in Moscou. — There, the Pss. of the Palace has already sent her first perfumed letter so I forward it to you. Personally I think she ought not to ask for him — what wld. it look like, both Paul's sons living lazily, comfortably at the *Headquarters,* whilst their comrades shed their blood as heroes.

I shall send you the boy's pretty verses to-morrow. If I were you, I should tell Paul about this letter, even show it to him, & explain that its too early to call him back — its bad enough one son not being out at the front & it would harm the boy in the regiment, I assure you; — after a bit of service he can be perhaps given a place as *courier* of one of the Generals, but not yet, I find. I understand her Mother's heart bleeding — but she must not spoil the boy's career — dont speak to Dmitri about it. — I must now write to Miechen & Aunt Olga, so to speak to invite them to the consecration of our microscopic Church — officially I cant, as the Church is too small, but if I don't, Miechen is sure to be offended. The Pavlovsk family (ladies) I must then too, as their soldiers are buried on our ground. —

Goodbye my Love, sweetest One, Beloved — I bless & kiss you without end.

Ever yr. very own old Wify.

Khvostov has asked to see me after the 5-th. —

No. 132.

Tsarskoje Selo, Oct. 3-rd 1915

My own beloved Darling,

A gloriously bright, sunny day — 2 degr. of frost in the night. What a pitty, nothing is written in the papers about your having seen the troops — I hope it will appear to-morrow. It is necessary to print all such things without mentioning of course what troops you saw. — Am eagerly awaiting details how it all was.

So silly, in Moscou they want to give *Samarin* an address when he returns fr. the country — it seems that horror *Vostokov* has sent him a telegram in the name of his two »*flocks*«, *Moscou* & *Kolomna* — so the dear little *Makari* wrote to the *Consistory* to insist upon a copy of *Vostokov's* telegram to *Samarin* & to know what gave him the right to forward such a telegr. — how good, if the little Metropolitan can get rid of *Vostokov,* its high time, he does endless harm & its he who leads *Samarin.* Moscou is in a rotten state, but God grant nothing at all will be — but they need feeling yr. displeasure. — Sweetheart, me misses you very, very much, I want your kisses, I want to hear your dear voice & gaze into your eyes. —

Thanks ever so much for yr. telegram — well Baby must have been pleased that he was present at the review. How cosy yr. beds must be in the same room. And a nice drive too. — I always give over by telephone all you write to *Vladimir Nikolaievitch.*

This morning I went in to the little Boy — he is fast sinking & the quiet end may come this evening. — I spoke with his poor mother & she was so brave & understood all so rightly.

Then we worked in the hospital & *Vladimir Nikolaievitch* made an injection to the new officer — probably to-morrow will be the operation.

Pss. Gedroitz has 39 & feels so ill — *eresypelis* in the head one fears, so she begged *Derevenko* to replace her for serious operations. *Nastinka* lunched, then I received generals *Prince Tumanov, Pavlov,* Benkendorf, Isa. The inauguration of the Winter-Palace hospital can only be on the 10-th as the red cross has not brought the beds etc. yet — our part is done — so you see I better keep quiet after that ceremony (& Bekker no doubt) & the 11 & 12 — if so, then I would be at *Moghilev* 15-th morning at 9 if that suits you? Thats a Thursday, just 2 weeks fr. the day you left. You let me know. That means I am the 13-th at *Tver,* 14-th other places nearing you. — A lovely bright moon, its 10 minutes past 5 & becoming rather dark, we took tea after a drive to *Pavlovsk,* so cold — the little ones are trying on & the big ones have gone to clean the instruments in our hospital. At 6½ we go to the evening service in our new little Church. —

In the evening we see our Friend at Ania's to bid goodbye. He begs you very much to send a telegram to the King of Servia, as he is very anxious that Bulgaria will finish them off — so I enclose the paper again for you to use it for yr. telegram — the sense in yr. words & shorter of course reminding them of their Saints & so on. — Make Baby show you *Peter Vassilievitch* envelope, its sweet. I shall also address my letter separatly to him, he will feel prouder. *Derevenko* has got our presents for him & can arrange them in the bedroom before your dinner. — Wonder, how you will feast the *Convoy.*

Now I must end my letter, Sweetheart. God bless & protect you & the holy Virgin guard you from all harm. Every goodwish for our sweet Sunbeam's Namesday.

I kiss you without end & hold you tightly clasped to my old heart wh. yearns for you ever, Nicky sweet, yr. very own wify

Alix.

No. 133.

Tsarskoje Selo, Oct. 4-th 1915

My own beloved Darling,

With all my heart I congratulate you with our sweet Child's Namesday — — He spends it quite like a little military man. I read the telegram our Friend sends him, its so pretty. You are in Church this evening, but I was feeling too tired, so went into *Znamenia* just now to place candles for my darling instead. — A glorious sunny day, zero in the morning, 3 at night. At 10 we went off to the Consecration of the dear little Church — last nights service was also very pretty — many sisters in their white headdress give such a picturesque aspect. Aunt Olga & we both were also as sisters, as its for our poor wounded, dead we pray for there. Miechen & Mavra & *Princess Palei* & many others were there. About 200 men of the *convalescent companys* stood round the church, so they saw the *procession with the cross.* — At 1 went to our hospital & *Vladimir Nikolaievitch* performed the operation wh. went off well — then we had dressings after wh. I went to see poor *Princess Gedroitz.* She had 40.5. temp., took Communion in the evening & felt calmer later — spoke about death & gave all her orders. To-day she suffers less, but its very serious still as descending towards the ear — *eresypeles.* But our Friend promised to pray for her. — Then we fetched Ania & drove to Pavlovsk, everything looked lovely, & to the cemetry as I wanted to put flowers on poor Orlov's grave — 7 years that he is dead!

After tea fr. *Znamenia* to the big palace to the poor boy. He recognised me, extraordinary, that he is still alive, poor child. Ania & *Lili Den* come to dinner. Yesterday we saw *Gregory* at Ania's — nice — Zina was there too — he spoke so well. He begged me to tell you, that it is not at all *clear* about the stamp money, the simple poeple cannot understand, we have enough coins & this may create disagreablinesses — I think me wants to tell the tail to speak to Bark about it. — One, of course, did not accept his wire to Baby, so I send it you to read to the tiny one, perhaps you will wire to me to thank. —

How do you find the news? I was so happy to get your telegram, Baby's & Mr. *G.'s* letters to-day — they warmed me up & I cld. picture all to myself. — So strange not to be with him on his Namesday. — His letter was sweet — I also write every day — probably with many faults too. — The big girls go in the evening to clean instruments. Its quite funny to have »*for the time being*« no affairs to write about, nor to bore you with. — Your bedroom is cosy? Did he sleep quietly & the creaking boards not disturb him? — Oh, I miss you both awfully. — Now goodbye my love, God bless you, protect you. I cover you with kisses my own Beloved, & remain yr. fondly loving very own

Sunny.

Sweety, I do not think it right that Zamoisky's wife is going to take appartments at the *Headquarters.* It was known her goings on at Varsovie with Boris, in the train, at the *Headquarters* & now in *Petrograd* — it will throw a bad light on the *Headquarters.* — Fred. admires her so wont disapprove, but please, tell *Zamoisky* its better no ladies come to settle down at the *Headquarters.* Therefore I do not either. Ania kisses yr. hand & congratulates you with *Alexei.*

No. 134.

Tsarskoje Selo, 5-th Oct. 1915

My own Sweetheart,

Once more many happy returns of this dear day — God bless our precious Child in health & happiness. I am so glad that one at last printed that you had seen troop and what you said — otherwise none out at the front would be any the wiser, as before. — And every bit of your movements to the troops, when known, will yet more raise their spirits & all will hope for the same luck. —

Glorious, sunny, cold morning.

We went to Church at 10, then I changed & we worked at the hospital till 10 m. to 2. After luncheon I drove with the girls.

Miechen came to tea, was nice & cosy, is so delighted that Plotho has been set free — now he gets transported to Siberia, but its quite different. — She goes with her train now, Ducky returned with a terrible cough — so she wishes to go, as its not far nor long — well, lets hope no bombs will be thrown upon it. — We have just returned fr. a *funeral service* in the new Church — the little boy in the big palace died peacefully this night & in *Maria's* & Anastasia's hospital one died too — so both coffins stood there — I am so glad we have got that little Church there. — I received still several officers & feel now mighty tired, so excuse a short letter. — Lili *Den* was very handsome yesterday evening & dear.

How sweet that you say prayers with Baby, he wrote it to me, the treasure — his letters are delightful. — I am so grateful, that you told *Grigorovitch* to send me every evening the papers — I eagerly read & then return them after having sealed them myself. — Sweetheart, beloved Treasure, I wish I had wings so as to fly over to you & see how you both sleep in wee bedybys — & would love to tuck you up & cover you both with kisses — very »*not necessary*«. —

Ever, my Treasure, yr. very own, tenderly loving old

Wify.

God bless & protect you.

At night 2 & 3 degr. of frost, nevertheless I sleep with the *little window* open. — Its so empty — miss you both terribly.

How does Paul get on? —

You may like to read *Putiatin's* letter, so I send it to you. —

No. 135.

Tsarskoje Selo, Oct. 6-th 1915

My own beloved Treasure,

A cold foggy morning. Have read through the papers, thank God, the news continues being good. I was glad to see, that one already speaks of changing the stamp money, thats good. — P-ss *Gedroitz* is happily better, the temperature less high. —

We have just returned from town. The school is really charming — 4 stories high so I was carried up, the lift not being ready; a part of the necessary things are at *Archangelsk.* — Really the girls have made wonderful progress.

I went through all their work-rooms weaving, carpets, embroidery, paintings, where they prepare the dyes and dye the silk threads and stuffs they make out of blackberry. — Our priest officiated the Te Deum. *Bark, Khvostov, Volzhin* and *Krivoshein* etc. were there, the later offered us 24,000 *Rubles* for keeping up the school one year. — Then we took tea at *Elagin,* — she looks well and thinks of going for a tiny visit to *Kiev* to see Olga whilst Xenia is away, wh. I find an excellent idea. — In the morning, I had much to do in the hospital. — Sweety, why did *Dzhunkovsky* receive the »*Preobrasentsi*« and »*Semenovtsi*« — too much honour after his vile behaviour — it spoils the effect of the punishment — he ought to have got army regiments. He has been continuing horrors against our F r i e n d now amongst the nobility — the tail brings me the proofs to-morrow — ah no, thats f a r too kind already to have given him such a splendid nomination — can imagine the filth he will spread in those two regiments and all will believe him. — I am sending you a very fat letter from the Cow, the lovesick creature could not wait any longer, she must pour out her love otherwise she bursts. My back aches and I feel very tired and long for my own sweet One. One keeps up alright, but there are moments when it is very difficult. — When sanitary trains pass do you sometimes have a look to them? Have you gone over the house, where all the small people of your staff work, take Baby with you and that will be a thanks to them for their hard work and serve as an encouragement; have the different officers of yr. staff been invited to lunch on Sundays? — Has the English Admiral arrived yet? — There is so much to do, people to see etc. that I feel mighty tired and fill myself with medicins. How is your health my Beloved? — Are no troops for you to see near *Orsha?* or *Vitebsk?* An afternoon you might give up to that? — You think me a bore but I long for you to see more troops and I am sure young soldiers pass by on their way to fill up regiments — they might march pass you at the station and they will be happy. You know our people often have the false idea of not telling you, as it might prevent your habitual drive as tho' one could not often combine all quite well. — What does Paul do of an evening? And what have you settled about Dmitri? — Oh Deary, how I long for you yearn after you both its horrible how I miss you. But I am sure, all seems different now the little man is with you. Go and have the regiment drill before you and let Baby see it too it will be a nice remembrance for you both my sunshine and sunbeam. The letter must leave. — Good bye my very own Huzy heart of my heart, soul of my life — I clasp you tight in my arms and kiss you with ever such great tenderness, gentleness and devotion. God bless and protect you and keep you from all harm. A thousand kisses fr. yr. own old

Wify.

No. 136.

Tsarskoje Selo, Oct. 7-th 1915

My very Own,

Sweetest Darling, I try to picture to myself how you sat answering congratulations. I also got from some of Baby's regiments (I collect his regimental ones for him during the war) & I answered that he was at the *Headquarters,* as I was sure it would rejoice their hearts to know Father and Son together. — Since yesterday evening it gently snows, but scarcely any remains lying — does seem so early already to have real winter beginning.

Lovy Dear, I send you two stamps (money) fr. our Friend, to show you that already one of them is false. People are very discontented — such wee papers flie away, in the darkness they cheat the *cabmen* & its not a good thing — he entreats you to have it stopped at once. — That rotten Bulgaria, now we shall have them turning against us from the south, or do you think they will only turn against Servia & then Greece — its vile. Did you wire to old King Peter, our Friend wanted it so much.

Oh my love, its 20 m. to 8 & I am absolutely cretinised have heaps to say & don't know how to begin. — 10½—12½ operation, & gips being put on — 12 — 1 *Krivoshein,* we only spoke about the *home manufactures committee* how to arrange it, whom to invite etc. Girls came late to lunch, had to choose cloaks for them, received officers — *Bark* for ½ hour, then to big palace. Then got yr. p r e c i o u s letter for wh. I thank you without end, you sweet One — I loved to get it & have reread it & kissed it & Tiny's too. — Our Friend is rather anxious about *Riga,* are you too? —

I spoke to Bark about the stamps — he also found the stamps wrong, wants to get the Japanese to make coins for us — & then to have the paper-money, instead of wee stamps, like the Italian lire, wh. is then really paper-money. —

He was very interesting. Then Mme Zizi, then young Lady Sibyl de Grey, who has come to arrange the English Hospital & Malcolm (whom I knew before, was at Mossy's Wedding, our Coronation as a fair curly young man in a kilt), both remained 20 minutes each.

Then Khvostov till this minute & my head buzzes from everything.

As remplacant of *Dzhunkovsky* for the Gendarmes he thought *Tatistchev* (Zizi's son in law) might do, discrete & a real gentleman — only then he ought to wear a uniform — you gave Obolensky one again & *Kurlov* & Prince Obolensky general governor of Finland — he asked me to tell you this beforehand so as that you should think whether it would suit you. He wishes to ask to be received next week by you & he told me the different questions he will touch.

To-morrow I'll try & write more, when can calmly shape all into words — I am too idiotical this evening. — Our Friend was very contented with yr. *decree* about Bulgaria, found it well worded. —

I must then end now. Thanks again over & over for yr. s w e e t e s t letter, beloved Angel. I can see you & the wee one in the morning & be talking to you whilst you half sleep. Bad Boy wrote today: *Papa made smells much and long this morning*. Too noughty!

Oh my Angels how I love you — but you will miss him shockingly later.

Just got your telegram. What news Deary, I l o n g to have some, it seems very difficult again, does it not?

Goodbye my Sun, I cover you with fond kisses. Bless you my Love.

Ever y r. v e r y o w n old

Sunny.

No. 137.

Tsarskoje Selo, Oct. 8-th 1915

My very own Love,

A grey and dreary morning. You too have cold weather, I see, its sad, as winter is so endless. — I am glad tiny behaves well, but I hope his presence does not prevent you from seeing troops or anything like that. Am I a bore, always mentioning that? Only I have such a longing you should go about & see more & be seen. Do not reserve regiments stand at Vitebsk, or are only the horses kept there? Baby writes such amusing letters & everything that passes through his head. — Does he speak with the foreigners, or has he not the courage? — I am glad his *little lamp* does not keep you from sleeping. — Well, about the Tail. I spoke to him concerning flour, sugar, wh. are scarcely & butter, wh. is lacking now in *Petrograd* when cars full are sticking in Siberia. He says its *Rukhlov* this all concerns, he has to see & give the order to let the waggons pass. Instead of all these necessary products, waggons with flowers & fruit pass wh. really is a shame. The dear man is old — he ought to have gone himself to inspect all & set things working properly — its really a crying shame, & one feels humiliated before the strangers that such disorder should exist. Could you not choose somebody & send him to revise it all & oblige those to work properly out there at the places where the waggons stand & the things rot. *Khvostov* mentioned *Gurko* as a man to send and inspect as he is very energetic & quick about all — but do you like such a type? Its true he was unjustly treated by *Stolypin* but some energetic means ought to be taken. — I wrote to you about *Tatistchev* for the gendarmes only I forgot to tell *Khvostov* that he is terribly against our Friend, so he ought to speak to him upon that subject first, I think. — Fancy, how disgusting, the warministery has its own detective work to look out for spies, and now they spie upon *Khvostov* & have found out where he goes & whom he sees & the poor man is very much upset by it. He cannot make a row, as he found it out through a clerk (?), I think, who told him all about it, his *Uncle* also had heard things wh. came from the side of *Polivanov* — the latter continues being *Gutchkov's* friend & therefore they can harm *Khvostov.* One must have a firm watch over *Polivanov.* — *Bark* also dislikes him & gave him a smacking answer the other day. But perhaps you are satisfied with *Polivanov's* work, for the war. In any case when you find he needs changing, there is *Beliaiev* his aide, whom everybody praises as such a clever, thorough worker and real gentleman & utterly devoted to you. — All the papers against our Friend, kept in the ministery of the Interior, *Dzhunkovsky,* took copies of (he had no right to) & showed them right & left at Moscou amongst the nobility — after he was changed. — Once more Paul's wife repeated to Ania that *Dzhunkovsky* gave his word that you had given him in winter the order to have *Gregory* severely judged — he said it to Paul & his wife & repeated it to Dmitri & many others in town. I call that dishonesty, unloyalty to the higest extreme & a man who deserves no recompenses or high nominations. Such a man will continue unscrupilously doing harm & speaking against our Friend in the regiments. *Gregory* says he can never bring luck in his work, the same as *Nikolasha,* as they went against him, — against you. — What a delightful surprise, your dear letter was brought me so early — I thank you for it over & over again my Sweetheart. That is right, Dear, that you have at once ordered those 3 generals who were at fault, to be changed; such measures will be lessons to the rest & they will pay more attention to their actions. I wonder who the 3 are. —

But God grant *Riga* wont be taken, they have enough.

What an idiot I was to wrongly number your letters, please correct the fault. Tiny does love digging & working as he is so strong, & forgets that he must be careful — only watch he should now not use it — wet weather can make it ache more. I am glad he is so little shy, that is a great thing. — I am not going to the hospital this morning & shall only get up for luncheon, because my back continues aching & I feel very tired, but must still go to town, its necessary, as people are so very unfriendly & misjudge one — then one must just show oneself, tho' its tiring.— I am astonished the little Admiral did not answer yr. letter — I think a change of air will do him & his wife good; A. went to see them, as I begged her to — at first he was stiff — he had not seen her for a year & never enquired after her when she had the accident, but afterwards he got alright, talked a lot about the *Headquarters* & the good change since you are at the head.

Well, I am tired. In town I received the Baroness Uxcull of the Kaufmans hospital — it is the first time I saw her & we had a charming talk. She is very fond of our Friend. Then I went with the 2 little ones to Css. Hendrikov, whom I had not seen for a year — it was indeed »fatiguing«

with her, poor soul. — Then the big girls joined us and we went to the *Noblemen's assembly.* — By chance I fell upon a day when they were all assembled at a sitting — *well, let them,* perhaps all the better & will make them amiable.

We had tea in the train. Upon our return I found yr. sweet telegram for wh. tenderest thanks — how glad I am that our attack near *Baranovitchi* was successful. — Ella wired that my Grodno hospital with Mme *Kaygorodova* has settled down at Moscou, in a nice, new house. —

Then I received *Volzhin* with whom I talked for 3/4 of an hour, he made me a p e r f e c t impression, God grant all his good intentions may be successful & he have the strength to bring them into life — he indeed seems the right man in the right place, very glad to work with energetic young Khvostov. — In going away he asked me to bless him, wh. touched me very much — one sees he is full of best intentions & understands the needs of our church perfectly well. How awfully difficult it was to find the right man — & you got him I think. — We touched all the most vital questions of our Priesthood *refugees Synod* etc. — Günst comes at 9 to say goodbye, she is going to *Bielgorod* to join her mother. —

Now Lovebird I must send off my letter. God bless & protect you & keep you from all harm. I kiss you my both Treasures over & over again.

Ever yr. very own old

Wify.

I send you some of the postcards I ordered to have made, they cost 3 *kopeeks* & are sold for 5, so *Massalov* proposes I should use the money for some charity organisation & it must be printed on the back, so I shall think out for what. —

No. 138.

Tsarskoje Selo, Oct. 9-th 1915

My own precious One,

It is snowing — the men were cutting the grass this morning & raking it away under the falling snow, I wonder why they waited so long. — Well, I have had again a day. The morning I had *Rostovtzev's* papers to read till 11, then dressed, went to *Znamenia* called on Ania & at 12 was at hospital till 1. *Mordvinov* lunched with us, then I had Prince Galitzin, Rauchfuss, had to see about coats — then Ania came & read to me (as I cant talk the whole time), the head is so tired as so many things to remember — *caviar,* wine, postcards to the hospital — our prisoners — Babies etc. Then Ania has heaps to tell after all her conversations & her humour today is not famous (as I go away). Then after tea officers, *Duvan* fr. *Eupatoria,* again papers & lots more people to see before leaving & all must be fitted in. Our Friend is with her, & we shall probably go there in the evening — he puts her out by saying she will probably never really walk again, poor child, better not to tell her with her caracter. —

I am going to see *Zhevakha* to-morrow — to hear all about the Image, it will be interesting to hear all — it would be good to draw him to the *Synod* as worker. — I wonder how Baby's arm is — he so easily overtires it, being such a strong child & wanting to do everything like the others — you know Lovy, I think I must bring Marie & Anastasia too, it would be too sad to leave them all alone behind. I shall only tell them on Monday morning, as they love surprises. — Mme Zizi wants to come as far as *Tver* as its her old town & she knows everybody, so she can be of much help to us. — Lovy, wont you go to *Vitebsk* with Baby, before we come, so as to see the army-corps wh. stands there, its interesting to see, *Mordvinov* says — or let us all go there together & from there you leave to the south somewhere to *Ivanov*. Think that over — it would be a w f u l l y interesting to see the troops, only 2 versts from Vitebsk by motor — our Friend always wanted me also to see troops, since last year till now he speaks of it — that it would also bring them luck. You speak it over with *Voyeikov* & let us go a l l t o g e t h e r. We arrive 15 th morning at 9, I think & then you say for one or 2 days. — What intense joy to meet again, I do miss you both so dreadfully! Yesterday it was a week you left us, our precious sunny ones! —

Beletzky presents himself to-morrow. It seems he spoke very energetically to *Polivanov* & told him, that he knows his detectives work & spy & so do his watch, & that rather upset him. *Mordvinov* was full of best impressions of all he had seen — oh what good it does being out there, far from these grey, nasty, gossiping towns. —

Forgive my bad writing, but I am as usual in a hurry. — Shall see our Friend this evening at 9 at her house.

Sweetheart, how are things working near Riga, who are the 3 generals you cleared out? —

I cannot imagine what *Nikolasha* does, now he has taken *Istomin* (who hates *Gregory)* who was *Samarin's* aide, as the chief of his chancellery.

Miechen is off with her train. *Igor* returned very ill, inflammation of the lungs & pleurisie — now he is out of danger, poor boy — he lies in the Marble palace — what bad health they all of them have, I pitty poor Mavra.

Now my Sunshine I must end. My longing is great for you & I eagerly count the days that remain still. God bless & protect you, guard & guide you now and ever. I cover you with tender kisses, my Treasure, & remain yr. fondly loving v e r y

Own.

I send you some flowers again. — I always kiss & bless your cushion morning & evening.

No. 139.

Tsarskoje Selo, Oct. 10-th 1915

My own beloved Darling,

Snowing and one degree of frost and grey; but still I slept with an open *window.* — What a lot of prisoners we have made against, but how is the news near *Riga*, that point disturbs one. — Our Friend, whom we saw last night, is otherwise quiet about the war, now another subject worries him very much and he spoke scarcely about anything else for two hours. It is this that you must give an order that waggons with *flour*, butter and sugar should be obliged to pass. He saw the whole thing in the night like a vision, all the towns, railway lines etc. its difficult to give over fr. his words, but he says it is very serious and that then we shall have no *strikes*. Only for such an organisation somebody ought to be sent from you. He wishes me to speak to you about all this very earnestly, severely even, and the girls are to help, therefore I already write about it beforehand for you to get accustomed to the idea. He would propose 3 days no other trains should go except these with flour, butter and sugar — its even more necessary than meat or amunition just now. He counts that with 40 old soldiers one could load in an hour a train, send one after the other, but not all to one place, but to *Petrograd* — Moscou — and stop some waggons at different places, by lines and have them by degrees brought on — not all to one place, that also would be bad, but to different stations, different buildings — if passenger trains only very few would be allowed and instead of all 4 classes these days hang on waggons with flour or butter fr. Siberia. The lines are less filled there coming towards the west and the discontentment will be intense, if the things dont move. People will scream and say its impossible, frighten you, if can be done and »will hark« as he says — but its necessary and tho' a risk, essential. In three days one could bring enough for very many months. It may seem strange how I write it, but if one goes into the thought — one sees the truth of it. After all one can do anything, and one must give the order beforehand about these three days, like for a lottery or collect — so that all can arrange themselves good — now it must be done and quickly. Only you ought to choose an energetic man to go to Siberia to the big line and he can have some others who will watch at the big stations and embranchments and see the thing works properly, without unnecessary stoppages. I suppose you will see *Khvostov* before me, therefore I write all. He told me to speak it to *Beletzky* and to morrow to the old man, so as that they should think about it quicker. *Khvostov* says its Rukhlov's fault, as he is old and does not go himself to see what is going on, therefore if you send somebody quite else to see to the thing, it would be good. — If one looks at the map; one sees the branching off lines and from *Viatka*. Also one ought to get sugar from *Kiev*. — But especially the flower and butter wh. overflows in *Yalutersk* and other districts — old men, soldiers can be used as there are otherwise not enough men to pack up and load the waggons. — Make it spread like a notwork and push on them and fill up — there are sufficient waggons. — Well, please, seriously think this over. — Now enough of this topic. — A. is very put out He wont let her go anywhere, *Bielgorod* for instance, whilst we are away — and when I encouraged her to go she found her house so cosy, that she did not wish to leave it; its always the same thing and it does not improve her mood and spoils ones pleasure when one rejoices to see you Darlings soon. — He finds it necessary to remain on here to watch how things are going, but if she leaves then he will too, as he has nobody otherwise to help him. Yes, He blesses you for the arrangement of these waggons, trains. — Again I cannot go to the hospital, as have four people to receive before luncheon; and each will have a lot to talk about. At 2.20 we go to the *Winter Palace* for the opening of the hospital. — I take the 4 Girlies — Mother dear will be there too and heaps of people — if there is time I shall pass through the *Store*. At 6 I receive again — its madning. — In the train I must speak with *Ressin* about our journey. — I am so tired and M. Becker will be coming too. — Here we are back again from town. The hospital in the *Winter Palace* is really splendid — a marvel how quick all the works have been done — one does not know where one is with rooms made in rooms quite excellent, and the baths, any *amount* of them. You must come and see it some day, its certainly worth while seeing. From there we went to the *Store* right through. — *Beletzky* told me, that you are leaving to-day or to morrow for *Tchernigov, Kiev, Berditchev,* but *Voyeikov* only mentioned yr. name, therefore I wired about Baby, because he can remain in the train when necessary and appear too sometimes — the *more* you and he show yourselves together, the better it is and he does love it so, and our Friend is so happy about it; and so is your old Sunny when Sunbeam accompainies sunshine through the country. Wee God bless you, my Angels. — We think of leaving monday evening at 10½ — reaching *Tver* at 9—9½ and remaining there till 3 or 5 — the next morning, Wednesday at 8½ at *Velikia-Luki* for several hours — and in the evening 8½ at *Orsha* where we can see several establishments of *Tatiana's* committees — its too late to go on to *Moghilev* so shall spend the night there and be at 9½ at *Moghilev* Thursday morning. You will then tell us how long we are to remain. It will be such a joy! *Zhevakha* is charming and we had a thorough talk about every thing — he knows all Church questions and the clergy and Bishops à fond, so he would be good as a help to *Volzhin*. The latter spoke well at the *Synod* it seems. — *Beletzky* pleased me, another energetic man. — Now I have been talking to the American Mr. Hearte for 1 h. and 20 m. about our prisoners in Germany and Austria and he brought me photos I'll show you. He helps a lot now he goes again to visit the Germans and Austr. here. — Well my Sunshine, Goodbye and God bless you. If you see Olga kiss her tenderly from me — my prayers follow you everywhere so tenderly. —

Very tender kisses. Sweatheart fr., yr., own deeply endlessly loving old

Wify.

No. 140.

Tsarskoje Selo, Oct. 27-th 1915

My very own Sweetheart,

There off you are again my two treasures — God bless your journey & send His Angels to guard & guide you. May you only have beautiful impressions & everything go off well. What will the sea be like? Dress warmly

Lovy, its sure to be bitterly cold — may it only not be rough. — You will take Baby on some ships — but not out to sea & perhaps to the forts, depending how you find his health. I feel so much quieter for you knowing that precious child near you to warm & cheer you up with his bright spirit & by his tender presence. Its more than sad without you both. But we wont speak of that. — See that he dresses warm enough. — I wish the old man wld. stay at home — I find it a shame he goes with you as you will feel nervous on his account — but insist upon Feodorov being severe with him. — Give me news whenever you can, as shall anxiously follow your journey; I know you wont risk anything & remember what He said about Riga. — Sweet Angel, God bless & protect you — ever near & with you my own Sweets, its such pain every time & I am glad its in the evening at least, when one can go straight home to ones room.

Yr. warm caresses are my life & I always recall & remember them with infinite tenderness & gratitude. —

Sleep well, Lovebird — Holy Angels guard yr. slumber — tiny is near by to keep you warm & cheer you up. —

Ever yr. very own, endlessly loving

Wify.

No. 141.

Tsarskoje Selo, Oct. 28-th 1915

My own sweet One,

Such tender thoughts follow you both darlings everywhere. I am glad you saw so many troops, I did not think you would at Reval. How I wonder whether you will go on to *Riga* & *Dvinsk.* — So bitterly cold, but bright sunshine. Miss you both quite horribly, but feel much quieter for you as sunbeam is there to cheer you up & keep company. No need to motor with Fred. & *Voyeikov* now. Do have the old man always watched, our Fr. is afraid he may do something stupid before the troops. Let somebody follow & have an eye upon him. — A. gave me this paper for you — she forgot to tell it to me, probably not grasping what it would mean to us about Baby's health & the great weight lifted at last fr. ones shoulder after 11 years of constant anxiety & fright! —

Forgive me bothering you already with a paper, but Rostovtzev sent it to me — *Voyeikov* can send the answer to Rostovtzev — that would be best.

I was not long at the hospital as had much to read. We had *Valia,* Iza, Mr. Malcolm & Lady Sibyl Grey to lunch — they are such nice people (arranging the hospital in Ella's house — the operation room will be in the room of Ella's with the 3 lights wh. you used to watch). — Then I received our 3 sisters, who go to Austria & *Kazbek* my lancer. Please remember about *Kniazhevitch.* — Went straight to bed fr. the station, sad & lonely —

saw yr. sweet faces before me — my two St. George's treasures. — Goodbye Sweetheart! God bless & protect you now & ever. Cover you with kisses & yearn for yr. embrace.

Ever yr. very own old Sunny.

I wonder whether this goes to the *Headquarters* or *Pskov,* wh. wld. have been cleverest. — Am so glad I know now where & how you live & the drives, country around & Church — can follow you everywhere. All my love.

No. 142.

Tsarskoje Selo, Oct. 29-th 1915

My own beloved

I just received yr. wire from Venden, wh. came fr. 10—11.5, so now I suppose you are at Riga. All my thoughts and prayers surround you my darlings. How interesting all you saw at Reval — can imagine how enchanted the English submarines must have been that you inspected them — they know now for whom they are so valiantly fighting. The manufacteries and ship building yards are sure to work doubly hard and energetically now. Wonder whether Baby accompanied you and what you did with the old man. — Here too its a little bit warmer, 5 degree of frost and sunshine. I remain in bed till 12 as heart a little enlarged and aches as does my head (not too bad) since yesterday. Then I have several gentlemen to see with *Reports* and that is fatiguing when the head is tired. — I shall finish this later, as may have more to tell then. Sweety, again I come with a petition, wh. the widow Mme *Beliaieva* brought me to-day. — *Groten* came to *Ania* to-day, in despair to be without a place — he is well now and will go to the regiment to give it over and then he has to go to *Dvinsk* with *Reserves* — but perhaps you will think about getting him a nomination. His eldest officer got a regiment and now a brigade already. — I am quite ramolished after all the people I saw. Mlle Schneider was interesting and talked like a fountain — we just arranged with her to keep *Krivoshein* in the new *Home Manufactures* committee, as he can be most useful. Excuse such a beastly dull letter, but am incapable of writing a decent letter. I bless and kiss you over and over again — sad lonely nights and don't sleep very well. God be with you.

Ever yr. very own old Wify.

Remember about *Kniazhevitch.*

No. 143.

Tsarskoje Selo, Oct. 30.th 1915

My precious Darling,

It is thawing, raining and terribly dreary and dark this morning. Many thanks for last nights telegram again from *Venden.* I am happy you managed to go beyond Riga — it will be a consolation to the troops and make the town inhabitants more reassured. — Was Baby excited to hear the distant shooting? How different your life is now, thank God, with nobody to keep you from traveling about and showing yourself to the soldiers. *Nikolasha* must now realise how false his ideas were and how much he personally lost by never having shown himself anywhere. Old Mme *Beliaieva* told me yesterday, that she had a letter from her son yesterday from England (all 6 serve in the artillery). He is attached to Kitchener and has to see about our orders being executed there. — Georgie received him and spoke about you just that you are with the troops and *Kitchener* wont allow him to go wh. is a sure point. *Beliaiev* answered him, that here there is a great difference, we are fighting on our own territory wh. he would not be doing. This simple answer seemed to console him and *Kitchener* was very contented when *Beliaiev* repeated their conversation. I was sure it wld. torment Georgie — but he does visit the troops in France from time to time. —

Markosov is off to Sweden to meet Max etc. and speak over the questions of all the prisoners. M. just returned from *Tashkent* as he wanted to see how they were cared for there, and found 760 Austrians, officers, but only 15 intelligent people to look after them, to answer their questions etc. — I think he can be of use, as he is very just, wh. people are not inclined to be now. But one sends him without any instructions wh. is foolish, and its the business of the red cross who sends him to do so. — Thank goodness the *Epaulets* have been restored to the officers. — I hope, Deary, that as soon as you reach the *Headquarter* one will print in the papers where you have been and what you have seen. How does the old man get on? I hope Feodorov keeps an eye upon him and that he want gaffe before the foreigners. Strange at the *Headquarters* without us? The noisy girls not there. *Eristov* wrote to Ania, that you will be receiving a petition from *Molostvo's* widow, to receive a yearly substitute. It seems he left her scarcely a penny and she is in an awful dilemma. *He squandered his small capital sold his estate to his brother and the crumbs which remained will with difficulty cover the debts which were left after his death. Unfortunately the victims of an epidemic have not the same privileges as those who fell in Battle.* He is delighted that *Afrossimov* has been advanced as General, and in the suite, an honour to the regiment. — Would *Groten* have done for yr. lancers, how do you think? I had old *Shvedov* for ½ hour and I told him I shall go one day and see where the young men work. *Sazonov* is a nuisance — always jalousie de métier, but in my *Imperial academy of oriental sciences* we have to prepare good consuls who know the languages, religions, customs etc. of the east. — Isa lunched with us — then I received 3 young officers returning to the war after wh. we went to the big palace — the hospital exists since a year, so we had lots of groups taken. Later I received Joy Kantakuzen who talked a lot, her husband is delighted to command yr. curassiers. Then P-ss Galitzin of Smolna, then I read — A. went to town and returns only at 9½ (with *Groten)* as they dine at Mme *Orlov's* in town. —

I do so wonder whether you reached the *Headquarters* to-day or went to *Dvinsk*. Sweet Angel, goodbye and God bless and keep you, endless passionate kisses fr. yr. old

Wify.

Massages to the old man and *N. P.*

No. 144.

Tsarskoje Selo, Oct. 31st 1915

Beloved One,

I am so glad that you saw the splendid troops at *Vitebsk* you have done a lot in these days — such joy Baby can accompany you everywhere. — Its grey thawing, raining; I remain at home as my heart more enlarged and don't feel very nice all these days. It had to come sooner or later as I had done so much and still a lot ahead to be done.

Olga only got up for a drive and now after tea she remains on the sopha and we shall dine upstairs — this is my treatment — she must lie more, as goes about so pale and wearily — the Arsenic injections will act quicker like that, you see. — All the snow has melted away.

I just heard through Rostovtzev that my lancer *Baron Tiesenhausen suddenly died on his post as a guard* — it seems to me very strange — he had no heart complaint. His young wife died this winter.

Our Fr. is happy you saw so much, says you walked all *in the clouds.* Isa lunched and bid us goodbye, she leaves to-morrow early fr. town for Copenhagen, to see her Father for 5 days, after 2 years' separation. —

Do you look at our names on the window sometimes! Paul is better but I think *Varavka* speaks of an operation wh. *Feodorov* dreaded on account of his heart. The wife says he cannot take any food, only a cup of tea. —

Alas, no Church for Olga and me — and I cannot go on Monday to the *Supreme Council,* it had to come, I had overtired myself — and I do so miss you my own Treasures. — Well Love, Goodbye and God bless you.

I cover you with tenderest kisses and remain yr. very own old

Sunny.

What is Greece up to? Does not sound very encouraging — hang those Balkans all. Now that idiotical Roumania, what will she do?

No. 145.

Tsarskoje Selo, Nov. 1st 1915

My own precious Darling,

I just got Baby's letter and enjoyed it thoroughly, he does write amusingly. What a pitty there was such rain and mud — but then at least the *Dvina* wont yet freeze.

Am so anxious about Roumania, if its true what *Vesselkin* wired *(Grigorovitch's* papers) that at *Rustchuk* one says Roumania has declared us war — I hope it is unfounded and that they only spread such news to please the Bulgarians. It would be horrid, as then Greece I fear will turn against us too. Oh, confound these Balkan countries. Russia has only been as an ever-loving helping mother to them and then they turn treacherously and fight her. — Really you never get out of worry and anxiety. —

I read the whole description of your journey in the papers — what a lot you did; and then Mr. *Gillard* explains all nicely. — Last night we dined upstairs in the corner room — horribly sad and empty without Sunbeam — I prayed in his room afterwards — no little bed! And then I remembered that where he is now he has another beloved Being lying near him. What a blessing that you can share all together, its so good for him to be your little companion it developes him quicker; — he is not too wild before guests, I hope. He writes so happy to be again at the *Headquarters*. — To-day I bid goodbye to my *Crimean, Gubariov, Vatchnadze* and *Botkin's* son, who all return to the front. The *Crimeans* all are anxious to reach the regiment as they are sent to the new front. — Grey, rainy weather. — The heart is better this morning, but does not feel nice, so I wont go out, nor to church, I must put myself to right again. — I send you a touching telegram from Alexei's *Georgians;* I answered them and said I should forward it to him — so perhaps you would thank them in his name again.

How did you find poor *Kanin,* not too bad I trust. Sister Olga wrote she is so happy in her work — Motherdear runs about all day in hospitals and finds Olgas especially cosy and nice. —

Beloved, I have popped into bed after seeing *Khvostov* who begged urgently to be received. Well, our good old Fred. had gaffed' quite colossaly again, wh. shows that one must no more tell him anything serious or wh. is not to be repeated. *Khvostov* got a letter fr. (his former brother in law) *Drenteln* — he will bring it to you, for you to see in what terms it is written. He tells him that Fredericks sent for him and told him that he wishes to know why *Khvostov* judges *Dzhunkovsky* so unjustily etc. *Drenteln* furious, sees in it the result of that black force (one understands our Friend) and that he pities you and Russia if *Khvostov perverts* all *orders* in that way. — *Khvostov* told Fred. that one must beware of *Dzhunkovsky* because of his different actions, police etc. Moscou meeting of the nobility, making himself out as a martyr because of *Gregory* and so on, and finding that in the society and clubs one ought to pay attention to his talks — and not let him receive a nomination in the Caucasus. Oh, that awful gaffeur — now that runs the round of the »*Preobrazhensky*« reg. and the Governors excomerades and hinders *Khvostov* terribly. He begs you not to tell anything to Fredericks, who will make it yet worse, nor *Drenteln,* who will be furious that I saw the letter. Such an unfortunate affair and binds *Khvostov's* hands. The regiment is not, alas, famous and hates our Friend, so he hopes you will soon promote *Drenteln* — give him an army brigade, so as that he should not yet more influence the regiment. *Drenteln* writes that *Orlov* sent for

Dzhunkovsky (soit disant his brother being very ill) — *Nikolasha* proposed him to become *hetman of the Tersk troops* but *Dzhunkovsky* refused. According to »spied upon« correspondance *Nikolasha* intends proposing him to be his aide. For God's sake don't agree, otherwise we shall have the whole lot of evil doers brooding harm and mischief there. Give him any command in front rather, he is a dangerous man pretending to be a martyr.

I said in future *Khvostov* is to address himself to *Voyeikov* in stead of the old ramoli gaffeur — no its too, too bad. Tell it *Voyeikov* if he promises to hold his tongue until he has seen *Khvostov*. He begs you to receive him one of these days for affairs. He will send me his answer to *Drenteln*. — I begged him to well think it over, as many will read it, and he must still explain reasons wh. can be told. — Then as not enough waggons move, thought it wld. be good if you could a t o n c e send a senator *(Dm. Neidhardt)* who has often been — does not matter he has Miechen's committee and its not for long to make a revision about the c o a l in the chief place. Masses are heeped and must be moved on to the big towns and if you send him directly it wont be an offense to the new minister. He does not know *Trepov*, many are against him as being a very weak and not energetic man. Our Friend is very grieved at his nomination as He knows he is very against him, his daughter told it to *Gregory* and he is sad you did not ask his advice. I too regret the nomination, I think I told you so he is not a sympathetic man — I know him rather well. His daughters were cragg and tried to poison themselves some years ago. The *Kiev* brother is far better. Well, one must oblige this one to work hard. —

400 waggons ought to come a day with flour, but only 200 do — one must set about things quicker and more energetically — the idea of the revision I think excellent, *Senatorial Revision* for the c o a l — if we get that people wont freeze and keep quiet — to send him out to the chief coal places fr. where one forwards it here. — I am sorry to bother you with so many things. I enclose a petition fr. my *Galkin* for his son. He made Ania write to several Generals and all say it concerns General (cant spell his name) the little one, *Konazarovsky*. Perhaps you would tell *Kira* to give it him fr. me. He is a good officer was in the artillery academy, I believe, and Costia knew about him — so funny for *Galkin's* son. — *Leo* is better, I am glad to say — Isa lunched and bid us goodbye, she leaves to-morrow early fr. town for *Volkov* is now doing duty — I am ashamed I took him away fr. the *Headquarters*.

I do hope the dear little arm will be better by the time you get this letter and that it wont spoil the nights rest. —

Poor Serbia is being finished off — but it was her lot, had we let Austria do it, o u r n o w a l l the rest — nothing to be done, probably a punishment for the country having murdered their King and Queen. Will Montenegro now be eaten up too, or will Italy help? — Oh and Greece? What shameful game is going on there and in Roumania — I wish one could see clearly. My personal opinion is that our diplomates ought to be hung — Savinsky has a l w a y s been the greatest friend of longnosed Ferdinand (the same tastes one says) that he always said before he ever went there. Then *P. Kozel* has neither performed his duty and Elim I think a fool too. Could they not have worked harder? Look how the Germans dont leave a thing untried so as to succeed.

Our Friend was always against this war, saying the Balkans were not worth the world to fight about and that Serbia would be as ungrateful as Bulgaria proved itself. —

Hate yr. having all these worries and I not with you. I find *Sazonov* might have inquired fr. the Greek Government, why they do not stick to their treaty with Servia — beastly false Greeks. —

How did all the foreigners like being out at the front? — Must quickly end. I miss and long for you quite terribly and kiss and hug you with all the tenderness I am capable off and yearn for your arms to be around me and rest and forget all that torments one. —

Endless fr. yr. old

Wify

On Tuesday Olga will be 20.

No. 146.

Tsarskoje Selo, Nov. 2nd. 1915

My own Sweetheart,

I send you my very tenderest congratulations for our darling Olga's 20th birthday. How the time does fly! I remember every detail of that memorable day so well, that it seems as tho' — it had all taken place only yesterday. — It is grey and raining, most dreary weather. I wonder how Baby sweet's arm is, I hope no worse and does not give him too much pain, poor Agooweeone.

How anxiously one waits for news — in Athens an Austrogerman deputation was received, they work hard to attain their aim, and we always trust and are constantly deceived; — one must always be at them energetically and show our power and insistance. I foresee terrible complications when the war is over and the question of the Balkan territories will have to be settled — then I dread England's selfish politics coming in rude contact with ours — only to well prepare all beforehand, not to have nasty surprises. Now whilst they have great difficulties one must take them in hand. —

Yesterday *Andronnikov* told Ania that *Volzhin* sent for *Zhivakhov* and told that you and I wished him to be appointed, so he gave him the list of all the *officials* of the *Synod,* telling him whom wld. he wish to have sent away and replace, one with 8 children, or 6 and so on — of course *Zhivakhov* declined and the minister of the Interior will take him, not to loose such a perfect gentleman who knows everything about our Church à fond. Its downright cowardice and hideous. Why not take him as one of his aides? He told someone he feared us, but yet more the *Duma.* Worse than Sabler, how can one do anything with such a poltroon. If you have papers of his do write that you wish to know »whether you have already appointed *Zhivakhov*«. To you it may seem a *mere nothing,* but no Deary, he knows all the ins and outs and can be of immense help and he is decided and could support and counsel *Volzhin* tho' he is a younger man. Why send away a poor man because of him, why not as aide, only because we begged for him. Your first wish almost, and he does not fulfil it and no doubt will throw the fault upon Zhivakhov, oh, humanity, so dispisable only think of themselves, lots of beautiful words and when it comes to deeds — cowardice.

I enclose a charming telr. from the »*Erivantsi*«. I find Olga looks better since she lies more — less green and weary.

Now its snowing and raining together, such a mess. —

O Lovebird, thank you over and over again for yr. sweet letter. I was intensely happy to receive it, it means so much to me a word from you, my Angel. How interesting all you write. I am only rather anxious at Baby's arm, so asked our Friend to think about it. — He told me to let *Khvostov* know, not to answer *Drenteln's* letter, as it would only be worse, give rise to more talking, be shown about and so forth. He is not obliged, as it was an impertinence and insult writing thus to yr. minister. Ania gave it him over by telephone. She gave me a letter of Kellers for you to read through when you have a free moment; and then as usual a petition. — I am going to give Olga her presents in her bedroom as we dine upstairs. — Groten leaves in 2 days to his regiment to give it over and then will remain at *Dvinsk,* as he has been put en reserve (wh. makes him sad). He looks flourishing and young, can ride again. — To-morrow my *Vesselovsky* comes, *Vikrestov* and several petty officers who ran away. I must end now Deary, as I have heaps of papers to read through before dinner. —

Goodbye my Beloved, God bless and protect you.

I kiss you endlessly, lovingly and longingly. —

Ever yr. very own old

Sunny.

No. 147.

Tsarskoje Selo, Nov. 3-rd 1915

My very own beloved One,

Many happy returns of our big Olga's 20-th birthday. We are having a *Te Deum* at 12½ in my big room with the ladies — as it is less tiring for her & me. Such a foggy morning, Tatiana has gone off to the hospital. *Rita Khitrovo* was yesterday with Olga & touched me by saying, that the wounded are very sad I am not there to do their *dressings,* as the Dr. hurts them. I always take the worst. So stupid not to be able to work again, but I must keep quiet — one day the heart is more enlarged, the next less & I don't feel nice, so have not even smoked for days; receptions & *reports* are quite enough. —

Saw poor *Martinov* on crutches, the leg is 4 inches (!) shorter — its now soon a year & by May one hopes he may be able to serve again. Its a marvel that he is alive — how wonderfully he every time escaped, 2 horses killed under him being already wounded & crushed & both bones shot through, broken. — I spoke with Count Nirod about Easterpresents for the army — we did not use up the 3 million roubles you had given fr. the appanage & wh. have to be replaced by the cabinet. A little over 1 m. remains & with that we want to get & order things for Easter. Only each man will get much less, as everything is far more expensive & in such quantities as we need, not even to be had.

Then Mr. Malcolm came again with a proposition of a society of the suffragists, who have been working splendidly in France, to look after our refugees, especially the women who are expecting Babys — one can set them to work here under Tatiana's committee — Buchanan must still speak to *Sazonov* about it. I told Malcolm to see Olga, he is off to *Kiev* to-night & then Odessa — it would have interested you to have seen him, such a nice man & ready to help everywhere. He wrote home to Engl. begging one to collect for our prisoners — most kind, general Williams knows him. They have asked me to be the patroness of the hospital in Ella's house, it will be called after Aunt Alix I think. — Then I saw my rifles I enclose their names — 4 splendid men — one ran away before & was cought again — 50 have already returned — through Belgium & Holland — there they left one now at the Consuls to act as interprator — they were kindly cared for, fed & clothed, they went at night by the compass. They were made prisoners nov. 11 of last year — *Vikrestov's* brother is there too, but under another name & as a soldier, so as easier to run away. The one man, the *flag-bearer* says, that the bits of the flag wh. were not burned by the old *Sergeant,* different men kept — & the top too. — Then I saw Olga's commander too. And Alia came with her 2 children for 3/4 of an hour, wh. made me very tired. When you see *N. P.* alone, tell him to be careful about *Dzhunkovsky's* book, on account of *Drenteln(?),* who may make a nasty story of it — only that should never guess it came through Ania. — The tail & *Beletzky* dine at Ania's — a pitty I find, as tho' she wanted to play a political part. O she is so proud & sure of herself, not prudent enough, but they begged her to receive them — probably something to give over again & they don't know how to do it otherwise & our Friend always wishes her to live only for us & such things.

Sweetest Treasure I must end now. God bless & protect you & give you wisdom & help. What news about Roumania & Greece? I wish our »fliers« could do something in Bulgaria on the railway lines where so much is being in time & succeed. It would be a great thing.

Endless kisses of deepest devotion & great yearning.

Ever yr. very own old

Sunny.

No. 148.

Tsarskoje Selo, Nov. 3-rd 1915

My own Beloved,

I begin my letter this evening, so as not to forget what *Khvostov* begged Ania to tell me.

I. It seems the old Man did not propose the ministery in a nice way to *Naumov,* so that he found himself obliged to refuse. *Khvostov* has seen *Naumov* since, & is sure that he would accept, or be happy if you simply named him. He is a very right man, we both like him, I fancy *Beletzky* worked with him before. Being very rich, (his wife is the daughter of Foros *Ushkov)* so not a man to take bribes — & the one, whom *Goremykin* proposes, is not worth much — have forgotten his name.

II. Then about *Rodzianko* of the *Duma* — *Khvostov* finds he ought to receive a decoration now, that wld. flatter him & he wld. sink in the eyes of the left party, for having accepted a reward from you. Our Friend says also that it would be a good thing to do. Certainly its most unsympathetic, but, alas, times are such just now, that one is obliged out of wisdom sake to do many a thing one wld. rather not have. —

III. Then he begs the police master of Moscou not to be changed just now, as he has many threads in hand, having belonged to the detective force before. Our *Spiridovitch* won't do there, as it seems he has just remarried a former doubtful singer of gipsy songs — so that one proposes him a post far away of governor I believe. —

IV. Begs you not to have *Ksiunin* banished to Siberia, as 2 Generals gave him the false news about our disembarkment in Bulgaria (he will bring the names to you) — & the man writes well in the papers & a repremand might be enough. —

V. Did you get a telegram fr. a woman saying, that you must place Ella & me in a convent, as he heard something about it, &, if true, wants to have her watched & see what type she is. —

Thats all I think — he dreads meeting *Drenteln,* after such a letter finds he cannot give him his hand (ask him to show it you) — if you invite him he must — & if you dont people wld. be unkind & speak. Am so sorry for the poor man. — He brought yr. secret marcheroute (fr. *Voyeikov)* to me & I won't say a word about it except to our Friend to guard you everywhere. If only Kiril could succeed! — One thing our Friend said, that if people offer great sums (so as to get a *decoration),* now one must accept, as money is needed & one helps them doing good by giving in to their weaknesses, & 1000 profit by it — its true, but again against all moral feelings. But in time of war all becomes different. — Speak to *Khvostov* about *Zhivakha* (do I still spell it wrongly?) *Andronnikov* did not quite give it over as it happened.

Nov. 4-th. Thick snow fell over night, everything white, but zero. —

You will receive this letter a few hours before you leave on your journey — God take you into His holy keeping & may your guardian Angels, St. Nicolas & the sweet Virgin watch over you and Baby sweet. Shall be near you all the time with heart & soul. How interesting it will be. If you have the chance, give over a *greeting* & blessing to my *Crimeans* & the *Nizhegorod.* officers too, if you have the chance, through *Yagmin.* How I wish we were with you — so emotioning.

I read a short description in the »*Novoye Vremya*« of an eye witness at Riga, & could not read it without tears, so what must be the feelings of those 1000, that see you & Baby together — so simple, so near to them. Can imagine how deeply you feel all this, beloved One, oh the endless blessing, that you command & are yr. own master.

Here I send you some flowers to accompany you upon your journey — they stood the day in my room and breathed the same air as your old Sunny, fresias last long in a glass. —

If you see our beloved sailors & my giants, think of us & bow to them from us if there should be an occasion. — I hope it will be nice & warm & that will do you all no end of good. For sure *Olga Evgenievna* will watch you from somewhere, as she lives at Odessa. —

If you do get any sure news about Roumania or Greece, be an Angel & let me know. *Elena* fears for her Father, because if the worst should happen, he said, he would die with his army — or he may commit suicide.

Igor told us this at luncheon — he says one cant touch the subject of Greece with poor Aunt Olga. —

Miss you both this time more than ever, such an endless yearning craving for you, to hear your sweet voice, gaze into your precious eyes & feel your beloved being near me. Thank God, you have Baby to warm you up & that he is of an age to be able to accompany you. Carry this infinite longing alone in my weary soul & aching heart — one cannot get accustomed to these separations, especially when one remains behind. But its good you are away — here the »atmosphere« is so heavy & depressing, I regret yr. Mama has returned to town, fear one will fill her poor ears with unkind gossip. Oh dear, how weary one is of this life this year & the constant anguish & anxiety — one would wish to sleep for a time & forget everything & the daily nightmare. But God will help. When one feels unwell, everything depresses one more — others dont see it tho'. — Our Friend finds *Khvostov* ought not to shake hands with *Drenteln* after such an insulting letter — but I think *Drenteln* will of his own accord avoid him — am so sorry for the poor fat man. —

Gregory has asked to see me to-morrow in the little house to speak about the old man, whom I have not yet seen. —

I must end. God bless yr. journey — sleep well, feel my presence near by in any compartment, I cover you with such soft & tender kisses, every little bit of you & lay my weary head upon yr. breast, yr. own old

Wify.

Very fondest thanks my own Sweetheart for your very dear letter, I was more than overjoyed to receive. If you cannot wire details, I can still understand. If you say you saw »ours« — that will mean *Marine of the Guard* if »yours« — »*Crimeans*« if *Yedigarov* — »*Nizhegorodtsi*«, can always understand more or less — & then what weather — I have the towns & dates, you see, fr. *Khvostov* to go by & keep it to myself. —

I did not mean you should now take the *Pr(eobrajentzi)* away fr. *Drenteln* but later on. —

Read this before you receive *Khvostov,* — he wants me to prepare you to several questions.

No. 149.

Tsarskoje Selo, Nov. 5-th 1915

My own Angel,

How charming Alexei's photos are, the one standing ought to be sold as postcard, — both might be really. — Please, be done with Baby, also for the public and then we can send them to the soldiers. — If in the south, then with cross and medal without coats and in caps and if at the *Headquarter* or on the way there, near a wood, — *overcoat* and *fur cap.* — *Fredericks* asked my opinion, whether to permit that cinema of Baby and Joy can be allowed to be shown in public; not having seen it, I can not judge, so leave it to you to decide. Baby told Mr. *Gillard,* that it was silly to see him »faisant des pirouettes« and that the dog looked cleverer than he — I like that. —

We had Mme Zizi to lunch, she had a *whole report* about all sorts off petitions and ladies, who want to see me. — *Rostchakovsky* was interesting I told him to write me a *Memorandum* for you. It concerns the railway line to *Archangelsk,* wh. he says might work 7 times more than he does. *Ugriumov* sent him for affairs concerning P. works especially, but he profitted to ask to see me to tell me how difficult it is for *Ugriumov* to do anything, as he has no official power given to him all these months.

Now one says it will be under *Military law,* so as to give him help, but thats unnecessary, as they are quiet there, no stories or disorders whatsoever. Then he asked for some formal nomination as to see to the railways, the minister of war put it on to *Rukhlov* etc., if he had a special nomination, then he could give severer orders as he is energetic, the engineers wld. be obliged to listen to him, those who dont work he cld. change, those that are good reward. He could force more goods trains leaving, could hurry on the work of the broad gage and so on. He does not ask, but *Rostchakovsky,* for the good of the work spoke to me to say a word to you... General Gov. during the war, as its such a very essential place now and much depends upon all being regulated and sent off well and hurried up. — Do I bore you very much with all these things, poor sweet? — Then of course

I add a petition. — General *Murray* has not yet arrived, but when he comes I shall certainly receive him with pleasure. — Now I had P-ce Galitzin with his *report* about our prisoners. 4 times a week we send off several waggon loads of things. How stingy the *Synod* is, I asked *Volzhin* should send more Priests and Churches to Germany and Austria — he wished us to pay, but as it was too much, he made the money be given out of the military fund — really a shame in time of war. Their convents, especially the Moscou ones are so rich and don't dream of helping. He wrote to St. Serg. for them to give us little Images and Crosses and if they wont gratis we shall pay — and they dont even answer; I shall try now through Ella; — we have sent 10,000, but what is that wee number. — I wonder, where this letter will find you!

Isa arrived at Copenhagen and had a good passage. — *Maslov* sent a *Trumpeter* with a letter telling the details, of poor Tiesenhausen death — influenza and heartfailure; — so I told one to give him food and then called him upstairs — he talked nicely. 21 years in the regiment, was on the dear *Standart* with us. I gave him an Image and the envelope of the military-post letter with my name to bring back to the Commander.

Now sweetest One, my beloved, my Soul and Sunshine, brightness of my life I must end my letter. I miss you more than words can say and yearn for you my huzy love. I cover you with kisses caresses and undying love. God bless you my A.

Ever yr. very own old Wify.

Paul continues being very ill, lost in weight very much — the Drs. wish an operation and to take out the »*Gall Bladder*«, Friend says he will die then and I remember Feodorov saying he feared an operation because of the heart being weak, with wh. I agree. She says Paul won't hear of an operation; it looks bad their wishing to take it out, is there a bad growth? I should not operate him in the state he is now. —

No. 150.

Tsarskoje Selo, Nov. 6-th 1915

My Own,

Warmest congratulations for yr. dear regiment's feast. — It was an intense joy when your dear letter was brought me this morning & I covered it with kisses — thanks ever so much for having written. So comforting to hear from you when the heart is sad & lonely & yearns for its mate.

I am sending you *Rostchakovsky's* paper — its quite private, I begged him to write all out so as to have it clearer for you, & I am sure, that you will agree with the chief points. The man is very energetic & full of best intentions & sees that things might work far better with a little help & a few changes -- so please read it through. —

That is a good plan you intend sending the guards later to Bessarabia after they are reformed & rested — they will be perfection then. Well, may God help those miserable Serbians. — I fear, they are done for & we cannot reach them in time. — Those beastly Greeks, so unfair leaving them in the lurch.

Our Friend, whom we saw yesterday evening, when he sent you the telegram, was afraid that, if we had not a big army to pass through Roumania, we might be cought in a trap from behind. —

Alexeiev is worth 100 longnosed *Sazonov's,* who seems somewhat feeble, to say the least of it. —

Well Lovy, He thinks I better now see the old Gentleman & gently tell it him, as if the *Duma* hisses him, what can one do, one cannot send it away for such a reason. You thought out something with *Taneyev* for him, did you not? I feel sure he will understand it. If you get a wire from me — *all is arranged* or: its done — that means I have spoken & then you can write or, when you return, send for him. He loves you so deeply that he wont be hurt & I shall say it as warmly as I can — He is so sorry as venerates the old Man. —

But he can always be yr. help & counsellor as old *Mistchenko* was — & better he goes by yr. wish than forced by a scandle, wh. wld. hurt you & him far more. He spoke well & it did me good to have seen him. Coughs very much & worries about Greece. Your presence in the Army with Baby brings new life to all & to Russia, he was always repeating it. — He finds you ought to tell *Volzhin* you wish *Zhivakhov* to be named his aide — he is well over 40, older than *Istomin,* whom *Samarin* took, knows the Church far better than *Volzhin* & can be of the very greatest help.

Now old *Flavian* has died, ours ought to go there as highest place & *Pitirim* here, a real *worshipper.* —

I saw *Senator Krivtzov* this morning — he gave me his book — I cried reading of the horrors the Germans did to our wounded & prisoners — cannot forget the atrocities, to think that civilised people could be so cruel — during battle, when one is mad, thats another thing. I know they say our cosacks did horrors at Memel — a few cases of course there may have been out of revenge. Better to forget it, as I firmly believe they are better now — but when once we begin to advance & their needs become greater, then I fear our poor men may fare worse. —

»*Mother Elena*« sat with me for some time, she is intensely grateful that you allowed her with her 400 nuns & 200 children to live at »*Neskutchnoye*« where its so peaceful & quiet. They have only got the dining room on the midle floor as our furniture fr. *Bielovezh* & Varsovie are kept in the other rooms. —

All my tender thoughts dont leave you, Angel dear & agooweeone on your journey, oh I do hope the weather will be sunny & bright — do Baby good, dampness acts on him & makes him pale always. —

Precious One, I kiss you with deep tenderness & loving caresses, passionately love. God Almighty bless and protect you my huzy darling, my bright sunshine. —

Ever yr. very own old wify Alix.

When you are away, I always dream — shows what it is not to have Sweetheart near me. —

Bow to the old man, I do hope he wont hinder yr. movements.

Give the little Admiral & *N. P.* also my love.

Wonder, whether Dmitri is with your or not.

No. 151.

Tsarskoje Selo, Nov. 8-th 1915

My own beloved Nicky dear,

Precious one, my thoughts dont leave you. So grateful for yr. telegram yesterday evening fr. *Novomirgorod* — comforting to see so many military trains pass — God bless the brave souls!

I have nothing of interest to tell. Yesterday evening we dined at 7½ because the 3 youngest girls went at 8 to the *funeral service* of the young officer, who died in the big palace. From 9—9½ I went to our hospital to see one who is very dangerously ill & I could not bear the idea of not going to him for a little bit — & then I passed through all the wards to bid goodnight. I had not been for a week & was glad to find all the others looking & feeling much better. —

I had *Viltchkovsky* with a long *report, on account* of the year, money questions etc. & then Ania got me to sledge for ½ an hour the interior *Babol.*-park, where you walked near my little carriage — 3 degrees of frost, we went much at a footpace, as then it was easier for me to breathe. Mme *B.* has come just now!! —

Longing for a wire from Odessa, all thoughts there with you. — I feel my letter is mighty dull, but I have absolutely nothing interesting to tell. —

Sweet Angel, long to ask heaps about yr. plans concerning Roumania, our Friend is so anxious to know.

Bezobrazov is inspecting the young soldiers at Novgorod to-day. What now about poor Paul? I doubt his ever being able to take up his service, to my mind its a finished man, that does not mean that he may not continue living with care, but not at the war, & I pity him deeply.

Wont you give Dmitri over to *Bezobrazov* to use then?

Huzy mine, I long for you & love you »with unending true devotion deeper more than I can say, better better every day« — you remember that old song of 21 years ago?

God's blessing be upon you my Sweetheart, sunshine.
I cover you with kisses

Ever yr. very Own.

Its cosy to get back into the train after a tiring day? Is there still a chance of yr returning the 14-th or only later?

No. 152.

Tsarskoje Selo, Nov. 8-th 1915

My sweetest Huzy dear,

I am so glad that all went off so well at *Odessa* and that you saw so many interesting things and our dear sailors too, but what a pitty that the weather was not warmer. Here it continues, about 3 degrees and no sun. — I wired to you about poor *Echappar's* accident and operation, as I got the news this morning. I do hope he will pull through, tho' its a terribly dangerous place — oh those motors, how careful one must be. — And Fredericks keeps on alright? It costs our Friend a lot, and he finds one really must not take him another time, anything may happen — besides he might suddenly take you for somebody else (William for instance) and make a scandle — I don't know why he says this. —

Something has got wrong with my pen and my writing is queer. — Alas, again wont go to Church, but wiser not on account of B. — How glad I am, that you were so contented with all you saw at *Tiraspol* what good it must do them seeing you, and how refreshing and emotioning for you. I am sending you a telegram. He dictated to me the other day I saw Him, walking about, praying and crossing himself — about Roumania and Greece and our troops passing through, and as you will be at Reni to-morrow, he wishes you to get it before. He wanders about and wonders what you settled at the *Headquarters,* finds you need lots of troops there so as not be cut off from behind. — In the papers *Grigorovitch* sends (so grateful you let me get them as most interesting generally) one sees how many guns and troops they send to Bulgaria. Hang those submarines, who hinder ones fleet and any disembarcation and they have time to collect so much. —

When one day our troops will march into Const. he wants one of my regiments to be the first, don't know why. — I said, I hoped it wld. be our beloved sailors, tho' they are not mine, at heart they are nearest to us all. — I long for news about the Guard etc. — Ania's brother has arrived and its her mothers and Alia's birthday, so shall only see her this evening. Do send me a message once for her, she is sad to have none.

I am much grieved about *Echappar's* death. Georgi will be awfully sad and all who knew him except Minny. And for my train a great loss and I was just thinking about arranging for his train to go south, but perhaps I can let *Riman's,* wh. goes from *Kharkov,* go to *Odessa,* as one will need a good train there. — So tiresome that cannot go about again because of my health, had wanted to do a lot during your absence. — We had Nini and Emma to tea and we talked long about their Father and how to keep him back next time. —

I am going this evening at 8½ for half an hour to our hospital to see the one who is so bad, as they say he is better since he saw me, and perhaps it may help again. I think its natural, why those who are so very ill feel calmer and better when I am there, as I always think of our Friend and pray whilst sitting quietly near them or stroking them — the soul must prepare itself when with the ill if one wishes to help — one must try and put oneself into the same plan and help oneself to rise through them, or help them to rise through being a follower of our Friends. —

Now Lovebird, I must end. God bless and protect you and keep you from all harm. Oh h o w one longs to be together at such serious times to share all.

Endless blessings, fondest, tenderest kisses Nicky sweet, fr. yr. deeply and passionately loving old Wify

Sunny.

No. 153.

Tsarskoje Selo, Nov. 9-th 1915

My own beloved Sweetheart,

Grey, thawing and very dark. Well, I went yesterday evening to our hospital, sat some time near the bed of *Smirnov* temp. still high but breath quieter — said goodevening to the others — 3 were lying on their backs playing on guitars and quite cheery. —

Xenia telegraphed, that Olga is going to her for a few days, I am glad as it will do her no end of good, as her nerves seem to me rather down, ever since she came to *Petrograd* and one filled her ears with horrors, and *Kiev,* wh. *Militza* and *Stana* had spoiled by wicked talks. —

In one of the copies of a German newspaper they write, that whilst the allies are wasting time discussing about Roumania, we and the Bulgarians are not wasting time making our preparations — yes, they never dawdle and our diplomates do most piteously. I wonder whether energetic Kitchener will manage anything with Tino. — Could one but get hold of the German submarines in the black sea, they are sending out more of them and they will paralise our fleet completely. Interesting all *Vesselkin* will have to tell you, I hope they are all well fortifying etc. all along the Roumainian-Bulgarian frontier — always better to calculate for the worst, as the Germans seem to be collecting all their forces down there now. It sounds absurd my writing all this, when you know a 1000 times better than me what to do; — I have nobody to speak with on such subjects; — but what a lot of men they send down there, wish we could hurry up a bit. — How glad I am that you are satisfied with all you saw at *Reni* and that *Vesselkin* works well, how proud he must have been to show you his church — may it only not suffer on have to be taken away. —

I received *Altfater, Pogrebniakov, Rumella* and *Semenov* of the *1-st artillery brigade of the Body-Guards* as its their feast, and the touching people gave me 1000 — Olga 150, and Tatiana 150. — I went with *Tatiana* to the *funeral service* for *Echappar* — *Baranov* was there, *Kotzebu* grown quite grey, *Yakovlev, Schulenburg, Kaulbars,* and *Kniazhevitch* and all the ladies. As my train stands without work at *Dvinsk* have told it to bring his body. —

General Murray is enchanted with all he saw, Anias brother took him about a lot. — Excuse a dull letter, but am tired and achy as slept very badly these last 3 nights. —

Very tenderest blessings, fondest, warmest kisses, Precious One, fr. yr. very own old

Wify.

No. 154.

Tsarskoje Selo, Nov. 10-th 9115

My own beloved One,

It seems to be darker every morning — nearly all the snow gone & three degrees of warmth. — Now the letters have to leave much earlier, the trains have changed it seems. — By the by did you settle anything about a senator to inspect the railways & coaldepots & see to set all moving, because really it is a shame — in Moscou one has no butter & here still many things are scarce & prices very high, so that for rich people even it is hard living — & this is all known & rejoiced at in Germany as our bad organisation, wh. is absolutely true. —

Such a nice surprise Baby dears letter from Odessa & Mr. Gillards — of course you cant write, I can imagine how even in the train you are bothered with papers. — Perhaps, if you do send me a word, you will give a message of thanks to A. for her letter, because when I said you wired thanks for letters, she said it meant ours. — I suppose, this letter will find you at the *Headquarter.* Nini understood you were probably arriving here on the 14-th, to me it does not seem very likely, as after such a journey you will for sure have lots to speak to *Alexeiev* about. — Stupid heart is enlarged again & the old pain in the legs was very strong — nevertheless have many people to receive to-day, — ex lancer *Kniazhevitch* too, don't know what shall have to tell him. —

Our Friend told me to wait about the old man until he has seen Uncle *Khvostov* on Thursday, what impression he will have of him — he is miserable about the dear old man, says he is such a *righteous man,* but he dreads the *Duma* hissing him & then you will be in an awful position. — Is the *Zemstvo reform which Nikolasha* wants to bring into the Caucasus a good thing? The people and many different nationalities, can they grasp this — or do you find a good reform? My personal weak brain does n o t find it yet time — you will see «*Novoye Vremya*» page 7 below of Nov. 10-th. —

What hideously dull letters I write! Forgive me sweetest.

The Austrian sisters have arrived, one is a good acquaintance of Marie Bariatinskys from Italy. Mme Zizi will beg Motherdear to see them & the Germans when they return, then I can too; & one must do such things, its for humanity's sake then they will be more willing to help our prisoners too; — & if she sees them one cannot find fault with me. —

Volzhin will need a good deal of «picking up» from you, he is weak & frightened — when all is going to be well arranged about *Varnava,* he suddenly writes to him privately that he should ask for his dismission — young *Khvostov* told him it was very wrong — but he is a coward & frightened of public opinion, so when you see him, make him understand that he serves you first of all & the Church — & that it does not concern society nor *Duma.* —

Princess *Palei* says Paul eats a lot now but looses daily in weight — he weighs less than Anastasia now, at night sometimes screams from pain & then again feels better. The *gall bladder* is becoming *atrophied* & therefore the *gall* spreads everywhere, tho' he has not become yellow . They want him to be operated at once upon yr. return, in some *hospital station* — they say its the only thing to save him, & our Friend says he will certainly then die, the heart not being strong enough. To-day *Tchigaiev* is to see him. His colour frightened me, the same as Uncle Wladimir had the last months, & Uncle Alexei before he left abroad then, & looking so like Anpapa, hollow under the eyes. He receives nobody, not wishing them to see how he has changed, but as soon as am better want absolutely to see him; am so awfully sorry for him — at last all his wishes achieved — & nothing of any avail. —

Now goodbye Lovebird, God bless — & protect you. Ever such tender, passionately, loving kisses, Nicky sweet, beloved huzy, fr. yr. very own old wife

Sunny.

How is the little Admiral? What have you settled about Dmitri? Love to the boy.

No. 155.

Tsarskoje Selo, Nov. 11-ths 1915

My own beloved Sweetheart,

I am so glad you saw the Caucasian cavalry — I got a charming telegram afterwards from *Yagmin.* — Can imagine their enchantment at last to have seen you; & the «*Tvertsi*» Baby for the first time. —

Dark, windy, snowing, 1 degree of frost — the shortest days, so dreary. —

Yesterday afternoon dear Lili *Den* came to us for tea, on her way from Helsingfors to the country. She saw her husband, & he told her many interesting episodes of their fighting, firing from sea on shore. —

Oh, my dear, I received Olga Orlov, on purpose I had Olga & Anastasia in the room & all went well, but when I got up she begged to speak to me alone & then went off about her husband & what I had against him & that she hoped I did not believe all the calumnies spread against him etc. I was sorry for the woman, but it was horribly painful, as I could not offend nor hurt her — I got through somehow, but I dont think she went away any the wiser — I was kind & calm, did not fib — well I wont bother you with the talk & thank God its over — one has so to pick out ones words, that they should not be turned against one afterwards. —

The Russian motor sanitary *detachment* of Verolas wh. is under my protection, worked splendidly in France, a while ago I got the telegrams from him & Mme Isvolsky & today I read a description in the «*Novoye Vremya*» — the one motor got holes. —

Then I saw *Prince Gelovani* to speak about *Eupatoria* wh. he looked after for me. Now he goes for 10 days to his family to the Caucasus & then straight to the regiment. He is delighted the Css. Worontzov has been taken away as the harm she did was very great. About the *Zemstvo* he is very contented & says its obligatory to be arranged as they must see to the state of the roads & railways & so on; — he is such a nice, cosy man, with his amusing Russian.

Poor Petrovsky sat for nearly an hour with me & we talked over the question of his divorce without end all so complicated. —

A week to-day that you left us — but it seems much longer & I have such a yearning for you my two Darlings. —

Wont you have a lot to tell us!

I continue receiving daily, my heart is still enlarged so do not go out & miss my hospital, but I want to get decént for your return.

Olga looks better and less tired, I find. —

Well Deary, I saw *Kniazhevitch* & found him looking very well, fresh, good look in the eyes & nothing about him like last year. Feels well, so of course I could not say anything. He leaves at the same time as this letter for the *Headquarters*, Alexeiev told him to be there on the 14, well he will be already the 13-th. He has good complexion — his wife finds him also quite alright — so I really do not know what you will think to do with him — perhaps it was a momentary weakness — I should not personally listen to Erdeli, as he is not famous & a jealous nature — Georgi heard such strange things too — but you will see he is just now looking flourishing & bright too. — He thinks, that perhaps *Arseniev* may receive our brigade, that w o u l d be lovely. —

Goodbye, Beloved, God bless & protect you.

I cover your sweet face with kisses and tender caresses.—

Ever, Huzy love, yr. very own wify Alix.

How is the old man Fred.

In town one grumbles again so awfully against dear old *Goremykin* so despairing. To-morrow *Gregory* sees old *Khvostov* & then I see him in the evening — He wants to tell his impression, if a worthy successor to *Goremykin*, — old *Khvostov* receives him like a petitioner in the ministery.

No. 156.

Tsarskoje Selo, Nov. 12-th 1915

My own beloved Nicky dear,

Is this the last letter to you, I wonder. One says the »*Erivantsi*« are preparing for the 17-th when you go to see them — the guard awaits you too — you arrive only this evening at the *Headquarters* so, that it seems to me impossible you should leave the 13-th — besides *Bark* awaits you at *Moghilev,* and for sure heaps of work.

In case therefore if we do not see each other the 14-th, I send you my very, very tenderest loving thoughts & wishes & endless thanks for the intense happiness & love you have given me these 21 years — oh, Darling, it is difficult to be happier than we have been, & it has given one strength to bear much sorrow. May our children be as richly blessed — with anguish I think of their future — so unknown!

Well, all must be placed into God's hands with trust & faith. — Life is a riddle, the future hidden behind a curtain, & when I look at our big Olga, my heart fills with emotions and wondering as to what is in store for her — what will her lot be.

Now about affairs again. *Groten* suddenly turned up, he bid his regiment goodbye & was touched to tears by their kindness & the regimental farewell. He went to the *Headquarters* presented himself to General *Konazarovsky,* who did not receive him over amiably & said he could not tell him anything as you were away. He, the stupid, left again for the country instead of patiently awaiting yr. return. He is perfectly well & can serve — wonder what brigade he will get? As regiment I believe the *Horse Grenadiers* are free, my fat Toll, I fancy, receives the *Pavlogradtsi* (not a beauty, but one says thorough). — Does *Dobriazin* get a brigade? *Kussov* waits for a regiment — The «*Severtsi*» are free too, I believe. Heaps of questions, you see — But get work for *Groten,* he is young & strong & its no good his sitting in the country *in the reserves.*

I sleep abominably, get off only after 3, and this night after 5 — so dull. Heart still enlarged. — Ania walked on her crutches guided by *Zhuk* from *Feodorov* hospital through our garden to *Znamenia,* of course far to much, already twice, & now feels very tired. —

I received again yesterday, to-day I have *Rostovzev* & I read already a fat *report* of his this morning. At midnight I got yr. telegram yesterday about *Kherson* and *Nikolaiev* — it took 4 hours coming & I was beginning to get anxious without any news. —

It will seem strange to live in a house again, I am sure, after your long roaming about. —

Fancy, Olga Orlova telephoned to her friend Emma (she has broken with Nini for her finding *Voyeikov* at fault in everything), that she had seen me & not spoken a word about her affairs — such a lie! And when she gave her word of honour to me she had never said anything against me, the old Css. says she did speak against me, & he said nasty insinuations at *Livadia* against me to his friend Emma & she, *Olga Orlova* says he never did, nor wld. try to harm a woman's reputation — one nest of lies — they don't touch me, because I know both be liars, only I hate words of honour, when one does not know how to answer. —

Now my sweetest love, I must end my scrawl. Let me know about when to expect you. God bless and protect, guard & guide you. —

I kiss you with deepest tenderness and boundless love & devotion, & long to rest my weary head upon yr. breast. —

Ever, Huzy mine, yr. very own old Sunny.

P. S.

Darling, I forgot to speak about *Pitirim, the metropolitan of Georgia* — all the papers are full of his departure fr. the Caucasus & how greatly he was beloved there — I send you one of the cuttings to give you an idea of the love & gratitude one bears him there. Shows that he is a worthy man, and a great *Worshipper,* as our Friend says. He foresees *Volzhin's* fright & that he will try to dissuade you, but begs you to be firm, as he is the only suitable man. To replace him He has nobody to recommend, unless the one who was at *Bielovezh,* I suppose thats the *Grodno* one? A good man he says — only not *S. F.* or *A. V. Hermogen,* they would spoil all with their *spirit* there. —

Old *Vladimir* already speaks with sorrow, that he is sure to be named to *Kiev* — so it would be good you did it as soon as you come, to prevent talks & beggings fr. Ella etc. —

Then *Zhivakhov* he begs you straight to nominate as help to *Volzhin,* he is older than *Istomin* so age means nothing & knows the Church affairs to perfection — its your will & you are master. —

There, that was a long post scriptom. —

W.

No. 157.

Tsarskoje Selo, Nov. 13-th 1915

My own beloved Husband,

21 years that we are 1, sweet Angel, I thank you once more for all you gave me these long years, wh. have passed like a dream — much joy and sorrow we have shared together, & love ever increased in depth and longing.

Last year, I think, we were neither together; on that day you had left for the *Headquarters* & Caucasus? Or no, you were with us at *Anitchkov?* All is so mudled up in my brain. — Congratulate you with Motherdear's birthday — our Olga's Christening day. — I shall choose a present & the children can take it to-morrow. —

I was to have gone to Paul to-day, but my heart being more enlarged it would have been unwise. I have asked *Botkin* to find out the exact truth fr.

Varavka — I always fear cancer, & the french Drs. some years ago thought, that he had the beginning of cancer. By telephone one told me that *Tchigaiev* is of the same opinion as *Varavka* & that to-morrow he is to be looked at through Röntgen rays — now that shows, that they think there is something wh. might appear, because to be fed every 2 hours & decrease in weight shows that things are bad.

Our Friend entreats there should be no operation, as he says Pauls organism is like that of a wee childs — & Feodorov then told me, that he would not like an operation, fearing for Paul's heart. Now if it is cancer in the liver, then one never, I believe, operates — in any case I fear he is a doomed man, so why shorten his days & he does not often suffer.

I only think they ought to let little Marie know how bad he is, as the Child is devoted to him & might have cheered him up. The Prss. (Palei) continues her long walks twice daily to become thin, & I do not think realises how seriously ill poor Paul is. —

I see *Bezobrazov* to-day.

What are you going to do now, you will have to think of another man now instead of Paul, as were he to recover, in any case there would be no question, alas, of his serving at the war. — Remember to nominate *Groten* somewhere. —

Well, I saw our Friend from 5½—7 yesterday at Anias. He cannot bear the idea of the old man being sent away, has been worrying & thinking over that question without end. Says he is so *very wise* & when others make a row & say he sits ramoli with his head down — it is because he understands that to-day the crowd howls, to-morrow rejoices, that one need not be crushed by the changing waves. He thinks better to wait, *according to God* one ought not to send him away.

Of course if you could have turned up for a few words, quite unexpected at the *Duma* (as you had thought to) that might change everything & be a splendid deed & it wld. later be easier for the old man — otherwise better he should be ill a few days before so as not to personally open the *Duma* not to be hissed, but he thinks better to wait until you return, and when I said I should, it was a weight lifted fr. his mind — & I know you think so too.

He saw the old tail, very dry & hard, but honest, but not to be compared with *Goremykin* — one good thing that he is devoted to the old man — but is obstinate. —

Emma saw him afterwards & like a child poured her whole heart out to him. — He thinks Greece wont move & Roumania neither, then the war will last shorter — He hopes not more than to spring. — Would to God it were true!

Do you know a Count *Tatistchev* from Moscou (banks)? — I think a son (or nephew) of the old General a. d. c., a most devoted man to you, says you know him. Likes *Gregory* much, disapproves of the Moscou nobility to wh. he belongs — is an older man already. Came to Ania to talk, sees very clearly the faults *Bark* made, about the *loan* I believe & the fatal results it may have.

Our Friend says he is a man to be trusted, very rich & knows the bank world very well — would be good, if you could have seen him & heard his opinion — says he is most sympathetic. I can make his acquaintance, only my brain I am sure would never grasp money affairs — I do dislike them so.

But he might put things clearly to you, & help you advise.

Just this moment got Mr. Gillard's letter of the 8-th describing the day at Odessa — that was nice that you rode & Baby drove with the old man — he wired home enchanted too. —

I shall have a *mass* to-morrow in the house at 12½ for Olgas & me, the others will go for 11 oclock to *Anitchkov.*

Now I must end.

Goodbye & God bless you, my Treasure. Live through these days 21 years ago with tender, grateful love, I kiss you without end in deepest love & devotion caressing you gently. I bless you & commend you to our Lords' care & the Holy Virgin's love.

Ever yr. very own old Wify.

Will *Bezobrazov* take Dmitri? If my Commander General *Vesselovsky* receives a brigade, please, let his successor be *Sergeiev,* he is the eldest in the reg. & commanded when *Vesselovsky* was wounded.

No. 158.

Tsarskoje Selo, Nov. 14-th 1915

My own sweet Treasure,

Every loving thoughts and prayer are with you, all my love and caresses. So sad to spend this day apart, but what is to be done, we can only thank God for the past and that up to now we spent that day always together. Foolish old wify cried a lot this night. — A bright morning, the sun rose beautifully behind the kitchen, 10 degrees of frost — a pitty the snow has all melted. — Once more, Huzy mine, thank you for all during these 21 years! What a lot you have to do for sure now after your journey — wonder how you spend this day! Is Baby-kins not too tired from all the walking? Mr. Gillard's letters are so interesting, as he relates about all you saw — and what splendid French, it makes me quite jealous. — I am sending off the 3 youngest girls with Mme Zizi to Church and lunch to *Anitchkov* and Nastinka also meets them there. The rest of us will have a *Te Deum* in my big room at 12½. I have not been to mass since you left and it makes me so sad. —

I am so glad, that you have named *Naumov* definitely and am full of hopes, that he will be the right man — he always pleased me, I like his frank eyes and he always spoke enthusiastically and eager about his governments and all the work to be done and went into all the details, so it is knowledge he has gained personally by work. *Bezobrazov* came to me yesterday and we had a nice talk — you saved him as he says. — Then the Dr. of my train, who brought poor *Eshapar's* body, presented himself to give me all the details, and then a wounded officer returning to his Siberian regiment No. 13, wh. you must have seen near Riga. — Slept badly, again heart still enlarged and head rather aches, still shall have to go to Pauls, as he begged to see me. I asked *Ania* to invite Rita and *Shah Bagov* and *Kikinadze* and *Danelkov* for the Children at 4½, to spend a cosy afternoon, as they dont go to the hospital to-day and would have missed their friends. — I wonder how *Shvedov* is, he fell ill again at the *Headquarters* — A. wired to *Zborovsky* on his namesday, asking about *Shurik,* but got no answer — perhaps private telegrams are not let through.

Its quite strange to see the sun again after these dark days, such a consolation. —

My letter is dull and must now come to an end. God bless and protect you, my very own Darling, my Beloved, my One and All. I cover you with tender kisses and hold you tightly in my yearning arms.

Ever yr. very own old

Wify.

No. 159.

Tsarskoje Selo, Nov. 15-th 1915

My own Beloved,

Heart and soul were overjoyed to receive your dear letter, and I thank you for it ever so tenderly. Everything you wrote was most interesting and did one good to see how contented and well pleased you are with the state of the troops you inspected. Can imagine the wild joy of your »*Nizhegorodtzi*« and all the rest scampering after you — their dream fulfilled, to see you during the war! —

And perhaps you will be home on Wednesday, oh wont that be too lovely, after 3 long weeks. I have never been separated so long from Agoowee one — now it seems already s u c h ages. —

Now, before I forget, I must give you over a message from our Friend, prompted by what He saw in the night. He begs you to o r d e r that one should a d v a n c e n e a r R i g a, says it is necessary, otherwise the Germans will settle down so firmly through all the winter, that it will cost endless bloodshed and trouble to make them move — now it will take them so aback, that we shall succeed in making them retrace their steps — he says this is j u s t n o w the most essential thing and begs you s e r i o u s l y to order ours to advance, he says w e c a n and we must, and I was to write it to you at once. —

Then from *Khvostov.* He says *Trepov* is very much against the revision you ordered Neidhardt to do, and does not wish him to mix in his affairs, but *Khvostov* begs you to stick to yr. order and insists upon it, because the well-thinkers and in the *Duma* too are delighted, as they see that will save the situation and clear much up. *Khvostov* read delighted telegr. about it and that will touch different commissions, entre autre *Gutchkov* will be shown up, and its absurd *Trepov* being against it. I have a paper (copy) of *Shakhovskoy's* begging *Khvostov* to take energetic measures otherwise he cannot guarantee for the result — *Trepov* ought to be glad — no fault touches him as he is new and is also trying his best. *Khvostov* thinks it wld. be v e r y advisable if you had the pay of the *railroad men* augmented, as with the post, the result was glorious gratitude towards you, boundless, a stop to strikes — given by you personally before they had time to ask for it. He came on purpose to dine with Ania and *Beletzky,* to-night, so as that I should write this for you to read before *Trepov's report* on Monday. — Lovy, you wrote me that the railway line to Reni is old and rotten, please order it categorically to be at once improved to avoid accidents, as our sanitary trains, amunitions, provisions and troops will need it. Cannot you quickly have small lines branching off laid, to facilitate the communication, as we sorely need more lines there, otherwise our communication will stick, and that can be awful during winter battles. This I write of my own accord, because I feel sure it could be done and you k n o w, alas, how very little iniative our people have — they never look a head until the catastrophe comes suddenly right upon us and we are taken unaware. Several short branches towards the Roumanian frontier and Austria, have sleepers for broad gages prepared beforehand, you remember what trouble it was to reach *Lemberg.*

I was at Paul's, he lay in their bedroom, is allowed to move about in the room and sit a bit on the armchair — terribly thin, but not those dark spots on his cheeks I disliked, voice stronger, talkative, interested in everything. I begged him to put off having Roentgen photo taken till Feodorov returns, as Dmitri wired *Feodorov* begged it — she hurrys things too much. He puts all his trust in *Feodorov* and leaves it to him to decide about the operation, he of course hates the idea, but if *Feodorov* insists, of course he will do it; I should not risk it. — I felt rotten all day with my heart. Received my Toll (lancer), who gets a regiment, one says yr. *Pavlograd Hussars* — but he does not know for sure. *Samoilov* is also a candidate for a regiment and *Arseniev* for our brigade. — Paul imagines he will be well enough to go, she says — I told her I doubted it, I did not speak reassuringly when we were alone, as she was so cool about it and eyes so hard. You know its strange, the eve before he fell ill, he had a discussion with *Georgis* at the *Headquarters* about our Friend. *Georgi* said the family call him a follower of *Rasputin,* where upon Paul got furious and said very strong things — and fell ill that night. Her niece heard this from her — told it to *Gregory,* who said, that no doubt God sent it him because he ought to have stood up for a man you respect and his soul ought to have remembered that he received everything fr. you and brought a letter fr. his wife she had asked *Gregory* to write to me begging for them. — Our Friend was struck by this. —

It was a sad day without you — Sonia and *Irina* lunched, Olga fed Sonia and I lay as usual on the sopha. Your letters were then brought to me and I have reread them more than once since and kissed them tenderly — your sweet hands rested on the paper and Baby's too. —

Good old Rauchfuss died yesterday morning, a great loss for my society »*Mothers' and Infants*« as his head was marvelously fresh for his great age. —

Botkin is not well, so can't come this morning. — Ania manages to walk half an hour on crutches through our garden — how strong she is, tho' complains at being a cripple — nearly daily shaken by motor to town, climbs up to the 3rd story to see our Friend — her back aches especially in the evening. But I feel its the hope of meeting you in the mornings that gives her the strenght to walk. — *Zhuk* accompanies her now again, as it wld. be dangerous her going alone, she might fall and then, the Drs said, she wld. be sure to rebrake her leg. — Her brother returned for 6 days. —

Mavra is going to the country as she feels her nerves so shaken and cant sleep a bit, poor thing. Tatiana has gone to the Caucasus for the 6 months of her husband's death and then returns again from *Mskhed.* —

The old man is coming to me to-day, but I don't know why. — Such glorious sunshine! Remember about *Riga!*

And now goodbye and God bless you my sweetest husband, love of my soul.

Endless kisses fr. yr. own wife.

Alix.

Went to sleep after 4. —

No. 160.

Tsarskoje Selo, Nov. 15-th 1915

My own beloved Darling,

I began my letter already to-day, but I saw old *Goremykin* just now & am so afraid of forgetting what I am to give over, by to-morrow. — He was to have a sitting of all the ministers this evening, but had to put it off as you sent for *Trepov* — he will have them Wednesday evening & begs to see you on Thursday. He is perfectly calm for the interior quiet, says nothing will be. The young ministers, *Khvostov* & *Shakhovskoy* he finds get a bit excited before anything is the matter, to wh. I answered better foresee things than sleep, as one generally does here. —

Well, its the question about calling the *Duma* together now — he is against it. They have no work to do, the budget of the minister of Finances has been presented 5 to 6 days late & they have not begun the preliminary works, wh. are needed before giving it over to the whole *Duma.* If they sit idle, they will begin talks about *Varnava* & our Friend & mix into governmental questions, to wh. they have not the right. (now *Khvostov* & *Beletzky* told Ania, that the man who intended speaking against *Gregory* has taken back his paper & they say that subject won't be touched) — well, this is the old man's council after long consideration & yesterdays talk with a member of the *Duma,* whose name he begged not to mention. He would advise you writing two rescripts, one to *Kulomzin* (I find you might change him) & the other to *Rodzianko,* giving as reason that the budget has not been worked through by the commissions & therefore too early to assemble the *Duma,* that *Rodzianko* is to make his *report* to you when they are ready with their preliminary work.

I am going to ask Ania to quite privately speak of this to our Friend, who sees & hears & »knows much«, to ask what He would bless — as He thought otherwise the other day. *Goremykin* wants me to write all this to you before seeing you, so as to prepare you to his conversation. Always calm, only very wretched about his wife who suffers now from asthma beside all the rest & therefore can scarcely take her breath. —

From *Khvostov* he heard that all your orders to *Polivanov* or his papers to you are all shown to *Gutchkov* — now that cannot be stood, simply playing into yr. enemy's hands. He told me you had mentioned *Ivanov* to him — the same thing also our Fr., I believe, & *Khvostov* said — especially our Friend — then all would be perfect in the *Duma* & everything one needs, pass through. *Beliaiev* is a good worker & the old man's prestige would do the rest. And he is tired at the war — & if you have a man to replace him, perhaps it would be good now. — Then he touched other questions of less interest to you. — But our Friend said last time, that only if we have a victory, then the *Duma* should not be called in, otherwise yes, that nothing will be said so bad — that the old man must be ill a few days so as not to appear there — & that you should turn up unawares & say a few words. — Well, when we meet I'll tell you what he now says. —

Lovy mine, is this really the last letter, & are you coming on Wednesday? How lovely. — A. had a charming letter fr. *N. P.* telling all about the journey & his impressions — full of the beauty of the troops, as tho' they were fresh & never been to the war yet. — All this gives you strenght for your work & a clear mind. —

16-th. Goodmorning Lovy.

Cold & windy. Feel very tired after again a badish night & everything aches rather — so have been lying with shut eyes this morning — I have a *report* with Senator Pr. *Galitsin* about our prisoners & then see *Kolenkin* & hereafter the 3 Austrian Sisters. —

I hope your cold has passed & that the cocain helped well. Pitty no long walks for you, with the roads covered in deep snow. — I suppose you come for barely a week if you must be back again for the St. George's feast — how will that be, I wonder.

Oh what joy, God grant, if I shall have you home again in two days — to-morrow 3 weeks that you left! Such a longing for you, my Treasure. —

Well, goodbye my Love, I bless & kiss you over & over again with deepest love and tenderness,

Ever Nicky mine, yr. very own old Sunny.

P. S. I reopened my letter — she spoke to our Friend who was very sad & said, it was quite wrong, what the old man said. One must call the *Duma* together even for quite short, especially if you, unknown to others, turn up there it will be splendid, as you had thought before of doing — that there wont be any scandals, one wont make a row about him, *Beletzky* & *Khvostov* are seeing to that & that, if you do not call them together, it will create unneccessary displeasure & stories — I was sure He wld. answer so, & it seems to me quite right. Probably one frightened the old man that he would be whistled at, its people who were sorry personally for him — because I understand having sent them away when they did not expect it, one cannot again uselessly offend them — of course he loathes their existence (as do I for Russia). Well, one must see to their at once & quickly sitting to work over the Budget. I feel sure you also will agree to *Gregory* sooner than to the old man, who this time is wrong & been frightened about *Gregory* & *Varnava.*

No. 161.

Tsarskoje Selo, Nov. 25-th 1915

My own precious One,

Off you will be storming when you read this note. My tenderest prayers and thoughts will as ever follow you everywhere. Thank God, I had you 7 days — but they flew by, and again the heartache begins. Take care of Baby, don't let him run about in the train, so as not to knock his arms — I trust he will be able to bend his right arm alright by Thursday. — The idea of having to let him leave you alone afterwards, makes me sad. Before you decide speak with Mr. Gillard, he is such a sensible man and knows all so well about Alexei. —

You will be glad to get away from here with all your receptions, worries and *reports,* — here life is no rest for you, on the contrary. —

Your tender caresses warmed up my old heart — you don't know how hard it is being without you both Angels. — I am glad, that I shall go straight to Church from the station at 9½ in the darkness and pray for you — the home coming is always so particularly painful.

Sleep well and long, my Treasure, my one and all, the light of my life! I bless you and confide you unto God's holy care — tightly I hold you in my arms and press tender kisses upon yr. sweet face, lovely eyes and all dear places.

Goodnight, rest well,

Ever yr. very own old

Wify.

No. 162.

Tsarskoje Selo, Nov. 25-th 1915

My very own beloved One,

Your sweet note, you left me, is a great consolation, I read it over and over again and kiss it and think I hear you talk. Oh I hate those goodbyes! We went straight to church, upstairs, so I remained in my *prayer-room* — service had already begun, so lasted quite short. What pain in the soul! Came home and went to bed very soon, could not want to see A. I prefer being alone when the heart is so sore.

10 degrees this morning. Wonder how Baby's arms are — am a bit anxious until he will be quite right again — only careful in his movements. — Alek is arranging something in the *People's House* for to-morrow St. George's heroes. Now I can congratulate you too, my Angel, and do so with heart and soul. You deserved the cross for all yr. hard labour and for the *rise in spirits* you bring the troops. Regret not being with you and our little St. George's cavalier, Baby sweet, to bless and kiss you that day. —

I went to *Znamenia* and placed a candle for you — service was going on and they just brought out the *cup*. Then went to the hospital and spoke to all. We are lunching and this letter must be sent at once.

Goodbye my own precious Darling, I cover you with tender kisses.

God Almighty bless and keep you —

Ever, Huzy mine, yr. very own old Sunny.

The Children kiss you. Had you an answer from Georgie. —

No. 163.

Tsarskoje Selo, Nov. 26-th 1915

My own beloved Darling,

I wonder how all is going off at the *Headquarters* to-day, great excitement, I am sure. Hope, Baby dear's arms are much better. —

Am going later to Church with Olga, last night I went alone, upstairs in my *prayer-house* — Church is my consolation. Stupid heart rather bothers me. — Saw M-me *Poguliayev,* M-me *Manskovskaya,* — fancy, her sister is young *Khvostov's* mother — he asked to see me today, I don't know why.

Our Friend dined with him yesterday & was very contented. —

5 degrees & so dark. —

Ania just got a wire fr. *N. P.* about his nomination & that he is off to Odessa. I am a w f u l l y sorry he wont be any more with you, was s o quiet for you both — we shall miss him a w f u l l y — but its a splendid nomination — but you will be so lonely! — Our Friend is in all states that leaves, as one »of his« & ought to be near you, as have few such true, honest friends as He says only Ania & *N. P.* — wished me to telegraph to you, but I declined & begged Him neither to — I know what this means to him &

his comerades, tho' he will horribly suffer leaving us, who are his nearest & dearest as he always says! —

What news from Georgie? How delighted Orlov & Drenteln will be that *N. P.* leaves — their jealous hearts will be contented. — And 3 of yr. players at once gone, whom can you get?

Silaiev is quiet & nice & utterly devoted. —

Came to half of mass & *Te Deum.*

Had a long telegr. fr. *Mekk* about all my *flying stores* — M-me Hartwigs is at *Rovno* — have put our *camp.* Church & twice daily there are services for the passing troops. The I-st *disinfection unit* & motors stand also at *Rovno.* Our *flying detachment of the store is 40 versts north, on the new line near the front.* Then our *Bacteriological disinfection unit* works for all the army, another *supply train* at *Podvolotchisk,* another at *Tarnopol,* but he moves it to *Kamenetz-Podolsk* where the *Bacteriological Section* will have more work. I only tell you this in case you pass any. —

Goodbye my Lovebird, the man leaves earlier. —

Blessings & kisses without end & great yearning. God bless you.

Ever yr. very own old

Wify.

No. 164.

Tsarskoje Selo, Nov. 27-th 1915

My very own Huzy,

I am glad everything went off so well yesterday — Georgi telegraphed that it had been one of the finest sights he had ever seen in his life. How emotioning. One says it was splendid at the »*People's House*« — greatest order — 18.000 men — sat together according to the wars — got heaps of food & were allowed to take their plates & mugs home.

In each hall their was a Te Deum — *Valia* was there.

I spend yesterday afternoon reading„ the Children were out & Ania only returned from town at 4.20 — but I liked the calm, only the air in my big room was stiffling they let on the hot air — & out of doors the glass on 1 of warmth. So after tea & having seen officers, I sledged for half an hour with Olga — it was mild & snowing.

This morning there are 10 degrees — those ups & downs are so bad for the ill.

A. dined with us — all worked, even she at last, then they sang churchsongs & Olga played. *Khvostov* did not come yesterday as he felt unwell.

My letters are dull, I have nothing interesting to tell you, & the thoughts are not gay — its lonely without Sweetheart & agooweeone. —

I feel my heart enlarged, but still I want to go to our lower Church, as little Metropolitan Makari is going to serve, simple, without pomp — its the feast of *Znamenia.* So in the afternoon I hope to go in & place a candle for you & I believe our Friend wants to see me at 4. —

Just back from Church, little Metropolitan served beautifully, so quietly — looked a picture, all gold, glittering, & the golden Church round the Altar & his silver hair. I went away before the *Te Deum,* Olga to the hospital, & I to finish my letters, receive Isa & then *Valia* before luncheon. — Goodbye my Angel sweet, my Treasure, my Lovebird. God bless & protect you — 1000 of kisses, Nicky love, fr. yr. old wife

Alix.

Any idea about your plans? —

I sent for Joy & he lies at my feet — a melancholy picture, as he misses his little master

No. 165

Tsarskoje Selo, Nov. 28th 1915

Darling Sweetheart,

Ever such very tender thanks for yr. dear letter, wh. I never expected. I am delighted that the St. George's feast was so splendid — I just read the description and all yr. lovely words in the papers. Fancy *Navruzov,* my *Hooligan* as I always call him, and *Krat.* having been there, that is nice. Well, yr. 2 *Nizhegorodtzi* must tell us about it — we shall eagerly await them.

I saw our Friend for 3/4 of an hour — asked much after you, goes to-day to see the old man. Spoke about *N. P.,* regrets terribly he wont be near you, but that God will protect him and that after the war (wh. he always thinks will be over in a few months) he must come back to you again. —

Please dear dont let *Spiridovitch* be named as *Chief of police* in *Petrograd* — I know he and *Voyeikov* (whom *Spiridovitch,* sorry to say, holds in hands) want to place him there. It wld. never do, he is not enough gentleman, has now made a useless marriage and then on account of *Stolypin's* story at *Kiev,* it would not be good.

One proposed him to be governor at *Astrakhan* (yes?) and he refused, — and one thing more, why I do not know, but *Spiridovitch* puts *Voyeikov* up against *Khvostov,* with whom everything went so well at first. Now one must get *Trepov* to work in harmony with *Khvostov* — its the only way of setting things to rights and making work go smoothely. —

The dear little Metropolitan Makari came to me after luncheon and was sweet. — *Loman* had feasted him and all the clergy — Ania and Mme *Loman* were there too. — Then I saw two German sisters; Countess Uxkull had been to Wolfsgarten before coming, but she is still going to visit more places; — the other is from Mecklenburg — she asked me whether one could not let home to Germany old men and children fr. Siberia, whom ours transported there fr. Eeast Prussia, when our troops were there. Does it concern *Beliaïev* or *Khvostov?* I should say, the latter. — Can you tell me as then I can ask about it — off course only the quite old men and tiny children — she saw them in Siberia, Samara. — I went to *Znamenia* and placed a candle for you. Then I got *Loman* so as to speak about a wee *camp.* Church, I want to send to the *Marine of the Guard* as our priest is with them. I am remaining quiet this morning, as don't feel very famous. — One of our wounded officers died last night — yesterday he was operated — he was several times at death's door — I used to go to him in the evenings when he was so bad — but I think he never could have recovered — his soldier is an Angel. —

This evening *Shavelsky* officiates in our Church. In the evening *Nik. Dm. Dem.* and *Victor Erastov.* come to Ania's at 9, to say goodbye to the latter; so sad we shant see *Shvedov* before he leaves. — All ones dear friends go off at the same time to the war!

11^0 of frost and thick snow.

I am sending you a paper of Rostovtzev, I think it concerns *Alexeiev* and can be quicker done through you, if you agree — I saw the wretched officer and yr. Mama too. —

Ortipo is lying on my bed and sleeping fast. —

I have sent your letter to Malcolm to give over to Georgie — he leaves to-morrow. —

Now my sweetest One, my sorely missed and deeply yearned for Huzy, Goodbye and God bless — and protect you. Endless tender kisses do I press upon yr. sweet lips and beloved eyes.

Ever yr. very own old

Sunny.

No. 166.

Tsarskoje Selo, Nov. 29th 1915

My own beloved Sweetheart,

Only the 5th day since you left, and it seems already such ages. Dark, snowing 11 degr.; last night 16. — yesterday evening *Shavelsky* served, it was so nice and I like his voice. He is kindly going to take two *Communion Cloths* with him, as I am sending the *Marine of the Guard* and 4 rifles *camp Churches* for the 6th. —

Marie P. came to tea — looked really pretty when she took off her *scarf,* her short hair had been curled. She has greatly improved and becoming so different to what she was before. To-day she returns again to *Pskov,* but does not know when Dmitri leaves. — In the evening we went to Anias and there were besides us, *Demenko* and *Zborovsky.* It seems *Alexei Konstantinovitch* has also come, so shall see him before his departure for the war. This morning *Bulpa* comes to bid us good bye: — Pss. Lolo D. lunches with us and after I see *Sandra Shuvalova* with her *Report.* —

Every day somebody to receive and affairs and nothing interesting to tell you.

My jaw has jumped out and I eat with difficulty.

I enclose a letter fr. A., perhaps you will in your wire say I am to thank her and for the present. —

Beloved one, I do wish yr. letter had come, now the man is always late. —

I bless you over and over again my one and all and kiss you with all the fervour of my love —

Ever, Nicky mine, yr. very own old

Wify.

No. 167.

Tsarskoje Selo, Nov. 29 1915

Sweet Beloved,

I begin my letter already to-day, so as to thank you ever so fondly for yours, wh. I just received. That is nice, that you will spend your namesday with the troops, tho' sad we cannot be together, am glad you will spend that big feastday in yr. army and may St. Nicolas send special blessings to all and help. — I don't like Georgie's answer, to my mind its quite wrong. —

How interesting you saw *K. Krutchkov;* its snowing so hard, A's train left an hour late from here and took a whole hour to town, she fears sticking on her way back. *Ira, Larka* and *Sandra* leave tonight for *Alupka* as the old Count had a stroke. She has four St. George's medals. It looks so strange on a smart dress. Mme Orjewsky is going to propose to your Mama that one should send her to see the prisoners here, wh. I find perfect, as there are things one must see into. Our government gives enough money for food but it seems its not given as ought to be, I fear, dishonest people keep it back and that wont do; I am glad she and I had the same idea — I have no right to mix in, and she can advise. Thank God, Baby is better, so I hope he will get through the journey alright. — Does *Drenteln* take over the regiment now, or how is he arranging?

I have got a fly buzzing round my lamp, reminds one of summer; but the wind is howling down the chimney. Oh sweet Love, I long for you so terribly — thank God you have Sunbeam to keep your heart warm. — What do you do in the evenings, have you anyone for domino?

Navruzov and *Chavtchavadze* took tea cosily with us — it was awfully nice seeing them again after so many months and to get news of you both. You see us 5 taking tea with 2 officers, but with them it seems somehow so natural. They also are enchanted that Vorontzov left the Caucasus. — I am sending *Grabbe* on Tuesday 170 Images, 170 little books, 200 ordinary *store* post-cards, 170 packets for officers — to *Zborovsky* and Shvedov I shall give the things myself. And then a small Image of St. Nicolas for the *company,* you can bless them with it, Deary.

Well, our Friend was with the old man who listened to him very attentively, but was most obstinate. He intends asking you not at all to call the *Duma* together (he loathes it) — and *Gregory* told him it was not right to ask such a thing of you, as now all are willing to try and work and as soon as their preliminary work is ready it would be wrong not to call them together — one must show them a little confidence. —

Nov. 30th

I am lunching and writing. At 10 I went to the *memorial liturgy* for our officer, the children came for the *Requiem.* Then sat in the hospital, *Navruzov* turned up, he leaves tonight again for *Armavir. Ravtopolo* turned up, looks flourishing!

Its 2 of warmth and pouring. — The guard officers heard, that the promotion did not count for them. —

Do you return straight to the *Headquarters* or over *Minsk?* The *Erivantsi* were asking. *Melik Adamov* turned up fr. *Eupatoria.* —

Have to receive and so must end and swallow my food. —

I bless and kiss you over and over again with unending deep devotion.

Ever, Sweetheart, yr. very own old

Sunny.

No. 168.

Tsarskoje Selo, Dec. I-st 1915

My own Beloved,

Dark, cold, II° of frost. Sonia has fallen ill, very weak, a noise in the lungs & dozing state, scarcely speaks & when does, scarce to be understood. I had *Vladimir Nikolaievitch* to come & he will bring his brother too. *Vl. Nik.* put *cuppings* on whilst I was there — she took no notice & hung like a lump in the 2 maids' arms — pittyful sight this paralised body. In the night she was worse so they got a sister fr. the big palace to make camphor injections & then the heart got a bit better. I know she likes to take holy Communion when so ill, so shall try & get *the priest.* She only said yesterday „like Mama", she always thinks of her mother's death when feels ill. Mitia *Den* & Isa sat long next door — I shall go up soon this morning — still when ill, she is accustomed to have me near her always.

Only since yesterday morning everything, & at once so weak & *broken* & yesterday only 37.3 & pulse 140 — today 38.7 & pulse 82 — 104. — I had Pss. Gedroitz for a *report* 1½ hour yesterday about *Eupatoria,* where I sent her to clear up things wh. were going on. — *Shurik, Victor Erastov.* & *Ravtopolo* were in the evening at Anias, — Nastasia's eyes glittered fr. joy. — I hear *Erdeli* let the staff know you have said my *Andronnikov* is to be aid to *Viltchkovsky.* Well, then we must add a place as second aid, as have already one. —

Tchitchagov was at Ania's & told her that he leads *Varnava* 's story today & that today the *Synod* issues the *glorificate decree* of *St. John Maximovitch*

Tchitchagov found a paper at the Synod, wh. the metrop. & all had forgotten (scandal), in wh. the *Synod* asked you to permit his *glorification* (a year ago or a little more) & you wrote *„agree“* on the top — so they are at fault in everything. — Shall finish this during luncheon, must go up to Sonia, when dressed. Sweetheart, m e w a n t s you. —

Are lunching in the p l a y - r o o m to be nearer to poor Sonia. Lovy, she is very bad. Inflamation of the lungs, but whats worse the paral. is creeping round the muscles of her heart wh. is very weak — there is little hope & she looks so bad. At 3 she will take holy Communion. Does not speak to-day, hears when I tell her to drink & cough. Eyes always shut — bad complexion — They say her left *eye-ball* does not react. Her Aunt *Ivanova* & a sister fr. the *Alexander hospital Station* (fr. the *convoy)* have come to look after her. —

For yr. beloved letter, endless thanks, always an intense joy, Sweetheart.

Excuse short letter, but am worried about Sonia. Our Friend says better for her she shld. go & we all feel it — I am very calm, seeing so many going off, dying, makes one realise the grandeur of it & that He knows best.

Sun shines.

Endless blessings & kisses fr. own

Wify

No. 169.

Tsarskoje Selo, Dec. 2-nd 1915

My very own sweet One,

One more true heart gone to the unknown land! For her I am glad that all over, as in the future life might have been a yet worse phisical trial to her. Want so quickly that one cannot yet realise it — she lies there like a wax all, I cannot call it otherwise, so unlike the Sonia full of bright life and roy colours we knew. God took her mercifully without any suffering. I wrote to you during luncheon yesterday, then just began *report* with *Viltchkovsky* and I was called to her, heart very weak, 39,7 and was taken Holy Communion (2½), she could not open her eyes — the only thing she said, was to me, and »forgive« — that was all and then no more heeded when one told her to swallow, the end began. I asked *the priest* to read the prayers and give her the last unction — it brings peace into the room prayers and I always think helps the parting soul. She changed rapidly. At 4¼ her Aunt begged me to go and rest — so I lay in Isa's room and there we took tea — at 5.10 they called me — *the priest* read the prayers for the dying and she quite peacefully went to sleep. God let her soul rest in peace and bless her for all her great love to me through these long years. Never did the child complain of her health — even paralised, she enjoyed life to the end. — It was the heart wh. failed, they gave her camphor and other strong injections, nothing acted upon the heart. What a great mystery life is — all waiting round for the birth of a human being — again all awaiting the departure of a soul. Something so grand in it all and one feels how small we mortals are and how great our heavenly Father. Its difficult to express ones thoughts and feelings on paper — I felt as tho' were giving her over to God's care alone now, wanting to help her soul to be happy — a great awe and holiness of the moment overtakes one — such a secret, only to be fathomed yonder. The girls and I went at 9 to the *funeral service*. Now they are going to place her into her coffin in her sittingroom, but I shall spare my forces the evening, to accompany her out of our house to *Znamenia*. I scarcely slept — too many impressions! I am quiet — calm — numbed feeling you know fr. crushing all in. *Botkin* for the first time turned up this morning — begged me to keep quiet because of the enlarged heart. I want to go to holy Communion to-morrow morning — *Christmas Fast* and now it will be a help. — A. will go to *Pestcherny Chapel* at 9. So Sweetheart, I tenderly, lovingly beg your forgiveness for everything — word and deed — bless me Lovy. It will be a comfort, as you leave on your journey to-morrow, to pray for you there. God grant all will go well. Sad you won't see the *marine of the guard*. After your letter yesterday, we arranged to send *Popov* to Odessa with my Church and *Andreiev* with the one for the 4-th reg. to *Zhmerinka* or wherever they are. It will be interesting you go on further. — I send you a small present to-day (the letterbox awaits your return) and you open it the 5-th evening. Its a photo taken out of a group last year and enlarged. — I send it today, in case it might not reach you on the 6-th and in any case also my very tenderest blessings goodwishes and kisses for your precious Namesday. Heart and soul ever with you my beloved Angel, also a few flowers — the others must have faded, as yesterday it was a week that you left us. God grant you a good journey in every respect. — Ania kisses you. — Yr. Mama is coming to the *funeral service*, so I must go to it, because *Olga* and *Tatiana* are obliged to go to town, they cannot put off a big committee and *receipt of donations*.

God bless and protect you my Love, 1000 fond kisses fr. yr. own old

Wify.

No. 170.

Dec. 3-d 1915

Sweet precious One,

It was a great consolation to go to Holy Communion this morning and I carried you in my heart. So peaceful and lovely and our singers sang beautifuly — nobody was in Church — only Olga dear came. Ania went with me — but everywhere one misses and thinks of Sonia — how I used to wheel her up to the *Czar Gates*. — We took a cup of tea, then Ania went to town and Olga and I a moment to place candles at *Znamenia*. A nun was reading, — she was covered right over and only her faithful servant stood there — so lonely.

As nobody thought, of 40 days mass, I had it ordered. — Yesterday the officers of the *United Regiment* carried her in the house down the stairs and in Church, in the street the servants, *Tatiana* and *Maria* followed on foot I drove behind with *Olga* and *Anastasia* — snow — so quiet and quick all. But one cannot grasp that being so full of life is lying there so still — yes, the soul is gone indeed. —

Ania had confession in our bedroom too, it was simpler for *the priest.*

I had wanted to go this lent and now it came as a great consolation — one is a bit tired from more than a years suffering and that gives one new strength and help. —

To-day its the anniversery of *Botkin's* son's death. Sonia died the same day as my Mother 34 years ago; — she was much pittied and loved and heaps of people came.

During the *funeral service* in the house, I kept near the bedroom door so saw nobody, wh. was easier. Kind little Mother dear came, as she wanted to see her in her own room still, and then she told me she wants all those pictures of Zichy's taken out of the frames again and put in a map and sent to her, as they are remembrances of the journey and she says were before at *Gatchina.* I shall get *Stcheglov.* to do it, only after one has taken Sonia's things away and put order.

It's cold and snowing — I wonder how you are getting along on your journey, my sweetest sweets. Such an intense longing for you, but I am glad you are not here these sad days. *Petia* comes to tea. —

I had Mme Zizi, as there was a lot to talk about and on account of the funeral too. —

Its snowing away the whole time. Lovebird, treasure, how I think of and lovy you and my Sunbeam.

God bless you and your journey and bring you safely back again I cover you with very tenderest kisses, and remain,

Huzy Love, yr. very own old

Sunny.

No. 171.

Tsarskoje Selo, Dec. 12-th 1915

My very own,

Sweetheart, beloved Darling, its with an aching heart I let you go — no Baby sweet to accompany you — quite alone. Tho' I suffered without my Child, it was a great consolation to give him to you and to feel his sweet presence would be ever near to brighten up your life. And no *N. P.* anymore to accompany you — I was quiet when I knew him with you »*He is ours*« as our Friend says so rightly and his life is so knitted to ours since all these years, he has shared our joys and sorrows and is quite our very own and we are his nearest and dearest — he too dreads the long absence now from us all, I do hope you will see him with the battalions, it would be a blessing for his new work. —

Thank God, your heart can be quiet about Alexei and I hope, that by the time you return, you will find him as round and rosy as before. — He will be very sad to remain behind, he loved being with you alone like a big fellow already. Altogether separations are horrid things and one cannot get accustomed to them. Nobody to caress and kiss you for long now — in thoughts I will be always doing it, my Angel. Your cushion gets the morning and evening kisses and many a tear. Ones love always grows and the yearning increases.

God grant you may have fine and warmer weather there to the south. Its a pity all has to be crowded into one day — one cannot so thoroughly enjoy all one sees, nor have enough time to talk, as one would wish. — May your precious presence bring them great blessings and success. —

I wonder, whether you will return for Xmas or not, but you will let me know as soon as it is settled, now of course you cannot tell. — My own, my own, I hold you tightly clasped to my heart and cover you with kisses — feel me with and near you, holding you warm and tenderly . The first hour will be horrid in the train without Baby — so silent and you will miss the prayers too. Sweethearty mine, oh me loves so deeply, deeply »with unending true devotion deeper far than I can say«. — When you are away, there is a feeling of the chief thing in my life missing — everything has a sad note, and now I keep Agoowee one, its worse for you by far. Sleep peacefully my Love, God send you strengthning sleep and rest. —

I have given the Image for the *Chasseurs regiment,* the bag is lined with their ribbon they gave and our Friend blessed on their Feastday 1906 at Peterhof. The rest of it I have kept; but He said it would be in a war and they would do great things. Now He cannot exactly remember, but said that one must always do what he says — it has a deep meaning. Perhaps you wont wish to give it personally, not to hurt the other reg. (as this one has nothing to do with Baby or me) — then have it given them fr. me when you leave, — Remember Georgi's good idea of having all yr. a. d. c. to do service 10 days — then you will hear fresh news and they will get a rest. —

Goodbye my own Huzy, my Own, own, very Own, my Life, my Sunshine, God bless and protect you, St. Nicolos hear our prayers.

Kisses without end.

Ever yr. very

Own.

No. 172.

Tsarskoje Selo, Dec. 13-th 1915

My own Beloved,

It was a lonely night and I miss you awfully — but for you its far worse and I feel so much for you my Sweetheart. Was so hard parting! God bless and protect you now and for ever. —

I slept midling — its snowing since the evening, 12—15 degrees only, such luck and I hope you will find it much warmer on your journey. —

Just got a wire fr. *Zhukov,* very touching, before their departure and one from *N. P.* from *Podvolotchisk,* that they arrived there safely yesterday — so I hope he will still see you there. — Dined upstairs and then a letter from Paul was brought me and one to him from Marie all about *Russky,* despair etc.; after a talk of hers with *Bontch Brujevitch,* who complained of course that one protects the Barons here — that when he sent away the 2 of the red cross, *Beletski* got them back — that *Russky* is against this plan of *Alexeiev* to the south and abuse of *Alexeiev* — so, as Paul left it to me to choose, whether to send his and Maries letters to you — I returned them to him with a few explanations — as I disagree with all she writes. As tho'one simply sent *Russky* off, after his letter to *Polivanov,* wh. soi disant the latter never showed you — lots of rot. — Tiny slept well, 37, but left arm rather stiff, no pain. — As heart a little better, and not so cold, am going at 11 to mass — *Pitirim* serves and I will feel grateful to pray in Church, tho'miss you there quite awfully. —

God bless you Lovy, I must get up, and dress. I feel still your goodbye kiss on my lips and hunger for more. Goodbye my Angel, my Sunshine. I cover you with tender fond kisses. —

Ever yr. very own old Wify.

Toughts don't leave you, nor my prayers with endless yearning. —

No. 173.

Tsarskoje Selo, Dec. 13-th 1915

My own Sweetheart,

I begin my letter this evening, as shall not have much time for writing to-morrow morning, as the dentist awaits me & Ella arrived. Excuse another ink, but the other pen is empty. Baby has been quite alright — we lunched, took tea & dined with him & after seeing Benkendorf & Sonia's Aunt *Sister Ivanova,* I remained with him. The Metropolitan *Pitirim* served beautifully, & at the end said a few warm words & prayer for you, Lovy dear. *Loman* gave him a big clerical luncheon at wh. Ania also assisted. It was comforting praying in Church with our dear soldiers. — Ania, *Voronov* & wife took tea, Baby was delighted to see them. He leaves cn Thursday to join the *crew* with his 160 sailors, over Moscou, as that way to *Kiev* seems quicker. —

He says poor *Melnovetz* has grown terribly thin & his lungs are in a seriously bad state. — To-morrow is already the anniversary of *Butakov's* death — how the time flies! — Then I had a Pr. Obolensky, brother of M-me *Prutchenko,* tho' she hates Ania on account of our Friend, he came to me through A. to bring me photos of the frescos in the Ferapontievsky monastery, wh. he is helping to restore — they need still 38.000, so I told him he must wait to the end of the war, now all sums are needed elsewhere. Then Pr. Galitzin came with his *report* of my committee for our prisoners. —

Then I rested an hour. Ania dines too, as I shall see her less these days, tho' Ella leaves again Wednesday evening & will spend half her days in town & I with the dentist. Alas, I cannot go to the consecration of the little Church — its too tiring & I am not fit yet; in ten days Xmas & so much to be done before that. — It was warmer, so the children drove to *Pavlovsk,* — met the *Countess Palei,* son & little girls on snowshoes. Now I must try & sleep.

Dec. 14-th. 17° of frost.

Good morning, Sweetheart,

Babykins slept well, I not famously. — I wonder whether my letters catch you up on the way back or whether you will only find them upon yr. return to the *Headquarters;* well, as they are numbered, you wont make any confusions. — The pink sky behind the kitchen & the thickly covered in snow trees look quite fairylike — one longs to be an artist to paint all. — I told Benkendorf about the gospels to be sent to you through Rostovtsev.

Ella comes at ¼ to 12—3½ & then goes to town for *Acathistus* & evening service before to-morrow's consecration & dines at *Anitchkov.* And I have the dentist before 11 in consequence. —

His arm is alright again & 36.6 & gay.

All my thoughts follow you the whole time and ernest prayers — miss you greatly, my Sweetheart & long for your tender caresses to warm me up. — There, Ortipo jumped upon my bed, Tatiana has gone off to the hospital, Anastasia was at the dentists. — *Leo* is still alive — ups & downs, poor man. —

I kissed one of o u r little pink flowers & enclose it in this letter. — Now I must get up — such a nuisance — & end my letter.

Goodbye my Beloved, I bless you & kiss you without end.

Ever Husy sweet yr. very Own.

No. 174.

Tsarskoje Selo, Dec. 15-th 1915

My very own sweet Darling,

All my thoughts are with you, wondering how all is going on. — We have again 20° of frost, and glorious sunshine. — Such a fidgeting from early morning on, hundreds of questions about Xmas presents for the wounded and personal of the hospitals — the number always increases. — The 900 gospels, images and postcard-groups have been sent to Kyra. — I only saw Ella a second at 9 before she flew off to church — it is 1, and she has not yet left town again. Sat with the dentist for an hour. — Heart more enlarged this morning. — Baby slept till 11, alright, but still has a cold. — Had Sophie Fersen for nearly 2 hours yesterday, and we had such a nice talk — such a pleasant, good woman. —

I send you a petition of Prince *Yurevsky's* sister-in-law, a not good person, you will do as you like with it. —

Css. *Rebinder, Kharkov,* wrote to Ania, that her brother *Kutaysov* got the news of his nomination there: »*At first he would not believe in his good fortune, and now he is aflame with the desire to prove his worth to bear the insignia of his beloved Monarch and ready to sacrifice for him all his powers, all his life.*"

She says he has become quite another man since — God bless you for what you have done to him, Sweetheart.

How glad I am you saw Xenia too. — A. sends you her tender kisses, she has left for town at 1, over night. — Must send this off now. —

Blessing and ever such warm, tender, fond kisses, Lovebird fr. yr. very own little

Sunny.

No. 175.

Tsarskoje Selo, Dec. 16-th 1915

My very own Darling,

I was so happy to receive your dear telegram last night from *Podvolotchisk* and to know, that all had been so beautiful. Our Friend prayed and blessed again from afar. — *N. P.* wired after 4 already, that you had promoted him after the review and that he was awfully happy — I am glad you saw him before the battalion. —

We made Baby tell Ella all about *Volotchisk* and your inspections there and the Pss. *Volkonskaya* — he told it very well and with lots of details. — Ella had been there a year ago in autumn. Her humour and looks are excellent, quiet and natural — of course has to rush every morning to town and receives besides here still. She leaves again to-morrow evening — to-day I am going to look at the china and drawings from the fabric with her and *Strukov.*

26^0 of frost again, so that and my enlarged heart keep me quietly home. Ania was yesterday at the Metropolitans, our Friend too — they spoke very well, and then he gave them luncheon — always the first place to *Gregory* and the whole time wonderfully respectful to him and deeply impressed by all he said. —

You have only left us 5 days, and it seems to me such ages already Oh Lovy, Baby and I are already thinking of your loneliness at the *Headquarter* and it fills us with great sorrow »You really mustn't« I find, precious Angel mine.

Now I must dress and go to the dentist, after wh. I shall finish my letter. —

Here I am upstairs and he is arranging my (false) tooth — we spoke about the big military Sanatorium, wh. is being finished with yr. sums and now he hears the *Yalta* medical society (wh. the »*Union of Cities*« helps) wants you to give it over to them — he finds it principally quite wrong (belongs himself to the society), therefore I warn you not to agree if you get such a petition, — speak it over with me when you return, please — one needs it for those *tubercular patients,* who must be kept separately and have no place at *Yalta* — and it must be y o u r s. — Now I am sitting next to Alexei's bed and he is writing to you — *Peter Vasilievitch* watches how he spells. »*Joy*« lies sleeping in the floor. The sun shines brightly — I am giving an Image of St. Nicolas for Ella to bring Prince *Chir.-Chakhmatov* from you, as thanks for his work, — he was ill and could not be at the consecration of the Church. —

I fear my letter is very dull, but I have nothing of interest to tell you. Now it is time to go down to luncheon. —

Goodbye, my very own beloved Sweetheart. The empty house at the *Headquarters* will make you sad, poor Lovy mine and you will miss our Sunbeam. God help you, Deary.

I cover you with tenderest, fondest kisses, blessings.

Ever yr. very own old

Wify.

No. 176.

Tsarskoje Selo, Dec. 17-th 1915

My own Darling,

Again no time to write even a decent letter. I had to read through any amount of *reports,* must get up at 10½ to go to the dentist — then *Viltchkovsky* with a *report,* in the evening Khvostov I don't know why, and my heart more enlarged and hurts and I ought to keep quiet. —

22⁰ of frost. — I send you a paper Ella brought from *Kursk* — she tought you would perhaps send someone with medals. The other is to remind you whom to telegraph for Xmas — it's no good my sending them, as we are not together. — Baby hopes to be up and dressed to-morrow if his temp. keeps normal to-day; the cold had thrown itself unto his tommy, so that he has to keep to a diat. — Ella leaves this evening, as has much to do — her visit was cosy, calm and homely and, I think, will have done her good. — I got a telegram fr. *N. P.* that he comes on the 20-th fr. *Kiev,* no, not true, thinks of leaving the 20-th, but why the wire comes fr. *Kiev* and he writes »*not well*«, perhaps cought cold — rather unclear. —

Ones thoughts are »out there« wondering how all are moving along. — Your lonely homecoming to the empty house makes me sad — God help you.

Blessings and v e ry tenderest kisses without end fr. yr. very own old

Wify.

Excuse short letter, but really have no time — when Ella leaves and dentist finished, shall he free'r — but all is worse before Xmas wh. is in a week. —

How was and is the old Man?

No. 177.

Dec. 18-th 1915

My own beloved Sweetheart,

Glorious bright sunshine, 8 of frost in the morning — the dentist finished with me for this time & the teeth ache still. Yr. loneliness makes us sad — fancy yr. dreary walks in the garden, call *Silaiev* or *Mordvinov* to come with you, they have always something to tell. And the empty bedroom! Come back quicker & we shall warm you up & caress you, Lovebird tenderly longed for. — The amount I have to do these days makes me wild, so as that I have not even time to write to you quietly. I am smoking because my teeth ache so more the nerves of the face. — Alas, I must bother you with papers, a thing you dont like. I enclose Miechen's letter, its simpler than writing out all the story about Dellingshausen, & when you have read her explanation, you will see whether anything can be done for him — she is very careful whom she asks about, but also wants us to help set right things if one can, & if an injustice has been committed through people having hastily judged people. — Manus never died, it was simply a game of the bourse wh. made the papers rise & fall — an ugly trick. —

My conversation with the Tail I shall write to-morrow, to-day I have no time & my brain is too tired. —

Things to settle for Xmas are always tiring & so complicated. —

Baby has got up & will lunch in my room, looks sweet, thin with big eyes. — The girls alright. Tell me to thank her for letter & goodies & send a message. — Must end. Blessings without end & 10 000 of very, very fond kisses

Ever, Huzy mine yr. very own old

Alix.

No. 178.

Tsarskoje Selo, Dec. 19-th 1915

My own Sweetheart,

You cannot imagine what a joy & consolation your precious letter was. I miss you quite terribly, & all the more knowing how intensely lonely you must feel, & no soft kiss to warm you up, no little voice to cheer you. Its more than hard knowing you all alone & not even *N.P.* near you.

How I wonder what news you have from the front, is the move going satisfactorily — black crows croak with whys & wherefores, in winter such an undertaking — but I find we have no right to judge, you & *Alexeiev* have your calculations & plans & we only need praying with heart & soul for success — & it will come to him who knows how to wait. Its bitterly trying & hard, but without great patience, faith and trust nothing can be achieved. God always tries one & when least we expect it sends His recompense & relief. And how different all will be interiorly when once our arms are crowned with success. —

We talked a lot about the *supply question* with *Khvostov,* he says the ministers really try working together (puting *Polivanov* & Bark beside), but its the *Duma's* fault wh. hung comissions with 70 members onto them & the Minister of. Interior's powers consequently are greatly diminished & he can take no particular measures, without it having passed through the commission. Certainly with one's hands tied like that, little can be achieved — he told it at the *Duma* the other day & they held their tongues. He therefore asked me to remind you of his conversation with you when he begged you to give an o r d e r — to the Council of ministers (I think) for the people to know, that you are thinking of their needs & wont forget them — it wont be much of a help, but as a m o r a l link, to show them, that tho' you are at the war, you remember their needs. I fear, I explain things badly, but my head aches — I had such masses to read through — yesterday was dead tired 2 hours looking trough Sonia's things with her brother & choosing Xmas presents & receiving. To-day I shall only have V. Kotchubey about the Eastergifts & a fond he is thinking we might found. —

One person, whom not only the tail, but many good intentioned people are against & find not at the hight of his place is *Bark.* He certainly does not help *Khvostov* — ever so long one has asked for money for him to buy the „*Novoye Vremya*" partly (the ministers, alas, told *Bark* to do it instead of *Khvostov* who wld. certainly have succeeded, whereas *Bark* dawdles for his own reasons) — & the result is *Gutchkov* with Jews, Rubinsteins etc. buy up the paper, put in their own mendacious articles. He himself does not feel his sitting very firm since he signed that letter with the other ministers, who partly left since & so tries to get on with the party of *Gutchkov* more or less. They say a clever Minister of Finance cld. easily catch *Gutchkov* a trap & make him harmless, once he wld. have no money from the Jews. Now this *Prince Tatistchev* whom I saw (was in the Cavalry school, no, Cadetcorps, I think, which *command.* is a great friend of his) is a very competent man, knows & venerates our Friend deeply & gets on to perfection with *Khvostov;* a sort of relationship besides between them — a m o s t l o y a l man & only wanting yr. & Russia's good.

His name is in many mouths, as a man capable of saving the financial situation & the gaffes Bark made. He is a man with an opinion of his own & seeks nothing personal, is rich, a prince, & an enemy of the *Tjutchev — Samarin set — he is one of our own men, ours, and will not betray us, as Khvostov* says, & l o v i n g o u r F r i e n d is certainly a blessing & gain. Do think about him & when you see *Khvostov* speak about him, as he of course has not the right to meddle in the affairs not concerning him — but they wld. work harmoniously together. He hates *Gutchkov* & those Moscow types — made a really good impression upon me. It was *Andronnikov* who spoke without any reason, nastly about *Tatistchev* to *Voyeikov,* & he confessed this afterwards — fancy, Pss. *Palei* knows even this (Ania pretended utter innocence & no knowledge of anything) — & said what good one says of *Prince Tatistchev.* — I enclose a paper about him, I asked *Khvostov* to write down for me. —

In his *Luzhskoye* estate he has just found a sulphour (?) spring & coal, this I only tell you for a point of interest. — Do see him when you come & have a quiet talk. — Certainly if the Cabinet becomes always more united, everey thing will work better & they will besides stick up for our Friend from love for you & veneration for him.

Baby has written you a French letter, you send him a telegr. it will rejoice the child.

Now I must end.

Goodbye my own precious Husband, heart of my heart, longsuffering Darling. I cannot think of you quietly, the heart draws itself together from pain. I long to see you at last relieved from worries & anxieties — seeing people honestly fulfilling yr. orders, serving you for your own precious self. You have so much to carry. —

God indeed has laid a heavy burden upon yr. shoulders — but He will not fail you, will give you the wisdom & strength you need & recompense your unfailing patience & humility. I only wish I could be of more use to you — all is so difficult, complicated & hard now — and we cannot be together, that is the worst of it.

Do you think there is a chance of yr. coming soon? —

God bless and protect you, comfort you in yr. loneliness & hearken unto yr. prayers.

I cover you with tenderest warmest kisses, press you tightly to my heart & long to rest upon yr. breast & keep quietly so, forgetting everything that tears the heart to pieces.

Ever, Sweetheart yr. very own

Sunny.

No. 179.

Tsarskoje Selo, Dec. 20-th 1915

My own Sweetheart,

Well, that was a surprise receiving yr. second dear letter, and I thank you for it with all my heart . I am glad you are off and away again, you will have less time to feel lonely and then those troops have been so long waiting to see you. It is also less cold now, wh. is a good thing for inspections. Fancy the old Sinner having ridden past at the head of his Squadron, — thank God it went off well; — but I hope he otherwise does not bother you in your active movements. —

What joy you can be here on the 24-th, then you drink tea in the train and we can light the Children's tree when you come — we shall have finished the servants and ladies trees by then too. Ones head goes round from all there is to do and I feel rotten — still I want to go for a bit to Church as *Lili Den's* Boy becomes orthodox this morning in the lowerchurch — and upstairs will stand during mass and go to Holy Communion for the first time in his life — my Godchild. As Drenteln lunches at Isa's we have asked him to come down after, to bid him goodbye, as probably he won't think of doing it himself. —

Fancy yr. being English Fieldmarshall! That's nice. Now I am going to order a nice Image of the English, Scotch and Irish Patron Saints, St. George, St. Michel, St. Andrew for you to bless the English Army with — St. Patrick is the Irish au fond. — I saw in the papers to-day what you wrote about our advance to the south till the wire-lines and so forth. God bless the troops with success.

I wonder what *B. (Botkin?)* told you about Mama.

10^0 — of frost this morning and the trees as thickly covered in snow as when you were here. Sunbeam is at last going out and I hope he will quickly regain his pink cheeks again. — To-day it's 20 days that Sonia died! One has no idea of time now — it seems like yesterday and then again as tho' it had happened ages ago — one day like a year at these serious times of suffering and anguish. —

Lovebird, I must be getting up to dress for Church. Goodbye my very own beloved, my joy, my life, my one and all. I bless and kiss you tenderly as it is only possible and cuddle close to you. —

Ever, Sweetheart, yr. very own old wify Alix.

How nice if you see the »*Erivantsi*« *Georgians* and the other Caucasians now — perhaps my Siberians? I got a very pretty telegram from the *Chasseurs of the Guard* thanking for the Image and ribbon.

No. 180.

Tsarskoje Selo, Dec. 21-th 1915

My own Sweetheart,

How glad I am that you were satisfied with all you saw yesterday, and that the weather was not too cold. To-day we have only 3^0— and Baby enjoys his outing twice daily in the garden. — I went to mass yesterday — the latter half, because I wished to be present when Lili Den's boy took holy Communion for the first time — he is my Godchild. She became orthodox yesterday morning. The discription of her journey with *Groten* last time from here to the country — is delightful — please, they slept in one compartment, he over her head as there was no other place — good it was not *Ania.* —

Erdeli comes to me to-day, I don't know why, perhaps after the false order he gave in your name and wh. he wants to clear himself probably, but I don't see how he can. — Yesterday *Drenteln* took leave of us — eyes full of tears — he leaves the 26-th evening and hopes to have a chance of bidding you before goodbye. Won't yr. days here be madning, 3 days Xmastrees in the manège there are such masses!

Then I had Mitia Orbeliani to look through little Sonia's jewels and devide them according to her wish — painful work seeing all her little things she was so fond of. —

Tudels is such a bore, never remembers anything, asks hundred times the same things, and that does not make my writing better. Head and heart bother me and I am awfully tired. For the other's sakes I went to Ania's house yesterday as there were 2 of the Childrens wounded friends and Marie's fat fellow-so I had to keep Ania company. —

Beloved Darling, I must say goodbye now. Keep well, heart and soul never leave you. Blessings and kisses without end, Huzy mine, fr. yr. own old

Wify.

No. 181.

Tsarskoje Selo, Dec. 22. 1915

My own Lovebird,

I congratulate you with our little Anastasia's namesday. It was sad giving her the presents without you. We have a *mass* in my room at 12½ & perhaps after I shall go for a little airing, as there are 2⁰ of warmth & no wind, from time to time a little snow. The first day that snow has fallen from the trees & they are quite uncovered. —

Our Friend is always praying & thinking of the war — He says we are to tell him at once if there is anything particular — so she did about the fogg, & He scolded for not having said it at once — says no more foggs will disturb. —

Alexei & Shot have just gone off into the garden, it does him such good these walks. — *Vesselovsky* telegraphed, that you saw my *Company* on the 20-th — I am so glad for them, our wounded *Kunov* may also have been there or the other wounded *Maleiev.*

I saw *Erdeli* — well! the story is most unclear to my mind, as he protests ever having spoken to you personally about *Andronnikov* & that he never wrote such a telegr., he thinks at the telegraph they did it, to wh. I firmly protested, as they never would invent or use your name & for what reason besides. Then says its *Maslov's* fault, may be the idea was a mistake of his — but I told him to find out in the staff in town who wrote & who got the order fr. *Erdeli* & »by your order« — I honestly believe *Erdeli* did it, because he told me other words & tho' my name were mentioned — bosh, — you know I don't like him nor his shifty eyes & manners. Then he told me good things about *Groten* (looks upon him as my protégé & Ania's no doubt, as *Erdeli* was awfully rude the last years, during his great friendship with *Stana,* towards Ania).

My lancer *Guriev* sat an hour with me (also spoke well of *Groten* & *Maslov)* & was nice, interesting, excellent *spirit* — the thing for a young officer. —

How strange it must have seemed to you to see our troops in the places you knew from the old Headquarters. Do we at all advance there, or have we stuck fast since the retreat? — To the south we seem to be making lots of prisoners and slowly but firmly advance. —

I have been making up things for *N. P.* — we sowed him a silk shirt, I knitted stockings, then got india rubber basin & jug like those I gave last Xmas to *Rodionov* etc. —

Seeing the troops must be refreshing. I suppose you go by motor & walk — not possible to get your horses there. —

Sweetheart, I must now end, I bless, & kiss you without end, caress & love you beyond words. —

Ever yr. very Own.

Khvostov told Ania that he, *Naumov* & *Trepov* have made a plan for the *food distribution* for 2 months — thank God, after 15 months, these have at last worked out a plan. —

M-me *Antonova* returned from *Livadia* — I enclose a violet, snowdrop & other smelling buds from there. —

No. 182.

Dec. 30-th 1915

My very own beloved One,

Off you go again alone & its with a very heavy heart I part from you. No more kisses & tender caresses for ever so long — I want to bury myself into you, hold you tight in my arms, make you feel the intense love of mine. You are my very life Sweetheart, and every separation gives such endless heartache — a tearingaway from one, what is dearest & holiest to one. God grant it's not for long — others would no doubt find me foolish & sentimental — but I feel too deeply & intently & my love is fathomlessly deep, Lovebird! — And knowing all your heart carries, anxieties, worries, — so much that is serious, such heavy responsibilities wh. I long to share with you & take the weight upon my shoulders. One prays & again with hope & trust & patience the good will come in due time & you & our country be recompensed for all the heartache & bloodshed. All that have been taken »& burn as candles before God's throne« are praying for victory & success — & where the right cause is, will final victory be! One longs just a bit quicker for some very good news to quieten the restless minds here, to put their small faith to shame. — we have not seen each other quietly this time, alone only ¾ of an hour on Xmas Eve, & yesterday ½ an hour — in bed one cannot speak, too awfully late always, & in the morning no time — so that this visit has flown by, & then the Xmastrees took you away daily — but I am grateful that you came, not counting our joy, your sweet presence delighted several thousands who saw you here. The new year does not count — but still not to begin it together for the first time since 21 years is still a bit sad. — This letter I fear sounds grumbly, but indeed its not meant to be so, only the heart is very heavy & your loneliness is a source of trouble to me. Others, who are less accustomed to family life, feel such separations far less. — Tho' the heart is engaged, I'll still come to see you off and then go into Church & seek strenght there, & pray for your journey & victory. —

Goodbye my Angel, Husband of my heart I envy my flowers that will accompany you. I press you tightly to my breast, kiss every sweet place with gentle tender love, I, your ownlittle woman, to whom you are All in this world. God bless & protect you, guard you from all harm, guide you safely & firmly into the new year. May it bring glory & sure peace, & the reward for all this war has cost you. I gently press my lips to yours & try to forget everything, gazing into your lovely eyes — I lay on your precious breast, rested my tired head upon it still. This morning I tried to gain calm & strenght for the separation. Goodbye wee one, Lovebird, Sunshine, Huzy mine, Own!

Ever your unto death wife and friend.

( ) a big kiss imprinted here

Sunny.

This little calendar may still be of me to you.

No. 183.

Tsarskoje Selo, Dec. 31-st 1915

My own Sweetheart,

This is the last time that I write to you in the year 1915. From the depths of my heart and soul I pray God Almighty to bless 1916 quite particularly for you & your beloved country. May He crown all your undertakings with success, recompense the troops for all their bravery, send victory to us — show our ennemies of what we are capable. 5 m. the sun shone before you left, and so has even *Shah Bagov* also noticed it each time you left for the army & to-day it shines brightly, 18 of frost. And as our Friend says always to pay attention to the weather, I trust that forsooth it is a good augury.

And for interior calm — to crush those effervescing elements, wh. try to ruin the country & give you endless worry. — I prayed last night till I thought my soul wld. burst, & cried my eyes out. I cannot bear to think of all you have to carry, & all alone away from us — oh, my Treasure, my Sunshine, my Love. We went straight to *Znamenia* from the station, Baby dear also placed his candles. I don't know how we shall meet the new Year — I likes being in Church — it bores the Children — my heart is worse, so I cannot make up my mind yet, — in any case, its very sad not to be together & I miss you quite horribly. —

And yr. empty rooms without our Sunbeam, poor Angel; such endless pitty fills my heart for you & such a craving to hold you tightly in my arms, & to cover you with kisses. — Baby has just gone off into the garden. — Now I must end — Once more every blessing and goodwish for the coming Year.

God bless you, Lovy sweet, beloved Angel,

I kiss you without end, & remain yr. deeply, deeply loving, loving very own old Wify

Alice.

A. sends every blessings, goodwish, love & kisses for the New Year. — Just got yr. wire, so sorry you did not sleep, for sure too hot, övertired & worried & sad. My humour too is of the saddest.

No. 184.

Tsarskoje Selo, January 1-st 1916

My own beloved Angel,

The new year has begun & to you I send the first words my pen traces. Blessings & boundless love I send you. We had a *mass* in the other side of the house at 10½ & then I answered telegrams & got to my prayers before 12 — I heard the Churchbells ring lying on my knees, crying & praying with heart & soul.

Sweet Lovebird, what are you doing? Have you been to Church? Alone in yr. empty rooms, a sad sensation!

One happy man I saw this evening, that was *Volkov,* as I have named him my 3-st page, the others beeing old & so often at death's door — he cried when thanking me — we remembered how he brought us in a present at Coburg, when we were engaged & I remember him yet before at Darmstadt. — I cant write any more to-night, my eyes are too sore. Sleep well, my precious One, my Sunshine.

Goodmorning Huzy, my own!

22 of frost, bright weather. Slept badly, heart ached — this morning more enlarged so have to spend the day in bed — sorry for the children — if better, shall get over onto the sopha in the evening to have this room aired.

Got a telegram from *Sandra* from town, glad poor little Xenia not alone, as she feels so very unwell.

Longing for news from you, as only had a wire upon your arrival 24 hours ago & my thoughts dont leave you, — As Baby has a wee bit scratchy throat, he remains at home. — The others have gone to Church. — Darling treasure, I trust this bright sunshine will bring many blessings to our brave troops & dear country and shine into your life with bright hope, strength & courage. — Have any amount of telegram to answer. — Yesterday I received Mme Khvostov (wife of Minister of Justice) & pretty daughter, who marries next week, before the young Artillery officer returns to the war — he had 7 wounds. Then received 4 wounded officers, *Viltchkovsky* & a *Kalmyk* & Priest of theirs, who ask me to send wounded earlier in this year to their hospitals for *mare's milk* — they want to arrange also a *sanatorium,* wh. wld. be splendid. — Well, in bed one wont get at me & that will be perhaps better & help getting my heart sooner into order. — A. spent the night in town, she went after 5 already — & after her telephone, by our Friend's order. She told me what to tell you at once about the trams. I know, Alek once tried to stop it & at once there were rows — what general gave the order now? It is perfectly absurd, as they have often to go great distances, & a tram takes them there in no time. It seems an officer, because of the order, kicked a man out of the tram & the soldier tried to beat him — its bitterly cold too — & really, gives rise to nasty stories — our officers are not all gentlemen, so that their ways of explaining things to the soldiers are probably often „with the fist". — Why do people always invent new reasons for discontent & scandal, when all goes smothely. — *Beletzky* got hold of a gang & brochures, wh. were being printed for the 9-th, to make filth again knowing our Friend, God will help them serve you.

The children are lunching next door & making wonderful noises. *„Engineer-Mechanic"* has arrived unexpectedly & so prevents med (icine) wh. is a bore. —

This instant, quite unexpectedly your sweetest letter was brought — oh thank you Lovy mine, thank you tenderly for yr. s w e e t words wh. warmed up my aching heart — the best gift for the beginning of the new year. Oh, Lovy mine, what good it does a tender word like that! you don't know, how much it means to me, nor how terribly I miss you — I yearn for your kisses, for your arms, shy Childy only gives them me in the dark & wify lives by them; I hate begging for them like Ania, but when I get them, they are my life, & when you are away, I recall all your sweet looks & every word and caress. —

Baby received a charming telegram fr. all the foreigners at the *Head-quarters* in remembrance of the little room in wh. they used to sit & chat during »*Zakuska*« (hors d'œuvres).

Ania brought a flower from our Friend for you with His blessing, love and many good wishes. —

Goodbye my Angel Dear, I bless & kiss you over & over again yr. own

Wify.

No. 185.

Tsarskoje Selo, Jan. 2-nd 1916

My own beloved Darling,

Nice bright sunshine, 20 of frost. Did not sleep well as head continues aching, so excuse short letter. Was on the sopha yesterday fr. 9—11, but the head began aching thouroughly then — therefore I remain again in bed to-day, as head & heart ache more when I move. *Maria* & *Anastasia* went for an hour to church, because of Ania, who takes Holy Communion the others were in the hospital & now they are lunching next door. No news from the front — shows the weather has not yet changed for the better. — I made a mistake, Sandro is not here, it's the other one who telegraphed to me. Sergei too is in town again. *Nikolasha* wired from his family. — My Beloved, my lonely

Sweetheart, my old heart aches for you, I s o well understand that feeling of emptiness, tho' there are many people around — no one to give you caresses. When A. speeks of her loneliness, it makes me angry, she has Nini near whom she tenderly loves, twice a day comes to us — every evening with us four hours & you are her life & she gets daily caresses fr. us both & blessings; you have nothing now — only all in thoughts and fr. far. Oh, to have wings & fly over every evening to cheer you up with my love. Long to hold you in my arms, to cover you with kisses & feel that you are my very Own, whoever dares call you »my own«, — you nevertheless are mine, my own treasure, my Life, my Sun, my Heart! 32 years ago my childs heart already went out to you in d e e p love. — Of course you are your country's first of all & that you show in all your deeds, precious One. — I just read what you write to the army & the navy as New year's greeting. — have you let know about W's birthday, that they may feast it in the same way as yours was? Baby began writing his first diary yesterday, — Marie helped him, his spelling is of course queer. — Cannot write any more to-day. — Every thought is with you. I bless you fervently & sent warm »soft« kisses. Ever Huzzy mine, very own tenderly loving, deeply devoted little

Wify

I reread your letter & love it. —

No. 186.

Tsarskoje Selo, Jan. 3-d 1916

My very own Sweetheart,

This morning only 5 degrees — such a great change. Scarcely slept this night — after 4—5½ — after 7—9 — head better, heart more enlarged, so remain in bed again. Yesterday was up from 9—11 again on sopha. —

Am sorry one takes Masha's Chiffre off, but once that done, there are gentlemen who allow themselves to say things, whose golden coats and aiguillettes can now in future well be taken from them. Give *Maximovitch* the order to pay attention in the club — *Khvostov* begged Fredericks to help him, but the latter could not or did not understand the necessity. — Alas, *Bor. Vassiltchikov* has changed much for the worse and many another — oh, they need to feel yr. power — one must be severe now. —

A. was awfully happy with yr. telegram and says she wrote a rotten answer with the Parents, tho' she did not add half the official things the old man wanted her to write. —

I send you a whole collection of letters. Excuse bad writing, I don't know why I cannot write evenly with this selffilling pen, because its so hard probably. I enclose a postcard made of Baby's photo by Hahn at the *Headquarters* when we were there — it's such a good one. — It's snowing. — How dull I write. But I am squashed and humour not bright, so cannot write nicely. The Children are eating next door, chattering and firing away with their toy pistols. — Oh, my Angel sweet — my Own, very own — do so long for your loving arms to be around me, to hold me tight. The consolation of yr. loving letter! I continue rereading it and thanking God that really I can be something for you — I long to — I do love you so intently with every fibre of my heart. God bless you my sunshine, my one and all — I kiss and kiss you without end, pray without ceasing, that God may hearken unto our prayers send consolation, strength, success, victory, peace, peace in every sense — one is so dead tired and weary fr. all the misery. —

Ever Huzy mine, life of my life, the blessing of it, the gratitude for every second of love you have given me.

Yr. little woman, Yr. Wify.

No. 187.

Tsarskoje Selo, Jan. 4-th 1916

My own Sweetheart,

It was such an unexpected joy to receive your sweet letter yesterday afternoon, and I thank you for it with all my deeply loving heart. My day passed as usual, Ania read to me a little in the day. Got on to my sopha from 9—12, *N. P.* came to tea from 10—12 — had not seen him since last Monday, missed you, Lovy, as never had him to tea without you, but he leaves probably the 8-th, according to the day he has to meet Kirill at *Kiev.* To-night he leaves for 1 day to bid his sisters goodbye. He told us how touchingly kind Motherdear was to him; kept him half an hour, talked about the *marine of the guard,* politics, the old man whom she finds honest, but a *fool* because he offended *Buligin* — said how deeply she regretted *N. P.* was leaving her son, such a true and honest friend, fished an image out of her pocket and blessed him — he was awfully touched by her kindness. — It seems *Sablin* 3 (whom other believe, alas, to be his brother) spread the story about his being sent out there, away fr. you for having spoken against our Friend, such a beastly shame and it has made him again less willing to go to *Gregory,* as tho' now it would look as if he went to beg for himself; and he ought to see him before going to the war, his blessings can save him fr. harm, I shall see him again and then beg him to go — its a subject one has to handle gently — Manus did all the harm then. —

Ebikin saw him several times and will do all about getting the men, I think they look at them together before he leaves. K. begged *Grigorovitch* to ask *Kanin* to send officers from the »*Oleg*«. They have sent for *Kozhevnikov* to prepare the men for his *Company* — that goes together with 3 weeks leave, — then *Rod.* and so on they got no leave till now, since easter, as had to be always ready at Sebastopol and Odessa. — *Gutchkov* is very ill — wish he would go to yonder world for you and Russians blessing, so its not a sinful wish. — The Children went to the *Silaievs* yesterday, *Olga* and *Tatiana* and enjoyed them. — I slept so badly, heart enlarged and head aches rather, so remain in bed. — *Ania* »rushes« about arranging her *refugee-home,* as wants to take some men in on the 6-th — I scrape up things for her too and order others she needs. They say the house looks so cosy, *Tatiana* went to look at it! — 15 degrees of frost to-day. Bichette wrote in despair to Mme Zizi to crave your forgiveness, that her son was not at Nieswicz when you went there. Since 17 months he had not left, and only then went for 2 days to see his mother and Grandmother, who was feeling ill. Had they known you were coming, she too would have flown to meet you. —

Baby seriously writes his diary, only is so funny about it, — as little time in the evening, he writes in the afternoon about dinner. — Yesterday as a treat he remained long with me, drew, wrote and played on my bed — and I longed for you to be with us — oh, how I want you, beloved One, but its good you are not here, as I am in bed and I should never see you, as they have the meals next door. — Very windy and cold, Baby remains in, because of his cold, and *Poliakov* says he must never go out above 15 degr. for some years still, tho' I sent him out before to 20. Olga and Anastasia also have colds, but go to hospitals and drove yesterday — sledged in a sleigh driven by three horses. *Papa-Feodorov* and *Olga Evgenievna* have come to town and hope to see her. —

How is the little Admiral, and do they get on with *Mordvinov* at domino? What news has *Grabbe* from our dear *Convoys.* The Children are eating and firing away with their rotten pistols. Xenia feels still very weak fr. her influenza — Felix has got the mumps. —

Sweety, are you seriously now thinking about *Sturmer,* I do believe its worth risking the German name, as one knows what a right man he is (I believe yr. old corespondent lady spoke of him?) and will work well with the new energetic ministers. I see they have all gone off in different directions to try and see things with their own eyes — a good thing — also that communication will soon be stopped between Moscou and *Petrograd.* I am glad you enjoy the book, am not sure; but fancy you gave it me once to read, did not *Sandro* give it you? —

Now my Sunshine, my joy, my Husband beloved, Goodbye. God bless you and protect you and help you in everything.

I cover you with tenderest gentlest and yet passionately loving kisses, Lovebird. Ever yr. own unto and beyond death Wify.

No. 188.

Tsarskoje Selo, Jan. 5-th 1916

My own Sweetheart,

What joy, I received your sweet letter from the 3-rd this morning — nice snowstorms must have retained the trains. We all 6 are intensely happy over our letters and thank you for them as tenderly as we only can.

A bright, sunny morning, 15 degrees and a very cold wind. Thats good you found a spade to work, get *Mordvinov* to come and help you, otherwise this solitude must be distracting, and I can feel how you miss sweet Sunbeam everywhere.

I slept a little better this night and my heart too is better, tho' aches a good deal and I feel still rotten, so keep to my bed. Have not yet been able to begin my medicines. — Hope poor, spineless *Valia* will soon be better — give him over my compliments. Anastasia has a cold, 37,5 and *Bekker,* and did not get to sleep till very late, Olga has a slight one too and Baby a tiny bit. —

How good the things go well in the Caucasus — what *Grigorovitch* papers say fr. German and Austrian sources of course is always different — and as tho' on the Roumanian frontier they had good luck and we terrible losses — but the latter you knew still here, yes? And not too terrible, therefore you stopped. — *Gutchkov* is better!! —

How nice that Harding wired from all — yes, how things do change in this world. —

The 3 eldest are off to church — long to go, get consolation and strength there. — Oh my Lovebird, »me loves oo« quite terribly! —

Here I send you card from Louise. — Your sweet letters are s u c h a joy to me and I reread and kiss them incessantly.

Dearly beloved One, sunshine of my aching soul, I wish I were with you, far from all these worries and sorrows, quite by ourselves and the wee ones, to rest a while and forget all — one gets, oh, so tired!

Mita Benkendorf told at Paul's, that Masha had brought letters from Ernie, Ania said she knew nothing, and Paul said it was true — who told him? They all found it right the chiffre was taken from her (I personally find, that *S. Iv. T.* and *Lili,* who behaved so badly and were my own personal ladies ought far sooner to have suffered, and other men too) — it seems a letter fr. a Pss. Galitzin, to her was printed, a horrid one, accusing her of being a spy etc. (wh. I continue not to believe, tho' she has acted v e r y wrongly fr. stupidity and I fear, greed of money). — Paul is still offended about Rauch — whenever I see him, I shall certainly explain things to him wh. are as clear as day. —

I saw in the papers that nice *Tkatchenko* died at *Kharkov* — am so sorry — many a remembrance of the peaceful, happy bygone are linked with his name!

An old friend of the Standarts. — *Kilhen* (I thought it was written with a »g«) has died — such a shame they cleared him out from Bessarabia because of his German name — I never heard that name before. There are german names here wh. do not, I believe, exist elsewhere. —

I read an endless letter fr. Max to Vicky, wh. he wished me to read — he tries to be just, but it was more than painful, as many things, alas, were true about here and the prisoners —; I can only repeat that I find one must send a higher placed official with Mme Orjewsky to inspect our prisons, especially in Siberia. It is so far away, and certainly people, alas, in our

Country, do but rarely fulfil their duties well, when out of sight. The letter hurt me, much truth was in it and also things that were wrong, and he says ours wont believe things said against the treatment here (— neither do they vice versa) — I saw what the sisters had told him, also about the cosacks. But all that is too painful, only I find in that he is right, when he says they have not enough food to feed their prisoners much, as all cut off their food from outside (now fr. Turkey I think its great gain for them) — and we can give more food — and more grease they need, and in Siberia the trains go alright — and warmer barracks and more cleanliness. Out of humanity sake and that one dare not speak badly of our treatment to the prisoners one longs to give severe orders, and that those who don't fulfil them will be punished — and I have not the right to mix in as a »German« — one, some brutes, persist on calling me so, probably so as to hinder my interference. Our cold is too intense, with more food one can save their lives, 1000 have died — our climate is so terribly trying. — I hope *Georgi* and *Tatistchev* will inspect on their way back and thoroughly — especially the small towns and poke their noses well into everything, as one does not notice all at first sight. — *Fredericks* might have wired a cypher to *Georgi* with yr. order, only yr. Mama and I begged him to go and look. — He must not say it before hand, otherwise they will prepare things on purpose — *Tatistchev* can be a help as he speaks German well and will know how to be with the German officers and found out the real truth about their treatment and whether they have really been beaten, as thats disgusting if true and may have happened out there — as better for us, they too will do things more humanely, as Max intends helping in his mother's memory — so if Georgi does, it wld. be excellent; and send someone else also here about, and Mme *Orjevsky* to Siberia to meet *Georgi,* — these are wify's ideas. — Why dont you, now that you are, free'er, prepare all for the old man's change — I am sure he feels he has not acted wisely latterly, because he long has not tried to see me — he realises he is, alas, not in the right. —

Precious One — I have sent Baby to church for the blessing of the water — he had masters before.

Such sunshine! —

I am so glad Ania has that work to do about her »*home*«, — several times a day she goes there to see to all, to order things, and what a lot one needs for 50 invalids, sanitarys, sisters, doctors etc. *Viltchkovsky* and *Loman* and *Reshetnikov* (fr. Moscou) help her — I think she has 27,000 — all been given to her, not a penny yet of her own. Its so good at last she has something like that to do, not time to have »the blue devils« and God will bless her for this work. She has lost a pound this week in consequence, wh. delights *Zhuk.* To-morrow she takes in her first soldiers .—

So you, Sweetheart, also only got my letter this morning -- is it possible so much snow or our railways once more at fault — when will there at last be order, wh. in every sense our poor country needs and wh. is not in the Slave nature!

I read one has evacuated Cetinje and their troops are surrounded — well, now the King and sons and black daughters here, who wished so madly this war, are paying for all their sins towards you and God, as they went against our Friend knowing who He is! God avenges Himself. Only I am sorry for the people, such heroes all — and the Italians are selfish brutes to have left them in the lurch — cowards! —

Baby will write to-morrow, he slept long to-day. —

I bless you and kiss you without end, with fervent love.

yr. very own little Wify.

The Priest I hear is coming to bless the rooms, so I must put on a teagown and crawl back to bed — its nice he remembered to come, tho' Church is not in the house to-day.

No. 189.

Tsarskoje Selo, Jan. 6-th 1916.

My very own Treasure,

It was such a joy having two letters to reread ever so often yesterday and to cover with kisses. I was in bed at 2½ and only got to sleep after 3½ (as usual now) and reread them again and hovered over every tender word. The heart is again enlarged, tho' I twice took my adonis yesterday — I told *Botkin*, I need a moments fresh air — so he said I might go unto the balcony, there being only 5 degres and no wind. Poor Anastasia has 38 this morning and slept very badly. At first I feared it might be the beginning of measels, but they say that no — so I suppose only influenza — Marie will sleep this night with the big sisters, its better. They went to Church at 9 and now are in the hospital, Tiny is going there too. — I miss my hospital so much — but whats to be done. —

Ah yes! I often think how lovely it would be in your free hours to sit cosily by yr. side and chatter away calmly, with no ministers etc. to bore us — it seems as tho' all difficulties and sad things come together for you. — Our friend is sad about the people of Montenegro and that the ennemy takes everything and is so pained that such luck accompanies them — but always says the final victory will be ours but that with great difficulty as the ennemy is so strong. He regrets one began that movements I think without asking him — he wld. have said to have waited — he is always praying and thinking when the good moment will come to advance, so as not to uselessly loose men. — Please, thank General Williams in Baby's name for the pretty cards — it is interesting for him to have the collection. — Anastasia has bronchitis, head is heavy and hurts her swallowing, coughed in the night, she writes about *Ostrog(orsky)* »*Although he said that I look a litttle better than yesterday, but I am pale and my appearance is foolish in my view*« just like the »*Shvibzik*« to say such things; — such a bore I cant sit with my Beloved Darling, I think of you so endlessly lovingly and suffer over your loneliness — Nobody young and bright near you, a thing one needs so much to keep one going when worried and hard-worked. — Just collected 10 simple Images for Ania's Invalid-house, she takes in her first men to-day. Well, I lay for 1/4 an hour on the balkony — nice air, heard the bells ringing — but was glad to get into bed again — still not feeling famous. — I send you a petition from our Friend, its a military thing, He only sent it without any word of comment and then again a letter from Ania. —

A week to-day that you left us — to me it seems very much longer, wify misses her own, her Sunshine, her one and all in Life and longs to caress and cheer him up in his loneliness, Sweetest of Sweets. I have nothing of interest to tell you, as I see nobody. Had a wire from *Miassoyedov Ivanov* yesterday thanking for pretty *Regimental book* I send them — they have moved on to *Belozorka* wherever that may be. —

Malama wrote a card to Ania saying that they leave »*for business and go on that account West. The place is not especially pleasant, to rest in a hole is also not well, but not for long. Yesterday went to the dance arranged by the detachement, the whole village »monde«, was there I enjoyed myself much and am arranging a similar affair tonight.*«

Now my Beloved, my Angel, my one and all I hold you tightly in my arms, gaze long and tenderly into your sweet loveley eyes, kiss them, and every bit of you — and »me« alone has the full right to this — true?

God bless and protect you and keep you from all harm. Ever yr. very own old

Sunny.

Lovy, you burn her letters so as that they should never fall into anybody's hands?

No. 190.

Tsarskoje Selo, Jan. 7-th 1916

My very own beloved Darling,

I received your sweet letter after having sent off mine — thanks for it with all my heart. It is lovely that you can write to me every day & I devour your letters with such endless love. —

N. P. dined with A. & then spent the evening with us. He was disgusted with Moscou & all the filth one says there & it took him lots of trouble to clear up many horrors his sisters had heard & false opinions they had. Here he avoids the clubs, but friends tell him lots of things.

The train fr. *Sebastopol* was late, so he stuck at Moscou station from 2—4 in the night, & reached *Petrograd* at 5 instead of 2. — He says about Manus its not true about his wishing to change his name, enemies of his spread things about him, because they are jealous he got that rank & he had a row with *Miliukov,* who wrote lies about him & now people want to set the little Admiral against him out of spite. *N. P.* went in the train with old *Dubensky,* who spoke very frankly to him about the old *Headquarters* & all the stories & »nice« things about fat *Orlov* & plans he & others had, coinciding with what our Friend said, I'll tell you when we meet.

Have you any plans in view or any journeys, as you have less to do now & it must be so dull at the *Headquarters.*

Lovy, I don't know, but I should still think of Stürmer, his head is plenty fresh enough — you see *Khvostov* a tiny bit hopes to get that place — but he is too young — Stürmer would do for a bit, & then later on if you ever want to find another you can change him, only don't let him change his name »it would do him more harm than if he kept his old & venerated ones« as you remember, *Gregory* said — & He very much values *Gregory* wh. is a great thing. You know *Volzhin* is an obstinate nuisance & wont help *Pitirim* wont give into things unless he gets yr. special order — frightened of public opinion. *Pitirim* wishes *Nicon* (the brute) to be sent to Siberia, you remember & *Volzhin* wishes him to go to *Tula* & the Metropolitan finds it not good he should be in the centre of Russia, but further away, where he can do less harm. Then he has other good plans about paying the clergy & *Volzhin* wont agree & so on. Shall I ask *Pitirim* to write me a list of the things he finds neccessary & then I can give them you to order *Volzhin* to fulfill. *Pitirim* is so clever & largeminded & the other just not, fr. fright.

Anastasia's temp. in the evening was 37, she spoke with me by telephone. Alexei came to our dinner already in his dressing gown at 8.20 & wrote his diary wh. he is sweet about. Your message came in time, as he was already beginning to get a bit bored about it, not knowing when to have time to write. —

Such a craving for your caresses, yearning to hold you in my arms and rest my head upon your shoulder, as in bed & to cudle up close & lie quite still upon yr. heart & feel peaceful & at rest. So much sorrow & pain, worries & trials — one gets so tired & one must keep up & be strong to face everything. I should have liked to see our Friend, only never ask Him to the house when you are not there, as people are so nasty. Now they pretend he has received a nomination at the *F. Cathedral* wh. obliges him also to light all the *lamps* in the palace in all the rooms! One knows what that means — but that is so idiotic that any sensible person can but laugh at it; — as do I. —

You don't mind my seeing *N. P.* often now? But as he leaves in a few days (his friends left), the whole days he is occupied & in the evenings quite alone & downhearted. After all these talks here & in Moscou that he has been sent away because of our Friend — its not easy for him leaving you & us all, & for us too its horrid to have to say goodbye — one has so few real friends & he is our very nearest. He will go to our Friend, thank God. Ania spoke lots to him & then I did all about the great change this summer — he did not know that it was He who kept you & us up to the absolute necessity for you, our & Russia's sake. I had not spoken to him alone for months &

was afraid to speak about *Gregory,* as I knew he was doubting him — it has not yet quite passed I fear — but if he sees Him he will feel calmer — he believes so in Manus (I don't) & I believe he set him against ou Fr. & now he calls him *Rasputin,* wh. I don't like & I will try & get him out of this habit.

So much milder, 1° in the evening only — those changes are bad for the health. —

What do you say about Montenegro? I don't trust that old King & fear he may be up to mischief as he is most untrustworthy & above all ungrateful. What have the poor Servian troops done wh. had gone there? Italy is disgusting to my mind & so cowardly, she easily might have saved Montenegro. — Bow to nice old Po from me & to General Williams & Baby's dear Belgian. — I am sure the blessing of the waters must have been very fine — such a pretty place down by the river, the steep street & mild weather.

Anastasia is better, 36,5, feels clearer in the head & the cough already less — it seems only the tops of the bronchi were touched. —

I slept most rottenly & feel idiotic, so will go out on the balcony — 1° of warmth — & Isa will keep me company.

Am sorry to bother you with petitions, but *Bezrodny* is a good Dr. (he knows our friend already long) & only you can help, so write a word on his *memorandum* (there was no petition) to say one is to give him the divorce & sent it to *Volzhin* or *Mamantov.*

Then there is a paper from a *Georgian, Gregory* & *Pitirim* know & ask for — well you can send it to *Kotchubei,* tho' I doubt he can do anything for this *Prince David Bagration-Davidov* — or do you know him? — Then a paper from *Mamantov (Gregory* knows him many years) — it seems an injustice was done, can you just look it through & do according to what you think right with it. Sorry to bother you, but they are for you — simpler ones I send straight to our *Mamantov* without any commentary. Baby's throat is a bit red, so he wont go out — it's the real weather for catching cold — these great changes. —

Did you repeat the order about William's birthday being allowed to be feasted the same as yr. namesday was? — Did you think over again, that people of the *Duma,* such as *Gutchkov,* shld. no more be allowed to go to the front & speak to the troops? He is recovering, honestly I must say, alas! One ordered *services* for him at the *cathedral* & now he becomes yet more of a heroe in the eyes of those that admire him.

Here is a letter from *Alexei.*

Sweetheart, me thought so quite particularly of you this sleepless night & with such tender longing & compassion! — How is you?

Now Goodbye, my Sunshine, my long-loved Huzy, God Almighty bless and protect you & help you in all yr. decisions & give you great firmness of caracter.

Kisses, tender & passionate without end, fr. yr. very own fondly loving

Bow to *Mordvinov:* & *Silaiev.* Wify.

Where is Misha, no living sign fr. him since he left in Dec.

No. 191.

Tsarskoje Selo, Jan. 8-th 1916

My own Darling,

Very tenderly do I thank you for yesterday's precious letter. — The end was so sweet and full of tender meaning — lady thanks for the caress wh. she returns with great love! —

Well Babykins went up after luncheon with a heavy head, rather red throat, ached swallowing, so I told him to lie down and get a compress on. Later he had 38.4. but the head got better. I no more saw him, we only spoke to him and Anastasia by telephone, she felt better, 37.2. — Ania coughed 2 days and was feeling feverish when she came in the afternoon, so I made her measure her temperature, 37.9. so I sent her home instead of to her wounded, *Akelina* remains the night with her, the Dr. gave her medicine, she drank hot red wine blessed by our Friend — I hope she will be better by to-morrow. She wrote in a very sad mood — and begged to say she kisses you. — I remained on the sopha after the balkony till 6 — and then up for dinner again — feel weak all day and not very nice. *N. P.* came after 9 and kept us company and the children tried all sorts of music for the gramaphones I want for our, and Ania's hospital. He says one sends *Rodionov* now instead of *Kozhevnikov,* and as soon as he arrives, Saturday or Sunday, he supposes Kirill and he leave. If you are at the *Headquarters, Kirill wanted to pass* there for 2 days, then *N. P.* thought better to join him at *Kiev* so as not to look pushy at *Moghilev,* but if you are away, as *Dubensky* hinted to him you might be, then he and Kirill will go straight fr. here to-gether. He bought masses of shoes for their horses and nails etc. and things without end the others of *Kozhevnikov,* and as soon as he arrives, Saturday or Sunday, he supposes, the son of ours) Koni and the other names he had forgotten. It freshens one up to see him — its lovely — to-day a week that I am so to speak in bed and one does not feel bright nor over gay — and neither does my own Lovebird. — Its been raining and »dirty« weather. — Am so glad *Trepov's* and *Naumov's* journeys were useful and I hope they woke up everybody thoroughly — one must go about oneself and poke ones nose into everything, then people work harder and feel that one is watching them and can turn up any moment. How good you have a cinema for all the children and then they can see you nicely too.

Anastasia slept well, 36.8, *Alexei* only woke up twice in the night, 37.6, is in the playroom, in bed and very gay. I hope to go upstairs this afternoon to see them both. In the morning I am to lie on the balkony again. 2 degr. of warmth, rainy, windy, dark, dull weather shall get Isa there again to speak over affairs.

Did not sleep again very well and had nasty dreams, head aches rather, heart too, tho' just now not enlarged. Ania slept very badly, to wh. she is unaccustomed, coughed much, head aches and 38. Olga has gone there for a little and Marie will at 12 — stupid I cant. Perhaps you will tell me to give her your love to cheer her up. — All about people have influenza, rotten thing. — Could you not have got *Sturmer* to quietly come to the *Headquarters*, you see so many people, to have a quiet talk together before you settle anything. — Look here, when you see *Dubensky* cleverly draw the question to speak about fat *Orlov* and make him tell you things about him — if he has the courage to show up the man's vileness wh. drags in others too high placed of the old *Headquarters* — *Feodorov*, I think, knows it too. Me, he always spoke of as »she« — and that he was sure I wld. not let you come soon to the *Headquarters* again after they had forced »their« ministers upon you, — ask about *Drenteln* too, who had the convent in view for me ultimately — *Dzhunkovsky, Orlov* ougt straight off to have been sent to Siberia — after the war is over you ought to have a *punishment* made — why should they go, free with good places, when they had prepared all to have you changed and me shut up, and who did all, to be nasty to yr. wife — and they wander about and other people think they were unjustly cleared out, as they went scot'-free. Its vile to think of the falseness of humanity — tho' I long knew and told you my feeling about them — thank God, *Drenteln* has also gone — now these are clean people round you, and I only wish *N. P.* were of their number. We spoke long about Dmitri — he says that he is a boy without any caracter and can be lead by anybody. 3 months he was under the influence of *N. P.* and held himself well at the *Headquarters* and when in town with him, kept himself like the other and did not go to ladies companies — but out of sight — gets into other hands. He finds the regiment perverts the boy, as their coarse conversations, jokes are horrid and before ladies too and they draw him down. Now he is used as aide de camp. —

»Shvibzik« (Anastasia) just wrote one of her funny notes — to-day she has to keep still in bed. —

I spent my time writing notes to all the invalids. Ania had a letter from dear *Otar Purtseladze* — tell it to *Silaiev*. He sends lots of good wishes, feelings, love to the *family;* — and is happy we have seen his wife and boy. Learns French and English — gets up and goes to bed early — does not say how kept or fed nor any details — only in despair to be there instead of serving at such a time.

Now Sweetheart, Beloved, my Own, My very Own, I bless you —, kiss you, press you tightly in my arms, with infinite love and gratitude for 21 years perfect happiness for wh. morn and night I thank God.

Oh, how I long for you and yr. tender caresses — I send you all, all, all, the same as you did.

Ever yr. own old Sunny.

Does the paper smell good!!!

No. 192.

Tsarskoje Selo, Jan. 9-th 1916

My own Sweetheart,

Mild, snowing, raining and dark. The 2 little ones slept well, have 36.3 and 36.4. I shall go again up to them in the afternoon. — Have been reading *reports* and Isa came to help about a few questions and yesterday evening too. — The Children went in several times yesterday to see Ania — and Tatiana late, still after cleaning instruments in the hospital. She had people all day, her Father, then our Friend and nice Zina, then her Mother, then Axel P. who has come for 3 days, and *Zhuk.* The *Metropolitan* hearing she is ill, wants to see her too — awfully kind and she does not know what to do. Her maid last night 40.2, *Angina,* so the Dr. took her off to the hospital and her old *Zina* came in to help *Akelina.* She did not sleep the night because of her cough — now she is better no doubt, as has not let me know about her temp. — She said to kiss you and beg for yr. prayers, therefore I had to wire and also what our Fr. said about *Sturmer* not to change his name and to take him for a time at least, as he is such a decided loyal man and will hold others in hand, — let one scream if one wishes, they always will at any nomination. *N. P.* spoke by telephone: Kirill sends him off to-night to Helsingfors to see *Kashin* and the staff — because *Grigorovitch* told Kirill they make difficulties about fulfilling your orders to K. — so the quickest and best was to send *N. P.* to explain matters and that K. got the order from you, — its not *Kashin* but others in the staff and he fears *Timirev* may be disagreable as he is offended with the *Marine of the Guard,* wh. he left. — Ania slept from 8—11 and has 35.8 — so feels very weak. *Sergei* goes to the *Headquarters* soon, I hear — better not, keep him there long, as he is always a gossip, alas, and such a sharp, criticising tongue and his manners before strangers are not edifying — and then there are very unclear, unclean stories about her and *bribes* etc. wh. all speak about, and the artillery is mixed up into it. — Just got your letter, 12 o'clock nice and early, such an endless joy to have news fr. you, you cannot think what your sweet letters are to me and how I kiss and reread them ever so often. Such a treat to get them now daily, they warm me up, as I miss my Treasure quite terribly and kissing your cushion and letter is still not quite satisfying to a hungry wify. Ah, My Angel, God bless you for your marvelous love and devotion, wh. I am not near worthy enough of. — Bless you for it, sweet One. You too, Huzy mine, know what you are to me and what dephts of love my old heart is capable of — these separations kindle the fire yet more and make the great love yet more intense. — Will you be moving about to the other corps as you have less work now? Its good you let the ministers come out there to you. Oh, how I wish you could get rid of *Polivanov,* wh. means *Gutchkov* — old *Ivanov* in his stead, if honest *Beliaiev* too weak — all hearts in the *Duma* would go out to »*grandfather*«, am sure, but perhaps you have no one ready in his place. — To-day 40 days little Sonia died. — In a few days its Tatiana's namesday; to-day the famous 9-th. — How much we have lived through together and what hard times and yet God never forsook one and kept us up — and so he will now, tho' we need great patience, faith, trust in His mercy. And your work resignation and humility must be recompensed and God I feel will do so, tho' when, we cannot guess. — Yesterday evening I laid patiences, read, saw Isa and played with Marie. — Took tea with the little ones upstairs — the three then stood still and their beds were in the middle of the room — Anastasia looks green with shades under her eyes, but he — not bad. My Love, I send you just one paper to do what you like with. —

You must get the old man out and calmly tell him yr. decision — now its easier as you dont agree quite and he did not have that circular printed (showing he is a bit old and tired and cant grasp, alas, everything, dear old man) — you have time to speak, and its better the other shld. have time before the *Duma* is called in to have sittings with the ministers and prepare himself — and *Sturmer* being an older man, won't offend *Goremykin:* and then you give him the title of old *Solsky,* not of course Count (wh. is rotten), but the other thing I should calmly do it now at the *Headquarters* and not put it off any longer, believe me Deary. —

Well, now goodbye, Sweety mine, Husband of my heart and soul, light of my life — I hold you in my arms and clasp you tightly to me, kissing yr. sweet face, eyes, lips, neck and hands with burning tender kisses, — »I love you, I love you 't is all that I can say« you remember that song at Windsor 1894? on these evenings!! God bless you Treasure.

Ever yr. very own unto death   Wify.

Hope my flowers will arrive fresh and smelling good.

No. 193.

Tsarskoje Selo, Jan. 10-th 1916

My very Own,

Warm & snowing again. Our Friend's Namesday. — I am so glad, that thanks to measures having been taken, all passed quietly in Moscow & *Petrograd* & the strikers behaved themselves. Thank goodness, one sees the difference of *Beletzky* & *Dzhunkovsky* or *Obolensky.* I hope you dont mind I wired about *Pitirim,* but he wld. so much like to see you quietly (here you never have time) and tell you all his ideas & improvements he wld. like to make. He sat near Ania 's bed yesterday, kind man. She slept only for about 4 hours this night, (so did I) coughed much, 36.8, & Becker, & tired, & *Gregory* wanted her to come to-day, but she really has not the strength to go & it would be utter folly fr. the human point of view. — Anastasia slept well, 36,3. Alexei still sleeps. The big ones are off to Church. — I lay in their room yesterday fr. 4½—6½ — Baby was playing bezigue with Mr Gibbs, who spent the day with him. —

Eugeni Sergeievitch turned up, his foot was better & found my heart enlarged this morning too, but I knew that — so must take more Adonis & other drops to quieten the heartbeating. — I have absolutely nothing of interest to tell you, am so sorry — but I see nobody & hear nothing. Xenia feels still very weak and is only half dressed, & up half. —

How well our cosacks »worked« near Erzerum! —

Anastasia may get up in her rooms only on Tuesday, its a bore, but wiser & she does look still green. —

Baby slept very well till after 10, woke only once. 36.2. —

Why, there is the sun out for our Friend, that is lovely indeed, had to be so for Him! —

Ania thanks for yr. love & sends a letter, asks me whether you will be angry, I answered she must know better than me whether you allowed her to write often. —

Isa lunched with us — shall spend afternoon again quietly & alone till go up to the pets. —

Just got precious letter for wh. endless thanks, Sweetheart.

You are right about *Sturmer* & a »thunderbolt«.

Glad you will manage to see troops. Kiss & bless you without end, press you to my big, aching heart, yearn for yr. tender kisses & caresses wh. mean so much to yr. very own little Woman yr. wife, yr.

Sunny.

Who lives by you & whose Sun and light you are, purest & best One.

No. 194.

Tsarskoje Selo, Jan. 11-th 1916

My own Sweetheart,

A brighter day at last & 2 degrees of frost & the dear sun shining — its a pitty you too have such »dirty weather«. — Is the English General nice? I suppose he was sent to you from the army to welcome you as fieldmarshal? — But there is nothing you can give Georgie in exchange, as he does not command, & one cannot play with such nominations. —

I don't quite understand what has been going on in Montenegro — it says the King & Pietro left over Brindisi for Lyon, where he is to meet his wife & 2 youngest daughters & that Mirko remained to try & unite with the Montenegrian Servian & Albanian troops. Only now Italy has landed 70 000 men in Albania — an ugly game theirs. But if the King surrendered, how about his troops? Where are Jutta & Danilo? Why does one allow him to go to France — all most uncomprehensible to me. — Ania was up an hour on the sopha in the evening & spoke with quite a strong voice — she is already dreaming of coming here — what a strong health after all, to pick up in a second, after she thought she was so fearfully ill & miserable! —

Now don't think me mad for my wee bottle, but our Friend sent her one from his namesday feast, & we each took a sip & I poured this out for you — I believe its Madeira, I swallowed for his sake (like medecine), you do it too, please, tho' you dislike it — pour it into a glass & drink it all up for His health as we did — the lily of the valley & wee crust also are from Him for you, my Angel Sweet. One says heaps of people came to Him & He was beautiful. I wired congratulating *from all of us* & got this answer. »*Inexpressibly overjoyed — God's light shines on you, we will fear nothing.*«

He likes when one is not afraid to wire to Him direct, I know He was very displeased she did not go, & it worries her, but I think He goes to her to-day.

The little ex Xmas-tree smells so deliciously strong this morning! All have good temperatures this morning. —

I am sorry my letters are so dull, but I hear nothing & see nobody. — *Vassilievsky* telegraphed so happy to have received the brigade in wh. my regiment is, & *Sergeiev* enchanted to have taken the 21 reg. fr. him as he has served there so long. — I had to take another pen, as there was no more ink in the other one. — Slept better, so far heart not enlarged this morning. I shall go & lie for a bit on the balcony as had no air since two days. —

Thoughts & prayers never leave you, Sweetheart & I think of you with intense love, tenderness & longing.

God bless you, 1000 kisses fr. yr. very

Own.

Ania just writes that *N. P.* returned fr. Helsingfors & that she would like to come with him to dinner, that her Dr. has allowed her to go out in a shut carriage in the evening — I find Drs queer, or she is wonderfully strong & when she wants to do a thing she always does it & somehow succeeds — Youth & strength. —

Very tenderest thanks for sweetest letter — what joy if you come end of the week home again!!

No. 195.

Tsarskoje Selo, Jan. 12-th. 1916

My very own Treasure,

Tenderest good-wishes for our Tatiana's Namesday. She and Olga have flown off to the hospital and at 12½ we have a *mass* in my room — sad you are not with us, sweetheart. —

I can so well realise the utter boredom of your daily walks in that tiny garden, better cross the bridge in a motor and at the end of the town walk — or near the train on the big road; you indeed need air and exercise, but soon I suppose the snow will quite melt in yr. parts. — What joy if you can really come end of the week, sweet Angel mine! — the time seems long and weary when you are not here. —

Well, Ania and *N. P.* came to dinner, she remained only little over an hour, looks stout, rosy, tho' shades under her eyes. I had not seen either since last Thursday.

He had lots of difficulties at Helsingfors, they dont wish to give the quantity of officers needed, so now Kirill must work on at it. *Rodionov* arrived, and they both will come at 9, so as give *Tatiana* pleasure too on her Namesday. — Anastasia and Alexei are allowed to be dressed and up, but not to come down yet to-day — Baby slept till nearly 10 — 36.2. Its much better he us up, as felt well and did such awful nonsence in his bed and could not be kept quiet. —

The Germans are evacuating *Pinsk?* I wish one cld. »pinch« them before they have time to. —

At last 2 nights that I have slept quite nicely and the heart has not been enlarged in the morning. —

Such a surprise, both the little Ones turned up and may lunch with us — and really its much better. Both look rather thin and green still. —

Now Goodbye Sweetheart, Beloved. God bless you, kiss you ever so tenderly and fondly, and remain, Nicky mine, yr. very own old

Wify.

P. S. Just received yr. sweet letter, thanks 1000 times my very, very own Beloved, cover you with burning kisses. Oh how dull to sit with the old man!!! Wish it were me, wld. not Boyxy like lady? She wanted him frantically.

No. 196.

Tsarskoje-Selo, Jan. 13-th. 1916

My own Sweetheart,

Grey, dull weather, 2 of warmth again & very windy. — Lay out on the balkony yesterday for half an hour. The little ones are so happy to be able to come down again, but look pale. —

To-day the two eldest lunch at *Anitchkov,* have committees, *receipt of donations* & tea at Xenias. It seems Motherdear was not quite well, & so was lonely & could only go to Xenia once. —

It was cosy having *N. P.* & *V. N.* yesterday from 9¼—11.50 — they talked much about there. *N. P.* lets him live in his appartments as nearer to the *escort.* He & Kirill leave Saturday evening, I believe. There is still masses to be done — people are so obstinate & wont do things — he goes to *Grigorovitch* this morning. —

How dull, poor Angel, to sit near the old man at the cinema — why, its to run up the walls. I am glad the new English general is nice. — What are the stories going on about the Montenegrians? As tho' he had sold his country to the Austrians, therefore one wld. not receive him in Rome nor in Paris — or is this all gossip — he is capable of anything for money's sake & his personal profit, tho' he loved his country I thought — in any case I understand nothing. —

I want to go in the little sledge in the garden, tho' strong wind, with Marie, & enter into *Znamenia* for the first time in 1916, & place candles there & pray for my own sweet Lovebird. — Nice Zina, who likes our Friend sat for an hour with me yesterday.

Now goodbye my Sunshine, my one & all. I bless you & cover yr. beloved face with ever such tender kisses.

Yr, very own little

Wify.

Fancy *Raftopolo* being at *Moghilev,* he wrote to *Ania* he was sent there from the regiment.

No. 197.

Tsarskoje Selo, Jan. 14-th 1916

My very own Lovebird,

Very windy, mild, sun shone a little. Feel rotten as had such pains in my tommy in the night and such faintness, even rang for Madeleine to fill up my hotwaterbottle and give me opium. Probably it comes from Adonis. But I feel so weak to-day. — *Olga Evgenjevna* lunches and then I receive *Yagmin,* who came to hurry his wife, at last. —

How nice that *Raftopolo* lunched with you — *Silaiev* will have been delighted — it was the boy's sisters namesday too on the 12-th. To-day is Williams birthday! There now its snowing. — I wonder whether this is my last letter and you return on Saturday or not? —

The Children found Motherdear rather thin, they lunched with her upstairs — then after their committees they took tea at Xenias, who neither looks flouroushing. — Yr. friend *Plevitskaya* brought *Olga* money fr. the concerts she had given. — She had sung to *Olga* at *Kiev* where by chance *Mahalov* (*»Rosotchka«*) was, and he accompanied her and *Rodionov* came with her here. — Ania read some stories out of yr. book to us, about Children, whilst we were laying patiences — she has brought a new book for you for yr. return. — Cannot write any more, feel too idiotic. —

Goodbye my Sweetheart, God bless and protect you now and ever and help you in all the difficult moments of your life. —

I cover you with tenderly caressing, yearning kisses, and remain, precious One, yr. very own fondly loving old wife.

Sunny.

No. 198.

Tsarskoje Selo, Jan. 15-th. 1916

Sweetheart,

Only a few lines as feel very rotten. Slept well, but head aches still, difficult to keep eyes open, feel so weak, fievrish, nasty, 37. 1, but will probably rise, heart enlarged — as tho' I were going to have influenza, so *Botkin* said I was to remain all day in bed. Yesterday also felt nasty and cretinised.

Olga Evgenjevna the same as always, begged to send her compliments. *Yagmin* has news the regiment is well into Persia now.

Ania and *N. P.* dined — I felt too rotten to fully enjoy them —

Sunny day, 6 of warmth in the sun. —

Such happiness you come Sunday, but want to be well by then.

Hope good weather — all will go off well, see dear Cosacks. —

How was it a beastly Zeppelin came as far as *Rezhitsa?*

Children well, tho' Olga was sick in the night without any reason.

Beloved, I cant write any more, eyes ache and are so heavy.

Poor Css. Worontzov — she will miss her dear old husband — but for him it must be a relief. — How is Feodorov?

Blessings and kisses without end and great longing to have you back again, Lovebird, sweetest of Sweets —

Press you tenderly to my heart —

Ever yr. own old wify

Alix.

You will get this no doubt at *Orsha.*

No. 199.

Tsarskoje-Selo, Jan. 16-th. 1916

My Own,

I hear that a messenger leaves even to-day still to worry you — so I write a few lines. Bright sunshine, calm & 2 of frost.

Went to sleep after 3, feel a bit better to-day, but still a strange feeling in my inside & I keep a hotwater bottle on my tommy — but heart by chance this morning not enlarged. —

I got up for dinner yesterday & lay on the sopha till 11 — laying patiences as usual, as less tiring than working. —

Sandra is with her mother, *Ira* & *Maia* here in town. — Such consolation you return to-morrow, lovebird. Yr. dear letter made me so happy. — But how strange *Chelnokov* having been with you — can imagine that he felt small & not sure of himself — he ought to have stood all the time, doublefaced man! —

Fancy *Voyeikov* also having fallen ill — you have had to wander from one to the other. What a dull letter! Excuse my not coming to the station, but have not the strength to stand about there. —

Kiss & bless you my own Love & am more than happy to clasp you soon to my breast again.

Ever yr. very own old

Wify.

No. 200.

Tsarskoje-Selo, Jan. 28-th 1916

My very own beloved Sweetheart,

Once more the train is carrying my Treasure away, but I hope not for long — I know I ought not to say this, & for an old married woman it may seem ridiculous — but I cannot help it. — With the years love increases & the time without your sweet presence is hard to bear. When I could be about & nurse the wounded it was more bearable. For you its worse, my Own. I am glad you see troops already to-morrow, that will be refreshing & to all a joy, I hope you will have the same sunshine as there is here to-day. — It was so nice you read to us & I hear your dear voice now always! And your tender caresses, oh how deeply I thank you for them — they warmed me up & were such a consolation; when the heart is heavy with care & anxieties, every tenderness gives one force and intense happiness. Oh, could but our children be equally blessed in their married lives — the idea of Boris is too unsympathetic & the child would, I feel convinced, never agree to marry him & I should perfectly well understand her. Only never let Miechen guess other thoughts have filled the child's head & heart — those are a young girls holy secrets wh. other must not know of, it would terribly hurt Olga, who is so susceptible. That conversation has made me feel far from cheery, & as it is I feel very low at yr. going & my old heart cramps itself in pain — cannot get accustomed to our separations. — Here, Baby's note will amuse you.

The lilies of the valley are to brighten up yr. writing table. You will talk seriously to Kedrov, wont you — because the joy & honour of this journey comes almost like a recompense & so as to cover the reprimand he so rightly deserved.

Why you saved him being judged again &, tho' a nice man, needs to be held in hand, the Admiral ought never to be so familiar with him — he is terribly ambitious. But you take him for short, I suppose. — What rejoicings there will be, when you get rid of *Bontch-Bruievitch* (can't spell his name) — but he ought to be made to understand first the wrong he has done & wh. falls upon you — you are too kind, my sunny Angel, be firmer & when you punish, don't forgive at once & give good places — one does not fear you enough — show yr. power, one profits of yr. marvelous kindness & gentleness. — Sad I cannot take you to the station, but I am not up to it, the heart being enlarged — & the »*engineer-mechanic*« came.

My Own, my light, my love, sleep well & peacefully, feel my tender arms encircling you, & your dear sweet head rest it in thoughts upon my breast, (not upon the high cushion you dislike). —

Goodbye, my Treasure, my Husband, Sunshine beloved, God bless & keep you, holy Angels guard you & the force of my intense love. Oh my Boy, how I love you! Words cannot express it, but you can read it in my eyes.

Ever yr. very own old

Wify.

yr. Own.

Oh, the lonely night!

No. 201.

Tsarskoje-Selo, Jan. 29-th 1916

My own Treasure love,

I thank you very, very fondly for yr. sweetest letter you left me as a consolation — over & over again I have reread it, & in the night when I could not sleep & my eyes ached fr. crying. — We went to bed at 10½ — bad night & head aches this morning.

Have just finished heaps of papers from Rostovtzev.

It is gently snowing — 2⁰ of frost. Ania peeped in a second on her way to town & she begged me yet again to thank you fr. the depths of her heart for the money. She telephoned it to our Friend, & He said it would bring you blessings — & that she is to put it aside in the bank to be a fund she must collect for building the home for the cripples. — I shall see whether we cannot give her a bit of ground — it would be good if it were not far from the Invalid House, as then they could profit of our *bathhouse* & *shops.*

I wonder whether you will begin the French book, you will see how exciting it is. —

How did my Lovebird sleep? How I miss my Sunshine!!

Do think about *Ivanov,* it would indeed be a splendid change — & clean beginning for 1916 — *Polivanov* needs no place to bother you about, *Stcherbatchev* can replace *Ivanov* & then somebody energetic in his place. What a bore old *Ruzsky* is not yet well enough. —

How glad I am that you have got *Sturmer* now to rest upon; one who you know will try & hold all the ministers together.

Now I must be getting up for luncheon. Later *Benkendorf* wishes to see me & Mme *Volzhaninova* from the Crimea.

The Children want to see *Rodionov* to-morrow evening, as he wishes to go to our Church for service. —

Sweetest of Sweets, then now goodbye & God bless and protect you. I cover your beloved face with very tenderest kisses, & remain

Ever yr. own wify

Alix.

Fedorov slept well, coughs less, 37.

Mme Zizi feels better, 36.4, tell this to Kira, who does not think enough about his mother. — Have a quiet talk with *Mordvinov* about Misha's story & then about Olga & ask what sort of a man her *N. A.* is.

No. 202.

Tsarskoje-Selo, Jan. 30-th 1916

My own Sweetheart,

We were so happy to get yr. telegram during tea, and to know that all went off so well — how nice that you had a guard of honour of your »*Cabardintzy*« at the station. — There must have been heavy fighting as Baby's train brings 15 wounded officers and over 300 men from *Kalkuny — Drissa,* that is where *Tatiana's* regiment is and where you will be, it seems to me. —

All looks so white to-day, a good deal of snow fell yesterday — 3⁰. of frost — Had a bad, restless night, went early to bed — head ached and continues to, heart the same. — I saw Mme *Volzhaninova* fr. the Crimea — *(wine-makers)* you remember her I am sure, she met me on the pier with flowers, lunched at *Livadia* and sold at the bazaars. You made acquaintance with her old mother (over 90) at the opening of a childrens' sanatorium beyond *Massandra* — Mme *Zheltukhin* born *Ilovaiskaya,* daugther of the hero of *Borodino.* Her property near *Bielovezh* was completely destroyed and she had no time to save anything and she possessed many historical things. You are the 5 Emperor she has seen.

Our Friend is very happy that you see the troops now again, he is quiet about everything, only anxious *Ivanov* should be named, as his presence in the *Duma* can be of much help. —

I have again several officers waiting to be received — that continues the whole time — and I do feel so tired. Wish I could at last get to Church again — not once in the month of Jan: — and I long to go and place my candles there. —

Old *Professor Pavlov* died — he got poisoning of the blood, after an operation he had performed, I think. —

Lovy sweet, I miss you awfully. The evenings are dull — A. is aggravated we all lay patiences, but it rests the eyes after much working and to sit with folded hands is awful. She likes reading aloud, but gabbles awfully — but one cannot sit and talk all day, and I have nothing to speak of — I am weary. Dear Sweetheart, I am not boasting, but n o b o d y loves you s o intensely as old sunny — you are her life, h e r O w n!

God bless you Precious one, I cover you with tender, passionate kisses and long to have you back into my arms again.

Ever, Nicky mine yr. very own old girly

Wify.

No. 203.

Tsarskoje-Selo, Jan. 31-st 1916

My own sweet Treasure,

Tatiana was delighted that you saw her regiment and found it in good order. I had always hoped to go about more, in sanitary trains too, and to have the chance of seeing at least one of my regiments. — *Rodionov* was in Church yesterday evening, dined with Ania and then came to us. He leaves to-morrow. Again they stand in a new village, he said, only 8 *versts* fr. *Volotchisk* and all the officers together in a *landlord's estate* — they have changed already four or five times. He showed us some groups he had made and of some of them on horseback — *Mlassoyedov's* horse looks quite antidiluvian. —

A grey morning, 5 degrees. Got to sleep late, but then slept alright, head scarcely aches, but heart and eyes do, and I am writing in specks, so as to tire them less. — I saw one of my *Crimeans* yesterday — now they all deeply regret that *Drobiazgin* leaves them — all stories had finished, and now they appreciated him and much regret the change. — We receive *military cadets* to-day who will be promoted to-morrow I believe, and then leave. Then *Varnava, Archbishop Seraphim, — Kuptsov (Erivanets)* who was here on leave and wants to see me before returning to the regiment, then *Alek!!* what can he want? probably to talk about *Gagri,* but then I shall have to tell him about *Skalon.*

At 6 comes *Captain of the 1-st rank Schultz* (such a purely German name, alas), who leaves for England — suppose its the one with the long beard who commanded the »*Africa*«, if I don't invent, occupies himself with hypnotism, and his sister was nurse in my hospital during the Japanese war and died later at *Kronstadt.*

One of the wounded I received yesterday, gave me a charming collection of photos, he had taken at *Eupatoria* — some lie out taking sunbaths, others covered in mud, others in baths, having douches, being electrified — quite amusing. —

Yesterday was the silver Wedding of the *Putiatins.*

I am trying to give you all the news I can, tho' its not interesting. alas. —

Sweetheart, I wonder whether you get my letters on the way, probably they will await you at some big station — I wish I were in their place and could feel your sweet lips upon mine and could gaze into your beloved eyes. Sorely do I miss my own Sweetheart and his tender kisses, wh. mean so much to me. — Well, Lovy, I will end now. Goodbye and God bless you now and evermore.

Endless kisses fr. yr. very own old

Sunny.

No. 204.

Tsarskoje-Selo, Feb. 1-st 1916

My very Own,

Colder this morning, 7 degrees & snowing. Scarcely slept this night & heart aches more this morning, head alright. I send you a little snowdrop from *Livadia.*

Miechen wrote again yesterday begging for Baron Dellingshausen to be let free. He is kept in the prison *Kresti* at *Petrograd, Viborg side.* His son, the dragoon may visit him. But its such a hideous shame that can only be helped by having him quickly let out by telegraph. One wont know how to look him in the face later on. —

Alek did not say anything particular to me — only it seems is not contented with the wounded officers — then those that have to be sent to the south (fr. Moscou by the commission), stick there for 2 months without leaving — disorder wh. he is going to try and set to rights; — then he spoke about the prisoners he visited — indeed one must think of having some moved as they die from illnesses, the climate being unbearable fore them. — Many people find it wld. be good if you had, for a time only, given over the *food supply* question to Alek, as really it is scandalous in town & the prices are impossible; he would poke his nose into everything, fly at the merchants who cheat & ask impossible prices & would help getting rid of Obolensky who is really no good whatsoever and does not help one bit. Our Friend is anxious if it continues still for 2 months that we may have disagreable rows and stories in town — & I understand it, as its shameful making the poor people suffer so — & the humiliation before our allies!! We have got everything in quantities, only they wont bring it, & when they do, the prices for all become unattainable. Why not ask him for 2 months to take all in hand, or one month even, & he wont allow cheating to go on. He is excellent in any place to set order, shake up people — but not for long. I write this to you, as you will be seeing him I believe on Tuesday. — *Schultz* was charming, we talked for half an hour upon every sort of subject — he is the brother of the black one who still commands the »*Africa*» & all the *divers.*

To-day I have *Shvedov* with a *report,* & M-lle *Schneider* & that will be endless as we have much to talk over about the artschool, & reorganisation of my patriotic schools — & the *Home Manufactures Committee* wh. it seems to me *Krivoshein* has forgotten all about. — Then the Commander of the »*Erivantsi*« asked to see us, he was here on leave & returns to the regiment. —

How you will miss Baby sweet again at the *Headquarters,* — your lonely life begins once more again, poor precious Angel mine! —

The Children enjoyed themselves at Anias yesterday & the soldiers too — I suppose *Tatiana* will have discribed all. Anias namesday is on the 3-st in case you care to send her a telegram. —

Tatiana is bidding *Rodionov* goodbye by telephone & I shall too.

How awfully difficult the fighting in such terrible cold in the Caucasus, Alek says less men have frozen feet, 1 per cent, & officers — 8, — to lightly dressed, going south they no doubt thought it would be warmer. —

Now Sweetheart I must end my letter. God bless & protect you, precious One & keep you from all harm. I cover you with tender kisses & clasp you to my breast. —

Ever yr. very own loving old

Wify.

Has »everything« passed with you & do you no longer need the things. I gave you? I do wish you could take more exercise, it would be the best thing for you. Tell boyxy that lady sends him her tenderest love & gentlest kisses & often thinks of him in lonely, sleepless nights. —

Loman drinks again heaps & is most crazy, Ania simply dreads him — he ought absolutely to be sent to Finland to a sanatorium for 2 months complete rest — otherwise I assure you he will shoot himself or others. The Drs also find he needs a change & rest, he had a nervous stroke already. —

This green ink smells abominably, hope the scent will take the odour away. —

No. 205.

Tsarskoje Selo, Feb. 2-d 1916

Sweet Angel,

Excuse a short letter to-day, but I am cretinised, did not sleep all night from pain in my cheek wh. is swollen and looks hideous. *Vladimir Nikolaievitch* thinks its from the tooth and has wired to our dentist to come. I had a compress on all night, changed it too — sat smoking in the sitting room, wandered about. Good you were not there for me to disturb. It is not as bad as those madning pains I used to have, but hurts quite enough and incessantly. I made all dark from 11—1 but without any result and the head begins to ache and the heart is more enlarged. I have begun my medicines again to-day. —

4^0 of frost, tiny bit snowing. *Gorodinsky* of Xenia's reg. said you saw the reg. thanked them and they were awfully happy. In to-day's papers there is a description of yr. inspections, but am not up to reading it, so shall keep that number.

Yesterday I had *Shvedov's report* for 3/4 of an hour and Mlle Schneider 1 1/2 hour till I was quite done for.

Beloved Sweetheart, I thing and long for you and cover you with very tenderest kisses. God bless and keep you.

Ever yr. very own old

Wify.

The Children kiss you; they were in church and hospital. —
Shall keep in bed till teatime and see then how I feel. —
Beloved One, think incessantly of you.

No. 206

Tsarskoje Selo, Feb. 3-d 1916

My own Sweetheart,

I got to sleep after 4 — the cheek is less swollen — yesterday evening I looked too ridiculous one had to laugh at this croocked face. Olga and Ania read to us *Avertchenko* stories about children and I laid patiences, tho' head ached and felt cretinised. — Baby was sweet, when I told him yesterday that there wld. be blinis for him for luncheon as he loves them — »how, when you have got pain you order me blinis, I wont eat them on purpose — it is not necessary« but I said it would just please me and it seems he ate a lot. — We played douratscki before he went to bed. —

5^0 of frost and snowing. —

Our Standart officers and *the priest* wired her their good wishes, so touching, and *Rodionov* from the way too. —

N. P. writes: *I am happy that I have enough work even for 24 hours a day; I don't know whether it is good or bad, but I push myself everywhere, yesterday I even picked horses for every carriage — this I was taught to do by the senior officers, but indeed I thus learned everything. My brother visited me, spent with me a whole day — it is unimaginably easy in his regiment, he has been a month here and leave is given him again — this is because in his regiment instead of 29 officers there are almost 89 — cannot understand it — what is happening in our army regarding officers is not right — this is my deep conviction.* Your 3 *Sharpsbooters* dined with them and they had music and singing and my »*giant*« *Petrov* is the *choir-leader* and splendid......

There, my letter became quite long, as personally I have nothing interesting to tell you, only that love you intensely and long for your tender, soothing caresses.

How was *Alek?* What answer about *Shumilov's* paper? Can the young man be sent to the army? What about Dellingshausen?

God bless and protect you. I cover you with tenderest kisses.

Ever yr. very own old

Wify.

You wld. laugh at my face! — Glad you took a longer walk. How good we have taken so many of the forts around Erzerum. —

Are you reading the French book? Will you be here by next Monday? Oh that will be too beautiful my own sweetest Treasure, my shining One! Just received yr. precious letter for wh. e n d l e s s thanks Sweetheart — such a joyful surprise. And all you saw — so good. Yes, get quickly rid of *Bontch-Bruievitch* only dont give him a division if he is so hated. And what about *Ivanov?* Try and take a glass of quite cold water after yr. breakfast it may help yr. tommy working.

No. 207.

Tsarskoje Selo, Feb. 4-th 1916

Beloved One,

With all my heart I congratulate you that Erzerum has fallen. Splendid fighting it must have been, & how quick it went. Such a comfort — & to the others a good moral crush. May it only remain in our hands now. —

Now a perfectly private question of m y o w n — as one reads always that the germans continue sending & artillery & troops to Bulgaria, if, when we advance at last, they come from behind through Roumania — who covers the back of our army? Or does the guard get sent down to the left of Keller & to protect towards Odessa? These are my own thoughts, because the enemy always finds our weak points — they prepare everywhere & for all emergencies always & we very superficially as a rule, therefore lost in the Carpathians etc. as had not sufficiantly fortified our positions. Now, if they force their way through Roumania upon our left flank — what has remained to protect our frontier. Excuse my bothering you — but involuntarily all such thoughts come. — What are our plans now that Erzerum has been taken, how far off from us are the English troops? Wonder whether Aleks antigas is of any good. — Thanks deeply for having saved that poor fellow's life — out at the front he can prove his thanks — poor civilian tho' he is. — 4 »*Plastuni*« officers have been brought to our hospital & some to the big palace. I have not been to our wounded since Dec. 23 & ages not to the big palace. I miss them all so much, & the work I love.

Baby's right arm is swollen, but does not hurt, so its difficult for him to write. —

Got to sleep late, but then the night was alright — face less swollen, but not yet normal & feels still stiff. —

Fedorov is getting on well, tho' temp. not quite normal — in a few days he hopes to leave the house. Mme Zizi feels still weak. —

Here is a fat letter of love for you fr. the cow!!

2° of frost, gently snowing. To-day its a week we parted, my Sunshine, & to me it seems such ages already. My life has been very monotonous & dreary this week — & still the days flew & the nights dragged. —

O, Love, I do so terribly miss you — the light seems gone out of everything when you are not here. Oh, my Own, my one & all, I long to clasp you to my heart, I am sad and weary & want yr. caresses.

Goodbye Lovebird, my own & not hers, as she dares to call you, God bless you little One and keep you from all harm, guide you to success & ultimate glorious, yearned for peace. Girly covers you with kisses, Huzy Sweet.

Ever yr. very own old

Wify.

Whom have you named instead of *Pleve?* What is longnosed Ferdinand doing in Vienna?

Now I must dress for luncheon, have invited Ania as she found she scarcely saw me yesterday, as had masses of people. —

No. 208.

Tsarskoje Selo, Feb. 5-th 1916

My own Sweetheart,

Zero this morning, windy, — snowing hard. Thank God Baby's night was on the whole good — woke up several times, but not for long and did no complain. His both arms are bandaged and the right ached rather yesterday — but our Friend says it will pass in two days. The last nights his sleep was restless, tho' painless and he did not complain about his arm, tho' could not bend it. Probably hurt himself holding on to the cord of the sledge when several are tied together. But *Derevenko* says he is quite cheery, so don't worry, Lovebird. We dined upstairs, so as that he should be in bed and move less. The quieter he keeps, the better. — Olga and Tatania go to town for T's committee. —

I got to sleep after 4 — scarcely swollen, but felt it still and the head whole time strange and jaw too — more like a chill in the head, without a cold and difficult to open the mouth again in the jaw. — Heart aches all these days and don't feel nice — do hope that Alexei and I shall be decent for your return. —

It may interest you to know, that the sums my *store* and chancelry received since June 21. 1914 — Jan. 31. 1916 — 6. 675. 136 80. Given out 5. 862. 151 46. — Remains 812.985 34. Immense sums of it goes to my Moscow, *Kharkov, Vinnitsa, Tiflis stores,* to my 6 *supply* trains, sanitary trains etc., regiments etc. But the big *stores* collect sums and things too. *Supreme Council* gave me big sums — then yours all along you get and from English flag days. —

Why have our troops again evacuated Galicia? It seems to me so from *Rebinder's* account as so many officers of the reg., wh. have gone back fr. *Galicia,* come to *Kharkov* to my *store* and ask for linnen and »*individual parcels*«. I cannot understand, what happened down there or they are being more concentrated together and these are the troops ready to defend one rear to the south? —

Ania makes her excuses for bad writing yesterday, but was in an awful hurry — and she forgot to tell you that she had a dear card of congratulations fr. Olga. — She lunched with us yesterday and stayed till 5 — read aloud and even played cards with me. — Shall go up to Baby in the afternoon — remain lying till luncheon, as feel still rotten. — Eagerly awaiting yr. letter yr. telegram announced. — Do hope you are really coming and wont put off this joy of a few days happiness. —

Are you quite content with Alexeiev, energetic enough? How is Ruzsky? Some here say that he is quite well again, but I dont know whether its true or not, wish it were, as Germans fear him. —

Fancy only, I saw Miss Eady yesterday, Dona and Loos nurse. — She had to leave Darmstadt to *Ernie's* and Onor's deep sorrow, last Nov., the ministers found it necessary she shld. leave — they all were wretched. Poor woman cld. get no situation in England, as she had been at Darmstadt — even in England they are quite unnormal — so she came over here, as must earn her living, keep up her old mother (4 brothers and many nephews at the war). She is at the Osten-Sackens *(Voloshev)* here and the change fr. Darmstadt is very great. I told her to come often to Madelaine and us, so as to feel less lonely. — She told Madelaine how sad many were, Ludwig had to leave and that they greatly venerate him and go after his plans. The first ideas of his at the outset of the war, they did not follow, and now have seen how wrong they were and deeply regret it. It was so nice seeing her — reminded me of old home and all and of Friedberg and Livadia especially. She hears from them sometimes. But in Engl. one got angry with her because she wld. not speak against the Germans but she had only received greatest kindness in Germany.

This war seems to have acted on all the brains. — Just read in the »*Novoye Vremya*« the *heroic deed* of the *senior under-officer* of Baby's Siberian reg., his portrait is there too — yes, we have many a hero in the army and were but our Generals as perfect, we might do marvels! — I see Misha has not yet left, do get him to the army, I assure you its better he should be in his place there, than here with her bad set. —

Sweetest of Sweets, just this minute, 12 o'clock, your precious letter was brought to me and I thank you for it with all my tenderly loving heart. Oh Lovy, what joy to have you even for two days. — God bless all yr. undertakings, yr. appearance will do wonders I feel sure, and God will inspire you, with the right words — and to see you — is already immense — you yourself do not half realise the power of yr. personality wh. touches every heart, the worst even.

I am glad you will have the council of war, to thoroughly go into all questions — you wld. not have sent for *Ruzsky* for that day, as he commanded nearly the whole time and is such a capable man, and tho' often disagrees with *Alexeiev,* it wld. just be advisable to have one who perhaps sees things differently and then you can choose the right way easier — and as God grant you can have *Ruzsky* back when he is well again, he ought to know and share all the plans, I shld. say. —

How splendid what you write about Erzerum; — marvelous troops indeed! —

Yes, I too admire those men who go on working at these vile gases and risking their lives. Oh, to think that humanity should have stopped so low. They find it splendid technics — but the »Soul« where is it in all this? One can cry aloud at the misery and inhumanity this ghastly war has provoked. —

You will get this letter somewhere on the way. I wonder at what hour you arrive on the 8-th? This letter, no doubt, is then the before last.

Goodbye, my Own — I bless and kiss you with unending love and tenderness, and remain, sweet Nicky yr. very own old wife

Alix.

No. 209.

Tsarskoje Selo, Feb. 6-th 1916

My Treasure,

The men are cleaning the roof, making a great noise as they clear the snow away — 2^0 of frost. —

Baby woke up several times, but did not have pain, so I hope will be quite alright for yr. return.

Oh how lovely it will be to see you again, my Sweetheart, I do miss you so terribly! They will be tiring, those 2 days here.

Xenia writes that *Sandro* arrives on Wednesday for a few days — I am so glad for her. She walks a tiny bit in her garden & Motherdear goes to her daily. —

What did you do about poor Dellingshausen? —

I read yr. telegram & answer to the Moscou nobility & to the widow of the former governor of Erzerum — strange feelings for her, who saw the last fall of the fortress 38 years ago. —

Have nothing interesting to tell you, my Sunshine. —

I am glad you took a good walk at last, it is sure to have done you good — as going round & round in the little garden must have been distracting. — *The Karangozov* wrote to Ania that in Odessa the weather was lovely, 12 in the shade, the ladies walk in light dresses — from there he went to Kiev — into snow.

His regiment got only leave to the south, not to *Tsarskoje Selo* so his mother & sister arranged to meet him at Odessa. —

I wonder when & where you see the first Siberian corps. — Goodbye Lovebird, God bless yr. journey & bring you safely to us.

I cover you with tender kisses & remain yr. fondly loving old

Wify.

All the children kiss you warmly.

No. 210.

Tsarskoje Selo, Feb. 10-th 1916

My own precious Sweetheart,

It has been such a gift this flying visit of yours, beloved one — & tho' we saw little of each other — yet I felt you were here. And your tender caresses have warmed me up again. — I can imagine the deep impression your presence at the *Duma* & *Council of the Empire* must have made on everybody — God grant that it will be a stimulant & make all work hard & in unity for the blessing & grandeur of our beloved country. — To see you, means so much! — You just found the right words. —

We, Ania & I, had gone through very trying days because of this story against our Friend — & no man near to advise — but she was brave & good about it all — even stood a hideously rude talk with *Vojeikov* on Monday. I really feel rather anxious about her now — as she saw through an ugly story one was trying to drag in *Khvostov* with — the jews — & just to make a mess before the *Duma,* so tendencious all. —

Seeing you — has given one again courage & strength as humanity is so low especially around us & the »*rear*« minds are ill still. — All my prayers & thoughts will surround you to-morrow — a great thing you are doing & such a wise one — & all the chiefs can speak out their thoughts honestly & give you a clear picture of everything — God bless their work under yr. guidance. Sleep well, my Treasure — I shall miss you again most awfully — you brought such sunshine to me & I shall live in remembrance of yr. sweet presence. Soon again, lets hope, I shall have you home again. — God bless & protect you, my own Lovy dear, my husband, my Own — a thousand tender kisses fr. yr. very own little Wify.

No. 211.

Tsarskoje Selo, Feb. 11-th 1916

My very own precious One,

Bright & sunny, 12° of frost. All my tenderest thoughts are with you, beloved Sweetheart, & I hope, the great military council will go off well & according to yr. wishes. — I can imagine how refreshed you will feel to be amongst military people, as these days here have not been of the pleasantest & you must have been delighted to get away again. You generally have some painful impressions here — Tuesday brought splendid good — & then that wretched story about our Friend. She will try her best with him — tho' in his present humour he screams at her & is so awfully nervous. But its sunny wheater & so, I hope, he will have changed again into what he always was. He is frightened to leave, says one will kill him — well, we shall see how God turns all! —

All this gave you pain & worry & you could not get any joy out of yr. visit, beloved Sunshine — but you warmed up old Sunny & she feels your last kiss still upon her lips! Yr. visit was like a dream — so empty now again! — I have nothing to tell you yet to-day.

Yesterday evening we worked, laid patiences & Tatiana or Anastasia read aloud — but my thoughts were with you & not in the book. —

Precious Sweetheart, I must get up now as Prince Golitzin comes at 12½ with his *report* about our prisoners, & after luncheon *Viltchkovsky.*

Goodbye & God bless you my own Love.

I cover you with kisses & remain, Ever yr. very own

Wify.

No. 212.

Tsarskoje Selo, Feb. 12-th 1916

My own Sweetheart,

A bright, sunny morning, 7 degrees of frost, last night 12. I wonder how the generals all spoke — nice they met you. So refreshing such talks, however serious & difficult they may be. But I hope that they are contented on the whole with the amunition, or is there still a great scarcity of rifles?

I had a nice long letter from Victoria, she is now in London — Ludwig & Louise are going north to see Georgie & she will go later. They have been having great gales & very cold weather & when the New Zealand was out cruising last month, the sea washed right over her & one wave came into Georgie' turret through the gun openings & washed one of his men down a liftshaft & Georgie had to crawl in after him & found him wedged in at the bottom halfdrowned & with his legs broken.

Some of the sailors have been allowed to go & see the fighting in France & a ship's corporal of the N. Z., who was of the lot, was in a trench, when a German mine exploded under it & killed the men of the machinegun — whereupon the bluejackets promptly manned it under their corporal

& did such good work, that he has been decorated & the ship is very proud of him. — Dickie & the cadets of his term are not to go straight to sea after easter, but to the engineering college at Kegham (Plymouth) first. The best 26 or 30 of them will go to sea in June, & as his place in the term is about 15-th always, he hopes to be one of the lot. Of course he is disappointed at the delay, but I feel selfishly grateful for it. —

Alice writes that the english are liked at Salonica, the officers are courteous, the men well behaved; with the french, I am sorry to say, she says it is the other way round, & in one small town they have behaved as horribly to the women, as the Germans in Belgium, whilst the officers at Salonica, from the general downwards, are insolent & rude even to Andrea. —

Louise is enjoying her holiday at home, she will probably go back to Nevers at the end of this month. —

Sandro is at the *Headquarters?*

Little Marie lunches with us to-day & before & after I have receive.

Precious Treasure, Goodbye & Good bless you, many a tender, longing kiss fr. yr. deeply loving old wife Alix.

No. 213.

Tsarskoje Selo, Feb. 13-th 1916

My own Sweetheart,

2⁰ of frost & gently snowing. I happily sleep well now, wh. is a rare treat — also cough a little like Baby. — Saw *Nekliudov* yesterday — he speaks alright, only from time to time becomes an affected diplomate, wh. is distractingly aggravating. Then I saw Dr. Brunner who gave me an account of how the German & Austrian are kept in Siberia — satisfactorily!

Then a Psse Françoise Woroniecka (born Krassinsky) who organised many hospitals at Varsovie & got the medal there. Her husband & 2 sons remained at Varsovie & she rarely has any news of them.

She seems most energetic, tho' looks rosy, plump & comfortable in highest narrowest heals & funny little cap to her sister's dress. —

To-day I have Pss. Gedroitz — probably to grumble. —

Lili Den & husband came for an hour & evening tea — she is a real dear & so amusing always — but his foolish laugh rather trying. — Is he going to receive the »*Variag*«?

I am so glad that you are contented with the result of the military council — it is a beautiful thing that you called them all & gave them the chance to speak together in your presence. — Little Marie lunched with us, looks quite well, only covered in pimples — she says Dmitri arrives to-morrow — pitty, as he will get into a bad set again & ways.

How I wish somebody wld. speak to him seriously — I know *N. P.* did many a time & kept him several times fr. evening escapades — the boy behaves according to the person whom he for the moment cares for. —

The oftener I think about Boris, the more I realise what an awful set his wife wld. be dragged into. His & Miechen's friends, rich french people, russian bankers, »the society«, Olga Orlov & the *Bielos.* & all such types — intrigues without end — fast manners & conversations & Ducky not a suitable sister in-law at all — & then Boris' mad past. Miechen gave into H. Wladimir's ways so as to share all together, but she found pleasure in that life — with her nature that was easy. — Well, why do I write about this, when you know it as well as I do. So give over a well used half worn out, blase young man, to a pure, fresh young girl 18 years his junior & to live in a house in wh. many a woman has »shared« his life. Only a »woman« who knows the world & can judge & choose with eyes open, ought to be his wife & she wld. know how to hold him & make a good husband of him. But an inexperienced young girl would suffer terribly, to have her husband 4,5-th hand or more — a woman could put up with this of course easier if she loved. —

Therefore Dmitri ought to be held light in hand by you too & explained what married life means.

Now I must end. — Goodbye my Angel, my Lovebird. Holy Angels guard you — God bless you. Endlessly tender, yearning kisses fr. yr. very loving old

Wify.

In the *Duma* one makes horrid speeches — but they fall flat, nobody picks them up. *Purishkevitch* made an awful one — why to be so mad always. But you brought great good there, as the speeches have no effect.

No. 214.

Tsarskoje Selo, Feb. 14-th 1916

My very Own,

Your sweet letter made me intensely happy & I read it over many a time & tenderly kissed each page wh. yr. dear hand had touched. I am a foolish old woman, yes? But a deeply loving one who sorely misses her Sweetheart.

Poor Pleve, fancy his having become such a wretched little being — before the war he was already pityful to behold.

I am glad that they all spoke themselves well out & even squabbled — its the very best thing & clears up all misunderstandings & pictures the caracters far better. —

The big girls go to a concert in our hospital, & the 3 youngest to Ania's *refuge* this afternoon for a concert & old *Davidov* wanted to come too, so as to see Baby. Her Parents will also be there, so as to cheer them up, after a vile letter her mother got fr. Mme *Rodzianko* full of vilest abuse of Ania. And *Nicolai Dmitrovitch D.* & *Irina Tolstoy, Vladimir Nikolaievitch* & Mr. Gibbs. I cannot go, am not famous, cough rather & 37.3 this morning — to catch things without going out is really too bad. — Greyish morning calm, $3\frac{1}{2}^0$ of frost. —

I receive then people.

Poor Isa is very depressed as one wrote nasty things about her Father in the papers — my ex Stern they also accuse of being a spy — & altogether I find people somewhat unbalanced, to say it gently. — Mme Zizi is still not yet fit to come out here. —

I got the french book alright — when you finish the English one, I can send another. Such innocent lecture is a rest to the tired brain & gives one other thoughts. —

I hope you will get some good walks again.

Have you arranged about yr. aide-de-camp doing two weeks service at the Headquarters? Now whilst things are calmer you could get commanders of regiments even, tho' there are scarcely any more. But it would be a great gain to you, they could tell you many truths wh. the generals even don't know, & I am sure be of help to you .

And all will try their best & work harder, if they know that one of their officers will be at the *Headquarters* & have to answer frankly to all yr. questions. They notice more things than others do — & then it is a constant living link with the army. —

Alexei got a wire fr. *Eristov* fr. yr. lancers. —

Now, my Sweetheart, I must end my letter.

God Almighty bless & protect you. I cover my Huzy love with fond kisses.

Ever yr. old

Sunny.

The Children kiss you very tenderly.

No. 215.

Tsarskoje Selo, Feb. 15-th 1916

My very own Beloved,

Ever such tender thanks for yr. sweet letter, I received yesterday. You have indeed had busy days & I am glad you at last got a good walk yesterday to freshen you up. —

Fancy only, Esi lunches with us to-day! I have not seen him since he left for the war, & he asked to present himself as G. a. d. c., so I thought better to invite him to luncheon. It will be rather stiff work making him talk, & without you to help me. —

A glorious sunny morning, 8° of frost. A. begs me to go out every day, but I know it wld. be folly with my cough. Did not sleep very well as it disturbed me. Sometimes don't cough for long & then it goes off again, just like Baby. Marie has a cold. — To-day they all go to the big palace to see small theatricals for the wounded — »*Krivoye Zerkalo*«.

Old *Goremykin* was with me yesterday. I gave him all the news I have of you, & was happy to hear of yr. military Council. His wife had just been taking leave of her »hospital« when she got an access at the heart from emotion, & they had to leave her the night there — poor old people, I am so sorry for them. He looks alright, but the first days he had suddenly no work to do, he was in a constant half sleep — after the great strain of these heavy months.

When he says goodbye, it always seems to me that he thinks it may be the last time that he sees one — at least the kind old eyes have that look.

The French are having a hard time round Verdun, God grant them luck, how one longs for them & the English at last to advance. —

What was Fillimore's impression of *Archangelsk?* Does he now realise our difficult position there & does he find one is working hard? A foreign critical eye can always be of use. — *Zuiev* comes to-day, as he leaves on Wednesday for England — France. — Emma Fr. was at *Sashka's* marriage, says the bride's profile is pretty, en face the nose too aquashed, fine eyes, very black hair — not tall & plump. —

Irina (Drina) came to me in despair that *O. Lamkert* has been told to leave after all these years. The money affairs he put into splendid order, after having received his place wh. was deeply indebted. *Sturmer* comes with his own candidate *(Gurlin* I think or *Gurland),* who has already much work to do, so wont be able even personally to lead this. If I see *Shakhovskoy (?)* whom I expect to ask to be received because of the *supreme Council,* I shall ask him about it. —

I am glad you like my nicely scented letters — I want them to remind you of your old girly who longs for you so much, so much! —

In thoughts I tenderly press you to my heart, hold you tightly in my embrace & cover your sweet face with loving kisses & caresses. —

Now goodbye my Lovebird. Ever so many blessings & kisses fr. yr. own old

Alix.

Been reading through some of my letters to Sonia & tearing them up — quite like diaries & bring back the past so vividly.

To-morrow would have been her birthday.

No. 216.

Feb. 16-th 1916

My own Sweetheart,

A bright, sunny morning again, there were 6° of frost. I dont venture on to the balkony yet, because of my cough. — At 12½ I have Witte with his *report,* then after luncheon still people & at 6 — *Sturmer.* To-day would have been Sonia's birthday — so sad, I have not once been to her grave. —

Yesterday evening we had *A. P. Sablin,* he was not in the least bit shy & quite natural. He returns to-morrow again to the terrible mud of *Proskurovo* — he talked away cheerily. — Olga made nonsence, sitting on a tiny table, until she happily smashed it. Its so funny, he has some of his brother's movements; a refreshing change to see him, as one dries up in sorrows & worries. —

I am eagerly awaiting yr. letter, wh. you wired about — does it bring news of your return, that would indeed be lovely; me wants Sweetheart badly. —

Mme Zizi is still not famous, went out in town in a close carriage, & felt worse after.

I must stop a little, my eyes ache, as I have written a long letter to Victoria for *Zuiev* to take to-morrow. —

Excuse my dull letters, Lovy, but life is very monotonous & I myself am not of the gayest — & what I hear is nothing to cheer one up. —

It will be interesting to hear fr. you, your opinion upon the Generals & what was spoken of & settled. I long to hear about military things, of wh. I of course cannot, except from you. — Just got yr. sweetest letter, a big kiss for it. So this is my last. Oh what joy! Thursday home again, this is indeed splendid news — to-morrow just a week you left us. How good to have you back, & the Children are free the last 3 days so will be wild of joy you are home & I hope Baby can go out by then again. Wish you heartily a good journey. God bless & protect you. Cover you with kisses,

Ever yr. own old

Wify.

No. 217.

Tsarskoje Selo, March 2-d 1916

My own Sweetheart,

I cannot tell you what joy it has been to have you here, tho' to you it brought again worry without end and was tiring. Its hard you cant come home to feel quiet, but on the contrary — therefore I have even to be glad for you when you leave. Such a blessing we could go to Holy Communion together. — These last days my horrid pains cretinised me, so that I was good for nothing — and many a question before parting I should have liked to touch, and could not remember them. —

Am so wretched that we, through *Gregory* recommended *Khvostov* to you — it leaves me not peace — you were against it and I let myself be imposed upon by them, tho' fr. the very first told Ania that I like his great energy but that too selflove and something not pleasing to me; and the devil got hold of him, one cannot call it otherwise. I wld. not write to you about it last time not to bother you — but we passed through trying times, and therefore wld. have been calmer if, now that you go, something could be settled. As long as *Khvostov* is in power and has money and police in hands — I honestly am not quiet for *Gregory* and Ania.

Dear me, how weary one is! Your beloved presence and tender caresses soothe me and I dread your departure. Do remember to keep our Friend's Image near you as a blessing for the coming »move forwards« — oh how I wish we were always together, to share all, see all! Such an anxious time is ahead! And when we shall meet again — is a vague thing. All my prayers will incessantly follow you, sweetest love. God bless you and yr. work and every undertaking and crown it with success.

The good *will* come and you are patient and will be blessed, I feel so sure, only much to be gone through still. When I know what the »losses« of lives mean to yr. heart — I can imagine Ernie's suffering now. Oh this hideously bloody war! —

Excuse bad writing, but head and eyes ache and heart feels weak after all this pain. —

Oh Lovy mine, beloved, precious Sunshine — its *so* depressing when you go — you are yet far more lonely, so I ought not to complain — but to feel yr. sweet being near me is such a consolation and calm. —

Goodbye Sweetheart, love of my soul — God Almighty bless and protect you and keep you fr. all harm, guard and guide you on all yr. ways and bless all yr. undertakings.

May He *help* you find a good successor to *Khvostov* too, so that you should have one worry less. —

Farewell Sunshine. I hold you tightly clasped in my arms and cover you with tender kisses. Beloved, and remain yr. very own girly,

Wify.

Am glad *S. Petr.* is with you — *prefer* him to *all* the rest who accompany you and good *Mordvinov* too. *N. P.* also became good friends with *Feodorov* just because he is so devoted to you — *Voyeikov* is selfsure and gets blown about by the wind sometimes, is better for him personally.

Thank you over and over again for all yr. love, wh. is my life.

No. 218.

Tsarskoje Selo, March 3-d. 1916

My very own Sweetheart,

Oh its lonely without you and I miss you awfully. So sad to wake up and find an empty place beside me. Thanks tenderly for yr. evenings telegram. Such sorrow without you, every moment one expects you to be looking in. — I slept well, the effect of the medicine still acts, — and I feel my heart not nice in consequence. *Vladimir Nikolaievitch* continues electrifying the face. The pains only come from time to time, but I feel rather gidy and nasty and have to eat carefully, not to bring on the pains in my jaw. — Olga and Anastasia have Becker. — Ania coughs worse, so remains home and will only come in the afternoon, wh. is much wiser. —

Here is a petition fr. the *Athos* monks living at Moscou. I send it you, hoping you will forward it to *Volzhin* with a strong resolution upon it, that you insist (once more) that all are to be allowed to take Holy Communion and that the priest may personally serve. *Volzhin* is somewhat a coward, so you personally write *your order*, not a wish, upon the petition. Its shameful to *get on* as one does with them. You remember *Metropolitan Makari* allowed it them and you too, — and the *Synod* of course protested. —

N. P. just telephoned to Ania that he arrived this morning and leaves again this evening, — so will come to us this afternoon; is in despair you have left, as come for affairs with the 6 officers for the »*Variag*«. Seems in a wretched state, that had to give up good officers and 400 men, — things all must better be finished off, that cannot continue command the battalion with again less officers and men. He goes to talk to Kiryll. I shall have a good talk with him, as I think all can be managed, tho' I understand its more than depressing when you have well organised a thing, to have to break it up again. I personally find they ought to talk to *Grigorovitch* and both go straight off to you and explain matters and ask yr. wishes. I shall do my best to quieten him. I felt it wld. be so, when you told me of it a few weeks ago. Already then they lacked officers and how they have to give up their best, — but as they are in the reserve they wld. have time to get and prepare men fr. here, only where to get the officers from. A sort of bad luck and preventing them going with the guard. —

I shall tell you all to-morrow after have seen him. —

The Children are alright. *Sturmer* has asked to see me on Saturday, — he asked through Ania and told her that all is now in his hands, — nothing is of course as yet in the papers. —

How are you getting on with the book, is it not exciting, — it was so sad and dull without your reading yesterday. —

I see your beloved, sad eyes still before me, when you left, — its an awful wrench each time. O Lovy, thanks again and again for all yr. tender caresses wh. warmed me up and were such a consolation.

The heart is so heavy and sad and when phisically run down, one gets yet more depressed. I try not to show it to others. —

Very mild to-day again.

Sweetheart, I must say Goodbye now and God bless you. I cover you with tender kisses and remain your fondly loving, endlessly devoted, own old

Sunny.

Ania is sad she never had an occasion to see you alone, — personally I think she gets calmer and more normal, less aggressive when she has less chance, — because the more one has, the more one wants, — if you need talks, then of course its another thing. But she gets over those things much better now, — you have trained her and in consequence her temper is calmer and we have no stories. She was killing about telephones and visits and stories about our Friend, flinging her stick about the room and laughing — Oh how I long for you!!!

No. 219.

Tsarkoje Selo, March 4-th 1916

My very own Sweetheart,

I can imagine how lonely you must feel again at *Moghilev,* poor Sweetums, — wify too misses you terribly. — I am glad you also found mild weather there. Is the book not palpitatingly interesting; when you return again you must finish reading it aloud. —

Well, *N. P.* came in the evening. They had a long & serious talk & now go to you to ask for the decision. Over 400 men have been taken — the lists sent fr. here, so that the best men who are accustomed to the *Machine-guns* are taken, — to form new ones takes a long time. But with the men things could be arranged, if it were not, that in a month one will again take 400 away for the «*Svetlana*«, then the work is bitterly hard — to form all well & then have it picked all to pieces. You gave the order 6 officers were to be given to the battalion — they never were, & 6 have instead now been taken, so that now Babys *midshipmen* command the *companies* — they know nothing & the sailors of many years service know better than them & can find fault & judge all their actions. *Voronov* is to replace *Popov* here — *Koshevnikov, senior officer* »*Variag*« — *Kublitzky, Taube, Lukin.* I forget the other two. Like that the battalion cannot remain, as it will not be what it was, & not what you could expect it to be. So you will have to decide (don't ask the ramoli Admiral's advice as he councils badly) — better now give away the men already for the »*Svetlana*« & then have two small battalions, wh. anybody can command & wh. won't have much significance. Its a sad thing after puting one's soul into a work to have it picked to pieces. *N. P.* of course brought the officers, & men all as ordered. The men of course are enchanted to go, a comfortable ship, no marching & much better pay. For them its harder serving now in the army with smaller rations after what they were accustomed to for years — in the army most men are new & young. Therefore they need also older officers to keep them in hand & explain things. — I only tell you this as I see how terribly it has worried *N. P.* He is quiet & sad & awaits yr. decision when they come & what will become of him too.

I asked about *Lialin*. Kirill is also in despair the Admiral recommended him. When *Miassojed.-Ivanov* wrote & asked *Lialin* to join the battalion, as they needed him, he declined as got more pay & prefered the ship in the black sea or living without work in town. They were horrified with him. And he, who was in no war before, now did nothing, received such a splendid nomination. *N. P.* you remember one said was too young to receive the Standart, tho' had been in the war & had commanded the »*Oleg*« during some time & was yr. aide-de-camp — *Saltanov* or *Den* were far more worthy of it. Now she does not go to sea. Kirill & all hoped *Schir. Schachmatov* wld. be named as such an excellent man, but the Admiral hates him. Alas, more than ever one feels the admiral takes no interest in the *crew* how much he could have helped, — & he does the contrary & presents the things to you as he chooses. I wish you had another in his place; and he dislikes *Grigorovitch* as much as *Kedrov* hates him too. Very interesting all he told about where they stand — they followed the »*Preobrozhentsi*«. — he left Wednesday evening & arrived Thursday morning here. — I felt all this would come when you told me about the »*Variag*«. — He returns this evening to *Rezhitsa* & probably fr. there to you & meets K. Tuesday.

Css. Kleinmichel who married the Dr. came to Ania looking young & handsome. I am really anxious about Ania; once a man was capable to try & buy others to kill our Fr. he is capable of revenging himself upon her. She had an awful row by telephone with *Gregory* for not having gone to-day, — but I entreated her not to — besides she has a terrible cough & Mme B. Then the woman came & made a scene to her for not going to town & he sort of predicts something is going to happen to her wh. certainly makes her yet more nervous.

This war has made everthing topsy turvy & turned all minds. — I saw by the papers you have said *Sukhomlinov* is to be judged, — thats right, — have his aiguillettes been taken fr. him. One says there will come out bad things against him, — that he took bribes, — thats her for sure, — its so sad. Dear me, what bad luck one has, no »gentlemen«, thats what it is — no decent bringing up & inner development & princips wh. one can rely upon. — One gets so bitterly disappointed in Russian people, — they are so far behind still we know such masses & yet when one has to choose a minister, — none is capable to hold such a post. — Remember about *Polivanov*.

Have you talked with *Feodorov*, wld. be interesting for you — he is so devoted & he has nothing to gain, has received all & can have no higher position to aim after. —

A mild day again. — Have been reading through heap of papers from *Rostovtzev* & feel cretinised. My head & eyes became weaker since these pains, the jaw is so heavy & pains still continue, tho' at times almost pass, — but it makes me feel good for nothing.

How does Po (Pau) look upon the state of affairs in France?

Oh, my precious One, all my thoughts are with you & tenderest prayers. Lonely without sweet Huzy dear's caresses. — I hope you can take good walks. *N. P.* enjoyed riding a good deal. They stand in the different villages all about, he is lodged in a splendid house of a millionaire — friend of M. *Ivanov* — beautiful rooms, hothouse, garden, stables, carriages — watched fishing with the nets under the ice. —

I said goodbye to a young wounded officer who returns to his regiment. Now I have no more news to give you. I wrote out our conversation for you to have an idea in yr. head when they come to you next week for yr. decision — one thing well done better than many bits unsatisfactorily — well, they will tell you all their ideas & you will know what is best. —

Goodbye my Sweet One, God bless & protect & help you in all your decisions & undertakings.

Fondest, tenderest kisses fr. yr. very own old

Bow to *Feodorov* & *Mordvinov* if you have an occasion.

Wify.

Mr. Dodd's book is an example of how history is made?

No. 220.

Tsarskoje-Sello, March 5-th 1916

My Sweetheart,

Very tenderly do I press you to my loving old heart wh. is ever full of deepest love and yearning. Thats good you took a nice walk, it will make you feel much fresher, and the time will pass quicker. Are you reading now the french book »La Dame au parfum«? I had a collection of English ones brought me to-day, but I fear there is nothing very interesting amongst them. No great authors already since a long time & in no other country either, nor celebrated artist, or composer — a strange lack.

One lives too quickly, impressions follow in rapid succession — machinery & money rule the world & crush all art; & those who think themselves gifted, have ill minds. —

I do wonder what will be after this great war is over! Will there be a reawakening & new birth in all — shall once more ideals exist, will people become more pure & poetic, or will they continue being dry materialists? So many things one longs to know. But such terrible misery as the whole world has suffered must clean hearts & minds & purify the stagnant brain & sleeping souls; — oh, only to guide all wisely into the right & fruitfull channel.

Our Friend came to Ania yesterday, he finds it a good thing that the *Putilov Plant* has been taken by the warministry & doubts that there will be any more troubles — others set the workmen on to strike. He thinks you will return here still before our attacks begin, as there is still such deep snow. When *N. P.* left beginning of Jan. he said that he would be back in less than three months, & so it turned out too. —

Lovy, have an eye on *Nilov*. Nini finds his influence upon her husband not good — says they are inseparable & that he sets *Voyeikov* up against Ania. I know the little Admiral gets himself under bad influences. — I had a vile anon. letter yesterday — happily only read the 4 first lines & at once tore it up. Fancy *Andronnikov* & *Khvostov* used to occupy themselves writing anon. letters sometimes. — our Friend got one a month ago & is convinced *Andronnikov* wrote it. What a vile thing it is — Ania continues getting them & with black crosses on them & telling her what dates she must fear, — so cowardly!

Its again mild & grey. I receive *Mekk* & *Apraxin* as they are off to inspect my *supply trains*. *G. M. Gurko* of the 5-th Army wired fr. *Dvinsk* thanking me for my *supply train*, wh. stands there & is such a help to the regiments, — its a comfort to know that small organisation of Mekks works so well. — I had to name *Apraxin* now my *chief manager* of the 5 trains, — over Mekk as people were so unkind & jealous of the young man (in Moscou). I tell you all this in case you hear of him travelling about. —

Eagerly I am awaiting your promised letter to-day — beloved Huzy mine, sweet Treasure! Already a week to-day that we went to Holy Communion — how the time flies. — *Molostvov* comes to present himself — he has one of my waggons (Mme *Sukhomlinov's)*, wh. takes linen & presents to the front & brings back wounded or sick. —

Such a bore I have nothing interesting or amusing to tell you, — »me wants oo«. Are you going to find some work for Igor to do, as Mavra hoped you would use him so that he should not dawdle about, — & to keep him from drinking — he got into a rather too wild life, it seems, when he lived in town. Its sad she has so many worries with her children, — one sees the father never occupied himself with them & Mitia was not the man to bring them up & Mavra was not permitted to say a word, — hard lines on a mother. — Sweetheart, your precious letter has just been brought to me, & I thank you for it with all my heart. Such happiness to hear from you. That was nice you saw some of the »*Lithuanians*« passing.

So nearly all is ready for to advance, must just get the snow to melt a bit first.

I daily have my face electrified for 1/4 of an hour — the pains are rare, only such a stiff feeling in the jaw — am sure its gouty.

Now Beloved, I must end. Many a fond kiss & blessing fr. yr. very own old wife

Alix.

How is *Feodorov* feeling?

No. 221.

Tsarskoje-Selo, March 6-th 1916.

My own Sweetheart,

I reread your precious letter with such happiness & feel warmed up by it. — You say you felt so tired in the train — I am sure it was the result of 3 hours daily standing in Church the first week, & moral worries wh. pulled you down. Now being amongst military people, it will set you up again. — Dull, grey weather continues — 2° of frost this morning, Baby has just gone out before Church. He & some of his sisters go for an hour to A's hospital to see a conjurer in the afternoon.

The face continues improving. — The heart still a little enlarged, saw *Sirotinin* as he came to *Tsarskoje-Selo* for Ania. —

Well *Sturmer* sat with me nigh upon an hour. We talked about the strikes — he finds the fabrics ought to be militarised during the war, & that paper is a long time at the *Duma,* but does not get looked through as they are against it. He is rather adverse to Pr. *Tumanov's* wish of very strong measures & would prefer *Kuropatkin* naming some cleverer man in his place. — Of course that *food committee* makes his despair & they had a strong talk about sending representatives fr. the committee to London, as *Russin* brought the invitation. Judging by the example ob the behaviour of those delegates in America, its clear one cannot permit them to go as they act against the Government. *Polivanov* & *Grigorovitch* & *Ignatiev* (the liberal!) are for it — but *Grigorovitch* only because *Russin* brought the invitation.

Polivanov is his despair — and longs you would change him, but understands you cannot do so without having a good successor. He says his one aid is such a bad man & does such harm — have forgotten his name, a very firm man but not good. *Polivanov* simply treacherous, the way he repeats at once all that is spoken over in secret at the Council of Ministers — its too hideous. — Spoke of the ***responsible*** government wh. all scream for, even good ones who do not realise we are not at all fit for it. (As our Friend says it wld. be the utter ruin of everything.) —

Then, how weak Obolensky is. (Fancy, his wife, born *Princess Mingrelskaya* went to *Gregory* to beg her husband shld. not be changed — think of that, Lili's sister-in-law!) *Volkonsky* he finds no good in his place, also disapproves of his running about behind the scenes at the *Duma.*

Well we went through all the ministers, & his aids.

God help him in his great task to serve you & his country well — makes him also sad that such a capable man as *Khvostov* should have gone so utterly wrong. —

It seems there was a horrible article in the »*Retch*« against Ania — how vile people are to drag a young woman in like that! —

I am glad you find the new governor a nice man — where was he before? — Oh you dear one to have written to me again, thanks ever so tenderly & with many a kiss.

I saw the nomination & changed came out this morning in the papers, — yesterday at 6 *Sturmer* did not know yet when he would get yr. paper back. — Yes, *Khvostov* told *Sturmer* he did not understand why he left, if on account of that story — the other did not answer anything particular. In any case he did not come up to what you expected of him, did not work properly, — was most promising at the beginning & then all changed. Now he does certainly not behave as a gentleman. He showed about Ania's letter to members of the *Duma,* in wh. she asks to see that one shld. make no ***search*** in *Gregory's* rooms a certain night »if its not again a chantage story«, she wrote. No harm in the letter, but ugly to give others to read — he was to return the letter to *Sturmer,* as the parents heard of it — but *Khvostov* did not, — now a friend of his said it was untrue, he was shocked one sh. say such a thing & that he had just n o w found the torn fragments in his basket!! (he got it m o r e than a week ago) & that he wld. glue them together & return them her tomorrow. Can only be a big lie this answer of the basket — hang that dirty story & I am glad you are put of it. — The Children have gone to the big palace to see the wounded.

Now I must end.

God bless you, Sweetheart. Many a tender kiss, precious One, fr. yr. deeply loving old wify

Alix.

No. 222.

Tsarskoje Selo, March 7-th 1916

My own Love,

Its gently snowing, grey, 2 of frost. Feel my heart still and face — not pain, but heavy, stiff. — I am going to see *Grigorovitch* today with photos. of the naval Sanatorium at *Massandra* — I asked that he should bring them, as have not seen him for more than a year. Then I see Mme *Ridiger* (widow of a *Georgian* Reg. officer), who will look after my Sanatorium at Massandragates, below the naval one. Its a very big building and we can send wounded there in a week, I am so glad. We collected the money for it with bazars, then as there was not enough, you allowed the *estate* to finish building, as we had not enough money (later I hope we can by degrees pay it back). It was to be for usual sick who come to *Yalta* and have no place to live, below richer ones and at the top poor, tired out school-mistresses, dressmakers who can't pay much. Now of course it goes only for the military and I gave it over to the »*Zdravnitsa*« to keep up. — *Nikolai Dmitrovitch Dem.* comes to say goodbye. Then *Yakovlev* about Marie's train; one of our wounded returning to the army and Kaulbars. —

Always people to see. —

You have much to do and so could not write yesterday, poor Darling, but I hope you are contented with the way things are going and the preparations, wh. are being made for the great advance.

Had a letter fr. Irene, (in german) asking about some prisoner officers. Bobbie will be promoted officer in summer (he is Tatianas age, Toddie was yesterday 27, Louise will be the same already in July) — she says the boy has seen already many trying things — was he out on a ship, I do not know. She sends love to all. —

Then Daisy kindly wrote and asks for prayerbooks for our Priests in Germany for lent and easter services and she will forward them, so as that it should go quicker. —

I read a most exciting english book yesterday, wh. we must read aloud with you later on.

I end in haste.

Every blessing and kiss, Treasure, fr. yr. very own old

Sunny.

No. 223.

Tsarskoje Selo, March 8-th 1916

My Beloved,

Quite cold, 10 of frost, but in consequence lighter. I had the woman for the first time to masse round my heart, — gently stroking to make the muscles stronger (did not like it) and then she did my face because of the continual aching, and the back of my nape of the neck and shoulders wh. was agreable — felt tired after it all. — Sweet Lovy mine, I do so miss you, no sun without you, tho' I have a Sunbeam in the house and bright girlies, but my Own, my one and all is ever missing and I yearn for yr. consoling, tender caresses! —

Yesterday evening, after they had dined at Anias, *Lili Den* and husband — *Kozhevnikov* and *Taube* spent from 9—11 with us. Sad saying goodbye to them, — so far away, endless voyage they and we without news. Awful to be away from home at such a time. All our Friends spread away, all over the place. *Den* has managed to get 20 officers and is enchanted. He and *Lili* and the most of the officers leave to-day — the kitchen follows a few days later with the men. For *Lili* it will be awfully hard — she has already grown thinner and the eyes all the time swim in tears. — Oh this hideous war!! —

I had the American Harte for 2 hours yesterday — he is off to Germany now. He told several things wh. decidedly can be done here and I begged him to speak again with G. Rüdiger.

To-day I have *Viltchkovsky* with a long *report* and other people.

My Lovebird, to-morrow its a week you left us! How lonely you must feel. I am glad you will see *N. P.* to-morrow, it will remind you of the time when he lived with you at the *Headquarters.* Wonder what you will settle? —

A. just brought me in a big letter for you, so have to use a large envelope to stick it in. She is quite well and the cough has passed and walked even — strong health, recovers so quickly.

Georgi at *Pavlovsk* has got the mumps, poor boy! —

Yakovlev with Marie's train was ordered to Riga yesterday. Look here, do a clever thing and tell Kirill you strongly disapprove of Boris having that beast Plen. His reputation — vile, — kicked out of the navy, sent away by Kirill, received into Baby's »*Atamantzi*« — honour far too great to wear that uniform and covered with war decorations and high rank — for no military bravery and service — but some private dirty service. Speak to Kirill and *N. P.* about him, all are horrified, and *Petrograd* talks enough about it, — (also Miechen's ambition to get him nearest to the throne is well known.) Much dirt everywhere. — So sad the lowness of humanity — Sodom and Gomorrah verily, — many must still personally suffer through the war and only then will they be loitered and change. Its all very painful and one can have so little veneration or respect of anyone. —

Has *Kuropatkin* at last cleared out *Bontch-Bruievitch?* — if not, do have it done quiker. Be firmer and more authoritative, Sweetheart, show yr. fist when necessary — as old *Goremykin* said still the last time he came to me: »the Emp. must be firmer one needs to feel his power« and its true. Your angelic kindness, forgiveness and patience are known and one profits of it — show you alone are the master and have a strong will. —

Oh, my Angel love, I long to be near you, to hear yr. beloved voice and gaze into yr. lovely, deep eyes! God's holy Angels guard and protect you and bless your life and works and send success. Thousand tender kisses do I press upon yr. lips and press you fondly to my heart. —

Ever yr. very

Own.

Just got yr. sweetest letter for wh. fondest thanks. How good you saw those Engl. and nice *Yudenitch* gets a decoration from Georgi. Wonder for what occasion *Alexeiev* will be made General a. d. c.? — So one has probably talked to *Piltz* already against our Friend, pity. — Glad you had a conversation with *Feodorov.* She will be happy with yr. kiss. — God bless you. Endless tender kisses. —

No. 224.

Tsarskoje Selo, March 9-th 1916

My Love,

15⁰ in the night, now 12⁰, snowing finely & one sees too, sun wishes to appear. Once again winter seems to have set in, but not for long. —

How strange it is what one reads in the Naval Minister's paper fr. foreign news, that every little success we have, they call theirs, really it would be interesting to print the announcements next to each other, to see the difference. I am sorry I did not heed the story of the Moewe & so missed what they did. —

I slept alright, only had rather strong pains in my face till I smeared it with a new mixture & wrapped my whole head in a thick shawl. —

Lili Den's boy comes to Ania for two days & 2 nights, I am so glad for the lovely child, & I shall get him to come to me too & the children can take him into the garden.

The big ones go to town for a committee, *donations* & tea at *Anitchkov.* Xenia again is feverish & does not go out — a wretched winter for her — she & Motherdear ought to go to *Kiev* for 2 weeks to get a change & have their rooms, wh. are full of microbes, throughly aired. —

I have people to see again & reports. Sturmer again too, don't know why. — He had a long talk with *Viltchkovsky* — one sent our »station« at *Luga,* two hospitals fr. *Rezhitza* & yet another comes, military ones, as of course the greater mass will come straight to us. There is much to do to prepare things before hand. — What a wind & snow! Now you will be having yr. talk with Kirill & *N. P.,* — always I try to live my life with you & wonder how you are getting on. I send you again fresh flowers, as yours have for sure already faded — a week that you left — I lie in the corner of my big room in the afternoon, as its lighter & we took tea there too. —

Sweetest of Treasure, heart of my heart, Goodbye & God bless & protect you. Endless tender kisses my Own, fr. yr. deeply

loving old wife

Sunny.

In case *N. P.* is still at the *Headquarters* when you get this, give him our love. —

No. 225.

Tsarskoje Selo, March 10-th 1916

My own Sweetheart,

Snowings, blowings of frost. Little Titi came to me yesterday afternoon for an hour — we looked at books together, took tea with us and played with

Alexei. Now he has begun speaking English quite nicely, a tall, clever boy for 7½; writes alone to his mother in Russian. He spent the night at Anias and we hope he will come again on Saturday. Had *reports* and received. *Sturmer* came to speak about that story as things must be seriously cleared up and I had to give him over letters fr. Iliodor relating everything and he will have investigations made still as to the truth of what he wrote, — alas, it seems truthful. — Then he told me to warn you that *Nikolasha* wants to have Uncle *Krivoshein* as a help. During *Vorontzov's* time there was a *Nikolsky*. He has to represent *Nikolasha's* interests when necessary in the *Duma* and *Council of the Empire* and it wld. be impossible *Krivoshein* filling such a place. It would be the ruin of the Caucasus, he cleverer than anybody and unscrupulous now — friend to *Nikolasha* and fat *Orlov* and *Yanushkevitch* — would be awful. As it must come to you for yr. approval, I warn you. —

Its madness of *Nikolasha* to take a man you sent away and who did all the harm then. — *Sturmer* was much less shy and quite open this time — one sees what a real love and veneration he has for you. — Is worried about the *Convention* in Moscow wh. will be soon, is sending for the General fr. there to speak over matters, personaly I fear that *neurasthenic Shebeko* will be a useless rag there, if there should be any stories. Of course he also finds a General Governor must be there, without having any man in view. — He wishes I could show myself often in town and go about and to *Kazan* Church — but my stupid heart and now face prevent and I know it would be good. Motherdear neither can and Miechen is playing a popular part in town and going about a lot and to musical evenings and acting her part as charmeuse. The Benkendorfs are also in despair about this, the Css. told Ania. They came back quite sick after a few days spent in town.

Everyone horrified by *Khvostov*. — She took tea at Pauls (after ages again) — good humour. The boy goes about quite green as returns to the regiment to-day. The terrible, forced drinking in the Hussars made him ill and acted on his heart. They and the Garde à cheval continue drinking colossaly at the war, its loathsome and d e g r a d i n g before the soldiers who know that you prohibited it. — If you have an occasion, tell *Bezobrasov* to have an eye on the regiments and make them understand how hideously unmoral it is at such a time.

The Css. Benkendorf is shocked with Dmitris goings on in town during the war and finds one ought to insist upon him returning to the regiment — I fully agree, town and women are p o i s o n for him. —

Just read in the papers about our advancing — thank God its going quietly, steadily well — God grant this may change the rotten minds of the »rear«. —

To-day Css. Carlov comes to me, as she leaves for Tiflis for 3 months. as her daughter is expecting — then Mme *Nikitina* (ex Odessa) and a lady of my *store*. —

Tatiana is at an operation of one of our officers this morning. —

Poor old *Zaltza* died yesterday — a remembrance of our young married days here. Dear me, how much we have seen and lived through in these

21½ years of married life — but all is so distinct and clear in my memory — oh how lovely the times were, Sweetheart, Sunny's love ever increases, fuller, richer and deeper and she dreams of our youthful happy love in the bygone, how mad we were! — Precious one, I bless and kiss you without end and y e a r n for yr. tender, consoling caresses more than ever. —

One just brought me your beloved letter for wh. very tenderest thanks. So, my Angel also kisses my letters as I always do yours, every page and more than once. To-day it smells of cigarets. —

I see now why we advance, it being again winter here, I did not think it wld. be thawing yet there.

In the papers to-day the news is so good about our advance, 17 officers and 1000 men taken etc. oh, God bless our troops, I am sure he will and its good we waste no time, before they profit attacking us. All are so happy and full of it here.

I am glad the cinema was amusing as well as interesting. Did Kiryll and *N. P.* not turn up yesterday as I thought they intended to?

No, those English books have not yet come. Motherdear finished the 2-nd, so I sent her the French book you read.

Now I must end and get up, as the oculist comes to see to my aching eyes. —

Sweetheart, goodbye and God bless you over and over again and all yr. undertakings and our beloved troops. Ah how full the heart is and our prayers must be redoubled.

I cover you with kisses, my Huzy, and remain yr. very own

Wify.

Belarminov says I need stronger specks to read with, eyes overtired and the aching comes also from gout — the same as my face nerve pains too — but he is contented with the eyes themselves and says they are very good, only I overtask them. I am glad to have seen him, as the pain is often very strong and that acts on my head, and I see worse for reading. (I personally know they get bad fr. much crying) and fr. many unshed tears too, wh. fill the eyes and that must drink themselves up again — this all I did not tell him.) Then he gives me an ointment to rub in exteriorly if they ache much. —

No. 226.

Tsarskoje Selo, March 11-th 1916

My very own Sweetheart,

At last glorious, bright sunshine — what a difference it makes. I have ordered service in the house as its Friday & I have such a longing to go to church. All ones thoughts & prayers are with our troops & one flies to read the news every morning. Should there ever be anything quite particularly good, perhaps you wld. send me a short wire? one feels so anxious — but God will bless the troops & send success, if we only all pray enough. All our sanitary trains have been called out & heaps of *units* & 15 hospitals have gone to *Dvinsk*

I got yr. wire that you settled that question once for all with Kirill & *N. P.* & am anxiously awaiting what conclusion you came to. — Have again ladies to receive. Excuse my having wired about M-me *Nikitina's* husband, but she entreated me to, — of course you will do as you think right. She thought he was the oldest general with the St. George's cross who could fill that vacancy! —

The children say the tower in the garden has become quite magnificent — I long to go & look at it — hope to soon, if can risk with my face. — Beloved One precious Darling, you feel wify holding you tightly in her arms, caressing you tenderly & gently? Oh, hard not to be together at such times. —

There are rumours that some guard reg. have already had great losses, — but have they already been used?

Oh, the beautiful sunshine! Beloved, I must end. Heart & soul with you. God bless & proctect you & help you, give strenghts & energy & success. More than ever I pray for you. I want to see you blessed, happy, successful, I want to see the recompense for all your endless heartache, sorrow, anxiety, work, & that the prayers of all those who fell for their Sovereign & Country shd. be heard.

My Own, endless kisses from your own old

Sunny.

No. 227.

Tsarskoje Selo, March 12-th 1916

My own Lovebird,

I scarcely slept this night from pains in my face again. It began in the evening, just after I had told *Vladimir Nikolaievitch* that I thought I was quite rid of it & might go this evening to Church, — *the Cross-Worshipping Sabbath,* so disappointing. Had massage again this morning, smeared the face with all sorts of things. It is a little better now, but aches & the eye is half shut. Have again sent for the poor dentist — have seen so many other Drs. now, that I think he better come & have a look & perhaps change a filling there may be a new cavity. Of course feel cretinised & have to receive *Mrasovsky* & our three Sisters who returned fr. Austria & have a lot to tell. — Two of our sanitary trains are returning with heavy wounded. Is it true our losses are very heavy? Of course attacking, it cannot be otherwise — still we made many prisoners & took a lot (whilst the Germans said they did not let us advance one step, that we have immense losses & that they took 17 officers & 800 men prisoners).

Sweety, remember you have that special telegrapho-telephon, or however you call it & if anything particular let *Vojeikov* speak to *Ressin* or you to me. One feels so anxious & longs for more news than waiting 24 hours for the papers. — *N. P.* came yesterday fr. 7½-9 (such a pleasant surprise). A joy to get direct news. He was sad for you that very dull atmosphere around you, no young, fresh a. d. c. & you seemed so lonely. Its that wh. worries me too. He told me about all yr. decisions, & hurried off last night back to *Rezhitza.* — It is provoking that lack of officers. —

He says the Admiral spoke again very much against *Grigorovitch,* wh. always hurtes him, as he venerates him very much & sees N. wants to fight him out. —

He said he had a good talk with *Feodorov.* & about *Polivanov* too. *Maklakov* was at Ania's & entreats to see me also b e s e e c h i n g that I shld. i m p l o r e y o u quickly to get rid of *Polivanov,* that he his simply a revolutionist under the wing of *Gutchkov* — *Sturmer* begged the same. They say that in that odious *war-industries committee* they are intending to say horrid things, they come together in a few days, & *Maklakov* says therefore quickly clear out *Polivanov,* any honest man better than him. If you cant *Ivanov,* why not honest, devoted *Beliaiev* & give him a good help. *Sturmer* much dislikes the other help of *Polivanov,* says such a very bad man, I did not catch the name.

Lovy mine, dont dawdle, make up yr. mind, its f a r too serious, & changing him at once, you cut the wings of that revolutionary party; only be quicker about it — you k n o w, y o u yourself long ago wanted to change him — h u r r y u p Sweetheart, you need Wify to be behind pushing you. You above all need an h o n e s t l y d e v o t e d man, and that *Beliaiev* is, if *Ivanov* is too obstinate. Please, do the change at once, then propaganda & all can at once be stopped energetically. *Maklakov* adores you & spoke to her with tears in his eyes about you & so I shall see him soon. Promise me you will at once change the M. of War, for your sake, your Sons & Russias, — & it is high time — otherwise I shld. not have written again so soon about this question. You told me you wld. be soon doing it & who knows if God won't sooner bless our troops if this »choice of the old *Headquarters*« is at once cleared out. *Rodzianko* & *Gutchkov* knew well why they & *Janushkevitch* made *Nikolasha* propose him to you & fat Orlov behind all. *Maklakov* loathes Orlov says he is a man to stoop before nothing, the same as *Khvostov.* —

Saw *Shebeko* yesterday & had a good talk; & my ex lancer *Vinberg.* —

Our Friend leaves to-morrow, cld. not get any tickets for last Wednesday. — I wish my face did not ache so, long to write a lot more & can't, & want to ask heaps about the troops. —

Heart & soul with you longing to be together. —

There, your sweet letter has just come, thanks ever so tenderly, Sweetheart. — So you think *Shuvaiev* the right man (tho' less of a gentleman than *Beliaiev*) & is he really the right type? I only once spoke to him when found him most obstinate, so cannot judge. But who to succeed him? In any case — hurry up, Lovebird.

Excellent that you intend attaching *Ivanov* to yr. person, as all down there complain of the dear man being so tired & »getting old«. — Cannot understand why Keller & *Brussilov* always have hated each other & when he can *Brussilov* is not just — & the other in return abuses him (privately). Wont the ministers be happy when *Polivanov* leaves? Oh, the relief.

Alas, *Ignatiev* is neither a man in his place, tries to play the popular man & is left, alas, as too *Boris Vas.,* his brother-in-law, — the smart set.

Can imagine how palpitatingly interesting the work now is, & long I were near you to follow all together on the map & share anxiety & joy with you. From far we all do, heart & soul. — Yes, that frost is despairing for the troops. *There is nothing to be done, — God will help.* God bless, & protect you my Angel, my Own, my Love, my Huzy Sweet — guard & guide you. Endless tender, passionably loving kisses fr. yr. own old

Sunny.

No. 228.

Tsarskoje Selo, March 13-th 1916.

My very Own,

Warm & lovely sunshine, so God grant our troops have the same weather. Our train is just beeing emptied out & Maries comes later in the day with very heavy wounded. Despairing not to be able to go and meet them and work in the hospital — every hand is needed at such a time. Slept alright, but the strong pain in my eye continues, the cheek gets better when *Vladimir Nikolaievitch* electrifies it, so I do it now twice a day. Baby went out already early before Church. Ania goes for the whole day to town, as *Gregory* leaves, then she sees her parents & dines at the Css. Fredericks. —

My poor Rostoftsev's twice-sister has just died from cancer & one says he is quite wretched — is ill himself the whole time but goes on working. — Little *Titi* played on the snowtower with the children yesterday & enjoyed it, today he returns again to town. —

I am thinking so much about *Shuvaiev* & do greatly wonder whether he can fill such a place, know how to speak in the *Duma,* as one time one abused him & the *ordnance department* — but is that alright now? My eye aches so writing — I could not use it all day yesterday, & whilst I was receiving it was distracting — as if one stuck pencil into the centre & then the whole eye aches too, so better stop now & finish later on. —

So anxious for news. The children were all in Church & are now going out, hot sun, wind, frost in the shade, last night rain. — You cannot imagine how terribly I miss you — such utter loneliness — the children with all their love still have quite other ideas & rarely understand my way of looking at things the smallest even — they are always right & when I say how I was brought up & how one must be, they cant understand, find it dull. — Only when quietly speak with T. she grasps it. Olga is always most unamiable about every proposition, tho' may end by doing what I wish. And when I am severe — sulks me. Am so weary & yearn for you. — There are also many things wh. A., with her bringing up & being out of another set, does not understand & many a worry I would never share with her — I used to with *N. P.* because he, as a man with inborn tact, understood me. — We all have our ways & thoughts & I feel so horribly old at times & low spirited — pain pulls one down & perpetual anxiety & worry since the war goes on. Your precious calming presence gives me strength & consolation — I take things too deeply to heart — try to master it — but, I suppose, God gave me such a heart wh. fills up my whole being. Forgive my writing all this & pay no attention to it, I am only a bit down. Oh, I must be off to *Vladimir Nikolaievitch* to electrify myself. —

I bless you, kiss you over & over again & press you to my yearning heart, Sweet Angel, Treasure,

Beloved!

Ever yr. very own weary old

Sunny.

No. 229.

Tsarskoje Selo, March 14-th 1916.

My own sweet Treasure,

I send you an apple and flower from our Friend — we all had fruit as a goodbye gift. He left this evening — quietly, saying better times are coming and that he leaves spring-time with us. — He told her He finds *Ivanov* wld. be good as Minister of War on account of his great popularity not only in the army, but all over the country. — In that He is certainly right — but you will do what you think best. I only asked He should pray for success in yr. choice, and He gave this answer. —

I spent the whole long afternoon from 1-4 alone, reading with an aching eye. It seems Neidhardt is ill with the same pains and high fever. The dentist has left the Crimea yesterday evening. — The girls went to see Marie's sanitary train whilst half full still — it left to the front in the evening again. Three trains came.

Forgive my having seemed to grumble in my last letter, its a shame — only I was feeling so low and wrongly forgot to hide it. Such constant pains pull one down a bit. Oh yes, yet another thing he said to tell you that the Metropolitan told him, the Synod wants to present you a wish of theirs that s e v e n metropolitans should be in Russia. *Vladimir* very much for it — but our Friend begs you not to agree as its certainly not the moment and we cant even find scarcely 3 decent ones fit to occupy such a place. How utterly absurd of them. *Nikon* is still here, too bad. —

One says Uncle *Khvostov,* hopes to whitewash his nephew, tho' all are against him and wants to drag *Beletzky* in, who really seems quite innocent concerning the *Conspiracy* and wishes him no longer to be Senator, but then you must be just and have *Khvostov's* courtrank taken away — I deeply regret it was left him — as in the *Duma* they say — if he wished to get rid of *Gregory* because he did not suit him, he can do the same with any of us who may displease him. I don't like *Beletzky* but it wld. be very unfair if he suffered more than *Khvostov.* He has forfeited *Irkutsk* through his imprudence, but thats enough. The other tried to instigate a murder. — Enough of this story.

Excuse this ink, but my other pen is empty and needs refilling. —

What a pitty you cannot get out more, I know how wildly you long for the sun and air towards spring — so was I in the bygone, could not live without air and then through being ill everything changed and I learned to be weeks without air and never any walks. — And you do so need it with all the work you have to do. How vile that they shoot again with explosive bullets. But God will punish them. —

Sweetheart, if you only knew how yr. little wify longs for you and now we shall for sure long not meet again. There is nothing to be done but you are s o lonely, Lovebird and I long to caress you and feel yr. sweet tenderness. Precious one, you feel wify's love enveloping you with fathomless tenderness? You feel my arms round you and my lips pressed to your warm ones with such utter love? God keep you, my one and all, my own Sunshine. —

Got to sleep late, because of the aching — its not any longer madning pain, but aches and these last day's especially my right eye.

4 of warmth this morning — the sun did not shine long. — Its the feast of the *Feodorovska Holy Mother* and consequently of our Church. *Igor* comes to present himself as yr. a. d. c. and lunches with us. I also receive the commander of my *Crimeans* — I wonder what he is like.

Alia has asked to see me as she drives here to-day, so will come to tea. All that with these pains is not gay, but difficult to refuse.

Now Lovebird, Goodbye and God bless you. I cover you, sweet Nicky, with very tenderest kisses,

Ever yr. very

Own.

The Children are alright — Tatiana busy at the hospital — Olga has gone there on foot with *Shura,* Anastasia after her lesson is off for a run with *Trina* as *the priest* officiates in Church this morning. Marie is writing to you. Baby is out. I must get up for my electricity. —

It does not concern me, but whilst I could not sleep, I was thinking over what you said about *Kedrov;* — wld. not *M. P. Sablin* be better instead of *Planson,* — such a serious, q u i e t man and not an ambitious »Streber«. Tho' *Kedrov* is clever and talented, yet he is somewhat an *insolent fellow,* judging by his letters to the Admiral — and the other so discreet and an older man for such a place. This is my very own opinion, not prompted by any talk with *N. P.* as you might think. We never mentioned his brother last time, there was no time even. —

Poguliaiev such a young admiral and in yr. suite — colossal honour, the couple wild of joy and he is going to fly off to the old Father to present himself — he is also ambition itself and *insolent* and therefore has luck and both these men turn the Admiral round their little finger. Eberhardt needs a serious help and I find a man f r. t h e b l a c k s e a is the one just to occupy such a place. Pardon my interference, Sweety, but in the long, lonely night I thought of this and felt I must write it honestly to you, — tell me whether you don't agree. —

Paul told Ania he takes over the command in April, can it be true? I personally strongly doubt his succeeding and honestly find it not right his insisting, as after all he is quite out of everything since ever so long and one cannot be sure of his health. —

Now I really must get up. Farewell my Angel. — A bow to *Feodorov* and Gen. *Alexeiev.*

No. 230.

Tsarskoje Selo, March, 15-th 1916

My own Sweetheart,

There, glorious sunshine with 10 of warmth, but windy — and yesterday afternoon and evening it snowed hard.

My head and eyes go on aching, the woman has been masseing my face and head, neck and shoulders and soon I go up to my electricity. I dare not risk going out until have seen the dentist and to be sure my cheek wont swell up. — Lovy, I send you here a letter I got from *Rostchakovsky* when read through and if you agree, wire to me »all right« and I shall have it wired on to him. He is a strange chap, not like others — but certainly devoted and energetic and as he so funnily writes, must be used. — I wish you could shut up that rotten *war industries committee* as they prepare simply anti-dynastic questions for their meeting. —

I have *V. P. Schneider* with a long *report* — I like her as she is so energetic and understands half words already — only my head is not fresh at all. Later *Emelianov* comes to bid goodbye before returning to my regiment. — Last night Baby's train came. It seems of the 20-th Sib. reg. only 5 officers have remained — fearful losses. But are you on the whole contented? of course in attacking heavy losses are inevitable.

Mme Zizi has at last returned here and I shall see her this afternoon. —

So tiresome I cant take medicines now, something came on 8 days too early.

Am eagerly awaiting yr. promised letter.

Excuse bad writing. —

One says Dmitri is still scandalling about in town such a pitty! He wont become a better husband for that. —

Did you see the Sultan received the fieldmarshal's staff from William, such mockery. —

Missy has sent another pretty fairytale book of hers to Olga. —

Beloved One, I kiss you, oh so tenderly and wish I could share yr. loneliness; you have not a soul to talk to, to feel near you, who understands you and with whom you can talk about anything wh. comes into yr. head; — sad *N. P.* is no longer with you — he had shared our life so much and knew and understood so many little things, wh. the other a. d. c. dont.

Wont you have them on duty change about with you? Would be good for them and interesting for you.

Thanks tenderly, my beloved One, for yr. sweetest letter, am glad you have settled all about *Polivanov,* God grant *Shuvaiev* may be the right man in the right place, in any case a b l e s s i n g you are rid of him.

I shall read through *Gregory's* telegr. with Ania when she returns from town and then explain it to you. —

Hang those Generals, why are they so weak and good for nothing, be severe to them. You have indeed been busy, Sweetheart.

But I must end now. God bless and protect you.

Warmest, tenderest kisses, Huzy mine fr. yr. very own old

Wify.

No. 231.

Tsarskoje Selo, March 15-th 1916

My own Lovebird,

I begin my letter to you this evening. It was such happiness hearing from you & I can imagine how comforted you feel to have at last settled the question of the minister of war. God bless your choice with success, & may he prove himself worthy of your trust.

Is it true that things are going very bad with *Sukhomlinov* — *Igor* had heard as tho' he wld. have to be shot — but I don't know where he got the news from. Certainly he had his great faults — but his successor is yet a greater traitor to my mind. I return *Gregory's* telegram to you. He means *Beletzky,* because he does not find just that he, who has scarcely been to blame, should so severely suffer & the other got off better, who committed the greatest sin. —

My eye has been hurting me madly all day (& head too) — its from the *triplex nerve* in the face. One branch to the eye, the one took the upper row of teeth, the other the lower, & the knot before the ear. I have heard of more people suffering now fr. these pains — Neidhardt had it so bad, that the Drs. send him to the south for a rest. Its fr. a chill in the facial nerves, the cheek & teeth are much better, the left jaw goes popping in & out this evening, but the eyes ache very much — therefore I wont write anymore now. —

Here is a letter fr. *Poguliaiev* for you to read through, & copy of a telegr. fr. the »*Tvertzi*« Baby got to-day. —

»On March 7-th the 3-d squadron of the Tver Regiment named after your Imperial Majesty penetrated into the ranks of kurdish cavalry body more than three times as large as ours and sabered many, thereby extricating our infantry from a dangerous situation — I am happy to felicitate with this our Worshipped August Chief.

Colonel von Harten.

(Field Telegraph branch 116.)

One says *Khvostov* is at Moscou talking away & saying he was sent off because wished to get rid of the German spies near our Fr. — so low. Ah, indeed he ought to be judged or his embroidered coat be taken fr. him. He said you ought to punish those that talk in the clubs. — Ania continues getting anon. letters, her Father & poor *Zhuk* too, telling him not to go with her, otherwise he will die a violent death with Ania. She spoke to *Spiridov.* & he will have her guarded, knows one is after her. Begs her only to walk in our garden, not go on foot to Church nor in the street, to get quicker into her carriage — certainly this makes her nervous. *Sturmer* told the Father he has her safely guarded in town. —

I wish one cld. stop *Ignatiev's* popular (left) speeches in the *Duma* about universities wh. one needs all over Russia etc. — he will break his own neck seeking for popularity. —

March 16-th. Again splendid sunshine, 13 in the sun & thawing hard — strange you had such a thick fogg. Slept alright, but the pains gently continue tiring me. I have the dentist after luncheon. Titi will walk with the children & before tea I shall have his hair cut — *Lili* could never make up her mind because his standing out ears were hidden by his long hair — so she let me do it, it wld. be less painful to her & I am sure he will look much nicer, being such a big boy. To-morrow he leaves for Reval to live with her relations. —

I am sorry, as he is a nice boy for Alexei to play with.

The big girls go to town as Olga has a committee & then they take tea at *Anitchkov*. Sweetest Love, its two weeks to-day, that you left us and I miss you quite terribly. Its good you have much to do, so that you cannot feel the loneliness so much. Only the evenings must indeed be sad & dull, poor Sweetheart. I send you again some lilies of the valley & the little sweet-smelling blue flowers you like — I have kissed them & they bring you my love, wh. is deep and tender. —

I don't read at all now, so as to rest my eyes wh. ache so & in the evening lay patiences with Marie, in the daytime Ania reads sometimes aloud to me. I shall send Motherdear an exciting book again. My »*Buian*« has come back again to the big palace & this time wounded. — I got telegrams fr. *Yalta,* my Sanatorium is quite ready — such luck as it gives us from 50—60 officers' places, than we can turn »*Kutchuk Lambat*« into a hospital only for soldiers, as the officers bored themselves to distraction there & always tried to go off to *Yalta* & there was no place for their wives to live, as its only a fishermens' village. —

I do so wonder how *Shuvaiev* will manage, is he energetic? What a blessing if he is the right man. — Yes, alas, our generals have never been very famous — what can it be? Clear them out then & bring forward young energetic men, as for instance Arseniev — during a war one chooses the capable men & does not go by the age & rank, I find, — its for the whole armie's sake & one cannot suffer men's lives to be shed in vain by blustering generals. —

I wonder what Admiral Filimore will tell you about the north? —

I had a letter fr. Malcolm expressing the wild enthusiasm all over England, about Erzerum — in the streets & clubs it was the reigning talk. — Unfortunately he did not succeed with the English red cross to get them to send their 3 sisters over to Germany as we did, & he is muchly disappointed.

Then Daisy arranged him a meeting with Max in Switzerland — when he got there, Max had fallen ill & cld. not meet him. He went over our organisation at Bern for the help of our prisoners & found it excellent.

I shall finish this after luncheon, as now must be getting up. I cover you with kisses, every sweet place & hold you tightly clasped to my heart — Treasure, sweetest of Huzys! —

We had Nastinka to luncheon & before that *Maklakov* sat with me for 3/4 of an hour talking hard. True, devoted soul. Intensely relieved you have changed *Polivanov* but he wld. have cleared out some others too. When we meet again I can talk over many things he said & I shall speak with *Sturmer* when see him, as some things are really true & need thinking over. — He entreats you not to agree with all the Moscou *demands.* Of course one c a n n o t sanction the *Unions of the Cities* etc. becoming legalized & stable institutions. Their money is governemental & they can use as many millions as they like & the »people« don't even know its crown money' — that must be made known officially.

Should they exist on later they wld. inevitably be the nest of propaganda & the workers of the *Duma* in the country. He was minister when you allowed it, as they came straight to you before *Maklakov* cld. make his *report* & then he begged you after o n l y to sanction it d u r i n g the war. Please, Lovy, remember this. You have now sent them a wire thanking for their work — but that must not mean that they should continue. If ever such sort of organisations are needed, it must be in the hands of Governors. — He is over disgusted with *Khvostov's* behaviour. He spoke like an honest, well-meaning, deeply loving & devoted loyal friend & servant of yours. —

Now for to-day I must end, the man leaves.

Goodbye & God bless & keep you, my Angel.

Tenderest kisses fr. all. Ever yr. very, very

Own.

No. 232.

Tsarskoje Selo, March, 17-th 1916

My Beloved,

A grey morning, 3 of warmth. How annoying that the fogg continues at *Moghilev* and such mud, swamps, inundated rivers all along the front. Really its bitterly hard all the difficulties our poor troops have to fight with; but God wont forsake them. Only Lovy, punish those that make faults, you cannot be severe enough — some firm exemples will frighten all the rest. —

Thats good yr. clearing away *Ronzhin* — he is the despair of all — and red *Danilov?*

Css. Carlov is furious her friend *Polivanov* has been changed and has at once offered him to live in her house — that pictures to you the state of many in society now. Formerly they would never have dreamed of doing such a thing — she with aplomb shows the opposition — her son in law is at *Tiflis, Nikolasha* chose *Polivanov,* thats all one and her unamiability when she came to me.

She is *Volzhin's* great friend and therefore sits upon the week man and crushes him. I know this all fr. Ania's Mother as the Css. and Sisters are her Father's relations and they have changed in their behaviour towards them too. —

Cannot one be more careful as to who gets put into the *Council of the Empire? Maklakov* says it makes all the good ones say, that many one does not approve of, find a home there, as for instance *Dumitrashko* whom *Trepov* wishes to get rid of and therefore begs him to be put there. One needs good men and not any body (else it becomes like the *retired officers).* It must be the loyal right. —

I never knew that nice *Pokrovsky* is a known left (their nicest luckily), a follower of *Kokovtzev* and of the »*Block*«. Wish you could think of a good successor to *Sazonov,* — need not be a diplomat! So as now already to get into the work and to see we are not sat upon later by England and that when the questions of ultimate peace comes we should be firm. Old *Goremykin* and *Sturmer* always disapprouved of him as he is such a coward towards Europe and a parlamentarist — and that wld. be Russia's ruin.

For Baby's sake we must be firm as otherwise his inheritance will be awful, as with his caracter he wont bow down to others but be his own master, as one m u s t in Russia whilst people are still so uneducated — Mr. Philippe and *Gregory* said so too. —

And another thing Lovy, forgive my bothering you, but its for yr. sweet sake they speak to me. Wont you give *Sturmer* the order he is to send for *Rodzianko* (the rotten) and very firmly tell him you insist upon the budget being finished b e f o r e Easter; as then you need not call them together till, God grant, when everything is better — autumn — after war. They want to dawdle on so as to come back in summer with all their horrible liberal propositions.

Many say the same thing and beg of you to insist they shld. finish now. And you cannot make concessions, an answerable ministery etc.: and all the rest they wish. It must be y o u r war and y o u r peace and your and our Country's honour and as no means the *Duma's* they have not to say a word in those questions. — Ah, how I wish we were together, I cant write all, I should like to, tho' my pen flies like mad over the paper and the thoughts tear through my head — its difficult to put all plainly on paper — and besides I have to get up and be off to the dentist. —

He is killing a nerve in my last tooth to the right, thinks that may calm the other nerves, because the tooth does not require the nerve being killed at all. He is quite put out about my pains. Head and eye go on aching to-day, but I slept well. —

My little *Malama* came for an hour yesterday evening, after dinner at Anias. We had not seen him for 1½ years. Looks flourishing more of a man now, an adorable boy still. I must say, a perfect son in law he wld. have been — why are foreign Pces. not as nice! — Ortipo had to be shown to his »Father« of course. —

Quite nice what they wrote about *Shuvaiev.* Must make Ania read what *Menshikov* says about *Polivanov* — am so relieved he has gone — the

»socie« of course will grieve, it interests me what Paul will say at tea to-day. — I must be off, shall finish after luncheon. —

Oh thank you so, so much my beloved Sweetheart for your precious letter wh. was joy to receive and every loving word warmed me up. —

Yes, thats Albert Grancy's son who told that — at least one told that — at least one who honestly said that the Germans began. —

Its most despairing thaw having set in at the front and that one cant advance and are deep in water. Such bad luck, but perhaps will pass quickly. Good, you have sent for the 3 chiefs to speak over with them. —

Sister Olga arrives on Sunday, to everybody's great surprise. I fear she comes to speak about her wishes for the future — what am I to say about yr. thoughts on that subject. The moment when all minds are so unpatriotic and against the family its hard she should think of such things and his part is unpardonable, and personally I fear *Sandro* has been egging her on — I may be wrong — but that story worries me very much and I don't find she ought to have brought up this theme now. Perhaps she wants to follow him to the Caucasus as one says his regiment goes off there — that would be more than unwise and give occasion for much talk and ugly talk.

I am so glad to hear that people are contented at *Shuvaiev's* nomination — God grant him success. —

Now my Darling I must close my letter. All the children fondly kiss you and I cover you with tender, gentle kisses and deep love, sweet Huzy mine.

Ever yr. old

Wify.

No. 233.

Tsarskoje Selo, March, 26-th 1916

My very own precious Love,

Once more the train will be carrying you off from us, when you read my letter. This week has flown; it was an unexpected joy you came & you can tell *Alexeiev,* with kind messages, that I think of him with a grateful heart. I am glad Dmitri accompanies you now, it will make the journey brighter & less lonely. The idea of your going off all alone again, is great pain. If I feel this terrible loneliness everytime, tho' have the dear children, what must yr. sensations be all alone at the *Headquarters!* And Passion-week & Easter approaching, those lovely services, you will be sad standing all by yourself in Church. God help you, my own Lovebird. —

You never can come here without there being some story to pain you or make you anxious & give worry, now poor Olga's intentions & plans for the future have assailed us & I cannot tell you the bitter pain it causes me for you. Your own sweet sister doing such a thing!

I understand all & don't & cant grudge her longing first for liberty & then happiness, but she forces you to go against the family laws, when it touches ones own nearest, its far worse.

She, an Emperor's daughter & sister! Before the country, at such a time when the dynasty is going through heavy trials & many countercurrants are at work, — is sad. The society's morals are falling to pieces & our family, Paul, Misha & Olga show the example, not speaking of the yet worse behaviour of Boris, Andrei & Sergei.

How shall we ever stop the rest from similar marriages? Its wrong she puts you into this false position & it hurts me its through her this new sorrow has been inflicted upon you. What would yr. Father have said to all this? We have been far to weak & kind to the family & ought many a time to have thundered at the young ones. — Do, if only possible, find an occasion of speaking to Dmitri about his goings on in town, & at such a time. — I, wickedly perhaps, did hope *Petia* would not give the divorce. It may seem cruel & I don't mean to be so, because I tenderly love Olga, but I think of you first & that she makes you act wrongly. Nice sunshine, I hope it will shine upon yr. way too. Please give many messages to Count Keller fr. me, ask after his boy (second marriage) he had him with him a time, I know. —

I hope to go to Church to-night when you have left, it will be a comfort to pray for you with all the rest. I hate goodbyes & the awful separations. You have warmed me up again with your tender, loving caresses, they soothe the constant aching heart. All my deepest, warmest, unceasing love surounds you, all fervent, burning prayers, heart & soul undying together through all eternity. My Own, my Life, my Treasure!

God bless & protect you & give you success in all undertakings, guide & guard you fr. all harm. Passionately I press you to my heart & kiss you with infinite tenderness, eyes, lips, forehead, chest, hands, every tenderly loved place wh. belongs to me.

Goodbye, Sunshine, my happiness, God grant the separation may not be too long. The chief thing is missing when you are not here & the evenings are sad & we try to get early to bed. Ever, Nicky mine, yr. own true wify

Alix.

Your Own. —

No. 234.

Tsarskoje Selo, March, 27-th 1916

My very own Lovebird,

Glorious warm sunshine, do hope you have the same weather. Such a sad feeling when I awoke this morning & turned to kiss you & found the dear place empty »Me don't like dat« at all. And the evening was melancholy, laid patiences & talked.

Went to evening service & prayed hard for my lonely One whom I had just parted with in great pain. *The priest* preached about *Maria of Egypt.*

Baby wrote his diary with grumbling.

They all go to Ania's hospital this afternoon to hear singing & see conjurers, she wants me to go, but do not feel up to it. After Church must finish this, then must look at some of *Stredlov's* pictures, change & go to the big palace hospital, where I have not been since about 4 months, & then for a drive, as they say the roads are better. — Isa lunches with us. Now I must quickly get up. — Always in a hurry, so my letter will be short.

Have you got on with the book? Oh, my Sweetheart, h o w I miss you & long for you. I cover you with tender kisses. God bless & protect you. The Children kiss you over & over again.

Ever, my Angel love, yr. very own old

Wify.

No. 235.

Tsarskoje Selo, March 28-th 1916

My own Sweetheart,

Another glorious morning with splendid sunshine, I am glad, then the snow will sooner melt & the roads become better. We drove yesterday at *Pavlovsk* I am so disaccustomed to the movement in a big carriage & driving quickly, that it makes my back ache & gives me a not very pleasant sensation (the moveable heart & kidneys), but after a while that is sure to pass. I so very rarely drive these last years. —

At Ania's hospital it was quite nice, fancy my having gone for an hour, I watched everything with a sort of interest, heart & soul being far away from all that. 2 tiny children played remarcably well on the gicelyra, that wooden instrument with wooden hammers. Then Mme Beling sang, very pretty voice indeed. The soldiers were enchanted. Nini sat next to me and was a goose. —

I saw *Kotchubei* about presents for the »*Plastuni*« from Baby, he will give the money & then our *store* can make the things for the 6-th of May, as they cannot possibly be got ready for Easter.

To-day I see the Priest of the Standart. He came here for the men's devotions on board & now goes back to *Rezhitsa*. Then *Shagubatov* presents himself. — I found 4 »*Alexandrovtsi*« & 2 *Crimeans* in the big palace yesterday, also one of yr. 1-st Siberian regiment, I had seen him wounded after the last war; he said the losses a week or 2 ago were terrible in yr. regiment nearly all the officers again killed or wounded, — such a cauchemar.

In the afternoon we went into *Znamenia* & placing candles & praying there reminded me of the last day we knelt there side by side, as one. Oh, my Lovy sweet, if you knew the solitude without your precious presence! Such a yearning besides in my arms to close them around you & press you to my heart & feel peaceful & calm in yr. great unfailing love.

I must stop now because of the masseuse & then I go to our hospital. —

Ania spends the day in town till 5, so I shall be free to visit another hospital & take Isa for a turn perhaps.

Three new officers arrived fr. *Tarnopol* & I made their *dressings.* One old one had served many years in Baby's »*Lithuanians*« & remembered seeing me when I arrived 22 years ago at *Simferopol.*

We are going to the *Maternity Hospital* after luncheon.

One brought me quite charming Images painted by wounded soldiers, who had never drawn before, & the *setting* made by them too. I am writing during luncheon, as have to receive after. Just got yr. wire from *Zhmerinka,* glad you have spring weather, hope you can take a little walk upon yr. arrival this evening.

Now goodbye my Nicky sweet, my own Huzy. Endless kisses & blessings

Ever yr. very own old

Sunny.

No. 236.

Tsarskoje Selo, March, 29-th 1916

My Beloved,

I have no idea when and where you will receive my letters. Just now one brought me yr. wire from *Kamenetz-Podolsk,* wh. came in half an hour only. Here too its grey this morning & dull.

Do so wonder whether you will see my *Crimeans* anywhere, they are at 20 versts about from where you spent the night. —

Poor little *Nikita* had *an operation* done yesterday, but I don't know the details, — the ear, — anyhow the Drs. seem satisfied. —

The Children worked in the ice & I sat in the sun for 3/4 of an hour looking on. — Dr. *Zuiev* has returned & I hope to see him, he went to Victoria to Darmouth to bring her my letter. Dicky walks on crutches, he broke his leg some time ago toboggaining. He spends easter with his parents at Kent House. Easter falls together this year. Louise is in France in the hospital again. —

Ania read to us yesterday evening, poor girl, she does not read well & makes endless faults in English. —

Lovy, do have that question stopped about the lot of new metropolitans, it is again being discussed in the Synod believe me, its not right, we have not the men & it will only do harm to the Church.

First our Bishops must be better men before we can think of making them metropolitans, its too early & will do much mischief & bring yet more frictions in the Church. — Have been to Ania's hospital & dressed the wounds of three of the worst. Now I am going to my lancer hospital, & before that, must receive. —

Tatiana Andreievna comes to tea; alas, Olga says she cannot come to us, so sad, as I had hoped to have a talk with her. — Goodbye, my Angel, God bless & protect you.

I cover you, my own sweet One, with very tender kisses & such craving

Ever yr. very own old

Wify.

No. 237.

Tsarskoje Selo, March 30-th 1916.

My own Sweetheart,

I am writing, to you during luncheon, as had no time in the morning. Read through my prayers, had the masseuse, went to our *Pestcherny* Church for service (thought so much of you) and then to our hospital, where I made 10 *dressings,* — now am tired. Have to receive. At 4 go to the red cross and I give the *graduates of the courses* their papers and they get the cross. Then A. Olga, Mavra and Helene dine with us, as I have not yet seen them this year. — A grey day, wanted to snow but not cold, so shall dine with the girls to freshen up my brain. A. has gone for the day to town, saw her in Church .—

I was awfully grateful to get 2 telegr. from you yesterday, Lovebird. We are enchanted that you saw our *Company.* —

3 people of »Paté« come to bring *Alexei* an apparatus and some films. — Baby improves playing on the *balalaika, Tatiana* also had a lesson yesterday, — I want them all to learn to play together, it wld. be charming.

Sweetheart, I must end now. God bless and protect you and keep you fr. all harm. I cover you with fond, longing kisses. —

Ever, Huzy love,

Wify.

No. 238.

Tsarskoje Selo, March 31-st 1916.

My own sweet One,

I hope you will find this letter upon yr. arrival to-morrow. How glad I am that all went off so successfully and that the weather got warmer. —

Mavra and Hélène dined, A. Olgas chill prevented her coming, — Christophor arrives to-day. Hélène read to us a most interesting letter she received fr. Vera, all about the last terrible days they went through in Montenegro and their marvellous escape. She writes so cleverly and full of life, — a regular nightmare, poor thing. — Mavra wanted you to send for *Igor* so as to get him away from a bad, fast set here, Ella Benkendorf etc: she will speak again to *Varavka* about the boy's health. — A lonely homecoming to the *Headquarters* again, poor agoo wee one, I long to hold you tightly in my arms and to cover you with kisses, — and you? —

Now I know *Vladimir Nikolaievitch* and *Danini* are working out plans for this institute of *Feodorov* and the plans will be sent to him and *Voyeikov* to choose, — but please, tell *Feodorov* that I must see them, as may have ideas to propose, — and I beg of you to i n s i s t upon Ania being permitted to buy that bit of ground she chose (10 to 12,000) and wh. *Voyeikov* knows about. Only he wont stand up for Ania, he is not a real friend of hers when it does not suit him. You give him and *Feodorov* your and my order that she is to be allowed to buy that bit of ground now they need not have it, only have ample place next to it. Its opposite the photographers, where the Baron fell into the water, a little higher up and she could have some green there. *Voyeikov* arranged the buying and selling of those grounds with a man and is obstinate and very angry that A. and *Putiatin* spoke about it and looked at the ground and arranged with the man that they (she) would like to buy it for her invalid hospital-house. Before she has the money for building, she can already plant vegetables, wh. will be a profit to her *refuge.* I dont want *Vladimir Nikolaievitch Der(evenko)* and *Feodorov* to be greedy. So you give that order — *Feodorov* will remember it. Both things are under my protection, — so *Voyeikov* can give *Kharlamov* (I think thats the man's name) the order to sell the bit Ania chose already before we had thoughts of that ground for the medical Institute (and there is ample place still), so as that she can buy it now and he can write to her, we both wish her to have that ground to buy (or we can give for Easter it to her, 10 to 12,000, as you think) — only please have it done at once, and don't let them cheet her. —

Excuse my bothering you, but I know she is in all states about this ground and its good she has that work to think about and the plans and the planting etc. —

We leave the house before 10, as at 10½ is the consecration in town of the little church in my school *Popular Artcraft.* Then 12½ lunch at *Anitchkov.* At 2 Olga has a committee and receives offerings. I shall probably go to the *store* with *Tatiana* or hospital in the palace, or to *Nikita.* He is getting on alright. —

A bright morning, — I wish had not to go to town, its always so tiring such an expedition. —

You will feel dull when Dmitri leaves again. Css. *Palei* wrote me a long letter, begging you to keep him away fr. the regiment, because his health is so bad and he so sad to go.

If one could find him work of some sort to do, or send him to a sanatorium for 2 months complete rest in good air, — only not town, or dawdling about. —

Now must get up and dress, Goodbye, my very own Treasure, my joy and sunshine, my very own Precious One.

God bless and keep you. I kiss you with unending true devotion and remain, yr. own old

Sunny.

No. 239.

Tsarskoje Selo, April 1-st 1916.

My own sweet One,

Now you are back again at the *Headquarter* & I fear, will feel awfully lonely. And to stand all alone during those lovely Church services will be sad, — have you at least got Georgi with you? —

I have the window a little open & hear a little birdie chirruping away, at *Gatchino* the first little blue flowers are out; its beautiful this sunshine & so calm to-day.

Olga wrote to you all about our doings in town, — I must only add where Tatiana & I were, whilst Olga was in the Winter Palace. We drove to the new little *Bari* Church of the »*Skoroposlushnitsa*« & saw the lovely Image there, — such an ideally sweet face & one has such a nice feeling when praying before it, — I placed a candle for you there & at the *Kazan* Virgin too, where we went. I send you a tiny Image I brought back from there, — you have already many, but when you read the inscription behind, it may help you in your heavy tasks. — Then to the *store,* went right through it, — alas, not very many people. — Sat then at Xenias, — for years I had not been to her & so found changes in her room. Nikita is getting on alright.

Have not slept very well, that happens when I am overtired & everything aches, therefore shall remain lying this morning. —

Had news from *N. P.*, says its spring there, lots of birds, 25 storks even arrived. Kirill spent a week with them & seemed sorry to leave. In the mornings they rode to the different *Companies,* wh. are several versts away, — watched the shooting. They have not yet been excercising as the roads are impossible & everything under water. After luncheon they walked in the garden & then went off again, — & in the evening bridge. The *Companies* make their devotions by turn, — my little Church is in a *barn* & so quite cosy & not cold & can stand without caps. *The priest* is happy to have more services, as *Polushkin* did not much care about it, — & on board ours are accustomed to it. I am going to get a small *holy winding sheet* for them & my lancers to send out. —

He is awfully happy that old *Ivanov* will be with you. — I remember him always hinting to me how good it would be. — If all is quiet, hopes to come about the 16-th for 5 days. — *Groten* turned up for a few days here & *Kussov* too it seems. —

Passed *Linevitch* in town, — *Dobriazgin* in a vile, small *fur-cap.* Oh Lovy, how sad the »*willows*« all alone! I hate to think of you without any of us, — those at the war have all their men & comrades around them, — you carry all the weight & have such dull people with you. I yearn after you, miss you more than I can say, my One & all, my Life, my Sunshine, — my Own, very, very Own. —

Shall sit in the garden this afternoon whilst the children work & before that go in to *Znamenia,* — feel quieter when have carried my prayers there to her, for you, my Angel.

Lovy, why dont you get a. d. c. from different regiments to come & do their duty with you for 2-3 weeks, it would be an honour to them, times are still quiet & they could tell you interesting things during your walks, — gayer than *Valia, Kira* & even *blissful Mordvinov* & selfsure *Voyeikov,* — please squash the latter sometimes, he needs it, is too awfully contented with himself, it puts me out every time I talk to him. Dont let him again speak against our Metropolitan, & pay less attention to what he says, — there, I meddle again, but he is a man

I always found needs holding in hand, & being watched. He is not amiable enough to others & thinks of his personal safety, position I mean, first.

Goodbye my Manny dear, my Boysy sweet, Huzy love. Feel my loving warm presence & prayers near you when you kneel with your candle & »*willows*« in yr. hand. I cannot imagine our not spending these great days together.

May yr. life & reign also turn from anguish and misery to glorious sunshine & joy & holy Easter bring its fathomless blessings. —

Farewell, Sweetheart. We shall make our devotions as usual, — but it will be awfully sad without you.

I gather you to my breast & hold you in tender embrace kissing every loved place, with fondest, most complete devotion. God bless you

yr. Own.

No. 240.

Tsarskoje Selo, April 2-nd 1916

My own beloved Sweetheart,

Oh, what an unexpected joy it was when Madelaine brought me yr. precious letter, I never thought you would find time to write. — How deadtired you must have been yesterday after that endless war-council. I hope you were contented with all the plans. — As you liked that sweet English book, I am sending you another by the same author, wh. we also like. It is also charming & interesting; tho' not as sweet as the Boy. Yes Lovy, it reminds one of 22 years ago, & I would give much to be alone with you in such a garden, its so true; every woman has in her the feeling of a mother too towards the man she loves, its her nature, when its real deep love! —

I love those pretty words & how he sits at her feet under the tree & he has such a lovely, sunny soul, »my little boy blue«.

We all of us read the story with wet eyes. —

Paul comes to us to tea to-day, I suppose Dmitri will turn up to-morrow, if it does not bore him.

I lay out on the balkony yesterday & Ania read to me, — to-day I'll sit near the children whilst they work.

Marie is in a grumpy mood & grumbles all the time & bellows at one, she & Olga have B. — Olga has become better humoured I find, it shows she is feeling stronger. —

I feel still awfully tired after town & ache all over. Must be back at 4 for a *report* with *Lili Ob(olensky);* amongst others, I saw *Baron Kussov* for 10 m. yesterday, full of questions, looking brown & well. —

Shall read over your letter lots more still.

Through *Groten* am sending to-day 3 small *winding-sheets* for his regiment fr. Baby, for the lancers & *Guard Crew* fr. me. — Shall think of you quite particulary this evening when we get our »*Willows*«, oh sweet One, God bless & protect you, all my tenderest, passionate love fondly surrounds you & I long to hold you tightly in my arms & let your head rest upon my breast like in bed & feel your sweet loving presence, & to cover you with kisses. Ever Huzy mine, yr. very own old

Wify.

No. 241.

Tsarskoje Selo, April 3-d 1916

My own Sweetheart,

Several times I have again reread and kissed your dear letter, I received yesterday, yes, — its like talking and a whole week without a word in your own handwriting was sad (tho' most comprehensible). —

How one would sometimes like to relive happy, peaceful moments as those when we were alone, together with our beautiful love, wh. every day brought new revelations. These constant partings wear out the heart, because one suffers so, but the sweet words in letters, wh. you, silly old Boy, are shy to use except in the dark, fill my heart with silent bliss and make me feel younger and the few nights we spend together now are so quiet and full of loving tenderness. Always being inseperable for years, one loose the habit of showing ones tenderness and feelings, whereas now one cannot keep them back they bring such untold consolation and joy. —

Marie wrote to you all about the nonsense on the ice. I went into *Znamenia* and placed candles and brought some flowers to the Virgine. — Paul took tea with us, to-day Dmitri and we have A. Olga and Christo for Church and luncheon. D. came with that rotten Marianna and A. in the train, in despair to go back to the regiment and all the more before the holidays, finds it no use being in the regiment, no work and constant drinking. Longs to go to the Caucasus, to be sent down there to see something else in a warm climate and with some order to fulfil. And disappointed not to have been left at the *Headquarters* with you. Oh these young men of the family with bad health and love of pleasure instead of duty! Felt so sad without you in Church, I was not last year either. The boys will only be out of quarantine for Easter I fear, — such a bore. But the men sang very well, masses of soldiers and people were in church, when we left there were still heaps waiting to approach the Image and receive their »*willows*«.

How was *Brussilov?* Did he speak out his opinions and did they seem good. I do wonder whether he is capable to fill such a responsible place, God grant it! —

How grateful we must be, that those aeroplanes were got to move off, you were in a precarious place, — hang them, they prevent you going further to the front and *trenches.* — The papers say William was wounded at Verdun by *shell-fragments,* is it true, I of course dont know. — Here I send you a petition (through Paul) fr. Mme Speier, perhaps one can help her a little? Paul begs you to remember General *Novoss.* — He longs for a place, hoped for Tougaku's place, but that is to great a one for him, I think, but as ex Garde à cheval, Paul asks for him some place.

You will be in despair when you see this big envelope, but its the *report* of Ella's *home for young volunteers* and she asks whether you would allow Alexei to be the *protector*. Therefore I send you the paper, only just to look through it, let *Mordvinov* read it and tell you if he finds all correct and then let me know, whether Baby may be named the protector and I shall send a wire to Ella for Easter announcing yr. sanction. The paper kindly return.

Aunt Olga was very sweet, Christo looks the same as ever, a big fat Boy. Came over London, Paris, Switzerland, Berlin, Sassnitz. — Says untrue all one said about Sophie, she kept herself very quietly and did not scream out her feelings, never left the country. Tino's wound has never healed up and every day the Drs. have to clean it and change the *tube*. A. Alix he found as well as ever, Minny very busy with her hospitals at Harrogate. — They were delighted with our Churches, showed them also the little one.

Glorious, warm sunshine, so we shall go for a drive. Dmitri comes to tea. Sweetest Love, precious Darling, Goodbye and God bless and protect you. Will you be going to Church twice daily? Do you make yr. devotions, or is it difficult at the *Headquarters?*

All my thoughts surround you in endless love, Treasure. Fondest kisses fr. yr. ever deeply loving and devoted old

Sunny.

No. 242.

Tsarskoje Selo, April 4-th 1916

My own Beloved,

I was so glad to get news of you through Dmitri, only we saw him quite short; he came at 10 minutes past 5 & left at 10 m. to 8. Hartmann is in town & he hopes he will allow him to remain on for the holidays. He wont ask, but he will make him understand his wish. Sad, how he dislikes going to the regiment & does not like the commander & the officers I think neither — all his comrades were killed. He looks better than when you left, & was in good humour. — We drove through *Tiarlevo,* the road already perfect — very little snow in the woods & one feels spring in the air — but there was rather a sharp wind. I fetched A. at her house, slipped on her balkony & came down with a great bang. Jumped up at once, but am bruised & achy — my hands were in my muff — too idiotic — & some wounding were standing opposite & saw the sight. But my hat, a very big one, did not move luckily — so absurd. — Mme Zizi sat with me for an hour. She does not feel famous, such *flow* of blood to her head, wh. make the back of her head ache, the whole left side of her face & arm, & she fears a stroke like A. Eugenie — it does begin so. So one gives her strong purgatives & she eats no meat — poor dear, it makes her so nervous & every worry makes her feel worse. — A. read to us in the evening whilst we laid patiences. D. said that the people on the railway said you would be coming for 3 days

— if true it wld. be too beautiful for words. — I know *Voyeikov* told Ania he could not understand why you wld. not do it.

Well, all lies in yr. hands & how you think right, & I will not meddle in any way.

Its grey this morning, & only 1 of warmth — I shall remain at home or lie on the balkony, don't want to be shaken about, as feel a bit achy fr. my fall, (a bump besides on the knee, wh. is most uncomfortable when I kneel) & the left arm feels heavy & uncomfy. — I am glad I have not... — there, I was disturbed, had to choose eggs & don't know what I wanted to write. —

Old Kundiger's brother, Heinrich died. — We have Church at 2 & 6½ as usual — the girls go before to the hospital. —

Will you make *Alexeiev* G. A. d. c. for Easter? — How is old Fredericks, not too gaga? How I wish we had somebody in view for his place. —

Do get yr. a. d. c.'s to do duty with you, now they have nothing to do, later it will be more difficult for the commanders of regiments to get free. I hate your loneliness at the *Headquarters* & yr. dull people. —

I cannot say how intensely happy I was to receive yr. precious letter, upon our return from Church. The sweet little blue flowers I put into my gospel. I do so love to get little flowers fr. you, they are a token of such sweet love. Not every husband wld. think of sending his old wife flowers. The first blue ones this year. I hope you get good walks & that one wont bore you too much this week. — Can imagine how lonely you feel with none of your own near you — if *N. P.* were near you I shld. feel quieter, as he is a man you are so accustomed to, can bang when you want, understands any joke — have lived so much together all these years — & your people are really such bores. — Am so happy & awfully touched that you wear my image, may it bring you blessings & helps & consolation & let you feel my presence always quite close to you. — Ah, I too have such a deep great love filling my heart for you & such a yearning to be together. Baby was in my *prayer-house* with me, the girls in Church. Ania outside at the door. Goodbye Lovebird, Sunshine — me is so sad & feel your absence intensely, & hate your loneliness. God Almighty bless & protect you. Endless kisses, Darling, fr. yr. very own old

Wify.

No. 243.

Tsarskoje Selo, April 5-th 1916.

My own sweet Treasure,

To think of you sitting all alone over a small puzzle, — its quite »*not necessary*«. Ah my poor wee One, it shows your loneliness. I understand after this heaps of work & reading you have to get through & people to see, — such a harmless occupation is a rest.

We don't either lay patiences now, & to-day I began drawing on wooden eggs, — with specks on. Cannot knit or hold my work comfortably because the left hand shakes & arm aches. Myself I smeared it for the night with white jodine & then put a hot compress on & bandaged it beautifully & tidily with my right hand, — I was quite proud of it.

All through the service I had to think of you, all the prayers & yr. favorite lovely passion-week singing, — I cant understand your not being near me, — & somehow I have the feeling that I carry you in my soul & bring you to God with all my love. — How Christ must suffer now, seeing all that misery and bloodshed around. He gave up His life for us, was tortured and calumniated, bore all & shed His precious blood for the remittance of our sins. And how do we all pay it Him back, how do we prove our love & gratitude? The wickedness of the world ever increases. During the evening Bible I thought so much of our Friend, how the *bookworms* & pharisees persecute Christ, pretending to be such perfections, (& how far they are from it now). Yes, indeed, a prophet is never acknowledged in his own country. And how much we have to be grateful for, how many prayers of His were heard. And where there is such a Servant of Gods, — the evil crops up around Him to try & do harm & drag him away. If they but knew the harm they do, — why He lives for His Sovereign & Russia & bears all slanders for our sakes. How glad I am that we went all with Him to Holy Communion the first week in lent. — You don't want a book so as to follow the service in? I can send you mine if you would care to have it, as I use the one wh. belongs to the *prayer-house* now. — I have had the foot-stool placed again next to my chair for Alexei to sit upon, — but on my right side the corner is, oh, so empty!

Our Friend writes so sadly, that as He was driven away fr. *Petrograd* there will be many hungry ones there this Easter. He gives such a lot to the poor, every penny he receives goes to them & it brings blessings too to those who brought Him the money.

A grey morning & slightly snowing.

I send you a petition fr. the wife of a *colonel Svetchin,* who asks her son to be placed as candidate for the pages corps. The boy's grandfather was promoted to general after he had left the service as a reward; the father commands the *6-th Finnish Rifle Regiment.* Your chancelry answered her it cld. not be done, so through Ania she sent this, as a last trial to see whether you wld. not allow it. Her husband has the gold sword & *Vladimir* 3-rd class.

Am sorry to bother you with these petitions, but perhaps you could write a word on them & send them to yr. chancelry. — The other is fr. a widow asking for help.

Here Lovy, I send you 8 Eastercards for the Children, Olga & A.; perhaps you would send them on Friday already.

I have sent still to *Uralsky* for eggs & shall make a small choice for you to-morrow, as it will give more pleasure if you send the eggs, and they will know they come fr. & were chosen by you.

For yr. precious letter my very tenderest kisses and thanks. Lovy mine, you can go to another Confessor when are in another place & *Father Alexander* wld. perfectly well understand it — if you do, wire it directly to me, & I shall tell it the Priest at Confession & yr. scruples, & I feel convinced he will only rejoice with you, as he knows how much you need that strength & blessing now, — & to go with *Alexeiev* & yr. people would be a special blessing to them & yr. work. If *Shav(elsky)* speaks about our Friend or the Metropolitan, be f i r m & show that you appreciate them, & that when he hears stories against our Friend, he is to stand up with e n e r g y against all & forbid their talks & they dare not say he has anything to do with the Germans — & he is generous & kind to all, as Christ was, no matter what religion, as a real Christian should be. And once you find His prayers help one bear one trials, & we have had enough examples — they d a r e not speak against him, you be firm & stand up for our Friend.

Do go to Holy Communion, we shall feel quite together then. — Thank God, things are going so well in the Caucasus.

What you tell about Misha is strange — I know Dmitri & he had some conversation & correspondence & they probably settled this together. One suffers in one's relations & their lack of feeling of duty — as poor Olga too.

Petia lunched with us & talked after & cried, poor Boy. He begs me to tell you, that he goes to-morrow straight to *Ai-Todor,* as wld. be to painful at *Ramon.*

Must end. Blessings & kisses without end. Tenderly do I beg yr. pardon for word or deed, wh. may have displeased or caused you pain & believe it was not done willingly. Ever Sweetheart, Treasure, yr. own old

Wify.

No. 244.

Tsarskoje Selo, April 6-th 1916.

My own sweet Darling,

I send you a book and collection of eggs wh. I think would please the children and Ania. — Several times I have reread your dear letter and kissed it over and over again.

Yes, it must be a fine sight, the inundated country before you and the immense river now. —

How splendid Trebizond has been taken by our splendid troops — I congratulate you with all my loving heart. It makes me sad that all the luck is down there — but the good will come here too in time. —

My arm is better, but aches still a bit — but its really nothing at all, and nobody notices it. Kneeling on the bruise has made it every colour of the rainbow.

Baby was awfully cheery and gay all day and till he went to bed — in the night he woke up from pain in his left arm and from 2 on scarcely got a moments sleep, the girls sat with him a good while. Its too despairing for words and he is already worrying about Easter — standing with candles to-morrow in Church, and holy Communion, poor little man. It seems he worked with a *dirk* and must have done too much — he is so strong, that its difficult, for him always to remember and think that he must not do strong movements. But as the pain came with such force in the night and the arm wont bend.

I think it will pass quicker — generally 3 nights pain, but perhaps God will mercyfully make it pass quicker — its too hard about Baby Holy Communion. I hope he will sleep now — she wires to *Gregory*. — I shall finish my letter after luncheon, by then can say more about him. Perhaps one can bring him Holy Communion upstairs.

Ania probably cant go before Saturday as B. came. *N. P.* telegraphed to her that they go to-morrow too; *Rodionov* is coming to town. — Grey morning. — The big ones are in the hospital and the little ones have gone to the big Palace hosp: so as to have the afternoon free to sit with Baby and we can paint up there our eggs.

Oh such thanks, Lovebird, for yr. sweet letter, tender words. Yes, indeed I shall think of you quite especially during confession and Holy Communion. Its more than sad we shall not be together this great moment but our souls will be. Once more Darling, forgive me for everything, everything. — Feel awfully sad and lowspirited to-day and cried like a Baby in Church. Cannot bear when the sweet Child suffers and know what it costs you. But Mr. Gillard said it came as sudden and terribly strong as on board — and then it passes quicker. — He is sleeping. — We had a bit of the Metrop. choir in Church *(The Priest* and A's doing, I did not want, as knew they wld. sing differently, and so they did). But our boys are ill all the time — really they might separate ours for *Tsarskoje Selo* fr. the others, when there are such a lot of them. —

How nice going up the river must have been — always nice beeing on the water — I hope *Grabbe* photographed. I have not been out these days, so as to keep quieter on account of Church. —

Now my own beloved Treasure, Goodbye and God bless you, I kiss you without end — and shall feel you so, so near me. Oh how I love you, long for you, beloved One. — Think of Coburg and all we went through these days.

Ever yr. very own old

Sunny.

No. 245.

Tsarskoje Selo, April 6-th 1916

My own beloved One,

I begin my letter still to-night, after once more having reread your sweet letter. The afternoon I spent in Baby's room painting, whilst Mr. G. read to him or held Foen. He suffered almost the whole time, then would half doze for a few minutes & then again strong pains. Eat next to nothing. Reading is the best thing, as for a time it distracts the thoughts when the suffering is less great. I hope he will have a pretty calm night. He confessed with the two youngest & *the priest* will bring him Holy Communion like last year. A. dined with us & remained till ten — she had been all day in town & motored back. — Sat with Tiny after dinner, poor wee one. The swelling is not much & less than in the night, so I hope it will soon pass. Seeing him suffer makes me utterly wretched. — Mr. G. is so gentle & kind with him & knows exactly how to be with him. — We had confession at 10 — sad without my Angel & I miss you quite horribly — do wish you had gone to Holy Communion & *the priest* agreed. — After, I read through *the reports* & arranged some Easterpackets. There was a colossally thick fogg this evening. —

Now its very late, so I better bid you goodnight. I know yr. prayers will be with us & I carry you with me. God bless and protect you. I cover you with tender, yearning kisses — in thought clasp you tenderly to my loving old heart, stroke and caress you & whisper of deep love. —

April 7-th. Ever so many fond thanks, my own sweetest Darling, for your beloved letter and telegram. Missed you awfully in Church this morning. Service was lovely & such a blessing & I prayed & longed for you quite unspeakably. The sun was shining splendidly & drove the fogg away. — Then *the priest* brought Baby the Holy Communion. Thank God, he slept much better, woke up only once, or twice for a short time. He would not touch anything even no water before Communion, wh. he partake only towards 11½.

He is far brighter to-day — we took tea with him & are going to lunch there too. I lay upstairs painting, whilst Mr. Gibbs read to him & then came down to finish my letter & change. After lunch shall go for a short drive as the air is so divine & go into *Znamenia* to place candles for you, sweetheart, & our Sunbeam.

Fancy, *Silaiev* receiving the »*Erivantsi*«*!* Yesterday I asked *Vishinsky* & he said he did not know who his successor would be. — They had hoped for a guard officer, as for one fr. there its difficult generally, as they either side with the Russian or *Georgians*. But I am glad for *Silaiev* & as his health is now better on the whole; at least if he can have the honour to command for a time. — Precious One, more than ever shall I think of you to-morrow, the 22-nd anniversary of our engagement — dear me, how the time flies & yet how vividly one remembers every detail. Unforgettable days & the love you gave me then & ever since. Its sad not to spend that day together & feel your warm kisses & live through all again. God bless my One & all & thank you over & over again for yr. endless, tender love wh. is my life. —

Goodbye now Lovy, Huzy mine, the letter must go.

I cover you with kisses & remain yr. very, very own

Bridy.

All the children kiss you awfully tenderly.

No. 246.

Tsarskoje-Selo, April 8-th 1916

Christ has risen!

My own sweet Nicky love,

On this our engagement day all my tenderest thoughts are with you, filling my heart with boundless gratitude for the intense love & happiness you have given me ever since that memorable day, 22 years ago. May God help me to repay you hundredfold for all your sweetness.

Yes, verily, I doubt there being such happy wives as I am — such love, trust & devotion as you have shown me these long years with happiness & sorrow. All the anguish, suffering & indecision have been well worth what I received from you, my precious bridegroom & husband. Now-a-days one rarely sees such marriages. Your wonderful patience & forgiveness are untold — I can only ask God Almighty on my knees to bless & repay you for everything — He alone can. Thank you, Sweetheart & feel my longing to be held in your arms tightly clasped & to relive our beautiful bridal days, wh. daily brought new tokens of love & sweetness. That dear brooch will be worn to-day. I feel still your grey suite, the smell of it by the window in the Coburg Schloss. How vivid I remember everthing; those sweet kisses wh. I had dreamed of & yearned after so many years & wh. I thought, I should never get. You see, as even then, faith & religion play such a strong part in my life. I cannot take this simply — & when make up for sure mind, then its already for always — the same in my love & affections. A far too big heart wh. eats me up. And the love for Christ too — & it has always been so closely linked with our lives these 22 years. First the question of taking the orthodox faith & then our two Friends sent to us by God. Last night gospels made one think so vividly of *Gregory* & His persecution for Christ & our sakes — everything had a double meaning & I was so sad not to have you standing by me.

Last year I was in the afternoon near Ania's bed in her house (our Friend too), listening to the 12 *Gospels* — a part of them.

To-day at 2 *the carrying out of the winding-sheet* & at 6 *the burial. Loman* begged upstairs instead of the night, as then none of the soldiers can go.

And you alone at the *Headquarters* — ah Sweet One, I cry over yr. solitude!

Baby slept well, woke up only 3 times &, I hope, will be up to-day, as he badly wishes to come to the *morning*-mass but without you I cannot imagine that great and holy feast. Think its Wify kissing you 3 times in Church, I shall feel yr. kisses too & blessings. —

I send you the petition of one of Aunt Olga's wounded men. He is a Jew, has lived since 10 years in America. He was wounded & lost his left arm on the Carpathians. The wound had healed well, but he suffers fearfully morally as in August he must leave, & looses the right of living in either of the capitals or other big towns. He is living in town only on the strength of a special permit, wh. a previous minister of the Interior gave him for one year. And he could find work in a big town. His English is wonderfully good, I read a letter of his to little Vera's English governess & Aunt Olga says he is a man with good education, so to speak. 10 years ago he left for the United States to find the opportunity to become a useful member of human society to the fullest extent of his capabilities, as here it is difficult for a Jew who is always hampered by legislative restrictions. Tho' in America, he never forgot Russia & suffered much from homesickness & the moment war broke out he flew here to enlist as soldier to defend his country. Now that he lost his arm serving in our army, got the St. George's medal, he longs to remain here & have the right to live wherever he pleases in Russia, a right the Jews don't possess. As soon as discharged fr. the army, as a cripple, he finds things have remained the same as before, & his headlong rush home to fight, & loss of his arm has brought him no gain. One sees the bitterness, & I fully grasp it — surely such a man ought to be treated the same as any other soldier who received such a wound. He was not obliged to fly over here at once. Tho' he is a Jew, one would like him to be justly treated & not different to the others with similar losses of a limb. With his knowledge of English & learning he could easier gain his bread in a big town of course; & one ought not to let him become more bitter & feel the cruelty of his old country. To me it seems one ought always to choose between the good & bad jews & not be equally hard upon all — its so cruel to my mind. The bad ones can be severely punished. — Can you tell me what decision you write on the petition; as Aunt Olga wanted to know. —

4 big eggs are for:

1. *Father Shavelsky,* 2. *General Ivanov,* 3. *General Alexeiev,* 4. *Admiral Nilov (Fredericks* already has one).

12 small eggs:

1. *Voyeikov,* 2. *Grabbe,* 3. *Dolgorukov,* 4. *D. Sheremetiev,* 5. Silaiev, 6. *Mordvinov,* 7. *Kira,* 8. *Feodorov,* 9. *Zamoi,* 10. *Pustov.,* as he works with you always.

Our Friend wired to me »*Christ has risen, is a holiday and a day of joy, in trials joy is brighter, I am convinced the church is invincible and we, its children, are joyous with the resurrection of Christ.*«

My head goes round, & during my writing one interrupts me & I have to choose eggs & write cards, so as to send off most things to-day — after all lots have to get things — & now must get up for luncheon at 12½, & after that shall finish my letter. — I send you my little Eastergifts — the bookmarker for the novels you read. — We lunched near Baby's bed in the big room, he feels rather giddy fr. his medicines — but will get up later. — The Image I thought you would perhaps all kiss in Church & then it will be a double remembrance. The egg is ***hand-made,*** can hang with yr. war Images in Church if you don't know where to put it. Its grey & now raining. — Your sweet blue flowers are too nice, thanks a w f u l l y for them, the Children & I love them & I gave some bunches to the ladies, who were quite delighted. — Baby fears he cant go to-morrow night & that worries him.

1000 thanks, Lovebird, for yr. sweet letter — I shall at once let Aunt Olga know about the Jew. *Sturmer* comes to me this evening. —

Yes, me loves oo, my little Boy Blue & already 31 years & belong to you 22. —

Now I must end.

3 Easter-kisses, blessings without end, my own lonely Angel, whom I love so endlessly — oh, your sad Easternight — shall miss you more than words. —

Ever yr. very own old

Wify.

I send you a »Sketch« of Baby for you to keep at the *Headquarters* — later can have it a wee bit arranged — & I send you *Stredlov's* photos he made, lovy.

I shall tell Ella you find the work very well done, only please, wire to me at once, may Baby be Protector, then shall telegraph it to her to-morrow, or will you, — please. —

Must be off. These flowers bring all my love. —

No. 247.

Tsarskoje-Selo, April 9-th 1916

Christ has Risen!

Sweetest Darling,

Three very tender Easter-kisses & blessings. I do so wonder how you will spend these feast-days — all alone amongst heaps of people. All my thoughts incessantly surround you, & I do wish we were together to meet this great holiday, but the joy of your precious letters must be my consolation.

I send you a matchbox fr. Mme. *Khitrovo.* The big egg is from the *Stroganov* school — they sent me an ideal one too — perhaps Fredericks might wire Globa thanks from us both. The picture Ella ordered a little painter to do for you & she hopes you will have it always with you when you travel. — The verses on the card I send you are written again by Mme *Gordeieva.*

My brain goes spinning round fr. all there has been to do again — sorting out things, the services, tho' I sat or knelt were also very tiring, tho' lovely — & I have a slight cold. —

The sun peeps in and out to-day — I want it to remain out & let Baby get some air. I fear this night will be too tiring for him & yet he longs to go. —

Rodionov came for four days & leaves to-morrow — so we asked him today to tea. *N. P.* lets them all off for a few days now.

Tchistiakov sent a postcard fr. where they live — & his staff, in a lovely property wh. originally belonged to *Koublitzky's* wife's family; now very rich people have it. Big lake, terraces & steps down to it. — Now they have put my little Church on the terrace & there they took holy Communion on Thursday whilst aeroplanes were flying over their heads & our artillery & the *Crew's machine-guns* were firing at them, but the shells burst far away. Every day they fly & they threw bombs onto the town, not far from the bridge. During service masses of storkes promenade about close by & marry before all eyes — *the priest* forbids the sailors looking about during service (wh. is most tempting there), so they tease him, that he at least looks through a chink of the little Church. —

They say its so warm & *N. P.* says you wld. enjoy ideal walks in the woods & along the roads & rowing on the lake. They heard & my lancers too that you are going to inspect the guard now. — Does *Silaiev's* nomination come out to-morrow? —

Babykins is going out & then intends colouring eggs, is very cheery — hope, the little sketch will have pleased you.

For the 6-th I intend another picture being made, & you must choose fr. the photos more or less wh. pose pleased you best — tell me the No. only. Of course one must never do completely en face, as no face is completely regular & one eye is bigger than the other. —

Ania goes to holy Communion this morning. *Sturmer* in town too. —

I must end now as shall be having to get up for Church — I shall go half an hour later, as service is very long to-day. — Excuse dull letter, but am cretinised.

I bless & kiss you without end, my own sweet Sunshine, my Joy & Life, dearest of husbands. —

Ever yr. very own old

Wify.

General-M. Fok who died from wounds, was he not the hero at Port-Arthur on the railway engine?

When was he wounded?

The relief & joy was great yesterday, when I read that our dear troops had arrived safely at Marseilles & just for Easter.

God bless them & may they do great deeds & have immense success on French soil. —

Do wire to our Friend for Easter, *Novy, Pokrovskoye, the government of Tobolsk.* 1000 tender, touched thanks for yr. awfully sweet words on the card — I shall wear it in my dress against my heart in Church to-night to feel your love, blessing & kisses with me. —

No. 248

Tsarskoje-Selo, April 10-th 1916

Christ has risen!

My own sweet One,

A blessed Easter to you, peace in heart & soul — strength for all your work & success & rich blessings.

I kissed your photo three times last night & this morning — the big Image, on wh. you are three times. — Your card lay on my breast during the whole service — cannot tell you how unutterably sad I felt the whole night, such pain in the heart & with difficulty kept back my tears — your loneliness is too hard — God bless & richly recompense you for all your sacrifices.

Just got yr. beloved letter & dear flowers. — Fancy that sinner *Rostchakovsky* having turned up — yes, I also found him calmer & much older — his wife is an angel of goodness & patience, A. Olga says — as his character is trying. —

You sweet ramoli, you forgot what I wrote out to you on an extra paper, that Ella asks whether Baby can take over the protectorship of that school of little hero boys of the war. —

How did you like the picture of *Alexei,* the sketch of *Stredlov?* How nice that you 4 carried the *winding-sheet.* —

Oh Pussy, *M. B.* is sure to come to-morrow! —

The 5 Children walked round last night & I sat on the top of the stairs (in a chair, not on the Churchsteps) — a lovely sight, only I dont like fireworks & crackers whilst the Priest is singing & saying prayers before the entry. Baby had lovely pink cheeks as he had slept before. He went home after the Easter service & broke fast with *Derevenko* & *Nag.* — we did with Ania after mass, 10 m. to 2. — One had to wake him at 10½ he was sleeping so fast this morning. The *Easter congratulations* was fr. 11—12.

Now Maria & Anastasia go to their hospital, & then I go with the 4 girls to our hospital — Olga is the whole time grumpy, sleepy, angry to put on a tidy dress & not nurses for the hospital & to go there officially — she makes everything more difficult by her humour. *Tatiana* helped me with the eggs & yr. men — so unnatural all without you. — Can you kindly give over the eggs I sent you.

Ania wore yr. egg & was enchanted with it & yr. card. — Must end.

Goodbye & God bless you. 1000 tender kisses fr. yr. very tired old

Wify.

No. 249.

Tsarskoje Selo, April 11-th 1916

My very Own,

Sweetheart mine, I wonder whether it is true that you are arriving on Wednesday at 3? *Voyeikov's* officer Rostovtzev told it privately to Nini that her husband is returning then. Nini told me the guard had been warned you were going to inspect them one of these days, so Sophie F.'s boy was recalled to the regiment yesterday evening. These are all the »*rumors*« wh. buzz around, but fr. the chief person, you Lovebird, I know yet nothing, so wait quite patiently & send this letter. — . . . .

Three days I am fighting with a cold — beastly nuisance, as it may make my face ache again.

Again grey weather, the second day already. Am tired & head rather aches, so have not gone to Church — this afternoon at 2 *Easter kissing* in the big palace, over 500 people & then below in the hospital. — It went off alright in our hospital yesterday, we remained there an hour.

To-morrow I must go to the red cross & *Matthew Hospital.* — So tiring when not well & cannot keep the heart up with medicines.

Sweet Angel, fancy what joy if you really do come now, the best treat of all my heart, my Sunshine, my radiant Love!

Easternight Baby kissed all the clergy in Church — & will his 101 officers (I hope) to-day. — I am dreading saying goodmorning & congratulating the men to-day. Probably in a smaller hall, as I said. — The blue flowers look charming in a big flat bowl. — You remember the primroses we picked these days at Rosenau? Oh, yes I remember *U.* Alfred dropping granny's stick & being rather »tired«. —

I live in the past & the poetry of it all — & long for the hero of those days to return, to clasp him tightly to my bosom & cover him with kisses. *Olga Evgenjevna* wrote & begged me to give you over her best Easter-wishes. — Thats good you get your rows on the river, good exercise at least. — Georgi met Easter with my lancers — such a nice idea! *Taube & Shesterikov* said, that your 1-st rifles were full of hopes that you would see them on their feast day. Everybody wants to see my Treasure, & I understand them & share that wish. — Morning & evening & when I rest in the afternoon I kiss the words on yr. Easter-card — your hand lay on it & you wrote all those dear words to your little woman & they must warm me up. Cant' bear your being alone, such pain. —

There is that lovely little French song I have, wh. Emma F. gave me. »Partir, c'est mourir un peu, c'est mourir à tout ce qu'on aime« etc. — so true — one feels an inner death when bidding goodbye! —

Baby slept splendidly again — woke only at 9 & continued till 10. — He has grown paler fr. the pain & no sun, feels very sad without you! —

Now sweetest of Husbands, my very own Treasure, Lovebird mine — my bridegroom that was — goodbye & God bless you. Ever yr. very own wife

Alix.

1000 burning kisses. —

Yr. card & telegram rejoiced her heart colossally & she loves the egg — I enclose her thanks. —

Endless thanks for yr. sweet letter & heavenly news that you are really coming, oh what bliss indeed, joy untold. — Excuse vile writing, I am eating, they are making an unearthly row & teazing the wolf atrociously. —

Fancy our beloved Standart's being there. Yes, for the soldiers the monogram eggs are best — tho' they love the flowers too. — Hope you can without hurrying see the guard in different places, more interesting & less stiff.

Goodbye my Manny — my Angel love, I kiss you without end, every tenderly beloved sweet place & the beautiful big eyes — write it I may, you cant stop me. —

No. 250.

Tsarskoje Selo, April 24-th 1916

My very own Beloved,

Sweetheart, I cannot tell you what your dear presence has been to me, the light & calm you brought to my heart, as without you everything is harder to bear & I miss you always beyond words. Your tender caresses & kisses are such balm & such a treat — I always yearn for them — we women long for tenderness (tho' I do not ask for it nor show it often) — but now that we are so often separated I cannot help showing it. I live afterwards upon the sweet remembrances. — God grant we shall soon be together again — you tell it privately to *Voyeikov*.

Please, see the guard before as they are so impatient to present themselves — & then to go together to the south would be splendid.

Now you will get a certain sort of rest, as these days here are really a torment to you — people fr. morn. to night with you, fidgeting & bothering. I am so glad our Friend came to bless you before leaving. I think He will return home as soon as A. has left. — What weather! O my Love, my Own, my Soul, my Life, my One & all — fare well. I hold you tightly clasped to my heart & cover you with kisses. God bless & keep you & guard you fr. all harm.

Ever yr. very own

Wify.

No. 251.

Tsarskoje Selo, April 25-th 1916

My own Boy Blue,

How do you like that, my sweet One? Yes, I love the book & shall bring it with me & read the tender passages when sad & heartsick. — I do miss you so, so much, Lovy mine — yr. lonely journey is yet worse. — Marvelous weather again they are putting up the marguin outside — it will be darker in the rooms, but the sun spoils the furniture. —

We went all over Baby's train, you had seen it already & there is a little commemorative plate on the wall. Schmidt was there & persisted in speaking French, *Trepov* too — we had to wait till 3 as the train had been sent to the *Alexander* station to wait. Very clean — a sweet little Church with bells too — 299 wounded soldiers & 6 officers — I gave medals to the worst. — Then I lay on the balkony till 6. — A. came for an hour — her humour is rather aggressive, aggravated to see me little these days, that has much to do, people to see, that did not scarcely see you; so that in some respects it will be a relief when she goes. —

We dined out & then I motored with the Children to *Pavlovsk* — heard the first nightingale.

She came back from town in the evening. — I am writing with another pen, as am in my mauveroom. Was ever so happy to get yr. dear wire fr. *Smolensk*. — Our Friend told Ania about one having shut up *Sukhomlinov that »it is a bit not well«*. — Such marvelous weather, our wounded all lay & sat out on the balkony & in the garden, even the worst, the sun being the best cure, & then morally it does them good. — Sweety, you won't forget to speak to *Voyeikov* about *Bressler* (Ania gave you her private letter fr. him about his brother). —

We are going to the hospital of the *Alex. community station* in the barracks of the *convoy* & I shall give medals to the worst. Visiting hospitals in the heat is somewhat fatiguing & the heart beats hard. —

Must end, my Sunshine, my joy. — We all kiss & bless you. I cover you with kisses & miss you horriblly, my Angel — you did take the fortress, you sweet Boy Blue & she was like yr. very own

Wify.

No. 252.

Tsarskoje Selo, April 26-th 1916

My very Own,

Another splendid day, such a blessing; but the night was cooler & there is a breeze this morning. —

We had *N. P.* & *N. N.* to dinner & sat out on the balkony till 10½ — at 11 they left to catch their train at the *Alexander* station. Missed you so much, reminded one of the bygone. — In conversation *N. P.* told me of an idea one had proposed (probably banker, but to my mind excellent) — that one should a little *later* on make a loan in the country for a milliard to build railways of wh. we are in sore need. It would be covered almost at once, as the bankers & merchants, who are colossaly rich now, would give big sums — as they understand the gain.

Then by this one would find work for our *reserves* when they return fr. the war, so as not to let them at once return to their villages, where discontent would soon begin — & all must try to avoid histories & disturbances by thinking out means of occupying them beforehand & for money they will be glad to work. The prisoners can begin all. — And thus one can find heaps of places for wounded officers along the line, at the stations etc. Don't you agree with the idea — you & I once had it, do you remember?

May I speak of it to *Sturmer* when next I see him, so as to work out a plan how it might be done & he can speak to *Bark* about it? — We had an operation — appendicitis to-day. — This afternoon I shall remain, on the balcony, as my heart is tired. — As you finished the Rosary, I send you the continuation, you will find the same people again in this book. — When do you go to the guard? Have you thought about our journey?

Is it not beastly the Breslau shot at *Eupatoria* — our wounded must have got a good fright. — Sweetheart, I must end now. I miss you more than words can say & yearn for your kisses. God bless you.

Ever yr. very

Own.

Noo. 253.

Tsarskoje Selo, April 27-th 1916

My own beloved Sweetheart,

My heart leaped with joy when Tudels gave me your precious letter upon my return from the hospital.

The air was terribly heavy, my heart ached & made me cough so, & left arm ached; felt the thunderstrom wh., thank God, came, and passed by, heard it twice in the distance & it poured, all has become much greener. It will lay the dust for A's journey & all our wounded, — when the train leaves is still not yet settled, they change every minute on account of the movement of the other trains — probably at 7. —

Great excitement in the hospital & Ania full of fidgets. —

Placed my candle for you at *Znamenia.*

Petrovsky came to the hospital to say goodbye. —

Yesterday *Tolia B.* came & did not know what to do, whether he would find yout at *Moghilev* or not.

So glad, you can row again on the river — that one arranges a tent in the garden. — When do you go to the guard? Heart & soul l o n g for you. —

You cannot imagine how wildly my face ached again yesterday, whole afternoon & evening ever, — since the motor drives it has been preparing. Today its better. —

Goodbye, Sweetheart, I bless you & cover you with passionate kisses. What joy to meet soon, I hope! —

Blessings & thousands of kisses, Huzy mine.

Ever yr. very, very

Own.

No. 254.

Tsarskoje Selo, April 28-th 1916

My own precious Darling,

There we are into winter again — everything white and snowing hard, I am so sorry for trees and bushes, wh. after yesterday's rain had become so green. — It will be less tiring for going to town, that is true. I take the four girls with me to see the English hospital in Ella's house — in the evening their *unit* leaves for the guard. — Then we take tea at *Anitchkov.* I cant take Baby as his left leg is bent all these days and one must carry him — he has no pain at all and its getting better and he is careful on account of the journey. —

I wonder, why you have not left yet for seeing the guard, they are all so impatient — and now the weather has suddenly changed. —

I send you the report about the little Dr. *Matushkin* of my 21 Siberian regiment — last winter he was in our hospital. Cannot he present the papers again to the *St. George Cross,* as it seems to me most unjust he did not get the cross — tho' he is a doctor, he did the work of an officer. —

Well, that was a *trial* for Ania yesterday — never could one settle when my sanitary train wld. get to *Tsarskoje Selo* from town to pick her up, — after endless changes, we at last took her off there after 6 and went all over the train, found lots of our and big palace hosp. officers, and from town, Gebel's son too — and soldiers → 5 of Ania's poor wretches too and 5 sisters going to *Livadia* to rest, and some wives accompanying their husbands. — *Viltchkovsky* went too so as to look at all the sanatoriums of the Crimea belonging to our *Tsarskoje Selo station* and *Duvan* went. Ania had a whole court to accompany her, *Zhuk, Feodor Stepanovitch, Korenev, Loman* takes the train. She is placed in his charming compartiment with her maid in the sisters waggon — her wounded are right at the other end. At 7½ at last they left (she was utterly wretched) — and when going to bed I got a letter from her fr. town, saving that they would stick there till 10½ — God knows when they will reach *Eupatoria*. She sends you many loving kisses, but had no time to write these last days of fidgeting.

No, what a snow. — I did not sleep well, something went wrong with my minister of the interior. —

We spent our evening working, and Olga and I read aloud change about an English story we had begun long ago and forgotten all about it.

What do you say to *Nikolasha* having presided the opening committee *»on the question of Zemstvos in Trans-Caucasia?«*

I see by the papers that *Grevenitz* has died — what will become of Dolly, I wonder. —

Just got your beloved letter, my Treasure, and I thank you for it with all my heart. Yes, Lovy certainly we shall take the marcheroute reaching *Moghilev* at 2, otherwise we should have no quiet time before Church. What joy to meet in a week!

That is good *Feodorov* watches your pulses, as all hearts are not equally strong and too much rowing against the current may harm them — they need gentle training.— You say, Motherdear probably leaves Saturday — here nothing is known, so for safety sake Ressin sends the soldiers and cossacks off to-day — *Zina* neither knows and all are in trances, as its difficult to arrange quickly, especially now. —

Ah my Boy Blue, me's coming soon to gather him to my breast and to cover his sweet face, eyes and lips with tender kisses!!! —

Oh, those 2 poor dogs! Do you remember *Iman* and *Shilka* at *Peterhof*, when we saved them?

Its after 12 and still snowing and blowing, the sun tries to break through, but has not yet succeeded. —

How is it you dont go to see the guards yet? Will one arrange to stop at *Vinnitsa* on the way south, so as that I can see my *store* there?

If I know the date beforehand, I can let *Apraxin and Mekk* know to be there then. — If you have any rough plan, let me know please, as we must calculate for our linen and clothes; and then can we go to Eupatoria by train, not all the waggons fr. *Simferopol*, one wld. be less tiring and we could lunch in the train, see the Sanatorium and Ania.

Have you thought about giving the order that the *Vladimir* Virgin fr. the *Uspensky Cathedral* should be brought to the *Headquarters?* Now I must get up and dress. — Goodbye and God bless you Sweetheart, little wify misses you terribly. I cover you with burning kisses and rest yr. head upon my breast.

Ever yr. very own old

Sunny.

No. 255.

Tsarskoje Selo, April 29-th 1916

My own Boy Blue!

Warmest thanks my treasure for yr. dear letter just received & for poor little Olga's. I fully understand & deeply feel for her — but had to put all before her, for your sake. Of course one can only long for her happiness at last — but will she gain it thus.

May I ask our Friend, of my accord, whether he would think it better for all reasons it should be now or after the war? I shall see him to bid goodbye a second in Ania's house, as he wants to bless me before the journey; & then you can answer her. I saw Xenia at tea yesterday, — she also leaves south on Saturday & wont probably see me before the talk. *Volodia Volkonsky* told her now & to *Petia* he said better after the war — he is such a man, tries to please all parties, the same as he does in the corridors of the Tauride. Been snowing hard all morning & very damp indeed, the wounded & my cheek feel it. I went to our hospital this morning, now must receive. Then shall go to Ania's hospital & then *reports* — always busy. Baby's arm is also swollen (does not hurt) fr. the damp & the leg is not yet quite right. Pitty about the guards, but you have your reasons no doubt. — Excuse short letter but must receive. —

Precious Boy Blue, me loves oo, oh, so much & so endlessly. — God bless & protect you. I cover you with very, very tenderest kisses.

Ever yr. very Own.

Motherdear looks well, but thin & longs to get off, as perpetual receptions tire & bother her. She leaves on Sunday — so we all now disperse. —

No. 256.

Tsarskoje Selo, April 30-th 1916

My own precious One,

Very tenderest thanks for dear letter & the progr. of our journey, it seems quite good, shall I only have time to see any hospitals & *store* at Odessa? What a nice journey together — hang Becker for wishing to accompany me then. You better find out whether that rotten Plen has nothing to do with Boris' behaviour — do get that man away. —

To-day at last finer, warmer, the sun peeps in & out. — Baby looks thin & pale, left arm also wont bend well, but no pains & as soon as its warmer, its sure to pass. — Sat in the hospital, worked & continued teaching my little *Crimean* English & *Taube* talked like a waterfall. —

Christo comes to tea & *Tatiana's* Children, as I have not seen them since last summer.

The children are eating & talking bosh & laughing. —

Went all over Ania's hospital from top to cellar, kitchen & stables.

In the evening we work & read. — *Nikolai* has asked to see me — alone. — Cant imagine why, so shall see him to-morrow & *Sturmer* too.

We go to the big palace — (so dull). Sweetest Treasure, beloved Darling, I do so long for you & your tender caresses. —

Awfully busy, tho' heart tired — strange enough, don't miss her a bit, can't understand how that is. — Pss. *Odoevsky* comes to me now & two wounded officers who return to the front. What real news from the front?

Goodbye my Treasure — sorry dull letter. —

Metropolitan was very nice yesterday, shall tell you our conversation, nothing particular. —

Fondest kisses, Huzy mine.

Ever yr. very, very own old woman

Alix.

No. 257.

Tsarskoje Selo, May 1-st 1916

My beloved precious One,

From all my loving heart do I send you these lines again. Yesterday, no, to-day a week that you left us — it seems ever so much longer & I am counting the days when we shall meet — 4 have remained.

I again did not sleep famously & my left »*ternary*« *nerve* of the face began aching, an awful nuisance — now its better. — Were in church yesterday evening, its so empty without you, but I feel our prayers are together & all our thoughts.

Fresh, windy, sun & rain change about — for Baby sunny weather is so essential, he is quite pale again — you both need the sunny south. —

Excuse my bothering you with petitions, but our Friend sent them me. —

Ania arrived last night at her destination. —

I have nothing interesting to tell you, perhaps after *Nikalai M.* has been — he asked to see me alone, cannot simply imagine why. — Then I have *Yoantchik* & *Putiatin* with the plans for the Church.

The last days there is always so much to do & see to & finish off before leaving.

»Do you love his mouth, his eyes, his hair«. Yes, my little Boy Blue, I do, & I long to press my kisses tenderly & passionately upon them. — Sweet Boy Blue, with that deep true love! —

Tenderest thanks Sweetheart, for yr. precious letter. What a nuisance you have so much to do, my Treasure, & I too am disappointed for you, the guard- & *N. P.* who were longing for you to come.

Snow, rain, hail & sunshine, strong wind, nuisance & my face aches. — Find it a shame about Souchoml. as if he wld. dream of running away. — Thanks for sweet forgetmenot. —

Well I had Nikolai for an hour — very interesting about the letters he wrote you etc. & he wants me to talk all over with you. I am very tired after it, but he meant & spoke well (tho' I don't like him). Now I must send this. Its snowing hard & we are going to Maria & Anastasia's hospital.

Goodbye, Sweetheart, Boy Blue — ah, could I but help you more & be an adviser & of real, real use to you.

I bless & kiss you without end, my one & all.

Ever yr. very own old

Wify.

No. 258.

Tsarskoje Selo, May 2-nd 1916

My own beloved Treasure,

Grey and windy, despairing weather as my cheek continues aching — the left one now, and I slept badly notwithstanding a compress & it is a little swollen. In my sisters *kerchief* it hides it. —

Last evening we were for two hours in our hospital to cheer them up, as our departure grieves them. —

Well, *Sturmer* found the idea about the *loan* for railways ingenious & just the right moment, as all grumble now about the railways & will sooner give money. He will send me *Bark* at 5. — Then I spoke of *Sukhomlinov* — he said Frederiks got a letter (like mine probably) fr. the wife, but he said it did not concern him to speak to you of it & gave it to *Sturmer,* who showed it to the Minister of Justice. The latter wrote a whole answer why it had to be, & *Sturmer* thought of bringing it to you now but I said you wld. have no time to receive him these days & he will ask for an audience after yr. return, he has never been at the Headquarters. He did not wish to grieve you about *Sukhomlinov* as he knows you liked him. So I asked him to speak again to *Khvostov* whether one could not keep *Sukhomlinov* in another place at least, not there & *Khvostov* comes to me at 4½. Look at me with all the ministers suddenly. —

Sturmer has nothing in particular — only if you receive *Rodzianko* (one sees he goes to you) do tell him you wish insist the *Duma* to finish her work in a month & that its the place for him & all the rest to be in the country & see to their fields. — He does not approve of the question of *Zemstvo* for the Caucasus as is sure they will always fight — the different nationalities — I thougt you did not agree, but according to yr. answering telegram to *Nikolasha,* you wish them luck. — Paul took tea with us yesterday, — is waiting for news, so I said you have sent for *Bezobrazov* to talk over things concerning the guard. — Ania writes she lies on the beach in the sun, that its like a dream, like paradise, people bathing all round. Am going to our hospital — hang the cheek! —

1000 thanks lovely card, sweet words — so you too have cold weather, disappointing. I am bringing *Vladimir Nik.* till the 7-th (except Mr. Gillard of course) — for safety sake as we travel for 27 hours its safer, tho' his right arm is again alright, the left leg also much better. — Fondest blessings & warmest, tenderest kisses, Lovebird.

Ever yr. very

Own.

Soon, soon together.

No. 259.

In the train, May 17-th 1916

My own Beloved,

In a few hours we shall part — our lovely journey together at an end! Oh, I hate saying goodbye to you my both treasures, sunshine & sunbeam & feel already a heavy, sore heart. But its a comfort to know that you are together & so you will feel less lonely & Baby will bring life into yr. so dull life. —

The lovely south did him good — you get him to play in the sand without making too strong movements.

Wonder, when we shall meet again?

Sweetest One, it has been a dream, these 10 days & so cosy being next to each other — & such sweet remembrances of all your love & tender caresses wh. shall sorely miss at *Tsarskoje.* — Our hospital will be my consolation; if only the weather is nice. —

Goodbye, my Angel, my own Sweetest of sweets, little Boy Blue with his great big heart.

God bless & protect you & Babykins — kiss him very tenderly & think of me when you say prayers together.

I hold you tightly & yearningly in my arms & cover you with kisses.

Ever yr. very, very own little

Sunny.

A kiss.

No. 260.

In the train, May 18-th 1916

My very own Sweetheart,

All my heart's thoughts are with you my both treasures; miss you sorely — had my lonely luncheon wh. was very quiet & sad without Sunbeam's lively prattle. — Its nice the book, is it not? I am glad you know so many of them now, they do one really good, so healthy, simple & warm up the lonely heart. — When I got up yr. dear telegram was brought me. It was horrid saying goodbye!! — Spent the whole afternoon & evening till 10¼ with Ella, who then went to try & get some sleep till Moscou — 2. 15. — I took tea with all, so as to be able to speak with her people. At *Kursk* I received the handsome new governor. —

I have finished my third piece of embroidery since this 2 weeks' journey & feel quite proud. — The 2 youngest & Olga are grumbling over the weather, only 4^{0} & they said one saw one's breath out of doors, — so they play ball, to get warm or play on the piano — Tatiana sows quietly. But the sun shines at least brightly. —

Yesterday, whilst still warm & Tudels was arranging my compartment, we sat in the saloon — the girls sprawling on the floor with the sun shining full upon them so as to get brown. From whom have they got that craze? Now you like the heat, but not when you were their age; & I run away fr. the sun — tho' the air in the south did me good I think, as there was always a breeze. —

Our last stoppage now & *Valuiev* has come — the platform close & the exact hight for all to look in, so I quickly had to draw the curtain.

I am not yet dressed & quite in bed till 2, so as to thoroughly rest. — Babykins I am sure keeps you all gay & now 2 sweet campbeds stand cosily together. —

I shall give this to the Feldjäger who goes on to town, then it will reach the other in good time. — I slept well, thank God & got throught this journey much better than I ever expected. —

To-morrow Tatiana & I have our regimental feasts. — Lovy, tell *Sturmer* to come now, speak about the railway loan; & let him know to bring *Sukhomlinov's* journal & letters to his wife, wh. are compromising, better you should see for yourself & judge rightly & not only go by their words — they can have read in another sense than you will. — Then, remember please, both the Metropolitans with *Volzhin,* upon yr. return here. Tatiana's birthday May 29, Anast. June 5, Marie 14-th — now Heart of my heart, my Own, my Sunshine sweet, whose caresses I yearn for — Goodbye & God bless & keep you. 1000 of endless, tender kisses.

Ever yr. very, very

Own.

The 4 girls kiss you very much. —

No. 261.

Tsarskoje Selo, May 19-th 1916

My own Beloved

Ever such tender thanks for yr. dear sweet words on the card. Bless you, my Treasure. I miss you 2 quite awfully, therefore am glad to be in our hospital instead of at home. Well, yesterday *Vespers* in the hospital itself ½ an hour, & then sat & talked with all. Spent the evening quietly working. This morning 9½ to the hospital Church & then to our wounded. *Karangozov* turned up, *Anushevitch, Yedigarov* — last moment, so have invited him to dinner — leaves to-morrow & came only so as to see us, such a dear — we were all shy & silent, meeting after 15 months, — here it will be better. — After luncheon went to *Te Deum* & cup of chocolate to my lancers' hospital. All the ladies were there, *Baranov, Trubnikov* & one or 2 old ones, but not one active one, all are in the regiment. Then to *Lianosov* hospital to see *Silaiev;* have told him by your order to go to *Sebastopol* for a cure at the *Rom. Institute,* 2—3 weeks; he wanted to return to the regiment, wh. I told him, was absolute folly — so by yr. order he will go in a few days. Its quite essential I find. —

1^0 of frost in the night — sunny & cold — small oakleaves, lilacs not thinking of coming out. Must quickly send this off, else the man wont catch the train.

Blessings & tenderest kisses, sweet Angel, fr. yr. very own little

Wify.

Tenderly I clasp you to my breast with endless love. —

No. 262.

Tsarskoje Selo, May 20 1916

My own Beloved,

Ever such tender thanks for yr. dear card I received upon my return from the hospital. I do wish it wld. get really warm at the *Headquarters* — to-day its better.

I have a long *report* with *Rostovtzev* & then *Shvedov,* so fear I shall again not have time to go out. I placed a candle for you my Sweetheart at *Znamenia, Yedigarov* was very dear, kept him for 2 hours & he told us a lot of interesting things. Dear me, how difficult & hard it is for them in that terrible heat, & the wretched horses suffer awfully & never any rest.

We bid him goodbye this morning at the hospital, *Raftopolo* & *Shah Bagov* also were there; — I photographed them all. — I send you 3 photos. I took in April when you were here. Its so nice being with them all & I feel the loneliness less than here in my rooms. —

Botkin was an hour with me & has still not yet finished all about *Livadia* & *Yalta* hospitals, to-morrow morning he will continue his *report.*

Irina lunched with us. —

How do you spend your evenings? Always reading, poor wee One? But Tiny must be a consolation & bring life into your solitude, I am sure.

Happily I keep alright, so can get about more, this fresh weather keeps me up. — Sweetest of Sweets, dearly beloved One, I cover you with tender, burning kisses. God bless & protect you & help you in all your undertakings.

Ever yr. very

Own.

The girlies all kiss you very fondly; — they have gone out driving with *Irina.* Bow to *Igor* fr. me; — speak to him about his sister Tatiana. —

No. 263.

Tsarskoje Selo, May 21-st 1916

Sweetheart beloved,

I cover you with kisses & thank endlessly for precious letter. Yes, Lovy, its true what you say — when apart one doubly realises that one has not sufficiently appreciated the many marks of love, wh. one has taken as natural & usual. Now every caress is a double treat & terribly longed for when not to be had. —

I send you & Baby each a pansy. Dear, can you give the enclosed paper over to Frederiksy — poor M-lle Petersen has really nothing to live upon — her old Aunt left her 50.000 — that means 2000 a year for lodging, food & clothes — if she could have got 2000 yearly fr. you, *Katia Ozerov* says it would be a Godsend.

Can you have it done as an exception — they did behave too badly sending her off without a penny & nowhere to live — life so expensive now. — What is the news about the English naval battle — awfully anxious to know whether Georgi was out too on the New Zealand & wh. English ships were sunk. —

Maries & Babys trains have been sent for to *Pskov*. Olga says she has much work now, many wounded again.

Sorry, you have again such a lot to do. —

Were in hospital — operation.

Zizi lunched, now *Mekk* comes with *report;* — so must end. —

Blessings & very tenderest kisses, sweet Angel, fr. yr. very, very.

Own.

No. 264.

Tsarskoje Selo, May 22-d. 1916

My own Sweetheart,

From all my loving heart I send you thanks for yr. beloved letter — how I love all you write! Me too longs for Huzy's fond caresses and soft, warm kisses! —

Its warm, grey and trying to rain. We were in Church, then Isa and Nastinka lunched. After my letter we go to the big palace and at 2 to the *Cross Procession* i. e. to the *Te Deum;* one has brought the miraculous Image of St. Nicolas fr. *Kolpino.* — Yesterday we spent the evening cosily in the hospital. The big girls cleaned instruments with the help of *Shah Bagov* and *Raftopolo,* the little ones chattered till 10. — I sat working and later made puzzles — alltogether forgot the time and sat till 12, the Pss. G. also busy with puzzle. — Its more cosy than at home now. — I am sorry to bother you again with a letter fr. Mme *Sukhomlinova.* — The other paper is fr. one of the wounded who returns to the war, but is anxious to know about his decoration. —

Silaiev leaves to-day. We took chocolate with them yesterday — his brother and wife (hideous) too, *Shah Bagov* and *Raftopolo* too. —

Shuvaiev comes after — Betsy *Sh.* —

Always heaps to do. —

Heart bleeds to think of all the losses at sea — all those lives done for — oh such a tragedy! —

Now must end. Goodbye, my one and all.

Blessing and kisses without end, Nicky mine fr. yr. very, very own

Sunny.

One says Kitchener comes the 28-th here or to the *Headquarters.*

No. 265.

Tsarskoje Selo, May 23-rd 1916

My sweetest Treasure,

Over and over I thank you for yr. precious letter. I always get them when I return fr. the hospital and read them at once, and then still later on several times and kiss them with fond love.

We at last lunched on the balkony — ideal weather — everything now quite green at last. —

I drove with the big girls to *Pavlovsk* yesterday and the smell of the birches was divine — now I am going again with 3 of them, whilst *Tatiana* rides (I envy her this joy). — I just saw Misha Grabbe. — Yesterday Betsy sat with me for an hour. One says you wished her to be one of the sisters to go to Germany and this disturbs her as she cannot speak German and is tired and does not find herself capable for such an undertaking. I told her I was convinced you never chose her, but that one proposed her and you said yes, and that you wld. perfectly well understand her not going — and that I wld. write you all this. She was much consoled. —

Our Friend begs very much that you should not name *Makarov* as minister of Interior — a party wants it, and you remember how he behaved during the stories of Iliodor and Germogen and never stood up for me — it would indeed be a great mistake to name him. —

I spent yesterday evening in the hospital. — Have Mlle *Schneider* with a *report.*

Must end now, Lovy dear. God bless you, my One and all — I cover you with kisses,

Ever yr. own old

Sunny.

To-morrow I shall be 44!!!

No. 266.

Tsarskoje Selo, May 24-th 1916

My own precious Huzy,

Tender thanks for your sweet letter. — I think Fred. is mistaken about Mlle Peterson. Her sister is married to a Bavarian (Monjelas, I believe) and this is her son who is our prisoner here, to whom she therefore sent presents (very natural) and no brother at all. They behaved very badly to her, thanks, Darling, for saving her. —

Very hot indeed, I am roasting on the balkony and ramoli — had 2 reports fr. $1\frac{3}{4}$—$3\frac{1}{2}$ and am cretinised.

The operation was rather long but went off well, I gave the instruments.

Thats nice Sweety, that you told *Shavelsky* about the Image to be brought now, — thank God the news was good — such a comfort! Wonder, whether my *Crimeans* have been fighting?? —

Touching *Shipov* sent me a soldier with flowers he picked on the 14-th under fire, had blessed them and sent for my birthday. —

Of course you cannot move now, I felt sure it would be so — well, we had our treat together and my old birthday does not matter — its really to-day.

Very sad I am, you wont probably see the guard, why did they keep you fr. seeing them before they were moved off! —

What about Paul I wonder? He comes to tea. —

Beloved, I need no present yr. love is m o r e to me than anything you might have given me — yr. letters are such a joy to me. — Yesterday afternoon we drove to *Pavlovsk,* to-day I prefer keeping quiet. — Now I must end, heart and soul are with you in endless love and prayers.

God bless and protect you, give you strenght and success.

Ever, my One and all, yr. very own old

Wify.

I cover you with burning kisses. —

No. 267.

Tsarskoje Selo, May 25-th 1916

My own beloved Angel,

Quite grey, colossal downpour — will refresh the air. Lunched on the balkony. Ever such tender thanks for your dearest letter, Sweetheart.

All your loving words warm me up, I miss you sorely — such lonely nights! -- How awful about Kitchener! A real cauchemar, & what a loss for the English. Were in Church — to tea come Miechen & Mavra.

Paul took tea yesterday, is full of hopes to get his nomination.

Going to Church met Misha, stopped, talked a minute & than he went back to *Gatchina,* — not a hair on his head, completely shaved off. —

Excuse dull letter, am cretinised. —

Mary congratulates you many times. Children are driving, I must answer telegrams. At 7 see our Friend in little house.

Believe *Kolenkin* has new nomination; all hope very much, that the *Horse-Grenadier* (of course have forgotten his name), who has been a year in the regiment, will receive it — you know him. —

Ania has sent you photos. Let me know if you got them safely, as she was anxious about them. —

Must end now — blessings without end.

S o happy good news — God grant will continue.

Kiss you fervently with ever increasing love, my Boy Blue, yr. very

Own.

No. 268.

Tsarskoje Selo, May 26-th 1916

My very own Sweetheart,

I send you my tenderest thanks for yr. dearest letter. We saw our Friend yesterday & he is so happy over the good news. Was delighted that we had fine weather & several showers yesterday, says its a particular blessing of Gods on ones birthday — repeated it several times.

He had just returned fr. Moscou — saw *Shebeko* & had a good impression of him, thinks he will be good in his place. —

Begs very much if you receive *Volzhin* & *Vladimir,* also to send for *Pitirim* with them. Says the peasants, cannot choose a suitable priest, that one cannot allow. — Says for Ania wld. have been good to have remained on still a bit at E. only if she continues fretting, it will do her more harm, than good. I fear she returns in a week. Its noughty to say so, but its been a holiday without her as I cld. do what I liked without having to combine & arrange things & hours to suit here. She dislikes our hospital & disapproves that I go often so how I shall do when she returns & will want her afternoons & evenings above all with me — I don't know. The Children make grimmaces already. — Miechen was in a vile humour she left last night for Minsk with her train & then to inspect her organisations in other towns. — for ever jealous with Ellas organisations, & tries to do the same things wh. don't concern her & make too many alike. — Fine days but clouds. Going to big palace & for a drive. — Blessings & endless, longing kisses fr. old

Wify.

Sending you flowers & for the table & Williams.

No. 269.

Tsarskoje Selo, May 27-th 1916

My own Beloved,

The good news makes my heart rejoice for you quite especially, such a comfort and recompense for all yr. hard work and patience. To me its like a second war we are beginning again and may God bless it and all act with wisdom and forethought. —

In the hospital one says after they have read the papers they scream hurrah with joy — they only all long quickly to get back to the war to help their comrades. —

Yesterday afternoon went to the big palace and then for a drive. At 6 I went for ½ hour to Ania's hospital to see them all and give her news. Keep the photos till we meet, they were for your album, Deary. —

Mine succeeded too and I have ordered duplicates. — Dined in as cooler and damp and I was afraid for my cheek. Spent the evening in the hospital. — Fancy yr. having made Baby *corporal* on the 25-th, its too sweet! — Botkin left for *Livadia* via *Eupatoria* fetch his daughter for his son's marriage at Abaza's estate. — Why do all your people fly off at once?

Benkendorf is delighted to have been called to the *Headquarters* and to be nearer the news — one longs for more details wh. of course cannot be given. I am glad Baby lives through these days with you — such great moments for his whole life. — I am, oh, so, so happy for you, Angel beloved. Endless love and tenderness surrounds you and in thoughts I cover you with kisses and press you to my heart wh. burns for love of you. —

A grey morning, the weather cannot make up its mind to rain or to let the sun break through the clouds.

With greed one throws oneself every morning upon the papers and with heartbeating — too much at times for the human — the joy and anxiety. —

It is true new regiments are being formed to send to France? —

How does Baby like *P. V. P's* letters, does he quite understand them? Yr. enemy, the crows, are making a vile noise opposite to my window. I must be getting up and dressing for the hospital — shall place my daily candle at *Znamenia* with tenderest love for you my one and all, my joy of joys, my Huzy dear!

The weather became quite divine. Sat in the hospital garden working whilst some played croquet. Now Tatiana rides, Maria and Anastasia are going to dig out weeds in the little garden, as they are spoiling the lilies of the valley; — Olga and I are going to a hospital and then to drive. —

Endless, tender kisses and fervent blessings Sweetheart, fr. yr. own old

Sunny.

Sturmer comes at 6.

No. 270.

Tsarskoje Selo, May 28-th 1916

My own Beloved,

I don't know how it happened, that I did not discover yr. letter till the afternoon when I opened all the big envelopes with *reports*.

My joy was all the greater when I read yr. sweet words. — No time for much to-day. For an hour having been reading *reports* & writing & now must be getting up & go to the hospital — have two heavy *dressings* to do. — Fred. & wife lunch, then must go to opening of a hospital for *refugees* children — & then look over the *Drozhdin lying in hospital* etc. to settle what hospital to build. — Ella wired the *Cross procession* with the *Vladimir* »*Holy Mother*« *(icon)* was most touching, great crowds. —

What good news again, ones heart rejoices & to-day interesting fine facts are mentioned, wh. is a good thing.

Glorions weather. Yr. group at the *Khadji Liman* succeeded very well, M-me *Sosnovsky* sent it me. — Drove yesterday afternoon with Olga — whilst picking daisys, Pss. *Palei* turned up — she has a birthday present just come for me fr. Worth (dressmaker in Paris) & wants to bring it me — what next? Wish she wld. leave me in peace. —

Now beloved I congratulate you with *Tatiana* who will be 19 to-morrow! How the time flies! — I kiss & hug you, press you to my yearning heart & whisper words of deepest love & devotion, Treasure Dear.

God bless you & yr. undertakings.

Yr. own old

Wify.

Tenderest thanks for beloved letter. —

No. 271.

Tsarskoje Selo, May 29-th 1916

My own dearly Beloved,

I congratulate you with our sweet *Tatiana's* 19-th birthday — how the time flies! Well do I remember this day at the farm. — The heat is quite tremendous — the rooms are far cooler, but I am lying on the balkony. My heart feels the heat & protests. Church-bells are ringing — service lasts so long to-day. —

Many thanks, Lovebird, for your dear card. Thank God, all continues well — where on earth are we to put these masses of prisoners — in Siberia there is ample place, only give orders that all should be quickly & decently, hygienically arranged for them, so as to be safe from epidimies. —

Such a surprise when *N. P.* telephoned that he had come for the day for affairs — so we got him to tea for a short hour, looks well & much thinner. They are standing in front of all the rest, told lots of interesting things, asked much after you; — wont return probably for very long now — was here 5 weeks ago with *Rodionov* who will also be coming soon for a few days. Says Kirill intends going out to see them soon. —

Zizi comes to tea as she leaves to-morrow for the country. —

I feel quite cretinised — have, alas, to go & look at a »*home*« & future hospital to give my orders. — Spent the evening in the hospital, but I lay back in a comfortable chair in one of the wards as was very tired. —

Excuse the unutterably dull letter. I bless & kiss you without end, my Own, my very Own. God be with you. —

Ever yr. old

Sunny.

Have you been able to bathe in the river? — Do you know how great our losses are? —

My tommy becomes impossible in this heat as every summer & gives me no peace. —

No. 272.

Tsarskoje Selo, May 30-th 1916

My own Sweetheart,

Very tenderest thanks for yr. precious letter. Really the good news fill ones heart with endless gratitude. How good you send the Image out to the front, may the holy Virgin give strength & wisdom to all to bless the final successes. What are our losses? Two of my *Crimeans* are wounded & they told a lot. — The heat yesterday was quite unbearable, so I took a refreshing bath at 6½ before resting. Early this morning there was rain, so that to-day it is quite ideal. We went to service in the hospital Church; as early & could do our *dressings* afterwards. — Shall go for a drive with the big girls now. Ania leaves *Simferopol* this evening at 8 o'clock — am sure she will miss the lovely sea, peaceful calm & all *Duvan's* kindnesses but she is mad to get home. Her Father leaves with the grandchildren to-day to the country. —

Mme Zizi took tea with us yesterday & has now gone off to her country-place for the whole summer. — Just now *Nikolaiev* (former *Crimean)* bid me goodbye, he is off to his 4-th *Ulans* again (near Segewoldt). He was so happy to have seen you at *Eupatoria.* — I suppose you have not yet begun the «Wall of partition» — I don't read a bit now, only work. —

Beloved Angel, heart & soul never leaves you. God bless & protect you & give you success — I cover you with tenderest caresses & warmest kisses. —

Ever Huzy mine, sweet Boy Blue,

yr. very own old

Wify.

No. 273.

Tsarskoje Selo, May 31-st 1916

My own Beloved,

From all my heart I thank for sweetest letter & tender words. I too have such a yearning after yr. caresses & love! —

Really the news is beautiful! Idiotical *Petrograd* does not nearly enough appreciate it. God bless you & our heroes — so glad the Image was gone to bless them all. The *mass* must have been very touching before the house — she brings them yr. love & prayers too & they will feel how near you are to them. A glorious day & cooler, wh. is a great boon after the colossal heat. — Placed my candles, worked in the hospital, now am going to drive with 3 girls whilst Tatiana rides. — Was *Purishkevitch's* train alright, please, tell me which Number, 1 or 2, as my *Crimean Sedov* has a sister in Number 2, & it interests him so much to know wh. you visited. — I have nothing of interest to tell you. —

When about will the guard be advancing? —

Beloved Treasure, prayers & thoughts ever surround you. I miss you, oh, so much. To-day its 2 weeks we parted at *Kursk!* How horrid it was. — God bless & protect you. I cover you with tender kisses, Huzy my Love, & remain yr. very

Own.

No. 274.

Tarskoje Selo, June 1-st 1916

My own beloved Treasure,

Ever such fond thanks for yr. sweet letter. Its a comfort to know our losses have not been so very great in comparison with what we have gained in every sense. That we have the weak point in the centre is comprehensible, but with care & reinforcements it will, with God's help be alright. — All think of you in the joy of victory, first thought of all the wounded is, — how happy you must be. Such a recompense for your intense suffering, patient endurance & hard work.

Its much cooler to-day, rained a bit. The big girls have gone to town, as Olga receives *offerings,* &, then they go to Tatiana.

The little ones are in their hospital & as soon as I have finished writing I shall fetch them for a drive. Ania comes to tea, she arrived to town alright. —

We worked in the hospital & then I went with Marie to the cemetry as there was a funeral *service* for little Sonia — already six months since her death. The birds were singing so gaily, the sun lit up her grave covered with forgetmenots — it made a cheery impression & not sad. — Pss. *Palei* came yesterday & brought me a very pretty chiffon thing to wear. She says Paul is full of excitement & quite well & the Drs. are perfectly quiet about his health. —

I too have had no time for reading, as were so much in the hospital, then received, drove, work & wrote. — I congratulate you with sister Olga. Two weeks that we returned & five that Ania left fr. here — the time simply flies. —

To-morrow shall have to be going for service to town, anniversary of Costia's death! — Think of my Huzy with great longing & intensest love. I cover you with tender kisses & press you to my heart.

God bless you my Angel. Keep well — am always near you.

Ever yr. very own old

Sunny.

No. 275.

Tsarskoje Selo, June 2-nd 1916

My own precious One,

A very tender kiss and thanks for yr sweet letter; how I love hearing fr. you, it warms me up to read yr loving words and I try to imagine I hear you saying all those dear words to lonely wify. —

Little sun to-day, but it was better for town. In the morning went for ½ hour to bid all good morning in the hospital. Like Babies they all stared at us in «dresses and hats» and looked at our rings and bracelets (the ladies too) and we felt shy and «guests». — Then with Olga and Tatiana to the fortress to mass. Oh, how cold that *family vault* is, difficult to pray too, one does not feel its a church at all. — Now are going for a drive with A. too. —

Yesterday afternoon M. A. and I got into a colossal downpour, so were out quite a little. In the evening I went to Ania for 3/4 of an hour and then joined the Children in the hospital. They were wild of joy as did not expect us at all.

The good news is such a boon and helps one to live. — Really Miechen! She can drive one wild — I have to see Witte to-day to speak over all, on her account, as she really is very pretencious — only one does not wish needlessly to offend her, as she means well, only spoils all by her jealous ambition. — Don't let her come bothering you and above all give her no promises. —

Sweetest Angel, I clasp you to my breast and hold you long and calmly there, whispering tender words of deepest love. — God bless and protect you. Holy Angels guard and guide you.

Ever, Nicky mine yr. very, very own old girlie

Alix.

Saw *Leo* the other day — looks very thin, but not so bad — wanted to begin his service, but I told him to wait still and pick up more strength. *Kondratiev* serves again, also very thin — I don't let him help at table so as that he should walk about less. — your Own. —

Ania was very happy over telegrams.

No. 276.

Tsarskoje Selo, June 3-rd 1916

My Sweetheart,

Please, change the N. in my yesterday's letter, I made a mistake, it ought to have been 507 only. — Fine & sunny & then suddenly clouds. — Spent the evening quietly. Ania sat with me, showed photos, & read to me, the children were in the hospital. She proposed to me to go, but I said I was tired from town & wld. remain quietly with her. — Had a long letter fr. Irene, Gretchen, Anna Rantzau. My poor Friend Toni's boy has been killed at the war (only 19, my godchild, went in 1914 already as freiwilliger) — was an excellent officer it seems already & received the iron cross — too sad for words, she adored the boy. — Aunt Beatrice also wrote & sends you her love — she imagines I am at Livadia, resting. —

Now I must get up & dress for the hospital.

I send you & Baby my photos, I took. The water is fr. the black sea, Ania had it filled for you & Baby & sends it with much love — the goodies are also for you from her. —

Please if you settle any thing about Miechen, have it written to *Senator Witte* or *Sturmer,* as it concerns the *supreme Council* & I feel she intends making a mess in going to you behind my back — a revenge wh. is ugly. —

I had just *Professor Rein* & a long talk — I have told him to ask *Sturmer* to receive him, to explain all, because really his work ought to be begun as you said, & Alek said you said all was to be put off. — Would you let him come to you some day, as when you are here you have yet less time. — Pouring cats & dogs. — Such warm thanks for sweetest letter. How charming the photos are, I have kept one. Goodbye, my Angel Love, God bless you. I love & kiss you without end. Yr. very, very

Own.

No. 277.

Tsarskoje Selo, June 4-th 1916

My own Lovebird,

From all my heart I send you tender thanks for yr. precious letter. Ania forgot to tell you, that our Friend sends *his blessing to the whole orthodox army*. He begs we should not yet strongly advance in the n o r t h because he says, if our successes continue being good in the south, they will themselves retreat from the north, or advance & then their losses will be very great — if we begin there, our losses will be very heavy — He says this is an advise. —

Becker has just come. I too throw myself upon yr. letters & devower them up & the children stand by, waiting for me to read aloud what is for them of interest — & then later I reread & kiss the dear pages.

Thats good the music passes through the streets it brightens up the spirits. — Am trying to get hold of *Zborovsky* (wounded through the chest, not too bad), *Shvedov* typhoid, *Skvortsov* wounded — with my sanitary train, *Yuzik* will help through *Kiev,* I told all to *Grabbe.* — How glad I am at what you write about the trains at last moving quicker with the troops — I assure you «where there's a will there's a way» — only not too many cooks to spoil the broth. — Just had long wire fr. Apraxin — my little trains are working hard at *Lutzk, Rovno, Rezhitsa, Tarnopol, Trembol., a branch of the Vinnitsa store at Tschertkov* all grateful, the military say they could not get on without us, thank God for helping us succeed. — Yes, Angel, we can fly to you some day to cheer you up with joy. — Pouring. — Emma, her Father & Ania lunched. — Spent evening in hospital, today at home. Endless kisses, burning love

God bless you. Yr. very Own.

No. 278.

Tsarskoje Selo, June 5-th 1916

Darling beloved One,

I congratulate you with our little girlie's birthday — fancy her being already 15, its quite sad — no babys any more. — Such cold, rainy weather only 7,8 degrees — we drove in thick coats and Olga is freezing. — From all my heart I thank you for your sweet letter. Shall send you still more photos, as soon as get them. — Really one cannot let Miechen mix up in things wh. do not concern her — she has become so grasping — military things are not her business. — Am sorry about Rein — he is right and Alek quite wrong, I see it clearly. — Ania has just left for Terioki to see her family and will be back by Tuesday afternoon. She forgot to tell you, that our Friend says its good for us that Kitchener died — as later on he might have done Russia harm and that no harm papers were lost with him. You see he always fears about England at the end of the war when the peace-negociations begin. —

He said that *Tumanov* is excellent in this place and has no wish to leave and is better than *Engalitchev* — I did not know he was to be changed. —

I asked *the priest* to have thanksgiving prayers, wh. he did after a short good sermon about our successes and the *Potchaiev* monastery being again ours, and how God harkened unto all prayers and so forth. —

Yesterday evening Ania read to me, whilst they were in the hospital. *Anna Alexeievna Korovtchuk* had a daughter 3 days ago, and I am going to christen it to-morrow. — Must send this off now. All thoughts, longing love, kisses, blessings, great yearning, Sweetheart.

Ever yr. very own

Wify.

Sweet Boy Blue!

Just got enclosed wire fr. my 21 Siberians — poor (?) am awfully sorry — such a nice man had St. G's.

No. 279.

Tsarskoje Selo, June 6-th 1916

My own Sweetheart,

I congratulate you with all my heart for our successes and the taking of *Czernovitzy* — thanks be to God Almighty. Only that we don't rush too wildly foreward — are we laying small railway lines to bring provisions and amunitions nearer to the front? I made *Tatiana* at once telephone the news to the hospital — the joy was immense. We spent the evening there. The little ones play games, the big ones with *Raftopolo* and *Shah-Bagov* prepare material for the *dressing-station,* I sometimes play a little and wander fr. ward to ward, sitting with those that lie — then rest in a comfortable armchair in little *Sedov («Crimean»)* room and work and talk, and then *V. Viltchkovskaja* brings a stool and sits at my feet and its very cosy à 3. Now another youngster who suffers awfully, lies next door and wants me also to bring my work and sit there, so that I shall be torn to pieces now. — Have little Mme *Kotzebu* (ex-lancer) after lunch, then the christening *Korovtchuk* and to see Olga's (Caucasian nobility) train. — Shall give medals to the worst and go through the whole train. *Princess Tzeretelli* (ex *»nizhegorodetz«)* is at the head of it. — Such loving thanks, Lovebird, for your very sweet letter and the delicious white acacia. I am glad my rifles also wired to you, brave fellows! —

Oh what weather! cold, grey, rainy — autumn simply. Excuse short letter but must receive. All my thoughts are with you and love of the deepest, deepest, Sweetheart. God bless and protect you. Cover you with tenderest kisses.

Ever, Nicky mine, yr. very own

Sunny.

No. 280.

Tsarskoje Selo, June 7-th 1916

My own sweet Angel,

Very fondest thanks for yr. dear letter. I think so, oh so much of you, my Pet, in yr. loneliness, tho' Sunbeam is with you. I miss you both more than you can guess and live over all your sweet tenderness. — The good news keep one up. Thank God the dear Siberians have been so brave again. —

At last sunshine and warmer so we could lunch on the balkony. Mavra, *Vera* and *Georgi* too as they leave for *Ostashevo*. She asked whether *Igor* was going to be sent out somewhere to the war in the warmer parts as you had once thought. — Worked in the hospital. The Commander of the *Tekintzi* my ex *Alexandrovetz* is with us. He was wounded in the foot during their splendid cavalry attack. He always wears their tiny cap. Interesting all he tells, he is very deaf fr. contusion and the heart enlarged. —

To-day at 4 we have the cinema you saw of *Sarokomisch* and *Trapezund* in the manege for all the wounded. —

Ania returns at 5 fr. *Terioki.*

Sweetheart, I press you to my heart and cover you with very tender kisses, God bless you — I love you b e y o n d words.

Ever yr. very own little

Sunny.

Zelenetzky brought me 96 r. from our sailors again, too touching. —

No. 281.

Tsarskoje Selo, June 8-th 1916

My own Beloved,

Many a tender kiss & warmest thanks for your sweet letter. I understand perfectly well that you wont be coming now for some time, your presence is too much needed. Thanks for the news about the plans, of course I wont repeat them. —

Sashka lunched with us — he has 3 week's leave & lives at *Tsarskoje Selo* with wife & mother — he has remained the same & teased Olga as usual. — Were in the hospital, now are going for a little drive. Yesterday evening I spent at home & Ania read aloud to me whilst I worked. The weather is so changeable, & my cheek in consequence is rather swollen. In my sister's dress its not seen & I can drive with a black shawl over my headdress — but to-morrow at the *supreme Council* I wont be very pretty. — The roses I send you come from dear *Peterhof,* the sweetpees fr. here, they smell so deliciously that I must send you some. — I think of you so much, my joy & happiness & cover you with passionate, tender kisses. — The cinema of *Erzerum* & *Trapezund* was interesting, some pictures very pretty, others so dark that one scarcely saw anything; — must have an amusing one once for all, so as that the men can laugh; — heaps looked on. —

Now my Huzy dear, my Own, Goodbye & God bless you. Excuse my dull letters, but, alas, have nothing interesting to tell you. —

I send you all that is tender & fond — clasp you in thoughts to my breast & let you rest yr. sweet head upon my heart.

Ever yr. very Own.

No. 282.

Tsarskoje Selo, June 9-th 1916

My own Lovebird,

Tender thanks for yr. dear card Benkendorf just now brought me; I am glad he found you both looking so well, tho' the weather also bad & even out at the war. — We are off to town directly to the *Supreme Council* & back to tea, as Paul comes to bid us goodbye, he leaves to-morrow. — Were in the hospital, yesterday evening too, so I sat an hour with her before as she seemed rather hurt I went — tho' understood it, — this evening she will spend with me. —

I see by the papers Motherdear goes about, has been to the old Branitzkaia at *Belaya-Tserkov,* I think. — To-morrow our prayers will meet at *Tobolsk.* Lovy, I told *Zaiontchkovsky* to tell *Volzhin* to go, they got no answer fr. you (he wrote too, I find) & I said I was sure you wld. wish it, as it is *customary* for the *Over-Procrator* to go & not the *assistant* — I hope it was right I said so; — he ought to have known that, but as its far, he thought you might need him etc. Ella, alas, has not gone, I was sure she would not. — Lunched on the balkony, but rather cold — weather not inviting. Such a strange summer.

Yes, dear Walton! What lovely, sweet, tender & passionate remembrances — ah, dear, how intensely deeply I love you, more far than I can ever say — you are my life, my sunshine, my one & all. —

God bless & protect you. I cover you with tenderest kisses, ever Huzy mine,

yr. very own old girly Alix.

No. 283.

Tsarskoje Selo, June 9-th 1916

Beloved sweet Angel,

Before going to sleep I begin my letter to you. I have told A. to write to you, as she was told to give over 5 questions to you, & its easier for her to write them, who must remember. Do you wish me to send for *Sturmer* & speak to him about these subjects to prepare them, if so wire at once to me: «agree to yr. question», then shall see him on Sunday, speak over all & tell him to ask when you can receive him. Our Friend hoped you could have come now for 2 days to settle these different questions, wh. he finds most essential should be thought of quicker, especially about 1 — the *Duma* — I remember I told you He begged you should say, that they were to finish quickly & go to the country & watch the fieldworks. —

Only send for *Sturmer* soon, as things do dawdle so. You can show him Miechen's paper just to look through. —

2. Obolensky to be changed — why not name him governor somewhere — only who is the right man to replace him? He has never gone against *Gregory* so he is sorry to ask for him to be changed, only he says he really does nothing — & one must seriously begin the collecting of provisions quicker — people file along again in the streets before the shops. —

3. That wld. it not be wiser to give over all that question about food & fuel to the minister of Interior, whom it concerns more than the minister of Agriculture. The Minister of Interior has his people everywhere, can give orders & direct instructions to all the Governors — all are under him after all & *Bobrinsky* took it out of greed into his hands & — I don't want to insinuate worse things. I remember young *Khvostov* also thought it wld. have been better in the Ministry of the Interior. This is one of the most serious questions, otherwise fuel will be too awfully expensive. —

4. About the *Union of Cities*, that you should not thank them any more personally. That means should be found for now publishing all about what they do and saying especially that you, the Government, give all the money & that they spend it largely — its yours & not theirs. The public must know this. I spoke it over several times with *Sturmer* how it cld. be made known — by an order of yours to *Sturmer* or a paper fr. him to you — shall talk it over with him as they try to play too great a part & it becomes a political danger, wh. now must already be taken into account, otherwise too many things will come at a time to settle. — No. 5 — she could not remember what He told her. —

The *Supreme Council* lasted fr. 3—4½ — *Rodzianko* & *Tchelnokov* talked a good deal, & Miechen's Neidhardt aggravated me — *Stichinsky* spoke well, not famously Boris Wassiltchikov. *Trepov* gave me over yr. messages, thanks Lovebird. Am sorry had no time to see Mitja Den before he left — heard of it too late. — Dear old *Goremykin* was too at *supreme council* so tiny, very thin with big eyes — said the heat at *Gagry* had disagreed with him, whilst his wife, on the contrary, has greatly improved & her eyes are better. —

Paul & Marie came to tea (she covered with pimples again) — he leaves to-morrow. Seems Dmitri is here several weeks & up & down to Moscou — has not shown himself once — cannot understand the way he serves! — Olga & I drove in my *droshki* & as service was going on at *Tiarlevo* we got out & went there till we kissed the Bible & then returned home. A nice, cosy

Church. The other 3 & Isa went for a walk. The evening A. spent with me. — Yr. first acacia lies in my gospel, this one will go into another prayerbook. Now I must put out my lamp, shall finish to-morrow. We have Church at 9 *(St. John Maximovitch* now) & then go to the hospital for an operation. Saturday shall see our Fr. in her house to say goodbye — he leaves next week home. — Sleep well my Treasure, I always, morn. & evening bless & kiss your cushion — its all I have! Why on earth this ultimatum to Greece, for sure England & France are at the bottom of it — to my simple mind, it seems unjust & hard — cannot imagine how Tino will get out of it & it may harm his popularity. One more thing I was to tell you, that *Gen. Selivanov* is the judge of *Sukhomlinov* & one says he cannot be *unbiased as he had formerly been discharged by Sukhomlinov from Siberia and that it would be better to appoint the member of the Council of the Empire, General Shumilov.* I only tell you this as He wished me too, but I told Ania I doubt yr. mixing in this affair.

10- h. Warmest thanks sweetest letter, so happy to receive it, my Angel. Were in Church, then an operation, 7 new officers were brought to us, *Ingermanlandians, Hussars of the Belomorsky, Beloozersky regiments etc.* Now saw *Malevsky-Malevitch* — glad to be back fr. Japan as has both sons serving in the *Preobrazhentzi.*

He longs to be presented to you, but knows you have no time. — Thanks for wiring to *Silaiev.*

Endless, burning kisses & many blessings fr. yr. old

Wify.

St. John Maximovitch may He send you both & our Country His blessings. —

No. 284.

Tsarskoje Selo, June 11-th 1916

My own beloved Angel,

Tenderest thanks for yr. dear card. — Its pouring as usual. Were at the hospital, then *funeral service* for poor *Zhukov* — what can have induced him to commit suicide? —

Then I saw my *column of ambulances* wh. are going off to army where he needs them!

Now saw *von Harten* Com. of the *Tvertzi* and he begs to be allowed to be presented to *Alexei,* so I told him to go to the *Headquarters* and ask *Voyeikov.* — Had a wire fr. my Siberian rifles — again many losses amongst the officers, heaps heavily wounded — one of ours again, now 2 wounds in the head. »*Killed as a result of extraordinary heroism the senior under-officer of the unit of reconnoitring infantry, B. P. Jakimov, formerly a naval lieutenant.*«

Zborovsky has already arrived (my train hunts for him) and comes to the Children hospital — they have gone off there in great excitement. I sent

Viltchkovsky the names of the Cosacks we must get here. To-morrow I think my train arrives, it has been picking up in different towns. — Has Georgi arranged himself cosily? — Despairing this perpetual damp — for Baby too. The dentist has arrived and will soon be worrying me. —

We see our Friend a moment this evening in her house to say goodbye, as he leaves. *Suslik's* telegram is really killing. —

Beloved of beloveds, I bless and kiss you without end and yearn for you.

Ever yr. very

Own.

Where has the *Marine of the Guard* gone off to again? Dmitri in good spirits and funny as usual.

No. 285.

Tsarskoje Selo, June 12-th 1916

My own dearly Beloved,

For yr. sweet letter my very tenderest thanks. How tired and weary you must be of all those people bothering you, and I with my tiresome letter the other day too. — Yesterday I had the joy of seeing our Friend in the evening in the little house before going to the hospital. He was in excellent spirits and so affectionate and kind — happy over the good news, asked much after you. It did me good to see him and I was glad to go to our wounded straight from him. The poor old Colonel is so bad, but I hope, with God's help that we can pull him through. He took Holy Communion this morning as I proposed it to him — I always put all my hope into that blessing. — The hospital is very full, we have 23 officers. — Olga and Tatiana are working and abusing each other that they »skull«, absurd girls. We came back from a drive after having been at the little ones hospital. *Victor Erastovitch* looks brown and alright, pretends he has no pains, but one sees his face twitch. He is wounded through the chest, but feels the arm. — A. has gone for the night to Finland. Our exhibition opens to-day at the big palace, like last year — the works of all our wounded of here — and our own things we do. —

Were in Church. — Have *Sturmer* and then Rostovtzev with a long *report,* as he leaves for 6 weeks rest to Finland.

The weather is finer, warmer, but scarcely any sun.

Beloved Angel, I long to press you to my heart and to whisper words of endless l o v e and tenderness, Sweethearty mine!

I cover yr. dear face and eyes and lips with burning kisses. God bless and keep you.

Ever yr. very, very

Own.

Thanks, my Pet, for the wadding!!! —

Excuse such a dull letter. —

No. 286.

Tsarskoje Selo, June 13-th 1916

My own sweet Angel,

Such a lovely day, and the birds are singing away so merrily enjoying the sun — but there is a strange light, a sort of haze in the sky — can it not be from all the shooting? Beloved, I thank you very very fondly for your sweet letter. Thank God the news is good and that Keller behaves so splendidly. — More wounded are being brought. We had to operate the old Colonel — it was serious, thank God his heart so far bore it alright, but its still very grave. I feel tired, it lasted 50 m. and I stood all the time so as to give the instruments quickly and be ready for anything. Css. *Vorontzova* sat a long time with me — begs to be remembered to you. Lives here, has grown very old indeed, friendly and kind. Now the dentist is going to worry me (just when its fine) then a long *report* with *V. P. Shneider.* The evening remain at home, Ania returns fr. *Terioki. Gardinsky* turned up for 2 days — always feels still the results of the railway accident. —

Lovy, excuse my bothering you, but can you ask Alexeiev, is it absolutely necessary to give up Baby's splendid hospital of mine (ex *Sukhomlinov's)* at the Military Accademy — it's such a splendid one, you remember, and beautifully arranged, one of the very best in town. *Alexeiev* says he wishes to *renew his studies,* as needs more off. for the *General Staff.* — Are they so much needed now, don't the *line* officers do yet better and understand all more during the war. They even ask us to have 50 beds for these officers who are to learn there. Its more than a pitty as I doubt our ever finding an equally suitable big house anywhere. Be an angel and ask *Alexeiev* quite sure again, must we clear out — can he not have us there? Kindly answer me as all are very anxious about it. Thank *Gillard* for his letter, he finds Baby not quite so well and therefore the lessons are not quite so good — I think it is owing to the weather being so damp and unsettled. — Must end and fly off now. Saw *Sturmer* told him all, he wrote down the questions all, will prepare everything for when you send for him. Hopes the *Duma* will finish 20-th. —

I bless you, kiss you without end in yearning love and adoration. —

Ever, Huzy mine, yr. very own old

Wify.

As the Pss. has left with a wagon to the front to fetch wounded, I feel responsable for the hospital and they turn to me as their head. —

No. 287.

Tsarskoje Selo, June 14-th 1916

My own beloved Darling,

Warmest, tenderest thanks for yr. sweet card. Such lovely weather, a real treat. All our wounded lie out on the balkony and enjoy the beautiful air. *Taube* lay in the sun under a parasole, so as to have a sunbath for his poor stump. — Now we are directly off to *Maria's* and *Anastasia's* new hospital, next to their old one, and there will be a Te Deum. I warmly congratulate you with our big Marie — she is overjoyed with yr. dear letter. — Our Friend hopes there will be a good victory (perhaps *Kovel)* and if so, he begs on that account you should have *«release on bail Sukhomlinov»*. Give the order privately, without much ado, to *Khvostov,* or the *Senator* who looks after him — and let him live at home under the trust of 2 others. He is old — of course the judgement remains, but it will make the heavy load easier for the old man to bear — He begs you to do it, if we have a big victory. —

The cigarets came to an end, so *Tatiana* fished out a little box as you had told her to. — I am glad you can lunch out again, we also with gratitude take our meals on the balkony. *Titeriat* will bring you flowers again. — A. came to the hospital in her little pony-carriage to see all our wounded — such a sunny friendly smile must cheer them up. — After my *dressings* were over, I embroidered (always for our exhibition-bazar — and the things sell splendidly) and *Gardinsky* and *Sedov* helped me sowing. — I fear the Colonel is dying, so sad! —

To-day 4 weeks we parted — ah, my Love, I love you so intensely, my own my very own Boy Blue and cover you with kisses. God bless and protect you now and ever

yr. very

Own.

No. 288.

Tsarskoje Selo, June 15-th 1916

My own Beloved,

Ever such grateful thanks for yr. sweet letter. —

I send you a paper fr. *Duvan* wh. Ania told me to give you with her love, and a petition fr. Ania's future sister-in-laws Mother, *Princess Dzhordzhadze.* Olga and Tatiana have gone to town, as *Tatiana* has a committee — I shall drive with the little ones. Every day the dentist worries me and my cheek aches in consequence rather. — Our poor old Colonel died peacefully this night — we shall bury him on our *fraternal cemetry,* the wife agrees to this; she and the daughter seem to feel it less than his touching soldier who never left him. —

What a downpour! Will refresh the air. —

A. has gone for the night to Finland to see her brother, (after 8 months) who has come for 3 days. —

Miechen lives now here!!

Thanks dear for the paper about the ex Naval officer. —

Heart and Soul ever near you with burning love and yearning.

How the Ministers must bore you, my Angel. I kiss you as only wify knows how to, true? God bless you.

Endless kisses fr. yr. own

Sunny.

No. 289.

Tsarskoje Selo, June 16-th 1916

My own beloved Sweetheart,

Warmly do I thank and kiss you for your sweet letter. Excuse my bad writing, but I have a compress and bandage on my first finger. When we operated the poor colonel, I pricked my finger and now have a gathering. — Its splendid weather, but I think a thunderstorm is in the air, my heart felt so bad in the hospital. — I receive to-day our sisters who are leaving to-morrow for Germany and Austria — Mme Orjevsky does not seem to be of the number. — Then *Sister Kartzeva* (Mme Hartwig's sister) I send to *Eupatoria* as *inspectress* and *senior sister,* so as to put all in order there and to better look after everything. Olga is working here on the balkony — the 3 others have gone riding. —

Ania returns fr. *Terioki* where she spent the night with her whole family. —

I forgot to tell you that our Friend begs you should give the order that one should not augment the prices of going in town in trains — instead of *5 kopeeks* now one must pay *10 kopeeks* and thats not fair upon the poor people — let the rich be taxed but not the others who daily have often more than once, to go by train. — Write it on one of yr. papers to *Sturmer* to tell Obolensky, who I suppose gave this foolish order. — It will be nice to go and see you afterwards. If we do, *Gregory* begged me to take Ania — I said its not convenient as there are always guests and foreigners — then he said she need not come to the meals and remain in the train, but he said it would be kinder to give her that joy; — I should bring Nastinka this time and then the 4 Girlies. —

Beloved Angel, I must stop now. My heart is full of very deep, great love for my Angel love and I cover you with kisses. — God bless and protect you, Nicky mine.

Ever yr. very own old

Sunny.

I use Baby's envelope again, it will amuse him to see it. —

No. 290.

Tsarskoje Selo, June 17-th 1916

My own beloved One,

Still a bad writing, because the finger disturbs me. From all my heart I congratulate you with the good news again, over 10,000 prisoners. — This morning I got a telegr. fr. Keller fr. *Kimpolung «Fulfilled the given task, cleared southern Bukovina of the enemy. Was wounded to-day in the other leg by a bullet the bone has not been shattered but splintered. With the help of God I hope soon to return into the ranks for further service to Your Imperial Majesty.»* — Ania's brother told her much about him, how the soldiers adore him and when he goes to the wounded, how each tries to sit up to see him better. He rides, followed by an immense *banner with the image of the Saviour,* and 40 cossacks, of wh. each has 4 St. George's crosses, otherwise they dont guard him — they say its an imposing and emotioning picture. How glad I am for him — he always yearned for this great chance to prove to you his intense love, loyalty and gratitude. So prettily he told Sergei *Tan.* that he (Keller) and Ania serve us alike, each in our place and therefore he is so fond of her. — So I told Ania to ask our Fr. to pray for him, I told her last night to give it over to-day (he leaves for *Tobolsk* and home) — and this morning I already had a wire he is wounded — but thank God seems not serious. —

Splendid weather. Spent the evening with Ania, sent for the dentist in the evening (3-rd time in one day) to take out the filling, because of the pain, you see the *inflammation of the periosteam* makes the treatment so difficult.

I must get up now so shall finish this after luncheon. We have a French *cinema* at 4 in the manège, a Count shows it — our troops arrival in France — Verdun, fabrics where they make cartridges and amusing pictures. —

Sweetest Angel, my thoughts forever suround you with yearning love. —

Yes, One begs you should n o t a l l o w the *districts (Metropolitan)* wh. *Volzhin* wishes to bring in now with *Vladimir* its not the time and *Gregory* says would have fatal results. She goes to see him of this morning. —

Forgive my bothering you with the enclosed paper, but He wished you to know it. —

I hold you tightly in my arms and whisper words of infinite tenderness and love. —

Heartfelt thanks my treasure for yr. dear letter; none came fr. Baby or *Zhilik* thanks for Alexei's telegram, shall show it to *Rita* and then return it for *Derevenko* to keep. — Hang Miechen on 60 apple trees!

So uncomfy writing with this bandaged finger. I cut the thing open with an operations-knife. —

Ah my big wee one, I kiss you endlessly — the balkony is so empty without you and *Tiny.* —

God bless and protect you my Own, my Sunshine, my life's joy.

Ever yr. very own

Wify.

No. 291.

Tsarskoje Selo, June 18-th 1916

My ever beloved One,

Ever such tender thanks for your precious letter, my Treasure. Such heavy air, in the distance a thunderstorm happily. Finger is a little better, and I nevertheless work, but my writing is ugly. — Again good news, they say such a necessary place has been taken for the railways. — I wired to you about *Shakhovskoy,* because *Gregory* begs you to see him, they have been thinking over things together, and he has got propositions to make, where to get things one needs, wh. you wrote about. — When you see all the ministers he begs you to be very firm with them. *Sturmer* is honest and excellent, *Trepov* seems rather against him. — *Petrovsky* is awfully happy you have sent for him — I saw him to-day. Get *Sashka* another time too. — The dentist bothers me daily, it goes so slowly on account of the inflamation of the periosteam. — Drove with Ania yesterday evening to *Pavlovsk,* — no, what ugly ladies one sees, its extraordinary — dresses! — Miechen asked to take tea, I said I could not (have *Kostritsky* and later Church). — *Gregory* says Keller will soon be well again. —

I feel my letter is beastly dull, so sorry, my Angel. — Thats nice you bathe, so refreshing. — Am quite ramolie — *Valia* waits to see me and another officer. — The cinema was interesting, only too long. — Have said Witte *(Supreme Council)* is to tell *Iljin* to look through Miechen's paper. —

Beloved, I long for you and yr. caresses. Keep well and of good cheer. I kiss you with endless, tender love. Holy Angels guard and God bless you

Ever yr. very, very

Own.

No. 292.

Tsarskoje Selo, June 19-th 1916

My own beloved One,

Such fond thanks for yr. sweetest letter I found after church. Shall think of you when Fr. will give me over yr. kiss, that will make it bearable. Ah, Sweetheart, — how long this separation is! Both of you far away — but we are doing it for our country and when the news is good, one stands it better. All my very most fervent prayers will be with our beloved troops on Tuesday — God Almighty help and send them strength, courage and wisdom to have success! — We are on the balkony, working, *Ania* and Anastasia glueing photos — one thunderstorm after the other, but not heavy air! Were in Church. — I wired to *Konzarovsky,* to ask about *freight trains Mekk* needs. You see, my tiny *supply* trains fetch the wounded far in front and take them to *Novoseltzy* etc., were real sanitary trains await them — our motors are not enough — and we shall arrange barracks to bind up their wounds before sending them on. *Brussilov* agrees, as he needs our help. In 1 *day* we can 4 times transport the wounded, thats good is it not? — Brinken wired my *ambulance column* (of my train *Loman's)* arrived alright, he needed it — the first year we helped the guards and now *Stcherbatchov* wanted us. — Such a comfort to know that thanks to *Mekk* I can help our troops so much.

How its pouring! —

A. goes for the night to Finland — Now, beloved Huzy, Goodbye and God bless you. I cover you with yearning kisses and love you beyond words.

Ever yr. very, very own

Sunny.

No. 293.

Tsarskoje Selo, June 20-th 1916

My own sweet Angel dear,

Warmest thanks for your precious letter. Again a thunderstorm and raining, the air was so heavy this morning. Frederiks lunched and gave «the kiss» on my «*grain de beauté*». He begs to be remembered to you. Found him fresh and looking well; will live here and go every day to town for *reports. Rita* just heard that her brother has now been wounded and already operated at *Voronezh* — she and her Father leave at once this evening, anxious as don't know what operation has been, I have wired to the Governor. — I saw *Sturmer,* who begs to come a little later, as the *Duma* finishes to-day, the *Council of the Empire* closes the 22-nd and then he has to see lots of people — but wld. like to see you before all the Ministers as has several questions and things to say beforehand. Says now he will be energetic, that it was difficult until he had quite got into the work and the *Duma* only hampered him in everything — he has got answers to all those questions I put to him and told you about. — One thing I this time forgot to remind him about, was what Nikolai mentioned and wh. is most essential — now already to choose people to study and work out ideas for the future congress, when the war will be ended — they must already now thoroughly prepare and think over all — speak over that please, its so urgent. — I am glad my poor Siberians can rest now. — The regiment has just sent for *Korovtchuk* to come, probably after their heavy losses, so he comes to say Goodbye. Have the amusement of Miechen to tea! — and twice the dentist — such a nuisance. — Congratulate you for to-morrow feast of yr. yellow Curassiers. — Beloved, I must end now. God bless and protect you. I cover you with burning kisses.

Ever yr. very, very

Own.

Do speak with *Vladimir Nikolaievitch* as he fidgets so much about mud for Baby, cld. one not have arranged the mud compresses at the *Headquarters,* because it seems cruel to take him fr. you now.

No. 294.

Tsarskoje Selo, June 21-st 1916

My own Sweetheart

We just received *Lavrinovsky,* who came to congratulate in the name of yr. curassiers — he reminds one very much of the poor brother who died, only that he is fair. —

All my thoughts are out at the war — God help them.

The news fr. near *Baranovitchi* was good yesterday. If there is anything particular, do let it be given over to me by the straight telegraph-telephone, wh. comes in 5 m. — Two of my *Alexander* officers are wounded at *Novoseltzy,* — shows, they have been sent down there now. Does the guard take part yet, or not? Forgive these questions, but I am interested for my lancers and the *Crew.*

Strange sky, looks as tho' there wld. be a thunderstorm again. — Ania had a slight heartattack yesterday, wh. frightened her and she of course thought the end was coming. I spent the evening near her bed. She will lie out in the garden and we shall take tea with her, *Victor Erastovitch* and *Yuzik.* — Fancy, poor little Lady Sybil being wounded in the face — it does seem horrid. — Miechen was most amiable and did not say a word. — Remember to wire to Toria on Thursday for her birthday. — Baby writes sweetly. »*I have no more money, beg you to send the allowance — I entreat (its me).*« His notes are often too dear, precious Child. — *Zhilik* finds he develops very well and that the life with many people does him much good — I too am sure of it — yet miss you both, sorely. — I suppose we better come a little later, as you wont be seeing the ministers so soon? Pss. Gedroitz has not yet returned.

Blessings and very tenderest kisses, my longed for Angel, fr. yr. very own old

Wify.

Thats good you send Georgi about again. —

No. 295.

Tsarskoje Selo, June 22-d 1916

My own beloved One,

Such tender thanks for yr. dear letter. I am glad *Petrovsky* is with you, a nice cheery young fellow wh. must brighten up yr. walks. — Get *Eristov* and others too change about. —

I find you ought to send for *Boris* and wash his head — how dare he say such things — can think what he likes, but to have the impertinence of speaking to an Englishman before others, is rather strong — you must have him reprimanded, he dare not behave so, *the insolent fellow.* —

I just saw the *Mufti* of Orenburg and he said all sort of nice things, prayers and wishes for you. — Such heavy air to-day, rained a tiny bit too. —

My little trains and transports are working hard at *Vinnitza,* only the distances are great, they brought in 6 days 839 wounded 90 versts awful roads, so the horses are in a sad state and the *changing of carts* acted on the horses, 4 fell ill, one died, thats why I asked for light *freight wagons* and *Konzarovsky* promised them. — *Shuvaiev* comes to-day to speak about the Academy. I want him to try and get us a decent big house for our hospital. — *Derevenko's* photos of Baby were sweet, please ask him to send me 12 of each still, with his gun, running, learning in the tent, and you in the boat, as I have to glue albums for our exhibition and have mostly old photos. — He might send me some other nice ones he did before of Alexei and you, please. —

I shall give her yr. letter, she will be wild of joy. Am just going to drive with her and Olga, — Tatiana is riding and the others are in their hospital.

Lady Sibyl feels alright one says. —

Most uncomfortable writing with such a swollen, stiff finger. —

So anxious for news. —

Goodbye my Sunshine, my joy, my life. God bless and protect you. 1000 of tender kisses fr. yr. own old

Sunny.

No. 296.

Tsarskoje Selo, June 23-d 1916

My own Sweetheart,

Ever such tender thanks for yr. precious letter. I understand that our Generals make you wild when they act stupidly and make faults. — It was a mistake of *Mekk's* — its 2 «*Crimeans*» and not «*Alexandrovtzy*», who were wounded. — Nastinka lunched with us as its her birthday, then I receive *Belosselsky* — the dentist for an hour, perhaps Ania brings her brother and sister to me. — At 5½ *Sturmer* and the dentist again for 1½ hour. — There is a *rumor* that Sergei M. is to be at the head of the question for provisions in the country — such rot. — *Sturmer* has a good idea about all that if you give it over to his ministery where it has been for hundreds of years and only sly *Krivoshein* took it to himself. In the Ministery of Interior its all easier as he has all the necessary people and influence and can put a good, energetic man at the head of a special commission. Now I hear as tho' *Naumov* keeps it, that wld. be a real pitty, as he is not energetic enough and thinks too much of the *Duma's* opinion and *the Zemstvo Union*. *Sturmer* thought of a Pr. Obolensky (Gov. of *Kharkov),* who could head the commission and travel about and see all and go energetically into all the details. I don't know, why he comes to-day — he begged so much you should send for him before the other Ministers so as to talk over quietly with you all the questions you allowed me to tell him. —

Very warm again. Must end now Deary. I long for you and cover you with burning kisses. God bless and keep you. —

Ever yr. very, very

Own.

I cover yr. letters with kisses and try to think, I hear you talk, ah, me misses you madly!

No. 297.

Tsarskoje Selo, June 23-d 1916

My own beloved Angel,

It is 12½ already and I am just in bed, but I want to begin my letter whilst I still remember my conversation with *Sturmer*. The poor man was much disturbed by rumors, wh. had been brought him fr. people who had been at *Moghilev,* but as *Rodzianko* pounced upon him, he began to get quite surprised. As tho' there was to be a military dictatorship with Sergei *Michailovitch* at the head, that the Ministers wld. be changed etc. and *Rodzianko* the fool came flying to ask him his opinion on the subject etc. etc. He answered that he knew nothing whatsoever and therefore could not form any opinion. I consoled him, saying that you had written nothing to me upon this subject and that I was convinced, that you wld. never put a Grand Duke at such a place and least of all *Sergei Michailovitch,* who has enough to do to try and put his business in order. We discussed it being possible that Generals think it advisable a military man being at the head of such a commission *(food)* so as to unite everything for the army and to be able to take military measures for punishments — tho' certainly the Ministers wld. be placed in an awkward position. — Then we spoke of *Naumov,* who again said to him, that he was tired of his work and did not feel well and wld. like to leave. (He does not agree with the Government, looks at things quite fr. another point of view. Tho' being a loyal and charming man, he is obstinate and sticks to the ideas of *Duma, Zemstvo* etc. and trusts their work better than the Governments; this is not famous for a minister and makes work with him very difficult.) He wished *Sturmer* to tell you he wants to ask to be dismissed, but *Sturmer* protested and said he must ask himself, tho' he finds he has no right to ask for his dismission during the war — but for *Sturmer* it would be easier without him. Yesterday was the last sitting of the Conseil de L'Empire, *Golubev* presided. Nearly all the right were missing, had left some time ago as had enough of it — *Kokovtsev* lead the other party and is altogether an abominable element. — This party intended as bonne bouche to draw *Trepov, Shakhovskoy* and *Naumov* to account for things not being as they ought to and to insist upon their answering to all questions. *Trepov* and *Shakhovskoy* said they were ready with all documents, but agreed with *Sturmer* that questions might be touched, wh. they were not yet ready to answer — *Naumov* delighted said he would with joy answer everything and that there wld. not be one question he wld. not find his explanation to — it was very unpleasant but *Sturmer* insisted upon *Golubev* not allowing these questions to be touched at all — so when all came together it ended decently. —

Then another thing, *Sergei Michailovitch* twice already asked *Sturmer* that all the fabrics should be militarised — but *Sturmer* said during the *Duma* it cld. not be done — and now he has found a much better way out of the thing. One fabric (of course have forgotten in wh. town) is just an example, there were strikes, so one ordered at once all the people and work-men to be called in, and instead of sending them out to the war, make them work in the fabric as before, only being now soldiers, if they dare do anything wrong, they are judged by military judgement. This can be done smoother and with less noise than all the fabrics together — its the best example and all will tremble that their turn may come. — He is becoming far more energetic now and feels a heavy load off his shoulders now that the *Duma* has left. — What will that odious *Rodzianko* have spoken about — there is much chance he wont be reelected, because his party is furious he did the thing clumsily and asked you should shut up the *Duma* as they were tired — and *Sturmer* said no, that they of their own accord must go. — I beg your pardon for bothering you with all these questions, but I wanted to warn you beforehand about *Naumov* and what was worrying the good old man. —

I saw dear *Lili Den* at Ania's this evening — just back — and our ships gone off — God guard them. She spent 2 weeks in Japan as her husband was sent there. At Kioto she lived in the house and very room you did. She is full of Japan and managed to see a great deal. She created much surprise in the streets and little japanese women took a fancy to her and hung on either side of this giantess. She brought me an ivory elephant and each of the girls and Baby too, wh. I send him. Elephants are for luck and especially the number 7, so our elephants make 7, as Baby has two. — *Seriozha Taneyev* told lots about the war and Keller. — I had awfully much to do to-day and heaps of *reports* to read. I had a wire fr. the Commander of my 21 S. R. about the losses of the 13-th. — really terrible the mass of the old officers killed and lots severely wounded. Pss. Gedroitz saw them now. — Then I got at last a map and *report* fr. my *Crimeans* of 3 weeks ago. And this evening's paper mentioned my dear regiment in the announcement fr. yr. staff — am so proud — my 2 wounded are in despair not to be there now when work is going on hard. — Now its 1 o'clock, I must put out the lights and get to sleep and rest my weary old head. I would give much to have another precious and dearly beloved one lying next to me and to feel Sunshine's caresses. —

June 24-th.

Sashka V. lunches with us and says goodbye, as he returns to the front. His wife is expecting it seems. Then I have *Naumov, Prince Golitzin* and *Shvedov*. Just finished *Taneyev's* papers and must be getting up and dress for the hospital. *Sashka* lunched with us, he leaves on Sunday. — Thank you very tenderly, my Lovebird, for yr. sweetest letter. Certainly with joy shall see our dear Cossacks, was just thinking how to do it (rather shy work without my own Huzy and Baby).

I am glad that the *Home Manufactures Committee* has now understood what they must do, *Naumov* talked just now long with me — Witte helps him much — that man is a real pearl and is my right hand in everything, and *V. P. Shneider* gives useful advice and they want to unite it with the *Supreme Council*. Excuse my finishing in pencil, no more ink in the pen and I must quickly finish (and am on the balkony.) We shall interest the governors and spread it all over the country and for the wounded and then have art and taste in it like in my *School of Popular Artcraft*.

Oh Sweety, what a lot one can do, and we women can help so much, at last all have woken up and are ready to help and work — like that we shall get to know the country, peasants, governments always better and be in real union with all. May God help me in that way to be of some use to you, Sweetheart. And they are glad to work with me, you helped and set all going through giving me the *supreme Council and the «Infants' and Mothers Home»,* all goes together, all for the «people» wh. are our strength and the devoted souls of Russia. —

Must end now. Cover you with yearning, endless kisses and blessings.

Ever, Nicky mine, yr. very own old

Wify.

No. 298.

Tsarskoje Selo, June 25-th 1916

My own beloved One,

Thank you ever so tenderly for yr. precious letter. What colossal thunderstorm you must have had, *Zhilik* also wrote about it. —

How glad I am *Martinov* will be able to continue his military service. I enclose a wire I had yesterday fr. Count Keller. —

Thank God the news is good and you are contented. All that lie here are craving to get back. In the «*Novoye Vremya*» of June 24-th there is an article «*Armor-clad*» wh. describes the heroes who lies in our hospital — only he did not like how it was written, found one spoke too much of him and little of his officers and men who were splendid. *Siro-Boyarsky,* — he has got all the decorations one can have and one asked for him to get the 2 cross now for entering *Lutsk* first and how he continued firing, fallen under the bridge, lying on his dead comrade etc. — but they say its against the rules, he being too young (I don't understand there being rules for heroes.) — Were at the *Te Deum* and then saw the splendid *Sotnia* — said good morning, congratulated them for their safe return and gave all my hand and spoke to some with 3 crosses. — Colossal heat. Just had a long *report* with *Witte,* my head quite goes round. Fred. lunched and I send you the enclosed paper, about a feast *Miechen's* committee arranges. Why so colossally official — and before whom do our troops pass, before the German trophies or Miechen? Please, say what you wish, am I to assist or not, perhaps I must, else Miechen will play too great a part, only she has the medal. Tell me what you wish, as soon as possible please wire, because they await an answer and I don't know what to say, having no idea how you look upon the whole question. All the *St. George* knights will be invited one says. — And then later on, off into my Angel sweet's loving arms. —

Ever blessing and endless kisses, my Nicky sweet, fr. yr. very

Own.

No. 299.

Tsarskoje Selo, June 25-th 1916

My own sweet One,

I want to begin my letter this evening. Its still uncomfortable holding the pen — the skin of my finger is all pealing fr. the spirit-compresses I wore and there are blisters, so I cant well bend my finger. — Lovy, I forgot to tell you, that I saw the Metropolitan yesterday and we spoke over the question of *Hermogen,* who is in town since some days and receives reporters etc. He has no right to be here, as you never gave the permission, he received it fr. *Volzhin* and Metropolitan *Vladimir* in whose *Kiev house* he is living. Several papers speak about him, the «*Novoye Vremja*» writes that the *disgraced* bishop will probably soon be named to *Astrakhan* and in the same place they say the *Synod* allowed him to come. *Sturmer* also by chance heard of it and was displeased, so I asked the Metr. to go to *Sturmer* fr. me and beg him in his own name to tell *Volzhin,* that he cannot trouble you upon this subject, but that he finds it not at all proper, nor the moment for *Hermogen* to be here as one cannot forget, why you had him sent away and that stories may arise again; especially now all such things must be avoided — they chose the moment *Gregory* is away. That he lived already some days here and it was kept a secret even fr. *Sturmer,* to whom the police ought to have told it at once — is strange. I only write all this, in case you hear about it — he must be sent back to his place and I hope *Sturmer* told *Volzhin,* — you ask *Sturmer.* As long as *Volzhin* remains, things wont ever work, he is quite unfit for this place, is a handsome man of the world and works exclusively with *Vladimir.* On Monday I receive *Raiev* (brother of the Dr., son of old Metr: *Paladi)* — a professor I believe — an excellent man, knowing the Church by heart since his childhood. Write down to ask *Sturmer* about him, he found him very good indeed (his looks certainly not like *Volzhin* and wears a wig) — you probably know him — has the *ladies high* school under him, and when there were rows in all the schools and universities, his girls behaved beautifully. It interests me to see him as he is so well versed in everything concerning our Church. Please, remember to speak about him to *Sturmer.* —

26-th.

No, what a heat! Thank you my Angel over and over again for yr. sweet letter. I am so glad my long letter did not bore you and that you agree with all. — *Sandro L.* lunched — he leaves to-morrow to take over his regiment near Riga. — He has much improved, become so quiet and eyes too less nervous. — Poor *Olga* and *Tatiana* have gone off to town, Ania off to *Terioki* with Becker probably on the way. The little ones are in the hospital and I shall meet them and take them for a drive. — Well Lovy, if we go on the 3-rd to town, wh. I think wld. be right as its such a big military thing — who takes the review — who says good-morning, who thanks — without you I cannot imagine how things are done. —

Paul has wired for his wife not to come to him for his names day, wh. means the guard will probably move then. —

Had the dentist fr. 5—7 and to-day again, odious in the heat. —

Must end now — what joy if we soon meet — tell me about A. Can I bring her extra with me, as our Friend wanted it so much, she too wld. bring blessing for the troops as, He says, Wify does when goes there. —

God bless and protect you. Kisses without end fr. yr. own old roasting

Sunny.

Thanks, my Angel, for the sweet pansy.

No. 300.

Tsarskoje Selo, June 27-th 1916

My own sweet Angel,

I thank you very tenderly for yr. precious letter — such an intense joy to hear from you, its my recompense after working in the hospital. Pss. Gedr. returned with her wounded. She worked three days in a *front unit,* where there was no surgeon (just left) — made 30 operations, lots of *trepanning;* saw my poor dear Siberians. —

Apraxin lunched with us, told many interesting things, been with my *supply* trains, was at *Lutsk, Czernowitzy,* returns there soon again. Then saw Senator *Krivtsov* — oh, what a rottenly affected man he is with sweet phrases — makes me sick every time. *Raiev* made me an excellent impression. — Then *Col. Domashevsky,* my ex page, happy to have seen you. Now my brain is utterly gaga. Going to hear the artillery *balalaiki (guitars)* in our hospital — they leave Wednesday for *Lutsk* — then dentist. No brains for writing — and so awfully hot — quite ramolie. — Once more I ask about this tiresome trophy exhibition ceremony — why is it so official — ask Fred. and Minister of war about it. If we dont go, does it matter that Miechen does all? Only wire — don't go — or — better go to it, so as to be quite sure, please answer at once. — Shall think of you much to-morrow. Be energetic, lovy mine. —

Cannot write any more. Kisses without end.

Ever, Sunshine mine, yr. very own old

Girly.

God bless and protect you. — Hope, Baby's arm not too bad. —

No. 301.

Tsarskoje Selo, June 28-th 1916

My own beloved Angel,

Such tender thanks for yr. very dear letter. Poor one, so sad you have to see all those Ministers in this great heat. — In the distance there is a thunderstorm. We had awfully much to do in the hospital, I did the 11 new ones, who are very heavily wounded. The dentist every day is madning — I hope to finish to-morrow. *Emma* and *Nini* came to tea and then they leave for the country. Ania sends you both radishes, wh. her wounded planted. *Hermogen* has left. — Certainly *Zhilik* must have a rest — does he think Mr. Gibbs ought to go in his stead not for lessons, but to read more to Baby and to give him the chance of speaking more English. Please, ask him, and if he thinks it good, he can tell, write it to *Peter Vassilievitch,* or should *Peter Vassilievitch* come for a time, please, speak it over with *Zhilik.*

It will be lovely to come there — Becker will be about the 3-rd, so as to be the 11-th with you.

I must end now. Goodbye my love, my Sweetheart, whom I yearn after. God bless and protect you.

Endless kisses and passionately loving ones fr. yr. very

Own.

No. 302.

Tsarskoje Selo, June 29-th 1916

My own Sweetheart,

Warmest thanks for yr. dear letter. Glad, all went off well at the sitting, judging by yr. wire — it was dear of you still having written.

We went to the hospital Church for service and then did our work. Isa lunched — now a Colonel comes to her about this odious *holiday* — we take tea at Miechens and she is sure to speak about it too — I wont answer till yr. wired answer comes. I have told I. to ask details — because, if Miechen intends playing a part, its better we 5 go — because of the *St. George knights* who will all be there. Think it over again with Fred. Will you? Its only because of Miechen. Am as usual in a beastly hurry, as people are waiting to be received.

I send you a paper about *Zhuk; Ania* and *Loman* very much beg for him and he deserves this — write a resolution on it, and I can send it then to be done quicker. Excuse bothering, but they wanted Ania to ask for him. —

Becker came to *Tatiana* and me to-day, so kind before time, will be all the better for journey. — Ania will remain more in the train, not appear at meals — so we shall have time to be more to ourselves — she for nothing wishes to disturb, and never asked — our Fr's. wanted. — Lovely weather. Must end.

I hold you tightly in my loving arms and cover you with kisses. God bless and protect you yr. very own old

Sunny.

No. 303.

Tsarskoje Selo, July 1-st. 1916

My own Angel dear,

We had Georgi to lunch — he will be with you on Saturday. Aunt Olga goes for 10 days to *Kiev,* — Motherdear invited her — soon Nicky and Andrea arrive. — Had much work this morning, operated upon poor *Taube's* leg again. — Said goodbye to our 5 Cossack officers. Shall be to-morrow at 4 at the *Te Deum* before the *Feodor. Cathedral* — the men on horseback, as they go straight fr. there to the train. —

Excuse my always bothering you about that beastly feast on Sunday, but I fear one may think I don't want to come because of German trophies — Miechen you see goes — and one has gathered over 1000 St. George's cavaliers to be present. — Nice weather. — I finish with the dentist at last this evening. — Took tea at Miechens yesterday — most amiable, and touched absolutely no subjects. —

God grant soon, next week we shall be together — too lovely — not leave here before the 5-th — for how many days can we remain. I cover you with yearning kisses and boundless love. Beg yr. pardon for the smudges, the wind blew the page too — God bless and protect you — yr. very own old

Wify.

No. 304.

Tsarskoje Selo, July Ist. 1916

My own Darling,

Such endless thanks for yr. dear letter. *Zhilik* will dine with us and then shall get news of you all. — Can well imagine how tired yr. poor head must be fr. all the hard work — so difficult to remember always everything. I have told Marie to speak with *Zborovsky* and then we can arrange all — he had wanted to go to the Caucasus, I know. — I am glad you take iodine again, its so good for you from time to time. — Are going to bid our *Company* goodbye — there is the *Te Deum* before the big palace (so frightening all that without you). Am glad that need not go on Sunday, and that you have ordered off the military part of the feast. —

Now we have a little boy of 8 in the hospital, a nephew of *Jedigarov,* he lies with the officers, as they begged to have him with them and one big young hero was laying puzzles with him. «*You need'nt!!*» —

Taube is getting on nicely, tho' the leg hurts very much. —

Weather changeable to-day. — Ania sends you both radishes again. — Am sure Baby must feel sad without *Zhilik,* — that man is a pearl. —

How nice I shall see then *Daragan.* —

I also had a wire fr. *Gregory.*

Had letters fr. Victoria and Louise. — The red cross forbids the Germ. and Austr. sisters fr. inspecting the prisoners on account of the loss of the second red cross ship — I find it foolish and wont help a bit. — Sweetheart, goodbye now. I cover you with endless, burning kisses.

God bless and protect you. Ever yr. own old

Sunny.

Old Lolo D. will lunch with us to-morrow. —

No. 305.

Tsarskoje Selo, July 2-nd. 1916

My own Lovebird,

I am writing in my room by lamplight, as there is a colossal thunderstorm and rain — terrible loud claps as tho' it had struck near by. Pss. Lolo and *Valia* lunched — he will bring you this letter. —

Very tenderest thanks to you, my Angel dear, for your beloved letter. The photos *Derevenko* did are perfectly delightful, especially of you both my sweet Darlings. How big Alexei has grown, no more babies! Ah, h o w I miss you both!! The hospital is my real saving and consolation. We have many heavy wounded, daily operations and much work we want to get through before leaving. The «*Kakham*» has come and spent the evening at Ania's yesterday — to-day she has asked me to spend the evening with her and him and to hear him tell pretty stories. —

There, its clearing up. — One begged me to ask for *Bezobrazov (chevalier garde)* as the boy is still ill, but his term is up and he wld. have to leave the regiment unless I get yr. order that he may remain still 2 months, then they keep him in the regiment. —

Now my Sunshine, Goodbye and God bless and protect you. —

I cover you with very tenderest and warmest kisses.

Ever, Nicky mine, yr. very

Own.

No. 306.

Tsarskoje Selo, July 3-rd 1916

My own beloved Angel,

Ever such tender thanks for yr. sweetest letter. — God grant we shall be together by Thursday after luncheon. Wont that be too lovely, at last again together after 7 long, long, weeks? — We bring *P. V. Petrov* with us. —

So the guard moves! *N. P.* wrote that they were just going off, probably to *Lutsk.* So we shall be with you those great days — God almighty help our troops. *Gregory* said if I went to you, God wld. again send His blessing to the army — may it be so. — *Staff-Captain Liubimov,* com. of Baby's *Company* of the *Belomorsky Regiment* soon leaves our hospital, has never seen Alexei, so we told him to pass by the *Headquarters* ask to see Baby through *Valia* — he is such a nice little man. There is another I wish you could see — our hero, I wrote to you already once about him of the *armored machine-gun cars* — he has never seen you — thats why came to our hospital to see us at least — wld. be nice if he cld. also have passed the *Headquarters* (26 years old. *staff-captain,* father was in the Jap. war; commanded at *Poltava* the artillery and died there just before this war began) — *Siro-Boyarsky,* St. George's sword, cross all one can have, three times already wounded. May they pass like that, can I tell him anything (they never asked) — he leaves now for a week to his mother at *Poltava* and then returns to *St. Petersburg* for business; — if they come to *Moghilev,* whom must he ask, so as to be presented? One wants to give pleasure to such brave fellows, and you will listen with interest to all he tells. —

Glorious weather. Ania has gone to Finland for the night. Miechen is in town feasting with her medal. — I spent yesterday evening at Ania's with the »*Hakham*«!! Very clever, pleasant man — she has quite melted. —

Now must go to the big palace (such a bore)! —

S. N. Feodorov will be at the *Headquarters* about July 15.

Every blessing and 1000 kisses fr. yr. own old

Wify.

Shall come to you and leave Becker behind!

No. 307.

Tsarskoje Selo, July 4-th. 1916

My own Sweetheart,

Fondest thanks for yr. precious letter. *Petia* lunched and send his very tenderest love and good wishes for success. —

There was a thunderstorm. — Now we are bringing *Silaiev* with us — you will think me crazy, but I thought it best he should present himself to you and tell you all the details about the Dr's opinion, as it needs a long treatment still and he does not know what to do about the regiment, poor man. Writing up and down takes so long, and like this it is simplest you talk it over together and give him yr. orders. — The operation *hernial rupture of Yedigarov's* 8 year old nephew went off well — now I am going to the hospital to see the men, as many of my 21-st reg. have been brought. — Ania's *Raduta (refugee, nurse)* marries her sanitary and they have a feast in the hospital. —

There is nothing you wish me to bring you?

Shurik and *Victor Erastovitch* take tea with us. —

Now must end. Cover you with tender kisses and blessings

Ever yr. very, very

Own.

To you and Baby each a cornflower. Saw *Vera Volkova* who came for a few weeks and now returns to England.

No. 308.

Tsarskoje Selo, July 5-th. 1916

My very Own,

Such loving thanks for yr. last dear letter. To-day 7 weeks that we separated — it was a Tuesday. The heat is tremendous, I am perspiring and broiling. — Thanks so much about the officers, they will be wild with joy, all the more so, because they did not dare ask; — they will come whilst we are there so as to feel less shy. —

Groups were taken in the hospital to-day. — *Nastinka* has fallen ill, so we bring Isa, who is overjoyed. —

Sturmer comes to-day, and still others to receive. — What joy to feel I shall soon have you in my loving old arms again. —

Excuse rotten letter, but am ramolie and in a haste. —

God bless and protect you. I cover you with kisses.

Ever yr. very own old

Sunny.

Dediulin came to say goodbye, the regiment has sent for him. —

No. 309.

Imperial Headquarter, 12-th July 1916

My own Beloved,

Again goodbye, but thank God not for long — but nevertheless I hate leaving you and Sunbeam. Its so lonely without you and knowing yr. hard work and dreary life, makes it very sad. Thanks my Angel, for having let me be with you, for having sent for us, it was a joy and gives strength again to continue. We have enjoyed our holiday and go now back to our work. Thursday morning straight to *dressings* and then to receive the German and Austrian Sisters (I don't look forward to that). — She has wired to Our Friend about the weather and I hope God will bless the front with Sunshine. Please, wire this evening how Tiny's temp. is and to-morrow morning. We reach *Tsarskoje Selo* to-morrow evening at 8. —

Farewell, my Sunshine, my Love. I fear our visit was too fidgeting for you, so much running about and still yr. work to be done. I shall remember every caress with yearned longing.

God bless and protect you, give you strength, courage, success.

I cover you with endless, burning kisses,

Ever yr. very, very

Own.

No. 310.

Moghilev, July 12-th 1916

Lovy my Angel,

I have asked Ania to drop these papers for you to give *Alexeiev* to read and then to return me the *Report,* the telegram I dont need as have another.

What rain!

Do hope my Baby is alright, they let know he woke up and went to sleep again, hope the night was good — do say they are to let me know as soon as he wakes up, the temp. etc. then I can come up earlier to sit with him. I hope its nothing and a good sleep will set the sweet child to rights again. —

I cover you both with kisses yr. own old

Wify.

No. 311.

Tsarskoje Selo, July 14th 1916

My own beloved, precious One,

Such endless joy to receive yr. dear letter and I thank you for it with all my fondly loving old heart. Sweetums, every tender word of yours is my greatest, deepest joy and I carry it deep in my heart and live by it. Seems a dream, our journey. Had to relate heaps in the hospital, all full of interest and wanting to know everything. — The weather is very warm and a divine breeze, so that we are going for a drive. Just receive 6 German and 5 Austrian sisters — real ladies, nothing like our bad selection, wh. was sent. — They brought me letters fr. home and Irène and all send you their love. You must excuse a stupid letter, but am slightly cretinised. —

Went early to bed and enjoyed a bath. — Lovy, do say about *Sukhomlinov* being let home, the Drs. fear he will go mad if kept shut up any longer — do this act of kindness of your own sweet self. — My Siberians were so happy over *Sergeiev's* telegr. that they had succeeded again. —

I am so glad you took us everywhere, now we know how and where you spend your afternoons. —

Beloved Angel, now Goodbye and God bless and keep you. —

I cover you whit endless burning kisses and live in the past.

Ever yr. very, very

Own.

No. 312.

Tsarskoje Selo, July 15-th 1916

My own beloved Darling,

Very fondest thanks for yr. dear letter. — All my thoughts & prayers are with you and our dear troops — God help & send success — it will be very hard for them I fear, if you get news — let me know, feel so anxious. —

Weather fine, not too hot & now even grey, in the evening there were only 9 degrees. — To-morrow is Ania's birthday, please wire to her, if in the evening then to *Terioki, Estate of Mikhailov.* She leaves for there at 4 to-morrow & spends the night with her parents.

I saw *Maximovitch* this morning — I am glad the old man goes on leave again, it will freshen him up, as I found him pale, thin & not looking well. —

How is *Grigoriev's* health? *Derevenko* sends you photos, he took on the river. —

The bedroom is so empty & big after the train!! — Sweet Angel, soon we shall be back again with you & I long for your caresses & kisses. —

I have got to receive three officers now, who are returning to the front. Have nothing interesting to tell you. —

Goodbye Sweetheart, God Almighty bless and protect you; I cover you with fond kisses & remain,

yr. very own old

Wify.

My compliments to *Alexeiev.* All were wonderfully kind & amiable to Ania. —

No. 313.

Tsarskoje Selo, July 16-th 1916

My very own Treasure,

Warmest thanks for yr. sweet letter. Let me congratulate you with all my heart for the good news — what a surprise it was when *Rita* announced it to us this morning in the hospital — I had not had time to read the papers. *Brodi* taken — how lucky — the straight line for *Lemberg* & the *break-through* begun — the good is coming, as our Friend had said. I am so happy for you — a great consolation & recompense after all yr. anxiety & hard preparatory work! And how are the losses? Heart & soul are with you out there! —

Thats right you let Nicky speak himself out, it will have quietened him & I really think the other powers do not act fairly towards Greece, tho' its a rotten country. —

Heavy air, the rain did good, a tiny shower — good luck for Ania — she is 32 to-day. She begs yr. excuse for blotching her letter — now she is off to Finland till to-morrow evening. —

I have Witte's *report* at 5½ & to-morrow *Sturmer,* whom I must speak seriously to about the new ministers — alas, that *Makarov* has been chosen (again a man against yr. poor old wify & that brings no luck) & I must have our Friend guaranteed against them & *Pitirim* too. *Volzhin* does act so wrongly — *Pitirim* chooses the man to be at the head of his *Church* & *Volzhin* forbids it — he has no right to do so. —

Goodbye my One & All, my Huzy Love, my precious Sunshine. I bless & kiss you without end in fond & deep devotion. Yr. very

Own.

No. 314.

Tsarskoje Selo, July 17-th 1916

My very own Lovebird,

A kiss for yr. dear card I received to-day. So the guard has already taken part — *Taube* was very much interested to know about it. The amount of prisoners taken again is indeed splendid. — Darling, can you please let me know where my Siberians are just now, as one of my officers returns to them in a few days & does not know where to go & one looses so much time looking for one's regiment & I thought you might know — can you? —

We have just christened *Loman's* grandson, a splendid baby — old *Sirotinin* & I were the godparents. — Its pouring cats & dogs, so we shall be good & go to some hospital. In the morning we went to the lower hospital Church & then worked. Yesterday to the *Feodor. Cathedral* & evening in the hospital. —

I wonder how the weather is along the front. The glass has fallen a good bit. — Had a long letter fr. Olga, says Motherdear is well, in good spirits & enjoys herself at *Kiev* & does not speak about leaving; she sees her but rarely & works very hard since 3 months. In 3 or 4 days her friend goes back to the front & she thinks of it already with despair. He came for her

Namesday — he was somewhere with the horses the last 2 months. — How the papers are down upon *Sazonov*, it must be very unpleasant for him, after imagining he was worth so much, poor long nose. —

Now, my Sunshine, goodbye & God bless & protect you & keep you from all harm.

Ever yr. very own old

Sunny.

No. 315.

Tsarskoje Selo, July 18-th 1916

My own Angel dear,

Every tender thanks for yr. sweet letter. To-morrow already 2 years of the war — terrible to think. As its St. Seraphim's day too, we shall have service in the little Church below. — Yesterday evening Kirill came with the 2 telegr. I copied out for you — because *N. P.* told him I always wished to know all about them. —

We read them with great emotion. — Wonder, who the 16 men are who were killed — thank God no great losses. — *Generally* kindly let me know whenever you get lists of deaths & wounded — because the families all telephone for news fr. me. Several of our trains are down there — lots of 4-th rifle officers are wounded. One waits with such anxiety! —

Just had Apraxin — I told him he might pass by the *Headquarters* soon, to see the different Generals with whom he, *Mekk* & I have to do! —

Many showers to-day. Sorry cant write any more. We went to A. Olga yesterday, she was very dear — asked after you. —

God bless & project you. Ever such fondest kisses, my own Sunshine —

yr. very

Own.

No. 316.

Tsarskoje Selo, July 19-th 1916

My own Beloved,

All my thoughts and very tenderest prayers were with you this morning in our *Pestcherny chapel*. We ordered a service below for ourselves & afterwards there was in the big Church & *Cross Procession* & feasting & lunch in the Childrens' hospital. We had fewer *dressings* to-day. Your messenger came late — fondest thanks for yr. dear card, my Sweetheart.

Again quite cold, only 8 degrees & showers from time to time. — *Sturmer* spoke with me about the Polish question — one must inded be very prudent — you know, I like *Zamoisky*, but know he is an intriguer, so one must well weigh over this serious question. —

I deeply regret one made you rename Metrop. Wladimir for the summer session of the *Synod* — it ought to have been *Pitirim*. *Wladimir* belongs to *Kiev* & has only been a week there in all these months. He harms ours in everything, — not one thing can *Pitirim* do in his own town, for everything Wlad. must be asked, so that the clergy don't know who is the master, & its very unfair towards him. The other metrop. had the tact of remaining at *Kiev* more — one ought to do something for this poor one. — Now I must end. Heart & soul with you. — 2 years this awful war! God bless & help you. 1000 fond kisses fr. yr. own old

Wify.

No. 317.

Tsarskoje Selo, July 20-th 1916

Sweetheart mine,

Fondest thanks for yr. dear letter. I saw *Vladimir Nikolaievitch* yesterday & was glad to get news of you all. He thinks of quietly remaining here, as there is much work in the hospitals & we are daily expecting new trains.

Cold & grey weather, tho' the glass is rising — reminds me of autumn, we dine in coats — because its dull indoors. — Olga & Tatiana have gone to town for *donations*. Nicky has asked to see me, so shall probably to-morrow, if he is not with *Sturmer* — Saw *Voyeikov* who stank of cigars & is full of his millions & constructions & selfsure as always — absolutely positive the war will be over by Nov. & in Aug. now the begin of the end — he aggravates me & I told him God alone knows when the end will be & many have said it wld. be Nov. but I doubt it — in any case its unwise to be always so cocksure as he is.

Nektliudov of Stockholm's son has fallen *(Preobrajenetz)* & the son of Uncle *Mekk* — too sad! — Excuse a dull letter, but my head rather aches. Remember to wire to Miechen on the 22.

Goodbye, my Angel sweet, my Sunshine & joy. God bless & protect you. I cover you with tender kisses. Ever yr. very own old

Sunny.

No. 318.

Tsarskoje Selo, July 21-st 1916

My own Treasure

Again grey & cool & the glass is falling — really, where is summer flown to, we have seen so little of it. — Last night at 10 Anastasia's train arrived & I went all over it with her. Heaps of very heavy wounded — they had been endlessly long on the way.

There were several of her »*Caspian*« officers. — *Arapov's* grandson — the cousin of one we had 2 months before. Soldiers fr. Finland regiments etc. »*Belomortzy*« a few with many crosses — all fr. the Austrian front. I gave medals to the worst of wh. many were going to *Pavlovsk* to Aunt Olga's hospital. — We want to enlarge our little hospital, so as to be able to always have 35 officers — now 6 of them lie in the room we had for the men (where Ania lay).

We want to build out a wing with a room for 20 men, add a bathroom for them & rooms for sanitaries — they can do it quickly — last autumn we added on the large sittingroom. — The men love coming down to us, & its a pitty not to look after them.

Formerly we worked also in the big house — & this is more comfy.

Viltchkovsky & *Danini* come this morning with the plans & all are already deeply interested in it; it has become such a home to all & all the more so, since we spend the evenings with them. I shall finish this after luncheon, now must be off to *Znamenje* & our work. Thank God, that He has given me the strength to be of use again; — such consolation in one's work. —

Ever such tender thanks for yr. sweet letter. Our Friend's wire is comforting, as this constant rain & cold are sad for July & will make the movement again impossible. — Nevertheless I am going for a drive as my head is heavy. I think you better answer Olga's first question, that she ought to write a nice kind letter to the Pss. as she is so fond of her, & it will hurt less coming straight fr. her, thanking her for all these year's service, but that now she will no longer be in need of a lady in waiting & therefore must part with her. Tho' she remains a Grand Duchess, she may at times need a lady — she wont wish to appear at official occasions, but still there may be moments after the war, & when our Children marry & so forth — then Motherdear must lend her one — I suppose she of c o u r s e speaks to her about this question — she ought first of course to ask her advice.

Nicky will come to-morrow to tea, as he is now with *Sturmer*. We had news of *Yedigarov*, poor boy — fancy, the commander did not wish him to come to Russia even to find an occupation, but now he is coming. He wld. not give him yr. squadron, & this has been the great blow, as he ought by right to have got it.

What can I propose him to do? Go over to my *Crimeans* or what on earth. What can you council? —

Now must end. Congratulate you with Motherdear & our big Marie. Remember Minny and little Marie P.

God bless you. 1000 burning kisses fr. yr. own, very

Own.

No. 319.

Tsarskoje Selo, July 22-nd 1916

My own precious One,

There, a downpour again. Such tender thanks, Lovy mine, for your sweet letter I was so happy to receive. — We had service in the *Feodor. Cathedral*, Css. *Vorontzova*, Css. *Benkendorf*, *Princess Dolgurokova*, Mme *Nilova*, *Dediulina* & our ladies were there. —

Now I have Velepolsky — I rather dread it, because I feel sure I shan't quite agree with him — & think wiser one shld. wait a bit, but in any case not give t o o great liberties, otherwise when Baby's turn comes he will have very hard times to go through. —

Then to M. & A. hospital for a concert — a visit to Miechen — Nicky to tea, then *Sturmer* — between that Ania — & the Hospital begging me to come in the evening & I shld. like to — its the only thing wh. helps me now you are away. Yet I know, A. is sad — tho' she has Alia lying not well in her house & might naturally sit more with her, I find. Forgive therefore a short letter, as am in a great hurry & fidgeted (wh. I don't like). —

I cover you with kisses & count the moments till we shall be together.

God bless & protect you & keep you fr. all harm. Always miss & yearn for you —

Ever yr. very, very

Own.

Shall do my very, very best about the old man. —

No. 320.

Tsarskoje Selo, July 23-st 1916

My own Lovebird,

From all my heart I thank you for yr. dear letter — yes, I too am eagerly looking forward to our meeting on Wednesday.

What a nice wire from Tino — I also wrote to him, Nicky begged me to. He was very contented with his talk with *Sturmer.* It was a tiring day yesterday. Church, *Velepolsky,* — to the Childrens' hospital — to Miechen — Nicky — *Sturmer* — till 7½. A. dined & remained with me till 10 — then to our hospital. —

Cold, grey & windy. — We have to go to the big palace for a concert & before want to drive a bit. Are awaiting trains. —

We used to work in the big house & have heaps of men — & this will be much better near us. — Frederiksy cld. not come to lunch, not being well. Benkendorf is also still not well. — I am glad you like old, nice *Maximovitch.* — Now, sweetest Angel, wify's lovebird, I cover you with burning kisses & remain yr. own old

Sunny.

Ania's goodies will only be ready to-morrow, she begs pardon.

No. 321.

Tsarskoje Selo, July 24-th 1916

My own beloved Sweetheart,

From all my tender heart I thank you for your sweetest letter. — The train (I am ramolie) bringing mostly guard officers & men arrived to-day & we went over it — 2 sailors were there too — some remained here, others went on to town. The poor couple *Verevkin* (ex. gov. of *Kovno* — «*Preobrajenetz*») came to meet their son's body. We had service in the hospital & then did *dressings* — without any doctors, as they were all occupied at an operation of a lady upstairs. — At last! divine weather — our Friend has brought it, He arrived to town this morning, & I am eagerly looking forward to see Him before we leave. —

A., I think, is more than grieved I don't take her this time, tho' she does not say it in words — but He has come & Alia is ill in her house & its unnecessary this time. I think my going so often to the hospital in the evening puts her out, but really her sister is there & ill to sit by — & there I forget the solitude & misery & they warm us all up. —

Grabbe is coming with us, I am delighted, as Nastinka & *Ressin* are dull. —

Sweet Angel, goodbye & God bless & protect you. Ever yr. very own endlessly loving old

Wify.

Thousands of kisses. Am awaiting Becker for the journey — hideous nuisance! —

No. 322.

Tsarskoje Selo, July 25-th 1916

My own beloved Huzy dear,

Changeable weather — at moments lovely sunshine & then such dark clouds again. I am in bed this morning as my heart is a good deal enlarged, I felt it all these days — I overtired myself — so remain quiet today & only go to A. this evening to see our Friend. — He finds better one shld. not advance to obstinately as the losses will be too great — one can be patient without forcing things, as ultimately it will be ours; one can go on madly & finish the war in 2 months, but then thousands of lives will be sacrificed — & by patience the end will also be gained & one will spare much blood.

I bring *Botkin,* as he was anxious to let me go now alone — before B. its often worse — & then I worried rather much latterly over the nomination of *Makarov* & the Polish story — etc. — Endless thanks for yr. precious letter — this too is my last to you. — Ania wanders about with a long face & is aggressive — the hospital aggravates her because I so often spend the evenings there (my rest fr. talks & one needs other faces when the heart is heavy with anxiety & loneliness — very, very sad without you both & she, poor soul, does not brighten me up always — I prefer not speaking of the absent & remembering the past & cry over what cant be — our interests are different generally — when her sweetheart the *Caraim* was here and caressed her — she was splendid. But we get on calmly; & now I don't take her of course she is, I see, very hurt — forgets her sister is ill in her house & *Gregory* is here. —

Now its raining. Got grant in 2 days we shall be together!! 1000 kisses & blessings fr. yr. longing old

Wify.

We shall lunch in the train? & if heart bad I can dine home too, yes? —

No. 323.

Tsar's Headquarter, train Aug. 3-rd 1916

My very own beloved Angel,

Alas, the day of departure has arrived again, but I thank God for this happy, restful week. Now I can return with new strength to my work and live upon sweet remembrances of your tender love. Its very hard leaving you alone to yr. heavy responsability & masses of tiring work — wish I cld. be of more use to you.

I long to guard you fr. all useless worries & vexations, but often have myself to come with tiresome papers — but nothing is to be done. — Beloved One, God Almighty give you wisdom & success — patience for the others not to hurry obstinately forward & spoil all by useless losses — steadily forward, every step firm & no dashes with retracing again one's steps backwards — thats far worse. — If only *Alexeiev* has taken our Friend's Image in the right spirit, then God is sure to bless his work with you. Don't fear to mention *Gregory's* name to him — thanks to Him that you remained firm & took over the commandment a year ago, when all were against you, tell him that & he will understand the wisdom then — & many wonderful escapes to those he prays for at the war who know Him — not to speak of Baby & Ania. —

Sweetest One, heart & soul remain with you & all my passionate love. God bless you & precious Baby hundertfold — shall miss you both horribly — & you will feel yr. loneliness, alas, again. I cover you with burning, tender kisses, Sunshine of my life — & remain yr. very own old

Wify.

Sleep well, hold you both tightly in my arms. —

No. 324.

Tsarskoje Selo, Aug. 4-th 1916

My own sweet Angel

It is already 10 o'clock, but I want nevertheless to begin my letter to you to-morrow I shall be so busy. — We travelled alright & my heart behaved itself; I only took tea with the others, lunch & dinner I had in my compartment — lay the whole time & embroidered, whilst my thoughts were with you both treasures & I lived over that happy, peaceful week. Alone in my big empty bedroom, only your cushion to bless & kiss! Lovely moon & so quiet — the weather splendid to-day & not too hot. —

A. spent the evening with us — grown thinner this week, looks tired & one sees has cried much. Scarcely spoke — only after the children went to bed. She leaves on Monday with our Fr. & dear Lili for *Tobolsk* to pray before the relics of the new Saint. In despair to leave without yr. blessing for so far, & just when I returned, but He wishes her to go now, finds it the best moment. —

He asks whether its true what the papers write that the *Slavic war prisoners will be set free,* hopes not true, as wld. be a great fault (do answer this question). — Is grieved one says *Gutchkov* & *Rodzianko* have gone to give the order to collect copper — if true, says one ought to take the initiative from them, its not their business. Begs you to be very severe with the generals, that are at fault. You see, from all sides terrible cries against *Bezobrazov* arise, that he let the guard be slaughtered — that *Lesh* 5 days running gave *Bezobrazov* the order to advance & he always put it off & then lost all through his obstinacy. The wounded rifles & others don't hide their anger.

Ania got a most interesting, but sad letter fr. *N. P.* — writes about what they did too — but with despair about the Generals — *Bezobrazov* — now they know nothing, ordered the guard to advance where the bogs were known to be impregnable — & told to avoid other bogs where one cld. quite well pass — says, the worst impression — grieves to make me sad, but begs her to tell me this. — All here hope you will change *Bezobrazov*. — I hoped it fr. the beginning, surely not difficult to find a successor & at least one who is not as obstinate as a mule. The guard will never forgive him & wont be pleased you stick up for him, & that he profits as an old comrade. — Forgive me, but the more I quietly thought all over in the train what Paul wrote, Dmitri & others said, I honestly find he aught to leave, & it will be a glorious example of your wisdom. Its yr. special guard he has thrown sinfully away — & he will again disagree with *Lesh* & *Brussilov* — you kindly saved him after the story last year & gave him a glorious chance wh. he shamefully misused — one cannot act thus unpunished. Let him suffer & others be saved by this example. Regret, I did not speak more vehemently at the *Headquarters* & not to Alexeiev — yr. prestige will be saved — one will say you are weak & don't stand up for yr. guard wh. you always loved — & one can't risk another calamity. The generals know we have men in Russia still, & don't care about the lives — but these were so beautifully prepared & all — for nothing. I know how it has made you suffer — but be reasonable, Lovebird — listen to old wify who only thinks of yr. good & knows this step is the right one. — *Let Alexeiev* think otherwise — only better quite put him away, as you said a strong reprimand wld. make him nervous — do it for yr. brave guard's sake & all will thank you for it, they are too deeply hurt by his rashness in letting all their men be killed.

Ania told our Friend what I said about *Sandro's* despair & he was very much put out about it. He had a long talk with *Sekretev* on the subject & he says that he has heaps of things one cld. perfectly well use for the machenery of the aeroplanes. Don't you want to send for him & have a talk on the subject, or send him to *Sandro* to talk the question over — it wld. be in deed lucky if they cld. find a way of making the machenery here. —

Forgive me, if my first letter is already about affairs — but all concerning the army is so vital to us all & we live for it. —

By the watch I live through all you are doing all day, my own Lovebird. Only yesterday we were still together & it seems already much longer ago. Did you remember about putting off the calling in of the young soldiers till

Sept. 15 if possible, so that they can finish their fieldworks everywhere. — Isa came to the station but still looks ailing — *Trina* keeps to her room yet with a cold. Mme Zizi was there & asked where we came from!!! The Pss. *Palei* was there too — without a veil, but I did not kiss her. — I congratulate you with the *Preobrajensky* feast, my one & all. —

5-th. Ever such loving thanks for yr. precious letter, Sweetheart. Yes, the joy of being together is inconceivable & I live on remembrances now. For you its yet worse, poor Angel dear! —

Again lovely weather — got to sleep after 3. Worked in the hospital, lots of new faces. Pss. Gedroitz, *Taube* & *Emelianov* send touched thanks for messages. —

I enclose a paper about good *Manukhin,* — *Botkin* begs for him again & *Makarov* acts not fairly. —

Ania got a wire fr. *N. P.,* — he will be at the *Headquarters about the 12-th.* Sweety, I want to go to holy Communion this lent, so think Monday morning, as this evening is Church, to-morrow morning & evening, Sunday morning & then I'll order twice more — it will be a great consolation. Ania leaves Monday for — she does not know how long the journey will be. Wont you send her a card with wishes & blessing for the journey, only then write in time. — Lovely weather, are lunching on the balkony. —

I receive a lady now & then *Mekk* & Apraxin who goes to the front at 4 o'clock. — Lovy, you wont forget about the *decorations* for the wounded by bombs fr. aeroplanes. A. thanks for the teaglass. — Goodbye now, my Sunshine, my joy. In thoughts press you tenderly to my heart, cover you with burning kisses. God bless & protect you & help you in all yr. undertakings. — Think about *Bezobrazov*.

Ever, Angel mine, yr. very own

Sunny.

No. 325.

Tsarskoje Selo, Aug. 6-th 1916

My very own Sweetheart,

Fondest thanks my Angel for yr. precious letter. Yes, the blessing to be together is intense, & one feels the longing & missing quite awfully. Ah, your tender caresses, big sad eyes when we parted haunt me always. It is good to have a nice time to look forward to again, poor Ania hopes to be back by then, or the girl can catch us up at the *Headquarters,* it will refresh her & then *N. P.* will be there & we all once more together. Remember to give him the yacht, that makes a good reason for his not being out there & he ought to have it. — Lovely weather again, so shall remain the afternoon on the balkony. Have 4 officers. Mr. Gibbs & Pr. Golitzin with a *report* & then Nicky to see — there cld. not finish, they come one after the other & now the Feldjäger must leave. Nikolasha begs to thank you again ever so much for everything. —

Beloved, we had evening service in the *Feodor Cathedral* & to-night again, this morning in our *Pestcherny Chapel* & to-morrow morning in the lower hospital Church. Hope to go on Monday morning to Holy Communion — heart & soul I beg yr. pardon my one & all for word or deed by wh. I may have unwillingly hurt you; — I am so glad to go, long for this moral strength — one goes through so much & has to give out such a lot. Confession Sunday evening at 10 — perhaps Ania may come too — otherwise I shall be alone, the girls don't care about going now. — Goodbye, Angel Sweet. I see our Friend in her house to-day, you speak about him to Mr. Gibbs. — I cover you with fondest kisses & bless you over & over again.

Ever yr. very own, deeply loving & longing old

Wify.

As interesting, I told Ania to write out about her Brother for you. —

No. 326.

Tsarskoje Selo, Aug. 7-th 1916

My own beloved Angel,

I thank you fr. all my heart for yr. sweet letter — understand its difficult for you to write when you have so much to do. —

A grey day — rained a little. Saw our Friend yesterday evening in the little house — sends you these flowers and much love. They leave Tuesday evening. Ania and I go to confession at 10 and to-morrow morning service at 9 in our *Pestcherny Chapel* — quite particularly shall pray for you, my one and all and carry you in my soul. I cover you with tenderest kisses and send you endless love. —

What news fr. the war? Pretty quiet?

Excuse a dull, short letter, but have no time for more. — I send you the «candles» — what a nuisance you suffer again fr. them. —

Goodbye, my bright Sunshine.

God bless and protect you. Ever yr. very own tenderly loving old

Sunny.

No. 327.

Tsarskoje Selo, Aug. 8-th 1916

My own Beloved,

Warmest thanks, my Angel, for your dear letter. What a nuisance you have to see so many people. — Colossaly hot to-day and such heavy air — also a wee breeze— shant drive, prefer remaining quiet. —

It was a great consolation and so calming to go to Holy Communion — carried you both with me in my innermost soul. Can pray so much better in our wee Church below. From there went straight to the hospital where they gave me a glass of tea; and then I did my *dressings.* The foundation work of our new wing is getting on nicely — hope it will be ready by the end of

October. On Wednesday 10-th, will be the second anniversary of our hospital and all want it awfully to be called *His Majesty's own Hospital* No. 3. — as there are for ever confusions between *Palace Hospital* and *Hospital of the Palace*.

Wonder, what you are doing about the guard, — will they keep quiet now for some time. — Our Friend hopes we wont climb over the Carpathans and try to take them, as he repeats the losses will be too great again. —

Tchebikin comes to me to arrange about a hospital in the new barracks of the 3-rd rifle regiment. —

Must end now. Goodbye my beloved Treasure, my one and all, my sunshine dear; cover you with burning kisses.

God bless you.

Ever yr. very own old

Wify.

No. 328.

Tsarskoje Selo, Aug. 9-th. 1916

My own beloved One,

Ever such fond thanks for yr. sweet letter. Shall ask our Friend to pray quite particularly on the 14-th.—15-th. to bless the beginning. They leave fr. town at 7. — Pouring and sun shining, very damp and hot. —

She is sorry she answered yr. wire so officially, but her mother was there. — Kaufmann is coming to me, as I want them to send an *unit* out with our troops to France and *Alexeiev* agreed to the idea. —

Lovy, I have forgotten what *Zelenetzky's* place is as aid to Kirill, you speak with him and think the question over together. — *Tchebikin* was very nice yesterday and most willing to help — and so I get another wing still for Alexei's hospital (ex Academy). —

Our Friend had a good, long and nice talk with *Sturmer* — he told him to come to me every week. —

Now I must end, Zikov is waiting to see me — always somebody and have to write in a hurry.

Goodbye, my Treasure Sweet — I cover you with tender, passionate kisses and remain yr. fondly loving old

Wify.

God bless you.

No. 329.

Tsarskoje Selo, Aug. 10-th. 1916

My own sweet Angel,

Ever such tender thanks for your dear card. Grey and rather fresh. Go again to the hospital at 2½ for *the Mass* and feasting the 2 year's anniversary of our hospital. It will be shy work and we do not look forward to it. —

Got a wire fr. *Vologda,* they are traveling alright — before leaving, she begged me to send you her blessing and kisses. —

You will think about sending for *Raiev,* won't you, to have a good talk with him. — *Shvedov* and then *Bobrinsky* come — every day have people to see. —

Just had a wire from *Sergeiev* with the names of my wounded Siberian officers, Aug. 1 and 8-th, — losses of men he does not give. Now have to receive a Dr., who has to do with my «*Infants' and Mother's Home*» he went on an inspection — its spreading well over all Russia. — Am glad Mr. Gibbs gets on nicely, he was awfully happy to go. —

Don't you think it would be good if I stopped a few hours at *Smolensk* to look at some hospitals — and then reach you probably for dinner on the 23-rd? Yes, dear? —

Now I must be off. — God bless you, my Angel, long for you and yr. caresses. I cover you with tender kisses.

Ever yr. very own old

Girly.

No. 330.

Tsarskoje Selo, Aug. 11-th 1916

My own Sweetheart,

Heartiest thanks for yr. dear letter. I am grateful you are changing *Bezobrazov,* — it wld. have hurt the guard sorely hat he remained, as all knew it was his fault the losses were so great and useless, alas!

One speaks good of the one brother Dragomirov — God grant he may be fit for that place and work in harmony with the other Generals. Only they must have a better *intelligence service* than he had, he knew next to nothing.

Have not seen Dmitri, yes, I suppose his nerves are again, alas, good for nothing, its indeed a great pitty. Don't let him go to that lady so often — such society is his ruin — nothing but flattery and he likes it and then of course service becomes dull. You must keep him firmer and don't let him be too free with his tongue either. —

If Fred. is not well enough, I can send for C. Nierod and tell him to go to *Siverskaya* and explain all to the old man and find out what must be done. Only have I to say any date for it to come out, please, answer by wire. Operation went off well and yesterday's feast too. Now Olga and Tatiana count as serving in the hospital. — Weather cooler. The girls have been photographed whole afternoon by *Funk,* as they needed new ones for giving away to their committees etc. —

Tender blessings and 1000 kisses fr. yr. old

Own.

No. 331.

Tsarskoje Selo, Aug. 12-th. 1916

My own Sweetheart,

Ever such loving thanks for yr. dear letter. I am glad things go well in the Caucasus. — Yes, its quite good if you have 2 a. d. c. doing duty a fortnight & then change them — but keep *N. P.* for a bit longer so as to have a naval one with you & he has nowhere to go for sure; — & for you I am much quieter, when he is there — one of ours; & his influence upon Dmitri is good.

Got news fr. Ania, she sends you a kiss; to-morrow they arrive at *Tobolsk* to-day they are on the river. — Weather finer. —

Sorry have nothing of interest to tell you; — have much to do in the hospital as such heavy cases, & daily operations. —

Irina's Baby is much worse again, lives here with the Grandparents — *Irina* at *Krasnoye* with an «*angina*» — always ill, poor girl. —

Am sure *N. P.* must have many interesting things to tell you about the battles.

Are remaining on the balkony so as to be near in case poor *Renshakh* has suddenly to be operated. —

Am sorry my pen produces such antics — they are always capricious at the beginning. —

Got a long & interesting «*report*» fr. my *Crimeans.* It will be a joy to be together again, tho' just now we are much needed in the hospital. — Goodbye, my Sunshine. God bless & protect you & help you in all yr. difficulties. Had an interesting talk with Bobrinsky. —

Cover you with fond & tender, longing kisses —

Ever yr. very own old

Sunny.

No. 332.

Tsarskoje Selo, Aug. 13-th 1916

My very own Angel,

Ever such fond thanks for yr. dear letter. I told all about Olga's affair to Benkendorf, who was going to give it over to Nierod, who after collecting necessary papers will tell all to the old man. —

Can imagine how interesting all is that *N. P.* has to tell you! —

The weather is not very nice & it rained too, so I remain on the balkony & then go to the big palace.

Dmitri has at last asked to come to tea. —

Sturmer begged to see me to-morrow. —

Had an operation of one of my young Siberians, & heavy *dressings,* so lunched only at 1½. —

Thank goodness the Roumanians will at last move — & what are our movements for the 15-th? —

Benkendorf finds I must give a luncheon for Prince Kanin in September — a bore during the war, but I suppose necessary. —

Well, are you thinking about *Beliaiev* as Minister of War — I think it wld. be after all a wise choice. — *Bobrinsky* finds things cant work well, whilst *Sturmer* has so much to do, he cannot give himself over to one thing properly & entirely as he ought to & our Friend found the same thing too. —

Now Sweetheart, beloved One, I must end. God bless & protect you. I kiss you with unending true devotion & love you more than ever.

Yr. very, very

Own.

No. 333.

Tsarskoje Selo, Aug. 14-th 1916

My own Beloved,

Warmest thanks for yr. sweet letter. Well, one hears much good of *Gurko.* God grant him success & bless his commandment.

More than ever my thoughts are & will be with you these days, & I have asked our Friend to remember & pray much. —

I send you my Image back again, I have had a little border & safe ring made to it. — Also foggy, grey & rather cold, a September day. —

Dmitri took tea with us yesterday — his heart is not in a good state, moves like mine also therefore of course has at times pains, feels weak & gets out of breath. He ought to make a cure, as it is only beginning & then he can be quite cured. — We went to our *Pestcherny Chapel* this morning. Afterwards we go to the *store* in the big palace for me to give jetons to all the workers. —

Irina & Felix take tea. — *Shirinsky-Sakhmatov* has died — probably he had cancer — am sorry for his wife. —

Dear Sweetheart, I long for caresses & to show you all my deep, unending love & devotion — its hard, always being seperated!

Goodbye & God bless you sweet Sunshine.

I cover you with kisses & remain yr. deeply loving old

Wify.

No. 334.

Tsarskoje Selo, Aug. 14-th 1916

My beloved One,

I have remained at home this evening as am very tired and want to go to bed at 10 and drink something hot, as am fighting a cold down. The weather is quite sad, raining and cold and so dark all day. — Went to Alia this afternoon and sat a while with her and her husband, she looks and feels very unwell, has lost 15 pounds since spring. Then I went to Ania's hospital, found all in good order. Afterwards — to give jetons to 70 people in the big palace.

Irina and Felix took tea — they were quite nice and natural, she very brown and he looking very thin, short hair and as page looks much better and holds himself properly. — Then to rest had *Sturmer* (therefore this big sheet of paper). If only I can write clearly and properly with a stupid, tired head. — Well, to begin with, it was a great blow to him that *Beliaiev* has been dismissed, as he had given him the question over about the prisoners whom one must have for coalmines, etc.: all over the country, and wished him to speak with the Commanders of armies to arrange with them how many they can spare etc: — he gave him over this necessary and urgent commission for the *food* questions. Now he is no longer in the ministery, not liked by *Shuvaiev,* will no longer be able to help him, and he really is a capable man and works far more than *Shuvaiev,* who never appears at the Council of Ministers but sends his representants. I so much hoped you wld. name him minister of war — is a real gentleman and knows all questions, and a really able man, tho' *Shuvaiev* cld. not appreciate him. — We spoke long about the *food* question and wondered, whether it wld. not be more advisable to choose a military man (for example *Shuvaiev* himself, who cld. manage for sure that question well as it resembles all he did so well for the *Quartermasters Department* — instead of being minister). *Alexeiev* does not care for *Sturmer,* has clearly let other ministers feel this, perhaps because he is a civilian, and a military man wld. be more welcome. He wld. have to have the rights of Minister, wld. remain what you named him, at the head of it all, wld. see that all work together, help the ministers — and you wld. not have to change anything. He is not tired of the work nor affraid of it, only we thought perhaps you might prefer a military man to do it. So I said I shld. find out, and in case you wish to speak it over with *Sturmer* and please send for him — he does not wish to bother you and wld. wish the initiave to come fr. you. —

Then about *Volzhin* he will give him the paper now — and wont you see *Raiev* to have a good talk with him and see whether he suits you — I believe that he, with *Zhevakhov* as aid wld. really be Godsend for the Church. If you wish to see him, wire the date to me, without mentioning the name and *Sturmer* will let him know. The other candidates I find quite unfit and knowing next to nothing about the church.

When I spoke with *Bobrinsky,* he also found a special man ought to be at the head of the *food supplies* and who wld. have no other thoughts in his head and only live and think of this. — The old *Khvostov* comes to present himself to-morrow.

So sorry to bother you with such a letter, but the old man always feels relieved, when he can pour out his heart to one and is glad, when I go to the *Headquarters.* I daily pray God to help me be of use to you and come with right advice, our Friend encourages *Sturmer* to speak with me always, as you are not here for him to talk over things with. — I am touched the old man has confidence in yr. old woman. —

Why was *Beliaiev* cleared out? Does it make it now easier for you to name him Minister? —

I got 2 wires fr. Ania with lovely impressions fr. *Tobolsk,* where she has prayed for us all. To-night they already leave again, to-morrow are on the river and 16-th reach *Pokrovskoye.* I shall finish this letter to-morrow. Sleep well Sweetheart, beloved Angel, my one and all, my dear patient sufferer. —

My prayers and thoughts are at the front — for sure they begin at 4 in the morning as usual — God help them and the holy Virgin, whose great feast it is — may she bless our troops. —

15-th. Good morning my own Treasure. Fondest thanks for yr. dear letter I found upon my return from the hospital. I am sorry you have not such a very high opinion of *Beliaiev,* he seems always so exceedingly willing and does try his best, but I think it has been more than hard for him working under these 2 last Ministers of war — and he was going to help *Sturmer* now so much and he intensely regrets he wont have his help now — Perhaps independant he might be alright? —

I had a letter fr. *Olga Evgenievna* — you know she is always so grieved her husband no longer has his »eagles«. Now she read the Commanders of Military ports (rear or vice-admirals) — order 26/5. 1916 and of course her hopes and apetite arose, she begs m e o n l y to know this — but I mention it to you feeling, I must say sure, you cant do anything and *Nilov* I know is against him and laugh at the idea of her wanting *Papa F.* to get the »eagles« back again. —

Not nice weather, raining and grey, the sun tried twice to break through the clouds, but without any success. — We were in our *Pestcherny Chapel* and then in the hospital — little work by chance, so had more time to sit and embroider and then fed some of those who cld. not eat alone. — Tho' I went early to bed, 10, only got to sleep after 2½ and woke up for good again at 7½. — Remaining on my sopha, so as to rest more. —

Now sweet Angel, Goodbye and God bless you. Endless tender kisses fr. yr. very loving old.

Sunny.

Poor Pr. *Shirinsky-Shakhmatov* died. —

No. 335.

Tsarskoje Selo, Aug. 16-th 1916

My own truly Beloved,

A big kiss for yr. dear letter. Benkendorf will bring you the papers about Olga in a few days. It continues pouring, wh. is really depressing. — Had an operation & many heavy *dressings* with tears & moanings! —

Saw *Maltzev* a moment, he says their guns help immensely & the aeroplanes keep away. They are at *Lutsk* & helped at *Rezhitsa* — he has come for a few days. — I am sending Marie's train off & have asked the *Headquarters* to say where it is to go, quite to the left or to the guards. —

Siroboyarsky has been sent south, passed the 8-th to the 11-th Armycorps for whatever place needed.

My *Crimeans* are not very far fr. *Halicz,* — *Sedov* reached them alright. — I hear *Sandro L.* intends marrying an awful woman, Ignatiev, born Coralli, former cocote with a dreadful reputation — her sister is ruining old *Pistolkors* for 3 years. I do hope it can be prevented — will only bring the foolish boy great misery. —

Ania & *Lili Den* reached *Pokrovskoye* this night. — Miechen took tea & was alright, enjoyed her visit to *Belaja Tserkov* & to Antoinette (Josef) Pototzky.

Real summer weather, everybody bathing & in summer dresses. —

Have to go now to the big palace to be photoed with the wounded — dull. —

Spent the evening in the hospital, lay there also on a sopha so as to rest more.

Goodbye my Treasure Sweet. God bless & protect you. Very tenderest kisses fr. yr. own old

Girly.

How nice the photos of Alexei with the boys. — So Germany has declared war to Roumania, I thought as much. Endless kisses lovy.

No. 336.

Tsarskoje Selo, Aug. 17-th 1916

My own Sweetheart,

Warmest thanks for yr. dear letter — can imagine how awfully tired & weary yr. poor head must be. Sunny will come & freshen her Treasure up with caresses. God grant we shall be together Monday at 5½ for tea in the train, yes? Am yearning for my 2 Beloved ones.

Rain continues, still hope to get out at last if clears up a bit. — Now La Guiche comes to me. — Am sending *Yedigarov* off with *Yakovlev* in Marie's train to-morrow to see if he can manage. If he went to another regiment he wld. sit on the head of others. — Lady Muriel Paget takes tea with us this afternoon. Always daily people to see & many *reports.*

Of course its sad for you about *Bezobrazov,* but you saved him once, gave him this beautiful chance — & he was not fit for it — whats to be done — one cannot keep one & loose thousands because of his obstinacy. —

Yes, send for *Sturmer* & speak to him about *Raiev.* — Really I think *Beliaiev* wld. be a good choice & *Shuvaiev* more capable for the *food question,* as he managed the *Quartermasters Department* well — & *Sturmer* remains at the head still, so will watch that the Ministers do what the other asks. —

Must end now. Cover yr. beloved face with tender kisses & remain yr. deeply loving old

Wify.

God bless & protect you & help our troops & send success — all prayers & thoughts with them. —

No. 337.

Tsarskoje Selo, Aug. 18-th 1916

Sweetest Lovebird,

Very tenderest thanks for yr. dear letter. —

Grey weather, but warmer. Do you manage still to lunch out, do hope so. — Lady Muriel Paget goes out to the guard again, she was there during the battles and had much to tell — envy her. — Also got a wire fr. *Tiumen to-day. »A bad tree will fall whatever be the axe which cuts it. St. Nikolas is with you — by his miraculous appearance he always does wonders.«*

So glad you are contented with *Gurko* — is it the one who lay at us and whom Pss. Gedroitz saved at the Japanese war?

Worked hard this morning, now must go to the blessing of Olga's wagon, arranged by Thekla *Orlova Davidova.* Fancy, poor *Petrovsky* wrote to Ania that *Sandra* had a son in July — not his certainly and he has no idea who is the father (may be several) and it counts him so to speak as they are not divorced — poor boy, am so sorry for him, he had no idea that she was expecting — she has been for months in the country. —

Must end now. In four days, God grant!! Of course Becker will catch me up at the *Headquarters,* am furious. —

Goodbye my Sunshine, God bless and keep you!

Endless tender kisses fr. yr. very

Own.

No. 338.

Tsarskoje Selo, Aug. 19-th 1916

My own Treasure,

Always in a hurry. Fondest thanks for yr. dear letter. Glad you are over yr. conversation with *Bezobrazov.* — Just had a good talk with *Zhilik* about Baby's lessons and ideas I have and he is writing them to Mr. Gibbs. We bring Ania with us. — Then I had *Sekretev* — a long and interesting talk — so grateful to you for having saved him in *Polivanov's* time, a young general of 38, so energetic — we spoke about the aviation question — that I'll all tell you when we meet. — Frederiksy asked himself to come to-day to tea.

Now I must fly to the red cross — then Pr. Golitzin. — Great grief for. many over *Beliaiev's* demission — for me and *Viltchkovsky B.* did everything so quickly and through Rostov. too and never made difficulties. —

To-morrow *Sturmer* asked to see me. — I thought you wld. send for him. Must end. Excuse untidy flying writing.

God bless you — endless kisses fr. yr. own old

Sunny.

In 3 days!!!

No. 339.

Tsarskoje Selo, Aug. 20-th 1916

My own Beloved,

This is my last letter and again written in flying haste — *the confusion* of the last day. Fondest thanks for yr. dear letter . What joy if we are going to enjoy sunshine and warmth — we only have rain, its pouring since the morning and the leaves are turning yellow. Had a lot to do in the hospital, then Mme Zizi lunched and Dmitri, has asked to come to tea. *Bezobrazov* came and talked much — I shall repeat all to you. — Poor *Masha Stenbok* has died, I regret it for the poor lovely *Orlov* boys — she managed well for them and I fear for Alexei without her to keep him fr. a foolish marriage. Now *Sturmer* comes — then must put my things together and arrange some paper, say goodbye to Alia to whom I go every second day and who also looks upon me as a second mother. My «Children» augment and so many like to pour out their hearts to old me. —

Thanks God for the good news, oh how lovely it is and now the 23-rd comes!

Am bringing *Botkin* as *S. P.* goes away. — Of course beastly Becker is coming — awful nuisance spoils everything. Feel rather rotten to-day and look forward to my »rest« with you, Sweetheart. —

Endless kisses and blessings

Ever yr. very, very

Own.

Poor *Liza Rebinder (Kutaissov)* died. —

No. 340.

Tsar's Headquarters, Sept. 4-th 1916

My own beloved Sweetheart,

Its horribly hard leaving you my both treasures again, tho' we were 2 weeks together, its never enough for loving hearts. And above all at such time when you have such a terrible load to carry upon your poor, dear shoulders. Could I but help you more — I pray so hard for God to give me wisdom & understanding so as to be a real help for you in every way; & to advise you always rightly. Oh, my Angel — God will send better days, luck & success to our brave troops — may He enlighten the Chiefs that they should leed them right & wisely. — You will be having the ministers now & speak on energetically to them — they do try, are only so slow & heavy to move. —

Only my Sunshine — please, I entreat you — do not hurry with the Polish affair — dont let others push you to do it until we get over the frontier — I fully trust in our Friends wisdom endowed by God, to council what is right for you & our country — He sees far ahead & therefore His judgement can be relied upon. — Your loneliness will be great — & so dull — no real friend near you — shall be quieter when *N. P.* returns again — he is one of ours, blessed by our Friend to be of use to you — & now he has learned & seen much in these months. —

What shall I do without yr. caresses & beautiful love! I thank you over & over again for all & for this holiday — shall live upon sweet remembrances. Keep well. God bless you. Cover you with endless, burning kisses & hold you tightly in my arms.

Ever Sweetheart, yr. very own old

Wify.

No. 341.

Tsarskoje Selo, Sept. 6-th 1916

My own beloved Angel dear,

I was intensely happy to receive your dear long letter & kiss & thank you for it over & over again. Oh, my Love, how I miss you, so empty here — but notwithstanding I slept like dead beat & did not wake up once in the night, wh. for me is a more than rare thing. A bright, sunny day — the leaves are so yellow & red — quite autumn — a great difference in these 2 weeks. Found our wounded all much better. Placed our candles at *Znamenje* & then did our work.

Taube & Pss. *Gedroitz* thank very much for yr. messages. — Paul has already asked to come to tea. *Colonel Maltzev* is coming now as wants to see me before returning to *Lutsk.* Saw *Yedigarov,* who went with Marie's train for a trial. He wants to get service now in Persia where is being formed a *cavalry unit* — against the Turkish gendarms or something like that — & I shall try & help arranging it for him. — Long talk with *Viltchkovsky* — affairs — & Isa to lunch as her birthday & now feel quite stupid in my head already.

Poor Countess *Renshakht Rit* came yesterday — holds herself very bravely, & then Ania. She showed me our Friend's wire to you. He says from to-day on the news will be better. The Image in the Monastery to wh. I several times went (He knows it, years ago prayed there when He walked all over Russia); says its a very miraculous one & will save Russia. — Do go to it once, its so close to the house — & the Virgin has such a sweet face. — He spoke with *Raiev* over an hour, — says he is a real God's send, & spoke so well about all Church questions & in such a *spiritual* way. — Is sad that heaps of people write nasty letters against him, *Gregory,* to *Alexeiev.* — We traveled well, it was so *cosy* having *N. P.* with us & reminded one of the *Headquarters* so much. — Had good long talks about all the serious questions. He is so grateful to you for all yr. great kindness to him. — Lovy dear, please dont let them present Mme *Soldatenko* to you — you remember I told you I had the conviction *Grabbe* wants to do it. And fancy that nasty man had the idiocy of telling Nini his friend, that he hoped I wld. not be going now to the *Headquarters* so as to get you acquainted with her & that she might become yr. mistress. What a vile, low thing to say — she was furious & gave it him nicely. (Thats, no doubt, why he gives you these exciting books to read.) Don't repeat this to him, but keep her away — she tried to get Isa to come to her, but she thanked & refused. Her reputation is very bad — *N. P.* knows with whom she »lived« before — this is her second husband — & he said he wld. not set his foot in her house. She tries to catch the grd. Dukes & suite — to play a part — I saw how she looked up at their box & found it strange she stood below when we passed — I told you then I felt sure they want to get her presented. — Its a dirty, mean thing of *Grabbe,* when we are so kind to him. — I should not have allowed her to remain living there — its a bad ton at the *Head-quarters* & will give rise to talks. To-day at the cynema she is sure to turn up again. — Excuse my writing all this but I want you to take care of *Grabbe*. Another thing he said to *Ressin* (know all this fr. Ania) that *Voyeikov* will be leaving & that one will propose his place to *Grabbe* who will refuse & then to Ressin & he begs him to accept, & he said he certainly wld. not, because he knows one wld. never propose it to him — this astonished *Grabbe* greatly. — Must hold him in hand — he plays the fool & is amusing with the Children, not clever but sly & not »clean minded«. — Forgive change of pen, but the other needs refilling — I have 2 such pens, only this one is thicker. — It was good having some cosy, calm talks in my compartment — only too little, on account of the boys. I live on the remembrances & thank God He lets us meet — 4 months is a very long time to be away. — Me too kisses oo sweet letters & reread them with a yearning heart. — Its cosy living in the train, I like it. But with joy I took my bath last night. — You know *Pustov.* is one of the men of yr. staff I like best — such kind, honest straightforward eyes. — Thank God, news better. Our-Friend wld. have liked if we had taken the Roumanian troops in hand to be surer of them. — We are going to drive.

Sad, already autumn before we scarcely had any summer here. — Must end. I send you some photos I did. — Love to Dmitri & *Igor*. — I bless & kiss you without end, long to feel yr. tender arms around me & kiss yr. sweet lips.

God be with you, Nicky mine. Ever yr. very own old

Sunny.

No. 342.

Tsarskoje Selo, Sept. 7-th 1916

My own sweet Angel,

Thank you from the depths of my heart for yr. beloved letter. I cover you with kisses for it, Lovy. —

Here one is always in a hurry. From the hospital to the *funeral hymns* of poor little *Zolotarev*. — His sisters remind one of him. His horse followed in the procession — & the men of his *squad* stood watching on crutches — so pathetic. — Then *Silaiev* & *Raftopulo* to lunch. The Prof. is very much against his returning to the front & spoiling his health completely — he agrees its unwise — but he wants to try & put order in the regiment & clear away bad elements. If you wld. let him try that & then say you will keep him in the suite, that wld. be best of course. His heart is in a bad state & he is so weak & unfit. He leaves to-morrow for the *Headquarters*. To my mind he wont stand it above a few days at the front. He can be of use to you always & such a perfect pure man, as one rarely finds — but no health, alas, any more; & so worried. —

Then I received officers — *Kazakevitch* too, who needs still treatment & hopes later to get service in the south. — Ania has just come & sends much love. — *Sturmer* comes at 5½ & I see our Fr. in the evening. — *Tatiana* worked for me & I sat & looked on, as must take care of my heart. — *N. P.* was with our Friend & He was contented with him & that through suffering had quite come back to Him & God. — Baby wrote a sweet French letter all alone, too nice; — I send him his money. —

I send you a petition of the widow of Sauvage — he died at the war — she is a nice woman, very poor, has two big daughters & asks for a bigger pension. —

The other 2 petitions are fr. a poor *official* who asks his son to be put into a cadetcorps.

Your dear letters are my joy — miss you oh, so, so much Sweetheart! — Now must end, beloved Angel. — Ah yes, I had Paul for tea & a long talk. Well, I think he will really be of use & has quite sound ideas. —

Seems again losses amongst our sailors, & a young officer (we dont know) wounded through the mouth. Do wish they wld. take them back, they are much to good to be wasted like that. —

Olga has a committee this evening. —

God bless & protect you. Remember wify to-morrow, Sept. 8-th — my day. —

If not too tired shall try & go to Church this evening. Very, very fondest endless kisses & boundless love, my Own,

Fr. yr. little

Sunny.

My love to Dmitri & *Igor*. —

No. 343.

Tsarskoje Selo, Sept. 7-th 1916

My own Sweetheart,

Tho' I am very tired I must begin my letter this evening, so as not to forget what our Friend told me. I gave yr. message & He sends His love & says not to worry, all will be right. — I told Him my conversation with *Sturmer*, who says *Klimovitch* must absolutely be sent away (he becomes senator) & then old *Khvostov* will go, as he cannot get along without him. *Khvostov* is nervous & feels ill (I know he dislikes *Sturmer* & so does *Klimovitch*, who is a bad man, hates our Friend & yet comes to him pretending & cringing before him). Now *Sturmer* wants to propose this Pr. Obolensky fr. *Kursk—Kharkov* (before that at the old *Headquarters* with *Nikolasha!!),* now works at the *food-question,* to become minister of the Interior, but *Gregory* begs you earnestly to name *Protopopov* there. You know him & had such a good impression of him — happens to be of the *Duma* (is not left) & so will know how to be with them. Those rotten people came together & want *Rodzianko* to go to you and ask you to change all the ministers & take their candidates — impertinent brutes.

I think you could not do better than name him. Poor Orlov was a great friend of his — I think *Maximovitch* knows him well. He likes our Friend since at least 4 years & that says much for a man — & this Obolensky is sure to be again of the other clan. — I don't know him, but I believe in our Friend's wisdom & guidance. He is sad you never come here — yr. presence is also needed here, even if only for 2 days, unexpectedly, they will all feel the *Master* has come to have a look. It would have been lovely, & not difficult for a flying visit & make people happy. — I told Him that *Sturmer* spoke to me about announcing officially about Constantin: — you know what you said to Georgi. He also thinks it wld. be good as it binds France & England before the whole of Russia & then they must keep their word after. — About Poland He begs you to wait, *Sturmer* too; only not before we cross the frontier — do listen to Him who only wants yr. good & whom God has given more insight, wisdom & enlightenment than all the military put together. His love for you & Russia is so intense & God has sent Him to be yr. help & guide & prays so hard for you. —

I told *Sturmer* again about having the paper about the money given to the *Union* to be printed — you told it him long ago — he said the ministers were looking it through — you remind him again. So as not to forget write out — or no, here I shall write out for you to remember, when you have him on Saturday. —

Our Friend finds it excellent to send out *units* with priests or monks fr. all the different monasteries — to be in the *front* hospitals & go out & burry our poor dead, where the regimental priests have no time — I shall speak to *Raiev* to-morrow. —

I must go to sleep now, its after 12 & I am very tired. Rested fr. 6—7 & then went to Church. — Goodnight & sleep well, my Pet — think of you so constantly — so empty & quiet here. 4 months we have not slept together — even more. —

Bless you, Lovebird, God give me strength to be yr. help & find the right words to give over everything rightly & to persuade you as our Friend & God would wish.

8-th My day. — Thank you my Huzy sweet for your precious letter. Such joy to hear fr. you. — That new Admiral, is he not the one Fillimore appreciates so much? God grant him success — one does need energetic ones & poor Kanin's ill health no doubt made him less capable latterly. —

Just saw Benkendorf about the Japanese. — The girls have gone driving with *Irina* & I take the others & Ania. —

Now must end. God bless you my Life & joy. —

I cover you with kisses & remain yr. own old

Wify

No. 344.

Tsarskoje Selo, Sept. 9-th 1916

My very Own,

Warmest thanks my own Sweetheart for your so sweet letter. -- Went to *Znamenje* for half an hour to the hospital & then to town with Isa & (Ania) to see poor Css. Hendrikov, who is quite dying — utterly unconscious, but I remembered she had asked me to come when she wld. die. *Inotchka* also just arrived fr. the country looking awfully ill; Nastinka very brave only cried when I went away. Then I placed candles in the *Kazan Cathedral* & prayed for you, my Angel. Back at 1¾. Lovely, sunny day. Too tired to go out.

Despairing that the losses of the guard again are so great — but have they advanced at least. — Paul has not a good impression of *Kaledin,* says he never seems sure of success — & that is not a good thing, as then he is less wise & energetic — wish they wld. spare the guard more. — Dear Sweetheart, all my tender, tender love & thoughts surround you with great longing & love — hate yr. loneliness.

You know deary, I shld. not have Dmitri & *Igor* on duty at the same time, am sure *Igor* feels he is at a disadvantage then — & notices the difference of ones treatment with Dmitri & then he comes more silly & his amour propre suffers. We had *N. P.* for tea yesterday — he left for 2 days to Moscou to see (only) his 2 sisters who had just come there — the widow with her boys & the youngest sister. — Miechen has gone off for 10 days to Odessa etc.!

Since Aug. 10-th my Siberians have 43 men killed, 281 wounded, 2 *lieutenants* killed, 2 wounded & 2 contusioned. — Had *Raiev* for nearly an hour — interesting & understanding so well all the necessary questions. *Zhilik's* letters about the »hand« are most interesting — can imagine how excited Babykins was. — A triumphal arch for the Japanese is being erected in town near the station — seems strange in war-time. —

Ania has begun reading an interesting English novel to me. I spend the evenings at home, too tired to go to the hospital. — Greek Nicky seems still to be at *Pavlovsk.*

Now sweetest of Loves, whom I miss so greatly & long to clasp to my burning old heart — goodbye. God bless & protect you & help you in all. A tender kiss fr. yr. old

Sunny.

Please, take *Protopopov* as minister of the Interior, as he is one of the *Duma,* it will make a great effect amongst them & shut their mouths. —

No. 345.

Tsarskoje Selo, Sept. 10-th 1916

My own beloved One,

Warmest thanks for yr. dear letter. So sorry I had to bother you about all those questions, only I wanted to prepare you. *Shakhovskoy* too good to be changed, & as *Khvostov* wants to leave & *Protopopov* is a suitable man, *Gregory* says — had to tell you — & that Pr. Obolensky would be again of the opposite clan & not a «friend». —

Such a busy day & feel so tired. — Two of my *Crimeans* came en passant, & told me about the regiment. — See old *Ivanov* — then an (American) *unit* under Tatiana's protection presents itself — then *Gussiev* (the younger one) who returns to the regiment. — Then go to a *Refuge* for Children (Olga's) in the hussar barracks or manege.

Then Pr. *Golitzin* — & at 8,20 off to town to a *funeral service* for Css. Hendrikov, who died this night at 4. —

I enclose a touching wire from old Frederiks — tear it when read.

Thanks for the English papers — don't you and Mr. Gibbs read them?

Baby wrote me his first English letter to-day. — Glorious, sunny day, orange & yellow leaves glitter beautifully, 15 in the sun, but I think, there was frost this night. — Sweet Angel mine, always in thoughts with you & so tenderly. — Cant understand why the guards loose so many & have such little luck — always worries for you. —

Ania has gone for the night to Terioki. — Must receive now. —

Goodbye & God bless you, my very precious Treasure, Sun of my life & love. Cover you with fond, burning kisses. — Ever yr. very, very

Own.

No. 346.

Tsarskoje Selo, Sept. 11-th 1916

My own beloved Angel,

Raining & grey. —

Very tender thanks for your precious letter, Lovebird & wire. Shall arrange then for my 7-th *supply train* to be sent to the Caucasus as soon as ready. — Sister Olga's sanitary train (off our *section)* has been much bombarded, the officers' wagon quite spoiled & the Apothecary Compartment much damaged, but nobody, thank God, hurt. — Did not go to Church as too tired. Then *Loman* begged me to tell poor *priest* that his eldest son (the favorite) had been killed & one had been obliged to leave his body. I had never had such a task before — he took it as a brave Christian with big tears rolling down his face! — Then I went to the hospital, made 4 *dressings* & sat knitting & talking long to *Taube*. —

Now have 5 officers to receive, then Mme Zizi, *Senator Witte*. Were yesterday evening at the poor *Countess funeral service* — she lies there with such a peaceful face — at last her long martyrdom has ceased. —

No, lovy, its my heart I feel & the whole body aches, so, so tired — It always comes fr. time to when I have been tiring myself. — Oh, I do s o long for you, my Boysy sweet — so lonely without you!

One hears nothing about the war, only sees by the death announcements the losses in the guard. —

Shall see Apraxin about my little *stores* — his wife is expecting her 5-th baby. — Goodbye now, my one & all, my Treasure dear. I bless you, God be with you. A thousand tender kisses fr. yr. very own old

Girly.

To-day a week we parted, seems much longer! —

No. 347.

Tsarskoje Selo, Sept. 12-th 1916

My own Sweetheart,

Warmest thanks for yr. card. Nice, sunny weather, so after a week am at last going for a drive. *Tatiana* & *Anastasia* have gone riding. — Went late to the hospital as felt too tired. — Just saw *Maslov,* begs to thank you ever so much for having made him general & kept him in the Suite — it came then so unexpectedly & he had no occasion to thank. — To-morrow is the funeral of the Countess — I think I must get out of it, too tiring — & yet its unkind not being near poor little Nastinka. —

My *Crimeans,* son of *Emanuel* arrived — slight wound, gained at that last attack of theirs. — I thought of giving the Japanese my photo in a very big fine frame of Faberge's for his wife — shall I add some Vases of the fabric *(factory)* too?

I think Kirill brought him to lunch to the farm in 1900? — Benkendorf tells me Frederiks let him know that Miechen arrives at *Livadia* 15-th for 3 days, (what confounded cheek) & we are to send linen, 2 servants & silver — I strongly protested & said first to find out whether she asked you — we have no Hôtel there — beastly impertinence, needs sitting upon — can live at *Yalta.*

Long for you my Sweet Sunshine — cover you with longing, tender kisses. God bless & protect you.

Ever yr. very own old

Wify.

Perhaps you will send *the priest* a wire to *Elagin.* — Nastinka sends touched thanks. Enclose a letter fr. A. —

What news fr. the front? So anxious to know. — Goodbye, agoo wee one. —

No. 348.

Tsarskoje Selo, Sept. 13-th 1916

My own Sweetheart,

A lovely sunny morning — am only going to the hospital again at 11, as too tired — Tatiana will dress the wounds for me. — We had *N. P.*

to dinner yesterday — so strange without you — he met all the Japs in Moscow by chance. —

So it seems you gave the permission to Miechen — hope she asked you personally — nevertheless, most incorrect she did not wire to me too — so impertinent. —

Such beautiful weather, that shall go for a little drive with the big girls. *Sturmer* has asked to see me to-day & *Schulenburg* & then I had wounded. Saw *Benkendorf* & then I told him better to invite the relations who are here, as they be offended if I dont. —

Paul & his boy come to bring me his poetry, wh. now been printed. — Sent for *Botkin* & made him give me pills, wh. generally did me good, as feel so rotten; — therefore the girls wld. not let me go to the Css. funeral. —

Went to the hospital at 11. — Very, very fondest thanks for yr. precious letter, Sweetheart. — Glad, all went off well with the Japanese.

You know Misha's wife was at *Moghilev!! Georgi* told Paul he sat near her at the cynema. Find out where she lived (perhaps wagon) & how long, & forbid strictly it happening again. —

Paul is sad about the guard's losses — one places them in such impossible places. Beloved Sweetheart, must end & send this off. —

God bless you — very tenderest kisses fr. yr. old

Wify.

Love to Dmitri. —

No. 349.

Tsarskoje Selo, Sept. 14-th 1916

My own beloved Angel,

A lovely sunny, fresh morning. I have not gone to Church, as too tired — was last night for 3/4 of an hour. Alia lunches & then I receive officers as usual & in the evening I see our Friend in the little house.

Yesterday had *Sturmer* & spoke alright — I begged him quickly to change Obolensky, otherwise we may have great disorders in the streets (on account of food) & he will at once loose his head & all are against him. God bless yr. new choice of *Protopopov* — our Friend says you have done a very wise act in naming him. —

Paul told me of the paper he has sent to the *Headquarters* after their decision where to get young officers, *lieutenants,* from. His boy is taller than he, goodlooking, reminds one very much of the Princess. —

The Children have gone to Church — I shall join them at 11 in the hospital — we have little work, so I leave it to Tatiana, except the 2 heaviest who feel quieter if I do it. —

I shall finish this later, after getting your letter. — Beloved Angel, fond thanks for yr. dear letter. Thank goodness, Miechen asked you still, tho' its very rude not to ask the *lady of the house* too, *in my opinion.*

Shall read through Mavra's paper & then tell you what is in it — *Emelianov* suddenly turned up again. — He brought me reports fr. the commander, with the map & read them to me. The sky is clouding over, alas, so we shall quickly go for a little drive. — Precious One, goodbye & God bless you. Very tenderest kisses fr. yr. own old

Sunny.

I got this wire fr. Daisy, what am I to do with it? To give it, or speak of it to *Sturmer?*

No. 350.

Tsarskoje Selo, Sept. 15-th 1916

My own beloved Darling,

Cold, sunny morning — am going to lie in bed till I receive the Japanese, as the heart is a little enlarged & I feel so tired. — I have chosen a lovely big pair of China Vases, wood in winter & summer & 2 high crystal ones with eagles — so a pair for each of them. —

Saw our dear Fr. yesterday evening in the little house. So happy that you named *Pokrovsky* — thinks it a most wise nomination, of course some may be discontented, — but for the next (not this) *Duma* he can influence for the elections. — He told me to speak to *Raiev* about the poor monks fr. *St. Athon* who may not yet officiate & die without receiving Holy Communion. —

I read the cutting Mavra sent — vile — the hell for Germ. & Austr. prisoners, who have to work to death with us — sensationally written & I feel full of lies. I shall tell *Igor* today, that you thank Mavra for her letter, then you need not bother to write. — He sends you much love. Begs quickly to change Obolensky & when the new man is named to tell him to give the order that in the breadshops they should already have everything weighed out beforehand, so that as soon as one asks, that piece already is ready according to price & weight & then the work will go quicker & those long tails in the street be sooner appeased — one must trust to the honesty of the men not to cheat the poor people & see that the police has an eye upon those shops & the *chief of police* must himself begin by looking himself to see all is honestly & quickly done. — Resting after the Japanese — headache, very tired — suppose B. soon coming too. He was talkative & nice, so no trouble. Was delighted to see Baby's 2 friends & talk to them. He gave me fr. the E. of J. two marvelous gobelins — such exquisite work & beauty of colouring. He was so touched by yr. reception & kindness, & Motherdears, & the crowd all along the streets to the Winter Palace. —

Countess Benkendorf was awful — much too badly died red lips — ghastly sight. —

Ducky too short velvet dress & badly coiffed, such a pitty. —

Very fondest thanks for yr. sweet letter. *Drenteln* — I shall return to-morrow. One must save & spare the guard. — We spoke with Kirill who was my neighbour at table, about the battalion — also finds it a good idea what you write. I told him to be more energetic with Admirals & Ministers to get the officers he needs as yr. order must be obeyed. —

Grigorovitch told me you gave him the order through Kirill about *N. P.* to be made Commander of the beloved »*standard*« & *Zelen.* — Commander of the port (which suits the latter very well he says) — does the little Admiral not rage? But I am glad its done — how happy dear Johnny wld. be that his son, as he always called *N. P.* shld. receive the yacht. — Head aches — can't write any more to-day. — Goodbye & God bless you. — A fond, fond kiss fr. yr. very own deeply loving old

Sunny.

No. 351.

Tsarskoje Selo, Sept. 16-th 1916

My own Sweetheart,

Grey, windy, rainy morning. The Children have gone off to see Olga's sanitary train — then to the hospital & at 12½ to a *funeral service* for *the priest's* son — he begged us to come. I remain in bed till luncheon as heart enlarged & dont feel well. Had hideous headache yesterday, but passed. *N. P.* dined with us & then we read *Drenteln's* letter together; & one he had from *Rodionov* — full of despair. 3 times in one day they were all obliged to attack (I think Sept. 4) & the place impregnable, the Germans were completely hidden & their maximguns fired without ceasing. A prisoner told them they have dug themselves down 10 meters, & somehow push the guns up & down as needed, so our artillery did them no harm — they (Germans) all know our guard is against them — they feel one sacrifices them for nothing. —

I begged our Friend to particularly pray for the success of your new plans, & he does so & hopes God will bless them. — All say the Comm. of the »*Pavlovtzy*« *(Schevitch)* is a real pancake & that regiment has no success & rarely advances. It seems to me our Generals are fearfully weak. Ah yes, He said I was to tell you, not to worry when you send a General away, if he has been innocent. You can always forgive him afterwards & recall him to service & him it will never do harm, to have suffered, as it makes him realise the *fear of God.* — Ania goes for 2 days to Finland as her Mama's namesday. — Do hope we shall have nice sunny weather when we meet again! —

Thats a good idea about the battalion — told *N. P.* you thought about it — only hopes they will not be in Odessa or *Sebastopol* but in some smaller place, to keep them better in hand & less temptations, than in a big town & to keep them up to work all the while. —

Just got yr. sweet letter, for wh. very tenderest thanks. — Tell Nilov to answer Dolly that she cannot receive the name (without any reason). What does she mean, that her marriage with *Grevenitz* did not count? She is cracked, I believe. The less one has to do with her the better — & Nilov can answer best — as she was a relation of his wifes & as Frederiks is not there. —

»Me« too is looking forward to our meeting with great longing — hope to feel better by then, now am really rotten. — Fancy, Greek Nicky is still at

Pavlovsk in an awful state of nerves they say. Cannot imagine why they dont let him home at last he cant help here, or perhaps its to show their good feelings towards us. —

I send you a paper about a general *Oganovsky,* read it through & do what you like with it. —

Now must end. Its cleared up, sun shining. Becker has come. — Feel rotten, blessings & kisses without end.

Ever yr. very own

Wify.

No. 352.

Tsarskoje Selo, Sept. 17-th 1916

My own dear Sweetheart,

Fancy, only 1^0 of warmth & yesterday evening 2^0 of frost — no sunshine. — I enclose a paper fr. our Friend for you, as I asked Him to think particularly of you to bless your new combinations. — Lovy, do tell somebody to go & see to the 4 heavy batteries, wh. stand since some time quite ready h e r e a t *Tsarskoye Selo* (one tells me) & nobody thinks of sending them off. They have munition (if not sufficient, can be sent after). If old *Ivanov* is still at *Petrograd,* give him the order to go & see & look at all in detail (officers told this to *Botkin* as they have seen them quite close). It wld. be good to get them off, because the men are not quite famous — several weeks ago there were stories & rifles were sent to catch them in a wood where they were occupied with propaganda papers. — These 40 guns stand w i t h o u t guard on the place — a young *lieutenant* has written paper after paper begging for men to watch them as every morning he finds some screw or little thing taken off, missing & nobody takes heed to this. I think a general u n e x p e c t e d l y being sent here by you to make an inspection wld. be best & quickest — we so sorely need them out at the war, but dont warn Sergei — let all be done unexpectedly — & then he will also see that ones eyes must be e v e r y w h e r e. He ought to move about more — & why does André stick here — is there no nomination for him anywhere out at the war — active, not as all these 2 years? — need not be in the guard as there are no vacancies — Misha also served elsewhere. — Make the family move about more. — In the battalion *Rodionov* wrote there have been 50 cases & more of dissentry — autumn — here Css. Nierod's child & one of our wounded too. — Lying till luncheon. Saw Bobrinsky yesterday — touched me. Asks to see you next week. — Now the sun is coming out brightly — but I shall remain on the sopha, must get decent again. — Fondest thanks, Beloved, for yr. dear letter just given to me. Lovy, it was *Grigorovitch* told me, not Kirill about *Z.* & *N. P.* Now I wish one cld. hang *Rodzianko,* awful man, & such a *insolent fellow. Kiknadze* has again been wounded & lies in our hospital — told *Tatiana* lots about our sailors. We have 4 new wounded besides him —

have not been to the hospital since Wednesday, alas. — Goodbye my Treasure, & God bless you. A big & tender kiss fr. yr. very own old

Wify.

Did you let *Petia* know he is free? What does *Sandro* say about Olga's intentions?

No. 353.

Tsarskoje Selo, Sept. 18-th 1916

My very own Treasure,

Fondest thanks for yr. sweetest letter. As I lie in bed in the mornings I get yr. letters much earlier to read, wh. is a very great joy. — Sun, clouds, snow change about — real autumn. This change may make Tiny feel less well; — but that weakness in the foot by a false movement or over exertion can easily swell up — thank God, that no pain. —

We can help glueing yr. photos in the evenings, if you like. — Put all my trust in God's mercy, only tell me when the attack is to begin, so as that He can particularly pray then; — it means too much & He realises your suffering. —

Lovy, I hear Pahlen's court rank has been taken fr. him because one read a private letter of his to his wife, where he calls the *ambassadors scoundrels* & I understand him saying so. But that surely is a mistake, one has hooked onto a German name again — & he really is so devoted to you. — Much sooner & with right one ought at once in winter to have taken off *Khvostov's* uniform — he behaved vilely & everybody knows it, only *Voyeikov* & *Andronnikov* (whom I again warned *Sturmer* against) stuck up for *Khvostov*. — Now a correspondance between *Alexeiev* & that brute *Gutchkov* is going on & he fills him with vile things — warn him, he is such a clever brute & *Alexeiev* will certainly, alas, listen to things against our Friend too — & that wont bring him luck. — Now my Sunshine & Joy — Goodbye & God bless & keep you.

Very tenderest kisses fr. yr. very, very

Own.

Must quickly get up & dress for luncheon.

Think of you incessantly with longing love & earnest prayers — soul & heart with you, Lovebird.

No. 354.

Tsarskoje Selo, Sept. 19-th 1916

My very own beloved One,

A cold morning, snow on some leaves & patches on the grass — its very early this year. — *N. P.* dined with us yesterday — he leaves to-day — had a blooming cold & cough. Was twice at our Friend's, I am pleased to say. Perhaps you will be able to find him some work to do for you? — One of the men just came from the battalion — says they are used very much. In the morning they are sent back & in the evening out again — I find it horribly anguishing they will take part in the big battles now — each man is in himself a perfection — the only bit of the whole army who has got men of so many years service — God spare them for work hereafter & in the «South». — Have got two *reports, Silaiev* & *Sturmer* to-day. *Trina* and Isa for affairs. — To-morrow *Raiev* etc. & so it goes on. — Heart still enlarged & tired, but lying much is resting me, the back & legs ache less. — I do so want to get quicker well again, have more work to do & all lies upon Tatiana's shoulders. Now it seems a most interesting young American Dr. with 3 sisters has been sent here by the rich Guld — we want to use them & put them up in the big palace. He will operate there & in any other hospital. To-morrow he does in our soldiers' ward. He cuts out & fits in bones with electric machine like a fine puzzle — one can never be so exact with the hand. I looked through a most interesting book with drawings & explanations. One Dr. went with such an apparatus to England, 2 to France (the inventor himself) & this one here. The red Cross did not need him & we accept him with delight — always good to learn & see new methods. Have forgotten his name. Worked in Servia a year during the war & so can speak a little Servian. For sure, Pss. *Shakhovskoy* will fall in love with him. We have by chance a French Dr. as patient in the big palace, but as not very ill, also helps *Vladimir Nikolaievitch*. How is the air now in the diningroom — I told it *Valia* a good while ago & repeated it to Benkendorf — but they dawdled over it, & its not so complicated to have the upper windows made to open upwards. — But when we come, cant we keep to the cosy habit of dining in the train — its so much less tiring & for you I think more refreshing too & *comfortable*. —

You must be feeling dull now, I am sure, as the walks are less inviting & soon I fear too cold on the river — we came in Oct. for the first time last year, & I remember it was very cold already, we went in closed motors & then you got out and walked — w h a t joy to meet again!

Ever such tender thanks, my own Darling for yr. very sweet letter. —

Those photos were fr. me for yr. album[1], lovy dear. — I think still you ought to let *Petia* know. *Sandro* can write him letter — or you a short wire. —

Yes, find out about those guns, do. —

Horrid weather. Paul's birthday is on Wednesday — they have asked us to chocolate — doubt I shall be up & about by then. —

Now goodbye my one & all. — Fondest, burning kisses — & blessings without end

yr. very, very

Own.

---

[1] Others were for Baby & the boys. —

No. 355.

Tsarskoje Selo, Sept. 20-th 1916

My own sweet Angel,

Grey, cold, trying to snow. Little Marie has arrived & comes to us to luncheon. Ingeborg's girls sent Tatiana an adorable postcard of little Lennard — such a sturdy, splendid, goodlooking boy with big, sad eyes — nothing of their family. How can she live so calmly without him all these years is to me quite uncomprehensible & most unnormal. — Had *reports* from 5—7 yesterday. *Sturmer* has not yet found a *Chief of police* for town — those he proposed wld. never do — have told him to hurry up & think again. — *Gutchkov* is trying to get round *Alexeiev,* — complains to him against all the ministers (egged on by *Polivanov) Sturmer, Trepov, Shakhovskoy* — & that makes things clear, why is so against the ministers, who are really working better & more together & things are getting better & we fear no real crisis if they continue thus. —

Please, Darling, don't let kind *Alexeiev* begin to play a part with *Gutchkov* as one did at the old *Headquarters, Rodziansko* & he make now one & are trying to get round *Alexeiev,* pretending nobody can work but they. He must only occupy himself with the war — the others answer for what goes on behind. — *Protopopov* comes to me to-morrow & I have heaps to ask him & some ideas wh. propped up in my own old mind to make a counter propaganda against the *Union of Cities* out in the army — to have them watched & those that one catches at cleared out; the *Ministry* of the Interior must get nice, honest people to be «his eyes» out there & with the military help, see what they can do — we have no right allowing them to continue filling their ears (the soldiers) with bad ideas — their Drs. (Jews) & sisters are awful — *Shavelsky* can tell you about them. — I told *Sturmer* to tell this to *Protopopov* & he will think it over till to-morrow & see whether anything practical can be done. I dont see why the bad shld. always fight for their cause, & the good complain, but sit calmly with folded hands & wait for events. — You dont mind my coming with ideas, do you deary, but I assure you, tho' ill & with bad heart, I have more energy than the whole lot put together & I cant sit calmly by. Bobrinsky was glad to see me so & says I am therefore disliked, because one feels (the left set) I stand up for yr. cause, Baby's & Russia's. Yes, I am more Russian than many another, & I wont keep quiet. I begged them to arrange (what *Gregory* said) that good, flower, butter, bread, sugar shld. all be weighed out beforehand in the shops & then each buyer can get his parcel much quicker & there won't be such endless tails — all agreed its an excellent idea — now why did not they think of it before. —

Shakhovskoy comes today, as I want to hear how about the watertraffic — I think he is quite calm about the wood, there will be enough — but I want to ask whether, before the rivers freeze, whether one cannot bring other provisions wh. are not of his ministery, down by water — as they must all help each other — & he adores you. He was with Ania yesterday. Then I see Bishop *Antony Guirysky* from the Caucasus. — You see, all day people —

at least have time to write the morning in bed. But I long to get back to the hospital work — love it so. — Just brought me yr. sweet letter for wh. fondest, fondest thanks, I am glad you had an occasion to speak about the artillery ready here. — About *Gutchkov* & *Alexeiev* I'll tell you to-morrow, *Sturmer* told me & *Shakhovskoy* has seen the copies of the letters — I'll tell you to-morrow after having personally spoken to *Shakhovskoy*. —

Certainly if one heeds privately letters between husband & wife — far more reason to watch others. Forgive me, but Fred. acted very wrongly — one dare not judge a man so severely because of private letters (opened) to his wife — thats mean, I find. I should have made Fred. understand this utterly wrong thing. *Khvostov* ought to have had his dress at once taken off — enough proofs & scandalous, dirty affair — & here quite private. I wish one cld. set it to rights for Baby's namesday — he is still happily Senator — & the punishment has lasted enough — spying at times goes too far — & I am utterly convinced that far more write like that & openly speak so — *Kokovtzev, Krivoshein* & many others got through scotfree — & they went in action, against Sovereign & country & the Pahlens quite privately — an awful gaffe of Frederiks & certainly because the man has a German name. You have not got the head for all such things, you are far too much occupied — & others are responsable for «putting you in» & that vexes me as they oblige you being unjust. —

You say I have numbered yr. letters wrongly, so sorry, cant you change them & add a No: to the letter I left you unnumbered last time?

Heart is better to-day the rest is doing me good. — But the weather is sad indeed. —

Fancy yr. having played old Nain Jaune again! — How I wish we could have gone off all together for a few days again to Sebastopol in October, how lovely it wld. have been.

An awful thing, sticking at the *Headquarters,* in town for so many months running; and now the long winter is setting in early. — *Silaiev* told me all, poor man. — Now he will go to *Sebastopol* & ask the Professor what he is to do & where to go & take his family if possible with him — the climate does not agree with them, they need sunshine for a few months & warmth. —

Now my very own Sunshine, life of my life, sweetest of dears, goodbye & God bless you. I hold you clasped tightly in my arms & cover you with burning kisses

Ever yr. own old

Sunny.

Does Mr. Gibbs read the English papers first?

No. 356.

Tsarskoje Selo, Sept. 21-st 1916

My own Sweetheart,

Goodmorning, my treasure! At last again sunshine — such a joy; but in the evening there were at my window already 3 degrees of frost. The leaves are falling, alas, so fast, I can well see the big palace Church fr. my windows. We still take our meals in my big sitting-room. —

Am sending Paul Vases and a note, as I cannot go to him, the heart being enlarged. A week I have not left the house to-day. I cannot yet take medicins, wh. is the bore. — Again received for 2 hours yesterday & before that 3/4 of an hour Apraxin & Uncle *Mekk* about the Caucasus. — *Raiev* (good talk) — *Shakhovskoy* (long conversation). It seems *Polivanov* & *Gutchkov* are working hand in hand again. I read the copy; of 2 of *Gutchkov's* letters to *Alexeiev* have asked for one to be written out cleanly to send you, to see the brute he is. Now I understand why *Alexeiev* rages against all the ministers — after every letter (there have been many one sees) he upsets poor *Alexeiev* & then his facts are often quite intentionally falsely put to *Alexeiev*. — The ministers all feel his antagonism at the *Headquarters* & now they see why. When I send you the letter, then have a serious talk with *Alexeiev* as that brute undermines the whole government in *Alexeiev's* eyes — really vile, & 10,000,000 times worse than anything Pahlen can have written to his Wife — one must pull away *Alexeiev* fr. *Gutchkov* fr. that bad, sly influence. Then I saw Bishop *Antony Guriysky* — charming impression, cosy *Georgian* intonation in his voice — knows our Friend longer than we do — was rector years ago at *Kazan*. He buried *Bagration* — have asked him to help me collect things, linen etc. in the Caucasus & to help Apraxin when I send him there next month. Speaks strongly against *Nikolasha* & them all (to Ania) — he is too harsh & rude against the *Georgians*. — Now I have found out who the Exarch is — you remember *Platon* fr. America — whom we saw at *Livadia*, & who spoke Russian with an American accent, was unsympathetic & terribly sure of himself, perfect for the Americans but not for the Caucasus — & now I grasp why *Nikolasha* wants him, to become Metropolitain!!! why the man was always ambitious & sly & clever & has already got round *Nikolasha* — one may have to send him away, if he continues being disliked so *Pitirim* they till now simply worship. — He came for the ordination of their priest as bishop Melchizedek (our Friend says he will be a marvelous Metropolitain in the future). But of course one must not have a Metropolitain now at *Tiflis* — they only want a court round them & everything grand, will soon ask for special ministers too. *Nikolasha* says because of the country we have vanquished — nonsense — Poland had none either. — Fancy, the *Synod* wants to present me with a *Testimonial* & Image (because of my work for the wounnded, I think) — you see poor me receiving them all? Since Catherine no Empress has personally received them alone, *Gregory* is delighted (I less so) — but strange, is it not, I, whom they feared & disapproved of always. Well enough about business talks. —

Yet more officers have been brought us — the *Varshavs Guard* etc. — despairing not to be able to work & see them. — The 3 big girls went to sister Olga's train & gave medals & saw lots. — To-day O. & T. go to town for Tatiana's Committee. — Our Fr. wishes to see me this evening in the little house (with his wife too), says I won't be any the worse for it. Says not to *worry too much,* God will help out at the war. —

To-day I see *Protopopov* & *Ilyin* — every day people & ones head has to work so hard, so many questions to ask & get clear into ones head. —

I also regret Olga wants to marry now — & how about her hospital then? And *generally* I cannot help deeply regretting this marriage, tho' want her to be happy at last. —

Little Marie lunched with us — looks well — has little to do, i. e. she does not nurse the wounded, but looks after the *economical managment,* wh. gives her not much work — & then she has taken over Ella's committee at *Pskov*. The summer she lived in a wee house near a monasters where a *recluse* lives she likes. — She made me a good, quiet opinion. Dmitri mocks at her & that grieves her & the rest too, that she is so hideous as sister, much better in her town dresses etc. — thats all so foolish — instead of being grateful, that the Child has found an occupation wh. satisfies her — what will be after the war, she cannot imagine. — I enclose a letter Ania received fr. *Bresler,* do tell me what one is to answer him — can he present himself or send you a petition through me? —

Madelaine just brought me yr. sweet letter — thanks fondly, my treasure. — I understand how worried you are, shall talk with *Protopopov* today & to our Friend. *Shakhovskoy* told me that they have brought ample fuel by the rivers for the whole winter — wood & coal — of course prices high — alas. He has received much money ahead, so as to already prepare the wood for 17—18 autumn too. — I asked about the bread. Says the peasants always sold their quickly, in time of peace, for fear the prices wld. fall — now they know that by waiting the prices rise, & they have no hurry for money as are well off. I said to my mind one ought to send people of the different interested ministeries to the most essential places for flour & bread & make them speak to the peasants & explain clearly to them. When bad people wish to succeed they always speak & are listened to, now if the good give themselves the same trouble, of course the peasants will listen to them. The Governor, vicegovernor & all their people must take part, shall speak to *Protopopov* & see what he finds to say. — The reason we have not enough sugar — you know. — Now butter gets sent in such colossal quantities to the army (need much fat as less meat) that one has not enough here. — Fish there is enough, not so meat. — It interests me speaking to a new man & we'll see what his ideas are. Oh, *Krivoshein* he has everything on his rotten conscience. But still, its not as awful as all that, we shall find a way out; & these brutes *Rodzianko, Gutchkov, Polivanov* & Co. are at the bottom of far more than one sees (I feel it) so as to force things out of the hands of the ministers. But you will see all soon & speak it over, & I'll ask our Fr.'s advice. — So often He has sound ideas others go by — God inspires Him — & to-morrow I'll write what He said. His being here makes me quieter, says things will go better — people less persecute Him, whenever they are more after Him everything goes worse. —

I hope such an endless letter does not make you wild, Sun of my heart? Wish I were with & near you the whole, whole time to help carrying all together. — I send some bits of cardboard back as am sure you need still lots. — Talked for an hour with *Protopopov,* — really good impression, I have told him to send you a wire he & *Bobrinsky* sent to all the governors.

Must end, 1000 kisses, fond blessings, old

Wify.

Verily think, God has sent you the r i g h t man in *Protopopov* & he will w o r k & has a l r e a d y begun.

I think now can have *food supply* in Governments hands, not need military.

No. 357.

Tsarskoje Selo, Sept. 22-nd 1916

My own beloved precious Darling,

I have a lot I want to speak about, but as I scarcely slept at all this night, saw every hour, 1/2 hour, except 5 o'clock, on the watch, (don't know why, as had spent a lovely, soothing evening) I don't know whether I shall find words enough. —

Its not easy giving over conversations, one always is affraid of using wrong words & thus making the sense different. To begin with I send you the copy of one *Gutchkov's* letters to *Alexeiev* — read it through, please & then you will understand the poor general gets beside himself — & *Gutchkov* is untruthful, egged on by *Polivanov,* with whom they are inseparable. Warn the old man seriously against this correspondance, it is made to enervate him — & they don't concern him, i. e. because for the army everything will be done & nothing missing. — Our Friend begs you not to too much worry over this question of *food supply,* thats why I wired last night again — says things will arrange themselves & the new Minister has already set to work at once. *Bobrinsky* will have told you about their united telegram to the governors which was a clever thing. One must make them realise their power & that they should make more use of it. —

I told *Protopopov* to write this to you — he said its against etiquette as he has not yet presented himself & did not wish to bother you. — I said that was quite the same, that you & I stick to etiquette for official things, but elsewise prefer knowing always everything. — Another fault is, *Protopopov* said & which I fully agree to, that from one government to the other things may not be exported — this is absurd — in one there is scarcely any cattle, in the other more than they need — of course one must let them get it & so on. — The landlords are to have all their woods confiscated, (other pen is being refilled) not fair, as some only live by their woods & life has become very hard for them — so must use one's brain & confiscate little in some properties — & others — more, who have other means beside wood for keeping up their properties — he told this to *Shakhovskoy.* —

We spoke for 1 1/2 hour — never before, & I did not even remember his face — *Brussilov's* sly face, when he puckers up one eye. Very clever, coaxing, beautiful manners, speaks also very good French & English, one sees accustomed to speak — wont sleep, he promised me (but needs being kept in hand our

Friend says, so as that pride should not spoil all) — I spoke very frankly to him, how yr. orders are constantly not fulfilled, put aside, how difficult to believe people, promises made & not kept; — I am no longer the slightest bit shy or affraid of the ministers & speak like a waterfall in Russia!!! And they kindly don't laugh at my faults. They see I am energetic & tell all to you I hear & see & that I am yr. wall in the rear wh. is a very firm one & with God's mercy I hope I may be of some wee use to you. *Shakhovskoy* has begged to come whenever he has important questions, *Bobrinsky* too & this one will also, & *Sturmer,* comes every week, so perhaps I can get them to stick together. I am obstinate & over & over repeat the same things & our Friend help with advice (may they continue listening to Him). — Things will & shall go, Lovy.

Protopopov is looking for a successor to Obolensky as its more than necessary — he thought of *Spiridovitch,* I said no, that you & I had spoken that over before, & find him better suited for *Yalta* than the capital. He has told Obolensky to come every morning to him, has given him orders about the *quebles* in town, to have the food measured out beforehand — to put the people under shelter, in courtyards, not out in the streets — till now he has done nothing — utterly unfit for his place — too grand to accept the place of governor.

Well, I wont repeat any more, its dull for you. But its a man who will work, has promised to be truthful, may he prove it (pen made me quite filthy). — But don't give it over into military hands — I fully believe *Protopopov* can cope with this question & will do all in his power to succeed. *Bobrinsky* is very devoted, but rather old — together they will manage, *Shakhovskoy* (goose, hoped to become min. of Int., our Friend told me & therefore is a bit against *Protopopov,* tho' an old friend of his) I shall keep him up to work with the others, begged me to do it (I had already on Tuesday). Lovy, all thats in my power I shall do to help you — sometimes a woman can, when men a wee bit look up to her — these know they have me to comit with as yr. guard, eye & ear in the rear. — Its better the *food supply* remains in the hand of the governm. civil — & the military all for the *active army.* All has been taken out of the *Minister* of *Interior's* hands & *Bobrinsky* has it now, therefore they will do things together, beginning by that telegram. Their aids were most displeased but the order was given to despatch the wire. One must not provoke — & unwillingly military measures might be too hard in the wrong place — & they could not give orders to Gov. vicegov. etc. — No, I believe you can be quiet now on that subject, & our dear Friend says so too. —

Had a lovely evening yesterday & we were very, very sad you were not with us, wld. have rested you, so uplifting! There was besides a bishop, an old man, a friend of his & »very high« therefore persecuted *(Viatka)* & accused that he kissed women etc. He, like our Friend & all people in the bygone, kissed everybody alike. Read the Apostles — they kiss all as welcome. Well, now *Pitirim* sent for him & he cleared him completely. He is much higher than the Metropolitan & with *Gregory* one continues what the other begins, & still the Bishop looks up to *Gregory.* There was such peace in the atmosphere &

I longed so for your sweet presence — such a rest after all yr. endless worries & work — such beautiful talks! —

They spoke of the Virgin — that she never wrote anything tho' so very clever — her very existence & being was enough of a miracle in itself — & needed no more, she wld. never speak of herself; *(and her life is known to our spirit)*. — Just got yr. precious letter — so, oh, so glad you feel less sad. I hate not being with you, you carry all alone, not a soul to share yr. worries — speak to *N. P.*, let him be of use to you, knowing our Friend makes him understand things easier — & he has much developed these last months with that grave responsability upon his shoulders. — Well, I suppose you are right to stop the attack & go at work fr. the south, we must push on over the Carpathians before winter now its already very cold up there. — The Commander of my Siberians is wounded & amongst others, a charming officer, who left us only two months ago — hope he will be brought here. — If we advance to the south then they will be obliged to take their forces down there — & we shall be free'r up here. God will help — just patience, but the enemy is a still very powerful one.

I enclose some photos for you — *Nastinka* or Isa did. — Nastinka comes to me this afternoon. — *A report* of *Rostovtzev* — yesterday had still Ilyin & I spoke about the shocking behaviour of many sisters (not real *community* ones) etc. We spoke with *Protopopov* about the methodists being called in (10.000 they are on the whole I believe) — we both found it unwise as against their religious convictions (& their number small) — so I proposed he shld. ask the Minister of war to give them as sanitaries & then take all sanitaries (whom they always are trying to take away) to the war; that wld. be good & they wld. be serving. — Or, our Friend says, use them for making *trenches* & picking up wounded & dead as sanitaries at the war. — Our Friend finds you ought to call in the *Tartars* now — such masses in Siberia everywhere — but explain it properly to them & not repeat that wicked mistake as in Turkestan. —

Then our Friend said: *General Sukhomlinov should be set free, so that he should not die in jail, otherwise things will not be smooth, one should never fear to release prisoners, to restore sinners to a life of righteousness — prisoners until they reach jail become through their sufferings in the eyes of God — nobler than we* — more or less His words. Every, even vilest sinner, has moments where the soul rises & is purified through their fearful suffering — then the hand must be reached out to save them before they are relost by bitterness & despair. — I have a petition fr. Mme *Sukhomlinov* for you — do you wish me to send it to you? 6 months he is imprisoned, enough punishment — (as no spy) for all the wrong he did — is old, brokendown & wont live long, wld. be awful if died in prison. Order him to be taken & kept closely watched in his own house, without much fuss — please, Lovebird. — *A day is an age now — there is need of wise administrators — the chief of police should be quickly removed* as does endless harm — one is looking for a successor. — Beautifully they spoke of God, reminded me deeply of the Persian book I love — Bogoutshita. *One must see God every where, in all things, in everything about us — then shall we be saved. »Be as holy as I am«, be like God in virtue.* — Its difficult to give over what He says — words are weak — it needs the accompanying spirit to enlighten them. —

Grey, rainy day & so dark, lie in bed with a lamp writing. — These mornings lying — do me good, look rather rottener than when *N. P.* last saw me — doing everything I can to get stronger, hope by to-morrow to begin my medicins again. Except when receiving — lie all day. —

Want badly to be decent by the time we meet. Sweet one, I miss you both quite awfully. Thoughts always with you. Cover you with tender, tenderest kisses.

God bless & protect you now & evermore

Ever, Nicky my Own, yr. deeply loving old

Sunny.

What on earth is going on in Greece — looks like a revolution impending, God forbid — the allies fault then, alas! —

No. 358.

Tsarskoje Selo, Sept. 23-rd 1916

My own beloved Angel,

A glorious, sunny morning — shall lie out a little in the sun. Sat out yesterday for 1/4 of an hour — as could not get any air, even kept the *ventilator* open all night. — Greek Nicky comes to tea — leaves on Sunday at last, poor boy. — Marie has gone out riding I am glad to say. —

Our Friend says about the new orders you gave to *Brussilov* etc.: »*Very satisfied with father's orders, all will be well.*« He won't mention it to a soul, but I had to ask His blessing for yr. decision. —

Very tenderest thanks for yr. dear letter, just received. Do hope *Brussilov* is sure & doing no folly & wont again sacrifice the guard in an impregnable place. —

Am glad you liked yr. talk with Bobrinsky. —

Baby wrote me such a nice letter, sweet Child. —

Have great, great longing for you, my one & all — am trying to get better — the air may help & now medicins. —

Excuse a short letter.

Fondest kisses & blessings fr. yr. very own old

Wify.

No. 359.

Tsarskoje Selo, Sept. 24-th 1916

Sweet beloved One,

A grey, foggy, pouring morning — slept & feel midling. *Schevitch* daughter (ex *rifles)* comes to be blessed by Paul & me — she marries Dellingshausen of the 4-th reg. to-morrow. Then I see poor *Kutaissov* whose sister *(Rebinder)* died so suddenly. — Lovy, our Friend is much put out that *Brussilov* has not listened to yr. order to stop the advance — says you were inspired from above to give that order & the crossing of the Carpathians before winter & God wld. bless it. — Now he says again useless losses. —

Hopes you will still insist, as now *all is not right.* — One of my wounded wrote to me in a way for me to understand, that its utterly in vain just now, the chiefs themselves not too sure & useless losses. So you see, something is not rightly managed; more than one tells the same story. It coincides with what Paul said about *Kaledin* not being sure at all of success; — why obstinately go against a wall, break yr. heart for nothing — & throw away lives like flies. — There is your letter! how beautifully early 10½. Thanks over & over again, Lovebird. So touched by all you write that will let me be a help to you — tried before, but the ministers I felt did not like me. —

Wish—I were only quicker a bit stronger again — as then the hospital does one good in between for the soul & rests the head. —

Had Mme Orjewsky 1½ hour yesterday & then Greek Nicky. He leaves to-morrow — hopes you got his last letter, as you never wired. Will write again to-day — I must say our diplomates behave s h a m e f u l l y & if Tino is kicked out, it will be our fault — horrid & unjust — how dare we mix into a country's p r i v a t e politics & force one government to be sent flying & intrigue to get a revolutionist back to his post. I believe if you cld. get the French Government to recall Seraille (this is m y private opinion) things wld. at once calm down there. Its an awful intrigue of freemasons, of wh. the Fr. General & Venizelos are members — & many Egyptians, rich Greeks etc. who have collected money, & have even payed the »*Novoye Vremya*« & other papers to write bad & forbid good articles concerning Tino & Greece. Vile shame! —

(Cant write any more to-day. — Red cross all say Miechen's papers, wishes of a *special department* — quite wrong, cannot be apart fr. red cross.)

Godbless you. Very tender kissis fr. yr. very own old

Wify.

This a s t r i c t l y p r i v a t e letter of Pahlens to *Taneyev* & as such I must still forward it to you — one has made you do an unjust thing. I honestly should give him back his rank, he undeservedly lost — *Gutchkov* does far worse things & is in no way touched or reprimended — & Pahlen has suffered innocently. Give it him back now, before I come, so as to show its you a l o n e who have done it — or if you seek an occasion, then Oct. 5 — but please, do it, Tell *Maximov* to write all to Fred. & have it quickly donc — so pleasant to set an injustice to rights — else *Taneyev* wld. never have sent me this private letter. He does not know I even send it you. —

No. 360.

Tsarskoje Selo, Sept. 25-th 1916

My own beloved Darling,

Grey, dull weather — yet more leaves have fallen, so dreary. —

Sweetheart, I saw *Kutaissov* yesterday & we had a long talk — then Paul told me about interesting letters fr. *Rauch* & *Rilsky;* — & fr. others I have heard — & all say the same thing, that its a second Verdun, we are sacrificing 1000 of lives for no-thing, pure obstinacy. Oh, give your order again to *Brussilov* — stop this useless sloughter — the younger ones feel their chiefs have neither any faith of success there — why repeat the madness of the Germans at Verdun. Yr. plane so wise, approved by our Friend — *Galitsch,* Carpathians, Roumanians. Stick to it, you are head master & all will thank you on their knees — & our glorious guard! — Those boggs, impregnable — open spaces, impossible to hide, few woods, soon leaves will fall & no saving shelter for advance. One has to send the men far round the boggs, the smell is so awful — the unburied comrades!! Our generals don't count the »lives« any — hardened to losses — & that is sin — when you are convinced of success, its another thing. God blesses yr. idea — have it executed — spare those lives — Sweety, I know nothing — but is *Kaledin* the right man in the right place, when things are difficult? —

Now other things. — Am hunting for a man in Obolensky's place (by the by, has asked to see me — very unpleasant, does not concern me to speak about with him) — would *Adrianov* not do? Is he still in the Suite? Was completely aquitted — does it matter he was under judgement? But he came out clean. If you have nothing against this idea — wire at once that you agree No. I; then shall propose him to *St.,* who can talk to the M. of Int. — not your order, but that you would have nothing against him. He was very good in Moscou, *Dzunkovsky* tried to break his neck & *Jussupov's* — of all, *Adr.* was the least at fault. But you can judge best. — Then to finish Obolensky, how wld. it be to give him *Komarov's* place — long, I doubt his living — even if life spared, will be an invalid. A splendid place, *Preobrazhenetz* & I think quite fit for such a place. If you agree to this — wire No. 2 yes. I have it written out on a paper you see, I shall probably see him on Tuesday, then if he makes a fuss, I cld. tell him that you think of him in future for the W. P. — he is in the Suite — & *Zeime* is not & he is more suited. —

The Children have all gone to Church — I am still unable to go — such a nuisance. —

Paul will be with you on Thursday, has a big *report* & wld. like to go to the guard (very good thing) & return to the *Headquarter,* if time, for the 5-th. — What have you done about *Gutchkov's* letter? At last our *Botkin* has fully understood what a man he is — they are relations — but only now he has fully understood the great evil in him — he & *Polivanov* tried to harm his naval brother. — You saved him now, by wiring to *Russky,* who did not wish to obey yr. order about *Botkin* before — but he was received like »a dog there«. —

Paul & I blessed the little *Schevitch* — pretty girl — to-day is her wedding — the mother, old, fat, with no teeth scarcely — & she is my age! — had a baby 3 years ago, happy woman. — Sorry, nothing interesting to tell you, dull letter. — Fondest thanks precious letter come so nice & early, can't imagine why mine are so often late. — Well, I am glad that *Br.* has sent *Kal.* south & given over all to *Gurko,* thats f a r the wisest thing to do — may he be reasonable & not obstinate, make him understand that clearly. Oh, I too yearn for you fearfully — soon, soon God grant again some happy days together. Babykins, you keep him in hand, see he does not play at table or put his arms & elbows on the table, please — & dont let him shy breadballs. 5 months from here — ah when shall you be able to get away fr. that old place & see something else again! —

Goodbye, sweet One, sun of my life. Kiss you e v e r so tenderly. God bless & protect you — yr. very own old

Wify.

Please pay attention to what A. has written about *rising the wages* to all poor *officials* all over the country. It must come s t r a i g h t f r o m y o u — there is always money had fr. some capitals — a check to all revolutionary ideas. — Our Friend says if you agree to *Adrianov,* then as *temporary prefect (hold. office).* — then nobody will have anything to say against him. —

No. 361.

Tsarskoje Selo, Sept. 26-th 1916

My very own Treasure,

There — you will say — a big sheet, means she is going to chatter a lot again! — Well, *Prot.* dined with A. — she knows him already a year or two — & he proposed my friend *K. N. Hagandokov* instead of Obolensky, i. e. *V. Volkonsky* proposes him. I have the whole *account* about him — tho' we know him — & that looks really so good. Now he is *Military Governor and Ataman (Hetman) of the Amur cosacks;* has been through Chinese campagne, Jap. & this war; *participated in the repression of the sedition in Manchuria* 1900 — probably my age or younger — *in service (officer)* 10 *aug.* 1890 has all military war decorations for his rank. Our Fr. says if the likes us — why not take him — I was much taken aback, never wld. have dreamed of him. Rank *major-general.* Perhaps this all is better than *Andr.,* who of course has enemies. — I think *Hagand.* told me he left because of his kidneys — & this service is not tiring, needs an energetic man — & his white cross will already make effect. —

Things were not very nice in Moscou yesterday, so *Prot.* sent off *Volkonsky* at once & made *Bobr.* sent off his aid there too to see into the affairs. He does not waste time — I am glad to say — & they & the military will let's hope at once quieten down all. But its sure to begin here, & Obol. will be absolutely no good — we sav what he was in the reg., where he might have stopped that story. —

I send you the petition of a *medical field surgeon,* who killed a man — just read it through — he begs to be a *field surgeon* out at the war — only you can change the judgement by mercifully letting him go — our Fr. gave it to me & Rost. says only you can help. My chancellry made the red marks. — Then I send you photos I did — also 1 for *Alexeiev,* 1 for *Maximovitch,* 1 for *Mordv.,* 1 for *Grabbe* & 2 for cosacks — give Baby to give them over if you cant, dear.

Protop. has asked to see you — wont you tell him to let *Sukhoml.* out, he says it can of course at once be done, he will tell M. of Justice, write this down to remember when you see him & also speak to him about Rubinstein to have him quietly sent to Siberia, not left here to aggravate the Jews — *Prot.* quite agrees with the way our Fr. looks upon this question. *Prot.* thinks it was *Gutchkov,* who must have egged on the military to catch the man, hoping to find evidences against our Friend. Certainly he had ugly money affairs — but not he alone. —

Let the man speak out frankly to you, I said you always wish it, the same as I do. —

He quite cleverly thinks of using *Kurlov* in some things of *food supplies,* wh. is right — not to waste the man. — He got the thing at once to be printed about the millions the *Union* got & wh. the others were dawdling over — only its not what I wanted — I did not want bare facts — they are bad enough — but it was to be cleverly written — this is too naked for my taste. One can cry to think of half a milliard has been thrown to the *Union* — when existing organisations could have done marvels with a quarter of the sum. —

I enclose it for you to read. —

Very, very tenderest thanks for your dear letter just received. So happy you have given that order about Pahlen, thank you for yr. justice. — How nice you had such warmth. This morning 1^0 of frost, but sunshine thats everything, so shall lie out on the balkony before luncheon — my heart is more enlarged again & its difficult breathing. Fear, I shant be good at much this time, I am sorry to say, for much motoring. And I do so want to get to the hospital — & cant — great nuisance. —

Fancy, Rosetti's son being with you — what a type! —

How lovely it will be to be with you again soon, sunshine & Sunbeam & old mother sunny! Miss you both horribly. These break downs come regularly 3 or 4 times a year — I fill myself with medicins. —

Now my Angel, goodbye & God bless & protect you. Kisses without end on every dearly beloved, very own place — yr. Own.

The *Synod* gave me a lovely old Image & *Pitirim* read a nice *paper* — I mumbled an answer. Was rejoiced to see dear *Shavelsky.* Our Fr. worries that one did not listen to you *(Brussilov)* as your first thought was the right one & a pitty you gave in, yr. spirit was right wishing the change. He took up the Virgin's Image & blessed you fr. far & said »*May the Sun rise there*«. A. just brought these messages fr. town & kisses you. — Obolensky's wife whole time bothers our Fr. in tears that husband leaves, begs for a good place. —

No. 362.

Tsarskoje Selo, Sept. 27-th 1916

My own Angel,

When I went to bed there were already 5⁰ of frost, this morning still 1 and grey. — As heart still enlarged, shall arrange to see nobody to-morrow & remain all day in bed — perhaps that will help more — so few days have remained — leave already in 5! —

Sweetheart, you are receiving the new M. o. t. Int. to-morrow — he is emotioned. — let him realise yr. power of will & decisiveness that will help & stimulate his energy. Let him talk with *Alex.* so as that the latter may feel he has to do with a clever man who wastes no time — it will be an antedate to *Gutchkov's* letters. — Speak to him about *Sukhomlinov* he will find means of doing it — the old man will die else in prison & we shall never be at peace about it. Au fond, to save *Kshess.* & *S. M.* he also sits there, & one dare not bring up that subject before law on account of those 2 — even *Adr. Vlad.* said as much to the *Rüdiger-Beliaiev* tho' he is *Kschess.* love Then speak about *Rubinstein,* he will know what to do. — Am so happy about Count Pahlen. — Your are right about *Adrianov* I suppose, just had a paper fr. *Prot.* showing he wont do — I only mentioned him like that as he came into my head. — If *Hagandokov* can be spared — may be good, at least all his military decorations let one hope it — still you may find another. *St.* proposed a *Meyer* who was years at *Varshaw,* but the name is to appallingly German for the wild anim. ears nowadays. — 10½ yr. sweet letter has just been given to me — endless thanks & kisses for it, Treasure sweet. — Shall bring A. too, our Fr. begged it, as the girl is good & so honestly helps when & how she can, & several of «us» together will bring more peace & strength. She can lunch in the train, as shy work in the room with many people — will enjoy the rest, nice air, drives, tea etc. — & we shall still be to ourselves — she does not fidget now. — I bless & kiss you without end in passionate love.

Ever Huzy mine, yr. very own old wify

Alix.

I return Nicky's letter to you — exactly as he spoke to me — please talk to *St.* severely about it — we are driving them into a republic, we, orthodox — its really shameful. —

Why cant you beg *Poincaré* (president) to recall Seraille & make Fr. & Engl. insist too (thats my idea) — & make them stand up for Tino, the King & not side with Venesuelos the revolutionist & free mason. Call out *St.* as its difficult to write — give him severe instructions, we are behaving most unfairly & understand poor Tino going half wild. —

Keep my little list before you — our Friend begged for you to speak of all these things to *Protopopov* & its very good if you mention our Friend that he should listen to him & trust to his advice; — let him feel you dont shun his name. I very calmly spoke of him — he came to him when he was very ill, some years ago. — Badmaev called him. —

Tell him to be warned against *Andronnikov* coming to him *(Prot.)* & keep him away.

Forgive my bothering you, Deary — but am always affraid as you are so terribly hard worked — that you may forget something — & so act as your living notebook. —

Sunny.

Speak to *Pr.* about:

1. *Sukh.,* order to find a way to get him out.
2. Rubinstein to send away.
3. *Prefect.*
4. Augment *wages* of the *officials* as your kindness to them, not fr. the ministers.
5. About *food supplies* tell him strictly, severely that all must be done to set it to rights — you order it.
6. Tell him to listen to our Friend's councils, it will bring him blessings & help his work & Yours — please say this, let him see yr. trust in him — he knows him several years already.

Keep this paper before you.

No. 363.

Tsarskoje Selo, Sept. 28-th 1916

My own Beloved,

Now, I said I wld. lie all day in bed & Apraxin, who was disgusted with my looks, also begged me to. Of course *St.* has just telephoned, begs absolutely to see me — so must of course at 6. *Schwedov* & Obolensky ask again — well I put them off to the next days — its always so, probably they have got wind that we are leaving & then each time all come flying. — Today warmer, poured, was a moment's sun.

Sweety, fancy only, Obolensky asked to see our Friend & sent a splendid motor for him (knows Mia, Obolensky's wife several years). Received him very nervously at first & then spoke more & more till at the end of the hour began to cry — then *Gr.* went away as He saw it was the moment the Soul was completely touched. — Spoke about all, openly, how had tried his best tho' it had not succeeded, that he heard as tho' one wanted him to *paint the roofs of the palaces* (probably somebody also imagined the same as we) — but that such a place he wld. not like — he wants work to wh. he is accustomed — & his great dream is to be General Governor of Finland — that he will always ask our Friend's advice about everything. Spoke all out against Ania, & was astonished when our Fr. said she was *from God* — & that she suffered so. — Then showed all the 20 letters our Friend had these years sent with petitions all tidily tied up — & said he had fulfilled when he could — when *Gr.* asked him about *bribes* — he said no, but his aid had taken much.

— I old. not get over the idea that he, that proud man, had come round, because in his misery he felt only with Him wld. he find strength. The wife must have worked hard at him —, & he to have cried! — Then our Friend says things wont go until yr. plan is obeyed. —

Just got yr. precious letter — kiss & thank over & over again for it. A. was just here, thanks & kisses tenderly. —

Am glad nothing has being going on at the front — was so anxious; that left move is the cleverest — near *Brody* even its so colossaly fortified & such heavy artillery to go against — a real wall.

Thanks, dear, for explaining about *Brussilov* — had not quite grasped before. — In any case our Friend says to go by y o u r i d e a s, your f i r s t are always the most correct. — Those meals outside are excellent for Baby — am bringing two camp chairs & pliable table for him too to take out with him — & I can profit to sit out then too. — There is a wonderful young, just ordained Bishop Melchizedek — whom *Pitirim* brought fr. the Caucasus — Bishop now of *Cronstadt* etc. Churches full were he serves — very high — (will in the future be a metropolitain) — fancy, he was several years *superior* of the *Bratsky* monastery at *Moghilef* & adores & intensely venerates the miraculous Image there of the Virgin to wh. we always go — please Love, go there with me & Baby — am bringing a *lamp* too to place before the Image, I promised it to the *superior* some time ago. — I am to make Melch.' acquaintance on Friday at her house, with our Friend — they say his *conversation* is marvelous; — it does one no end of good, lovely talks & helps the soul to rise up over the wordly worries for a time — but I want y o u here too always to profit with me. — We think of leaving Sunday at 3 — reaching M. for tea 5 on Monday — alright?

After yr. walk & then I can lie longer. —

What a joy to meet soon — in 5 days!! Seems incredible. — Cover you with tenderest kisses. God bless & protect you & keep you fr. all harm.

Ever yr. very own little

Wify.

Our Fr. says its v e r y much in the *spiritual sense* that a man, soul like shld. have quite come to him.

No. 364.

Tsarskoje Selo, Sept. 29-th 1916

My own beloved One,

Grey & stormy, barometer very low since two days — & all of us who have bad hearts feel it more. Lay on bed till 6 yesterday. — *St.* sat 3/4 of an hour — nothing very particular — spoke over many questions — told him strongly about my opinion of Greece — *Suchomlinov* — ministers — *dearth* — prisoners — *Gutchkov* — all & the *Duma* people know he corresponds with *Alex.* & it throws amongst good people a deep shade upon *Al.* — one sees the spider *G.* & *Poliv.* spreading a net round *Al.* & one longs to open his eyes & pull him out — you can save him — hope very sincerely, that you spoke to him about the letters. — Have nothing interesting to tell you — have my lamp burning, yesterday too, so fearfully dark dreary; — pouring. —

Such fond thanks, dear One, for yr. nice letter. Yes, *Alex.* told me the same thing about the Roumanians. As what does *Beliaiev* go there? With a letter or as counsillor? Hang them, why be such cowards! — And now of course our line is much longer again — quite despairing I find. Did you remember about mobilising the Tartars in Russia & Siberia?

How tired you must have been after yr. 2 hours *report* — but he does talk like a waterfall. Glad, had good impression — hope he spoke with Alex. — begged he should.

Sandro spoke by telephone to the Children, only few days here, some children not well, says cant come to me (he never does) & will see us on the 5-th as he brings *Andriusha* then as officer to you. —

Heart not enlarged, but aches.

Send you my very tenderest, softest kisses, Lovebird!

God bless & protect you. 1000 of caresses fr. yr. own old

Alix.

No. 365.

Tsarskoje Selo, Sept. 30-th 1916

My own Lovebird,

Warmest thanks for yr. dear letter just received. What about Obolensky & Finland? So glad your talk with *Protop.* pleased you — may he be worthy of the place you have confided him & work well for our poor, tormented country. You can write still on Saturday, because we leave on Sunday only at 3. — What a joy to meet soon again, my two dearest Treasures!! Am trying hard to get better. Heart not enlarged, filled with drops — but hurts very much. Still this evening go out to see our dear Friend & get His blessings for the journey. — Such a storm blowing, last leaves being shed — in between there were 5 m. rays of sun — not spoiled by sun this year — hope to find it at *Moghilev* — in every sense of the word. —

Made *Varavka* see A. — not at all contented with her heart (our Fr. neither), is glad she goes with us & hopes it will be a rest — here she runs about fr. morn. to night & has such deep shades under her eyes & breathes badly & feels giddy. — We all come to you to freshen ourselves up morally (after great yearning) & phisically — good air & no work.

Sad, we cant get off for a few days to the south. — Emma Fr.'s writes that her Father slowly gets better — when lies — no angoisse — but when up — begins again. *Voyeikov* has asked us to bring him to the *Stavka.*

Now Treasure, Sweetheart, goodbye & God bless & keep you. Endless kisses & love fr. yr. very own old

Wify.

Of course an affair again — its about yr. *Erivantzi,* read it through seriously.

Lovy, forgive my meddling in what does not concern me — but its the cry of an *Eriwanski* heart (on purpose don't write names) wh. has reached us. — They have heard »*admitted col. Georgian reg. Magabeli*« & they with anguish await, whether he is really to receive the reg. Mag. was promised to receive the first free regiment of the division, in every way a perfection dear men, respected, beloved by all these 37 years (but not in this case suitable). Several times he *temp. Commander* different of the reg. when the Commanders were ill, as for instance commanded a long time the *Mingrelian* regiment, whilst the Comm. was ill. Now that Comm. has been promoted General major — already 5 months & continues commanding the reg. wh. I believe is not correct in an army regiment; now give him a *nomination* & put Mag. there, as he knows the *Mingr. regiment* now so well — & all will be perfect. Alas, the *Eriv. r.* became free now first.

»Just now the regiment wants a real master — a commander, who could bring everything back to old conditions and who would be able to understand all personally, by himself, and put everything right, justly and sanely, as it ought to be by the law and it was formerly in the regiment. The commander must be quite unknown to the regiment, independent, from quite another milieu — everything will be quite clear to him, as a fresh man, and only then, only with that condition the regiment will again be like it was formerly — before Mdivani. God knows, what menaces our regiment, what dissensions, if just now the regiment will not have real glory. Col. Magabeli is an excellent soul, soft, easy, a general favourite of the whole division, modest and so on, — he was unceasingly with the regiment, makes part of it; but everybody, except himself will command the regiment. Besides he is more a friend, by his name, his family, his origin of »those« . . .

The Eriv. reg. ought just now to receive a commander who would tear up with the roots all contrast between »us« and »them« and would command our ancient regiment for its real glory and not for a definitive cleft.« —

Tell nobody about this letter — but it coincides with what Silaiev begged for an outsider now (of the guard perhaps), who cld. put a stop to the ruin of yr. beautiful, dear to our heart regiment — Mag. is an angel, but too gentle & a *Grus.* wh. just now is not the thing for the reg. wh. has parties . . .

No. 366.

Tsarskoje Selo, Oct. 1-st 1916

Yr. letters are late. Such a storm blowing. — Thanks for receiving the Metrop. & *Raiev* — they begged quickly, before Metr. Wladimir returns — only to bring the holy Image fr. the *Synod,* nothing else. — You must be tired, by the papers I see the ministers have been one after the other going to the *Headquarters.* I had Obol. for 1¼ of an hour — till I was dead beat — he talks like a wound up machene — only about the food *supplies* of *Petrograd* — touched nothing else, no time, as *Viltchk.* was waiting with a *report.* — Feel still rotten — hope change of air will set me to rights again. — Spent a quiet, peaceful evening 8½—10¼ with our Friend, Bishop Issidor — Bish. Melchizedek — talked so well & calmly — such a peaceful, harmonious *atmosphere.* From there I wired to you about *Pit.* & *Raiev;* — I wanted you to feel we were thinking of you. —

Poor *Sirobojarski* is again wounded — 3-rd time — shoulder, but bad or little, don't know, he wired to *Viltchk.* fr. *Tarnopol.* Never received his *Capit.* only yr. thanks (as in time of peace) — strange, how things are dis-honestly done — real great deeds receive no big recompense — small things in the *rear* big ones — how many suffer fr. injustices! — Such darkness. — Sweet Angel, this is my last letter to you — leave to-morrow at 3 o'clock. Going this evening to the hospital — shy after 2½ weeks & many new ones, but cld. not leave without seeing all. —

Warmest thanks & kisses for sweet letter. Glad *Beliaiev* at least used there. —

My last letter. — Goodbye & God bless you, my Angel, intensely rejoicing to meet & feel yr. warm kisses. —

Ever yr. own very

Own.

No. 367.

Moghilef, Oct. 12-th 1916

My very own Sweetheart,

Its with a very heavy heart I leave you again — how I hate these goodbies, they tear one to pieces. Thank God, Baby's nose is alright, so that is one consolation. Lovy mine, I do love you so beyond all words; 22 years have steadily increased this feeling & its simply pain to go away. You are so lonely amongst this crowd — so little warmth around. How I wish you cld. have come for 2 days only, just to have got our Friend's blessing, it would have given you new strength — I know you a brave & patient — but human — & a touch of His on your chest would have soothed much pain & given you new wisdom & energy from Above — these are no idle words — but my firmest conviction. Alex. can do without you for a few days. Oh Manny man — stop that useless bloodshed — why do they go against a wall, one must wait for the good moment & not go on & on, blindly. Forgive my saying so, but all feel it. — You need not receive any-body else, except *Protop.* wh. wld. be a good thing, or send for him again, let him oftener speak to you, ask yr. council, tell you his intentions, it will help the man immensely. — Its for yr. good & our dear countries I say all this, not from greed to see you (that wish you know will ever exist) but I too well know & believe in the peace our Friend can give & you are tired, morally, you cant deceive old wify! —

And at home its good they shld. feel you are sometimes near to all the interior work too — at this present moment you can be spared here a few days — you have the telephonogram for any question in 5 min. —

For all yr. endless Love I thank & bless you, I carry it all in my burning soul, wh. lives for you. Goodbye, my Sunshine, my joy & blessing.

God Almighty watch, guard, guide & bless you. I cover you passionately with tender kisses & hold you tightly in my arms. — I know there are people who don't like my presence at M. & fear my influence — & others who are only quiet when I am near you — such is the world.

Goodbye wee one, Father of my Children. —

I hope to go to holy Communion on the 21-st — how nice if you cld. have been with me in Church then, too good & lovely it wld. have been!!

Ever yr. very, very

Own.

No. 368

Tsarskoje Selo, Oct. 14-th 1916

My beloved Angel,

Thank you, thank you for yr. sweet little letter with l o v e l y news — cannot tell you what joy it is & what life & sunshine it brought to my sad heart. — Excuse also quite short letter — had *Protop.* for 1/2 hour, now Benk. waits, then Nastinka. This morning hospital. Only made 3 *dressings* & then sat with different ones — were at *Znam.* placed candles for you, Lovy. Glorious, bright, sunny weather. — Head stupid — Becker besides. — *Prot.* saw *Sukh.* — so happy. —

Very interesting talk was at the *Duma* this morning for 48 m. — Traveled alright, lay all day — this night slept badly — heart alright, especially since yr. letter. —

Endless blessings & kisses fr. us all. — Ever yr. very

Own.

Tell *Prot.* you are glad he goes & speaks with *Gr.* & hope he will continue. —

No. 369.

Tsarskoje Selo, Oct. 15-th 1916

My own Sweetheart,

Such fond thanks for yr. dearest letter. Hope Babykins is alright again — dont let them give him oisters wh. are not fresh. —

I feel quite different since I know you are coming for a few days — such a lovely prospect — after 6 months to see you here again. Then we can again all go to Holy Communion, if you feel inclined — & gain strength together & blessings. You don't need long preparations. — Then I suppose you wld. be going later to Reni etc. in Nov. — It will be good for you to get about again, & for the troops to see you. —

I am glad you told P. to speak to *G.* & *B.* — This evening I go to see our Friend. — He says the «*Maria*» was no *punishment* but an »*error*«. —

I shall keep Ella's letter to think about when you came. — Grey, hoar-frost covers everything, were 5 of frost. Shall go for tiny turn with A. —

Am prudent — did only one *dressing* & then sat knitting & had *Viltchkovsky's report.*

Vesselovsky has come, shall see him to morrow, has been 3 times contused — nerves shaken, Son in law died (or killed) & he wants to go for a rest to the Crimea. —

Beloved One, I bless & cover you with endlessly tender kisses & remain

yr. fondly loving old

Sunny.

No. 370.

Tsarskoje Selo, Oct. 16-th 1916

My own sweet Angel,

Very tender thanks for yr. sweet letter. Shall eagerly await you Wednesday afternoon; hope Babykins will be quite alright by that time. —

Had a nice evening at A.'s yesterday — our Friend, his son & the Bish. *Issidor.* As Obol. behaves well now & listens to him, he thinks it wld. be only good if *Prot.* had taken him as one of his aids — there he wld. have worked alright & so as not to kick him out of service. — Our Friend neither cares for *Kurlov,* but he is *Badmaiev's* bosom friend, & *Prot.* was cured by *Badm.* & so is grateful to him. — *Gr.* thinks it wld. be better to call in the younger men instead of those over 40, who are needed at home to keep all work going & to look after the houses. —

Warmer to-day but grey. Were in our lower Church for half the service & then went to the hospital. Saw *Vesselovsky* — sad many things he tells & other young ones — what goes on at the war — dear me, I understand their nerves give way, — no union, no confidence in the officers, orders, counterorders, disbelief in what they hear — very sad indeed. Ah this want of education is a misery — each for himself — never together. —

Merica & her Mother come directly — she leaves in a week to be married. —

Little *Ivan Orlov* is engaged to a Pss. Volkonsky — both such Children. —

Kiss you without end & bless you. He is so happy you are coming. —

Ever yr. very, very

Own.

No. 371.

Tsarskoje Selo, Oct. 17-th 1916

My Beloved,

Very heartiest thanks to you, my Angel, for your dear letter. — Worked in the hospital & then had a *Te Deum* in the corridor there for this day — was, so simple & nice. — 5⁰ of frost, bright & sunny, am going with Ania to see her bit of land & where one is going to begin to build. Yesterday I spent the evening at the hospital, calm & cosy. — To-day receive the Motonos who leave for Japan; Obolensky again — seems our Fr. is most contented, the man has so much changed for the better, & therefore he thinks it wld. be nice if *Prot.* took him as an aid. —

How lovely it will be to take Holy Communion all together, cannot say how greatly am looking forward to this blessing & joy; — & to have you once more home again!!

Do say that none of the family are to be on service these days.

Am so glad you wired to Tino, will help & give him courage. —

You will be glad even to get into the train again cosily after such a long time. One pen has to be refilled & this one — too much ink, — & my fingers are filthy. —

How are the Roumanians getting on? At *Orsha* you will see heaps of sisters at the station. They always came running to see one pass. —

Now, my Sunshine, goodbye & God bless you.

Soon, soon I shall have you tightly clasped to my breast again, — wont it be lovely!

I cover you with tender kisses, & remain yr. very, very

Own

No. 372.

Tsarskoje Selo, Oct. 25-th 1916

My very own Angel,

Once more we part again! I cannot tell you the joy & comfort it was to have you once more home again after 6 long months. Like old times it was — thanks for that calm joy, dear One. — I hate letting you go away to all your worries, anxieties & sorrows — here we at least share them together. — Every caress was a gift & I shall long hunger again.

For you, alas, no rest, so much hard work! And now this story about Poland, but God sends things for the best, so I will believe it will be for the best in some way or other. Their troops wont fight against us, there will be a mutiny, revolution, anything you like — thats my private opinion — shall find out what our Friend has to say. —

Sweetheart, goodbye & God help you. — I d o n t ' t like *Nikol.* going to the *H.-Q.* — may he brood no evil with his people. Don't allow him to go anywhere now, but streight back to the Caucasus — the revol.

party else will hail him again — & one was beginning to forget him; him & *Sazonov* we have to thank for the Polish question — forbid him to speak about it — get *Zamoisky* away when he comes. —

God bless yr. journey. My heart is very heavy. I cover you with endless, passionate kisses. Cannot bear yr. having perpetual sorrows & anxieties & being far away — but heart & soul are ever near you, burning with love. — Ever, Sweetheart, Sunshine mine yr. very own old

Wify.

No. 373.

Tsarskoje Selo, Oct. 26-th 1916

My own Sweetheart,

All my tenderest thoughts surround you — very empty, grey & lonely without sunshine & sunbeam. Long, lonely night — joy to get yr. two wires. —

Yesterday evening saw our Fr. with his 2 daughters in the little house, spoke so beautifully — was so happy to have seen you. Begs you to answer all who speak or worry you about Poland. »*I do all for my son, will be pure before my son*« & that will at once shut their mouths — strange, I said the very same to *Listopad* then too, only let none worry you & stop them talking — you are the master. — The Wedding in our hospital went off well — a handsome couple, I was his »Mother« & *Botkin* the »Father« of the bridegroom. Then the 4 girls & I motored half an hour to fresh one up, as I receive now Isa, *Kussov* (com. *Psk.* reg.) *Hagandokov, Bontch-Bruievitch, Vassiliev* (police) & three officers. Shall spend the evening cosily in the hosp. whilst A. is in town — she lunched with us. — Grey weather, lit up by the remembrance of yr. sweet presence. —

Kiss all at *Kiev.* God bless your journey. Endless tenderest kisses fr. yr. ever loving old

Sunny.

Tell Paul to be back when *Nikolasha* comes — better. —
Did you say about Obolensky? —

No. 374.

Tsarskoje Selo, Oct. 27-th 1916

My own Sweetheart,

A grey windy, warm day. — It must indeed seem strange to you at the platform without the girlies & *Mordvinov.* Wonder if you have sunny weather at least. —

Sonia Den lunched with us, looks awfully ill, green & thin, leaves to-day for Crimea — am glad for poor Xenia who seems to be sad & poorly. —

Rein comes later, wonder what he will have to say, shall beg him to get on better & more delicately with Alek, as you told me. — *Hagandokov* looked more like in old days, thinner & with a sly face — made me feel shy as left the talking to me. I only spoke about Siberia. — Its so dark in my room, I scarcely see to write on my sopha. — The Children have gone to the big palace.

Wonder, how all will be at *Kiev* — a bore Miechen will be there & you not alone. — Was nice in the hospital yesterday evening, sat in all the wards — at home its so sad & lonely without you, Sweetheart. Have your colds quite passed? Goodbye, my Love, & God bless & keep you. Many a tender kisses fr. yr. old

Sunny.

No. 375.

Tsarskoje Selo, Oct. 29-th 1916

My beloved Treasure,

All my tender thoughts are with you. — I have been reading what the German papers say about the Polish question, & how displeased they are William did it without asking the country 's advice & feeling it will be for ever a question of animosity between our 2 countries — etc. others look at it as not at all serious & most vague — & I think W. has made a formidable gaffe & will greatly suffer for it. The Poles will not bow down to a German prince & regime of iron under pretended freedom. — How many reasonable Russians, entre autre *Shakhovskoy* bless you for not having listened to those who begged you to give Poland freedom, when she no longer belonged to us, as it would have been absolutely ridiculous — & they are perfectly right. —

I saw Rein to-day & told him what you said & he will act accordingly. You know, the man is not sympathetic to me — something mocking in his way — but a clever, very ambitious man & must be held in hand. —

You know *Bontch Bruievitch* made a good impression on the whole upon me, & I was not favorably disposed to him after all one had said — & I told it him quite frankly. We had an interesting talk for nearly an hour. Now I shall mention some of the things & you profit of them & try & get things improved & changed, only don't say to *Alex.* you heard it from me — he did enough harm telling that lie to *Ivanov* — & I feel the man does not like me. — We spoke about black *Danilov* — he says he is a man only of chancelry work — not live work, always papers & not a good element, old *Ruzsky,* being rather delicate (bad habit of cocain in the nose) & lazy, needs a strong energetic right hand to make things work — good people have been sent away — & others have left as they wld. not continue under *Danilov.*

He told me why R. insisted upon Dan. being with him — protection, relation to his wife or something like that (have already forgotten what he said), but it was not because of his brains he took him. —

Under *Kurop.* the *enemy reconnoitring (deeply)* was almost quite abolished & very weak — they used to know all that went on in Finland, Sweden, Baltic Provinces — now know scarcely anything. *Hardly any counter-reconnoitring, only correspondence* — papers, papers, looking for laws in everything — no life. — Those 3 people, of the *counter-reconnoitring* in *Petrogr.* were formerly under *Bn.-Br.* with lots more & very good when guided & looked after, but when he was taken away that all ceased & these three are placed by *Alex.* & act as his personal staff *counter-r.* & according to his orders take people shut up etc. & then make their *reports* to *Moghilev* — thats not nice, & now I understand many things that happen not rightly. —

Fancy, *Ruzsky* & his staff have no *active operative plans.* I asked why they dont advance, as you had given *Kurop. and R.* the order to do so — he says perfectly possible, we have far more troops than the Germans. They train their young soldiers near the *trenches* to make ours imagine lots are there. *R.* is contented in his place, his ambitious wife wont let him lose it for anything in the world, & so he prefers sitting calmly — works only 2 hours a day — a good, honest man, but needs a strong right man to make him work.

They completely neglect the question of food supplies, say the Civil ministery must give it them — quite wrong. —

In complete neglect the question of civil administration in the front area. Can you make head or tail of what I write? — its so difficult to give over conversations. The points he wrote down for me as I was affraid to forget them. I can only say I am glad I made his acquaintance & heartily wish you could see him, he wld. tell you much I can't repeat, too complicated & long. He asks & wants nothing, only for your sake & the good he asked to see me to speak all out. Very clever & one can speak easily with him — but he said many sad things as one hears elsewhere. —

Such dishonesty everywhere. — But he says its most weak & disorganised all in that army, but he believes if the old man got a strong help, much could be changed for the good. And keeping the troops for months without moving when they cld. with success — says its demoralising.

Always contrasts — extremes. —

Now enough about affairs.

Grey, dull weather. Are off to town, O. & T. have a committee, & I shall go with M. & A. to the hospital in the W. Palace — 358 men just now. — If I did sleep at all this night, it was not more than half an hour — insupportable & without reason — nothing worried or hurt me; no dear »Animal warmth« any more to help me. —

Now goodbye & God bless you, my Sweet, I cover you with kisses tender & longing ones.

Ever yr. old, very own

Wify.

Fond thanks precious long letter.

No. 376.

Tsarskoje Selo, Oct. 29-th 1916

My very own Sweetheart,

It was an intense joy receiving yr. dear long letter yesterday — thank you for it with all my heart. How glad I am to see by yr. telegram that you could cosily lunch à 3 — wonder how you got rid of Miechen. And did you see Olga, or was she still ill? —

Warm, grey & raining & a fogg — real »dirty weather« as the sailors say. —

Slept ½ an hour the night before last & this one after 5½ till after 7 — insupportably tiresome. Shall go an hour later to the hospital to rest my legs & back still wh. ache after the Winter Palace hospital. It took us an hour — back they wheeled me through the empty halls. — I received *Protopopov* in town. Then we went to *Skoroposlushnitza* & placed candles — you wear that image I brought you once from there. Lunched & took tea in the train — at home received poor *Rebinder* whose wife died not long ago. And then Mme Zizi fr. 8½—9. —

To-day I receive *Volkov, Fedorov, Sturmer, Shebeko* fr. Moscou; ones head gets so tired — during the conversations I am fresh & energetic — but later on become somewhat cretinised. —

Now I must read still through heaps of *reports* — shall finish my letter after luncheon. —

Am going for a little drive to freshen up my tired brain, as have four *reports* this afternoon. —

I kiss you, my Angel, as tenderly & fondly as only possible. God bless & protect you, Lovebird.

Every yr. very, very

Own.

No. 377.

Tsarskoje Selo, Oct. 30-th 1916

My own beloved Sweetheart,

Forgive me for what I have done — but I had to — our Friend said it was a b s o l u t e l y necessary. *Protopopov* is in despair he gave you that paper the other day, thought he was acting rightly until *Gr.* told him it was quite wrong. So I spoke to *Sturmer* yesterday & they both completely believe in our Friend's wonderful, God sent wisdom. *St.* sends you by this messenger a new paper to sign giving over the whole *food supply* now at once to the minister of Interior. *St.* begs you to sign it & at once return it with the train 4½, then it will come in time before the *Duma* assembles on Tuesday. I had to take this step upon myself as *Gr.* says *Protop.* will have all in his hands & finish up all the *Unions* & by that w i l l s a v e R u s s i a , — that is why it must be in his hands; *though it is very difficult, it must be done.* In *Bobr.'s* hands it wld. not work. Trusting our Fr. He will help *Protop.* & *St.* quite agrees.

Forgive me, but I had to take this responsability upon myself for your sweet sake. The *Duma* wld. insist upon it being in one hand & not 3 hands, so better you give it straight beforehand to *Protopopov.* God will bless this choice. —

St. is very anxious about the *Duma,* & their paper is rotten, revolutionary — they (ministers) hope to influence so that the number will change — some of the things they intend saying. For instance that they cant work with such ministers — the colossal impudence of it.

It will be a rotten *Duma* — but one must not fear — if too vile, one closes it. Its war with them & we must be firm. — Tell me, you are not angry — but those men listen to me & when guided by our Friend — it must be right — they, *Pr.* & *St.* bow before His Wisdom.

My head aches & I feel stupid, so write unclearly, I fear. — Just get yr. precious letter fr. *Kiev* 1.000.000 fond thanks. —

So glad, all went off well. Kiss you without end with deepest, boundless devotion.

God bless & help you.

Yr. own old

Wify.

No. 378.

Tsarskoje Selo, Oct. 31-st 1916

My beloved Sweetheart,

Grey & rainy, depressing weather, scarcely slept again — one needs sunshine at last. — All thoughts surround you.

Concert nice yesterday — *Kuznetzova's* voice lovely & danced perfectly Spanish dances. *Lersky* I heard for the first time — & thought of you. — *Protopopov* has asked to be received for *very important business,* after that shall finish my letter. Then have several ladies — later *Shakhovskoy* & *V. P. Schneider* — every moment again taken up. —

Lovy dear, our Friend begs you absolutely to have *Sukhomlinov's* story stopped, otherwise *Gutchkov* & others have prepared nasty things to say — so do it at once, wire to *Sturmer,* I think it concerns him first? telegraph this:

»*Having got acquainted with the data of the preliminary investigation in the case of the former Minister of War, General Sukhomlinov, I find that there are absolutely no grounds at all for the charges, and therefore the case should be discontinued.*«

These things need being done before the *Duma* comes together to-morrow afternoon.

I feel cruel worrying you, my sweet, patient Angel — but all my trust lies in our Friend, who only thinks of you, Baby & Russia. — And guided by Him we shall get through this heavy time. It will be hard fighting, but a Man of God's is near to guard yr. boat safely through the reefs — & little Sunny is standing as a rock behind you, firm & unwavering with decision, faith & love to fight for her darlings & our country. Shall quickly motor for half an hour to clear up my brain for *Protopopov.* — God will help yr. — precious sake. —

I send you a paper about *Alexeiev's secret service* — because these people mix in things wh. do not concern them & it ought to be changed — I forgot to send it you before. —

Then about Rubinstein, the man is dying. Wire, or give *Alexeiev* the order at once to wire to *Ruzsky* to give over Rubinstein from *Pskov* to the *Ministry of the Interior* (best you wire yourself) then he will do all at once. — No time to write about our conversation, letter must go. They have managed to stop the *Duma* fr. giving their rotten *declaration.*

Endless kisses & thanks unexpected sweet letter. Blessings & kisses without end.

Yr. own old

Wify.

No. 379.

Tsarskoje Selo, Nov. 1-st 1916

My own beloved Treasure,

Such very tender thanks for yr. dear long letter with details of your stay in *Kiev.* I am glad you had cosy evenings with Motherdear & that you managed to do so much. Miechen's coolness is too bad — I hope you were stiff too, tho' I doubt that you succeeded to be anything but sweet & polite. —

So Olga will marry on Saturday — & where will that be & to what country place does she intend going? — Its much better Motherdear stays on at *Kiev* where the climate is milder & she can live more as she wishes & hears less gossip. — I am so sorry I had to send you that wire, ciphered by *Protopopov* — but the Minister all got so nervous on account of the *Duma* & feared that if it came out to-day, his nomination, that they wld. make a terrible row at the *Duma,* not accept him — & then *Sturmer* be forced to close the *Duma.* Whereas if put off a bit, then less harm closing the *Duma.* I disagreed with the paper & knew our Friend wld., so I sent *Protopopov* straight to him to speak it over together. Our Friend says its the Ministers' faults because they did not work all these days. Fancy, *Bobrinsky* never changed his aid, when it was written on that paper *Protopopov* showed you — that he should do so Now I asked *Sturmer* in his name to order him to do so. They are bad, *Bobrinsky's* men & sidle with the left parties. — I felt quite crazy yesterday receiving so many people. — *Shakhovskoy,* I did not agree with, he is against *Protopopov* (jalousie de métier). Then still *V. P. Schneider* and 1½ hour 3 ladies. —

Again got to sleep only after 5½ & not for long. — A. comes at 3, so shant close my letter before — she may have something to give over. My 3 cosy Lovings in the hospital are at an end.

What news have you about what happened at *Baltic port? Shakhovskoy* told me, that in the council of Ministers *Trepov* was most awfully rude to

Grigorovitch about that misfortune at *Archangelsk* & used very strong, ungentlemanly language. Really, they need smacking & being set to rights. —

I had a nice letter fr. Victoria — Georgi comes there to-day, to-morrow is the wedding & then they leave at once for the little house they have taken in the north & he goes to his ship. No leave now, but he hopes every day to see Nada for a few hours in their house. A difficult beginning for such young creatures. Victoria went to France to fetch Louise for a longish holiday — she has been working hard at the hospital & needs a rest. — To-day I receive old Schvedov & Mrozovsky, fr. Moscou. — Continually people to be seen. — On thursday our Olga will be 21! Quite a venerable age! — I always wonder whom our girlies will marry & cannot imagine what their lot will be — could they but find the intense love & happiness you, my Angel, have given me these 22 years. Its such a rare thing now a days, alas! —

How are things going on in Roumania? One hears so little now. — Am already busy about Xmas-presents for my »*station*« — its immense what masses of people — & so difficult to find anything suitable & not to abnormally expensive. —

Such darkness, never any sunshine — I hoped the colder weather would bring bright weather. — Miss you so much, my dear precious One, & long for your tender beloved caresses of love.

Our Friend is dreadfully angry with *Protopopov,* who out of cowardice wld. not have it announced that the *food supply question* shld. be in his hands now — on account of the *Duma* & our Friend had told him he could explain he had taken it & hoped in about a week to have arranged all satisfactorily. *Protopopov* wants to take it in 2 weeks only — wh. is foolish.

Gregory is not so much disturbed about the *Duma,* as they always scream *at anything.* I agree to this. — Ania sends tender kisses & was very pleased to have been in the country & to all the Saints in Moscou — *Skopin Shuysky* too, quite specially. — She went to the Metropolite, who begs to have no bishop as help, and our Friend finds it also. —

We all kiss you ever so tenderly. God bless protect & help you. —

Ever yr. very own

Wify.

Hope, you wired about dying Rubinstein. —

No. 380.

Tsarskoje Selo, Nov. 2-nd1916

Beloved Treasure,

Heartfelt thanks for your sweet letter. This morning I got yr. last night's wire — I was feeling anxious & sad, as I knew I must have upset you by my Russian one. I h a t e worrying you & begging you to change things you have settled, all the more so when I do not agree to what the ministers say. —

At last splendid sunshine — such a treat after long, dark weeks — our wounded feel all much brighter & several are going out driving — we too, tho' there were 7 degr. of frost this morning. I again only slept two hours — such a nuisance, perhaps with the change of weather I may manage better. Everything all in order at the hospital, tho' even there I receive architect, generals to speak about sugar & butter etc. . . .

One Officer suddenly had a small artery, wh. burst, so we had at once to perform an operation & sow it up — but it went off alright, Tatiana gave the chloroform for the first time. — Sad, you both wont be here for Olga's 21-st birthday. We shall have a *mass* in my room at 1½. — I am glad things are going better in Roumania — *Vesselkin* will have told you interesting things; — lucky we have such an energetic man there.

Now, Lovebird, joy of my heart — farewell. God bless & protect you. Ever such tender kisses fr. yr. own old

Wify.

Such longing for you!

Olga wrote she marries at 4 o'clock on the 4-th at the little Church *on the Dneper situated on the place, where the idol perun once stood.* God bless the dear & may *N. A.* really be worth of her love & sacrifice. —

No. 381.

Tsarskoje Selo, Nov. 3-rd. 1916

Sweetheart, beloved One,

Tenderly congratulate you with our big child. We had a Te Deum in the hospital & now in my big room. Your letters have not yet come. It was a joy to hear Babykins sweet voice — but one hears very badly, in a few days it will be better & I hope you will also once speak a tiny moment, just to hear the longed for sweet voice.

Victoria wired the wedding was lovely yesterday — Nada were our necklace. —

Spent a lovely evening with our Friend & *Isidor:* »*Calm Papa, write everything will be all right* (that *Protopopov* will get it into his hands quite — the *food supply) that all is in the future*«. They dawdled too long, & therefore cld. not name him so late — all their fault & it wld. have gone well. You are not to worry, yr. decision was right & it will be done a little later.

He is very sad *Nikolasha* will be at the *Headquarters.* Spoke beautifully, calmly & very heigh — you wld. have loved it. —

6½ of frost & bright sunshine — going for a short drive — difficult breathing in such cold. — Dmitri is coming to tea. — All thoughts & prayers with you. —

Lovy, wld you not send somebody to Oranienbaum to the off. school old General *Filatov* is at the head — about 300 officers learning for *Machine-Guners* & its very badly organised, great disorder, badly tought, so that many leave it. I heard this fr. officers where have been sent there by their regiments & they say its in a real bad state — unpractical & they are kept there ages & badly organised (*Karangozov* etc. spoke seriously to me about it & said it wld. be a blessing if it were changed & real order put). *Filatov* is an old professor & keeps to his oldfashioned ideas. I thought you wld. have it seen in to seriously by a competent general. Far too few *machine-guns* for them to practice on, 300 officers — as each must know all the work & go into every detail. Out of their worktime they privately study it, otherwise wld. know nothing. They have to listen to lectures about submarines etc. wh. dont concern them. —

Lovy, have you had Rubinstein given over to the Min. of Interior — otherwise he will die still at *Pskov* — please dear. —

Back fr. our drive, found your precious letter, for wh. warmest thanks. Glad *N. P.* only remained one day. —

Now Lovebird, I must end, the man must go. Blessings & kisses without end fr. yr. very, very

Own.

A. sits near & kisses you. —

No. 382.

Tsarskoje Selo, Nov. 4-th 1916

My own sweet Angel,

Warmest thanks for yr. dear letter just received. I read Nikolai's & am utterly disgusted. Had you stopped him in the midle of his talk & told him that, if he only once more touched that subject or me, you will send him to Siberia — as it becomes next to high treason. He has always hated & spoken badly of me since 22 years & in the club too (this same conversation I had with him this year). — but during war & at such a time to crawl behind yr. Mama & Sisters & not stick up bravely (agreeing or not) for his Emperor's Wife — is loathsome & treachery. He feels people count with me, begin to understand me & acre for my opinion & that he cant bear. He is the incarnation of all that's evil, all devoted people loathe him, even those who do not much like us are disgusted with him & his talks. — And Fred. old & no good & cant shut him up & wash his head & you my Love, far too good & kind & soft — such a man needs to be held in awe of you — He & *Nikolasha* are my greatest enemies in the family, not counting the black women — & Sergei. — He simply cld. not bear Ania & me — not so much the cold rooms, I assure you. I don't care personal nastiness, but as yr. chosen wife — they dare not Sweety mine, you must back me up, for your & Baby's sake. Had we not got Him — all wld. long have been finished, of that I am utterly convinced. — I am seeing Him a moment before *Sturmer.* Poor old man may die fr. the vile way his spoken to & of at the *Duma* — *Miliukov's* speech yesterday when he quotes *Buchanan's* words that *Sturmer* is a traitor & Buch. to whom he turned in the box — held his tongue — vile behaviour. We are living through hardest times, but God will help us through, I have no fear. *Let* they scream — we must show we have no fear & are firm. Wify is your staunch One & stands as a rock behind you. I'll ask our Friend, whether He thinks it advisable I go in a week's time, or, as you cant move — whether I shld. remain here to help the »weak« minister. They have again chosen *Rodzianko* & his speeches are quite bad & what he says to the ministers.

I hope Sweetheart's leg will soon be better. And *Alexeiev* ill — all worries at one time — but God will not forsake you & our beloved Country through the prayers & help of our Friend. — Am glad you arranged a place for Obolensky. —

Grey weather again, 4½ of frost — only two days sun. — Weary & sad.

No. 383.

Tsarskoje Selo, Nov. 5-th 1916

My own Darling,

Such fond thanks for yr. dear letter. What a nuisance for Babykins having to lie, but of course its the best thing for him to do — only that he should have no pain! — Thats good you send *Georgi* off, the more you make them move about, the better it is — no good sticking long in one place without any work. — *Alexeiev* ought to go off for 2 months rest & you get somebody to help you — *Golovin* for instance, who all praise very highly — only none of the Commanders of the armies — leave them quietly in their places where they are alright. Too much work for *Pustov.* & you alone & then you can't move & perhaps a fresh head might be very good with new ideas. A man who is so terribly against our Friend as poor *Alexeiev* is — cannot have blessed work. — his nerves, one says, are run down, & its comprehensible — the continual strain for a man of papers & not much soul to help him, alas. —

The wlaying of the foundation stone Ania's Church was nice, our Fr. was there, & nice Bishop *Isidor* — Bishop Melchisedek & our *priest* etc. were there — shall see *Gregory* a moment to-day. — *Sturmer* is very sad & unhappy they worry you so & that because of him too. I cheered him up & got calmer & full of good intentions. He finds *Rodzianko's* Court dress ought to be taken fr. him for not having those bad men stopped when they said such strong things at the *Duma* & bad insinuations — he told Fred. to give him a reprimand, but the old man misunderstood & wrote to *Rodzianko* that in the future he must allow no such things to happen. Won't you say he should have his Courtrank taken fr. him, or for the next thing he bets pass through wh. touches you again — horrid man! — What did »Misha the fool« mean, that he & Georgi got decorations fr. Georgs »*for my invention, which overjoyed me?*« — Our Fr. is so angry, Olga married — as she did wrong towards you & that can bring her no luck. Ah, dear me — I too more than regret this act of hers tho' understand her human craving for happiness at last. — Lovy, you will be careful not to be cought by *Nikolasha* into any promises or anything — remember *Gregory* saved you from him & his evel people. Don't let him go to the country, but straight back to the Caucasus where he must be — forgive me writing this, but I feel it must be so. — Be cool, only not too kind to him & *Orlov* & *Yanushkevitch* — remember for Russia's sake what they wanted to do — to clear you out its not gossip, *Orlov* had all the papers ready — & me to a Couvent — you won't touch the subjects — as they are over — only make them feel you have not forgotten & that they must fear you. They need to tremble before their Sovereign, — be more selfsure — God has placed you there, its not pride & you are an anointed one & they dare not forget this. One must feel your power, its time for the saving of your Country & your Child's throne. Beloved, goodbye & God bless you. I cover you with unending tender kisses.

Ever your old

Sunny.

I am ramolie.

Just seen our Friend — »*convoy to him, with kindness, a greeting.*« — He was very gay after the dinner in the *vetry* — but not tipsy — no time to write — says all will be well.

Kisses and blessings without end. —

No. 384.

Tsarskoje Selo, Nov. 6-th 1916

Sweetheart dear,

Very tenderest thanks for yr. dear letter. Thank God the little leg is better. To-day the sun is kindly trying to shine again. Were in our lower church, then worked at the hospital, now go to a soldiers hospital & to the very worst I shall give medals from you. — Later comes *Mekk* & then *Protopopov,* shall tell him one must take severe measures against the propaganda you wrote about — I shall make them work Lovy, & I shall tell Kalinin not to be so fidgety, & be firmer. —

Stupid head aches — no doubt Becker is coming.

I am glad N. M. did not speak as he wrote, — tho' it wld. have given you reason to wash his head & tell him to mind his own business once in a way. — I shall be anxious whilst Nikolasha is at the *Headquarters* hope all will go well & you will show you are the master.

Cannot help deeply regretting he will be with you remember to be cool to the bad set — hope *Nikolasha* will have the decency not to bring fat *Orlov.* Fancy *Poguliayev* wrote to me he is going to divorce — if she gives it him, he will marry a flame of his youth. She wrote quite miserable to Ania — wld. understand if he married a young person, but not one who is only two years younger than herself, & who would not have him before, he was not good enough — now he is Admiral, it suits her — I don't know her name, neither mentioned it. — Why did he ever marry and older woman — he needed a young one & children as he loves them. Now must end. Thoughts always with you & earnest prayers, kisses & blessings without end, Sweet one.

Ever yr. own old

Sunny.

No. 385.

Tsarskoje Selo, Nov. 7-th 1916

My own beloved Nicky dear,

From all my heart I thank you for yr. dearest letter. Of course its difficult writing, when you have such a lot to do. —

Again affairs:

I saw *Protopopov* a long time in the evening, short our Friend, & both find for the quiet of the *Duma* — *Sturmer* ought to say he is ill & go for a rest of 3 weeks. Its true (have just spluttered ink all over my sleeve) — he is really quite unwell & broken by those vile assaults — & being the red flag for that madhause, its better he should disappear a bitt & then in Dec. when they will have been cleared out return again. *Trepov* (who I cant help not liking) for the moment is the one who by law replaces him at the Council of ministers & will keep things going. Its only for a time. The *Duma* comes together again on Friday. If you wire to me you agree, I can do it for you; & kindly without hurting the old man — for his sake & the quiet, as I know it would be unpleasant for you writing & I want to spare my Sweetheart all I can. He can then ask you for leave for his health. — They will at once cool down & many know he is really not well.

So happy, Baby is better. — Would it suit you if we came the 13-th & what hour, 5, 4 or 4½? — Hope, shall find sleep there wh. I cant here. Receive awfully much & have still too these days. — All thoughts with you.

Blessings endless kisses fr. yr. own old

Wify.

No. 386.

Tsarskoje Selo, Nov. 8-th 1916

Lovy, my Angel sweet,

Such warm thanks for yr. precious letter.

Thank goodness *Nikolasha* brought decent people. — Thats quite right one sends *Alexeiev* away for a good rest to the Crimea, its absolutely necessary for him — calm, air & real rest! — I hope *Gurko* may be the right man — personally I am no judge as don't remember ever speaking to him — the brain he has — God give him the soul. Glad to see him now, I hope, when we come. — *Ressin* is in quarantine, Apraxin in the country, *Benkendorf* ill — whom am I to bring? — I take Ania & Nastinka, no *Botkin,* if necessary — *Vladimir*

Nikolaievitch, but thank God the little leg seems much better. — *Sturmer* has let me know he is going to the *Headquarters* & wants to see me before — so I shall gently tell him what I wrote to you (our Fr. begs me to) & if possible have it known b e f o r e Friday that he is going on leave for his health, as that day the *Duma* comes together & they are preparing a row for him that day — & his going on leave will quieten their boiling spirits.

I find *Grigorovitch* & *Shuvaiev* did not find the right note in their speech, but *Shuvaiev* did the worst thing — he shook hands with *Miliukov* who only just launched forth things against us. How I wish we had *Beliayev* (real gentleman) in his place. — *Gutchkov* has left his place, because he wants to get in with *Polivanov,* please don't agree to this paper wh. will come to you fr. the Cons. de l'Empire — *Polivanov* who aims at rebecoming Minister of War & promises freedom to the Jews, etc. he is dangerous & ought to have n o place in any committee & *Gutchkov* needs to be on a high tree. — *Andronnikov* will be also one of these days sent off to Siberia.

Now I must end. Last evening we spent at Ania's with *Yuzik, V. Erastov. Gromatin* & *Rita;* to-night go to the hospital. —

Blessings & kisses without end — intensely rejoicing for Sunday.

Ever yr. very, very

Own.

What a bore *N. P.* wont be at the *Headquarters* — shall we have that odious *Svetchin,* or nice *Kutaissov* at least.

Oh lovy mine h o w I live with you all the time — soul burns — head tired — weary — but spirits up & fight for you & Baby. —

No. 387.

Tsarskoje Selo, Nov. 9-th 1916

My own Lovebird,

Warmest thanks for sweet letter. — Our Friend says *Sturmer* can remain still some time *as President of Council of Minister,* as that one does not reproach him so much, but all the row began since he became Minister of Foreign Affairs, which *Gregory* realised in summer & told him then already that *this will be your end.* That is why He implores either he should go on leave for a month or a t o n c e to name another man in his place as Minister of Foreign Affairs for instance *Stcheglovitov,* as very clever (tho' hard) & a Russian name, or Giers (Constantinople), in that ministery, he is the red flag & at once all will be quieten if he is changed. But leave him *as President of Council of Minister* (if he goes on leave, *Trepov* by law replaces him) — All want that place, & they are not fit for it. *Grigorovitch* perfect where he is, — others & *Ignatiev* egg him on to take that place, for which he is unsuited. *Ignatiev* made him & *Shuvaiev* take the wrong note in their speach, wh. had been prepared alright by the ministers.

Now one calls Mme. *Sukhomlinov* before judgement on Friday & therefore I wired asking you to have *the Sukhomlinov case* at once stopped through Senator

Kuzmin. — Its vengeance because one let the poor old man out of prison. So horribly unfair! —

Just returned fr. *mass* at my lancers' hospital (I-st rifle regiments mass) — 2 years existence. Old Beckmann was there. 26 lancers, who had been ill or wounded & now return to the regiment. — So glad no conversations with *Nikolasha.* Baby's letter too amusing. — yr. letters came 3 hours late. — Weather, 3 of frost, grey. — What are you thinking about the St. George's feast, will you have it here, so as to lift up the *spirits* by yr. presence in this rotten part of the world. —

Now must end, Manny dear. *Gregory* hopes you will soon come here; yr. presence is much needed to keep them all in order. —

Sandro L. said *Nikolai Mikhailovitch* speaks awfully, all are furious what he says in the club, & he sees *Rodzianko* & company continually. Excuse only disagreable letters, but head weary from affair. —

Should I bring *Mordvinov* or *Kutaissov* for the journey, as have no gentleman? — 1000 tender kisses & blessings Ever yr. very, very, very

Own.

No. 388.

Tsarskoje Selo, Nov. 10-th 1916

My own sweet Angel,

The kitten is climbing all over my writing table, luckily through scarcely anything down — she climbs on the palme & whatever she can get hold of. — Been driving — it snowed & was wet. —

I received old *Sturmer* & he told me yr. decisions — God grant, all is for the good, tho' it gave me a painful shock you also take him away fr. the *Council of Ministers.*

I had a big lump in my throat — such a devoted, honest, sure man. Yr. kindness & trust touched him so much & the beautiful nomination. I regret, because he likes our Friend & was so right in that way — *Trepov,* I personally do not like & can never have the same fealing for him as to old *Goremikin* & *Sturmer* — they were of the good old sort. The other, I trust, will be firm (I fear at heart a hard man) — but far more difficult to talk to — those two loved me & came for every question that worried them, so as not to disturb you — this one I, alas, doubt caring for me & if he does not trust me or our Friend, thinks will be difficult. I told *Sturmer* to tell him how to behave about *Gregory* & to safeguard him always. Oh, may it be for the good & you have an honest man, in him to help you. You, Lovy, will tell him to come to me too sometimes — I know him so little & would like to «understand» him. —

Thanks, dear, for sending us *Voyeikov.* — Saw *Gregory* yesterday & then he wired to you, when I told him about the old Emperor's death — (Francis Joseph) he thinks it certainly for our good in every way (I too) & hopes the war may then sooner end, as there may be stories between Germany & Austria. Thanks for *Sukhomlinov,* — here is a letter fr. *S.* to you.

W h a t joy to meet soon — lots to talk over. Please, make *Nikolai Mikhailovitch* go away — he is a dangerous element in town. — Must end. 10,000,000 kisses & blessings fr. yr.

Own.

No. 389.

Tsarskoje Selo, Nov. 10-th 1916

Beloved Sweetheart,

Its one in the night & yet I begin my letter to you, as to-morrow have people all day long. Even in the hospital I shall receive a French Dr. as wants to speak about wonderfull tables he & other French Doctors take to Rumania. An electric battery & Röntgen apparatus under the table, so that during the operation one can the whole time see where the ball is & that colossally facilitates of course the extraction of bullets or bits of shells. Then an English consul from Riga I believe will bring me there 10,000 p. Then at 2 we go to my train to a *Mass* officiated by the Metropolitan, as they have newly arranged the church. Then receive somebody in *Ania's* house. Then Frederiks to an early tea. Then *N. P.* to real tea. Hereafter (no more ink in that pen) *Meliuhin, Nikolosha's* aid. Then *Protopopov, Trepov* & our Friend for an hour in the evening to say goodbye. He is very sad, *Sturmer* did not understand he ought to have gone for a rest. Not knowing *Trepov* of course he is anxious for you. But he thinks you ought to have another minister of roads & communication, finds it not good a man has two things to do, as then can never so well fulfil each place — & besides at the present time he must travel about & personally see to all, — would not *Valuyev* have — utterly devoted, good man (so found our Friend since a good time already). — Lets choose the Minister of foreign affairs together. I saw Princess Julie Branicka to-day, still so handsome, tho' full of rinckles — we saw her last at *Kiev.* Her husband died before the war. She is a niece of the old lady at *Belaya Tserkov* & saw Motherdear there. — Spent a cosy evening at the hospital knitting & chattering. *Elena* lunched with us — enjoyed the Crimea. She says Peter of Montenegro is fighting with our troops in France. — My head goes round from all the people I have to see — & all must fit in & enough time for each. Am greatly i n t e n s e l y looking forward to Sunday 5 o'clock!!! Now at last (thanks to our Fr.) since 3 nights sleep nearly perfectly well, such a comfort, as the head is then fresher. — Goodnight & sleep well — I have written this in 12 minutes.

N o v. 11 - t h.

Such fond thanks for Your letter, deary. Old man was wrong in not telling me about your other intention — they have put me a w f u l l y out. Forgive me, deary, believe me — I entreat you d o n t go and change *Protopopov* now, he will be alright, give him the chance to get the *food supply matter* into his hands & I assure you, all will go. *Sturmer* finds him fidgety, because *Sturmer* dawdled & did not answer quick enough & keep them all enough in hand.

Bobrinsky all the same if you change him, I find, only not *Protopopov,* now it is not good. Of course I m o r e than regret *Ignat.* sits there (very left) & that *Trepov* is at the head — but choose a new minister of Railrods & Communications — he c a n ' t do 2 things at a time, now when everything is so serious. — tho' of course he will say he can. — *Makarov* cld. be beautifully changed, he is not for us, but *Protopopov* is honestly f o r u s. Oh, Lovy, you can trust me. I may not be clever e n o u g h — but I have a strong feeling & that helps more than the brain often. D o n t c h a n g e a n y b o d y u n t i l we meet, I entreat you, lets speak it over q u i e t l y t o g e t h e r. Let *Trepov* come a day later or keep the papers & names back, Lovy dear — for Wify's sake. You dont know how hard it is now — so much to live through & such hatred of the «rotten upper sets». The *food supply* must be in *Protopopov's* hands. — Others are intriguing against him, he heard the news from the *Headquarters* some days ago. — Times are serious — don't break up all at once — *Sturmer* was a big act — now choose — *Trepov's* successor as minister & a younger one instead of *Bobrinsky* — but leave *Protopopov,* don't be angry with me, its for you I say all this I know it wld. not be good. Heart & soul are weary fr. suffering, but I must tell you the truth. Goodbye, my Angel. Once more, remember that for your reign, Baby & us you *n e e d* the strenght prayers & advice of our Friend. Remember, how last year *a l l* were against you & for *Nikolasha* & our Friend gave you the help & strenght you took over all & saved Russia — we no longer went back. He told *Sturmer* that he ought not to have accepted being Minister of Foreign affairs, that it would be his ruin — German name & one wld. say — all my doing. — *Protopopov* venerates our Friend & will be blessed — *Sturmer* got frightened & for months did not see him — so wrong & he lost his footing. Ah, Lovy, I pray so hard to God to make you feel & realise, that He is our caring, were He not here, I dont know what might not have happened. He saves us by His prayers & wise counsils & is our rock of faith & help. — M-me Taneyev said aloud that *Ignatiev, Krivoshein and Sazonov (?)* & c. intend breaking *Protopopov's* neck & will do everything to succeed. D o n t l e t t h e m. He is *n o t* mad, the wife sees *Bekhterev* for his nerves only. For *m e* dont make a n y changes till I have come, tell *Trepov* you wish to think it over a day or two & tell him you do n o t intend sending *Protopopov* & please, give him the *food supply question* as settled, — believe me, he will manage — in the country one feels it already (only vile *Petrograd* & *Moscou* speak against him). — *Quieten* me, promise, forgive, but its for you & Baby I fight. —

Kisses yr.

Wify.

No. 390.

Tsarskoje Selo, Nov. 12-th 1916

My own beloved One,

I am writing to you in our hospital in one of the wards — was too dead tired last night to think of anything & had to put my things together & arrange yr. letters. My head goes round in a ring so excuse if I write unclearly — so dark too & deary. You probably have a paper about *Viltchkovsky* being promoted general, please deary, do it, it will help him for all his *relations* with other generals & *commissioners,* who are a nuisance. — Lovy, my Angel — now about the chief thing — don't change *Protopopov.* I had a long talk with him yesterday — the man is as sane as only can, of course *Trepov* (as I was sure) said the same thing to me — its *utterly* false, — he is quiet & calm & utterly devoted which one can, alas, say of but few & he will succeed — already things are going better, & it would be folly at such a serious moment to change him. I will tell you details & intrigues when I come & you will see all clearly. Therefore I begged you to put of *Trepov* till we have met. Its the same story as last year — again against wify — they know he is completely devoted to me & comes to me as does *Shakhovskoy* (wants to change him too). Change nobody now, otherwise the *Duma* will think its their doing & that they have succeeded in clearing everybody out. And its bad to begin by sending all flying — others wont have the time to set to work in new places whilst the *Duma* sits. You know, I have no very good opinion of *Trepov* & I see by his wishing to clear out people devoted to me — the game. They will then be ministers as the last *Headquarters* chose, were all against me. They feel I am your wall & it aggravates them — ah, lovy, dont let them do this, its more serious than you think. It took you long then to realise that last year — & now its the bad party, who have got behind *Trepov* — *Voyeikov* also plays an ugly part with *Andronnikov* in this affair — he clings to this bad man. Its difficult writing & asking for oneself, I assure you, but its for yr. & Baby's sake, believe me. I don't care what bad one says of me, only when one tries to tear devoted, honest people, who care for me — away — its horribly unfair. I am but a woman fighting for her Master & Child, her two dearest ones on earth — & God will help me being your guardian angel, only dont pull the sticks away upon wh. I have found it possible to rest. *Trepov* will recommend him in *Shakhovskoy's* place — not if he says he is unnormal. Stick firm & send for *Protopopov* at once & have a good talk with him, if you like I'll be with you. Only when you tell *Trepov* you won't change *Protopopov* nor *Shakhovskoy, don't* for goodness mention my name — it must be your wise wish. If he says he cant work with them, then tell him you will keep him for the moment & then take another. Be the master — *Trepov* has a disagreeable character. I never care about people who use lots of words to explain their devotion, I like to see it in their acts — *Protopopov* proves it the whole time (another idiotic wounded stands & stares whole time & drives me wild — others make much noise in the corridor, wh. does not make it easier for writing).

I want you to read this before we meet — it will give you time in case *Trepov* comes before me. I am very hurt *Sturmer* did not warn me before. Lovy, its no joke, more serious, as its a hunt against wify. Categorically answer you have quietly thought it over & do not for the present intend changing any of your ministers. Leave old Bobrinsky even. Please, pay attention to all I write (now 3 more have come to make me wild). Its a lie when *Trepov* says *Protopopov* understands nothing about the ministery — he knows well, in the country one feels his firm hand — provisions are coming & its going slowly but rightly for the good. 10 days his papers were not read through by the ministers, such a shame. What joy to rest to-morrow in your arms to kiss & bless you.

Wify.

Darling, remember that it does not lie in the man *Protopopov* or x.y.z., but its the question of monarchy & yr. prestige now, which must not be shattered in the time of the *Duma*. Dont think they will stop at him, but they will make all others leave who are devoted to you one by one — & then ourselves. Remember, last year Yr. leaving to the Army — when also you were alone with us two against everybody, who promised revolution if you went. You stood up against all & God blessed your decision. I repeat again — it does not lie in the name of *Protopopov* but in your remaining firm & not giving in — *The Czar rules and not the Duma*. — Forgive my again writing, but I am fighting for your reign & Baby's future. God will help, be firm don't listen to men, who are not from God but cowards. Yr. Wify, to whom you are *ALL in ALL*.

True unto death.

No. 391.

Tsarskoje Selo, Dec. 4-th 1916

My very precious One,

Goodbye, sweet Lovy!

Its great pain to let you go — worse than ever after the hard times we have been living & fighting through. But God who is all love & mercy has let the things take a change for the better, — just a little more patience & deepest faith in the prayers & help of our Friend — then all will go well. I am fully convinced that great & beautiful times are coming for yr. reign & Russia. Only keep up your spirits, let no talks or letters pull you down — let them pass by as something unclean & quickly to be forgotten. Show to all, that you are the Master & your will shall be obeyed — the time of great indulgence & gentleness is over — now comes your reign of will & power, & they shall be made to bow down before you & listen your orders & to work how & with whom you wish — obedience they must be taught, they do not know the meaning of that word, you have spoilt them by yr. kindness & all forgivingness. Why do people hate me? Because they know I have a strong will & when am convinced of a thing being right (when besides blessed by *Gregory)*, do not change my mind & that they can't bear. But its the bad ones. Remember Mr. Philipps words when he gave me the image with the bell. As you were so kind, trusting & gentle, I was to be yr. bell, those that came with wrong intentions wld. not be able to approach me & I wld. warn you. Those who are affraid of me, dont look me in the eyes or are up to some wrong, never like me. — Look at the black ones — then Orlov & Drenteln — Witte — *Kokovtzev* — *Trepov*, I feel it too — *Makarov* —

Kaufmann — *Sofia Ivanovna* — *Mary* — *Sandra* Obolensky etc., but those who are good & devoted to you honestly & purely — love me, — look at the simple people & military. The good & bad clergy its all so clear & therefore no more hurts me as when I was younger. Only when one allows oneself to write you or me nasty impertinent letters — you must punish. Ania told me about *Balaschov* (the man I always disliked). I understood why you came so awfully late to bed & why I had such pain & anxiety waiting. Please, Lovy, tell Frederiks to write him a strong *reprimand* (he & *Nicolaï Mikhailovitch* & Vass make one in the club) — he has such a high court-rank & dares to write, unasked. And its not the first time — in bygone days I remember he did so too. Tear up the letter, but have him firmly reprimanded — tell *Voyeikov* to remind the old man — such a smack to a conceited member of the Council of the Empire will be very useful. We cannot now be trampled upon. Firmness above all! — Now you have made *Trepov's* son A. D. C. you can insist yet more on his working with *Protopopov*, he must prove his gratitude. — Remember to forbid *Gurko* speaking & mixing himself into politics — it ruined *Nikolasha* & Alexeiev, — the latter God sent this illness clearly to save you fr. a man who was lossing his way & doing harm by listening to bad letters & people, instead of listening to yr. orders about the war & being obstinate. And one has set him against me — proof — what he said to old *Ivanov*. —

But soon all this things will blow over, its getting clearer & the weather too, which is a good sign, remember.

And our dear Friend is praying so hard for you — a man of God's near one gives the strenght, faith & hope one needs so sorely. And others cannot understand this great calm of yours & therefore think you dont understand & try to ennervate, frighten & prick at you. But they will soon tire of it. Should Motherdear write, remember the Michels are behind her. — Don't heed & take to heart — thank God, she is not here, but kind people find means of writing & doing harm. — All is turning to the good — our Friends dreams means so much. Sweety, go to the *Moghilev* Virgin & find peace & strenght there — look in after tea, before you receive, take Baby with you, quietly — its so calm there — & you can place yr. candels. Let the people see you are a christian Sovereign & dont be shy — even such an example will help others. —

How will the lonely nights be? I cannot imagine it. The consolation to hold you tightly clasped in my arms — it lulled the pain of soul & heart & I tried to put all my endless love, prayers & faith & strenght into my caresses. So inexpressibly dear you are to me, husband of my heart. God bless you & my Baby treasure — I cover you with kisses; when sad, go to Baby's room & sit a bit quietly there with his nice people. Kiss the beloved child & you will feel warmed & calm. All my love I pour out to you, Sun of my life. —

Sleep well, heart & soul with you, my prayers around you — God & the holy Virgin will never forsake you —.

Ever your very, very

Own.

No. 392.

Tsarskoje Selo, Dec. 5-th 1916

My own Sweetheart,

From the depths of my loving heart I send you warmest, heartiest good-wishes & many tender blessings for yr. dear Namesday. May yr. patronsaint quite particularly be near you & keep you in safe guard. Everything that a devoted, unutterably loving heart can only wish you — Sunny wishes you. Strength, firmness, unwaving decision, calm, peace, success, brightest sunshine — rest & happiness at last after yr. hard, hard fighting. In thoughts I clasp you tightly to my heart, let your sweet, weary head rest upon my breast. With the candles my prayers rise in burning fervour & brightness for you — to-night shall go to Church, & to-morrow our fogies, court ones, will be there to congratulate after mass. — How can I thank you enough for the unexpected, intense joy of yr. precious letter — it was a ray of warming sunshine in my lonely heart. After you both left, I went to *Znamenia.* Later received *Ilyin, Vsevol.* of my *supply trains* — *Bagration-M.* of the »*Savage Division*« — will try & see you at the *Headquarters* — awfully interesting all he tells about the tribes under him — & the *Abreki,* who behave very well. —

After dinner went to the hospital — to forget oneself. — I thank God I could help you a little — you too, Sweet one, become firm & unwavering, show the masterhand & mind. Do not bend down to a man like *Trepov* (whom you cannot either trust or respect). You have said yr. say & had yr. fight about Protopopov & it shall not be in vain we suffered — stick to him, be firm, don't give in — as then never more any peace, they will begin worrying you in the future yet worse when you don't agree, as they see that by persistent obstinacy they force you to give in — as hard as they, I mean *Trepov* & *Rodzianko* (with the evil) on one side — I shall stand against them, (with God's holy man) don't you stick to them, but to us, who live only for you Baby & Russia. To follow our Friend's councils, lovy — I assure is right — He prays so hard day & night for you — & He has kept you where you are — only be as convinced as I am & as I proved it to Ella & shall for ever — then all will go well. In les »Amis de Dieux« one of the old men of God said, that a country, where a man of God helps the Sovereign, will never be lost & its true — only one must listen trust & ask advice — not think He does not know. God opens everything to Him, that is why people, who do not grasp His soul, so immensely admire His wonderful brain — ready to understand anything; & when He blesses an undertaking — it succeeds & if He advises people — one can be quiet that they are good — if they later on change that is already not His fault — but He will be less mistaken in people than we are — *experience in life* blessed by God. He entreats for *Makarov* to be quicker changed — & I fully agree. I told *Sturmer* that it was wrong he recomended him, that I told him that he is far from a devoted man, & now the chief thing is to find really devoted men — in deed & not only in words, & to them we must cling. Don't let *Trepov* deceive you about people. *Protopopov* & *Shakhovskoy* are only for us, I mean are above all things devoted & love honestly & openly. And *Dobrovolsky* too. — Should *Nikolai Mikhailovitch* turn (wh. God forbid), be hard & give it him for his letter & goings on in town. — I send you *Grigorovitch's* paper one sent me. —

Went at 11 to *Znamenia* (which I more than ever love) & to the hospital — sat much — Now receive 4 officers, then we all sledge. Paul comes to tea then *Poguliayev* then Church & in the evening see our Friend, who will give strength. My *spirit* is firm & live for you, you & you — my heart & soul. — I wonder, whether you will have a review of the St. George's regiment, wld. be so nice — if not the 6-th, then another day, — Ducky leaves to-night to see Missy & perhaps bring all the Children back, according to circumstances. —

Now I must end. Sleep well & peacefully, beloved Angel. The Holy Virgin guards you & *Gr.* prays for you & we do all so hard.

I cover you with tenderest, passionately loving kisses & caresses & long to be of use & help in carrying yr. heavy Cross. God bless & protect you, my Nicky. Ever yr. very own

Wify.

I hope you will like the book. The cushions are for yr. sopha, wh. is so empty. The ashtrays for the dinnertable or train. —

Always near you sharing all — the good is coming, the turn has begun.

No. 393.

Tsarskoje Selo, Dec. 6-th 1916

My own sweet Angel,

Many happy returns of the day — tenderest blessings & fondest good-wishes & deepest love. So sad not to be together for your Namesday — the first time in 22 years. But it was for the good you had to leave, so of course I don't dream of grumbling. — Nice snow covers all & 5^0 of frost. We sledged yesterday, but it humped still rather. B. came, hang him. —

Paul took tea & was nice. I wired to you about Papa *Taneyev* being 20 years at the head of yr. chancelry — she found it out by chance as they give him a big luncheon there. — Yesterday we spent the evening cosily, calmly in the little house. Dear big *Lili* came too later & *Munia Golovina.*

He was in good, cheery spirits — one sees how lives & thinks for you the whole time & that all shld. be well. Is anxious, *Trepov* come there, fears he will upset you again, bring false things, new's I mean & try to come with his candidats. — Take one instead of him for the railways — pitty you don't approve of *Valuyev* for that place — as such a honest & true man. Then get quicker rid of *Makarov,* don't dawdle (forgive me) & I wish you wld. take *Dobrovolsky* — the story *Trepov* told you seems untrue (there is another of the same name also Senator) — I send you a paper she copied about a story *Trepov* & good *Dobrovolsky* had — he thinks it may be a story of revenge. — But *Kalinin* — keep — keep him, my Love. I know I bore you, forgive me, but I would never do so, if I did not fear yr. wavering again. Stick to yr. decision — do not give in, how can one hesitate between this simple, honest man who loves us so deeply — & *Trepov* whom we cannot trust, nor respect or love, on the contrary. — Tell him that question exists no more & you forbid his touching it again & playing with *Rodzianko,* who wants *Protopopov* also to leave. He serves you & not *Rodzianko* & once you have said you keep *Protopopōv* you do not intend changing & he is to work with him. How dare he go against you — thunder on the table; don't give in (as you said, you wld. at the end) — be the master; listen to your staunch Wify & our Friend, believe us. Look at *Kalinin* & *Trepov's* face — clearly one sees the difference — black & white, let your soul read rightly. —

Its snowing away, but still we want to sledge & get a little air. The couple Benkendorf, Zizi, Isa, Nastinka, *Trina, Ania, Ressin* and *Apraxin* lunched with us & we drank to yr. dear heath. Paul was also in Church. The soldiers stood outside afterwards & congratulated.

No. 394.

Tsarskoje Selo, Dec. 6-th 1916

All my thoughts are with you — I fear a very dull day with heaps of people, but I hope you still can get a walk & Baby his game in the woods.

Congratulate you with all the regimental feasts. The eldest Colonel for the 4 rifles brought us bouquets. He says he has just received the 4-th rifle reg. & leaves soon. — Agoo wee one, big and small, he loves you beyond words. In the evening we shall go to the hospital. — Our Friend is so contented with our girlies, says they have gone through heavy »*courses*« for their age & their souls have much developed — they are really great dears & so nice now with Ania. They have shared all our emotions & it has taught them to see people with open eyes, so that it will be a great help to them later in life. Tiny feels so much in its little wide awake soul too — & I cannot ever thank God enough for the marvelous blessing He has sent me in you & them — we are one, which is, alas, so, so rare now a days — closely knit together. —

I received 2 lovely teleg. fr. *Archangelsk* from the *Monastery Patmi* & I answered with our Friend, & He begs you absolutely to allow the telegr. to be printed. Tell Fred. to give them the permission — & also their first & mine in the »*Novoye Vremya*« — it will open people's eyes & be a counteract against the Pss. *Vassiltchikov* letter (wh. M-me Zizi is quite disgusted & shocked with) — & a smack to old nasty *Balashov.* — The good is coming, & let »society & *Duma*« see that Russia loves yr. old Wify & stands up for her against them all. — Zizi admired their touching wire very much; I on purpose answered personally.

The snow is such a blessing too, St. Nicolas blesses my Sweetheart. —

Goodbye, my, Sunshine, my adored husband, I love you, love you, yearn over you, kiss & gently caress you, press you to my burning heart.

Ever yr. very Own unto death and beyond.

No. 395.

Tsarskoje Selo, Dec. 7-th 1916

My own Beloved,

You cannot imagine Olga's joy when she received yr. telegram — she got quite pink & could not read it aloud. She will write to you herself to-day. Thanks tenderly Darling, for having given her this beautiful surprise — she felt & her sisters as tho' it were her birthday.

At once she sent off a wire to the »*Plastuni*«.

Did you get news fr. Kirill? Till now no answer to my telegram I sent the 5-th evening.

It seems Irina is ill again & so Xenia had to put off going now to *Kiev,* so disappointig to poor Motherdear. My Siberians congratulate you & *Katia* Ozerov.

5 of frost & looks as tho' it wld. snow more, very grey. — Alas, we heard Baby's voice very badly by telephone. Mr. Gillard's is lower & so carries further. Hope you were not too tired & bored yesterday. — Have you begun iodine again, it wld. be good, think. — I go now always at 11 to *Znamenia* & hospital, as not many wounded & then I can finish my papers before. — Lovy, did you have a *reprimand* written to *Balashov?* Please, do its the very least you can do. — I cover you with kisses for yr. sweet letter I received, I never thought you would find time for a letter. — I saw *Kolenkin* in the hospital, had not been on leave for 9 months. They are off & on in their trenches. —

Cannot write any more to-day, Lovy my Angel. Only one thing, do put off seeing *Trepov,* am so affraid he will worry & make you decide things wh. in a quiet moment you wld. not agree to. Be firm about *Kalinin,* for our sake. —

Have you said about that nice telegr. to be printed, its a rarely touching one & will do good as *Taneyev* & others also say. —

Blessings & endless kisses fr. yr. very, very own

Sunny.

No. 396.

Tsarskoje Selo, Dec. 8-th 1916

My own beloved Sunshine,

Fancy, yr. having such cold weather — here are 5^0 of frost wh. fall to 3 in the day time. We think of going to Novgorod then, as I told you. Get into the train Saturday for the night, leaving very early — reaching then Sunday morning, spending a few hours, looking at Churches & I believe a few hospitals & home again, spending the night in the train & going fr. our wagon Monday morning to the hospital, then we miss no work. — I shall send for *Ressin* & tell him all — don't remember who the governor is — shall not keep it a secret this time, so as to see more people. But always so shy without you, my Lovy dear. — My nice old Princess Golitzin (committee for our prisoners) found the telegr. fr. *Astrakhan* lovely & begged they should be printed everywhere. Another Prince Golitzin (from *Kharkov)* spoke in the *Council of the Empire* & not at all well, & one congratulate this one for the speech, he was furious — also found that one ought to take off court dresses of such people. Pity you don't put *Stcheglovitov* now, he wld. tell you such things at once (if cld. not stop speeches even) & you cld. deprive them of their court rank — one cannot be severe enough now, therefore *Balashov* needs a strong rebuke — don't be kind & weak — forgive me Lovy. — Such very fond thanks for yr. sweet letter, Lovebird, such joy to hear fr. you. — We also several times thought it might be the bridegroom the »mysterious hand« — can imagine how excited all were.

But to have you back, what joy it will be, my own Sweetheart — only have the *Duma* cleverly shut — be firm as iron with Trepov & stick to *Kalinin* the truest friend. — Got dear letters fr. Victoria & Georgi, who thanks awfully for the present. —

Now goodbye, my Angel, sweetest of loves, treasure dear. I bless & kiss you over & over again, yr. own, very own

Wify.

Be firm — be the master. —

No. 397.

Tsarskoje Selo, Dec. 9-th 1916

My own Angel,

Ever such warm, burning thanks for your dear letter. I am glad you like that nice English book — its so refreshing amongst the sorrow & worries of this world. We see our Friend this evening, am very glad. Poor Ania's leg ached awfully yesterday, sort of Drachenschuss & ischias — screamed from pain — now has *B.* so lies to day in bed, dont know whether she can go to morrow. We take Nastinka *Ressin* & *Apraxin.* The girls rejoice, as they love sleeping in the train — but it will be sad alone. — Sleep so little when you are not there. — Am receiving *Rittich,* saw *Dobrovolsky* & spoke much about Misha's *Community station* & the senate. —

Poor General Williams, am awfully sorry for the poor man. — Please, bow to the Belgian fr. me. — How are things going in Roumania? & *generally* at the war ? Lovy my Angel, goodbye & God bless & keep you, cover you with very tenderest kisses. Y. own Wify.

Got a letter fr. Irène. Mossy lost two sons, & now the eldest couple of twins are out at the war. —

Ania saw *Kalinin* yesterday, who said that *Trepov* has combined with *Rodzianko* to let go the *Duma* from Dec. 17 — Jan. 8. so as that the deputies should have no time to leave *Petrograd* for the holidays & to keep them here in hand. Our Friend & *Kalinin* entreat you to close the *Duma* not later than the 14-th Feb., 1-st or 15-th even, otherwise there will be n o p e a c e for you & no works got through. In the *Duma* they only fear this, a longer *intermission* & *Trepov* intends to catch you, saying that it will be worse if the people return home & spreas their news — but our Friend says, nobody believes these delegates when *they are alone* in their homestead, o n l y have strenght when together. Lovy mine, be f i r m & trust our Friends advice — its only for your good & all who love you think aright. Dont harken, neither to *Gurko* nor *Grigorovitch,* if they ask for a short *intermission* they don't understand what they do. I wld. not write all this, were I not so a f f r a i d for you & yr. gentle kindness always read to give in, when not backed up by poor old wify, Ania & our Friend — therefore the untrue & bad hate our influence (which is but for the good). — *Trepov* was at *Kalinin's* cousins *(Lamsdorf),* not knowing they were his relations, & said he was going on the 11-th to you & wld. insist before you (brute he is!) that *Protopopov* should leave. Lovy, look at their faces — *Trepov* & *Protopopov* — can't one clearly see the latter's is cleaner, honester & more true. — You k n o w you are right, keep up yr. h e a d, order *Trepov* to work with him — he dare not be against your order — bang on the table.

Lovy, do you want me to come for a day to give you courage & firmness? Be the M a s t e r. One is against *Kalinin* for stopping assemblies of »Unions« he did quite rightly. Our Friend says »*that the confusion which was due in Russia during or after the war has arrived and if he* (you) *had not taken the place of Nikolai Nikolaievitch, he would now be thrown off the throne*«. Be of good cheer, the screamers will quieten down — only send off the *Duma* q u i c k e r & for l o n g e r — trust me — you know *Trepov* flirts with *Rodzianko* — all know it, & to you he slyly fibs its out of politics. — Go to the lovely Image & get strenght & power there — remember a l w a y s our Friends dream, it meens so, oh so much for you & us all. —

No. 398.

Tsarskoje Selo, Dec. 10th 1916

My own beloved One,

Always have to write in a flying hurry, heaps of *Rostovtzev's* papers I had to finish, then Ania's leg being bad went to her 3 times a day, & received, so that scarcely a free moment. But she hopes to go with us this evening. This morning first time 7 degrees, its brighter because of the snow, but we have no sun. —

I enclose a coin sent for you & an Image on silk; — & then some papers to read through from *Kalinin,* in case *Voyeikov* did not give you the duplicates. On *Manuilov's* paper I b e g you to write »*discontinue the case*« & send it to Minister of Justice. *Batiushin* who had to do with the whole thing, now himself came to Ania to beg one shld. stop it, as he at last understood it was an ugly, story, got up by others to harm our Friend, *Pitirim* etc. all that fat *Khvostov's* fault. General Alexeiev knew about it through *Batiushin* again later. Otherwise in a few days one begins the instruction & there can be very disagreeable talks all over again, & bring up that horrible scandle fr. last year. Before others *Khvostov* said the other day that he regrets that »*Tchik*« did not succeed to finish off our Friend. And his courtdress was left him alas, alas!

Well, please at once without delay send *Manuilov's* paper to *Makarov* otherwise too late. — Lovy, wont you quicker change *Makarov* & take *Dobrovolsky* — *Makarov* really is an enemy (of me absolutely, therefore of you too), & don't listen to *Trepov's* protests. He, of course, will speak against *Dobrovolsky* as has his own candidates — but is a devoted man which is much nowadays. — And why won't you have honest *Valuyev*, whom we know so well, honest & devoted as Minister of railways & *Communications?*

I enclose a letter from *Sukhomlinov* to our Friend, please read it through, as there he explains all clearly about his affair, wh. you must send for & not all to go to the *Council of the Empire* as then there will be no saving of poor *Sukhomlinov*. — He writes so clearly everything — do read it through & act according — why shld. he suffer & not *Kokovtzev* (who wld. not give the money) nor Sergei who on account of her has just as much fault. —

Just received your letter.

From all my heart I thank you for it very tenderly. Now *Trepov* is with you, & I feel so anxious. I just saw *Kalinin* — is so glad you got all the papers through *Voyeikov*, so I won't send them again to bother you. He is most anxious you shld. sooner send away the *Duma* & for longer — in 10 years they have never had a *recess* like this, so short & then one has no time to do things. The *Council of the Empire* is mad agreeing with the *Duma* about freedom of *censorship*. My head goes round & I seem to write bosh. — Only be firm, firm. — Thank God one stopped the meetings at Moscou, six times (*Kalinin* was till 4 in the morning at the telephone), but *Lvov* succeeded in reading a paper before the police got them in one place. You see — *Kalinin* works well & firmly & does not flirt with the *Duma* but only thinks of us. —

This letter must go now. *Zhevakhov* comes directly. — Shall give over your message to *Islavin* to-morrow — will be a nice change there; — only shall miss you awfully. You will in consequence get this letter on Monday.

God bless & protect you. Cover you with kisses & tender caress. Ever yr. very very own old

Wify.

No. 399.

Tsarskoje Selo, Dec. 12th 1916

Beloved Sweetheart,

For a precious letter & card my tenderest thanks. I am too happy you went to the dear Image — such peace there — one feels away fr. all worries that minute whilst pouring out one's heart & soul in prayer to her, to whom so many come with their sorrows. — Well Lovy, *Novgorod* was a success — tho' awfully tiring, the soul was uplifted & gave us all strength — I with my heart & Ania with her aching legs — we got about. — Of course to-day everything aches; but it was worth it.

I have *Anastasia* & *Olga* to write to you & *Anastasia* to Baby, as each describes differently; & I am a bad one at it. The Governor was perfect, kept us »going« so that we were everywhere in good time & then let the crowd come near too. What a delightful old town, only got too soon dark — lets go together in spring when there are inundations, then they say its yet better & one can go in motor boats to the monasteries. Passing the big monument of the 1000 years of Russia, reminded me of the big picture in the big palace here. — How beautiful the *Sofia Cathedral* is, only standing in front one could not see so well. The service lasted 2 hours (instead of 4) — they sang exceedingly well & I was happy to begin all with mass & pray for my sweethearts. *Yoantchik* & *Andriusha* went everywhere with us. — We *knelt* to all the saints. A pitty when one has to do all in a hurry & cannot give oneself enough to prayer before each — nor look at all the details. I give Baby the Image before which we stood (& sat). Bishop Arseni held an alocution, when we arrived — very touching, young bishop Alexei found himself very handsome *(a Scholar of the Lyceum)* they followed us everywhere, all day long. — Then after mass 10—12 we went to the hospital next door, *diocese* through the bishop's rooms, & to the museum of old church treasures, arranged since 3 years. Lovely old Images wh. had been lying in churches monasteries, hidden away, covered in dust. They have begun to clean them up & lovely fresh colours appear — most interesting & I should have liked to look at all another time in detail, you wld. love it too. — Back to the train the soldiers had already dispearsed (luckily). — I lunched on my bed & A. in her compartment. The children had *Yoantchik* & *Andriusha* & *Islavin*. We were received by his wife & daughter with flowers — bread & salt from the town. — At 2 we went off again to the *Zemstvo Hospital* small. Everywhere distribued Images. —

Then to the »*Dessiatinni*« monastery — relicks of St. Barbara are kept there. Sat a moment at the Abesses room & then I asked to be taken to the *old woman Maria Mikhailovna (Zhevakov* told me about her) & we went to her on foot through the wet snow. She lay in bed in a small dark room, so they brought a candle for us to see each other. She is 107, weares *irons* (now they lay near her) — generally always works, goes about, sews for the convicts & soldiers without spectacles — never washes. And of course no smell, or feeling of dirt, scraggy grey hair standing out, a sweet fine, oval face with lovely young, shining eyes & sweet smile. She blessed us & kissed us. To you she sends the apple (please eat it) — said the war wld. soon be over — »*tell him that we are satisfied.*« To me she said, »*and you the beautiful one — don't fear the heavy cross*« (several times) — »*for your coming to visit us, two churches will be built in Russia*« (said it twice) »*don't forget us, come again.*« — Baby she sent the *wafer* (too little time & fidgety around, else would have loved to speak to her), gave us all Images. Said not to worry about the children, will marry & could not hear the rest. —

Forget, what she said to the girls — I made *Yoantchik* & *Andriusha* also go up to her, & sent Ania in; — she will no doubt write about it. I thank God for having let us see her. — It was she who some years ago told people to have that big image of the Virgin of *old Russia* to be copied & sent to you — one would not, said too big — then the war began & she insisted & they did so & she said we would all be at the church procession & so it was when they brought her last year in July 5 (?) before the *Feodor Assembly* — you remember? And you had the immense Image kept at the 4 *Rifle Regiment* — I have a little book about her life an old servant of the *Marinsky Palace* gave me yesterday (her *spiritual son).* — She made me a far more peaceful impression than old *Pasha of Diveyer.* From there to the *Yuriev Monastery* (5 *versts* from town), yr. old *Nikodim* is there, adores & prays for you & sends you love. —

I think Olga writes all these details to you. — Such love & warmth everywhere, feeling of God & your people, unity & purity of feelings — did me no end of good & we are already combining ideas for *Tikhvin Monastery* with very venerated Virgin (Image) — 4 hours from here — & *Viatka* & *Vologda, Archangelsky* is going to find out. — Just combine hospitals with holy places, that gives strength. — All is so old & historical at Novgorod, one feels removed back to olden times. The *old woman* meets every one with »*be joyous uncrowned bride.*« —

We went to a little *home* for boys of *Tatiana's* committee — they brought little girls there from another one too. — Then we went to *Noblemen's Club* where the *Ladies' Committee* gave me 5000 *rubles* & saw their hospital — splendid big hall for the men, officers next door. Took tea, quite nice, the Governor's wife & Archibishop sat next to me — few ladies, all hideous — his daughter works there as sister. — Then to the *Znamenskaya church* — I send you an Image I bought of her, as so lovely & do hang her over your bed, her face is so sweet; & the *Bride of Christ's* (whom they hid fr. us), saw her that same day then, that she wld. help you. Then they brought a miraculous image of St. Nicolas for us to kiss — how lovely the church is! & *vault's* (such steep stairs) — no time to look at the »*Day of Jugdment*« on wh. Peter the Great & *Menstchikov's* portraits were painted by Peter's order. — Our motor stuck & the crowd pushed us off. From there to a wee *chapel* in a garden where on the *stove* of a holy bread bakery appeared (ages ago) the Virgin — it is intact & only covered in glass & with gems surrounded. Such awfully strong »perfume«, the girls & I noticed it. Carried you both everywhere in soul & heart sharing together everything!! —

(Write a little note to Ania as thanks, it will do her good as she shares so warmly everything — govern. so nice to her & *Nikodim).* — From there still to *Zemstvo* hospital, where wounded from surrounding places had been brought — & *City Hospital.* At the station received an Image & apples from the *Merchants.* The lancer's march was played by the *band* of *Reserve Regiment* of there. — Left before 6 — back here 10.20, slept night in train, morning off to hospital — now resting — evening our Friend.

— So lovely & restful, warming to the soul. Blessings & kisses without end fr. yr.

Sunny.

How odious about Roumania. —

No. 400.

Tsarskoje Selo, Dec. 13-th 1916

My own dearest Angel,

Tenderest thanks for Your dear card. Am so anxious (as you have no time to write) to know about your conversation with that horrible *Trepov*. I read in the paper that he told *Rodzianko* now, that the *Duma* will bee shut about on the 17-th till first half of Jan. Has he any right to say this, before the official anouncement through the *Senate* is made? I find absolutely not & ought to be told so, & *Rodzianko* get a reprimand for allowing it to be put in the papers. And I did so hard beg for sooner & longer. Thank God, you at last fixed no date in Jan. & can call them together in Feb. or not at all. They do not work & *Trepov* flirts with *Rodzianko* all know that, 2 a day they meet — that is not *decent* — why does he make up & try to work with him (who is false) & not with *Protopopov* (who is true) — that pictures the man. Old *Bobrinsky* loathes the *Trepov's* & knows their faults — & he is so utterly devoted to you & therefore *Trepov* kicked him out. My Angel, we dined yesterday at Ania's with our Friend. It was so nice, we told all about our journey & He said we ought to have gone straight to you as we would have brought you intense joy & *blessing* & I fear disturbing you! He entreats you to be firm, to be the Master & not always to give in to *Trepov* — you know much better than that man (still let him lead you) — & why not our Friend who leads through God. Remember why I am disliked — shows it right to be firm & feared & you be the same, you a man, — only believe more in our Friend (instead of *Trepov*). He lives for you & Russia. And we must give a strong country to Baby, & dare not be weak for his sake, else he will have a yet harder reign, setting our faults to right & drawing the reins in tightly which you let loose. You have to suffer for faults in the reigns of your predecessors & God knows what hardships are yours. Let our legacy be a lighter one for Alexei. He has a strong will & mind of his own, don't let things slip through yr. fingers & make him have to build up all again. Be firm, I, your wall, am behind you & won't give way — I know He leads us right — & you listen gently to a false man as *Trepov*. Only out of love which you bear for me & Baby — take no big steps without warning me & speaking over all quietly. Would I write thus, did I not know you so very easily waver & change your mind, & what it costs to keep you stick to Your opinion. I know I may hurt you how I write & that is my pain & sorrow — but you, Baby & Russia are far too dear to me. What about *Sukhomlinov* & *Manuilov*. I prepared all for you. And *Dobrovolsky* — a sure man —

& quicker get rid of *Makarov,* who, do at last believe me, is a bad man. God give me the power to convince you — its harder keeping you firm than the hate of others wh. leaves me cold. I loathe *Trepov's* obstinacy. There were lots of paris in the *Duma* that *Pitirim* wld. be sent away — now he got the cross, they have become crushed & small (you see, when you show yourself the Master) & more, & more one finds it right *Princess W.* was sent away. — You never answered me about *Balashov,* fear, you did nothing & Frederiks is old, & no good unless I speak firmly to him. — Such a mistake not to have closen the *Duma* 14 & then *Kalinin* could get back to his work & you wld. see & talk to him. — Only not *a responsible cabinet* which all are mad about. Its all getting calmer & better, only one wants to feel Your hand — how long, years, people have told me the same — »Russia loves to feel whip« — its their nature — tender love & then the iron hand to punish & guide. — How I wish I could pour my will into your veins. The Virgin is above you, for you, with you, remember the miracle — our Friend's vision.

Soon our troops will have more force in Roumania. — Warm & thick snow. — Forgive this letter, but I could not sleep this night, worrying over you — don't hide things from me — I am strong — but listen to me, wh. means our Friend & trust us through all — & beware of *Trepov* — you can't love or venerate him. I suffer over you as over a tender, softhearted child — wh. needs giding, but listens to bad advisers whilst a man of God's tells him what to do. Sweetest Angel, come home soon — ah no, you have the Gen., why not before, — I cant grasp; why the same day as the *Duma* — strange combination again. — And *Voyeikov,* has that also fallen through? —

Oh, dear, I must get up. Been writing Xmas-cards all the morning. Heart & soul burning with you — Love boundless, therefore seems harsh all I write — pardon, believe & understand. I love you too too deeply & cry over your faults & rejoice over every right step.

God bless & protect, guard & guide you. Kisses without end,

Y. truest

Wify.

Please, read this paper & Anias too.
If a lie — have *Rodzianko's* uniform taken off.

No. 401.

Tsarskoje Selo, Dec. 14-th 1916

My beloved Sweetheart,

7 of frost & thick snow. Scarcely slept this night again, remaining till luncheon in bed as all aches still & have a slight chill. Such loving thanks for yr. dear letter. *Trepov* was very wrong in putting off the *Duma* now & wishing to call it beginning of January again, the result being (which he, *Rodzianko* & all counted upon), that nobody goes home & all will remain,

fomenting, boiling in *Petrograd.* He came to you meekly, as then was sure to succeed with you, had he screamed as usual, you wld. have got angry & not agreed. Lovy, our Friend begged you to shut it 14-th — Ania and I wrote it to you — & you see, they have time to make *trouble* now about forbidding the »Unions« to unite — you got *Kalinin's* paper through *Voyeikov* yesterday. He also wrote to *Trepov* begging it shld. be behind closed doors, *Trepov* never deigned to answer him — so he wrote to *Rodzianko,* who did as *Kalinin* wished, only of course said by *Kalinin's* wish — coward *Trepov* wld. not take it upon himself — what ever you like, *Trepov* behaves now, as a traitor & is false as a cat — do not trust him, he concocts everything with *Rodzianko* together, its only too well known. —

That paper I sent you yesterday, *Rodzianko* himself wrote — he has no right to print & distribute yr. conversation & I doubt it being literal as he always lies — if not exact then be the Emp. & at once have his court-dress taken fr. him, don't ask Frederiks' or *Trepov's* advice, both are frightened, tho' old man wld. formerly have understood the necessity, now he is old. Already one spread in town *(Duma)* that the nobility in Novg. did not receive me, & when they read that we even drank tea together they became crushed. About *Kaufmann* one is very pleased — you see, yr. firmness is appreciated by the good — so easy to continue when once begun — forgive me tormenting you with these letters — but only read the 2 telegr. I wired to you, you will again see what the right say — & they turn to me to beg you. If you hear fr. *Kalinin* again & he begs to close the *Duma* — do it, don't stick to the 17-th — time is money, the moment golden, & if dawdled over difficult, impossible to catch up & mend again. — I do hope its not true *Nikolasha* comes for the 17-th — formerly it went perfectly without *Vorontzov* — that has nothing to do with the Caucasus, our front here. Keep him away, evil genius. And he will mix into affairs & speak about Wassiltchikov. Be Peter the Great, John the Terrible, Emperor Paul — crush them all under you — now don't you laugh, noughty one — but I long to see you so with all those men who try to govern you — & it must be the contrary. Countess Benkendorf was so outraged by Princess W.'s letter, that she made a round of visits to the older ladies in town, Princess Lolo, Countess *Vorontzov* etc. telling them her opinion & that she finds it a disgrace to what the society has come down to, forgetting all principles & begging them to begin by strongly speaking to their daughters who behave and talk outrageously. It seems to have had its effect, as people speak now of her, so they realise the letter was really an unheard of one, & not such a charming one as some try to pretend. Katoussia W. also wrote to me, but after reading I tore it. And here the contrast, telegr. fr. »*Union of the Russian People*« asking me to give over things to you. — One is rotten, weak, immoral society — the other, healthy, rightthinking, devoted subjects — & to these one must listen, their voice is Russia's & not society or the *Duma's.* One sees the right so clearly & they know the *Duma* ought to be closed & to them *Trepov* won't listen. If one does not listen to these, they will take things into their own hands to save you and more harm unwillingly may be done — than a simple word from you to close the *Duma,* — but till February, if earlier — they, will all stick here. I cld. hang *Trepov* for his bad counsels — and now after the papers *Kalinin* sent *Voyeikov* with those vile, utterly revolutionary *representations* of Moscou *Nobility* & »*Unions*«, wh. have been discussed at the *Duma,* how can one keep them even one day on still — I hate false *Trepov* who does all to harm you, backed up by *Makarov.* Had I but got you here again — all was at once calmer & had you returned as *Gregory* in 5 days, you wld. have put order, wld. have rested yr. weary head upon wify's breast & Sunny wld. have given you strength & you wld. have listened to me & not to *Trepov.* God will help, I know, but you must be firm. Disperse the *Duma* at once, when you told *Trepov* 17-th you did not know what they were up to. — I should have quietly & with a clear conscience before the whole of Russia have sent *Lvov* to Siberia (one did so for far less grave acts), taken *Samarin's rank* away (he signed that paper fr. Moscou), *Miliukov, Gutchkov* & *Polivanov* also to Siberia. It is war and at such a time interior war is high treason, why don't you look at it like that, I really cannot understand. I am but a woman, but my soul & brain tell me it wld. be the saving of Russia — they sin far worse than anything the *Sukhomlinov's* ever did. — Forbid *Brussilov* etc. when they come to touch any political subjects, fool, who wants *responsible cabinet,* as *Georgi* writes.

Remember even Mr. Philippe said one dare not give constitution, as it would be yr. & Russia's ruin, & all true Russians say the same. Months ago I told *Sturmer* about *Shvedov* to be a member of *Council of the Empire* to have them & good *Maklakov* in they will stand bravely for us. I know I worry you — ah, wld. I not far, far rather only write letters of love, tenderness & caresses of wh. my heart is so full — but my duty as wife & mother & Russia's mother obliges me to say all to you — blessed by our Friend. Sweetheart, Sunshine of my life, if in battle you had to meet the enemy, you wld. never waver & go forth like a lion — be it now in the battle against the small *handful* of brutes & republicans — be the Master, & all will bow down to you. — Do you think I shld. fear, ah no — to-day I have had an officer cleared out fr. Maria's & Anastasia's hospital, because he allowed himself to mock at our journey, pretending *Protopopov* bought the people to receive us so well; the Drs. who heared it raged — you see, Sunny in her small things is energetic & in big one as much as you wish — we have been placed by God on a throne & we must keep it firm & give it over to our Son untouched — if you keep that in mind you will remember to be the Sovereign — & how much easier for an *autocratic* sovereign than one who has sworn the Constitution. —

Beloved One, listen to me, yes, you know yr. old true Girly. »*Do not fear*« the *old woman* said & therefore I write *without fear* to my agoo wee one. — Now the girlies want their tea, they came frozen back from their drive. — I kiss you & hold you tightly clasped to my breast, caress you, love you, long for you, cant sleep without you — bless you

Ever yr. very Own

Wify.

No. 402.

Tsarskoje Selo, Dec. 15-th 1916

My own Beloved,

Please, forgive me for my impertinent letters — girly does not mean to hurt her Angel, but writes from deepest love — & sometimes driven to exasperation, knowing one cheets you & proposes wrong things. How can I feel ever quiet when *Trepov* comes to you? And still he succeeds in persuading you wrongly — only to find a successor — but many say, that once *Makarov changed,* he will become better on the whole. You see how he clings to *Makarov* (whom I continue saying is false to us) & wants him at head of the *Council of the Empire* — too bad. Put strongminded (hard) *Stcheglovitov* there, he is the man for such a place & will allow no disorders & bad things to go on. — I shall send you the papers back to-morrow when have studied them through. —

Thanks so much (& fr. A. too) for *Manuilov,* fancy nice *Malama* said at 5 yesterday there was no paper fr. you (the Messenger came early in the morning), so I had to wire. One had intended making a whole story, dragging in all sorts of names (out of filth, simply) & lots were going to be present at the *trial.* Thanks again dear one. — Our Fr. came to her, I did not go out of the house. He never goes out since ages, except to come here, but yesterday he walked in the streets with *Munia, to the Kazan and St. Isaacs (Cathedrals)* & not one disagreeable look, people all quiet. Says in 3 or 4 days things will go better in Roumania & all will go better. — How good yr. *order* is — just read it with deepest emotion. — God help & bless you, Sweetheart. *It is not necessary* to say poor old huzy with no will, it kills me — forgive me — you understand me I know & my allconsuming love — yes Lovy mine? Me loves too so terribly, terribly. — Little *Kazhevnikov* (fr. *Murman)* comes to lunch & *N. P.* to tea, to enjoy each separately. Do let *N. P.* get the yacht for Xmas, please dear. —

Our Fr. says *Kalinin* must be well now. Why don't you make him *Minister of the Interior* not *Acting Minister* (my idea) — that young *Rittich,* who only just began, already got his affirmation (to his own surprise). — Only slept after 4—6 this night, quite lost my sleep again — need you! —

The sun is trying to appear very thick snow, 6 of frost. Ania & I want to go to Holy Communion on Sunday, as its *Christmas Fast* — to get strength & help. — I am glad you liked the Image — is her face not sweet, tho' sad? I am sending 3 *little lamps* fr. the Children & me to *Novoye Znamenie* & to the *old woman* with an Image. Did you eat her apple? — So glad you told Frederiks to answer those nice telegr. from us both. Why on earth won't the Generals allow »*Russkoye Znamia*« (small patriotic paper) to be sent to the army, *Dubrovin* finds it a shame (I agree) & they can read any proclamations. Our Chiefs are really idiots. — That new Club *Trepov* has arranged (for officers etc.) not famous — am going to find out about it, off. of our *United Regiment* go there & they all met *Rodzianko* with manifestations & allocutions there — most tactless. — Lovy, *Dubrovin* asks to see me — may I or not? Please, tell *Trepov Duma* on leave till beginning of Feb. as they must have time to go home (here more mischief if they remain — *Rodzianko* & *Trepov* arranged it together) — believe our Friend's advice. Even the Children notice how things don't come out well if we do not listen to Him & the contrary — good when listen. *The path is narrow, but one must walk along it straight, in the manner of God and not of man* — one only needs to face all courageously & with more faith. —

Now, a miracle (all say) »*Variag*« arrived before all the others — *Storm, 40 knots* fr. Gibraltar to Glasgow. The water not simply washes over, but goes in & through, alas, everywhere, machine not famous, must be repared soon in England. Our Fr. was anxious when they left *Vladivostok,* but they were blessed & saved because *Lili* out of faith went to *Verkhoturie* & *Tobolsk* with *Gregory* & *Ania* in summer. —

Blessings, love, caresses & kisses without end, Huzy my Beloved, fr. yr. very, very Own.

Wish the telephone were not so bad. — *Kazhevnikov* was a dear & talked a lot, hope you will see him before he returns, he came with the *Adm.* they had 3 *accidents* on the new line. Probably in Feb. the »*Variag*« will have to go for 5—6 months to England for repairs, as its dangerous leaving her so, she is old & not safe. — The Engl. everywhere charming in all the ports helping where & how they could. Poor boy had to make speeches in England. Says *Den* a perfect capt., always calm, never looses his head. They rolled 42 — so that the guns sweeped along the sea sideways. Heat colossal in summer, they went 5 months. — So nice to see him — cld. not get over *Anastasia* being so fat & a big lady. —

No. 403.

Tsarskoje Selo, Dec. 16-th 1916

My own beloved Treasure,

10° of frost this morning & wee pink clouds — everything thickly covered in snow. — Slept five hours this night, quite a treat. *Botkin* turned up — I have not seen him for two months at least, because I know by heart what medicines to take when the heart is worse. Well, he gave me stronger drops as its so enlarged & of course said to keep lying, wh. I do. I only have *Shvedov* to-day, otherwise lie on the sopha. But still I want to go to Holy Communion on Sunday, if only possible & so now beg your forgiveness my Sweetheart for any word, wh. may have hurt you — I fear, I have been rough at times — but out of despair only & endless love & yearning to help you. Pardon me, Lovy. I want badly to go — am weary — but my spirits are up. Things a r e going better, & *Kalinin* has behaved splendidly. I told him to write openly to you about everything — he was shy to do so — I said it was his duty, once you show him confidence. It is only thanks to him the scandles were prevented in the *Duma — Trepov* was a coward, *Shuvayev* worse (wld. that *Beliayev* were in his place, a gentleman & not one to bow down to the *Duma* & seek to be popular) — & *Rodzianko* listened to *Kalinin's* letter & became small — bless the man may he continue being as firm & brave as he has up to now. Send him a word of thanks or encouragement, wont you? And affirm him as Minister of the Interior (its wify's idea, & I think the right one). — People said you would never stand up for him & *Pitirim* against everybody — & you have! Well done; Huzy mine! Only one thing just torments me, *Gregory* & *Protopopov* — the Duma not to be called together before Febr. so as to give them time to disperse, wh. is m o r e than necessary, they are in a »group« a poisenous element in town, whereas dispersed over the country nobody pays any heed to them nor respects them. — Olga had a Committee yesterday evening, but it did not last long. *Volodia Volkonsky,* who always has a smile or two for her — avoided her eyes & never once smiled — you see how our girlies have learned to watch people & their faces — they have developed much interiorly through all this suffering — they know all we go through, its necessary & ripens them. They are happily at times great babies — but have the insight & feelings of the soul of much wiser beings. As our Fr. says — they have passed heavy »*courses*«. — *N. P.* took tea, told heaps about Odessa & the battalion, *Olga Evgen.* etc. — Full of *Petrograd* horrors & rages that nobody defends me, that all may say, write, hint at bad things about their Empress & nobody stands up, repr. mands, punishes, banishes, fines those types. Only *Princess V.* suffered, all others, *Miliukov* etc. go free. Yes, people are not to be admired, cowards. But many shall be struck off future court-lists, they shall learn to know in time of peace what it was in time of war not to stand up for ones Sovereign. Why have we got a ramoli rag as Minister of the Court? He ought to have brought all the names & proposed how to punish them for slandering your wife. A private husband wld. not one hour have stood these assaults upon his wife. Personally I do not care a straw — when I was young I suffered horribly through those injustices said about me (oh how often) — but now the wordly things don't touch me deeply, I mean nastinesses — they will come round some day, only my Huzy ought really to stick up a bit for me, as many think you don't care & hide behind me. You won't answer about *Balashov* — now why did you not have him s e v e r e l y written to by Fred. — I am not going to shake hands with him whenever we meet, I warn you & I long to fling my fury into his face; little snake — I have disliked him ever since I set eyes on him, & I told you so. He thinks his high court rank allows him to write vile things — on the contrary, he is u t t e r l y unworthy of it. — Have you said that Prince Golitzin is to have his court rank taken fr. him — don't dawdle deary, do all quicker, its the Danish Bummelzug — be quicker in acting strike out people fr. court lists & don't listen to Fred. protests — he is frightened & does not understand how to deal at the present moment. —

Now forgive me, if I did wrong, in asking *Kalinin's* opinion about the list you sent me. As we trust him (he came for 1/2 an hour to her yesterday), I asked her to find out what he knows about the people. He promises to hold his tongue that he saw the names of the candidates. — Only a b o v e a l l begs *Makarov* to quickly leave, w i t h o u t putting him into the *Council* of *the*

Empire, others neither were put there, & don't need *Trepov's* letter, believe our Fr's advice & now *Kalinin's* too — he is dangerous & completely holds *Trepov* in hand, others, *Zhevakhov* for instance knows it too. — He spoke a while ago to *Stcheglovitov,* who finds *Dobrovolsky* whom he knows — excellent in that place. I think you would only be right in naming him. I know *Dobrovolsky* is much against the reorganisation of the Senate as projected, (I think agreed to in the *Council of the Empire* & now presented to the *Duma)* — says it will be as bad & left as the *Duma,* & not to be relied upon — he told me that, when I saw him. I only spoke about the Senate & *Georgie's* committee then. —

Send for *Kalinin* as soon as you arrive here & then *Dobrovolsky* to talk to & name *Stcheglovitov* quicker — he is the right man in the right place & will stick up for us & permit no rows. Yr. *order* has had a splendid effect upon all — it came at such a good moment and showed so clearly all yr. ideas about continuing the war. Fancy, poor Zizi was so upset, *Miliukov* in his speech spoke about *Lila Narishkin (Lichtenstein),* spies etc. & said she was a lady in high function at court confounding her with Mme Zizi. Poor old lady heard that it got into small papers in the country, the *Kurakins* came all flying & she had to explain to them — her *supervisors* full of horror, a general in the army, — how can we keep such traitors near us (always a bite at me & my people!!) — so she sent for *Sazonov (Miliukov's* bosom friend), & told him to explain all & to insist upon his writing in the papers that he was lead into error. It will appear in the »Retch«, & now she is quite calm again. They touch all near me. *Lila N.* is at Astoria, & being watched by the police. — Poor old *Stcheglov* died this night — better for him, he was so ill! I am going to get hold of Ressin one of these days & tell him to pay attention to his officers — *Komarov.* was always with them, he never, & the tone has become very bad & even left — its the most difficult reg. as so mixed & therefore needs a head to keep them well in hand & guide them, & one does not speak well of them at all. The men don't like him because he is hard — but the officers he does not a bit occupy himself with. — Just had old *Shvedov,* fancy, when he told *Trepov* he was to be a member of the *Council of the Empire* by your & my wish, he answered that it did not concern him what orders *Sturmer* got, he did not hear it from you.

He brought me the list on one paper of all the members & we can look at it together & strike out & add on new ones. Hates Kaufmann, says he said very bad things, strike him off — now one must come with the brush & sweep away the dust & dirt & get new clean brushes to work. —

Warmest thanks precious letter. Poor dear, will be tired to morrow — God help you — only military & no political questions. All wild about your *order,* the Poles of course intensely so. —

The kitten has climbed into the fireplace & now sneezes there. —

Glad, you saw *Bagration* — so interesting all about his wild men.

»*One must not speak*« — »with tiny will«, but a wee bit weak & not confident in yourself & a bit easily believe bad advices. — Now — I bless, hug, kiss you, my one & all. God bless & protect you.

Ever yr. very, very own tiresome Sunny.

No. 404.

Tsarskoje Selo, Dec. 17-th 1916

My own beloved Sweetheart,

Again very cold & gently snowing. Slept 5 hours this night, for me quite good — heart not famous & don't feel well. You see my heart for some time was bad again, but I did not keep quiet as ought to have by rights — but I cld. not — I had to be in the hospital to change my thoughts, had to see many people — the moral strain of these last trying months on a week heart of course had to tell — this lovely journey to *Novgorod* was phisically very tiring — & well, the old machine broke down. Hope to be decent for Xmas at least this year. Since the war I have not been to any trees in hospital or manège.— Shall think of you more than ever this afternoon — may all your thoughts & plans be blessed by God.

Hope you can go to the Image before. — I have ordered *an all-night* mass in the house — (& tho' very foolish) Church to-morrow at 9 in the *Pestcherny Chapel. Ania* goes too & we confess at 10. Once more forgive me for every pain & worry, beloved One — shall carry you in my heart & soul to-morrow. —

How is the new General instead of *Pustov?* The latter must have been sad to leave you — what a nice, honest & devoted man. —

I send you a paper with some ideas of *Sukhomlinov* about the *Duma* to read through in the train. —

I cannot grasp why *Voyeikov's* thing was not done 2 weeks ago as intended. —

Some gossips: *Ania's* Mother told her that *Krivoshein* & *Ignatiev* bless me for having telegraphed to you to leave all the *food supply question* in *Rittich's* hands — there, & not one single word of truth in the whole thing, ah, how people calmly lie & find it no sin!! —

You will finish the nice English novel in the train?

Oh the joy, the consolation of having you home again.

At such a time to be separated I assure you is at times absolutely exasperating & distracting — how much easier to have shared all together & spoken over everything, instead of letters wh. have less force, alas, & often must have aggravated you, my poor, patient Angel. But I have to try & be the antedote to others' poison. —

Has Baby's »worm« quite been got rid of? Then he will get fatter & less transparent — the precious Boy!...

We are sitting together — can imagine our feelings — thoughts — our Friend has disappeared. Yesterday A. saw him & he said Felix asked him to come in the night, a motor wld. fetch him to see *Irina.* — A motor fetched him (military one) with 2 civilians & he went away.

This night big scandal at *Yussupov's* house — big meeting, Dmitri, *Purishkevitch* etc. all drunk, Police heard shots, *Purishkevitch* ran out screaming to the Police that our Friend was killed.

Police searching & Justice entered now into *Yussupov's* house — did not dare before as Dmitri there.

Chief of police has sent for Dmitri. Felix wished to leave to-night for Crimea, begged *Kalinin* to stop him.

Our Friend was in good spirits but nervous these days & for A. too, as *Batiushin* wants to catch things against Ania. Felix pretends He never came to the house & never asked him. Seems quite a paw. I still trust in God's mercy that one has only driven Him off somewhere. *Kalinin* is doing all he can. Therefore I beg for *Voyeikov,* we women are alone with our weak heads. Shall keep her to live here — as now they will get at her next.

I cannot & won't believe He has been killed. God have mercy.

Such utter anguish (am calm & can't believe it). —

Thanks dear letter, come quickly — nobody will dare to touch her or do anything when you are here.

Felix came often to him lately.

& kisses

Sunny.

GENEALOGY AND INDEX

NICHOLAS I *m.* (Charlotte of Prussia)
reigned 1825–55 | Alexandra 1817–60

- ALEXANDER II, reigned 1855–81
  - Nicholas, *d.* 1865
  - ALEXANDER III
    - NICHOLAS II, 1868–1918, *m.* 1894 to Alix of Hesse-Darmstadt 1872–1918
      - Olga
      - Tatyana
      - Maria
      - Anastasia
      - ALEXIS
    - Alexander
    - George, *b.* 1871
    - Xenia, *b.* 1875, *m.* 1894 Alexander Mikh.
    - Michael, *b.* 1878
    - Olga, *m.* Prince Peter of Oldenburg
  - VLADIMIR
  - ALEXIS
  - Maria (Duchess of Edinburgh)
  - SERGEY, 1857–1905
  - PAUL, 1860–1918
- Maria
- Olga
- Alexandra
- CONSTANTINE
- NICHOLAS
- MICHAEL

CONSTANTINE (second son of Nicholas I), Viceroy of Poland

- Nicholas, *b.* 1850
- Olga, *b.* 1851, *m.* to the King of Greece
- Vera, *b.* 1854, *m.* to Prince E. of Württemberg
- Constantine (poet), *b.* 1858, *m.* Princess Elizabeth of Saxe-Altenburg
  - Ivan
  - Gabriel
  - Tatyana, *m.* to Prince Bagration Mukhransky
  - Constantine
  - Oleg, killed in the war
  - Igor
- Dmitry, *b.* 1860
- Vyacheslav

NICHOLAS (third son of Nicholas I), Commander-in-Chief during the Russo-Turkish War, 1877–8,
b. in 1831
m. Alexandra Princess of Oldenburg

Nicholas (Commander-in-Chief during the Great War, later Viceroy in the Caucasus), *m.* 1907, Anastasia Princess of Montenegro,

Peter *m.* 1889 Militsa Princess of Montenegro

- Marina *b.* 1892
- Roman *b.* 1896
- Nadezhda *b.* 1898

MICHAEL (fourth son of Nicholas I), Viceroy in the Caucasus, *b.* 1832
m. Olga, Princess of Baden

- Nicholas (the historian) 1859–1918
- Anastasia *m.* to the Grand Duke of Mecklenburg-Schwerin
- Michael *m.* Sophie Merenberg Countess Torby
- George
- Alexander *m.* Xenia Alexandrovna
  - Irena *m.* Prince Yusupov
  - Andrew
  - Dmitry
  - Feodor
  - Rostislav
- Sergey
- Alexis

VLADIMIR (third son of Alexander II)
m. 1874 Maria Pavlovna
Duchess of Mecklenburg-Schwerin

- Alexander *d.* 1877
- Cyril *b.* 1876
  - Cyril
- Boris *b.* 1877
- Andrew *b.* 1879
- Helen *b.* 1882 *m.* Prince Max of Baden (Chancellor of the German Empire, 1918)

ALEXIS (fourth son of Alexander II)
b. 1850
morganatic marriage with the daughter of the poet Zhukovsky

SERGEY (fifth son of Alexander II)
m. 1884 Elisabeth of Hesse (sister of Princess Alix)

PAUL (sixth son of Alexander II)

m. 1st, 1889 Alexandra Georgievna, Princess of Greece

- Maria
- Dmitry present at Rasputin's murder.

m. 2nd (morganatically), Mme Pistolkors, subsequently Countess Hohenfelsen and Princess Paley

- Prince Paley

INDEX

The following letters of the Empress are of special political interest :

Nos. 86, 87, 88, 89, 93, 96, 98, 99, 100, 107, 110, 111, 114–15, 116, 118, 120, 126, 128, 169, 187, 220, 229, 230, 236, 283, 286, 293, 343, 355, 362, 377, 378, 382, 383, 389, 390, 392, 396, 397, 400, 401, 402, 403.

"**Admiral,** the little." *See* Nilov.

Agafangel, Bishop. Opposed Rasputin. Under the Soviet he was named by the Patriarch Tikhon as his temporary *remplaçant* when the Patriarch was attacked by the Bolshevik Government.

Akulina Laptinsky. Exorcised by Rasputin and followed him about as a Sister of Mercy. Washed his body after death.

Alek. Alexander, Prince of Oldenburg, father-in-law of Olga Alexandrovna, sister of the Emperor.

Alexey. The Tsarevich.

Alexeyev, General M. V. Chief of Staff, South-western Front, 1914–15; the real conqueror of Galicia. Chief of Staff, G.H.Q., under the Emperor, who left him an entirely free hand 1915–17. Went on leave in late autumn 1916, probably in consequence of the Empress's suggestion. Commander-in-Chief after the March revolution.

Alia, Pistolkors, daughter of General Taneyev and sister of Anna Vyrubova. Married to a stepson of Grand Duke Paul.

Anastasia, Grand Duchess A. Nikolayevna, fourth daughter of the Emperor. *See* Schwibzik.

Andronnikov, Prince. A social and political adventurer of sinister reputation who became one of Rasputin's principal wire-pullers, but later appears to have been mixed up in Alexis Khvostov's plot to kill him.

Ania. Anna Vyrubova, daughter of General Taneyev, head of the Emperor's chancery. Married to Lieutenant Vyrubov and separated from him. Personal friend of the Empress and her intermediary for the instructions of Rasputin. Author of *Stranitsy* (*Pages*), 1923. *See* Introduction.

Anpapa. A variant of Grandpapa, used in the Imperial family.

Apraxin, Count. Private secretary to the Empress.

Balashov, P. N. Leading member of the Nationalist (Patriotic Conservative) Party ; sent a warning (of ten pages) to the Emperor.

Bark, P. L. Minister of Trade and Industry, 1912 ; Minister of Finance, 1914–17. Inclined to Liberalism.

Beletsky, S. P. Director of the Department of Police. Supported Rasputin. Outmanœuvred Alexis Khvostov and drove him from office by discovering his plot against Rasputin.

Benckendorff, Count A. K. Russian Ambassador in London. A great friend of England.

Benk, Count P. K. Benckendorff. Grand Marshal of the Court.

Bezobrazov, General. Commanded " Special " Army Guard Corps in the costly fighting of the summer of 1916. Grand Duke Paul served in his Army.

Bonch-Bruyevich, General. Chief of Staff on Northern Front, 1915–6; complained of his superiors to the Empress. Is now serving the Bolshevik Government.

Boris. Grand Duke Boris Vladimirovich, first cousin of the Emperor. At one time proposed for Olga, his eldest daughter, and was refused. Made to apologise for an insult to the English.

Botkin, Dr. E. S. Physician to the Tsarevich ; accompanied the family to Siberia and was murdered with them.

Brassov, Countess. *See* Misha's wife.

Brusilov, General. Commanded 8th Army with success in the autumn of 1914 and the South-western Front in the summer of 1915, making the celebrated offensive against the Austrians. Now serving the Bolshevik Government.

Buchanan, Sir George. British Ambassador to St. Petersburg, 1910–17. He warned the Emperor of his danger in February and October 1916. Author of *My Mission to Russia and other Diplomatic Memories.*

Carlov, Countess. Morganatic wife of Duke George of Mecklenburg-Strelitz.

Chelnokov, M. V. The Liberal Mayor of Moscow. Obtained an audience of the Emperor to represent public opinion.

Danilov, General Y. N. (" black "). Quartermaster-General at G.H.Q. to the Grand Duke Nicholas, 1914–15; Chief of Staff, Northern Front, 1916.

Dellingshausen, General. Imprisoned during the war, as of German race.

Derevenko. Sailor-guardian of the Tsarevich. Deserted him at the Revolution.

Derevenko, Dr. Vladimir. Assistant physician to the Tsarevich.

Dmitry, P. Grand Duke Dmitry, son of Grand Duke Paul, and first cousin of the Emperor. Present at the murder of Rasputin.

Dobrovolsky, N. First Procurator of the Senate; supported Rasputin; later the Empress's Minister of Justice from October 1916; entrusted with the investigation into the death of Rasputin; killed by the Bolsheviks in October 1918.

Dolgorukov, Prince. A Marshal of the Court; accompanied the Emperor to Tobolsk; murdered.

Dona. The German Empress.

Drenteln, Colonel. Preokrazhensky Regiment. A.D.C. to the Emperor; became antagonistic to Rasputin.

Dubrovin, Dr. Organised in 1907 the reactionary "Union of Russian People." Appeared with advice to the Empress on the eve of the Revolution.

Dzhunkovsky, General. C.O. of the Palace Guards, formerly City Prefect of Moscow.

E. S. *See* Botkin.

Eberhardt, Admiral. Commanded the Black Sea Fleet in the beginning of the war.

Elena, Mother. *See* Ella.

Eleonora. Grand Duchess of Hesse-Darmstadt.

Ella. Grand Duchess Elizabeth, widow of Grand Duke Sergey (uncle of the Emperor, died 1905) and elder sister of the Empress. Mother-Superior of the Community of Martha and Mary of Pity in Moscow; murdered at Alapayevsk in the Urals on July 17, 1918, by the Bolsheviks.

Emma. Invalid daughter of Count Fredericks, Minister of the Court.

Ernie. Grand Duke of Hesse-Darmstadt.

Evreinov. A Master of Ceremonies.

Felix. Prince Yusupov and Count Sumarokov-Elston; married Irena, daughter of the Emperor's sister Xenia. One of those who killed Rasputin.

Feodorov, Dr. S. P. The Emperor's physician.

Feofan, Bishop. Rector of the Theological Academy of Petrograd; Confessor to the Empress. He recommended Rasputin in 1905–7, disclaimed him in 1911, and was disgraced.

Fredericks. *See* "Old Man, the/Our."

Gedroyts, Princess. Surgeon at the head of the Palace hospitals; instructed the Empress and her daughters in ambulance work.

Georgi. Grand Duke George Mikhaylovich. Killed by the Bolsheviks in Petrograd, 1919.

Georgie. King George V of England, first cousin of the Emperor and of the Empress.

Girs, M. N. Russian Ambassador in Constantinople to 1914 and later in Rome.

Gibbs, Mr. English tutor to the Tsarevich; went with the family to Siberia.

Gilliard, Pierre. A Swiss; preceptor of the Tsarevich; author of *Le Tragique Destin de Nicholas II et de sa famille;* went with the family to Siberia.

Goremykin, I. L. Minister of the Interior, 1895–9; Prime Minister during the First Duma, 1906, and again 1914–16. Strongly Conservative. *See* "Old Man."

Grabbe, General A. N. C.O. Cossacks of the Imperial Convoy.

Greek Georgie. Prince George of Greece, first cousin of the Emperor; accompanied him on his journey to the East before accession and helped to save his life in Japan.

Gregory, Gr. Rasputin. *See* Introduction.

Grigorovich, Admiral. Minister of the Navy, 1907–16; supported the Liberal Ministers.

Groten. Colonel of Empress's Crimean Horse.

Guchkov, A. I. Leader of the Octobrist party; President of the 3rd Duma, 1910; Member of Council of State. Creator of the Central Munition Committee and the chief antagonist of Rasputin and the Empress.

Guriev. Served in the Ministry of Finance as Press expert.

Gurland. Professor of Law at Yaroslavl; served in the Ministry of the Interior in the Press Department.

Gurko, V. J. Assistant Minister of Agriculture, 1906–7; Nationalist.

Gurko, General. Did distinguished work in the war, and was *remplacant* of General Alexeyev as Chief of Staff at General Headquarters just before the Revolution.

Heliodore. *See* Iliodore.

Hermogen. Bishop of Saratov. Friend of, then enemy of, Rasputin. Acted with the monk Iliodore against him. Disgraced. Later Bishop of Tobolsk during the Emperor's captivity, and sympathetic to him. Murdered by the Bolsheviks.

Heyden, Admiral A. F. A.D.C. Married to a Lady-in-waiting of the Empress.

Hohenfelsen, Countess, later Princess Paley.

Ignatiev, Count P. N. Moderate Liberal. Minister of Education; one of the most enlightened holders of this post.

Iliodore. A wild, mystical monk. Disgraced with Hermogen. Threatened the Emperor with revelations in America. Alexis Khvostov sought to employ him to plot the murder of Rasputin.

Irena. Wife of Prince Henry of Prussia; sister of the Empress.

Irena. Daughter of Grand Duchess Xenia Alexandrovna and niece of the Emperor; married to Prince Felix Yusupov.

Isidor, Bishop. A supporter of Rasputin.

Ivanov, General N. Y. Commanded the South-western Front in 1914–15; honest, able and popular. Later retained by the Emperor at G.H.Q. as a military adviser. Entrusted with the task of marching on Petrograd during the Revolution.

Izvolsky, A. P. Liberal Minister of Foreign Affairs, 1906–9; supported the first Duma. The maker of the Anglo-Russian Convention of 1907. Dismissed in 1910. Ambassador at Paris, 1910–17.

Jemmy. Pekinese given to Grand Duchess Anastasia by Anna Vyrubova; was killed with the Imperial family at Ekaterinburg.

Joachim. Prince Joachim of Prussia.

Kalinin: Rasputin's nickname for Protopopov.

Kaledin, General. Commanded 8th Army, 1916. Hetman of the Don Cossacks. Committed suicide on their defection after the Bolshevik *coup d'état.*

Keller, General Count. C.O. Empress's Own Lancers. A great favourite. Later did distinguished work in the Carpathians (autumn, 1916). Killed by the Ukrainians in Kiev, December 1918.

Khan. Nakhichevansky, General. C.O. of the Horse Guards, and later commanded a cavalry corps.

Kharitonov. Moderate Liberal; Comptroller-General.

Khvostov, A. A. Member of the Council of State; Minister of Justice.

Khvostov, Alexis N. Governor of Nizhny-Novgorod; then Conservative Member of Duma. Strongly anti-German. Obtained, with Rasputin's help, the confidence of the Empress in autumn 1915. Minister of the

Interior. Turned against Rasputin and plotted against him. Finally dismissed on March 16, 1916.

Kirill, Grand Duke. Eldest son of the late Grand Duke Vladimir, who was the eldest uncle of the Emperor. Served in the Navy. Head of Naval Staff at G.H.Q. Apparently was concerned in a plot against the Emperor on the eve of the Revolution, and on its outbreak led the Guard Crew to the Duma. Married Victoria Feodorovna, sister of Queen Marie of Roumania.

Kniazhevitch. Formerly C.O. Empress's Crimean Horse.

Kokovtsev, Count V. N. Enlightened Conservative. Minister of Finance, 1903–October 1905, May 1906–September 1911. Also Prime Minister September 1911–February 1914. One of the few able statesmen in Russia. In March 1912 succeeded in bringing about the temporary dismissal of Rasputin. Dismissed in January 1916.

Korff, Baron. A Master of Ceremonies.

Kostia. Grand Duke Constantine Constantinovich ; a poet ; died in June 1915.

Krivoshein, A. V. Moderate Liberal. Minister of Agriculture, 1906–15. An able and enlightened statesman. Driven out by the Empress and Rasputin.

Krupensky, P. N. Member of the Duma. Conservative and almost Reactionary.

Kryzhanovsky. State Secretary (i.e. Head of the Chancery of the Council of State).

Kshesinskaya (Kchessinskaya), Matilda. Première of the Imperial Corps de Ballet. Her house became Lenin's Headquarters after the March Revolution.

Kuropatkin, General A. N. Minister of War 1904 ; Commander-in-Chief against Japan 1904–5 ; commanded the Northern Front in 1916 during the absence of Ruzsky through illness.

Kurlov, P. G. Formerly Assistant Minister of Interior. Reactionary.

La Guiche, Marquis de. French military attaché in Petrograd during the war to May 1916.

Lili Den (Dehn). Personal friend of the Empress ; wife of Naval Lieutenant Karl Dehn (an officer on the *Standart*), who was of Swedish origin ; author of *The Real Tsaritsa*.

Loman. Colonel in the Mixed Regiment of the Guard at the Palace. Starosta of the favourite church of the Empress, the Feodorov Cathedral.

Lvov, Prince George. President of the Union of Zemstva, the largest Red Cross organisation during the war. Did much work for munitions. Became Prime Minister of the Provisional Government after the March Revolution.

Madeleine, Zanoti. First dresser to the Empress. *See* Zanoty.

Makarov, A. Minister of the Interior, September 1911 to January 1913.

Maklakov, N. A. Minister of the Interior, January 1913 to the summer of 1915. Reactionary; was against the war; consulted and perhaps about to be recalled on the eve of the Revolution.

Maklakov, V. A. The most brilliant orator of the Duma (Cadet). Later Ambassador of the Provisional Government to Paris (1917).

Malama. An officer of the Empress's Own Lancers.

Maltsev, Colonel. Head of the Air Defence of Tsarskoe.

Mama. The Dowager Empress Maria Feodorovna.

Mama. A name used by Rasputin for the Empress Alexandra.

Manus. Banker and speculator; supposed agent of Germany; responsible for grave financial scandals before the Revolution.

Maria, M. Grand Duchess M. Nikolayena, third daughter of the Emperor.

Maria, P. Grand Duchess M. Pavlovna, daughter of Grand Duke Friedrich Franz II of Mecklenburg-Schwerin; widow of Grand Duke Vladimir, uncle of the Emperor.

Masha, Vasilchikova. *See* Vasilchikova, Maria.

Massalov, Mosalov. Assistant Chief of the Emperor's military chancery.

Mekk. Organised Grand Duchess Elizabeth's cottage industries and Red Cross work.

Menshikov. Brilliant leader-writer (Conservative) of the *Novoe Vremya.*

Miechen. *See* Maria P. Grand Duchess Maria Pavlovna.

Militsa, Grand Duchess. Daughter of King Nicholas I of Montenegro; married to Grand Duke Peter Nikolayevich. The first protector of Philippe and of Rasputin.

Miliukov, Prof. P. N. Leader of the Cadet party (Liberal) in the Duma; made the notable attack on Rasputin and the Government in the Duma November 14, 1916.

Misha. Grand Duke Michael, brother of the Emperor.

Misha's wife. Countess Brassov, formerly Madame Mamontov, then Madame Vulfert; married the Grand Duke Michael against the Emperor's wishes in 1913; lived ordinarily at Gatchina; expressed Liberal opinions.

Mishchenko, General. Distinguished cavalry leader in the Japanese War. Held an important command in the Great War.

Mordvinov, A. A. A.D.C. to the Grand Duke Michael and later to the Emperor.

Motherdear, Mama. The Empress Dowager Maria Feodorovna, mother of the Emperor and sister of Queen Alexandra of England.

Muftizada. An officer of the Empress's Crimean Horse.

N. M., Nikolay. Grand Duke Nikolay Mikhaylovich, grandson of Nicholas I; historian; Liberal. Warned the Emperor on the eve of the Revolution. Killed by the Bolsheviks in Petrograd, 1919.

N. P. S. *See* Sablin.

Naryshkin, Madame. Grand Mistress of the Court.

Nastenka. Countess Hendrikova. Lady-in-waiting. Murdered in Alapayevsk, June 17, 1918.

Neratov. Assistant Minister of Foreign Affairs under Sazonov and up to the Revolution.

Nikolasha. Grand Duke Nikolay Nikolayevich, born 1856; son of the third son of Nicholas I; married after a divorce Anastasia (*see* Stana); protected both Philippe and Rasputin. Head of the Committee of Imperial Defence, 1908. C.O. St. Petersburg Military District. Turned strongly against Rasputin. Commander-in-Chief July 1914 to September 1915. Then Commander-in-Chief in the Caucasus and took Erzerum.

Nilov, Admiral. Commanded the *Standart*; later at General Headquarters. *See* "the Little Admiral."

Nostitz, Count. General in charge of the Staff of the Petrograd Military District.

Obolensky, Prince A. N. Prefect of Police.

Old Man, The/Our. Count Fredericks (or Freederikz), Minister of the Court. An aged and knightly servant of his Sovereign.

Old Man, The. *See* Goremykin.

Olga, Aunt. The Dowager Queen of Greece.

Olga. Grand Duchess Olga Alexandrovna, married to Prince Oldenburg. Became a Sister of Mercy in the war.

Olga, O. Grand Duchess O. Nikolayevna, eldest daughter of the Emperor.

Olga, Evg. Bützow. Lady-in-waiting.

Olga Orlova. Wife of General Prince Orlov, Head of the Emperor's Military Chancery.

Olga Paley (Palei). *See* Paley.

Orlov, General Prince Vladimir. Head of the Military Chancery of the Emperor. Showed great courage in protesting against Rasputin.

Ortipo. Bulldog of Grand Duchess Tatyana.

Our Friend. Rasputin.

Palêologue, Maurice. Ambassador of France in Petrograd during the war (to May 1917) ; author of *La Russie des Tsars* (Paris, 1921).

Paley (Palei). Princess Olga, second wife of Grand Duke Paul ; earlier Madame Pistolkors, then Countess of Hohenfelsen, later Princess Paley. Authoress of *Souvenirs de Russie*.

Papa. A name used by Rasputin for the Emperor.

Paul, Grand Duke. Born 1860 ; the only living uncle of the Emperor ; married to Countess Hohenfelsen, later Princess Paley (second wife) ; killed by the Bolsheviks in Petrograd, 1919.

Petrov, P. V. Russian tutor to the Tsarevich.

Philippe, Mr., of Lyons. Unqualified doctor of neuro-pathology ; introduced by Grand Duchess Militsa. He had great influence with the Imperial family (1901–4).

Pitirim. Exarch of Georgia ; made Metropolitan of Petrograd by Rasputin.

Platon. Metropolitan of the Caucasus ; an enlightened opponent of Rasputin.

Plehve, General. One of the ablest Russian generals. Did brilliant work in Poland (autumn 1914) and on the Northern Front (autumn 1915). Died May 1917.

Pokrovsky, N. N. Assistant Minister of Finance ; Minister of Foreign Affairs, November 1918. Enlightened and honest.

Polivanov, General A. A. Co-operated for the War Ministry with Guchkov and the Duma, 1907–12. Succeeded Sukhomlinov as War Minister, June 1915. Very able and successful in reorganising the army training and supplies. Driven from office after repeated efforts by the Empress and Rasputin in April 1916, on the plea of his Liberalism.

Protopopov, A. D. Vice-President of Duma (Octobrist). Co-operated with Guchkov. Led the Duma visit to England for munitions in 1916. Then conversed with a German diplomat Lucius, Stockholm, abandoned his Duma friends and, on the recommendation of Rasputin and the Empress, became Minister of the Interior (October), which post he held to the March Revolution. *See* Kalinin.

Purishkevich, V. M. Brilliant Conservative Member of the Duma. One of those who killed Rasputin.

Pustovoitov, General. Quartermaster-General at G.H.Q., 1915–16.
Putyatin, General. Inspector of the Palace buildings.

Q. Helene. Queen Elena of Italy; sister of the Grand Duchesses Anatasia and Militsa.

Rasputin. *See* Gregory.
Rauchfuss, Dr. Called in to the Tsarevich.
Rennenkampf, General. Held high command in the Japanese War. Commanded the First Army, August 1914; failed badly, being partly responsible for the defeat of Tannenberg and entirely for that of the Mazurian Lakes. Failed as Corps Commander in Poland in autumn 1915.
Ressin, General. C.O. Mixed Regiment of the Guard at the Imperial Palace.
Rita, Hitrovo. Young Lady-in-waiting.
Rittich, A. A. The principal administrator of Stolypin's agrarian reforms (from 1906). Minister of Agriculture 1915–17.
Rodionov. Cossack officer; A.D.C. to the Emperor.
Rodzianko, M. V. President of the Duma. Moderate Conservative. Held Court rank. Very prominent in the work of munitions. Chairman of the Provisional Committee during the Revolution.
Rostovtsev, Count. Head of the Empress's Chancery.
Rubenstein. Jewish speculator; client of Rasputin; member of the German group before the Revolution, and with Manus responsible for grave financial scandals.
Ruzsky, General. With Alexeyev the most brilliant general of the Russian Army. Commanded the Third Army 1914, the Western Front 1914, the Northern Front 1915–17. Murdered by the Bolsheviks in October 1918.

Sabler, V. K. A follower of Pobedonostsev. Procurator of the Holy Synod in 1915. Reactionary, and adverse to the war.
Sablin, N. P. Naval Captain, friend of the Empress; appointed by the Emperor to enquire into Rasputin's orgy in Moscow in 1915.
Samarin, A. D. Marshal of the Moscow nobility. Conservative; Procurator of the Synod, summer of 1915. Driven from office by the Empress and Rasputin.
Sandro, Grand Duke Alexander Mikhaylovich; married Grand Duchess Xenia, sister of the Emperor.
Sasha, Aunt. Madame Naryshkin, widow of M. D. Naryshkin, natural son

of Alexander II. Shot by the Bolsheviks. Aunt of the Bolshevik Commissar Chicherin.

Saschka. Count Vorontsov Dashkov, A.D.C. of the Emperor.

Sazonov, S. D. Minister for Foreign Affairs, 1910 to July 1915. One of the chief builders of the Alliance. Moderate Liberal and advocate of autonomy for Poland. Driven from office on this issue by Stürmer and the Empress, immediately after his advice had been approved by the Emperor. He never received ordinary notice of his dismissal.

Schneider, Mlle. Reader to the Empress, and gave lessons to her children. Accompanied the family to Tobolsk.

Schulenburg. General, Empress's Lancers of the Guard; Controller of the Empress's hospital train.

Schwibzik. Grand Duchess Anastasia, fourth daughter of the Emperor.

Sergei. Grand Duke S. Mikhaylovich, General Inspector of Artillery; killed by the Bolsheviks at Alapayevsk, June 17, 1918.

Shakhovskoy, Prince. Minister of Commerce, 1915. Moderate Liberal.

Shavelsky. Senior Chaplain to the Forces.

Shcheglovitov, I. G. Reactionary. Minister of Justice, 1915; Leader of Extreme Right in Council of State. Was appointed President of the Council of State January 14, 1916. Supposed leader of the pro-German group.

Shcherbatov, Prince N. B. Moderate Liberal. Minister of the Interior, summer of 1915. Driven from office by the Empress.

Shirinsky-Shikhmatov. Church reactionary. Formerly Governor of Tver and later Procurator of Holy Synod.

Shura Tegelev. Maid to the young Grand Duchesses.

Shuvayev, General. Appointed Minister of War by the Emperor, April 1916. Honest but confessedly incompetent.

Sophia. Queen of Greece; sister to Wilhelm II.

Spiridovich, General. Commanding the special Okrana (protection) of the Emperor.

Stana. Grand Duchess Anastasia, daughter of King Nicholas I of Montenegro; married (1st) to Prince of Leuchtenberg, and after divorce (2nd) to Grand Duke Nikolay Nikolayevich. Helped to introduce both Philippe and Rasputin to the Imperial family.

Stürmer, B. V. Governor of Yaroslav. Reactionary. A Master of Ceremonies; Prime Minister by influence of Rasputin and the Empress, February–November 1916.

Sunbeam. The Tsarevich Alexey.

Suvorin, M. A. and B. A. The enterprising editors of the leading Petrograd paper *Novoe Vremya.*

Svetchin, Colonel. A.D.C. to the Emperor.

Taneiev. Head of the Emperor's Chancery, a post held in his family for nearly a century. Father of Anna Vyrubova.

Tatishchev, Ilya (Ilyusha). A.D.C. of the Emperor and earlier attached by him to the Emperor William. C.O. of Gendarmes, December 1916; picked by the Emperor to accompany him to Tobolsk; killed by the Bolsheviks at Ekaterinburg.

Timashev, Madame. Sent a letter of protest against the political activities of the Empress.

Timiriazev, V. I. Minister of Trade and Industry, November 1905, and again.

Tino. King Constantine of Greece.

Titi. The small son of Captain and Madame Dehn; godson of the Empress.

Toria. Princess Victoria of England.

Trepov, A. F. Minister of Communications, 1915; Prime Minister, November 1916; object of the Empress's most violent attacks. Conservative.

Trifon. Bishop; served in the first line in the 3rd Army.

Trina. Mlle Schneider.

Tudels. Louise Tutelberg, from the Baltic provinces, second dresser to the Empress.

Tyutchev, Madame. Governess to the Grand Duchesses. Objected to Rasputin entering the Grand Duchesses' rooms, which the Emperor then forbade. She left her post before the war.

Uexküll, Baroness. Head of the Kaufmann Community of Sisters of Mercy.

Varnava. A friend of Rasputin. Made Archbishop of Tobolsk. Consecrated a new saint (Bishop John of Tobolsk) without the Synod. Despite its opposition, he obtained direct approval from the Emperor.

Vasiliev, Director of the Department of Police on the eve of the Revolution.

Vasilchikov, Maria. Sent with peace proposals to the Empress from Germany, which aroused the Empress's indignation.

Vasilchikova, Princess Sophia. Wife of a former Minister of Agriculture

(1906); sent a letter of protest against the Empress's government on the eve of the Revolution.

Victoria, Princess (Marchioness of Mountbatten). Wife of Prince Louis of Battenberg and eldest sister of the Empress.

Vladimir. Metropolitan of Moscow before the war. Metropolitan of Petrograd in 1915, and opposed Rasputin, as President of the Synod; transferred therefore to Kiev. Killed by the Bolsheviks in 1918.

Voeikov, General. Commandant of the Imperial Palace. A supporter of Rasputin.

Volkonsky, Prince Vladimir. An upright Conservative. Vice-President of the Duma.

Vostorgov. A reactionary priest conspicuous for his political activity.

Volzhen, A. M. Procurator of the Holy Synod after the dismissal of Samarin, 1915.

Wassiltchikov. *See* Vasilchikov.

Welepolsky, Count. Master of the Emperor's shooting-boxes in Poland.

William. Kaiser Wilhelm of Germany, first cousin of the Empress.

Witte, Senator B. Head of the Commission on German Atrocities.

Witte, S. Y. Minister of Communications, 1891, and of Finance, 1893–1902. Opposed the Japanese War and made the Peace of Portsmouth, 1905. Prime Minister, October 30, 1905, to April 1906. Strong opponent of the war with Germany, and worked for peace up to his death in March 1915. Hated by the Empress. She hardly refers to him in these letters.

Xenia, Grand Duchess. Sister to the Emperor, married to Grand Duke Alexander Mikhaylovich.

Ysa. Countess von Buxhoewden, Lady-in-waiting; followed the Imperial family to Tobolsk and Ekaterinburg.

Yusupov, Prince. *See* Felix.

Zanoty, Madeleine. The Empress's chief dresser, an Italian who came with her to Russia from Hesse.

Zhuk. Sanitar in attendance on Anna Vyrubova.

Zina, Madame Z. S. Tolstoy, wife of an officer in the Horse Guards.

Zinaida. Princess Yusupov, mother of Prince Felix Yusupov.

Zizi. Madame A. A. Naryshkin, Grand Mistress of the Court.